YEARS OF HIGH HOPES

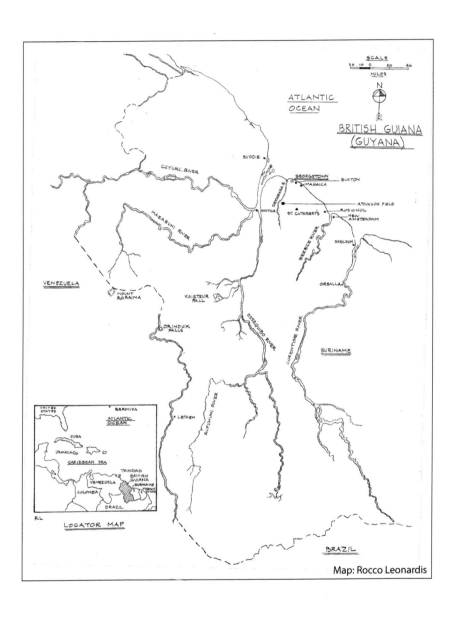

Map: Rocco Leonardis

YEARS OF HIGH HOPES

A Portrait of British Guiana 1952–1956,
from an American Family's Letters Home

The Letters of Marian and Howard Irwin,
Edited and with an Introduction by
Dorothy Irwin

First published in Great Britain by Hansib Publications in 2016

Hansib Publications Limited
P.O. Box 226, Hertford
Hertfordshire SG14 3WY UK

info@hansibpublications.com
www.hansibpublications.com

A CIP catalogue record for this book
is available from the British Library

Production by Hansib Publications Limited

Printed in Great Britain

For Rocco Leonardis, without whose unwavering encouragement all these years I could not have brought this project to completion.

CONTENTS

ACKNOWLEDGEMENTS

Abook like this does not come into being without the help of many people. First and foremost, it simply would not exist without the dozens of letters written by my parents. I am grateful to them for recording this unusual interlude of their lives so thoroughly, for preserving those records, and for entrusting them to me. I thank my sister, Liz Irwin Moore, for agreeing to let what is at times highly personal family history have a place within a much broader context. Friends and other family members also met my idea of the project with enthusiasm, sharing documents, reading transcripts of the letters, and listening as my notions of the book's structure took shape. For their unstinting encouragement and, most important, grasp of the endeavour's significance for me, particular thanks go to Lillie Caporlingua, Anne Irwin, Celia Maguire, Maggie Morth, and Thomasina Webb. I'm indebted to editorial colleagues who offered crucial advice: Stuart Bernstein, for suggesting that I broaden the scope beyond what my parents wrote; Joe Angio and Carla Davidson, for persuading me to cut back the introduction from an unwieldy "encyclopaedia entry" and reshape it into a coherent first chapter; and Marcia Schonzeit and Judith Sonntag, whose scrupulous readings (of the full manuscript and of chapters 1 and 7, respectively) saved me from committing any number of blunders and helped me achieve what I meant to say. Special thanks to Brian Molloy and Chris Beach for supplying scans, and to Rocco Leonardis for creating the map. The project's prospects received an inestimable lift from the Guyanese who so graciously contributed directly to its fruition—Raj Ramphal, for recalling his early encounters with my parents; Nigel Westmaas, for reading and commenting on the manuscript; Frank Birbalsingh, for recommending it to Hansib Publications and providing the foreword; and Arif Ali, for agreeing to publish it—but also from each of those who guided me to yet another person in the far-flung

Guyanese diaspora. For their supportiveness in helping to bring into being this record about our shared birthplace, I thank Terry Fletcher, Peter Fraser, Desmond Jagmohan, Michael Rose, Ronald Wilkinson and Ian Wishart. And to Marie-Hélène Fredericks, for demonstrating the book's potential appeal among Guyanese who've grown curious about their country's history—as well as for delivering an encouraging nudge whenever I needed one to keep the ball rolling—I extend my ongoing gratitude.

ABOUT THE AUTHOR

Born in Georgetown, British Guiana (now Guyana), Dorothy Irwin was raised in the United States and lives in Brooklyn, New York. She has spent her career in the publishing industry, first as a project manager for design studios and editorial packagers producing educational books, then as copy chief for such magazines as *Saveur, Bon Appétit*, and *This Old House*. As a writer, she has contributed to publications including *Saveur* and *American Legacy*. Her interest in the power of personal narrative to illuminate the past flourished during the ten years she worked with the editors of *American Heritage* magazine. *Years of High Hopes* is her first book.

PREFACE

"You'd be surprised what goes with you, once you leave a country like this."
             —Wilson Harris

One snowy winter not long after my mother died, I spent several weeks in my Brooklyn living room reading the letters she had sent fifty years earlier to her parents in the United States from Georgetown, British Guiana (now Guyana), where she and my father, Marian and Howard Irwin, lived for three and a half years. It was a slow process; some of the letters were handwritten in faded brown fountain pen, many others bore the faint typescript produced by a well-worn ribbon, and all were composed on onionskin that had been folded and tucked into envelopes now brittle with age. Most of the stamps had been torn off, destined to become part of my dad's stamp collection. Sometimes, as I removed a letter, tiny swatches of fabric fell out, or a four-centimeter-square snapshot (stamped "Bookers Photo Dept" on the back), or a yellowed newspaper clipping, or a handmade valentine or Christmas card. A direct link to another time, the letters that made up this cache of ephemera had been written when, other than costly telegrams, the mail was still the only form of overseas communication with British Guiana. Beyond my interest in my parents' efforts to get their bearings and make the most of their years in the colony, I was struck by the richness of life, Guyanese life, recorded in those pages.

After a brief visit to Georgetown in 1994, I'd begun reading novels by Guyanese authors, when I could find them. But this wasn't fiction; real relationships and interactions were portrayed, some humorous, some sobering, some of startling poignancy in their descriptions of misunderstandings or vulnerabilities, conflict or courtesy. The letters spill over with the messy immediacy of real life. The city they depict was recognizably the one I had seen a few years earlier. And, by sheer chance, they were written during a period that changed the course of the colony's history. I was sure it was wrong for this extraordinary record to remain unseen by anyone but the few of us who had written, received, or inherited it.

More emerged in a journal my mother kept during part of their stay. My aunt, Bee Jensen, contributed the letters she'd received. Then a year's worth of my father's letters to his parents surfaced. By virtue of his job and the greater mobility accorded to men, his accounts of goings-on around town (and well beyond) dramatically boosted the scope and level of detail.

Thus ensued the typing of transcripts, during which I quickly realized how little I knew about Guyana's history.

In fact, this book is a product of two eras. Fundamentally composed of those handwritten and typed pages, it would not exist in its present form without the mind-boggling access to documents of all kinds made possible by the Internet. Not wanting the book to consist solely of the words of Americans, I set out to quote, in footnotes and contextual extracts, Guyanese and others then on the scene, particularly during moments of upheaval. As a relative newcomer to the field, I'm sure to have inadvertently overlooked some people who should have been included, and I regret those omissions; still, I am astonished by how much was there for me to find. Searching haphazardly online, I chanced upon postings of obscure pamphlets, vintage newspaper articles (current ones, too), book reviews, declassified government documents, and essays in scholarly journals. I sought out memoirs and other books, and bit by bit, the complex mosaic of Guyana's past took shape.

At the centre of the book, as of my parents' years in Georgetown, is Queen's College, the colony's leading secondary school for boys, where my father taught biology. Some members of the staff—Guyanese as well as those placed by the colonial foreign service—would become friends; others are glimpsed in behind-the-scenes encounters at school or during extracurricular functions. Domestic arrangements are depicted in detail by my mother. There is also a personal side to her writing, as she muses about raising her firstborn, my sister, a child whose handicap made her prospects unclear, and goes on to describe my arrival toward the end of their stay. But my family is not the subject of this book.

Following a bitterly protracted campaign for independence, Guyana is still in the process of healing wounds that opened during the early

1950s. A number of books have focused on the political turmoil of that era, but I found few descriptions of the daily life in which it unfolded. My parents' letters include the milestones—the colony's first free election in 1953, its surprising outcome, and the calamitous aftermath—but those events take their place among movies screened, plays performed, concerts attended. Guyana's weather is nearly a character in the correspondence, as is Georgetown's notorious housing shortage, which inspired the book's organization. Interactions in Stabroek Market and Yong Hing's grocery, at the post office, the bank, and Bookers, on the streets and at home are given equal weight. By adding layers of detail to the record of everyday life in Georgetown, the book offers a nuanced look at how things stood as British Guiana reached toward a postcolonial identity.

The last chapter offers impressions from my trip to Georgetown in 1994 and thoughts about what transpired in Guyana following my parents' residency there. The epilogue supplies details about the lives and careers of some of the remarkable people they encountered.

It will be obvious that the correspondence in this book was intended solely for the reading of those to whom it was sent. While lightly editing the letters, mainly to reduce repetition, I decided not to delete the occasional disgruntled aside or unflattering anecdote (including those unflattering to the writer). I believe the historical value of the record as a whole supersedes those indiscretions, and I trust the reader will concur.

One final note concerns language. A decision awaiting every writer who addresses both the colonial and independent periods of Guyana's history involves the choice of spelling: Guianese or Guyanese. Because this book primarily covers the colonial period, I have retained the form then in use to refer to that era. References to the years following independence make use of the other spelling. Similarly, I have let stand East Indian, Negro, descriptions of grown women as "girls," and other language that was commonplace in the 1950s but has long since been retired.

FOREWORD

In September 1952, after our school had gone three years without a biology teacher, an American—Howard Irwin, "Mr. Irwin" to us boys—arrived at Queen's College (QC) in British Guiana (B.G.) to teach biology. Accompanied by his wife, Marian, and baby, Elizabeth, Mr. Irwin had come under a Fulbright teaching grant, and sixty-odd years after he left, in 1956, had totally faded from my horizon. So, in December 2015, when his daughter Dorothy (born in B.G. in 1955) contacted me saying she had edited a volume of letters her parents wrote to relatives in the US, it hit me like a bolt from the blue.

Years of High Hopes: A Portrait of British Guiana 1952–1956, from an American Family's Letters Home is a miracle of retrieval, a mysterious package from the past that invites wonder as well as curiosity. One hundred and ninety letters, the lion's share, are written by Marian (now deceased), and were collected by Marian's mother, a retired newspaper columnist. Marian's account of practical differences in social and cultural relations in B.G., as well as challenges with local maids, landladies, neighbours, and friends, is completely captivating, and Howard's record of his busy teaching schedule, music, extracurricular activities, and vigorous collection of botanical specimens is not far behind.

A fearless brand of American enterprise and energy shines through the letters, but what we relish most are glimpses of long-vanished customs and attitudes in a British Caribbean colonial outpost, and the ambiguous pleasure they offer us is like a jar of delicate preserves that we guiltily savour again and again. As Americans, the Irwins instinctively notice a lack of enmity between local Blacks and Whites; also, while Whites make up only 1.5 percent of the Guianese population, they account for 36 percent of boys admitted in 1952–53 to the prep form of our government-funded school; and other than the headmaster, Howard is paid the highest salary at QC, although many other staff members are much older and have put in much longer years of service. Best of all, ordinary Guianese betray strong (Hollywood) admiration of the US, even hinting at annexation.

Yet *Years of High Hopes* is no mere diary, journal, or travelogue; for the Irwins' visit coincided with a pivotal stage in the political development of B.G. when Guianese had achieved universal adult suffrage under a new, advanced Constitution first implemented in general elections in April 1953. But although the People's Progressive Party (PPP) won a resounding victory of 18 out of 24 seats, they were suspected of communism, the Constitution suspended, and their newly elected PPP government dismissed by the British, with support from British troops. Since this crisis is reported by the Irwins while they were briefly living in Atkinson Field, in close proximity to imprisoned members of the PPP, *Years of High Hopes* offers a rare, firsthand view of the start of a Guianese political conundrum that still defies resolution.

The pity is that Dorothy Irwin's indefatigable research and inspired, professional editing in *Years of High Hopes* pay homage to her parents after her mother passed on.

—Frank Birbalsingh

Main Street, 1950s

Chapter 1

THE PAST AS PROLOGUE

In the summer of 1994 I returned for the first time to my birthplace and walked right into a puzzlement. I was born in Georgetown, British Guiana (now Guyana), in 1955, arriving toward the end of the three and a half years during which my American parents and sister lived there while my father taught biology at Queen's College, the colony's premier secondary school for boys. Queen's marked its 150th anniversary in 1994 with an invitation to all "old boys" (alumni) and former "masters" to attend a celebratory program of events, and when my father asked whether I'd like to join him, I jumped at the offer. Even a brief, ten-day trip was bound to give me a better feel for this little-known place that figures so prominently in my family history.

What appealed to me immediately in Georgetown was the unassuming directness of its people, perhaps unsurprising in a capital of some 130,000 residents who don't see many tourists but noticeable to me, coming from New York City. Guyana fronts the Atlantic coast just above the equator, and the air is heavy and humid. Intermittently a Dutch, French, or British sugarcane colony, it was for centuries considered part of the West Indies and is the only English-speaking nation in South America. Because of my family's connection with Georgetown, I was fascinated by the extent to which the past was visible. The houses where my parents had lived were still standing. So was the building on New Market Street where I was born; formerly a doctor's small, private hospital, it had become by 1994 a hair salon. At the school compound, the Queen's College emblem, a three-masted Royal Navy barque, yellow-ochre on a black ground, appeared on a metal sign affixed to the wire fence at the entry gate. Across the yard stood the row of frame houses on pillars where, during my parents' era, the headmaster and several teachers had lived. The school itself, a cream-coloured, three-story wood structure whose walls were punctuated alternately with windows and broad louvres to catch the trade winds off the coast, had been constructed the year before my father's arrival, and from the outside it still looked much as it did in the photographs in our family scrapbooks.

But once Dad and I stepped inside the school and walked down the shadowy plank corridors, profound changes became apparent to us. The building was badly deteriorated. Windowpanes were broken; some were boarded up. Many louvres had been punched out. On the top level, a hole in the floor opened onto the classroom below. Downstairs, some of the rooms were flooded. A termite infestation had been left unaddressed, so the biology lab was unfit for use. Classroom furniture, much of it broken, was randomly stacked, askew. In the staff room I saw not a single book; only some piles of yellowing papers. It was hard to believe classes had ended within days of our arrival.

I was thoroughly baffled. In Guyana, as decades earlier in British Guiana, education was revered as a rare ticket to opportunity, which often involved emigration. Queen's College held a proud record in that respect. Yet the desolation we saw at Queen's was a sign of some other, overarching reality. Poverty was surely part of it. The country was among the poorest in the hemisphere, but the school's condition reached beyond neglect to vandalism. It suggested a deeper standoff, one that eluded me. The colony's path toward independence had been halting and rancorous. Britain granted it, finally, in 1966, nearly three decades before my visit, and yet the school's dilapidation seemed tied in some way to that event. Or was there more to it? I couldn't make out what was before me. I hadn't reckoned on Guyana's complexities.

Slowly it became clear to me that the country was still grappling with the fallout from events set in motion much earlier. Chief among those was the political upheaval that followed British Guiana's first free election, in April 1953. Never before had the vote been extended to those who didn't own property or meet a minimum income requirement; even to the illiterate. A new constitution for the colony called for a bicameral legislature: a State Council, with nine members, appointed, according to tradition, by the British colonial governor, and a House of Assembly, whose twenty-four members would be democratically elected Guianese. From among the latter, for the first time, an Executive Council of six cabinet ministers would advise the governor. Both the establishment of the bicameral legislature and the election were conceived as vital steps in Britain's plan for the long-neglected colony's improvement and eventual independence; still, other than roundly endorsing universal suffrage, many Guianese felt that the new constitution's provisions failed to go far enough. That was the opinion of the idealist, reform-minded People's Progressive Party, the first modern political party in the colony. Catching the British and even most of the party leaders themselves by surprise, the robust voter turnout favoured the PPP by a clear majority, and soon the brash new legislators took their places within the government. Chafing against the British aim of gradual decolonization, they brandished militant rhetoric that startled the Colonial Office in London; it also aroused the United States, then in the midst of the Red Scare. The following October, the colony's governor announced the suspension of the constitution to thwart what he and the Colonial Office charged were the PPP legislators' subversive, Communist proclivities. British troops were called in and remained for more than a decade. The fledgling legislators were deposed; some of them were arrested. That crisis drew, for a fleeting moment, the notice of the world. It rocked the colony and would soon fracture the PPP, and in some respects Guyana has never rebounded.

Queen's College, founded in 1844 as a school for sons of the privileged, had by the 1950s opened its doors to working-class boys throughout the colony, who won places by qualifying for government-backed scholarships. Its roster of high-achieving alumni includes the country's first prime minister, Cheddi Jagan (who, as it happened, was Guyana's president during my visit in 1994), and its first president, L.F.S. Burnham, both of whom were among the PPP legislators elected, and then ousted, in 1953. Queen's had moved to its new, modern quarters in 1951, and by then enrolment was up to 459, nearly triple that of twenty years earlier. But by 1994, I gradually came to understand, the school had become a political football. During the sesquicentennial program, the alumni and faculty seemed uncomfortable that the building was in such conspicuous disrepair, yet an uneasy silence surrounded its dereliction. A presentation in the vast auditorium brought together school officials and esteemed alumni who spoke at length about the stature of Queen's and its contributions, although, as one "old boy" would later write, none of the speakers had the temerity to mention that "it was a Queen's boy"—Burnham—"who was responsible for the miserable state of the school." We began to hear that the school had no books, that students left class at three o'clock to scrounge for them at the National Library or at another school, St. Stanislaus College. Only about a quarter of the teachers had college degrees. One teacher, with just a high school diploma, covered both physics and chemistry. Biology was no longer taught. Alumni had been pitching in to help pay teachers' salaries. In the 1980s, we learned, Queen's had suffered when President Burnham criticized its "elite" pedigree; he favoured instead the new President's College (which, I read in the newspaper slipped under the door of my hotel room one morning, had got running water and flush toilets only the week before our arrival). "Whether coincidentally or otherwise," stated an editorial in the *Stabroek News* during our visit, "pressure on [Queen's College] increased after it resisted changing its name . . . to something more in keeping with the nation's republican status, and also when it declined to abandon the ship symbol after being asked to redesign the school badge." Under Burnham, supervision of the school had gradually been transferred from its own authority to the Ministry of Education, which began hiring out the building, thereby cutting into the students' extracurricular activities. The physical structure, said the editorial, "came to be regarded as divorced from the school as such," which accounted for its ramshackle condition. Three years after our visit, Queen's suffered an arsonist's fire and has since been rebuilt.

For those who wish to trace the tumultuous events whose outcomes have long hobbled Guyana, some of which were encapsulated in what I witnessed at Queen's College, the letters that make up this book are an excellent place to start. The early 1950s, just preceding the political derailment of October 1953, are sometimes looked back on by Guyanese as a golden age. In the postwar world, hopes ran high. The British Empire was breaking up, education and employment restrictions had been loosened, technical and medical advances had begun to improve daily life, and optimism about further, desperately needed changes took hold. But in the post-election fervour of 1953 those hopes started to be checked, and for decades an impassioned, contentious, often violent, and at times downright corrupt stalemate hampered efforts toward positive change. Written from the perspective of outsiders, my parents' letters depict life in the colonial capital before, during, and after that first, rancorous turning point. I would have found the state of Queen's College in 1994 less perplexing, if no less poignant, had I read the letters before visiting Guyana. As it happened, I didn't read them until shortly after my mother's death, seven years later.

My parents had come to Georgetown in 1952 by way of the Fulbright program; my father was the first recipient of a Fulbright teaching grant to arrive in the colony. During their stay, my mother wrote her parents and sister at least once a week: in three and a half years, 190 letters, all of which were carefully numbered and saved by my grandmother, herself a sometime newspaper columnist who had a nose for a good tale. Rich in detail thanks to my mother's isolation, the letters were her only means of communication with people abroad. Overseas telephone service was primitive. In 1952 mail arrived from the United States twice a week ("after the plane comes in"), then was cut to once a week the following year. Her letters, combined with entries from a typescript journal she kept during the first twelve months and a selection of my father's letters home (fewer of which have survived), chart the family's daily life in a thoroughly unfamiliar place. My mother wrote from five addresses, each representing a distinctive facet of the colony's capital. By recording interactions large and small with neighbours, tradesmen, my father's school colleagues, and my sister's nanny, the letters offer an extraordinarily detailed portrait of midcentury colonial Georgetown. This close-up account brings to life a city of hard-pressed workers with meagre chance for advancement, people on the margins scrambling to keep from falling through the cracks, a slender middle class, and a small cadre of public servants who were kept perpetually on the move. Looking back at British Guiana during the early and mid-1950s, one can see what was functioning and what wasn't, the flagrant injustices imposed and protected by colonialism, and subtler though equally damaging habits of mind that took hold on both sides. As far as I have found, the sustained narrative of these letters, written to Americans by Americans describing the colony during that seminal period, is unique in the voluminous literature about British Guiana.

In September 1952 Howard and Marian Irwin were young—he twenty-four, she twenty-two; they had been married just over a year. Their parents had not supported their planned relocation with enthusiasm, especially objecting to the removal of their granddaughter, Elizabeth, then five months old. Among their reservations was concern about the baby's physical deformity—she was born without hands—which posed some questions as to her future independence and the possibility of surgical remedies or prostheses. Medical and technical advances at home suggested, in the view of the grandparents, that America would be a better choice than the rusticity of an obscure sugarcane colony. Acquaintances were bewildered about the family's destination; then as now, British Guiana was commonly confused with Ghana or Guinea. But as a student at the College of Puget Sound, from which he graduated in 1950, Howard had begun to envisage the practice of botany as a professional goal; in this he was encouraged by a professor, Dr. Gordon Dee Alcorn, who as a trusted adviser had also reassured his distraught former student after Elizabeth's birth. Tropical botany was then a largely unexplored specialty, and a post in British Guiana would position Howard to delve into it. While the couple's immediate incentive was Howard's job at Queen's College, the chance to further his career was equally enticing.

More personally, Howard and Marian each had something to prove. Marian had been a sickly child, overcoming serious bouts of strep throat and rheumatic fever when antibiotics were not yet in wide use. In her new life as wife and mother, she would emerge from a youth that had been somewhat sheltered, and living abroad would heighten the challenge. Howard, meanwhile, needed to make a fresh start, to compensate for his responsibility in a tragic car crash five years earlier, in which his younger brother had died, during the family's cross-country move from New York City to Seattle. Elizabeth's birth defect strengthened Howard's desire to put some distance between his young family and his anxious parents and in-laws. Neither Marian's health history nor the car accident are mentioned in the letters, but they added to the couple's eagerness to apply their energies in new directions.

Though they'd both moved frequently during childhood, they, like most Americans at the time, were not particularly worldly-wise. The trip to British Guiana, or B.G., was their first outside the United States, and the route, from Seattle-Tacoma to New York and then south to what was still known as the West Indies, made for an elaborate, three-day introduction to pre-jet air travel. "We didn't sleep that night," Howard wrote to his parents about the first leg of the trip; "it was so different flying—so painless that I cannot imagine our ever really fearing it." In New York they were met by friends of Howard's parents, and after a half-day of visiting they returned to Idlewild Airport (now J.F.K. International) to continue their journey. The seventeen-hour flight south involved stops in Puerto Rico and Trinidad.

Arriving in Georgetown, my parents soon discovered that some of those stationed in British Guiana considered the assignment a "hardship post," even though the city was very much a place of European creation, housing in its centre a Carnegie lending library, movie theatres, and a shopping district. The once flourishing colony was by the early 1950s poor, which meant that salaries were relatively low; some technical people had turned down appointments there, and among British foreign servants B.G. had a reputation for backwardness. It was farther from England than any of the other Caribbean colonies, and its isolation from them was palpable. A post in British Guiana lacked the cachet of one in Jamaica or Barbados, colonies that Britain had held some 200 years longer, since the 1600s, each of which had a far more established British elite.

And there was B.G.'s formidable, enervating humidity and heat, mitigated somewhat by the breeze off the coast. Howard and Marian had landed, they would learn, during a hot spell: 87 to 88 degrees Fahrenheit in the shade, with a humidity reading of 75 percent. "To be perfectly frank," Howard wrote, "it was hotter than hell when we disembarked and I was worried about Marian's standing up under the strain of three days interspersed with no more than a couple hours' sleep." The heat was variable, but the humidity remained constant. "All my slips are ripping in the back—I think it must be due in part to so much perspiration," Marian wrote after four months in Georgetown.

Just as the threat of flooding had led to houses' being built on pillars, so the humidity and high temperatures had influenced residential architecture. Within the white-painted wood homes, interior walls stopped about a foot shy of ceiling and floor to promote air circulation; exterior walls, just one partition thick, were largely formed of alternating sashes of jalousies (wood louvres) and glass casement windows, neither of which were screened. Those porous structural details made for a lack of privacy and a home life not firmly separated from the outdoors. In a letter, Howard described the din audible from within the couple's first "flat," on Parade Street: "We hear the chickens (4:00–6:00 a.m. and all day intermittently), the donkey's braying, . . . the thin exhaust sounds of the little British-made cars, the radio in the house two doors away blaring American music (Mitch Miller's 'Sparrows in the Tree-Top' at this instant), a yowling dog next door, footsteps overhead, conversation beneath us, and, occasionally, the sound of surf." Marian noted, "Everything needs constant attention here where windows are open all day and night, and dust blows in from the dirt roads." Rampant insects meant they slept under nets, and Marian swept out the large hardback beetles that flew in through the unscreened windows. The cold tap water in Georgetown was said to be potable (the city's system of piped water was completed in 1950), but after recurring discomfort my parents ended up boiling water for drinking; there was no hot water on tap.

The relatively raw domestic conditions were matched by the unfamiliar British colonial social structure and the customs common among the colony's largest ethnic groups, the African blacks and the East Indians (as they were then known, to distinguish them from the native Amerindians). All in all, the couple found that British Guiana took some getting used to. "In Tacoma, it sounded pretty glamorous to say that we were coming here for a year or two," Marian wrote six months into their stay. "Now that we're here, I find it almost anything but glamorous; certainly the life we lead isn't the gin-and-tonic-on-the-veranda life that many associate with the tropics."

In his first letter to his parents, Howard mentioned several accommodations that he and Marian would need to make "in order to become successful residents of British Guiana." Along with the climate and "a considerably slower pace," he described "a more significant and profound adjustment" concerning "the general acceptance by whites of the blacks as their equal." The letter was written in September 1952, when the United States was deeply divided along racial lines. Segregation, whether overt or tacit, was widespread throughout the country; the Supreme Court decision in *Brown* v. *Board of Education*, a cornerstone of early civil rights legislation, was still two years off. In B.G. Howard and Marian found a different reality. "In this colony," Howard wrote, "the blacks . . . have achieved eminence to a much greater degree than have the whites. Here we have the embodiment of a hope in the States— the proof that it can be a real working code. And we must admit rather shamefacedly that it's a little hard for us to accept. Yet our brief but rich experiences [here] have done much to help us see the way." These were first impressions: the British colonial social structure kept a tight rein on opportunities for advancement. Even so, the system stood in sharp contrast to what my parents had known at home.

Perhaps the greatest single lift to British Guiana's variable fortunes came with the arrival of DDT. Widespread awareness of its harmfulness would not emerge until the publication in 1962 of Rachel Carson's

Silent Spring, but the insecticide's short-term benefits were apparent immediately. Developed in Switzerland, it was manufactured prolifically during World War II by the British and American governments, which prized its astonishingly effective control of insect-borne malaria, epidemic typhus, typhoid fever, and dysentery among Allied forces stationed around the world. Its use in British Guiana, beginning in 1945, dramatically curtailed the incidence of malaria, which had been so endemic that it rendered the colony, in the words of the Guyanese anthropologist Denis Williams, "virtually a bridge to the grave." In his memoir, *Shadows Round the Moon*, the Guyanese novelist Roy Heath recalls his family's move in the 1930s from the village of Agricola to Georgetown as a bid to escape their "frequent debilitating bouts" of malaria. "At best an attack left us huddled beneath the sheet and blanket, our teeth chattering from the feeling of being held in an icy embrace. At worst we fell prey to hallucinations. . . ."

The insecticide was introduced in B.G. by Dr. George Giglioli, an Italian malariologist retained by one of the plantations in 1933 to study the illness, which routinely compromised the productivity of the colony's workforce. Years later, Dr. Giglioli told a company official: "When I first began to look at people working on sugar estates and I took their blood count, they were so anaemic from malaria that if you or I had the blood count they had, you would not have been able to walk up those stairs. I am not quite sure how they did it." DDT brought swift change. The incidence of malaria among schoolchildren was 60 percent in 1938 and 1945; in 1946 it fell to 18 percent. By 1950 the scourge had been eradicated from the colony. "The DDT campaign has been so effective," stated the background information supplied to Howard and Marian before their arrival by the Information Bureau of the Royal Empire Society, "that there are no carriers of malaria left on the coastlands and in other inhabited areas, so British Guiana may now be described as free of malaria." Marian's note after a week in Georgetown was more wry: "It certainly is a good thing there is no malaria here, or I would have it by now. There are, unfortunately, still mosquitoes and naturally they have discovered me. The bites are infinitely more annoying than the heat."

～

Today Guyana is sometimes known as the Land of Six Peoples, a nod to the ethnic groups whose descendants, along with those of the original Amerindian inhabitants and the European colonials, make up its population: the enslaved blacks imported from Africa and the indentured workers who came from India, Portuguese-held Madeira, and China. In a country about the size of Idaho but whose population, at 748,000, is well below half of that state's, the vast majority of people live on the coast, a fertile alluvial belt some 200 miles long and about ten miles wide, no more than a strip between the rain forest and the ocean. Guyana's interior— fully 80 percent of the country's landmass—is only sparsely inhabited. The country's name, from an Amerindian word meaning "land of many waters," is also telling: annual rainfall averages 100 inches (by comparison, Mobile, Alabama, the city whose rainfall is the highest in the contiguous United States, gets 67), the interior is more accessible via river than over land, and Georgetown lies as much as eight feet below sea level. Only the sea wall and an intricate system of sluice gates and canals, first engineered by the Dutch, then expanded upon and maintained by the British and the Guyanese, have kept the country's coastland arable. "Inhabited and productive British Guiana is an artificial man-made environment brought into existence by outside capital and outside technical skills," wrote Jock Campbell, who for fifteen years served as chairman of Booker Bros., McConnell & Co. By far the largest grower and processor of sugarcane in the colony, Bookers' presence there dated from 1815 to 1976, the year of Guyana's nationalization of sugar.

Sugar was British Guiana's economic mainspring. Workers who made their way out of the cane fields found limited opportunities. Well into the twentieth century, residents of Georgetown adhered to the "carefully structured, stylized constraints of life in a small colonial society," writes Noël Bacchus in *Guyana Farewell*, a memoir of his youth in British Guiana in the 1930s and 1940s. Bacchus's father had worked his way up in the civil service to become the registrar of deeds—the highest type of position to which black Guianese could aspire. (Even by the 1950s, East Indians, more recently arrived in the colony, held civil service posts only on an exceptional basis.) For decades, the civil service, writes Roy Heath, "represented the ambitions of a class, which saw in it a guarantee of material security, a second-best when resources to study medicine, dentistry or law were lacking." As Heath made plans in 1949 to distance himself from Georgetown's "stifling rule of parochial norms" by departing for London,

THE PAST AS PROLOGUE

his aunt "thought me foolish" to leave when "things were getting better in Guyana." At twenty-three Heath found her viewpoint eccentric, but years later he acknowledged that the political ferment and the eradication of malaria spelled positive change for the colony.

Visible change also came to Georgetown. Downtown, the city had undergone a transformation in the wake of a serious fire that occurred in February 1945. It broke out inside the manufactory of Bookers Drug Store, in the capital's central shopping artery, swiftly destroying more than twenty wooden buildings, which Heath describes as "some of the oldest and most attractive" in the city. The streamlined glass-and-stucco structures that replaced the louvred Victorian casualties in the heart of Georgetown seemed to usher in the modern age.

At Queen's College, boys of all religions and races were brought together with academics as their sole bond. Bacchus, who grew up in the capital, describes his first days at Queen's in 1947, when he encountered a number of "country boys" from outlying areas. "All we knew of each other was that most of us had won scholarships in the colony-wide, competitive examinations for admission," he writes. His previous six years of schooling had taken place in a single room, where reading and instruction occurred amid the din of recited lessons. "Something as simple as a separate classroom was a novelty after the open space and clamour of elementary school," he writes. At Queen's, he says, he and the other boys found the facilities and the coaching that enabled them to specialize in the fields of their choice and compete professionally on the world stage. Matriculation was for many a life-altering achievement. Even to acquire a secondary education was a feat, as compulsory education in British Guiana was limited to primary grades; to have the chance of becoming something other than a labourer was a distinct advantage. For one boy (and one girl) per year with a truly distinguished scholastic aptitude, that might take the form of a government-paid scholarship to a university abroad. British Guiana had no university-level facilities.

Even in the 1950s the reputation of Queen's as an "elite" school could carry an ambiguous connotation. Many Guianese criticized its favouring of the humanities over the sciences, a bias that had the double effect of promoting British cultural values and keeping Guianese unqualified for good positions. It was common practice in the colony to hire from abroad (at better salaries) any engineers, chemists, electricians, and mineralogists, and Queen's had not elected to help overturn that tradition to benefit locals. For the three years preceding my father's arrival, the school, lacking a biology master, had offered no biology classes at all, in a foreshadowing of what we found in 1994.

The curriculum taught at Queen's—and at Bishops' High School, its counterpart for girls—markedly favoured the Northern Hemisphere; it was keyed to the syllabuses of the Oxford and Cambridge Board intended for schools in Great Britain and used throughout the empire. "What is a birch, please, Miss?" Mona Williams asked her music mistress at Bishops' in the mid-1950s after learning a lyric in which the word appeared. "The lessons were fabulous and joyful, although they felt completely disconnected from my life," Williams recalls in her memoir, *Bishops*, where she also tells of being taught to cook with imported carrots, potatoes, cocoa, cream, and beef, all too costly for local budgets. The curriculum at Queen's was broadened somewhat in the 1950s when several graduates of the new University College of the West Indies, in Jamaica, were hired to teach history.

Wishing to protect their anxious parents, Howard and Marian omitted from their letters potentially worrisome news: about the escalating unease in Georgetown following the election, for instance, and the detail that my birth was attended not by Marian's physician, who was indisposed owing to illness, but by a midwife. I have appended my parents' later remarks when they are available. What else they may have left out I will never know. I might have wished for more awareness on their part in identifying what the writer (and Queen's alumnus) Frank Birbalsingh has called "the plight of Guyanese in being so deeply conditioned by colonialism as to mistake shadow for substance." But the workings of colonialism were new to them. Instead they arrived imbued with what Marian would describe much later as "naïve optimism," that strong current in midcentury America, which saddled them with any number of misguided expectations.

In the end, though, the letters are less about my parents than they are about the modest world in which the couple found themselves in September 1952. Its distance from their life in the United States then was vast and from our more global consciousness today is practically immeasurable. As Bacchus writes, "The opportunities that we considered special in that small impoverished British colony seem, in retrospect, so limited and inconsequential that it is difficult to conceive how important they were to us, our families and the society." Yet present-day Guyana makes no sense unless it is seen in the context of its past, and there is simply no substitute for a firsthand, on-the-ground account. My parents' letters are a portal to a moment that, however much it may still impinge on Guyana's progress, is no more, the character of its constraints, grievances, and small kindnesses nearly forgotten. Its evanescence is what makes the contents of this book so valuable.

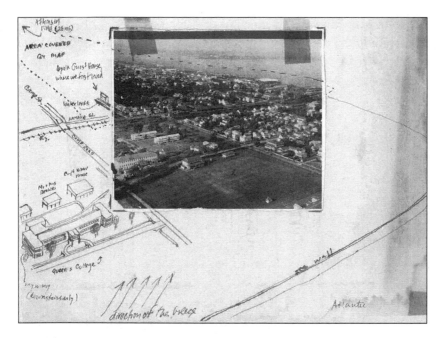

Above: Howard cut out a photograph from a tourist brochure to use as the starting point for a bird's-eye sketch locating the Loyola Guest House (upper left) and Queen's College (lower left). Below: The Biology labs were situated on the ground floor of the east end of the college, shown here from the north.

Chapter 2

1952: LOYOLA GUEST HOUSE
157 WATERLOO STREET

The couple's plans had fallen into place quickly. After receiving his bachelor's degree in biology in 1950, Howard began two years of postgraduate work in botany. He picked up an income by student-teaching at a high school, managing the apartment building on M Street in Seattle where he and Marian lived, and playing string bass in twice-weekly local dance band gigs. By June 1952 he had also earned a degree in education; still, he had a hard time finding a job. Veterans of World War II, having availed themselves of the GI Bill, competed with new graduates for employment, and many of those returning from duty in the Pacific had settled in the Seattle-Tacoma area.

That spring, Marian's sister, Barbara ("Bee"), working as a paralegal in a Los Angeles law firm, came across a flyer announcing twelve teaching positions available through the Fulbright Act, a cultural exchange program approved by Congress in 1946 with the aim of promoting international goodwill. The flyer called for American secondary-school teachers who would accept posts in colonial areas of the United Kingdom: Nigeria, Jamaica, Trinidad, Sierra Leone, Gold Coast, and one other place. "Opportunities in British Guiana: One male biology teacher for Queen's College, Georgetown. One woman teacher of physics and chemistry for Bishops' High School, Georgetown." Bee sent the announcement to Howard. He knew of the colony through his interest in philately; British Guiana was the origin of the "one-cent magenta," the world's most valuable rare stamp; and its current stamps, illustrated, like those of other British colonies, with realistic engravings of typical scenes, were among those whose artistry Howard especially admired.

According to the flyer, the teaching fellowships would be awarded for one year with the option of renewal for a second year. The assignments were to begin that fall. If approved, Howard would receive a salary from Queen's College; in addition, a grant would be paid in the host country's currency by the United States Educational Commission in the United Kingdom (U.S. Ed. Com.), based in London. The grant would cover an initial sum of £300 for incidental expenses incurred during the first year, plus a "maintenance allowance" (to "afford the grantee a professional standard of living in the community") of £300 per year, that allowance to be paid quarterly.

The deadline for applications was March 31, but things seemed to be running late; the position at Queen's College was still open in June. Howard applied, and after the couple met with a screening committee at the University of Washington, he swiftly arranged for the necessary medical exam. Then he waited with mounting anxiety as the weeks went by. After making several inquiries, he finally learned of his acceptance via Western Union on August 5. He and his family would leave Tacoma on the evening of September 8.

During their final weeks in Washington, he and Marian secured a passport and visas, made their travel plans, were inoculated against tetanus and typhoid, sold their car, and stored their furniture and many belongings at the Tacoma home of Tom and Anna Sterne, Marian's parents, where they also bunked after vacating their apartment. They packed linens and household goods in three 300-pound trunks, kitchenware and china in three barrels, and shipped it all by Moore-McCormack Gulf. Marian had three troublesome wisdom teeth extracted. Howard's wallet was stolen, and he had to quickly replace his driver's license. "We are going at such a mad pace," Marian wrote her sister on the Saturday before they left. "Here at Mother's, H. and I trip over some damn thing every time we walk into our bedroom. We won't be able to finish our packing until Monday, so we won't be able to clean it up before then. . . . Yesterday Elizabeth and I had our last shots, and my right arm is sore enough that I can't quite make our beds."

Howard had written to the American consul in British Guiana inquiring about local conditions. "As a rule," reads part of the two-page reply, "one must bear in mind that this is not a 'resort,' but a rather old British colonial city with a touch of the Victorian in dress and manners. Therefore, conservative dress is used. . . . American baby foods are not found in the local shops but similar British foods are available in limited varieties. The milk does not reach the United States sanitary standards, so powdered milk, available here, is usually prepared for babies." The letter went into some detail about clothing. "No ready-made suits are on the local market but material may be bought and made to order by local tailors. Ladies' ready-made dresses have just recently appeared on the local market in limited quantities. . . . From a pure dollars-and-cents standpoint, I would personally recommend that you buy clothing for the entire family in the States." And so the couple added clothes shopping to their list. "After a gruelling day in Seattle," Marian wrote Bee on September 6, "we came home with some gorgeous clothes for Howard—a beige suit (rayon) and a navy tropical worsted, quite dashing. Gray rayon slacks, three pairs of shoes, shirts in the summer weight material, shorts, undershirts, socks, hankies, etc. I have picked up a few more things for myself, too. . . . Naturally, we're almost broke, but elegantly clothed. For Elizabeth, we have purchased many pieces of dress material with trimmings, and three cute knit cotton sweaters." Marian's parents agreed to send things for the baby and other items as needs arose, and the young couple gave them access to a checking account so that they could reimburse themselves for the expense.

The Information Bureau of the Royal Empire Society, based in London, also offered tips. "The cost of living is high, largely because rents are high and many essential foodstuffs and household commodities are imported and subject to customs duties. . . . There is an acute housing shortage. . . . It is very difficult to get well trained servants." Only in hindsight do these remarks suggest the combination of rusticity and formality that Howard and Marian would find in Georgetown.

Aside from the details described in those sheets, and the mean temperatures and average rainfall listed in the *Encyclopedia Britannica*, the couple didn't know much about the place to which they were headed. They had, for example, little grasp of any Guianese antagonism toward the British or the drive for self-rule. They had never witnessed the kind of extreme poverty in which many Guianese lived. Howard and Marian had grown up in solid, comfortable households, protected from real want, despite their fathers' fears during the Depression, and without direct knowledge of racial strife. Equipped with the confidence and energy of youth, they observed and learned, and their letters abound with detail as Howard embarked on his career.

As for Marian, her chief goal, like those of many young women of her era, was to be a wife and mother. She hoped to eventually have six children.

After majoring in English literature, she graduated from Whitman College the spring before she and Howard married. Her secretarial job in a Seattle law office came to an end when Elizabeth was born—and four and a half months later the family was on its way to Georgetown.

September 10, 1952:

We arrived at Atkinson Field, British Guiana, about 3:30 p.m. and waited there close to an hour while our passport and baggage were checked. It was muggy and still: Howard likened the atmosphere to that of a greenhouse. There were few people about except the police officer who examined the passports and the customs official. Both were Negroes, the policeman dressed in khaki shorts and knee socks. As soon as we entered the shed-like building a man handed a note to Howard. This turned out to be a pleasant greeting from Mr. Hilary Beckles, the assistant principal of the college, who said he would await us at our guesthouse. Howard had to stand in line for ages while the poky officer looked at papers, but an official of some sort found a chair for me, and I accepted it gratefully as Elizabeth plus two diaper bags, my purse, and two coats were a load. My brown faille suit was plastered to me, and Elizabeth was damp all over with perspiration.

A taxi driver informed us that our fare into town had been paid, and as soon as our baggage was cleared he loaded it into the trunk of his little English car. Already waiting in the car were an American woman and her three little daughters (ages approximately one, three, and four). With the three of us added in, plus the taxi driver, we were really packed! After passing the swimming pool and buildings erected by the American army during the war,[1] we left the confines of Atkinson Field itself and started the 27-mile drive into Georgetown. The road we turned onto was narrow, made of red earth, and crowded with children and adults, cows and chickens. Our driver drove fast (probably only about 35 m.p.h. but the road was bumpy and the car small), honking his horn often as the people casually parted in front of the vehicle.[2] At one point we heard a scream and thought surely the driver had run over someone; however, it was only a boy calling attention to one of our bags, which had jounced out of the trunk.

By this time the one-year-old in the front seat was crying for her supper. Elizabeth, on Howard's lap, was perfectly quiet and probably too warm and tired to cry.

The houses we passed were horrible: shacks on stilts with newspapers on the walls and goats on the doorsteps, inhabited by the sugarcane workers who were then straggling along the road on their way home from work. Their children appeared ragged, sometimes naked, always dirty. The squalor of these huts was shocking and I think we both waited rather nervously to behold Georgetown proper.

The city grew gradually from ramshackle stores to modern structures, which we could barely glimpse on a nearby street. We reached Loyola Guest House at 5:30 p.m., sticky, tired, and hungry. Mr. Beckles met us at the gate, and his wife inside. Our first reaction was one of complete surprise, for Mr. Beckles is a Barbadian Negro and his wife a Dublin-born Irishwoman. They were both friendly and charming, and we asked some of the questions that had been on our minds. Elizabeth was placed in the little crib that the Beckleses had purchased, and after I washed her a bit she was fed and then much happier. She smiled and gurgled at the Beckleses but went off to sleep shortly. Soon after, the Beckleses left and we were served our dinner. Almost too tired to talk, we went to bed early, paying little attention to the novelty of mosquito nets and beds provided only with bottom sheets, just grateful that at last we were in B.G.

Thursday, September 11, 1952, Loyola Guest House

Dear Mother and Daddy—

Understatement though it is, it still seems impossible that we're here. Our trip was pleasant—very uneventful especially as Elizabeth slept most of the time. She ate little while on the plane but is certainly none the worse for the trip. Everyone was helpful with her. From Seattle to Chicago there were at least twelve children, about six of them babies. Such bedlam for a while! We were held up at Chicago nearly an hour while a fuel pump had to be replaced. None of us ever was the least bit sick.

We were met in New York by the Irwins' friends and had dinner with the two couples and their families. They were awfully nice and I really wished we could have spent more time there. We didn't see Times Square or Forty-second Street, but as we left the city the pilot flew over Manhattan as it was a very clear night. The spectacle was gorgeous—lights on the land as far as could be seen.

The tourist flight [to British Guiana] wasn't bad at all. E., H., and I had three seats with the baby in the center one. We were served meals (paper napkins instead of cloth), and our baggage allowance from N.Y. to B.G. was 66 pounds each.

When we reached this Loyola Guest House (boarding house), we were greeted by Mr. and Mrs. Beckles, two very charming and friendly people who certainly have been most helpful and kind. He is a native of Barbados and an Oxford graduate, and a black man—his wife is Irish and white. Such things are apparently taken with ease here, and it is most easy to understand, for we forgot any surprise after talking with them for a few minutes. He has taught Greek and Latin and won a prize for French at Oxford. They have a lovely sense of humor, and have certainly made our arrival here easier. He had purchased a crib here for Elizabeth, so I guess we will have H.'s mother stop shipment on ours at home and keep this one. E. sleeps a lot and is perfectly precious when awake. Everyone is quite smitten with her.

This place won't do permanently, but for a few days it is fine. Clean—neat but not gaudy. We have a living room, dining room (but eat our meals upstairs), bedroom, and bath; the food is good with the exception of some elusive flavoring that I can't quite take—last evening it was in the mixed vegetables, today in the meat. Otherwise it's fine, and we do enjoy our afternoon tea, which is as black as coffee. H. approves highly!

We toured the Botanical Gardens this evening with the Beckleses—H. nearly went out of his mind.[3] There is a zoo there with some wonderful animals, rather weird and ugly, but heaven knows interesting.

Everyone agrees that yesterday was extremely hot—today is considerably better, with a cool breeze all day. We have discovered that houses here are built on pillars in order to catch the breeze—our flat is in the basement and misses some of the wind. We may move upstairs as soon as possible, however there is only one large bedroom available there.

The college buildings were completed in 1951 and are wonderfully suited to the climate. There is a lovely large assembly and dining hall, now used by the masters who play badminton there Sunday mornings—the government can't afford electricity to run the all-electric kitchen! The government is really short of funds, from all indications. The driveway [on campus] into the five bungalows used as residences by some of the masters was so narrow that even one British-size car had difficulty negotiating the curves—finally the government was talked into widening the bad, sharp curves by about one foot.

We agree that publicity is not fair at all to B.G.—we toured the shops with the Beckleses this morning, and everything is here from Tide to Elizabeth Arden and Pepsi Cola. Also Evenflo bottles, thank the Lord—five of ours were lost yesterday on the Pan Am plane, taken out at San Juan with the empty refrigerator compartments. We have canned milk here produced in Holland that so far seems to agree beautifully with the baby. I'm waiting a few days to begin again on the solids.

Goodness—I just went into the bathroom to rinse out a diaper and met a spider about three inches across on the wall! There was a cute little pink lizard on the ceiling tonight at the Beckleses' but no one paid any attention.

This is very disjointed, but I'm too sleepy to think clearly.

We went to the bank today and opened our account. The manager reassured us about several things—shoes do not grow moldy overnight, and clothes don't rot providing they are turned out in the sun once in a while. After the bank we saw the stores and I see I forgot to continue along that subject. There is wooden and cane furniture available, all sorts of yardage from Japan, ready-made U.S. dresses, car seats for babies, Chanel No. 5, and Australian lamb. We are told inflation has boosted prices to three times those of a few years back, but the meat prices still looked ridiculously low to us. At Bookers, the store that has everything in one of its branches (grocery, drug, hardware, dry goods—all separate, sometimes blocks apart), I saw Libby foods, Cross and Blackwell, Colman mustard, and Black and White Scotch.

The baby is asleep so we shall retire. I'm sure I've left out a dozen vital points, but we shall do better when our typewriter arrives. H.'s school doesn't start till the 22nd, by the way. That may give us time enough to get settled!

Much love to you from each of us,
Marian

Friday, September 12, 1952

Dear Bee—

I'm still not sure I like the psychological aspect of plane travel—it transports you so darned quickly from one world to another, there's no time at all for any transition period! Our trip was fine—smooth flight except for a few bumps over the Rockies. My ears took a beating on landings and take-offs (E.'s, too, I'm afraid), but that was a small discomfort.

We are staying in this guesthouse only temporarily—it is a bit too crude for our tastes, but clean and reasonably bug-free. We have been in the assistant principal's home several times, and by comparison this place is not what we should be in! It reminds me of some of our beach houses—white paint over bare boards, linoleum rug in living room, sparse furniture, quaint plumbing. However, it is fine for now.

Well, it is now 4 p.m. and I have just finished my tea. We had visions of growing fat here on four meals a day, but good Lord—we're practically starving to death! It's all very sensible to eat small meals in this climate, but we aren't quite used to it yet. However, we bought "biscuits" yesterday and Mrs. Beckles gave us fruit today, so I doubt we shall die. The meals are a bit weird—frankly, that is one reason I would like to move. Yesterday for breakfast we each had a cold egg, fried earlier in strong-tasting coconut oil, served on a piece of wilting lettuce!

So far today I have done nothing more exacting than eat, play with Elizabeth, and fix her bottles. I haven't yet written Mother about the bottle situation because it is not ideal, but so far so good. Our water is drinkable so we wash the bottles in the washbasin (running tepid water, neither hot nor cold) and fill them with canned milk and boiled water, which the maid brings us in a thermos (called "flask" here—H. and I both did a double take when asked if we'd brought a flask). We have no refrigeration but trust to the lasting power of the evaporated milk, which we use up within the day. As I said, so far everything is fine and E. is happier than she'd been in quite some time, as her shots were troubling her a bit at home.

H. is at present being introduced to the college's board of governors. Of the three men on the faculty he has met so far, two are colored and one an East Indian. And I think we met the French master and his wife on Wednesday—if that is who they were, I believe they are English.

Prices are ghastly. I paid $4.95 yesterday for a dozen cans of milk and some biscuits, and over $3 for four bottles for Elizabeth. A four-page newspaper is eight cents. H.'s salary of £1,000 from the college really wouldn't be adequate without the £600 from London. I think we'll be able to live quite comfortably on that, but it's awfully hard to say this early. The Beckleses pay their maid, Mabel, $13.50 a month plus board, and say she is unusually honest, clean, etc. The salaries of the clerks are pitiful, and the squalor we saw on the road to town from the airport was horrible. Thatched huts looking ready to collapse momentarily; dirty and half-naked children; thin cattle and dogs—it was really a poor introduction to Georgetown.

By the way, E.'s nightshirt is ideal here and so is my fan. The pink nightgown will be, too, whenever it gets here. I just love it, Bee—so pretty and so practical. It is in one of the four bags that we had sent airfreight—much cheaper than as excess baggage. We didn't decide to do that until the last minute, so I hadn't packed them with that in mind. Result: I've three dresses here, one minus its belt.

According to the Beckleses, entertaining in Georgetown assumes grand proportions, with some parties lasting until 7 a.m. No doubt there is little to do other than to entertain.

Elizabeth is waking up so I shall close. We had fun in New York but still wish we could have seen you!

Much love,

Marian

September 12:

Archie Larthe, the French master at the college, called this morning to invite us for a drive. We were awfully pleased, as our life here in the guesthouse is a little dull. Howard walked to the Chronicle Stationery store for supplies and we spent most of the day writing letters and postcards.

At 3:30 Howard walked up to the college to meet the board of governors. We'd expected something quite impressive, but Howard says he was introduced to each, then someone started talking about a pillar in the college that is rotting away. That was all! One of the board members is Dr. Vincent Roth, who organized the zoo at the Botanical Gardens and is an authority on the interior and all the natural phenomena hereabouts; another (the chairman) is the Episcopal Archbishop of the West Indies.

The Larthes came by about 5, and we drove out along the sea wall and beyond. The sea wall road was choked with cyclists, nannies with their charges, small darting children, and strolling couples. This appears to be the most pleasant time of day: cool, breezy. Dorothy Larthe says the nannies bring children to walk by the sea wall every single day, until the children finally rebel when they're about six. I wouldn't blame them: There's nothing to see except the muddy Atlantic, the muddy beach, and the people. Of course it must be a wonderful spot for a visit among the various nannies.

We then went to the Larthes' home for a drink and met three of their four children. The oldest boy is thirteen and has been at school in England for three years now. Their other three are Jeremy, nine; Stephanie, six; and Timmy, four. They are all little devils; strong, sturdy, and freckled, and since the youngest two were born here, I don't think we need worry about the climate affecting Elizabeth's health.

Dorothy told us of her grim experience with a B.G. hospital when Stephanie was born. She was deserted for four hours in the delivery room; couldn't eat any of the food prepared there, and received little if any attention. In her words, she was "simply shattered." With Timmy, things were better, for she went to a different hospital where the care was excellent, food edible, etc. I think she must be quite a person: She came here from London in 1946, pregnant, with the two oldest boys and without Archie, who was already here. I don't think I could have possibly made it here with Elizabeth and without Howard!

We returned here a little late for dinner, and the proprietress made several uncalled-for suggestions about our keeping Elizabeth out at night. We don't care for the lady, as she seems to be vulgar, crude, and rather unclean. Hope we can move soon. The meals are becoming a trifle monotonous: soup, rice, potatoes, and meat with onions for lunch and the same for dinner, each day. We'll either grow fat from all the starch, or waste away from lack of vitamins.

Saturday morning, September 13, 1952

Dear Mother and Daddy—

Talk about the idle rich: We don't know yet if we're rich or poor, but we sure as hell are idle. It's 9:30 now and H. has gone to town for some necessities. I was planning to go along, but Elizabeth decided to take her morning nap, so this is a splendid time to write.

I shall tell you why I feel idle. Yesterday I got up, showered, ate breakfast, and played with E. until lunchtime. H. had an appointment at the college and then went on some errands with the Beckleses. We ate lunch, I wrote to Bee, fixed E.'s bottles, took a nap, entertained Elizabeth. About 5 p.m. Archie Larthe, the French master, called up and invited us to go for a drive.

Archie and Dorothy Larthe are, according to the Beckleses, rather "fast." However, we found them wonderful company and a bit livelier than the Beckleses, who are fifty-ish (no offense to you all!). The Larthes are both English, Roman Catholic, and in possession of a fine sense of humor. I imagine they're in their thirties. Howard tells me that Archie was in West Africa before the war, and that he married Dorothy after she was widowed with the two oldest boys. These two boys were his brother's children—he married his sister-in-law, in other words.

Howard glanced at the college salary schedule yesterday and found that he will be making more money than anyone else. The £1,000 he gets from the college is their high salary, and with the £600 from London we should be doing all right. We want to get a house, chiefly because in our position here we should have one. They are scarce, but the Sunday *Chronicle* carries a list of available houses and flats. Dorothy told me that a cook isn't needed if you can cook—the maid prepares the vegetables, serves, cleans up, etc. in addition to cleaning. She also recommended we get a "nanny" for Elizabeth who would do all our washing as well, but I think it will be quite some time before we find someone suitable for that. Dorothy said good servants are hard to get—the majority aren't honest, clean, or hardworking. I shall really need to have a house—this climate is not so enervating as to make plain sitting around a pleasure. I'll rot away in a month at this rate! Last night after dinner E. went to sleep, so we couldn't even take a walk. We had one four-page newspaper to read, and after that we were reduced to drinking water and going to the bathroom for entertainment. We really crave our own music and books and magazines—Elizabeth sleeps in the morning and afternoon as well as clear through the night, so I have quite a bit of free time.

H. talked to the physics master here who said our radio could be "rewound" if necessary, whatever that means. Consequently we are quite anxious to have the radio sent as soon as possible, by Christmas, I hope.

Also, when you can, will you please send to *The New Yorker* and *Time* for subscriptions? We forgot to do it, and I don't know quite what to do about paying for them from here. Please reimburse yourself from our Central Bank account. The college address is the one to use. Thank you!

Our airfreight bags are supposed to arrive tomorrow. I'm getting a bit tired of my one pair of shoes and two dresses.

There are some lovely homes here. The two most impressive that we've seen so far belong to a Portuguese who is in one of the department stores, and the other to the local Pepsi Cola man.

Howard doesn't have a uniform to wear at the college. We were quite peeved last night to learn from the Larthes that clothing is available and cheap here. Shirts are $2.98 B.W.I. [British West Indies] money, and Archie had just bought two suits with two pair pants each, English tropical worsted, both for $49.50! We don't blame the American consul [for steering us wrong], however, for he arrived just a few weeks ago—the one who left was a total loss, I gather. That explains the delay in his letter to us.

Later: Now we have had lunch and Elizabeth is napping, although she may eat again in 45 minutes. She looks as if she may have a little prickly heat. She's just a little pinkish on her face and around her neck.

Mr. Beckles stopped in before lunch, and we'll go for a ride with them this afternoon. Howard and Archie priced cars this morning and I imagine we'll get one as soon as our money starts coming in. A new Morris-Minor is about $2300 new ($1200 U.S.) and a 1950 Hillman Minx is $1800 ($1000 U.S.). The bigger cars are more expensive new but depreciate quite rapidly, whereas the little ones have very good resale value because of their low upkeep. There are several nice suburbs, but living in any of them is out of the question without a car. Howard says the garages will accept any down payment and any terms, provided the car is paid for in a year or so.

Mr. Beckles has a few flats [apartments] lined up for us to examine. One in the Tower Hotel at $255 per month he is sure we'd enjoy, but it isn't available until the end of October. Another, at the Woodbine [Hotel], which has good food and service, would be good, with the possible exception of some East Indian music that is played loudly and frequently from a neighboring house. The only way to do here seems to be to move often, each time securing something a bit more desirable until finally you acquire what you want. The Larthes moved five times in a year.

Oh yes—the Beckleses have a picture of Queen Elizabeth in their hall and Lana Turner in their bedroom. We haven't figured that one out yet. He is bringing us some murder mysteries tonight. This, from a Greek and Latin teacher.

Enough for now—I am going to take a nap, why I don't know.

Much love,

Marian

September 13:

There is a lovely girl staying here in the guesthouse, a native of the Rupununi district whose mother is Brazilian. She is quite beautiful, has a pleasant way of speaking, and adores Elizabeth. She is one of thirteen children, and evidently Elizabeth reminds her of her six-month-old sister. She dropped in this morning and we chatted a little. In her home village in the mountains near Brazil everyone has a jeep, she told me, and there are more passable roads in the interior than here. Each village has its own school, but she said it was far better to order clothes and goods from the Georgetown stores than to try to obtain them there. All the meat here in town comes from the Rupununi, where besides raising cattle they grow corn and a few other vegetables. She leaves Tuesday and is anxious to return home to her family.

Sept. 13, 1952

Dear folks—

Last evening we drove out along the shore road with Archie and Dorothy Larthe. The shore is not very inviting as it is entirely composed of brown mud and the water itself is of the same hue. Just outside the city limits along the shore road is the Carib, B.G.'s only nightclub. Archie explained that it is simply an inexpensive place to spend "a nice, wet evening," dancing, drinking, etc.—no cabaret or anything quite so lavish.

Just adjacent to the Carib is "Scandal Lane"—'nuf said!

Among other things, we discussed the matter of quarters with the Larthes. Frankly, we're not satisfied with this arrangement at the Loyola House and we hope to move before school is long under way. It's just a bit too crude. This place would remind you of a summer cottage where you would be happy to "rough it" for a couple of weeks, but not take up permanent residence—unfinished construction all painted a dead white, lights hanging by their cords from the ceiling, linoleum rugs, the barest scattering of furniture, etc.—and for this we are paying $12 per day ($6.40 U.S.) including meals (which are not too hot—literally and figuratively).

At any rate, one of the Sunday papers gives a more or less complete listing of facilities available, and we hope to find something more suitable either this weekend or next.

With Elizabeth (who is ultra-happy) it is something of a strain to live in a boarding house and to meet meal times, etc., although in this regard Mrs. d'Andrade, the proprietress, has been rather flexible but not without a price—free criticism of our methods of child-raising.

Another matter that adds to our displeasure in this place is the damned chickens. The people next door have their house elevated on ten-foot pilings (commonly seen in Georgetown), and beneath they raise chickens. The roosters, which about equal the hens in number, crow for over an hour in the early morning and the hens cluck all day, each going into a mad session when an egg is laid. We wouldn't mind them too much but Elizabeth is usually awakened and frightened by the dawn crowing of the cocks.

As for boiling drinking water, it seems to be a point of habit. Those who have boiled their water for years continue to do so, despite the fact that all pipe-supplied drinking water is treated with chlorine and precipitation inducers that remove the mud. Those of us who have come since the pure water project (here known as a "scheme") has been in effect (and have been inoculated against typhoid) see little reason to boil our water. However, we do boil Elizabeth's water.

We also discussed with Archie the matter of transportation. A car is a definite advantage in this town of numerous questionable districts. Nearly all the Europeans here have them. Larthe has a '39 British car that even today looks new according to style and condition. He bought it two years ago for $1000 ($550 U.S.). Although gas ("petrol") sells for 70 cents (38 cents U.S.) per gallon, most of these cars get 25 to 40 miles per gallon. As a matter of fact, the smaller and more economical they are, the more they cost!

Later: Just back from the stores, where I bought some prickly heat powder for E. and a market basket. The monetary system here is downright complex and it takes a good deal of savvy to get the hang of it. Although the units are nominally dollars and cents, coinage is entirely in British pence, shillings, half crowns, crowns, etc. Yet in a department store all prices are marked in dollars and cents, so the purchaser must make mental equality computations to relate one system to the other. Fortunately, the paper currency is in dollars. Unfortunately, the bills are shorter and wider than American bills, so they don't occupy the length of an American-made wallet but stick out along the top.

According to natives here, B.G. is in the throes of a spiraling inflation in the course of which prices have risen 225 to 250 percent since 1941. Yet most prices, when equated, are no higher and in most cases considerably lower than we were accustomed to [in Tacoma]. Australian beef (not "Argentine rot," as I was told) sells for 45 to 70 cents B.W.I. per pound, local beef around 36 cents B.W.I., all other meat proportionately lower, six tangerines, locally grown, for 1 shilling (24 cents B.W.I., 14 cents U.S.), twelve oranges for 18d (36 cents B.W.I., 20 cents U.S.), lemons six for 10d (20 cents B.W.I., 14 cents U.S.). Fruit is not as plentiful as you might think for it is not grown in the Georgetown area. Demerara County is predominantly sugar producing; Berbice, rice; and Essequibo, fruit (this is referring to the coastal regions of each). Transportation to Georgetown is entirely by water. In consequence, the fruit grown in Essequibo is picked before ripe and matures en route— exactly as in the U.S.

I have been to Stabroek Market twice now, and what a place! It's nothing more than a shed with a clock tower, enclosing scores of stands which have for sale everything from patent medicine to fish poison (some Indians spear fish with poisoned darts). The interesting thing about the place is that whereas most commodities in shops have fixed prices, those in

Stabroek are subject to dickering. Having been prepared by Larthe, I went there this morning to buy the market basket. I asked the price of one that seemed suitable and was told 95 cents, whereupon I countered with an offer of 85 cents. Then I was deluged with a tirade of higher rents, higher cost of help, higher, higher, higher! We settled on 88 cents (about 48 cents U.S.) for one big enough to accommodate four loaves of bread on end.

Yesterday afternoon I appeared by invitation before the board of governors of Queen's College for an introduction. There were three whites, three blacks, two East Indians, and one Portuguese. The men were very pleasant and wished us well here.

It's warm again today (about 88°) but the constant breeze from the ocean, which is just two blocks away, keeps us cool.

Love to all from all of us—

Howard

September 14:

Howard walked out to the Botanical Gardens this morning—it's quite a distance and the morning was awfully warm, but he is beginning to feel a bit confined here in the flat. I am, too—if it weren't for Elizabeth I would be bored to tears. Poor Howard returned in a few hours, dripping. He said he'd gone to the wrong gate at the garden, and upon asking a colored motorcyclist the correct way, was told to "hop on." Most of the people here seem to be very considerate and polite.

While Howard was out, Archie came by to say he'd seen a flat advertised in the paper. He gave me the address and later this afternoon Howard walked up to see it. Thinking the opinion of a longtime resident necessary, he went to the Beckleses for advice. After seeing it, they came by for me. It's a spacious place on the second floor with a long, narrow living room ("gallery"), which has three walls composed entirely of windows and wood louvers. There are two bedrooms, a dining room, kitchen, pantry, and the bathroom setup that seems to be standard here: separate cubicles for toilet and shower, with washbasin right out in the hall (that isn't exactly ideal, I admit). The whole place has just been repainted except the kitchen, but Mrs. Beckles said that as B.G. kitchens go, this one is excellent. The flat is supposedly furnished, but the owner hasn't finished yet, so we can't decide on it until we see what she puts in. If we do take it we'll have to buy our own stove and refrigerator as she refuses to buy them. The woman is asking $100 a month rent, which Mr. Beckles says is reasonable here.

The flat has its own door downstairs, complete with knocker and a rare mailbox. Inside the door is a little hall, cement floored and very rough but ideal for storing trunks and barrels.

Howard is calculating—seeing if we can buy a car, stove, and refrigerator and run a household.

Monday, September 15, 1952

Dearest Parents—

Elizabeth and I are taking advantage of our arduous routine and having a rest. She is wearing just a diaper, her customary costume here. When we're going out I put a little thin dress on her, and at night she sleeps in her nightshirt or a sacque. Otherwise, just the diaper.

I'm going to be reduced to similar garb if our other bags don't appear shortly! At the last word of an hour ago they weren't here in town, so who knows where they are. Probably sitting at the airport.

We think E. is going to have a tooth one of these days. Saturday she lost a bottle of milk right after drinking it, and on the next two she had great trouble sucking. I consulted the oracle, Dr. Spock, and following his advice we cut a larger hole in a nipple and filled her up with pears. Since then she's been very placid but she loves to get one of our fingers in her mouth to chew upon. She is sleeping until 7:30 a.m. when the maid wakes us up for breakfast, has a nap in the morning and afternoon, and goes to sleep about 9 p.m.

Howard is downtown again—I believe he's going to come home with a car. Unless our figuring is way off we'll be able to handle the cost easily. It's a cute car—light gray, with red leather upholstery.

Yesterday we looked at a flat that we hope to get. H. saw the owner this afternoon, and by tomorrow she will have put in the rest of the furniture. What was there yesterday was lovely—all newly refinished—and if the rest measures up, we'll take the flat. She says she can't afford to buy a stove and refrigerator for it, but if we buy them she will eventually buy them from us. If she doesn't, their resale value is excellent (as with the crib), according to the Beckleses. They went with us yesterday to confirm the price, desirability, etc., and thought it *quite* good.

If we do take it, we will have to stay here in this $12-a-day joint until the grant comes through from London, because we don't have enough for the stove and refrigerator down payments and the rent on top of it. When we do move in, we'll buy a pan and skillet, two plates and cups, and manage on next to nothing until our dishes and kitchen things arrive.

I believe I wrote once about the difficulty of finding good servants, "nannies" especially. We are simply delighted: Mrs. Beckles's girl, Mabel (age fifty-ish), took a great fancy to Elizabeth last Thursday when we dropped off E. (sleeping) at the Beckleses' and went downtown. Mabel, who works only from 8 to 11 for the B.'s, would love to come to us for a few hours in the afternoon, do E.'s washing, and take her for a walk. Mabel is everything a maid could be, according to Mrs. B.—and she and Elizabeth really took a shine to each other. Mabel is very black, seems intelligent, and is honest, clean, and industrious. At any rate, that would give me a little free time each day, and I don't want someone to take sole charge of Elizabeth, as I enjoy it too much myself. I would also like to secure a half-day maid to do the cleaning for me—maybe full-time but I don't know what she'd do all day, or me either! We'll see how it works out.

It certainly is a good thing there is no malaria here, or I would have it by now. There are, unfortunately, still mosquitoes and naturally they have discovered me. The bites are infinitely more annoying than the heat. There is a breeze almost all day, which relieves the heat and humidity both, and none of us are particularly uncomfortable.

When our records are packed, can you see that the copper bowl and the glass pieces from our shelves are included, please? I would love to have the Audubon pictures; however, H. says he doesn't believe they'd fit into the barrel. I'd also like the copper chafing dish, the silver pitcher, and the Swedish glass bowl.

Much love to you both,

"Itchy"

I would write more, but we're out of paper.

September 15:

We are getting desperate. Our four suitcases sent by airfreight weren't on yesterday's plane. Until they arrive, Howard has only one pair of slacks and I have two dresses. Everything is pretty dirty and utterly repulsive.

Received two letters from Mother—our first mail. Most welcome!

Howard made a deposit on a car today. It is a new Morris-Minor; naturally it's tiny, and we'd hate to have to go too far in it, the trouble for us being the difficulty of getting in and out without bumping our heads. The salesman took us for a short ride before Howard made the deposit. It rides well and will be delivered tomorrow.

Mrs. Ramsaran, wife of the English master, dropped in with their three-year-old, Susan, to invite us to have tea with them tomorrow. She is very English and seems not to enjoy it here too much. They've only been here four months and she says Susan is still not accustomed to the climate. Mrs. Ramsaran's mother, who is here with them, is also finding the adjustment difficult.

September 16:
Howard bought me a wonderful gift today—a flit gun. The ants, flies, mosquitoes, and roaches around here are more than a bit annoying. Last night there was a three-inch spider on the wall (H. said it was quite harmless); also fireflies, which are new to me, and a few mosquitoes, which have already discovered that I'm here. I feel much more secure with such a weapon close at hand. Especially after finding a hideous two-inch spider inside Elizabeth's netting this morning. That did it.

Our little car was delivered after lunch, and Howard zipped around doing a few errands. I doubt if I shall even attempt to learn to drive here; the roads are awful, and motorists, cyclists, and pedestrians alike behave in a completely unpredictable manner. No one signals, least of all the cyclists, who seem to get a delight from darting right smack in front of a car. Of course the right-hand drive doesn't help as far as we're concerned!

We drove to the Ramsarans' in great style and had a wonderful tea: bread with butter (our first here) and jelly, buttered scones, and a good plain cake. Tea with milk in it, and everyone seemed surprised when we both refused sugar. It was the first truly good food we've had: our proprietress is a marvelously consistent cook and is still giving us tepid eggs for breakfast and soup, potatoes, rice, bread, and meat for lunch and supper.

Mrs. McLaren, the mother-in-law, is very British and quite sweet. Susan is a pretty little girl with the dark skin and hair of her father, who is Trinidadian. He has a master's degree, one of the few at the college.

We left the Ramsarans at 6 to see the furniture Miss Osborn has put into our flat. We were supposed to see it, that is, but unfortunately she still hasn't taken care of it. What is already in place is nice: two Morris-type chairs, a settee, a rocker, and two little square-seated chairs that look strange but aren't uncomfortable. A good-looking buffet and chairs are in the dining room, but no table. It looks empty, and tomorrow I'd like to price wicker furniture, which would fill in the gaps very nicely. There is a little nook off the living room that has a higher ceiling than the rest of the flat and wonderful windows—but no furniture. People here put a coat of paint on the wicker to make it last better, and it looks fine.

All the windows in the living room open out, casement style, with glass panes and wooden louvers alternating in every other sash. Even with all windows closed it's quite cool, and I don't think we'll have to worry about ventilation there. Across the street and to the left are the Georgetown Militia barracks and parade ground. Their excellent band marches there several times a week, playing loudly. Directly across the street is the Princess Elizabeth Red Cross Convalescent Home for Children. And in front of our building there is a cement sidewalk, a rare wonder here, which adds greatly to the appearance of the street and will make life simpler in the wet season.

The college is just across the parade ground—a five-minute walk, so we will be conveniently located for Howard.

Mavis, the maid here at the guesthouse, is very excited about our car. Usually quite silent, she lit up beautifully this afternoon, said what a pretty car it is and could she please sometime have a little ride in it!

September 17:

We started early this morning—went downtown at 8:30 to buy shampoo (Palmolive, made in Australia, 90 cents), shoe polish, and insect repellent. I have a dozen mosquito and sand fly bites on each leg and am going crazy with them. Howard has one bite, Elizabeth none. Also bought a white plastic dish for Elizabeth's cereal and a cute pink plastic cup. Until now she's been eating cereal out of the previous night's fruit can, and I'm sick of it. All these things we purchased at Bookers, the fabulous group of stores that manage to sell everything including cars, groceries, clothes, and hardware. At slightly higher prices, we are finding.

At Wm. Fogarty's, across the street, we discussed furniture with a perspiring little man who showed us sets of wicker for $60, $90, and $120. The $60 set would do us beautifully, I'm sure. It consists of two chairs, a settee, and a small round table. Not exactly the latest in style, but comfortable and sturdy. The same nice man showed us some lovely American-made drapery fabric at $2.37 and up per yard. I still don't know what to do about curtains in our living room.

About this time I noticed that Elizabeth was asleep on my shoulder, so we started home.

After tea, we drove along the East Coast Road a ways toward New Amsterdam. The road is none too good. Part of it consists of lumpy pavement, part of red baked earth, and part of two cement strips poured down onto the red dirt. People drive like demons although the speed limit in the country is 30 m.p.h. The drivers seem to lack sense completely—to see them you'd think there wasn't a soul on the road. Usually, besides other cars, hazards include bicycle riders, motorcyclists (both crazy), pedestrians, goats, cows, sheep, chickens, burro-drawn vehicles, and men and women carrying huge loads on their heads. All of them seem awfully nonchalant about the passing cars—they step casually out of the way as if the oncoming car really weren't there. We continually ran off into the dirt to avoid hitting anyone.

Every few miles we passed a cluster of tiny weather-beaten houses in which we assume the estate workers live. The buildings were unpainted but looked in better condition than those on the road in from Atkinson Field.

The land is perfectly flat, with water-filled drainage ditches everywhere reflecting the sky. All the colors seem extraordinarily brilliant: the green of the trees and rice fields, the blue sky, and the red roads. Archie says the red dust has a bad corrosive effect on metal, but it adds greatly to the beauty.

We turned around after we'd gone what seemed to be quite a distance. Howard laughed and said we'd gone thirteen miles.

Thursday, September 18, 1952, 9:15 a.m.

Hi, dears!

This is just a note to tuck in with Howard's letter. We just came back from town, where Elizabeth fell fast asleep on my shoulder. Bless her heart, she really counts on her morning nap.

I guess the flat we've mentioned is ours. The furniture that the owner has put in it is very nice but sparse, so we priced wicker furniture this morning. We would also need a big old table and chair for H. to work at, perhaps a chest for E.'s clothes, and a rug or two. We still feel awfully funny about not being able to save money, and as soon as the grant comes through we're going to find out how much it costs to get home by boat (or plane: the most expensive, anyway) and add *that* to the amount we can take out, and keep that much inviolate. And spend the rest, I guess!

Yesterday we had tea with the Ramsarans, who told us tales of the cockroaches eating their clothes, especially silk or rayon as in suit linings. I fear for my beige suit. They say roach powder helps tremendously, though.

I was tickled to get two letters from Mother yesterday. Please don't worry about us! Of course we were tired when we left, but we've done nothing the least bit strenuous since our arrival. Granted our food here isn't the best, but as soon as we're in our own place we will eat very well.

Elizabeth loves that little rattle I bought. Sometimes in her crib she starts to fuss, and then bats the rattle as if working off all her frustrations. She plays with all her toys quite a bit now, and handles them better all the time.

Do write often—it's grand to hear from you.

Lovingly,

Marian

Sept. 18, 1952

Dear Tom and Anna,

We're writing to our respective in-laws this time as we thought a change of aspect would prove interesting.

Although we're with her constantly, Elizabeth seems to have metamorphosed before our eyes. She really enjoys her toys now and is content to spend a good deal of time with them, otherwise unattended. And, of course, she smiles and laughs even more freely. In the last few days she has required only four daily feedings—without waking up in the middle of the night for the fifth.

She has indeed caught the fancy of most everyone who has seen her, this, at times, not entirely to our pleasure. Mrs. d'Andrade, the proprietress of our present quarters, seems hard put to keep her hands off E.; we encourage distance here as Mrs. d'A. is not the cleanest soul in the world. We're developing a sort of "technique of recovery" when E. or we do not approve of prospective admirers.

Everyone here seems quite amazed with our, E.'s in particular, rapid adjustment to B.G. Apparently age is the qualifying factor (this deduction based on limited observation, you understand) for we noted in a visit with the Ramsarans yesterday that Mrs. McLaren, Mrs. Ramsaran's mother, has found it very difficult to cope with conditions here. Elizabeth, unaware, probably experiences a uniformly warm temperature that seems much to her liking!

We are startled by the lack of spirit of adventure shown here, particularly among the British and other importees. As yet we've met no one who has been to Kaieteur Falls, the stellar scenic attraction. Everyone *wants* to go, but no one progresses beyond that point of desire.[4]

Insects and their relatives have become our arch foes. This morning a spider of no mean size was found inside E.'s net enjoying a cricket that it had captured, Lord knows where. Spiders here (excepting the tarantula) are reputed to be harmless, but they never seem to embody any sort of aesthetic quality. Incidentally, they're not the web-spinning sort seen in temperate climes, but rather nocturnal hunters that stalk their prey. Marian has been rather uncomfortable from time to time with the bites of little sand flies. We purchased some insect repellent this morning in town and hope that will do the trick.

As Marian has noted in her enclosure, we have all but secured another flat—all I need do is sign the contract tomorrow. It's very spacious and nearly all of the outside wall area is made up of windows or louvers. It is rather general here that none of the inside walls of a residence meet the ceiling or the floor. Instead, there is usually a gap of eight inches or so to promote ventilation.

School starts Monday and it seems that much of the course ("form," as they call it here) work organization is left up to me as there is but one textbook for the four different levels that I'll be handling. This poses something of a problem as I'm not any too familiar with the local material as yet!

Incidentally, if this English form system is as puzzling to you as it was to me, it compares to our system in the following way:

English	Ages	American	Exam
Form I	10–11	5th Grade	School exam
Form II	11–12	6th Grade	School exam
Form III	12–13	7th Grade	School exam
Form IV-A	13–14	1st yr jr. high or 8th Grade	School exam
Form IV-B	14–15	2nd yr jr. high or Freshman	Oxford exam (prepared and corrected in England)
Form V	15–16	Sophomore	School exam
Form VI-A	16–17	Junior	London U. exam
Form VI-B	17–18	Senior	London U. exam

If, at the close of the Form IV-B term, a student satisfactorily passes the Oxford exams in the required subjects (English, Classics—only Latin here, French, Geography, Math, Biology, Physics, Chemistry, and P.E.) he is then eligible to take the matriculation exams at the university of his choice in England (or Canada or Australia). If, however, he chooses to make his preparatory work more substantial he may take two more years of study (often repeating courses in which he got low scores) and then take the London U. exams, which, if satisfactorily passed, permit him to enter the university of his choice without taking a matriculation exam.

There is a movement afoot now that would certify a student on a subject level rather than a general manner, as has been done for years. That is, for each course passed, a certificate would be received. Under the old system, a minimum number of subjects had to be passed for a general certification. There is much opposition to the new method.

As we indicated before, we are rather resplendent in the independence afforded by the possession of our new Morris-Minor car. It's an awfully tiny thing but everyone has agreed it's the best buy in the small-car field. And best of all—40 miles to the gallon.

Our bags did not arrive on Sunday's plane and we're getting mighty tired of the same old clothes. We're sending a prayer aloft that they'll be on today's flight. We're told that the only way to get service is to hammer away at the clerks until we've made such a nuisance of ourselves that they'll act to be rid of us. Or, we should go to the top and work from there. Mrs. Ramsaran said their trunks were here three weeks before they were so notified. Three more weeks and we'll be reduced to loincloths!

Let us hear from you often—Washington is still home to us.

With love,

Howard

September 18:

Yesterday's plane arrived at 5 a.m. today and our luggage was on it. The suitcases themselves took a beating, but nothing was broken. What a relief to have clean clothes.

Howard registered today at the American consulate. By funny coincidence the consul is from Kent, Washington [some fifteen miles from Tacoma]. He is a youngish man with a wife and a two-year-old daughter who is suffering some with the heat. He sounds like a rather indiscreet person: told Howard he doesn't like it here, suspects Communism in the college, etc. He gave Howard a few tips about the place, somewhat questionable since he's only been here three months himself. Howard was asked to report any Communism that he sees.

After tea we showered and put on clean clothes. Since we felt all dressed up, we decided to drive out to the Botanical Gardens. The weekly band concert was on, but we skirted it and drove along other paths. Saw some more of the lovely water lilies and the different types of trees, so new to both of us. Howard is trying his best to find a botanical manual for this area, with no luck so far.

We had our first rain this evening after dinner. It poured furiously for about fifteen minutes and then stopped completely, leaving the air fresh and cool. Smelled awfully good. I have yet to figure out what happened to the people in the street when the rain began. They seemed to disappear, and then were visible again the second the rain stopped.

Friday, September 19, 1952, 9 a.m.

Dear Mother and Daddy—

We have been up since about 6:15, Elizabeth's hour to wake up. It is lovely here between 6 and 7 a.m., and then it gets quite warm before the breeze comes up at about 10. At the moment I'm sitting in the sun trying to dry my hair—foolish me.

Do you remember once, Mother, telling me I might be lonely here? I know I would be, especially here at the guesthouse with so little to do, if it weren't for Elizabeth. She requires a third of the attention she needed in Tacoma, but when she's awake she's such fun to watch, play with, and talk to. She just fell asleep with the pacifier, after a very little quiet fussing—I didn't hold her at all. In the mornings now she is so good and content to play by herself—in the afternoon she takes a nap (yesterday from 12:30 to 3:00) and then plays a little, growing fussy only as she gets tired. She still wants her daddy to put her to sleep at night, but that is the only time of the day she cries hard or frantically anymore.

Elizabeth's prickly heat is almost gone. I powder her a dozen times a day, so it really doesn't have a chance. Since we've been here we've seen so many little children with rickets—it has impressed me greatly, and E. receives her vitamins daily.

By the way, Father, if our maid (when we get one) steals any silver, etc., as we are told they do (unless you get a rare exception), can we collect? This is a question important to my peace of mind! The buffet in the flat we've almost rented has drawers and side cupboards that lock, ideal for keeping the silver—but it still would be an easy matter to take something. I know

I'm not going to like this vigilance business. I guess we'll wait until we hear of some good maid who is available, and then try her.

I'm afraid I never did tell you of my experience with the laundress here. Last Saturday she asked me how I wished to pay her, by the day or by the week, and also how much. Naturally I had no idea at all what I should give her, but I said I thought by the day might be better since we didn't know how long we'd be here. She suggested I pay her $1.50 a day, which even in my great ignorance seemed a bit steep, so I stalled her off. That evening we consulted the Beckleses, who agreed that $3 a week would be correct. The funny thing was that she didn't complain at all when I told her the bad news—of course I did say that we had someone else lined up if $3 wasn't enough. The people here are desperate for work, and I'd feel awfully sorry for them if I didn't know how quick they are to take an advantage. We have been told to tell Mabel that for the amount we pay her ($13 per month, I guess) of course she will stay with Elizabeth any night we want to go out.

Speaking of going out, yesterday a well-dressed black gentleman (one of the residents here) came to the door and said he'd like to give us a pass to the Globe movie theater to see Humphrey Bogart in *Deadline–USA*. He said he owns the place (he and his brother own Globe theaters throughout the West Indies) and he thought we must be lonely here. I thought it awfully nice of him. I also chatted after dinner with a young missionary, American, who was returning to Brazil to his wife and three daughters. He has a six-month-old baby, and I guess seeing Elizabeth made him just that much more anxious to get back to her.

Howard and I have been eating lunch and dinner upstairs in shifts. It's just too warm to hold Elizabeth comfortably, and too often she's asleep, hungry, or otherwise unwilling to be held. Our breakfast and tea are served downstairs here in our flat.

Yesterday Howard called on the American consul. He gave H. a partial list of the duty exacted on things sent here: cigarettes, $4.20 per pound; confections, 60 percent; used clothing not exceeding $25, 4 percent; toiletries, 40 percent; medicines, 33 1/3 percent; and leather goods, 10 percent. We've heard that books are duty-free but haven't verified that yet. If they aren't, I think we should give up the idea of sending things back and forth. We still don't know what you'd have to pay for things we send—we shall try to find out soon. Just think—maybe we'll come home laden with two years' worth of Christmas and birthday presents!

The mosquito repellent worked quite well, and I have very few new bites, praise be. Such a nuisance.

Howard has gone to a masters' meeting at the college and should be back fairly soon. Schooling here is looked upon with great respect, and the majority of those who pass the entrance exams and can afford the tuition are seriously interested in their education. That in itself will be a treat for Howard, teaching students who want to learn.

I guess we will do without the Bernina [china] and the good crystal [wedding gifts]. I shall miss it, but from what we've seen so far, we needn't worry about "appearances" or "competition" among our friends and associates. Their furnishings are very simple—nothing lavish. Of course, they all make such small salaries and are expected to go to England on their leaves every three years. We will be so glad to see the brown-and-white dishes and to use our own linens again!

I'm hoping Howard will bring mail from you when he returns. We get batches of mail twice a week, after the plane comes in.

I don't know if you'll believe us, but we really aren't uncomfortably warm except for a few hours a day. Of course I've scarcely been out at all during the warm part of the day. Howard gets damp when he's running around, but he doesn't mind. And Elizabeth is happy as can be.

Much love to each,

Marian

Sept. 20, 1952

Dear folks,

Yesterday I received my teaching schedule for the fall term and although it's fuller than I had expected, I have no kick for no extracurricular activities have been added. This is a summary:

Nature Study II (ages 11–12) is a very general treatment of such things as insects, leaves, flowers, mammals, and birds.

Gardening III (ages 12–13) grew out of the war (as in the States) but is still maintained. Mostly practical work: getting the most from a selection of vegetables in a limited plot.

Biology IV-A (ages 13–14) marks the beginning of the study of the more theoretical concepts of the subject.

Botany IV-B (ages 14–15) limits the study to plant life, delving deeply into complexities.

Biology V (ages 15–16) corresponds to the type of work given in the freshman course in American colleges.

Biology VI (ages 16–17) is non-course work in category, more or less of an independent study program. I have none scheduled as yet.

It seems awfully strange to not even have a hint of fall in the air. It rained hard this afternoon—a thunderstorm. The rain falls in huge warm drops and in such volume that visibility is greatly restricted. The sky here seems to never really clear itself of clouds, but the clouds are the harmless, scattered white type that do little more than intermittently obscure the sun. When a rain does come up, the producing clouds simply appear—they don't seem to blow in. As it has been explained to us, the failure of the trade winds is what brings on showers this time of year. Ordinarily they carry away the warm, moist updrafts, but failure of these trades causes the warm, moist air to collect, condense, and then precipitate.

Our flat is nearly ready for occupancy. We decided to paint part of the kitchen. Previously, the upper half (five feet and upwards) was white and the lower half was in various shades of green (pea green, blue green, etc.—the result of several partial paintings, each from a different can). We left the upper part as is but painted the lower a pale yellow, dividing the two with a brown bar-line. The effect is light and pleasing, and, what's most important, clean! We won't be able to move in until the $1,800 grant fund is filed in the local Barclays Bank, part of this money to be used in buying a stove and a refrigerator (or "fridge," as they say here). We hope this comes about next week.

This evening we're off to see our first movie ("cinema") in Georgetown. Incidentally, the theater owner, who gave us the complimentary tickets, is from Afghanistan. B.G. is quite a melting pot!

Love to you all,

Howard

Sunday, September 21, 1952, 11:15 a.m.

Dear Mother and Daddy—

Last Sunday the radio blared out music all day long. Today: silence. Very disappointing! We will be tickled pink to have our radio here.

Howard just returned from the Botanical Gardens, where he says it was too hot to stay long: no breeze. I am sitting on my bed with Elizabeth, H. is sprawled on his. At the moment, E. is staring at Howard with great interest, stretching and kicking. At Bookers Drug Store there is a scale where everyone weighs babies. I shall weigh Elizabeth each month and keep you all posted. I'm sure she's gained. Yesterday I fed her (almost a complete can of pears, which she just gobbled down) at 5 p.m., and she was asleep by 7. H. and I went to our free movie, and Mabel came to babysit. We got home at 11 and Elizabeth was awake; had been for just a few minutes, Mabel said. Probably if we'd been home to put the pacifier back in her mouth she'd have slept clear through! I fed her, and she fell asleep by herself very shortly.

We enjoyed the movie—and the "newsreel" of the Democratic convention, Olympic Games, and Ascot races. Almost 30 minutes were devoted to previews. The theater is large, airy, and quite attractive. There are no curtains or draperies at all, and the auditorium is faced with beaverboard. The acoustics were excellent, as was the screen, which is supposedly very new, as it is lighted from behind. No popcorn, candy bars, or pop in sight—smoking permitted.

Yesterday we had a rip-roaring thundershower that caused six houses up in a creek valley to tumble down. The rest of the day was quite cool.

After lunch we went up to our flat to paint the kitchen. We wanted the walls from midway down to be a light yellow, with a brown stripe between that and the white upper walls and ceiling. The yellow turned out to be nearly orange, and even adding the white we had we couldn't tone it down. As the stores close at noon on Saturdays, we were stuck. However, Howard went ahead and painted the stripe and door trim brown, and I painted the scummy cupboards "golden yellow." I think that sounds much better than "almost orange"! It should look nice (clean, at least) once we've covered the hideous green with pale yellow. There are two open shelves above a nice stainless-steel-covered cupboard, and I guess I shall keep canned goods out in the open, and bowls and pans in the cupboard. There is another cabinet under the sink for dishpan, soap, etc., and a third that I haven't investigated. All are covered with stainless steel, which is good. There are no drawers in the kitchen, so what I'll do with kitchen silver is still a mystery to me. There is a portable cupboard in the pantry, with screen panels, for storing things that the varmints might enjoy, such as flour, sugar, bread, etc. As American kitchens go, it isn't too convenient (refrigerator is also in pantry), but we're told that according to B.G. standards it's darned good. Once it's painted I shall enjoy working in it. Good ventilation. Howard found a cockroach in a bureau drawer, so we placed a trap for it. We've decided to switch bedrooms with Elizabeth as only one has electrical outlets, and the wardrobe and dresser in it are in a little better shape. Also, in the room we were going to have, there is a window outside of which runs the stairway to the third-floor flat. The panes are frosted, but still, I think we'll enjoy our privacy and E. may enjoy the greater fresh air.

There was a great to-do this morning concerning our toilet. We have been using diaper liners for Elizabeth, and naturally we flush them away. It seemed all right since the pipe going outside was quite large. Anyway, things got a bit stuck, and it developed that the pipe outside, which should be about five inches in diameter, has been bent so that it's scarcely one and a half inches wide! Mrs. d'Andrade was in quite a rage, and we now have a wastebasket for the first time since our arrival. The maid will take our diaper liners, Kleenex, etc. each evening and "dump them in the big ditch." I don't really know what she meant by that. Howard and I are wondering now if all garbage is just dumped. Sounds impossible—too good a breeding place for mosquitoes, I should think.

I had a brilliant idea while eating my solitary dinner. If you can't send us any other gifts, how about subscriptions to a few more magazines? I have seen the international edition of *Life*, which has good world coverage in it. Reading material is scarce here. H. has been bringing me mysteries from the public library, but only one fiction book is allowed out at a time and the supply is quite limited.

Mother—once a week or so would you send me a few rubber bands? I need them for my hair and we don't seem to see them here. Parcels are wrapped in cheap paper and string—I have just realized the great amount of money it must cost to supply customers with paper sacks at home. Here everyone carries a basket to market because many things (fruit, for instance) just aren't wrapped at all.

We think you'll enjoy the enclosed newspaper [missing]. You see—it really isn't too primitive here!

Must fix E.'s bottles. She's sleeping again!

Much love and a hug to each of you—

Marian

You should probably start to use our new address: 124 Parade Street, Georgetown.

September 22:

First day of school. This is Howard's account of the proceedings: Everyone assembled in the large hall, where there weren't enough chairs for all the boys. The masters sat on the platform in a semicircle behind Mr. Beckles, who stood at the rostrum. Mr. Beckles wore his academic gown, as did others who possessed them. Everyone rose, sang two verses of a hymn unknown to Howard, the school song (three verses in Latin), then "God Save the Queen." There was a prayer, followed by announcements and introduction of the faculty. Mr. Beckles preached to the boys on what he expects of them. Then the last two verses of the hymn, the school song, and "God Save the Queen." That was it!

Before lunch, Howard bought some more paint, and we went to the flat as soon as we had eaten. The orange shelves were a bit too gaudy, so I went over them again with the chaste yellow while Howard started on the walls. We hate to spend so much money on paint but we may have to put on a second coat since the blue-green was mighty dirty.

Elizabeth was no help. She was fussy all day today, didn't nap more than an hour altogether, and cried a lot before going to sleep this evening. I can feel her tooth just under the gum: it should be through before long.

Sept. 22, 1952

Dear folks—

It was good to receive letters from both of you, yours on Friday last, Mother, and yours today, Dad.

To answer the questions in your note, Dad: Mr. Beckles is the deputy headmaster of Queen's College. Captain Nobbs, the headmaster referred to in the prospectus I received while still in Tacoma, has retired, effective last July, and is now on a trip to England. According to tradition in the British Colonial Service, Mr. Beckles, in his subordinate position, is not qualified to assume the headmastership left vacant by Captain Nobbs's retirement. The staff and board of governors of Queen's would like to see Mr. Beckles the headmaster, but it is expected that someone will transfer from another colonial school and assume the vacancy. In other words (and it does seem strange), in order for one to better himself in the Colonial Service, he must transfer to another area when the opportunity presents itself.

Yes, the faculty of Queen's College is predominantly not white. In fact, most of the racial categories present in the colony are represented: three of us are white; several are Barbadian blacks; three or four are East Indians (or "colored") but Christian; one is Portuguese; one is Chinese; and two or three are of Carib-Arawak (native Indian) extraction. I'm by far the junior member, most of the men being 35-ish or older—no resentment whatever, despite this. There is a little rather passive criticism of America, which is to be expected, but most of the faculty intelligently recognize the expected force of geographical propinquity to be shown—even in the newspapers, American news is at least on a par (as regards space devoted) with that from the U.K. Most movies shown here are American and at night, radio reception from Gulf cities is fairly good. Despite heavy duties, many American-made goods are available (Frigidaires, Lifebuoy soap, Heinz foods, etc.). Others bear American labels but close examination shows them to have been made somewhere in the British Commonwealth (Nestlé products from Wales, various American cars with right-hand drive from England, etc.).

There seems to be no innate enmity between blacks and whites whatever. Mixed marriages are quite common, mixed social groups are nearly legion, and black and white children play together in perfect harmony. At no time do children become aware of a racial barrier, and although it may seem a bit difficult to comprehend, it is truly a joy to live under such conditions of social harmony. We will be moving into a new flat within a week and below will be living a black family, above us a rather reputable East Indian couple.[5] We have so little awareness of race differences that we don't even think about people as belonging to one race or another. Of course, there are slum areas, regions of unrest, and under such conditions any distinction may be sought to promote some end, be it justifiable or not. Most of those in such areas are East Indians, and they live in utter squalor, receiving wages of a bare few pence per day's labor.

Economically, Georgetown is different from anything we've experienced in that there exists a tremendous range of income. The workers mentioned above may earn one shilling (24 cents B.G.) a day and I earn for the same period about $21 B.G.—I earn eighty-five times as much as the peon, and my salary by no means approaches the zenith.[6] Slums and apparently rotten luxury are inevitable with such a range. Elephantiasis is fairly common here, but most of those who contract it can't afford the cure. Rickets is a common deficiency disease solely because many cannot afford to buy the local fruit (sold for very little). Dental troubles are so prevalent that many make no attempt at dental maintenance and accept dentures as the inevitable termination of a score or more years of embarrassment and discomfort. All this because the rank and file cannot afford dental maintenance—they find the dentures cost less to keep up.

As regards the crib, Mr. Beckles's "drawing one out" referred to his purchase. As soon as the grant money appears (and, Lord knows, we need it!) we'll reimburse him. We had hoped you might stop the shipment of our crib from Seattle, but if not, no harm done. Our apartment-to-be is plenty large enough to accommodate it.

We were sorry to read of the Nixon problem.[7] I'd be anxious to get your off-the-cuff opinion.

We wanted to take some snaps yesterday, but, as luck would have it, clouds prevailed all day—and it rained most of today. This is the dry season! I wonder what the wet season is like.

Dinner is ready, so—

Love to all,

Howard

September 23:

All sorts of things happened today. First, I found a small bat on the wall in the living room when I was painting this afternoon. Howard left me at the flat on his way to school after lunch, and I painted happily for three hours. Having at last come to my senses I gave Elizabeth aspirin all day and she has been happy as a lamb. Bless her heart, she took several long naps and feels so much better that I feel terrible for not having thought of it sooner.

Second, we came home, and while Howard dusted off the car I showered. As I was combing my hair in the bedroom, the inevitable happened and Elizabeth fell off the bed. She yowled mightily for about three minutes, but recovered quickly and grinned at Howard who came dashing in to investigate the racket. Poor, dear Elizabeth—from now on we won't leave her alone on our beds.

The third thing happened after dinner. Howard was writing out some notes for a class and I was reading a murder mystery when I felt something splash on my forehead. There was a drip, drip, drip from the ceiling that was landing on a shelf right behind my chair. Howard swore mildly and went upstairs to investigate. It seems that one of the two house cats uses the doormat upstairs instead of a proper sandbox, and the doormat is placed right above the location of our drip! It was almost too much. We can't leave this place soon enough.

We're still waiting for Howard's grant to come through from London. Until it does we are stuck here, and hard put to pay our rent, too.

September 24:

Elizabeth is developing a bad habit of growing restless between 4 and 6 a.m. and rolling over enough to get all squeezed against the side of the crib. If she bangs and kicks enough, she wakes up—so I jump out of bed a few times and roll her back. It's a good thing we've been going to bed before 10 each night.

I went back to the flat after lunch and finished applying the first coat of paint. A second will be necessary, but our kitchen will be simply beautiful after that. The bat has left us, thank heavens. When we were there yesterday there was a three-inch-long dead cockroach on the kitchen floor. We didn't bother to sweep it up because we don't want to sweep until the paint is dry. Today the roach, carried by hundreds of tiny ants, was in the pantry, still being moved when we arrived. Thanks to the trusty flit gun, we wiped them all out.

Howard went back to the college after dinner tonight, trying to get his supply room into order. Apparently, when the new school was opened a year ago, things were brought over from the old building and just dumped. There are all sorts of surprises in connection with the school: Howard has three classes of eleven-year-olds, textbooks for only the oldest boys, no complete microscopes, and no slides. The boys are so polite it makes Howard uncomfortable. Each time one rises to speak he begins with "Please, Sir," and all the boys rise whenever a master enters the room. They also tip their hats to masters when they meet them outside.

At dinner we talked to the man who generally sits at our table, a Trinidadian who was born here. We don't know what his business is, but he has just purchased two wrecked cars to salvage them. He gave us a few warnings about night driving. Many of the donkey-pulled carts carry long timbers, with no lanterns or flags to mark them. Other wagons are left right in the road if something breaks down—again, without benefit of signal or warning. I guess we shall do our driving in the daylight, for a while at least.

Thursday, September 25, 1952

Dear Parents—

We got the letter you wrote Saturday, Mother, and were awfully pleased that you suggested a loan for the down payments in order to move sooner from This Place. Howard went right downtown after school and sent a cable—only we asked his parents for a loan instead of you because we didn't know where to reach you. According to your itinerary, you should have been between Salt Lake City and Yakima, but in a previous letter you mentioned going back to Boise. We decided that prompt action would be best as we have left just enough money to cover our bill here if we leave on Sunday ($12 a day adds up far too quickly), and we need some cash for rent come the 1st, etc. etc. Can't understand why the damned grant hasn't come through, unless the British government is just as pokey about such things as ours is. We should receive a reply [to the cable] tomorrow and we hope to move in Saturday with stove and refrigerator.

We have been giving Elizabeth aspirin now for several days, as it seems to help her sore gums. How long does it take to get all of one's teeth? Can we keep on giving her aspirin for months? At least she's happy. Her prickly heat comes and goes and never seems to bother her. She's changed so in the few days we've been here—I think she'll be an early creeper. We ran out of the fruits I brought along, and since the Nestlé baby foods cost 26 cents per can, we've been giving her (Heinz—made in England) carrots, beets, and beans (12 cents) the last three nights. She doesn't lap them up like she does the pears, but she eats them very willingly. Cereal is still a bore, not that I blame her. The little jackets you made for her fit her beautifully now. *Vogue* must think newly born infants are mighty robust!

Mabel is all signed up to come as soon as we move. Last weekend when she sat with Elizabeth, she arrived all dressed up and looking very nice in a yellow dress with big white polka dots, a white straw hat, and black shoes. When we got home, her shoes were off and she'd put on a clean white apron. She's tiny—Panamanian, she told H. Awfully nice.

Howard has picked up a drippy head cold. Luckily, I had Mentholatum, Sucrets (the ants were in them a little), and some old cold pills. Elizabeth and I are being exclusive. H. sounds miserable but says he doesn't feel too grim.

I'm going to love our kitchen in the flat. We will paint the baseboards the same brown as the mid-wall stripe, and touch up the windowsills with white. The stainless-steel counter tops are a filthy mess, but with cleanser, steel wool, and some hard rubbing they'll be fine. No linoleum on the floor—just old bare boards!

This morning at 3 while feeding Elizabeth I watched a two-inch cockroach meander on the bathroom wall and disappear into the shower. I must read "Archie and Mehitabel" again with my new understanding of the little monsters. After a few more weeks here, nothing will faze me.

I have plowed through an Ellery Queen, a Peter Wimsey, a Malone-Justus, and several other assorted mysteries in the last week. Howard says the public library is almost exhausted of such already—maybe I shall have to turn to more edifying literature.

We have yet to purchase a bottle of rum or anything else alcoholic. I guess we'll really celebrate when we acquire our refrigerator. Please forget the unusual seasoning I mentioned earlier—we've since decided the food was merely spoiled! The laundress gave me a long sad story the other day of how Mrs. d'Andrade keeps all the table scraps and tries to give them to unsuspecting boarders. We believe it—just this morning I got a piece of toast that looked slightly eaten around the edge. But Mrs. d'Andrade loves onions. We get onions as often as the rice, potatoes, and bread. Onions in our meat, on our meat, on our fish, in our rice—and once in our scrambled eggs. Lovely things, onions, at 7 a.m.

Thanks again for your offer [of a loan]. If the grant doesn't come through soon, we'll send you a cable!

Much love,

Marian

1952 Sept 25, pm 8

Western Union [Mr. and Mrs. H. S. Irwin, Sr.]
> Awaiting grant funds low please send dlrs 300
> Howard

Sept. 25, 1952

Dear folks,

I hope you weren't too shocked with our request for a quick loan, but things are getting a bit desperate here finance-wise. At this point we have just enough to pay our debt to Mrs. d'Andrade. We would like to move to our flat as soon as possible, for it is silly to maintain two places, but until we can purchase a stove and refrigerator we must remain here at $12 per day. And if ever a place overcharged, this is the one, so we've discovered. It seems it wasn't Beckles's idea for us to be here, but rather Captain Nobbs's ("Nobby," as they call him), probably for the reason which is its only saving grace, convenience to the college.

As for the initial grant, I suppose its delay in arriving here is tied up in more governmental gobbledegook. It does seem unfair, nonetheless, for there was no warning given. And I have complied with all requests. I've been to the bank twice just to be sure they haven't forgotten me.

The teaching year has begun and very interestingly so. Having eleven-year-olds is a twist I hadn't anticipated, but they are fun and the least troublesome of any of the ages represented.

Some aspects of the British system are puzzling to me. First of all, students here are hidebound by far more regimental wheel-spinning than are Americans. There are regulations to follow in nearly every nook and cranny of endeavor—homework in a given subject may be assigned only on certain nights; all notes are kept serially in one notebook for any series of related subjects. All assignments are kept in assignment books (so when an assignment is called for, a whole stack of books comes in, rather than separate sheets). Naturally, there are positive aspects to all this, otherwise they'd not be in use. The theory behind this sort of educational bureaucracy is that more time may be devoted to subject matter—and indeed the textbooks are written with that in view.

In my case, there are so many obstacles to overcome that this appointment is shaping into a first-class challenging opportunity. With the exception of the highest form, there are no textbooks. Although laboratory facilities are fine, materials such as dissecting kits, hand lenses, and microscopes are absent and, according to Mr. Beckles, prospects of getting them within the next six months are very slim.[8] Since biology has not been taught here to any extent for three years, nearly all the students are at the same level, yet they are theoretically to be treated as if they have had what they have not. As I may have mentioned before, a good deal of responsibility lies herein for, naturally, it is expected that the majority will pass the Cambridge-Oxford exams and subsequently the London University exams.

These are not complaints for I'm not at all discouraged. The worst I've felt is somewhat perplexed, but I know I'll catch on soon. The system, the people, and the country are all new—it takes time to adjust.

We live (at this moment) just a block south of the Georgetown-Rosignol Railway, and you'd really get a kick out of their rolling stock. The locomotives are quite contrasting—one a fairly up-to-date but small diesel unit, the other a 1900-ish cast-off steam job that had previously seen a normal span of service on the Bermuda Railway. There are about six wooden coaches and a dozen four-wheel stock cars. The Beckleses made a trip to New Amsterdam via the railway (60 miles), which took them eight hours. A derailment caused the delay, but since they are frequent, no one was upset!

Among the many discoveries we've made here the last two weeks, one concerns furniture. This piece is known as a Berbice chair, named for B.G.'s easternmost country. The armrest is composed of two boards, the lowermost swinging forward to become a sort of high-lift footrest. The upholstery is nothing more than a piece of carpeting stretched between the two C-shaped boards. Comfort: so-so; useless for reading, but excellent for complete relaxation. Perhaps that's all they do in Berbice!

If you have had difficulty in reading this, it's because I've been writing it in bed. I came home a little early this afternoon with a sudden head cold. Glad there's a weekend ahead for recuperation.

Love to all,

Howard

Thanks in advance for the loan!!!

September 26:

Howard has a repulsive cold. We had Mavis bring our dinners downstairs. We've moved Elizabeth's crib into the living room so she won't be so near, and we just hope she won't catch it.

The "movie man" upstairs has given us a pass to see *David and Bathsheba*, and although I don't care a bit about it, if we can arrange for Mabel to stay with Elizabeth we may as well go. The gentleman says his floating screen shows up best with Technicolor, and he's anxious for us to see it.

Finished another mystery a little while ago. I shall be so happy to have something constructive to do again.

September 27:

Howard felt ambitious enough to buy more paint this morning, so we completed the second coat in the kitchen. He touched up the white window sashes and sills, and I painted the floor of one cupboard brown. All that's left is to paint the baseboards. The paint has made a great difference—I know I shall enjoy the kitchen, with the stainless-steel counters once they've been scraped off and scrubbed. Miss Osborn had a man refinish some furniture, and he did it all in the kitchen, splashing stain on the floor and leaving great streaks on the cupboards and counters. I have also painted the toilet seat, which was a hideous green.

No answer to our cable. The Beckleses dropped by right after we returned from painting, and Mr. Beckles said, "Oh, don't worry." We don't know just what he meant. Mrs. Beckles has offered to lend us any "cutlery, crockery, or saucep'ns" we may need until ours arrive, which probably won't be until the first of November. Also linens. Thank heavens we won't need to buy all those things, for they're expensive here.

September 28:
We took a drive at 8:30 this morning—Howard wanted to collect some plants and water samples for a class tomorrow, so Elizabeth and I went along. We first stopped at the cable office, but still no answer. Then we drove all around the downtown area trying to locate Yong Hing's self-service grocery, the only one here, which has been open just a few weeks. Never did find it.

We headed out of town on the East Coast Road, our old haunt. And it is a risky ride on a Sunday! People drive like wild horses, staying in the center of the road until the very last possible moment. Others coming toward us passed cars when ridiculously close to us. What an experience. Howard took a few pictures of the landscape, and we both wish we could take colored ones. There is a purple bougainvillea near our flat that is gorgeous, bright and large.

On our way home a marabunta, or wasp, flew into the car via the wing [window] on my side. Scared me to pieces, since everyone we've met here has warned us about them. They are nasty-looking creatures, nearly two inches long, and have a reputation for bad stings. I was afraid it would sting Elizabeth, who was in my lap, clad in her customary costume, a diaper. Fortunately, Howard stopped the car and we managed to get rid of the thing before any harm was done.

I wonder why I brought plastic pants for Elizabeth. I only put them on her the first few times we took her out. I myself haven't worn stockings since our second day here.

Sunday evening, September 28, 1952

Dear Mother—

I am sending you thought waves like fury. At this point we have no grant, no answer to our wire to the Irwins, and we're awfully close to having no money. We owe Mr. Beckles for the crib, too. No doubt everything will come at once.

I've decided to put the glass items on a little shelf above our living room windows—they will add a nice bit of color. And I guess we will treat each wall of windows as one window, putting a drapery (short, perhaps sill length) at the end of each wall.

We finished up our kitchen today. The sink, unfortunately, is awfully low, but the counter tops aren't bad at all. Howard has figured out a pulley system for a clothesline, double-decker, between a window and a post outside. There is no space in the yard (no yard in back, concrete in front) for a line, so we will only do E.'s washing and, I suppose, the best underwear and dresses at home. H. had one pair of slacks cleaned and another laundered, for 78 cents. The cleaning job was poor.

Elizabeth is just fine. We've been really firm these last three days and have let her cry, certain she was all right. It's a new experience for her but does her no harm. She just goes to sleep after she cries, which hasn't yet been for more than 30 minutes. I shall be glad to be in my own clean kitchen so she can have her fruit again. I intend to buy canned fruit and strain it myself—26 cents each is ridiculous.

We expect to pay about $20 a month for electricity and $100 for food. Had I written that before? Other masters have been awfully nice about telling us what they spend, so we've been able to figure quite well. Now all we need is an income! Probably it will all be straightened out by the time you receive this, so don't fret.

E. sends her love and a gurgle to you both.

Much love,

Marian

Mon. 8 a.m.

This is an afterthought: Could you include in the next installment of goods to be sent the little fruit knives? We have had fruit as dessert here several times, and it would be fun for us to have the knives. However, if you have any qualms at all about sending them, don't. We can live very well without them.

It's pouring and has been since 6:30. The dry season this is, too. Reminds me of the Northwest. I'm even filled with ambition, but there's nothing to do. Thunder and lightning—whee!

Love,

Marian

Monday 8:00 a.m., September 29, 1952

Dear Bee—

Howard has been up since 5:30 for he had a gardening class from 6 to 7:30, and E. and I have been up since 6, the best hour of the day around here. H. is off to town now to buy shelf paper and a dust mop and to send a cable to Mother and Daddy.

We're really in a peculiar situation. H.'s grant from London has not come through yet, nor has he received any answer to two letters written to the office in London. Last Thursday we cabled H.'s parents for a bit of financial assistance— no answer! We're quite broke, have to pay rent on our flat on the 1st of October, car payment on the 8th, can't leave this place without settling our huge bill here, and can't move into our flat without buying a stove and refrigerator. H. is going to ask for a salary advance today—then we can relax a little bit.

Have I already told you about Mabel? As soon as we're moved she's going to come every afternoon to do E.'s washing and take her for a walk. We're lucky to get her. We're told that most servants turn out to be duds— dishonest, dirty, lazy, etc. Everyone says don't trust them—but Mabel is wonderful, according to the Beckleses.

I have worn the pink nightgown steadily since we've been here—wash it, let it dry, and wear it again. It's really more comfortable than clingy things.

I'm already hoping that you will be able to visit us here. You'd find it most interesting—a marvelous contrast to the States. Howard marvels at the harmony in his classes, where the majority of students are black, others East Indian ("colored"), Chinese, Portuguese, and one or two white.

E. is beginning to mutter, and I guess she's hungry or bored. Do write soon—at this point we've heard nothing from you, but it doesn't seem possible that you haven't written us!

Much love from all of us,
Marian

September 29:

Things are looking up. It seems we *did* receive funds in answer to our cable, which were sent promptly to the bank here. The bank notified us by mail, hence the delay. Also, Mr. Beckles discovered with great surprise today that Howard hasn't been paid yet by the school. Such a mix-up—we took it for granted that Howard would be paid at the end of the month, Mr. Beckles's secretary took it for granted that all of Howard's salary was paid through the Fulbright "scheme," and Mr. Beckles merely took it for granted that he'd already been paid!

As a result, we have told Mrs. d'Andrade we will move out after dinner tomorrow. Hallelujah!

The flat needs much scrubbing. All I did today was sweep. I'm beginning to think that we will need a girl to do the cleaning: everything needs constant attention here where windows are open all day and night and dust blows in from the dirt roads. To add to the mess, the floors are laid of uneven boards, none too well finished. Dirt collects in the cracks and chinks between the boards and is the very devil to sweep out. None of the lumber used in building here is really finished. Saw marks are visible, and some of our cabinets in the kitchen were actually splintery on the outside.

I am anxious to buy material for curtains. We need them desperately for privacy, for with so many windows we feel like a store's window display.

Sept. 29, 1952

Dear folks,

Well, the crisis is over—for the time being at least. It was in part due to misunderstanding and inefficiency. I say for the time being because although we received your loan (for which we are most thankful) and have since corrected a misapprehension regarding my salary from the college, the grant has still failed to materialize. In that regard I sent a rather crisp note to the Commission's finance officer asking for either money or acknowledgment. I had already sent two letters, neither evoking response. If this doesn't work I guess I'll have to bother my contact in the Federal Security Agency and have him find out just what the hell cooks in London! It's all so strange because I've followed instructions to the letter.

We took our weekly drive along the Georgetown–New Amsterdam road yesterday. I'm gradually getting the hang of this British driving routine—although every now and then I've found myself wandering over to the right side of the road and a couple of times in emergencies, when instinct rules, I've tried to avoid opposing traffic by getting over to the right—fortunately this happened downtown where things move rather slowly. Driving is terrifically hazardous, what with cyclists galore, breakneck drivers most frequently lacking "road sense," and occasional but utterly unnerving incidents with motorcyclists who lack all semblance of responsibility. We've come to the conclusion that the police act only when an incident has occurred—they make little attempt to prevent difficulty. I've seen scores of infractions witnessed by the boys in blue, but they just seem to ignore it all. They're not the roving patrolmen we're accustomed to but rather permanent fixtures on certain corners. Some ride bicycles, very few are equestrian, and I've seen only one P.D. motorcycle. The chief has the distinction of owning a 1937 Buick sedan—bright yellow!

I found among the completely disorganized mess known as the supply room at the college a rather ingenious plant press—complete with chains, springs, and blotters. On our little trip yesterday I made my first collection. The water hyacinth is a pestiferous weed in the drainage canals but awfully attractive. We've seen numerous times the huge Victoria water lily that has leaves four feet across and beautiful flowers a foot or so in diameter. The leaves are reputed to be broad and buoyant enough to support the weight of a baby—shall we try? Of course the palms are the very epitome of grace. Along the highway are numerous villages, all shaded with coconut and thatch palms. The sea wall, which extends many miles east of Georgetown, is simply a dike holding back a rather calm ocean. The land immediately behind the dike is four or five feet below sea level. The ocean would be truly beautiful but for its chocolate-brown color.

The crib Mr. Beckles bought is satisfactory enough for the moment, but we are now just not too sure if it will do for the next two years. It isn't as large as the one in Tacoma and the mattress seems to be made of straw, which has already become somewhat compact in the center. Now, we hate to even bring this up after reading of the devious and tortuous procedure you had to follow in order to keep our crib from being sent. But we may, in some months' time, ask that it be sent.

Tomorrow we move into our new flat and are we overjoyed! I was over to the Beckleses' this evening very briefly—Mrs. B. is going to lend us some bare essentials to tide us over until our trunks arrive—and Mr. B. presented me with my long overdue salary check, which covers the period from September 8 through October 1. It seems his secretary assumed I was being remunerated entirely from Fulbright funds [i.e., the grant due from London] and so made no effort to secure my government appointment papers from the Colonial Office. She felt very badly about the error and quickly sought to rectify it by performing what might well be considered a miracle in government circles: she not only secured my appointment papers but also had the colonial treasurer make out my check. These British officials are not accustomed to moving so fast!

You ask about the teaching supplies for which I was granted £300, but Mr. Beckles knows of no reason for me to spend a red cent on teaching supplies since the school furnishes everything to the masters in that regard. Of course, that term might have been an official shield for pure gravy—we hope so!

If we were to judge the food of B.G. by the fare we've had at this boarding house, we'd say it's pitiful. But having talked with a few intelligent homemakers, we are encouraged. By scanning the shops we can see that Australian beef is available for less than half the cost of beef in the States. Fruits and vegetables are not so plentiful as one might expect but still they seem dirt-cheap by our standards. Coffee is readily available in numerous qualities. Some of the locally cured stuff is akin to battery acid when brewed, but good standard types are available for 50 to 60 cents B.W.I. per pound. Imported dry goods are rather high-priced but still well below U.S. levels. The Bookers firm here has a healthy finger in every mercantile pie and even own their boats that ply between Georgetown and London. Bookers Drug Stores, Bookers Garages, Bookers Dry Goods Shops, Bookers Airline Agencies (Pan Am representative here), Bookers Insurance Association, Bookers Overseas-Surface Freight Lines, and Bookers Real Estate Agencies are all familiar sights to residents.[9]

As for school, my classes average about 30 students per. Some are a little larger and one has only nine. As I may have explained before, the trouble here is not the size of the classes but the brevity of time per period (only 40 minutes) and the inadequacy of supplies coupled with the difficulty in securing such supplies. Generally speaking, the situation is enjoyable, and how dull it would be if there were no opportunity for improvement!

Thanks muchly for the loan.

Love to all,

Howard

P.S. Needless to say, you'll eventually be reimbursed—we'll have Mr. Sterne [Marian's father] attend to it when the second $500 grant is made to our Central Bank account in Tacoma. —H.

September 30:

Naturally, the first thing we did today was go to the bank. After that we went to Sandbach Parker for wastebaskets, scrub brush, clothespins, and clothesline. All but the last item we acquired, and it seems that a clothesline with pulleys is just not to be found here. Our important purchases were the stove and refrigerator, which we bought at Fogarty's from the nice little man who showed them to us before. We met the assistant manager of the store, a huge, beefy Englishman with horrible-smelling breath. He did his best to be pleasant, bowed and scraped with great formality. We then went downstairs where Howard found a seat for me, and Elizabeth went to sleep. He and the little salesman scurried about collecting towel racks, trying to find a clothesline, etc. Elizabeth and I went back to Loyola and Howard went on to school.

I packed up all our belongings, and after lunch Howard and I brought it all to the flat. He dashed back to school and I spent a rather futile afternoon trying to put things away. Our drawer space is somewhat limited, and we will end up using our trunks for storing linens.

Went back to Loyola for our last meal, and if the meat wasn't contaminated with that same sweet-sour flavor we've had a few other times! Neither of us ate it, but the macaroni, rice, and potatoes were lovely.

There certainly are contradictions galore here. We'd asked to have the stove and refrigerator sent up this afternoon and the things from Sandbach Parker tomorrow morning. When we arrived after lunch, we found the stove on our back stoop, and the woman downstairs said our refrigerator would be brought back at 1:30. The refrigerator was delivered by five men, one in charge and four hauling, and it's just a little five-cubic-feet model! The stove will be connected tomorrow, we hope. The boy from Sandbach Parker brought the parcels shortly after noon, and yet if you want something done quickly, it's like asking for the impossible.

Howard bought some sheets today. One is 90x100 and cost $11.49, another is 70x108 and cost $8.89, and a "cheap" one to split for Elizabeth's crib was $6.[10]

ENDNOTES

1 Atkinson Field (9/10/1952 journal): The airbase came about as part of the Lend-Lease Act, through which the US contributed fifty destroyers to Britain's war effort in exchange for ninety-nine-year leases on sites in a number of British territories. Americans arrived in Georgetown in 1941 to construct the base. A US Air Force squadron that made regular patrols between Panama and British Guiana was stationed there, and the airbase was a refueling stop for the ferrying of munitions, other supplies, and newly purchased warplanes to Africa. After the war, the airbase was reduced to "housekeeping service"; it would be turned over to the British in October 1953. The terminal building was rebuilt in 1952 to accommodate civil aviation. Howard wrote years later of arriving in B.G.: "The airport building was small, barnlike, made of wood and was completely open to the tropical breezes."

2 Drive from airport (9/11/1952 journal): Howard's description to his parents: "The practice here is to not give the pedestrians even one-tenth of a break in the matter of right-of-way. The driver simply drove at 40 m.p.h. and somehow the road, cloaked with humanity, dogs, chickens, cattle, and mules, cleared just in front of the bumper and immediately swallowed our trail as we passed."

3 Botanical Gardens (9/11/1952): More than a pleasure garden, British Guiana's Botanical Gardens were conceived in 1879 as a place for botanical study. The grounds were an abandoned sugar estate in the city's southeastern corner. The largest such garden in any British colony in the Western Hemisphere, it featured an international collection of palm trees and outstanding native species, including vast trenches full of the mammoth *Victoria regia* water lilies. The zoo, which lies within the garden grounds, was opened, largely through the efforts of Vincent Roth, in 1951.

4 Lack of adventurous spirit (9/18/1952): A similar attitude was noted three years later by Michael Swan, an Englishman visiting the colony to gather research for a book. Swan attended a party thrown by colonials in Georgetown: "Hardly anyone in that room had been into the Interior. Most professed some interest in it and showed none. . . . For them British Guiana was two hundred miles long and ten miles wide; the Department of the Interior, run by eccentrics who 'liked that sort of life,' ran the Interior and that was that."

5 Such conditions of racial harmony (9/22/1952): As subsequent letters tell, this description isn't quite accurate. It was likely Howard's attempt to convey to his parents the sharp contrast between the US and B.G. concerning racial integration. His early impressions of interracial harmony in the colony would in time be tempered with a more nuanced understanding. For one thing, among the different ethnic groups in B.G. (as elsewhere), great store was put in shadings of skin tone. Roy Heath writes that "the light-skinned clerk, assured rapid promotion in the civil service, could avail himself or herself of innumerable advantages not available to his or her dark-skinned colleague." Howard would later recall that "store clerks and bank tellers were a uniform tan—Booker-tone, the Guianese dubbed it." Mona Williams writes that her employment in the 1950s at Bookers, the "company store" in Georgetown that was the retail arm of Booker Bros., McConnell & Co., caused a stir: "Portuguese, Chinese, and pale others as sales staff, yes; but a jet black girl? Come, come!" To land the position, she'd explained to the personnel director (a Bishops' graduate), in the plumy tones she'd learned at school, "I attend Bishops." That did the trick.

6 I earn 85 times as much as the peon (9/22/1952): In a letter to a college friend in May 1953, Marian wrote: "Our house here in Georgetown and the way we live are very

close to the way we'd be living in the States: comfortably, but with no frills. Last night we even figured up how Howard's salary here compares with what he'd be making at home, and it is just slightly higher. But here, we find ourselves in the strange position of making more money at Queen's than just about anyone save the principal. Some of the men on the staff have large families, and earn from half to three-quarters of the salary that Howard earns."

7 The Nixon problem (9/22/1952 HSI letter): Accusations had appeared in the US press that the vice-presidential candidate had received payments from a secret fund; in response, on September 23, Nixon delivered his "Checkers" speech.

8 Q.C. biology lab (9/25/1952 HSI letter): Marian later wrote that although the college had moved into its new building the year before, "the biology laboratory was not used or even equipped until Howard arrived. No books had been ordered. Old lab glass, charts, and models were still packed in boxes. Organizing this clutter was Howard's immediate priority. He frequently spent evenings contriving one workable microscope from two or three broken ones." From Howard's later recollections: "As biology had been suspended at Queen's for three years before I arrived, it had no budget and there were no books, no supplies, no equipment—just two bare rooms. . . . As the only duplication machine in the building was jealously guarded by the headmaster's secretary, Doris Wan-Ping, and was not for staff use, I wrote the day's notes on the blackboard in the unused adjacent room, and had students copy them whenever they had time to do so, and used the blackboard in my room for explanatory notes that were needed during the lectures."

9 Bookers (9/29/1952 HSI letter): The company had grown by means of acquiring, over 150 years, plantations and shops that defaulted through foreclosure. Its omnipresence, along with a legacy of resistance to reform and the longstanding abusive treatment of its workers and squalid conditions on many of its plantations, was a source of deep, widespread resentment among Guianese, spurring political unrest and the pejorative term for the colony, "Bookers Guiana." But its primary focus on B.G.'s sugar industry, the economic backbone of the colony, also put the company at considerable risk. "Nobody in their senses would have designed to involve themselves in British Guiana to the extent that Booker have done," wrote Jock Campbell in 1954, when he had been its chairman for two years.

10 Howard bought some sheets (9/30/1952): Marian's later note: "Like all imported goods, they were twice as expensive as what we were accustomed to."

The Irwins rented the second-floor flat, above, where the jalousies and windows opened onto Parade Street. Below, the sparsely furnished gallery, shown before the couple moved in.

Chapter 3

1952–1953: 124 PARADE STREET

Oct. 1, 1952

Dear folks,

We are in what we hope will be our permanent home. We feel so independent now, planning our own activities and not being restrained by the rigid meal times of the boarding house. Mrs. d'Andrade, the proprietress, is part Portuguese and seems to attract a good deal of Portuguese business (mostly Brazilians). When we ate, we were confronted with people talking in Portuguese about Lord knows what. At first, the seemingly excessive noise—overhead, outside, all over—bothered us, but now we realize it's that way throughout the city. When a chicken crows a few houses down the street, we are bound to hear it. What this new neighborhood lacks in chickens it has in dogs. Last night we were awakened several times by various dogs barking, but in time we'll become accustomed to them just as we have with the chickens.

We thank you very, very much for your loan, which made it possible for us to move in at this time. The receipt of your wire today made us think that Mrs. Sterne [Marian's mother] had contacted you concerning our wire to them. B.G. is *awfully* slow to act, and the Royal Bank of Canada, through which your transaction was made, saw fit to inform me by mail (this taking two days) rather than by phone. So we didn't get word until Monday at 11 a.m. Desperation forced us to send a wire to the Sternes meanwhile for we were really stuck and thought there might be some possibility of you folks not being home.

As I indicated in the last letter, Mr. Beckles's secretary had been operating under a misapprehension regarding my status at the college, and it happened that my salary from the college and your loan fell into our hands simultaneously, relieving our minds beyond description. At any rate, we're here and we're enjoying a normal routine, such as we haven't had for over four weeks.

We are still getting the hang of food shopping. A self-service market, Georgetown's first, opened only two weeks ago under Chinese management and although the selection is limited, there are the usual self-service advantages including lower prices. The best place to get fruits and vegetables is at Stabroek, distasteful as it may be to go there.[11] As yet we've not found a "pet" meat market nor have we heard of one. Bookers, needless to say, has one and for the moment we're dealing there. Stores, small ones particularly, are much more limited as to scope than we expected. A grocery handles tinned goods, bottled goods, butter, and a little meat. Fish is to be had at the fish stores, meat at meat stores, cigarettes and soft drinks at a "parlour." Liquor is sold at the city Ice House and at Bookers, and illegitimately elsewhere. There are very few stores.

Upon entering a store, we are often encountered by a floor manager or, in a smaller establishment, a clerk who quickly brushes aside any colored or black customers in our favor. I found this practice embarrassing and so now direct that he conclude his affairs with them before waiting on us. The clerks are usually very helpful about showing their wares, this probably being due to the limited variety in any category, and it isn't uncommon to hear "not available."

Oh yes, here's one of the novelties of B.G. life that we weren't too smitten with at first. There is a native lizard here that has a decidedly keen appetite for cockroaches (which are found in every house). The little devils are six or eight inches long, have adhesive pads on their toes that enable them to scamper up and down walls, and if you can encourage them to take up residence in your house, you're that much better off in your endless war against roaches. They're pretty little things, attempting to take on the color of their background (as chameleons do), and, of course, most active at night. I guess we're lucky, for as I have been writing, one just scampered up the wall.

Love to all,
Howard

October 1:
We began the day with a lovely breakfast of canned peaches, grapefruit juice, and "biscuits" (plain cookies). Ugh. I spent the rest of the morning painting the shower; the white walls were spattered and stained, and the fresh paint improves it tremendously. At least we'll know that the dirt that accumulates is our own!

A young man from Fogarty's came this morning, looked at the stove, and said he'd be back tomorrow to connect it. At lunch Howard said he'd called the electric company and that they were sending a man out. Fogarty's fellow came back shortly thereafter, said he didn't know how we'd be able to cook dinner without our stove, and set to work. It took him about two hours, one of which was spent waiting for a part to be brought from the store. The other electrician showed up then, but wasn't at all upset by the complication. People are all so polite: I could just hear an impatient American swearing and muttering over a delay or an unnecessary house call. But both of these men were completely courteous.

Sleeping last night without a net didn't seem to bother Howard, but I woke up with many mosquito bites. Howard and I couldn't see paying $20 for a net, so he bought the hoop, netting, and tape today. Tomorrow I shall see what I can do about making one.

We had mutton chops for dinner tonight—great big ones, for 66 cents. Our stove has three top burners; the element of one heats the broiler. So, according to the instruction booklet, you can use the top burners for three pans and broil your meat at the same time. Nothing like economy! Here it will be appreciated, since electricity is high. We are told the average charge in this flat is $18 to $20 a month, half of which would be from the stove.

October 2:

We had a surprise this morning. When Howard arrived at school he learned that Mabel had a maid all lined up for us, and that she was [waiting] at the Beckleses'. He brought her here, and she started to work. Her name is Evelyn and she is quite young. She scrubbed the shower floor (a job I'd been dreading) and the floor of the toilet, swept the whole flat, dusted, and washed windows. I suppose I shall have to keep after her a bit, for tonight Howard spotted dust under some of the furniture. She'll be a help, I hope. We will pay her $10 a month to begin with, and she will work from 8 a.m. to noon, seven days a week.

Taking advantage of Evelyn's presence, I tackled the mosquito netting. Using Elizabeth's as a guide, it was simple except for the sheer bulk of nine yards of netting six feet wide. I haven't hemmed it yet, but that can wait. I'm sick of the mosquitoes, and Howard still hasn't been bitten!

We performed a sacred rite this evening—had our first drink in our new home. Howard ordered three bottles of two-year-old rum and a case of lime rickey, all for $8.04 including the deposit on the lime bottles. Every two weeks the man will drop in to see what we need.

We had two drinks and then I started our dinner. I'll be so glad to see my cookbooks. We had a beef brisket, something I'd never even heard of before, so we decided to broil it. It was a bit rare and tough, but tasty. At this point, merely the fact that we have meat is enough, without worrying about the finer points of preparation.

Mrs. Beckles stopped by at about 11 a.m. to see how Evelyn and I were doing. She is so very considerate. She also inquired about my doing some Red Cross work here after we're a bit more settled. I think I shall—heaven knows I shall have the time.

Thursday, October 2, 1952

Dear Bee,

I'm starting this on the strength of a double rum, and guess what—Marian wants another one! What these tropics don't do. From the allusions you made in the first letter received from you we gather that we have not yet received (and may never) the first you wrote us.

We are now in our new quarters. We feel that the landlady was none too generous with furniture, but we are in a good district, only one block from the college and two blocks from the ocean—so you see we're convenient and breezy.

We don't have our trunks yet, and we don't expect the barrels until November 1. People and business in B.G. are so *slow*. We had something of a financial crisis here a week ago and, toward relieving it, we wired my folks for a loan. They obliged immediately, but the bank saw fit to inform me by mail (which takes two days) instead of by phone.

Shopping is interesting, complicated, and time-consuming. No trust is given a clerk by any store. As a result, when a purchase is made, even of a lowly toothpick, the clerk arranges the sale and prepares the sales slip. But this must be signed by a floor manager, so the clerk calls out, "Sign, please." We usually have a wait from a few seconds to several minutes before the proper gent makes his way to our slip. Finding the clerk's figuring correct, the reviewer rewrites the total and initials it. Then a "cash boy" takes your money and three copies of the sales slip to the cashier. The cashier stamps "Paid" on the slip, keeps one, and makes change. The cash boy returns your change and one copy of the sales slip, the final copy going to the clerk. Sales slips are all handwritten, none automatically prepared by the cash register. And then if a sale amounts to more than $10, a two-cent revenue stamp is affixed. In B.G. revenue stamps are merely postage stamps, canceled in ink. (In order for a contract such as the one I made between the landlady and myself to be official, it is necessary for both parties to initial the stamp—a fascinating bit of red tape.) In the meantime the clerk wraps the purchase with a scrap of paper and we're off.

School has been fine. I'm still amazed that black, yellow, white, and mixed can sit in the same room without the slightest semblance of racial feeling—all are equal. It's an ideal that has long been sought in the U.S., and here we see it's a working principle. I'm confused with the many levels I meet each week—each level takes biology, but in varying intensity.

B.G. is up-to-date in some respects. We hear daily the music of Billy Eckstine, Eddy Fisher, etc. and the orchestras of Ralph Flanagan, Percy Faith, Glen Miller (Beneke)—even David Rose now and then. Music on the radio is entirely American, news broadcasts are full of American events (including the Nixon incident). British portions include news from the BBC, and, of course, the announcers are very British. The local papers are miserable by our standards, full of patent medicine ads and news about birthdays. The first page is all that commands our interest, with the possible addition of the comics. The newspapers—*The Guiana Graphic*, *The Argosy*, and *The Chronicle*—have daily issues of eight pages each, Sunday issues of twelve pages, any copy costing eight cents.

One of the aspects of a place rarely written about in detail concerns sounds. In the more or less compact homes of temperate USA, the matter of outside noises seldom bothered us when we were indoors. Here we are at their mercy. Single-partition construction is the rule here (dead air space not needed for insulation) and in consequence we hear the chickens (4:00–6:00 a.m. and all day intermittently), the donkey's braying (pitiful noise), the Demerara-Berbice Railway (cast-off Bermuda Railway equipment), the rustling leaves of the palms, bananas, and the traveler's palm, the thin exhaust sounds of the little British-made cars, the radio in the house two doors away blaring American music (Mitch Miller's "Sparrows in the Tree-Top" at this instant), the yowling dog next door, footsteps overhead, conversation beneath us, and, occasionally, the sound of surf. These are the sounds of B.G. We are starved for Beethoven!

The place that tops all for noises is Stabroek Market. Inside on a Saturday morning you find hundreds of people of all extractions milling about restlessly, dickering with merchants, seeking bargains, comparing, mumbling, conversing. The merchants stand behind their makeshift counters or in their stalls or are seated right on the pavement, surrounded by their wares, barking their news for all to hear. By 10 a.m. bedlam reigns and all but the most robust start for home. The Stabroek as pictured on the twelve-cent stamp is typical of a slow day; on Saturday from the same vantage, all but the roof and tower would be obscured with buses, cars, and humanity. Superficially, it's an attractive market, painted white with red trim and roof, and if it weren't for the odors within, the interior would be equally attractive. Even so, the whole is exceedingly interesting.

Marian and Elizabeth send you their love, as do I.

Howard

October 3:

I really don't know about Evelyn. She worked hard this morning and scrubbed the gallery floors. But—she asked me for a baby bottle. I didn't understand at first, for we thought she was single. As it develops, she isn't married but has a six-month-old daughter. I couldn't very well say that we needed all six bottles, so I hedged and said I'd tell her later. I consulted Howard, and we decided to be charitable this time. We would like to help her, for $10 a month seems like nothing; on the other hand we don't want her to take advantage of us. I gave her a bottle (she reminded me of it before she left) and Howard bought another one for Elizabeth.

Howard learned this morning that we should give Evelyn a cup of coffee in the morning and a little lunch at noon before she leaves. She was a bit perturbed yesterday—hungry, I'm sure.

We took a drive this afternoon along the sea wall for a short distance, as the weeds were being burned down further out. Then we headed downtown and drove through some of the old, poor districts—houses crowded together on mud lots separated by muddy drainage ditches. The people looked fairly clean, surprisingly enough.

Saturday, October 4, 1952

Dear Anna and Tom,

I'll just begin this letter to give you the procedure I followed in preparation of our goods for shipment (assuming that in this case the radio will be crated and the records barrelled):

(1) You will need to go to the U.S. Customs Office, which is on the second floor of the Federal (P.O.) Building at the very end of the East Corridor.

Within you'll find a couple of government-type gentlemen and a secretary. If possible, try to have *her* do about the papers because she is familiar with the proper sequence, etc., and won't require *you* to fill in the forms. (It seems that there is some law which states that in customs declarations, the first or initial copy shall be prepared by the declaree—thus alleviating the clerk of interpretative responsibility. As yet they haven't rewritten the forms so John and Jane Doe can intelligently read them, so this girl will do the filling-in for you.) You might mention me and British Guiana—I'm sure she'll remember having done my two previous declarations. All you'll need to know for the declaration is the nature of the merchandise and the character of the containers. Ask Lyon or whoever does the packing to mark the outside thus:

H.S. Irwin, Jr.
Georgetown
British Guiana

Then indicate this marking system to customs—it aids in identification:

<1> for the first piece, and <2> for the second.

The street address is unnecessary because as soon as the goods arrive they must be inspected by B.G. Customs and it is at that point that the shipper's responsibility ends. (I'm well known at Bookers' shipping office, where Moore-Mac affairs are handled.) One of the blanks calls for a weight estimate of the two pieces packed—have the packer give you a rough approximation.

(2) Your signature will have to be notarized and I had that done across the street at J. B. Steeb & Co.'s office in the Perkins Building on the recommendation of the secretary.

(3) Either at this point or beforehand you should arrange with Moore-Mac in Seattle (Dexter Horton Building) for a bill of lading. (By having the customs business attended to first, a delay in the preparation of the bill of lading may be prevented.) They will need all four copies of the customs form. Assuming that the packer will transfer the pieces to Pier 88, Seattle, you should have nothing else to do.

I know this probably sounds involved, but doesn't anything that concerns the government?

I'm off to town so Marian will take over. Thanks muchly.

Howard

Saturday

Dear Parents—

I've been awfully lax about writing—and I shouldn't really say I've been busy, yet I feel as if I have been. We moved in Tuesday night, and things are only gradually being straightened out. Wednesday morning I painted the shower and put some things away. Thursday luck favored us, and Mabel turned up at the Beckleses' with Evelyn, who is now our maid. Howard brought her right over, and she scrubbed both the shower and w.c. floors, did windows, swept floors, etc. Yesterday she started scrubbing floors, which needed it desperately. I think she will work out well—she has initiative, works hard, and is very clean. I still don't know quite what to do with her, and yesterday she really threw me for a loss when she asked right out for a baby bottle. I ended up by giving her one, and she was grateful but not demonstrative. She has a six-month-old daughter, and Howard and I don't believe she's married. My feelings were torn—we only pay her $10 a month, and how she can feed a baby and herself on that I don't know. On the other hand it seemed a bit bold to ask for something right off the bat. Oh well—Mabel starts today, and Mrs. Beckles said to confide any troubles to Mabel. Howard and I are going to a movie tonight and Mabel will stay with Elizabeth.

H. bought an ironing board the other day—$7.50, it's only about four feet long, narrow and short. They were available *only* at Bookers. At least I can press my clothes now. Evelyn lined up a laundress for us—all H.'s and my clothes, our sheets, towels, etc. for $8 a month. Plus 38 cents a week for soap and coals for ironing.

So—my day includes cooking, washing dinner dishes, bathing and feeding Elizabeth, a little ironing—and oddly enough, it fills the day. We get up at 5:45 or so—E. is quite punctual now; are through breakfast by 7:30, and are ready for bed at 8:00 p.m. I hate to appear lazy, but I'm frightfully glad I don't have to do the floor scrubbing. With so many windows open all the time there is a quantity of dust—by morning the floors look awful, so they have to be swept well each day. All our floors need waxing—Evelyn informs me we hire a man to do that. We shall consult Mabel!

We bought a big galvanized tub for Elizabeth's baths—she has to sit up in it and has just enough room to kick her legs out straight. As soon as she can stand, I guess we'll introduce her to the shower. I put the tub on one of the kitchen counters with her towel beside it—she goes onto the towel for a soaping, then into the tub. I'm giving her orange juice now in the morning, and yesterday we experimented with an egg yolk. No rash—she liked it, too. I told H. we should try to complete our family while we're here, where help is so reasonable. Don't worry, it was just a thought! It is fun, though, having so much time for Elizabeth. A good thing, too, considering that she will take more time than an average child. She has developed all sorts of new sounds—a high-pitched, thin, sustained note that always makes me laugh. She is so contented now—yesterday, for instance, went like this: 6:15, cereal and milk; 6:45–7:30, play on our bed; 7:30–9, play and nap in her bed; 9, orange juice and vitamins, followed by bath and then milk at 10. Then she went to sleep and was out until 3:10, when she ate peaches, egg, and milk. Played and napped until 6:30, had milk, and was put to bed for the night. Her only crying was between 5:30 and 6 and even that wasn't serious.

Thursday Archie and Howard had haircuts (two shillings—48 cents), and made a deal to go shopping together every Saturday morning, alternating cars. Archie has given H. good tips on where to buy things—oranges at the government dock, occasionally a cent apiece!

Howard and I are drinking Klim [powdered milk] once or twice a day now. It has a creamy flavor that we don't care for too much, but H. says it is far better than the fresh milk (boiled) that he had once at the school. Canned milk is 30 cents per can, and as we figured it, the Klim is a little cheaper than either that or fresh, which is 24 cents a pint.

Mrs. Beckles's egg man is now coming to us, too. We get ten eggs for 96 cents, every Tuesday and Friday. They are small but are nearly all yolk. Very good, I might say. Howard bought a percolator yesterday, so we had coffee this morning. I used a tablespoon per cup and it was much too strong. Good flavor, though. Our canned goods are fascinating—grapes from South Africa, orange juice from New Zealand, corn and carrots from Canada, beets from England, etc. Rather than bring meat from the Argentine, the good old British get Australian lamb and beef. Grapefruit are very good—sweeter than those at home, coarser grained but tender, and certainly refreshing.

We learned yesterday that our trunks should arrive the first of the week. How we yearn for them—silverware, H.'s boots, our books—we'll have a grand time unpacking them. Did I tell you that Mrs. Beckles lent us all sorts of dishes and pans? All we've purchased so far are the percolator and a skillet, and I need a spatula.

By the way, you no doubt thought us to be hasty children, rushing in to buy things and then yelling for financial help. Really—we should have been well off! Only yesterday did H. receive a letter announcing that the grant had come through to Barclays Bank in London and should be transferred to our account here within a week. Heaven knows we were led to expect it would be here "shortly" after our arrival. The help from H.'s parents saved us from a minor crisis.

Evelyn is playing with Elizabeth. I must ask Mabel just how busy I should keep Evelyn. She wanted to finish the floor scrubbing Monday, but at 10 a.m. today she had nothing else to do—so the floors she did. Don't know what she wanted to do today—play with E., I guess.

Better close so H. can wedge his note into the envelope. Wish you could drop in over the weekend—we'd give you a lovely rum and lime rickey. Last night while drinking one of the same we were entertained by a small bat in our gallery. Ah, nature.

Much love—

Marian

October 4:

Howard and Archie went shopping this morning—they were gone for hours! Archie discovered he's been paying 40 cents more per pound for butter at Bookers than is charged at Yong Hing's. They were gone so long that Evelyn suggested that Mr. Irwin must have become lost!

Evelyn may do all right here. This morning she brought a little piece of metal to scrape off the putty on the floor, and also an old rag to use for scrubbing, instead of the baby's "nappies" that I gave her to use. Such treatment of good diapers must have horrified her as much as it did me.

Mabel arrived at noon and she and Evelyn put away the groceries. Archie had helped Howard pick out guavas that, he said, were "just right." Mabel clucked over them, said they were far too ripe, and disposed of most. The rest she cooked up for us. They have a lovely fragrance and a beautiful deep rose color—I haven't tasted them yet.

We decided to go to a movie, leaving Mabel in charge of Elizabeth. The picture, *Belle of New York*, was awful and we left wondering why a good cast had been wasted. Howard took Mabel home, then returned and did battle with a wasp that was fascinated by the light globe. I found a half-conscious roach and finished it off with a bit of flit. We have found several completely dead roaches around: our roach hives must be effective! They are such awful things. When I get up at 5:45 it's not quite light, and I'm sleepy so that I can't see too clearly. I'm always afraid I'll step on one of the damned things.

October 5:

Our next-door neighbor, apparently deaf, had her radio turned on full blast per usual, but it was such wonderful Sunday music—nice hymns. We let Evelyn go about 10, and then we three went for a drive out toward Atkinson Field. We drove over four rickety bridges "under repairs" and I held my breath each time. At one, we had to wait for three little donkeys to pull a greatly overloaded cart across—strictly one way. We didn't get more than halfway to the Field, and therefore missed much of the filth and squalor of the cane workers' shacks.

We stopped once for Howard to take a close look at the vegetation. Unfortunately, there were marshes on either side of the road. But we could see philodendron-like leaves that were easily a foot high and sedges that were ten feet high, a far cry from the eight-inch variety we're used to.

We dropped in on the Larthes this afternoon, interrupting their tea, and had a good chat. Archie is really a card, and Dorothy, too. They told us of their appalling experiences here when they first arrived. Housing was very bad during the war, and when Dorothy arrived with the two oldest boys, the only place Archie could find was downtown in the back of a printing press [shop]. Next door a house was being built by a Chinese man who installed and played a piano even before the house was finished. Nearby was a bee lover, and his homing bees found their way into the Larthes' flat every evening. On top of it all, the boys developed malaria and were very sick.

Mabel and Elizabeth beat us home by just a few minutes. Elizabeth looks awfully cute in the stroller and I imagine Mabel gets a bang out of taking her up to the sea wall.

Monday, October 6, 1952

Dear Mother—

I have reached a conclusion. Granted, I don't want particularly to do housework here. But women (white) seem to suffer from a lack of things to do. We spent a few hours yesterday with the Larthes, leaving Mabel to care for Elizabeth. A friend of theirs, Mrs. C., dropped in. She's the wife of the junior vet. of the colony, and while the Beckleses were on leave the C.'s lived in their house. According to Mrs. B., Mrs. C. broke dishes, broke springs in chair cushions, smashed the refrigerator, etc. etc. The C.'s have a small daughter, and the childless Beckleses may underestimate the normal wear and tear caused by children. At any rate, H. and I are frightfully glad we're not living in the college compound, where the Beckleses, Larthes, Ramsarans, and two other faculty families live. There seems to be a great deal of backbiting, general curiosity, and gossip among them—too close for comfort, we say. This Mrs. C. seemed to have a rather vicious tongue, and commented acidly on several of her friends, a recent party, etc. We felt reasonably certain we were being discussed after we left. Not that we are bothered by such nonsense. Contented as we are with each other, Elizabeth, and our home, we don't give two hoots about partying. We shall entertain mildly, one or two couples at a time, and they can believe us to be eccentric Americans if they wish. I do think the gossip angle results from not having enough to do. My goodness—with full-time nannies to care for the kiddies entirely, cooks and maids to do all the work, there's nothing left but partying! Since I'm not quite as social a creature as some, that doesn't appeal to me (nor to Howard). So—I'm going to use my fertile imagination and keep busy. Mrs. Beckles asked me the other day if I'd be interested in working for the Red Cross after we're truly settled. I accepted. (She says the uniforms are awfully smart—in fact, she introduced the subject by describing the splendid uniforms. Must think clothes are my main concern.) I shall end up an expert seamstress, or shall take to writing children's verse (I wish I could—it appeals to me, and I intend to try)—or something. I nearly had a fit yesterday. It suddenly occurred to me that it is *all wrong* for Mabel to feed Elizabeth when I am here and capable of it. With any other child perhaps I wouldn't feel so strongly. But my maternal instinct blew a fuse yesterday. In such a short time E. is going to want to feed herself. She can almost hold her bottle now. And of course I feel I have the patience and understanding (Mabel may have them too, but I'm E.'s mama!) to devise ways for her to feed herself. From the way she's learning to hold her bottle, I'm sure she'll be able to hold a little glass or cup. But it will doubtless be a messy bottle, and I want to be in on it. My—such a burst of feeling. From now on, Mabel can do E.'s washing with my blessing. And I'm thankful that she can take E. to the sea wall every afternoon (from 4 to 6). H. and I believe it will be good for E., even as young as she is, to see the other little children there. And it is grand to have a reliable person on call for afternoons and evenings if we want to go out. However—I cannot see this European business of leaving everything to the nanny!

We are really innocents abroad. The Larthes and Mrs. C. think we shouldn't be paying Mabel so much ($15; they said we should let her know she's the highest paid half-day help here) and that we shouldn't have to feed either Mabel or Evelyn. Dorothy did allow that Mabel is an excellent maid. People seem to think we're rolling in money, which we nearly are as far as B.G. is concerned. If they only knew! They are surprised to learn of the prestige attached to H.'s fellowship, and can't quite understand why we're here if we can't save money.

Evelyn is a bit presumptuous, but I think she's really trying to help. She just told me we should get linoleum put on the kitchen floor. Heaven knows it would make the kitchen, but a great expense isn't actually sensible for two years' stay.

The Larthes' "greens and floor man" is here now. He is waxing our floors, as he will do once a month as well as "bump" (buff) them every two weeks—for $3.50. There is a lot of floor space, I might say. Thomas is his name, and he has many lovely gold teeth.[12] He brought a basket of greens and I chose lettuce (leaf type), spinach, an avocado, a papaw melon, and icicle radishes. He had some funny little beans, red peppers, and a pitiful green tomato that I turned down.

Much love to you and Daddy—

Marian

This is later—after receiving numerous letters in today's mail. We can't understand how on earth the misconceptions were formed about money. We pay $100 (B.G.) per month for rent, about $50 U.S., and get over twice as much space as we had in Tacoma. We spend $27 for help, B.G. money. For stove and refrigerator, $40 for 12 months. I can't remember what the car payments are, but the down payment was one-third and it will be paid for in a year and a half. Howard received a letter Friday from London saying £375 had been deposited in our account. The bank here hasn't received it, or hadn't on Friday. If it hadn't been for the delay in H.'s salary from the school we'd have needed no loan—and we are awfully sorry you four are upset. H.'s parents had offered several times any help we might need, and I think his mother is upset mainly because she has the money here all confused. Things are expensive here according to B.G. standards, cheap according to U.S., and since H. is being paid top salary at the college, and gets the grants from London and U.S., too, we don't need to worry. The endorsed checks are enclosed, and I'm glad you sent it that way. As for the necessity of the car, H. might be able to do without it, but [in the heat] I don't honestly think I could walk the six or seven blocks each way to town and back! Most things can be delivered, true, but we have no phone and hence can't call cabs, order groceries, etc. Oh well, lah te da! I love you dearly, too!

Marian

Oct. 6, 1952

Dear folks,

I have just received yours of the first and Marian simultaneously got some letters from her folks, and after reading, we conclude that there should be some time spent in clarification.

First, I bought the car simply to spare myself and Marian the extreme social and physical discomfort of having to elbow among the drunkards, the paupers, the narcotic fiends, and so on all the way to town and back again. I haven't mentioned these matters in any detail to you because I didn't want to unnecessarily arouse your anxiety about our welfare. There is privation here in B.G. and in many respects it's most distasteful to say nothing of being unhealthful. Fortunately, our position permits us to be somewhat distant from it. We have not sold our lives away on a down payment—in fact, I offered to wait, but *truly* helpful, the manager urged that we have the convenience of the car's use for $200 down ($116 U.S.). We've paid no more since and shall not until our $1,800 is in hand—we're not expected to.

You generalize on the relative merits of new and used merchandise: true, in the States a good used piece often out-values new equipment on a short-use period. Here in B.G., used refrigerators, stoves, and cars are scarce. In my work in the field I couldn't trust the average or even above-average used car; they're so thoroughly beat up as to be worthless. Prewar cars are rare here (except for U.S. makes) simply because few endeavor to keep them up. As long as we maintain it in reasonably above-average condition (which isn't asking for much here), our car will market for $1800 B.G. in two years—a rather nominal depreciation.

And to finish up this none too pleasant discussion of tangibles and realities, we're not paying $100 U.S. for our present flat but rather $100

B.G., which is comparable to $58 U.S.—exactly what we paid at 901 North "M" Street in Tacoma.

We received a note from [Howard's cousin] today and he's still interested in shrunken heads. Can't help him!

As for school, my students, all 200 of them daily, are superior to Americans of a comparable age as regards academic background and academic zeal. However, many of them are "narrow," particularly those of English birth and upbringing, and seem interested in little else but schoolwork. Some are quite dull, but the overall average is high. I seem to be getting along with them satisfactorily thus far—no overt objections as yet.

I have joined (responding to invitation) the Master's Union, composed of senior government servants in the field of education. It's supposedly an honor to belong—needless to say, I'm by far the junior member. No meetings as yet.

I should close now for dinner.

Love to all,

Howard

October 6:

Our flat received a lift today from Thomas. After I took what I wanted from his basket of vegetables, he started in on the floors. I evidently misunderstood him on Saturday, for I thought he would bring the wax and turpentine. But I gave him six cents and he went out for kerosene. He also had to go out for more wax, but was so unconcerned and pleasant about it. He polished the floors with a heavy polisher that Evelyn could scarcely lift. The floors look lovely now—apparently they hadn't been waxed in ages.

With a little doubt in our minds we gave Evelyn a $5 bill so that she could buy a soft broom that won't scratch our floors. She also wants a short-handled broom or brush to dust the louvers, shelves, and windows. I believe she wants to be helpful—she did quite a few things today without being asked. I simply can't get over having someone handy to peel potatoes, wash dishes after us, empty the baby's bathtub, etc. She polished Howard's muddy black shoes beautifully this morning.

Evelyn tells me that Christmastime brings parties galore. The children dress up as monkeys, dolls, Mickey Mouse, and have a baby parade.

Mabel and I had a little talk about Elizabeth and other handicapped children today, as I felt she should know our feelings in case the subject is discussed at the sea wall. She is quite well informed, intelligent, and thoughtful, and I have no qualms at all. She says everyone admires Elizabeth and that several "European ladies" stopped to talk to her. Mabel is very proud of her charge, I am sure.

October 7:

I think we shall soon see some action on this grant business. Howard received a cable today from the U.S. Educational Commission in London asking us to confirm or deny receipt of the grant. Howard ran right downtown to the cable office and wired back "funds not received." So now we wait awhile longer.

Howard taught his early class this morning, and while I waited for him to return for breakfast I watched the motorcycle policemen across the street going through their paces. They start out sitting normally, rise to a standing position, raise one leg over the seat so that all their weight is on one side of the cycle, and then back they go. All this at quite a rate of speed. It looks as if they're playing follow the leader, but no doubt it is serious work. A few of them took both feet off the pedals and balanced their weight on their hands—quite an exhibit at 6:30 a.m.

We are missing two safety pins, one pink and one blue. I can't imagine what happened to them. I hate to suspect Evelyn of taking them, but I'm afraid I do. It seems like such a little thing, but I'd hate to lose something more valuable later on.

October 8:

An electrician appeared this morning to fix our light switches, and close on his trail followed Miss Osborn. She admired our floors and allowed us to keep the little table we were using in the dining room. Miss Osborn is definitely a character, and hard to understand as she speaks the local dialect very rapidly. Remembering that Howard wanted to ask her about using the garage behind the house, I brought up the subject. I offered her $5 a month for rent, which she accepted, but Howard said later I should have offered half that much!

We went downtown this afternoon and bought more soap dishes, a glass holder for our toothbrushes, a spatula, and other oddments. Also stopped by the library in anticipation of a weekend trip that Howard is planning. One of the masters' brothers is in the Agriculture and Fisheries Department here, and his business frequently takes him into the interior.

Mr. Allsopp has asked Howard to accompany him to the Mahaica settlement, where they will have a mission building to use as lodge and a sort of headquarters. Mr. Allsopp will examine the present state of the fish there, and Howard will have a chance to see some of the plants. It's a wonderful opportunity, all the better because Mr. Allsopp was educated at the University of Wisconsin and understands the American point of view. I shall meet him tomorrow when he comes over to discuss details and arrangements for the trip.

Almost the first thing Evelyn said this morning was that she knew nothing of the missing safety pins, except that something had dropped from the dresser while she was dusting and she couldn't find whatever it was. She offered to pay for the pins, and said she didn't want me to think she'd taken them. Besides, she said, her baby hasn't worn nappies since she was three months old! I declined her offer to pay for them and said we'd just see if they might not turn up. After all, what baby needs more than two safety pins.

October 9:

We are giving Mabel Thursday afternoons off, since she has to have some time in which to do her own washing. So—this morning I industriously washed diapers. Good Lord—how washing machines have revolutionized motherhood in the States!

Mr. Allsopp had said he would drop by this afternoon, but he didn't show up until after dinner. He is very pleasant, thirty-ish, a good-looking young Negro about Howard's height. He graduated from Queen's, then went to the U. of Wisconsin for fisheries work, then toured thirty-six of the forty-eight states. He's been in Washington State and has inspected and studied the fisheries school at the U. of Washington. He realizes the value of a U.S. education and likes the States very much—a refreshing attitude here, where the English don't understand or realize the U.S. educational system. He advised Howard to buy high-top tennis shoes, or "yachting boots" as they are called here, as a protection against snakebites. Howard is to buy a mess kit, a hammock, and blankets, and Mr. Allsopp has offered him the use of his mosquito net. He has charming manners and said he thought he could bring H. home safely! They leave Saturday morning at 7.

Evelyn found the missing blue pin this morning.

Friday, October 10, 1952

Dear Parents—

From yesterday through next week Jamaica and B.G. are involved in a cricket match, and school is dismissed at noon. Besides, Monday is a general holiday—a governor decided a few years ago that the cane workers and other laborers didn't have enough holidays, and so created one in each month—the second Monday of any month without a holiday such as Christmas, is a holiday.

Howard is taking advantage of the three-day weekend and will leave tomorrow morning to go into the interior with an official in the Department of Agriculture and Fisheries. My own preparation consisted of taking four books out from the library.

The library is really quaint. Nearly all the books I've chosen to read belonged formerly to the U.S. Army, which donated American novels, mysteries, and histories of most of the states, many of them missing pages—most irritating in mysteries. Other than that the library shelves are chiefly filled with ancient, uninteresting-looking books. In two years' time I shall probably get down to Religion and Woodworking, and I'm sure I shall read the books I've always intended, but never had the time, to read. Two books per card is the limit—one fiction and one non. I have a Sayres mystery, M. R. Rinehart short stories, *Best Plays of 1938–39*, and *Land Below the Wind*. Looked hard to find them, too.

Howard shopped yesterday—brought home artificial vanilla from South Africa; Royal baking powder, a Standard Brands Ltd. product; and Heinz vinegar, celery salt, and mayonnaise, made in England. Last evening we had lovely lamb chops from New Zealand, fresh native spinach, which tastes very close to our home variety, and broiled plantains, which are first cousins to bananas. They are grown for cooking, and baked or broiled are quite good. Firmer than a banana and with a little more flavor. Evelyn has brought bananas for us twice—gorgeous big ones, which she calls "apple bananas." Elizabeth loves them.

E. is doing just beautifully on her three meals a day. I still am astounded over her last month's progress, for she is now on a genuine Schedule. She does love her ride to the sea wall, and is very happy until she gets home, when she remembers she's starved. Mabel says Elizabeth is the only child there without shoes, and most of the babies wear diaper, plastic pants, slip dress, shoes and socks, bonnet, and sweater. Shades of the Victorian era—E. would die of prickly heat. Have I written that children of two and three years are still pushed up to the sea wall, where according to Mabel they are then allowed to run about? No doubt it's easier on the nannies than chasing them all the way, but I still don't like to see it. Many of the white children look too white—pale and colorless. The Larthes' three are an exception—they are all tanned and look very rugged. Mabel says Elizabeth "talks" all the time they're gone—she does so love to ride.

We agree, rather regretfully, about [the decision not to send] the radio. As yet we know nothing about what's available here, except that there are 33 1/3-speed machines and a few records in the markets, an innovation of the last month or so. Our machine is too nice to risk the journey, and yet not worth all that money. We were awfully sorry about the crib—such confusion. Now that I have calmed down, I imagine this little one will do all right for as long as we'll be here. The mattress isn't very good and I do grieve over not having the lovely big bed and pretty mattress—but I suppose a bed is a bed to Elizabeth. You'd be surprised at the number of times a day she ends up with both legs sticking out between the bars!

My morale improved tremendously after Mabel started washing E.'s diapers. The laundress at Loyola Guest House just didn't get them clean, and they smelled a bit musty. I believe now she must have used cold water, despite my instructions. Mabel gets them *white*, and they smell just as they should. We have a pulley clothesline between a kitchen window and a post outside, and the clothes are right in the afternoon sunlight. Our water is much better here, too—no more mud. By the way, the same old laundress never did get E.'s little white washcloths clean. They were the only ones we had at the Guest House, and with the muddy water there, the cloths got hideously stained. Mabel couldn't even get them clean. Yesterday I decided to boil them, and Lordy—the scum! They still aren't truly white, but they'll do. As yet, we've discovered nothing in the line of Clorox, although we hold out hope.

Still no trunks. Praise be, we didn't rely on having them immediately. And still no grant. H.'s letter from London saying the money had been deposited in London for transfer here was dated September 28, and crossed a letter from H. complaining about the delay. We received a cable Tuesday asking for a confirmation or denial of the money's arrival, and H. wired back Tuesday afternoon. Still no word—it certainly seems strange. Barclays Bank is rapidly losing my sympathy.

H. is enjoying his teaching. Mr. Beckles seems innocently vague about the lack of textbooks, and I believe a wire to London to order books was suggested by him. H. says the little boys are really cute, and many of the oldest ones very keen. Education is a serious matter here. If a boy is expelled from Queen's, he cannot enter any other British or colonial school. And here, unless one has graduated from Queen's or Bishops' (girls), the only jobs available are as laborers. Howard is by far the youngest on the faculty—most are about thirty. And his two degrees and five years of college are more than most have, since three years are required for a degree in England. A few men have master's degrees—not many. I'm running out of stationery.

Love from all of us—

Marian

October 10:

I don't know why we can never get downtown except at the hottest time of day. We left the house about noon and the heat and glare on the streets were terrible. We went right to Fogarty's and purchased a handsome hand-woven hammock, two cotton blankets the color of red dirt (Howard can be so practical!), an enamel cup and plate, and an inexpensive knife, fork, and spoon. These I packed in our market baskets together with flashlight, camera, raincoat, extra clothes, razor, and rum.

But the best news of all came today: Howard was notified by the bank that our funds have finally materialized. Such a relief! The plane from London carrying the message to the bank in Georgetown must have lost some of its mail cargo. Barclays Bank here was wired from London.

Mr. and Mrs. Beckles dropped in to see if I needed anything from the market. We were amused at Mrs. Beckles, who was rather ecstatic over some lettuce "which actually had white hearts!" We love the leaf lettuce we've had here, it has so much more flavor than what we get at home.

They stayed until about 8, and we were starving for our dinner. Evelyn bought fish for me on her way up to work, and we had that snapper with rice and [canned] Canadian carrots. For dessert, I'd made up a packaged pudding, so-and-so's "Jelly Cream," which had less flavor than cotton candy or plain old Jell-O.

October 11:
We got up at 5:30, even before Elizabeth was awake, and I tore around fixing Howard's breakfast, packing a lunch for him to take, and putting last-minute items in the baskets. Elizabeth woke up at about 6, and we took turns feeding her: I while Howard ate cereal, he while I fried an egg, and so on. And then we sat and waited. We both felt frustrated as we could easily have used more sleep. Mr. Allsopp arrived shortly after 8, and it seems he had a message sent to us that we just didn't receive.

Evelyn and I watched them go, and I decided to wash out some underwear to keep busy. It turned out to be a lovely day. Mabel stayed while I fed Elizabeth her supper, and we chatted about all sorts of things. Before she left she asked if I would be all right, and said she'd stay longer but it takes her an hour to walk home. She is a peach.

I felt a bit frivolous after putting Elizabeth to bed, so I brewed a pot of coffee to have with my dinner. The combination of good coffee and a good mystery novel is such fun. I enjoyed them together until the pot was empty, then washed dishes and went to bed.

October 12:
Naturally I miss Howard, but this change of pace is fun. Elizabeth was very obliging about my late hours last night, and slept until 6:30. I made a pot of coffee and began Agnes Newton Keith's *Land Below the Wind*, a fascinating story of her [first] five years in North Borneo. It makes me feel that Georgetown is frightfully civilized in comparison with Sandakan.

The Beckleses came by about 5 to check up on my welfare and brought a magazine for me. Awful stories, but I enjoyed it. The American ads looked good! They stayed until 7, and as I wasn't hungry I decided to be really gay and have a drink. Then I broiled my lamb chop, made another pot of coffee, and once again read until the coffee gave out, which it did about 10. I washed the dishes and just left them to drain, went to bed, and continued to read until 11:30. My eyes are scarcely open now, but this is a treat.

I saw a strange sight today. A Negro woman of middle age walked by the window dressed in a violent magenta dinner dress, full length. I couldn't imagine why until I saw her feet and legs, which were about the size of watermelons, encased in tremendous leather boots. Filaria.[13] The pathetic thing is, we hear, that it can be cured easily if caught early. But the people are generally too distrustful of doctors to be treated.

October 13:
I was awakened at 3 this morning by someone knocking on a door. It frightened me, but as it continued I decided to investigate. The door in question was to the house next door, thank heavens. After a little more prowling, I started back to bed but peeked in on Elizabeth and found a roach on her net. It made me mad, so I got the flit gun from our bedroom and gave him a shot. He fell to the floor, and I put a chair leg on top of him. My first fear of the little monsters is long since gone. Now they just irritate me.

This noon the maid from the upstairs flat presented me with a plate of lemons, "compliments of Mrs. Ina B. M. Ogle," whom we had decided was a bit of a snob. Evelyn made lemonade for me—very tasty.

Howard came in just as I started to feed Elizabeth. He is sunburned but ran into no snakes and has few insect bites. It seems the trip up to the settlement was hampered by delays caused by crossed wires, governmental inefficiency, and the unpreparedness of the boatmen. The men didn't reach the mission until 9:30 Saturday night, and at that there was a half-mile walk from the creek into the mission.

This noon we almost had a genuine domestic crisis: wiring difficulties with the refrigerator. Mabel dashed across the military road for Mr. Beckles, who advised us to call an electrician tomorrow. We had to leave it unplugged, hence no ice water, ice cubes, or chilled food. Disgusting!

Oct. 14, 1952

Dear folks,

I spent this past weekend in the interior with Herbert Allsopp, the deputy Fisheries officer. The opportunity to go came quite suddenly and, naturally, it was one not to be passed. We left early Saturday morning for Mahaica, a small town 25 miles east of Georgetown situated at the mouth of the Mahaica Creek. Upon arriving, we sought the local forest manager, with whom Allsopp had indirectly arranged to take us up the creek, but the gentleman was not to be found. Inquiry revealed that he knew nothing of the venture and so would not arrive before his usual 9:30 time. We awaited his time, met him, and after a whirlwind exchange of opinions during which the medium of verbal exchange lowered from rather decent English to barely discernible Creolese, we were on our way—three and a half to four hours late.

Our vessel was a river launch, which barely accommodated the four of us (we'd picked up a cook). After hitting a number of sand bars and getting into the wrong tributary once or twice, we arrived at the landing ramp of St. Cuthbert's Anglican Mission, 70 miles southeast of Georgetown—at 9:30 p.m.

The Indians there are Arawaks and were most accommodating, offering to do anything for us. They are a very short, stocky lot, slightly Oriental in appearance, and decidedly lacking in ambition. Their standard is quite low for they engage only in such activities as they must. The Anglican representatives (a black pastor and an East Indian teacher) exert the sole progressive influence, this much diminished by a paucity of funds and by their lack of faith in their subjects—a most unfortunate situation. And, too, the mission's economy is not the self-sufficient communal arrangement you'd expect. Instead the men and some women work for nearby rice growers as harvesters, sorters, etc., earning wages with which they purchase goods from Mahaica, 65 miles distant. When we arrived the men in the village were all so drunk on cassiri (fermented cassava juice) that they could hardly carry our gear inland to the settlement. We were so tired at that point we didn't care. They fixed our hammocks and we soon tumbled into them, only I tumbled too hard and landed on the floor—clothesline simply wasn't enough!

The next morning we bathed in the river and, of course, I was the object of much curiosity for white men seldom visit St. Cuthbert's. After breakfast Allsopp went to church and I set about collecting some specimens—a fairly productive undertaking. It was really hot, high 90s by 9:30 a.m., and there wasn't the breeze we all but take for granted on the coast. Nevertheless, I got two presses-full (this is the end of the dry season, and little is in flower). The only incident was the spectacle of a five-to-six-foot snake which, after sizing me up as a poor bet, took off into the bush (the word "jungle" is frowned upon here). Poisonous (striking) snakes are rare in B.G. but constrictors are quite common, their danger potential proportional to their size.

Hygienically, the people seem to be quite sound despite their very starchy diet. The men occupy themselves (when not harvesting rice) by cutting timber and raising some crops; cassava, which we convert to tapioca, is their mainstay. Women seemed to be eternally carrying water from the creek. Most of them were skillful in the preparation of raffia and the weaving of items. At any rate, they are a fairly active lot. Dental troubles

YEARS OF HIGH HOPES

are legion among them. Even little children were losing their first teeth to decay—too much starch.

Allsopp's attempt to have them collect fingerlings for shipment to fishless streams in the northwest probably won't succeed because of their inability to think on a level of colonial (rather than tribal) welfare. At any rate, the trip was most interesting despite numerous motor breakdowns and the oppressive heat (over 100 in the day; about 60 at night). At one point the river borders on the coastal savannah—a prairie or plain to us—relatively treeless and well adapted to cane and rice culture. Elsewhere the river appeared to be in a canyon of vegetation—not particularly tall (seldom in excess of fifty feet) but extremely dense. Among the mucca-mucca stems (a relative of Philodendron) we saw and heard an alligator slither into the water, and up in the trees above the din of the motor we heard and finally saw a few red howlers—arboreal baboons. To imitate their call, pretend you're preparing to gargle and then exhale quickly through your mouth. Magnify that sound 100 times and you may have some idea of what it's like. According to Allsopp, they take particular delight in annoying outdoor campers but seldom are they actually aggressive. The alligators—here called caymen—also seem to be tame or cowardly by reputation. Needless to say, the flora was all new to me. I hope to have that situation relieved in the near future with the acquisition of *The Flora of Trinidad & Tobago* (which is about one-third complete). Although we are some 400 miles from T&T, the floral picture there is much the same as here, so I'm told.

I've more or less decided to concentrate on the plants of the sand belt that extends from Atkinson Field eastward to the Corentyne River because it represents an interesting situation seldom encountered anywhere. The sand belt is actually an old coast, all the land north of it being alluvial in origin. The alluvium is now 50 miles wide, effectively separating this old coast from any direct oceanic influence, and so the once coastal salt-loving plants that inhabited this sandy shore have either perished or adapted to the new condition. Thus far I've found three plants here that occur in Washington—the common ordinary cattail, a low succulent plant called purslane ("parsley" here), and an insectivorous plant, the sundew, whose sticky leaves capture and digest insects for the nitrogen its roots seem unable to secure from the soil. This plant is common in Lake Kapowsin on floating logs, but here is found in a near-desertous situation. The area has sand whiter than any beach sand I've ever seen. This substrate makes aridity inevitable if any rainless period exceeds a few weeks in length. Mitigating this drought twice a year are torrential rains (totaling 80 inches), which inundate much of the region. So the plants inhabiting the district must adapt to aridity and inundation as alternating conditions, each occurring twice a year. That makes for a unique flora well worth separate study. [hand-drawn map] Above is a rough diagram showing the approximate location of the sand belt. I've also indicated a road of sorts extending from Atkinson Field to St. Cuthbert's Mission, entirely in the sandy belt. Certain hazards exist, such as the puma (South American edition of the cougar or mountain lion), large constricting snakes, and a multitude of pestiferous insects. But using precautions, there should be little trouble.

Love to all,
Howard

October 14:

A dull day. I spent a good part of the morning trying to wash rum out of the blanket, undershirt, T-shirt, pair of shorts, and socks that Howard brought back. One of the boatmen put the three-quarters-full bottle back into Howard's basket after they'd all had a little drink, but neglected to tighten the cap. Such a lovely bouquet!

Howard got hold of an electrician today who fixed our wiring. It was faulty wiring that caused the trouble, nothing to do with the refrigerator. Something wasn't strong enough, he said.

October 15:

Today [in Evelyn's absence] I worked: swept, dusted, polished, etc. I enjoyed it, except for the excessive perspiration, and debated with myself all the while whether I should keep Evelyn or do the work myself. It certainly made the morning pass quickly—but Howard tells me there would undoubtedly be days when I wouldn't want to do it, so why not take advantage of the situation. Heaven knows the flat needs to be swept every day. The dust that blows in settles on everything, taking the "newly dusted" look off in a few hours.

We went downtown this afternoon, first to the library for our necessary reading matter. Then to Ferreira & Gomes for jam and hard candy ("sweets"), and to Bookers for a small bottle of baby oil—$1.44. We went to Stabroek Market for fresh fruit, my first visit there. At stalls where fresh produce, drugs, pans, clothes, and such are sold, vendors simply display their wares on the ground, squatting beside them. The market is dark and awfully dirty; it has probably not been cleaned well in years. One of the more artistic sights is the enormous mound of baskets of all shapes, which rises halfway up to the roof and would fill a good-sized room. We bought lovely pork steaks from a man who chopped them off a huge hunk of pork, wrapped them in a piece of an old calendar, and handed them to us. Nothing is wrapped or put into sacks. We carried a basket, and into it put our bananas, oranges, grapefruit, and tangerines.

Next we went to Yong Hing's modern market, the only self-service grocery here. People seem to prefer the services of Bookers or Ferreira & Gomes, where a clerk runs to fetch an item as you point it out. Yong Hing's prices are for the most part lower than Bookers', and as it is the style of marketing we are accustomed to we really prefer it. Canned goods are available, but usually there is only one brand of each item. Flour, sugar, spices, and gelatine are all put up in little paper bags—no neat packaging here. Coffee is ground as you ask for it, and good coffee it is, too. Bacon, butter, cheese, and margarine are kept in three ancient refrigerators. There are some beautiful glacéed fruits in glass jars—I know I shall be tempted by them one of these days!

Thursday, October 16, 1952

Dear Mother and Daddy—

We do so look forward to Mondays and Thursdays, for the mail always brings a letter from either of you and Bee. Your letter came today, Father— awfully glad to know you are still around!

Elizabeth and I are on the double bed. Her one crib sheet (the other half of the big one I split is still being used as a curtain and I can't see spending $6 on another new sheet) is being washed, and she gets around so well now that I don't leave her alone, awake, on our bed. We're going to get a playpen in a few days as she will really need it before long.

Have I told you that our trunks should arrive on the 22nd? They sail from Trinidad on Monday on an Alcoa ship, so we expect them next week. You have no idea how we are looking forward to clean sheets, towels, etc. Typewriter, too!

Elizabeth's teeth don't seem to be troubling her anymore—the two lower ones are really through. She is so cute and so good. We haven't rocked her to sleep since we moved in here, and she doesn't even peep at night before she goes to sleep. She and Mabel return from their walk at 6, and Elizabeth yowls impatiently while Mabel removes the dress and puts on her nightshirt. I feed her, put her to bed, and in a few minutes she's sound asleep. Mabel feeds E. only if we have to go downtown or are otherwise away—she does give E. her afternoon orange juice.

We still haven't priced radios here, although I'm afraid they aren't cheap. Nevertheless we should hate to be without music for two years, so we shall find something, I'm sure. Will you be able to send our records—even just the LPs if the others would prove too heavy and expensive. We're considering the possibility of having things sent collect but there's probably a hitch somewhere.

Howard and I are both put out that this money situation got everyone in such a muddle! We never would have wired if we hadn't been told to if we needed to, and the only reason we wired you as well was because we were told we could expect an answer to wire No. 1 a day after it was sent. H. had great doubts of the efficiency of the cable office here, and when we didn't get an answer we figured our message had just been misplaced somewhere. We realize that you all think it is high time that we Accepted Our Responsibilities, etc., which, by George, we do! The only lessons we have learned from this are (1) whenever you move anyplace, take everything you own, dish drainers, garbage pails, and goblets included; (2) always remember that government red tape fouls things up for weeks longer than you'd expected; and (3) try not to disappoint parents whose feelings vacillate between "she (he) is my child and I want to help her (him)" and "why the hell can't she (he) grow up!" In line with (3), we shall endeavor to be strictly self-supporting from now on. Heaven knows you two have been most helpful—perhaps too much so. This muddle would never have occurred if we'd been left to fight out last year by ourselves—but then we'd probably not be here, either!

Being a lady here in Georgetown presents a paradoxical situation to me. I have always wanted to be a housewife, and now here I am with two maids who do almost everything. Yesterday, by arrangement the day before, Evelyn didn't come—her baby was sick and she had to take her to the doctor. So I swept and dusted and washed dishes. The morning went by more quickly than usual, and I was dripping slightly from the exertion when I finished. I do enjoy cooking, and eating, and I fear I am gaining weight. On days when Evelyn is here my most strenuous activity is washing out underwear.

I would be a prize chump to turn down help, but I do feel a bit useless. Of course, as H. says, we're really not settled, and I have curtains to sew, as well as unpacking and dealing with the trunks to do.

The Beckleses are helpful, but we are developing a strong urge to get Mr. B. to disagree with us on any single point, no matter how trivial. His chief expression is "Quite so, quite so." Annoying after a while. Mrs. Beckles is the only white woman I've seen here who wears stockings. I'm afraid her scope of interest is concerned mainly with movies, movie stars, and second-rate fiction. Still, they are very nice and have been so very helpful.

I must confess that not only have I ceased wearing stockings but I have also quit wearing slips with dresses heavy enough to be modest; and I hardly ever wear pants. They gave me prickly heat far worse than Elizabeth has ever had, and having a rash on one's stomach, sit-upon, and legs is a nuisance. Every afternoon I shower, then put on clean clothes and either the spectators or the white linen pumps you gave me, Mother. They are awfully comfortable and I'm very glad I bought that height heel.

Howard's trip into the bush was most educational, and he thinks he has found an area of interest on which he might base a thesis. I hope he can type out his weekend's experience next week or when his pictures are developed, as I couldn't begin to do it justice.

I'm glad neither H. nor I spent a large sum on our hats—no one wears them here but the Negroes. The little boys at Queen's wear pith helmets as part of their uniform, and all the colored women wear hats. (Mabel has one that is an awful lot like my fifty-cent wonder.)

Thanks muchly for the rubber bands. They don't last very long here.

H. is going to contact the radio hams [to see about the possibility of communicating with Marian's parents]. One name sounds familiar, and he thinks the man may be connected with the college.

We hear there was a picture in *Life* of someone feeding the manatees in the Botanical Gardens. Did you see it?

Much love to you both, and do take care of yourselves. Go to the beach!

Marian

Thursday, October 16, 1952

Dear Bee—

I have decided that the Tacoma city clerk has sent our absentee ballots by regular mail, and we wonder if we will ever get them. Darn it, we'd like to do our bit for Ike, too.

Elizabeth has two teeth! Naturally, you have to look closely to see them, but there are two teeth peeking through above the gum. Our discipline has abated only because it's no longer needed: no more sugar on pacifier, no more rocking to sleep, no more need for constant entertainment. She'll be crawling in another few weeks, and then we'll really have to watch her.

About books: the Georgetown library is worse than Tacoma's. Probably a third of its books belonged to the U.S. Army base here: histories of many of the states, adventure, mysteries, novels, etc. I've been having a lovely time reading. Yesterday I brought home *Of Time and the River* since somehow I've always overlooked Thomas Wolfe. Most of the books there are relics of the ages—dirty, battered, with pages missing. There is a relatively new set of *Remembrance of Things Past* so I may work up my courage one of these days and take it out, book by book.

As for movies, there are two theaters where the better people go—the Globe and the Plaza. Nearly all pictures are from Hollywood, and they're not as old as you might think. It costs three shillings (72 cents) to go, and the Globe, which is the only one we've got to, is really quite nice. No eating, but smoking.

We are still counting on your paying us a visit!

Much love to you,

Marian

October 16:

Once again, Mabel's day off, so I washed diapers as my chore for the day. We decided to take a ride this afternoon as Elizabeth would otherwise have been cheated of her daily outing.

As usual, we drove past Thompson's Ebony Parlour, out through Kitty, which is supposedly a good suburb but looks pretty crummy to me, and along the sea wall. Howard pointed out the faded red flags on tall bamboo poles, which the East Indians erect for each married child in their families.

At one spot by the roadside a man, a large woman in a purple dress, and three little pigs were lying down and apparently sleeping. On their way to market, I suppose.

Howard learned another strange custom last weekend. A motorist who hits and kills a goat, sheep, chicken, or other small animal may take away the body if he cuts off the head and leaves that behind. If you hit a cow, you are fortunate to get away with your own head intact, I gather.

We got home in time to hear the band as it drilled across the street. The band played several American marches, "Washington Post" among them. It is a strange-looking group, for the militiamen wear khaki shorts and shirts, and the policemen wear their regulation navy blue shirts and trousers. But they sound good, and it's fun being so close.

October 17:

Today was ghastly—no breeze at all. For the first time since our arrival, we were really uncomfortable, for the heat was oppressive without the refreshing wind.

Howard, free for the afternoon because of the cricket match, went on the prowl for a good, sturdy worktable and came upon a dandy, hideous one that was delivered this afternoon. It is a good-size table, ugly only because of the columns on which it is based. These columns are about six inches deep and twenty-four inches wide, and have doors with locks—caches for the family jewels, no doubt. Unfortunately, the keys have been lost.

We had a domestic incident today. I discovered that Evelyn has been using butter ($1.04 per pound) instead of margarine ($.50) on her bread, and asked her not to use the butter. She said she would eat her bread dry. Then at lunch, I put the butter back in the refrigerator after using it for Howard and me, leaving the margarine out for Mabel. "Is this for me?" she asked a bit querulously. I said yes, and she replied, "I don't eat it." So she ate her bread dry. I cannot believe they are used to butter and heaven only knows why they should be so uppity about margarine, unless they are just testing me!

October 18:

I threw a fit this afternoon over sheer lack of anything to do. We are still without curtains but feel we should wait for our rugs before purchasing material. Sitting and doing nothing or reading and writing letters is fine for a while. But after a few days it is awful. After my cookbooks arrive I can direct a little more energy toward cooking. It is a challenge here with meat limited to a great extent to lamb and mutton, and fresh fruits and vegetables none too plentiful.

The Larthes are coming over tomorrow, so I shall make some cookies in case they prefer tea to a drink.

We went to a movie—*Calling Bulldog Drummond* and *Golden Girl*. Double bills are almost too much, for we're used to being in bed at 8:45, when the first picture is just beginning. Mabel doesn't seem too keen on staying so late, but she is paid for it.

October 19:

Lord—what a day. Wesley Jorgensen, the American vice-consul, stopped by at 9:30 this morning and invited us to supper to meet another American couple who arrived in B.G. last Wednesday. He said 6:30, and we crossed our fingers and accepted, hoping we could count on the Larthes to leave at about that time.

I threw together a batch of cookies, baking them on the bottom of my one roasting pan and cooling them on a tea towel spread across two pans—despite the makeshifts, they came out well. While I was baking them Evelyn said, "Pancakes?" I told her, "No, cookies"—she thought that an awfully funny word, but said the one I gave her "was tasting delicious."

Dorothy and Archie came about 4:30 and Howard and I realized too late that they expected tea and not a drink. (They eat a huge meal at tea!) But we had the cookies and a drink made from sorrel[14] that Mrs. Ogle sent down for us to try. They are good conversationalists and we had fun, but I got nervous as the hour drew later. Mabel and Elizabeth returned from their walk; I fed Elizabeth and put her to bed. The Larthes left at five minutes to 7, when they had to go home to hear their children's prayers, and we snatched poor Elizabeth from her bed and tore out of the flat. Mabel couldn't stay on such short notice, unfortunately.

We arrived at the Jorgensens' and put Elizabeth to bed upstairs, where she howled lustily for a while. I'd lost her pacifier somewhere in all the rush, and she resented it. Downstairs we met Clifford and Betty Evans, both Ph.D.s, educated at Columbia and now connected with the Smithsonian Institution, where she is a researcher and he assistant curator of the archaeological division. They are here on a Fulbright research grant, the first to be given for this colony, just as H.'s is the first teaching grant, and they are leaving Friday for the interior, where they will begin their studies.

Talking to Americans was a real tonic! The Evanses have spent a great deal of time in South America and, knowing the continent as they do, insist that Georgetown is a more highly civilized city than most. They were as amazed as we were at the number of American products available here.

We don't care too much for the consul or his wife. He is quick to complain about situations here (he says Georgetown is considered a "hardship post"). Their house is enormous, very comfortably furnished (except for all their leather upholstery, which gave me prickly heat again) with American furniture. They lead a life that would kill Howard and me—either entertaining or being entertained every evening! Mrs. Jorgensen is a native of Aruba (Dutch West Indies), and they met while he was serving there. She wore a black taffeta dress, which looked frightfully warm, and stockings. I suppose she must, in her "position," but the mere thought of nylons appalls me now.

We both thought several times during the evening how much more fun it would have been without our hosts. Their conversation added little of interest, and we did enjoy hearing of the Evanses' travels. They live with the natives of the locales they study, and learn a great deal of native history, custom, etc. in that way. They are having much of the same trouble with funds as we did, but the Smithsonian is paying them as well as the U.S. Educational Commission, so they aren't desperate. They are about thirty or younger. We hope to take them for a drive some afternoon this week. Cliff told H. that he thought H. should do his research with a Ph.D. in mind rather than an M.S., which he said would be a waste of time.

We didn't get home until midnight, much too late considering Howard's 6 a.m. class tomorrow!

October 20:
Today our trunks leave Port of Spain, to arrive here on Wednesday—we hope! We decided to forget about waiting for the rugs before buying curtain material, so this afternoon (more cricket) Howard and I went to Fogarty's to look over their selection. We bought some lovely material for our dining room window: it is a provincial pattern with brown, rust, orange, green, and a touch of aqua. Very good-looking—I can just see our copper candlesticks with it.

We saw some brown material that would look fine in the living room, but we had to readjust our figuring from 54-inch material to 42-inch, so we couldn't buy it today. Saw nothing we liked for our bedroom, where we most desperately need curtains!

I have almost finished the first of the two dining room panels, and we are now wondering what people here do about curtain rods. We refuse to use string or wire, as the previous occupants evidently did.

As of today we're out of butter until the end of the week, so H. and I are using margarine because I refuse to buy more than one pound of butter at $1.04 a week. I fear I'm gaining weight, and I use too much butter anyway.

October 20, 1952

Dear folks,

We've more or less settled into a routine now that school is well under way and domestic issues have crystallized—and we've become accustomed to the climate. For the last few weeks I've been "all shot" at 3, when school dismisses, and have come home to read or do a little shopping, and then, upon having a rum and lime before dinner, I've sometimes all but collapsed, but now I feel as though I'm coming up and feeling my own.

The help situation, although superficially serene and a seeming luxury, still baffles us at times. The attitudes of those we have (and those others have) are sometimes puzzling. For instance, Marian has been giving Evelyn, our housekeeper, half loaves of bread that we don't need (we're gaining too much weight) and even an orange occasionally for her baby, but now she doesn't even thank us for the donations. In fact, we've just had to ask her to quit seeking handouts—she kept asking for butter, cheese, tangerines, etc.—things that are rather expensive and clearly beyond her buying power. Mabel, our "nanny," came to us highly recommended; just now Marian discovered that Mabel has helped herself to one of our plastic refrigerator bags and has put it in her own handbag. We do hate sleuthing but it seems necessary for self-preservation. At this point we've decided that if any more of this sort of thing occurs, we'll dismiss both of them and just forget about having help. Under this arrangement Marian finds she has to look for things to keep herself busy—at any rate, it seems decadent to be free of all responsibility, material and otherwise. She is busy now making draperies for our dining and living rooms and since all the stitching must be hand-done, a good deal of time will be consumed.

We had a rather busy weekend. We invited the Larthes over for Sunday afternoon and as soon as that date had been set (on Saturday), Wesley Jorgensen came by and invited us to their home Sunday evening. The Larthes are a lot of fun and have been here long enough to know something of the place. It came as a surprise to me, but Archie really despises teaching and seems to be shooting for an administrative post—and such is not available here. We are just a bit embarrassed, too, in regard to their visit for we think they came expecting tea, and we haven't really accepted the custom of having mid-afternoon tea as yet. Incidentally, "tea" means more than just tea. It implies the service of sandwiches, biscuits (cookies to us), jams, etc. in addition. In other words, a meal.

As soon as they left, we went to the Jorgensens' and met, in addition to Mrs. J., a couple from Washington, D.C., Clifford and Betty Evans. They plan on being in B.G. for seven months during which time they'll scout the interior for anthropological artifacts, fossils, and anything else that will shed light on the identity of the old aboriginal tribes that once flourished in B.G.

Cliff and I had a rather lengthy "on the side" talk about our respective projects. He more than intimated that whatever field research I do here in taxonomy should be applied to a Ph.D. or else separately published irrespective of any lower endeavor. Collecting specimens with the intent of publishing a flora (in this case, of a restricted area) is purely and simply an academic effort. Academic ventures are not yet known in B.G., which seems to be fighting tooth and nail for economic stability. In other words, there are few people here whose mentalities are broad enough to encompass the value of such work. That's why talking with Cliff left me more resolute than ever. He additionally said that Georgetown is unquestionably one of the most advanced cities in equatorial South America, exceeding Lima, Peru, and Bogotá, Colombia, in total offering. In fact, in his opinion, the only South American cities that exceed Georgetown are Buenos Aires, Argentina; Santiago, Chile; and São Paulo and Rio de Janeiro, Brazil. It seems so strange for B.G. does have so little on the ball as compared with the U.S.—we took so much for granted at home.

Love to all,

Howard

P.S. According to a fortnightly weather survey (of the previous two weeks), the temperature here has been 91°–93° each day (in the shade) and 72° at night— yet we've been perfectly comfortable. Good old breeze!

Tuesday, October 21, 1952

Dear Parents—

I keep thinking "I shall just wait for the typewriter and then write," but now I have convinced myself that there is only a small possibility of our trunks arriving tomorrow per schedule.

The enclosed scrap is the material for our dining room draperies. We have one window there facing a house only too close—so despite the fact that drawn draperies will cut some of the breeze, we're going to have draw draperies for privacy's sake. The print should look good with our dishes.

I have found some material downtown that I want for our living room curtains if the store can give me enough. It is dark brown cotton with a nice texture—I'll send a piece after we get it. There is some cheap pink gauze-like material with little bumps in it (I'm sure you know what I mean!) that would, I think, be sweet in E.'s room. Still haven't found what I want for our room.

We received our first two *Saturday Reviews* last week, and we've read every word in them. We are eagerly waiting for *The New Yorker*. American magazines are quite expensive here—most of them 56 cents (*Collier's*, *Life*, etc.). I'm really glad to have to do all the curtains by hand, as they will take longer to do. Efficiency and speed are not important factors here.

Yesterday I discovered a small eaten spot in the jersey dress you gave me, Mother. It's right next to the top button, but fortunately won't show much in the lovely splotchy pattern.

Since we like fresh air, we've been leaving all our windows open at night as well as during the day and even when we go out, as we felt awfully secure here on the second floor with no roofs or porches from which to gain access to our windows. Now we learn that everyone closes and locks all windows at night because burglars can, somehow, get into nearly any window. Last night I closed 15 windows, and reopened them this morning! We'll leave our bedroom window open as we do need a little air at night. Mrs. Jorgensen told us that she's heard of burglars who coat themselves with grease to avoid being caught and held, and who wear two shirts, one loose that will come off easily if grabbed.[15] After the family silver arrives I shall no doubt become nervous, but we will lock it up and hope for the best. By the way, nowhere have we seen so much as a sterling teaspoon yet—not even at the Jorgensens' (navy plate there, yet). I can't figure out why, since things tarnish here no quicker than anywhere else. Unless it is just the ease with which things disappear.

There is no doubt about it: Elizabeth is absolutely the cutest baby! She is also a ham and a show-off. You would have loved to see her last Sunday when she giggled at Dorothy Larthe for about fifteen minutes. She loves strangers and puts on quite a show for them.

I forgot to say that we've decided to cover the cushions on our living room chairs, as the present pink is not in tune with our favorite color harmonies. I call it slightly passionate pink; H. calls it whorehouse pink—it really isn't bad, but we prefer browns, greens, etc.

"I Wonder Why" is currently popular here, and I keep remembering *Call Me Madam* and the other wonderful tunes from it. We certainly enjoyed that weekend!

Much love to you both,
Marian

October 21:

How we are looking forward to having our trunks! Howard says our sheets are becoming unbearable, and our towels are utterly disgusting.

At least I have the curtains to keep me busy. I have finished the dining room curtains except for hems, which I shall put in after we hang them.

We are a little surprised to learn that Mr. Beckles's M.A. is a degree which, in effect, he merely bought. It seems that so many years spent in the colonial service, plus a certain amount of time spent in England, qualify a person for an advanced degree in the subject in which his original degree was taken. Those upon whom the degree is conferred are supposed to appear in person; if, however, that is impossible, the degree is conferred in absentia upon payment of £40. Sounds odd to us, but maybe we don't know the entire story. Degrees here mean everything: for instance, whenever the acting governor is mentioned in the papers, it is always as "His Excellency the Officer Administering the Government, Hon. John A. Gutch, CMG, OBE." We still don't know what the letters stand for.[16] Howard has received mail addressed to "Mr. H. Irwin, Esq., B. Sc."—which isn't correct, of course, but neither are the M.A.'s that appear after his name!

October 22:

You'd think we would know not to be so optimistic. Our trunks, Howard learned today, will leave Port of Spain tomorrow on the Alcoa ship *Tyra* and will be here Monday. So they say.

We continued our search for drapery material today and did quite well. The clerks weren't sure there was enough of the brown material I'd picked out Monday the 20th, but fortunately there was. We bought sheer pink material with dots for Elizabeth's room—can't think of the proper name, but it looks feminine. Also some aqua Indian Head for our room. It all came to a little less than $100, and the girl had to take the sales slip upstairs for approval since we already had some things on account and the store won't allow more than $100 to accumulate on a charge account. We were peeved but came home for the checkbook. Returning, we found the head of the department standing by our parcel, and he hastened to apologize profusely. We started to leave, but this time we were nearly mowed down by our friend Beefy, the assistant manager, who lumbered clear across the store calling Howard's name, even more apologetic than the other man. He nearly bowed from the waist, was so upset, sorry we were caused embarrassment, and so on. It struck us as funny yet distasteful to have this huge man treating us as if we had been offended royalty.

We have invited the Ramsarans to tea on Saturday. I told Howard I feel foolish asking an English family to tea, like coals to Newcastle. However, that's not the point, as it would be nice to see people occasionally.

October 23:
Curtains, curtains, curtains. I am getting a blister on my finger, but I still can't sew with a thimble. I ran up Elizabeth's pink curtains in a spare moment after I ran out of aqua thread. Howard bought another "reel" of thread for me, so now I have completed the first bedroom curtain and am halfway through No. 2.

We discovered that metal curtain rods cost a shilling (24 cents) a foot— way too much for us. Accordingly, Howard bought 100 feet of poling today and spent this afternoon cutting it into suitable lengths. At that, there isn't quite enough, and we need about 50 feet more. We hung the one curtain in the bedroom, and I finally removed the dishtowel-pinned-to-a-crib-sheet that has been shielding us from public gaze. Thank heavens!

October 24:
Spent most of the day finishing up the bedroom curtains. Somehow or other I miscalculated on the yardage, and the draperies are full enough so that we can draw them across the entire wall, adding an elegant air to the room.

Yesterday afternoon, to entertain Elizabeth while I sewed, I put her down on the floor on a blanket to let her try a little more creeping. Her creeping is just one-way, backwards at that, but she does cover ground. Now everything she sees interests her, from my pin box and thread and scissors to the tablecloth, dishes, letters, and magazines. We must be nearing the "no, no" stage. She is so cute with her two teeth, and she still wants to chew on everything.

October 25:

I started early today, and made sandwiches and then cookies for this afternoon. We had to borrow more cups from Mrs. Beckles, and H. bought paper napkins (he asked for plain ones, and was given holly wreaths!). It also seems that baking chocolate doesn't exist here; you buy milk chocolate and hope for the best, or use cocoa.

The Ramsarans came at about 4 and we had a most pleasant afternoon. We feel encouraged about the local social situation, since the Ramsarans seem to feel as we do about the cocktail-and-bridge parties that most people here consider a necessity. They abhor the gossip as we do, and are remaining as aloof as possible, considering their position there in the college compound. Mrs. Ramsaran said it irritated her to be told she had to have a maid and a nanny for Susan, so they've been here for six months and as yet have no servants. They don't drink at all but apparently don't object to others doing so. They left us with a cordial invitation to drop in anytime, for tea or just to chat.

Howard and I ate dinner, for which we weren't too hungry, and then went to see *The Wild North* with Stewart Granger, and I must say it was exciting. The snowbanks were refreshing, even if the wolves were too realistic. We arrived, as before, at 8 although the pictures don't begun until 8:30—we enjoy watching the people. Horrible songs are played over a loudspeaker system, American cowboy songs, twangy local records in calypso style, etc. We still can't figure out why the masses in the house seats downstairs refuse to stand for "God Save the Queen." Some even turn around and leer at those in the balcony who do. We are disillusioned: candy is sold! A girl walks through the balcony before the movie starts with a "confectionary box." I suppose they call it progress!

October 26:

E. has a touch of diarrhea, so she had only watered-down milk for supper tonight. Nothing serious, I'm sure. Mabel is sure it is just her teeth!

At lunchtime Margaret Ramsaran dropped by with Susan to offer the use of her sewing machine for the draperies. Good! She also asked if we would care to play badminton with them in the college dining room, but I declined that as best I could. Even if we wanted to play, I can't quite see getting so steamed up deliberately.

We took a little drive while Elizabeth and Mabel were out, past the Carib and then back through town. Drove by a large crowd gathered to watch the pulling-out operations of a car (postwar Plymouth) that had landed on its top in the roadside ditch. Pretty well battered.

Monday, October 27, 1952

Dear Mother—

Talk about "tomorrow and tomorrow and tomorrow"—this "petty pace" which is taken here is driving us crazy. H. was told this morning that our trunks will arrive tomorrow. I truly doubt it. They allowed him to make out a custom's declaration, so perhaps there is hope.

I'm still deep in yardage, but we are enjoying tremendously going to bed, eating, etc. in relative privacy. Living room yet to do.

Thanks muchly for rubber bands, clippings, etc. Had two letters from Bee—you can't imagine how hard we're hoping that she can visit us! Daddy might like it here, but I'm awfully afraid that if you came, you'd want to clear out the refrigerator and climb in. Don't worry about my modesty—I always check carefully, and wear more clothing than some do at that.

I liked the article about faith—heaven knows some inner resources are necessary here. We are repelled by the eager gossip that abounds in some gatherings. Saturday we had the Ramsarans to tea, and I do believe we shall enjoy their company. They are being beautifully independent about servants (have none at this point, although with both Mrs. R. and her mother to do the housework, they don't need anyone desperately). I loved Mrs. McLaren for saying that they'd had a "daily woman" for ten years in London but would never have considered calling her their maid! They resent, as we do, some of the whites who pedestalize themselves for no good reason except skin color. (We'd love to see them in the States, scrubbing their own floors!)

We are enjoying our legs of lamb and mutton and our chops so much. Howard found raw carrots again on Saturday, and for dinner tonight I shall roast them with onions and potatoes with our leg of lamb. We have had lovely pork chops, too—60 cents for three huge ones. Pork is purely local, of course, and when it comes from Stabroek it still has rind, bristles, etc. and is *filthy*. I cook and cook and cook it, and it is awfully good.

Elizabeth has learned the fine art of coughing. The first few times I heard her I was certain she was choking on her pacifier and rushed to her rescue, to find her lying contentedly on her back, coughing gently and looking very pleased.

Are you sending our LPs, and if so, how? We bought a secondhand table-model radio today and are going to get a portable record player later. Combinations cost $500 and up—they are ugly in design, too. So we couldn't see buying a new one. This is a Pye, a new name to me, and has good tone. We're simply starved for music.

I would love the address labels. My writing, I'm told, is none too clear at times.

Elizabeth sends a kiss and a cough! Love to you both—

Marian

Monday, October 27, 1952

Dear Bee—

I'm surprised we forgot to tell you of H.'s visit to the bush or interior, and now I can't remember if I wrote of our evening at the American consul's home. My mind is still on curtains, I guess. Howard went about 45 miles (65 boat miles) into the interior with a fisheries officer, and they stayed at an Anglican mission, St. Cuthbert's, on the Mahaica Creek. They sweltered at 9 a.m., and by 10 everyone was through with his daily chores. Nights were quite cool. H. collected two presses full of specimens and, most important, located a region for further study, research, and intense collecting. . . . He came back with a sunburned nose, no mosquito bites, and a basketful of rum-soaked clothes (a boatman forgot to put the top on tightly!).

We had the Ramsarans to tea on Saturday. They are such a nice family, and have remained, as we hope to do, apart from the social whirl with its late hours, drinking, gossip, etc. Too many women here do nothing but play cards, chitchat and party, and complain. Can't see it, myself! John R. teaches literature and English, is very quiet and pleasant, and is quite a scholar, interested as H. is (and few others) in continuing his own education.

Our trunks will arrive tomorrow, H. was told today. My hopes have been dashed to pieces too many times now to take it seriously!

Much love to you,

Marian

October 27, 1952

Dear folks,

I was glad to hear from you again, Dad, and I will undertake to answer your questions.

The preservation of collected plant material is more difficult here than in temperate climes but not at all impossible. I found at Q.C. a metal-lined herbarium case that will serve well to receive any specimens I may gather—a few ounces of calcium silicate on each shelf will absorb any excess moisture. Insects are legion here, but DDT still seems to be effective against most of the smaller ones and, of course, its latent effect is invaluable.

I understand from Herbert Allsopp, the fisheries officer with whom I made the trip to St. Cuthbert's, that the shipment of botanical specimens to the U.S. from B.G. is not difficult because of there not existing here any plant or other pathogens of which there is fear in the States. Climatic disparity probably rules out 99 44/100 of them, but I shall get official word from the Dept. of Agriculture and Wes Jorgensen, the American vice-consul.

As for the nature of my work, I am still a bit nebulous about the proper approach. A botanical collection of taxonomic specimens would serve merely as documentary proof of residence in work of this type, not as an end in itself. A new species may be uncovered here and there, but that is not the aim. My aim would be to relate the changes undergone by certain plants in adapting to a xerophytic (desert) environment from a halophytic (littoral) one. The question arises about the distinction between those which have truly undergone such adaptation and those which have come upon the scene as natural introductions. Here is the true test of taxonomic knowledge, for the only way to resolve such a question in respect to a given individual would be to seek out close relatives now known to exist as halophytes. That could not be done here because the present littoral zone is not at all like that which this sand belt once provided. B.G.'s shores are of mud (alluvial deposits from the geologically recent Orinoco River of Venezuela) and, in fact, the water itself is an unappealing mud-brown. In the very cursory examination I've given the sand belt, I've noticed some markedly different plants which I am at a loss to place in families (I once prided myself on this ability!)—I have no doubt of its botanical worth.

We still have not received our trunks. Both yesterday morning and this morning I went to the docks and the ship from Trinidad had not made port. This afternoon I am to call a bond clerk at one of the docks who said he'd give me the time it will put in, but we're not very hopeful. One thing you encounter here is inefficiency and irresponsibility. It seems to be a disease in every line of endeavor. At first it was annoying, then maddening, but now we've more or less accepted it.

Later—5 p.m.: Well, the ship has not yet appeared but is due to "soon," according to the dockmaster where I called. I do hope by the time I next write we'll have the trunks.

Our absentee ballots came a couple of days ago. We filled them out—straight Republican except for Sullivan—and they'll make the Pan Am plane to New York tomorrow. (Postage totaled $2.34!)

Love to all,

Howard

October 27:

Howard bought the radio, and this afternoon we picked up the three-speed Garrard record player. I waited in the car while he went in for it, and had a fright when a young black man put his hand on the car door and peered in at me. I reached over and put my hand on the horn, but before I pressed it he left.

Our absentee ballots arrived in today's mail, so at 3 when H. was through at school we drove down to Wesley Jorgensen's office to fill them out. Having done so we discovered that we are entered in different voting precincts [in Seattle], and couldn't remember which was whose. Although it didn't seem very legal, Wesley had us bring the ballots home and told Howard to return them tomorrow.

Our eyes really popped this afternoon when we watched a funeral procession go by outside our door. The hearse was a large, shiny, black carriage, drawn by two large, shiny, black horses. The driver actually wore a stovepipe hat. The mourners' carriage was also ancient and shiny and pulled by high-stepping black horses, and it even had a footman. The cars that followed were regrettably up-to-date.

The trains here look like antiques, too. All I can think of when we see them is an old picture of the driving of the golden spike that joined the continent at Promontory Point. The engines are tiny, dull black, steamy toys, and it would take at least two to equal our "iron monsters" in bulk.

October 28:

Still no trunks. What is more, no one accepts any responsibility for or affirms any knowledge of the ship's whereabouts. Bookers' dock and the government dock both are ruled out: officials said, "Oh no, Alcoa ships don't dock here." A man at Sproston's [steamer ferry service] said he'd look into the matter for us, but we're beginning to think that our trunks, the ship, et al. are mere fantasies.

An electrical inspector came this afternoon to look at the stove connection. He was a very pleasant and intelligent Negro, with a Portuguese (white) assistant. The inspector pointed at what he wanted done and the assistant hopped around to do it. He asked how long we'd been here, and at my reply said that wasn't really time enough to make any impressions. I told him we liked what we had seen, and he said he knew one English lady who had said she didn't like it here because it never changed, that there are no seasons. He said, "She was no student of nature. All she needed to do was look at her five fingers, none of which were exactly alike. One can't expect B.G. and the world over to be exactly like England!"

Howard and I went out to buy some lime rickey, and we drove by the sea wall but didn't see Elizabeth and Mabel. Some of the shrubs here are lovely. Hibiscus is used as a hedge, but we like it much better untrimmed. We saw some fuchsia-colored blossoms that were just beautiful. The bougainvillea up the street has had its fall and winter and is now blooming as lustily as it was a month ago.

October 29:

Oh, inefficiency! We can't help being exasperated by it. Howard learned today that our trunks have been here for eleven days. They didn't come on the Alcoa *Tyra* but on a ship that left Port of Spain earlier! Naturally, the nincompoops at the dock couldn't be bothered to notify Howard, even though he had left them his address. We hope to get the trunks through customs and carted here tomorrow.

Elizabeth is still bothered by diarrhea. Mabel said that often "teething humbugs the tummy," but I'm afraid that theory is passé. Tomorrow we will take her to a doctor if there is no improvement.

I went to the Ramsarans' about 1 p.m. to sew on the draperies. Got very little stitching done, but had a good chat with Mrs. McLaren, in whose room the machine is located. We had tea about 3:30 and then Howard arrived with the news about the trunks. We plan to take the R's for a ride next Saturday.

Undoubtedly one of the most valuable aspects of our stay here will be our friendships with people such as the Ramsarans. Both Margaret and her mother feel badly that they came out to B.G. "a year too soon," and will miss the Queen's coronation in June. According to Margaret, the pageantry of the State opening of Parliament is something that is thrilling and exciting to her even though she has seen it every year of her life.

Mrs. McLaren says the only reason the crowds in the theater's house seats don't rise is lack of education and respect in regard to royalty, and some Communistic influence which, many seem to agree, is present here.

October 30:

Howard made an appointment to see Dr. Kerry this afternoon, and he left school early so we could take Elizabeth at 1:30. The doctor is a tiny man— he would probably come up as far as my shoulder, if that far. He's East Indian and has a nephew at Queen's. He asked us what we feed Elizabeth, and when I told him he shook his head at the answer. "Typical American diet," he said. "We go a bit slower here." He told me I should boil her bottles for 20 minutes—and to think I didn't boil a blessed thing for three whole weeks at that guesthouse! I couldn't sterilize anything but merely had faith in Dr. Hellyer's statement that we wouldn't need to sterilize after four and a half months under "reasonable sanitary conditions"! But Dr. Kerry said her diarrhea didn't seem to be serious, and gave us a prescription for her.

We had it filled at Bookers, and I'm sure it is the same chocolate-peppermint-flavored stuff I had last Christmas. Howard also bought some arrowroot flour at Dr. Kerry's suggestion, for he told us to give E. only arrowroot cereal and glucose-flavored water until she's well. My Lord—the glutinous mass that resulted when I tried to cook the flour into a cereal! I tried two batches, gave up, and cooked some groats (a powdered oat cereal) for the poor child, who was yowling with hunger by this time.

And—we have our trunks now. Howard had a marvelous experience with the customs man who examined them. He was asked to open one trunk for inspection, and by chance he picked the one with his stamp collection and our silver in it, both dutiable items. The inspector had asked H. where he worked, and H. told him although he felt the question rather unnecessary. The man said, "Are you by any chance the new biology master?" and H. said yes. Whereupon the inspector very deliberately let it be known that he could use some coaching in biology for he is trying to pass the government veterinary exam. So he charged no duty and said he'd contact Howard at the college in a week or so!

Everything seems to be intact. We received a great thrill from each lowly ashtray as we delved into the trunks, and dinner tasted awfully good when eaten with our own silver. The rugs make our living room look lived-in, and our books, while still strewn about on the floor, add some character. Such a relief!

October 31:

This morning I gathered up all the tired and dirty linen we've been using and put our own bright towels up. Such a remarkable difference!

Elizabeth resents mightily the water we've been giving her in place of milk. Poor baby, she starts on her bottle so eagerly and stops after one or two mouthfuls.

After lunch I went back to the Ramsarans' house for more sewing. Finished one of the living room pairs, and we put it up this evening so I could pin in the hem. Looks good.

From the Ramsarans' windows we watched the college cadets drilling. Most of them seemed green and had difficulty keeping in step. After they finished, Mr. Hetram, the classics master and a lieutenant in the B.G. Militia, came up for a visit. I would call him quite a character: he seems to have few inhibitions and says whatever comes into his mind. He is married and has two children. Howard said he is quite brilliant and won a Guiana Scholarship to study in England.

November 1:

Mabel tells me the showers we have had lately herald the rainy season, which usually comes in November. I'd better buy an umbrella.

Today the Police Show was held across the street on the Parade Grounds. The mounted police put on a fine show, and the event was so well attended we could barely see the motorcycle corps performing the stunts they've been practicing so long. We watched from our windows: the crowd was large and we didn't particularly care to become involved in it.

At 4 we picked up John, Margaret, and Susan and drove out along the sea wall. Had the usual trouble with cattle and sheep—such poky, skittish animals. On the way back we stopped at the Carib and John bought us a refreshing drink.

Elizabeth is better and seems to have resigned herself to a diet of gruel and water.

Nov. 1, 1952

Dear folks,

Georgetown is an interesting city, even if disgusting at times. The happy-go-lucky attitude of so many people here lends a very casual air to the British stiffness. To this extent it isn't annoying, but rank irresponsibility such as we've witnessed many times in connection with numerous events is still very perturbing to us. We're told that in time we'll come to accept that just as we do the climate—I hope not.

In its physical layout, the city is an amalgamation of once distinct but proximal towns, originally plantation villas. One by one the plantations were abandoned; the villas grew and thrived on the income from commerce. The Demerara was truly the ideal river in B.G. for a port as it was deep but relatively narrow (only a mile or two across at its mouth). To the casual reviewer of a colony map, the Essequibo might seem more logical, but its width at its confluence with the Atlantic is 26 miles and at the same time it's very shallow. Under those conditions only small vessels could dock, and virtually without protection. Today the districts are all fused but they retain their original names: Queenstown, Bourda, Albouystown, Kitty, Subryanville, Alberttown, Stabroek, Kingston (our district), etc. Hunting an address from the seat of a car is nearly always futile because probably less than 20 percent of the houses have numbers posted and the numerical sequence changes radically from district to district even when traveling on the same street. Asking bystanders is the only way.

I am familiar with this as I just got us a radio last week by responding to a newspaper ad (here called an advert) and spent over two hours hunting an address that turned out to be only a few blocks from us. The radio, a Pye (British make), is a year old, and I whittled the fellow down to nearly half of what the set would retail for new. I'm getting pretty adept at this bargaining routine.

Although there is but one station here in B.G., government-owned Radio Demerara, we receive programs from Trinidad, Venezuela, Brazil, Argentina (in English no less), and BBC Overseas. According to some, Florida and New Orleans may be reached in favorable weather. Radio Demerara's programs display very clearly America's influence on the worldwide ether. We have singing commercials, children's serials (of the Jack Armstrong type, transcribed in N.Y.), *Music by Roth*, Jack Benny, *Andy Hardy*, *Dr. Kildare*, etc. It seems so incongruous to hear a "limey" introduce "Back Beat Boogie," long discarded from American radio record libraries. Some of the music is current but most would be passé in the U.S. On B.G.'s hit parade are Mario Lanza's "Most Wonderful Night of the Year," "No Other Love," "You're Just in Love" from *Call Me Madam*, and "Smile Awhile." There are two very formal, very British announcers, a man and a woman, on this station, which begins broadcasting at 6 a.m. and signs off at 1:30 p.m., resuming at 4 and concluding at 10:30.

John Ramsaran, senior English master at Queen's, does bimonthly book reviews on the air, and he approached me in connection with doing reviews of books on biological subjects. I gave him a conditional yes, the condition being the O.K. of the Commission in London, for in the Terms of Award it was rather plainly stated that I was to engage in no other activities for financial profit. According to John, the only profit in this case is the gift of the book reviewed, but it still merits the Commission's go-ahead.

One facet of B.G. life we haven't said much about thus far concerns food. We had a rude introduction to the matter at the Loyola House, but now, having done some cooking ourselves, we feel better able to discuss the subject without undue bias. First of all, there are four meals a day: Early Tea (our breakfast), Breakfast (our lunch), Tea, and Late Tea (our supper). For many, the main meal of the day is, strangely enough, Tea—meat, potatoes, vegetables, and, needless to say, tea. Our British friends tell us the four-meal system is theirs but the names given are strictly Guianese. John Ramsaran has done a bit of research toward explaining the origin of the terms and has come up with this: On the plantations it was usual practice for the people to rise at dawn and have a cup of tea (Early Tea). Then they would work in the fields until 11 or so, after which the heat was too much. At this time they would eat a fairly substantial meal (Breakfast). Siesta was observed until 3 or 3:30 (Tea) and then they would work until dark. The second real meal would then be eaten or sometimes just a snack (Late Tea). The only explanation for the current custom of eating a heavy meal in the later afternoon is the fact that among the poor, it is the only meal taken.

As for us, we eat at the same times we did at home—no tea (it spoils dinner). Food is generally good if you know where to buy. I've been very lucky in having experienced shoppers to show me the way, and now I feel confident. Meat is the most difficult item. Lamb and mutton are readily available in good cuts at Bookers Grocery, and pork can be had on Saturdays at one of the two public markets (Bourda and Stabroek). Lamb costs 84 cents (50 cents U.S.) per pound; mutton 60 cents (35 cents U.S.). Pork, while cheap—24 cents (16 cents U.S.)—is risky unless thoroughly cooked for the threat of trichinosis is much magnified in the tropics.

The greatest culinary adventures are in the realm of fruits and vegetables. For breakfast we each have half a papaya melon (long, somewhat cylindrical fruit that grows on trees; flesh about the color of cantaloupe but the flavor is more delicate, excellent when fortified with a sprinkling of sugar. Cost: 16 to 24 cents per), or half a grapefruit ("out of this world" here—juicy, sweet, never harsh or coarse-grained). I usually have a bowl of cornflakes (Kellogg's made in Britain with milk prepared from Klim), and then we have fried or scrambled eggs (eggs are usually smaller but with a greater proportion of yolk; five for 48 cents B.G.) with bread (two very tasty loaves delivered daily for 10 cents B.G.) and jam or jelly (frightfully expensive stuff imported from all over the world but very flavorful; locally made guava jelly is of course much cheaper and just as good). We usually have sandwiches and milk for lunch. Then for dinner Marian exercises ingenuity making it difficult for me to generalize. A type of spinach is grown here which resembles the New Zealand spinach we raised during the war. Carrots are raised locally but are marketed most often in tremendous size, nonetheless palatable. Potatoes, yams (gray when cooked), and sweets are all readily had for very little although the latter two are somewhat seasonal. Plantains, a type of banana, are fried or broiled (M. isn't too sure yet) and with some they are something of a staple, costing just 9 cents per pound. Rice is the staple of most lower-class families and is marketed here by the pint, quart, gallon, etc. (14 cents per quart). Bananas are nearly always on hand although the cost fluctuates according to supply (now about 12 cents for eight good-sized ones). Various flours are on display in the markets: wheat, rice, plantain, arrowroot, sago (palm nut), to mention those I remember.

Love to all,
Howard

Sunday, November 2, 1952

Dear Parents:

I was going to write you Friday but the typewriter was indisposed. The particular trunk in which it was packed took a beating and arrived a bit battered. The typewriter case is dented in and the carriage deal wasn't working properly, but I guess H. fixed it up all right. Also a little lever broke off, but we don't know how important it is because we can't find the place from which it came. Everything else was in fine shape.

Let's see—I am now boiling E.'s bottles for twenty minutes. Elizabeth is just about back to normal, and last night she had some watered-down milk for her supper. The doctor said she could have picked up a bug from an overripe banana if the skin had any breaks in it, and you know how easily the top bit is torn—I imagine that is what happened, since we are so careful about milk.

People's sanitary standards vary quite a bit. Margaret tells me that they boil their milk for about twenty minutes, and they wash all fruits and vegetables that are eaten raw in an antiseptic solution. Mabel says the Beckleses don't do that, but they do continue to boil drinking water out of habit. I think as soon as we can get hold of the crystals we, too, shall wash our lettuce and fruits in this solution. We've gone this long without being affected by any bugs, but with Elizabeth we can't take any chances. I truly get cold chills thinking about this sterilization business, and if I didn't care so much for Dr. Hellyer I would write him and tell him not to tell mothers such things so casually. Of course, it was up to us to learn what constitutes "reasonable" sanitary conditions here, but everyone seems to have different ideas on that subject.

I started this letter about 8:30, just after breakfast. Howard has gone out to the sea wall to wade around in the muck in search of whatever is interesting there. Elizabeth is taking her before-bath nap, and Evelyn is cleaning. Elizabeth will wake up shortly, as it is now about 9, and demand something to drink (usually orange juice, today it will probably be more glucose water!) and then have her bath. Now that we have the quilt Mrs. Orr gave her, we put it on the floor and Elizabeth plays there for several hours during the day. She does try so hard to creep, and when she gets disgusted with herself she starts to cry. If we turn her over on her back she goes right back to her tummy and tries again—I doubt if she'll be happy until she succeeds.

Isn't my typing horrible! To think I ever earned good money this way. The fact that I and others continued to work while pregnant really surprises and shocks people here. It just isn't done! I have been to the Ramsarans' twice to sew, and each time we have had such a good time comparing notes on England and America. Cooking terms, names of clothing, prices, etc.—all are so different. Of course, we all have a hard time deciding which phrases are English and which are native, and the

English think some of the strange terms are American when they are really native. Here, an undershirt is a vest, and a vest is a waistcoat. Biscuits and cookies, of course, mean different things to us than they do to the English, and if we want powdered sugar we have to ask for icing sugar, at 58 cents a pound. The English grill instead of broil, the same process under a different name. Their teaspoon is about the size of our demitasse, their dessertspoon is our teaspoon, but our tablespoons are about the same. Exchanging recipes here should prove interesting.

Elizabeth has had her bath, and is now on the quilt playing in some sunshine. I still haven't been able to find a toy that floats—I just don't think they have them here. I guess we shall have to buy a balloon ("bladder" here, unfortunately) for a bathtub toy. Bee sent a Magnin's pamphlet of exclusive toys, priced from about $10.95 up, all elaborate and beautiful items such as poodles with music boxes in their innards, 18-inch rag dolls, and wonderful sets of blocks. I hated to come right out and say that they were too expensive and fragile for Elizabeth, but I did say that E. could do more with something soft or of plastic that she can chew on or handle more easily—and which can't be broken! The duty would be quite a lot on an expensive toy, too. It sounds awful to say, "Please don't send Elizabeth any toys because we don't want to have to pay the duty," but it amounts to that. So—I hope Bee can find something that appeals to her for not quite so much money. We are told that some things take a beating in the mails, and that it wouldn't be wise to send anything as delicate as the music box poodle. The toys available here look like Woolworth's worst. They aren't at all up to the ones available in London, according to the Ramsarans, and most of them look awfully cheap and poorly made.

My goodness—it is now 12:30 and we've just finished lunch. Soup, of all things. We have so many good bones left from our roasts, and I can't bear to throw them out without making soup from them. I add the liquid from our canned celery, an old carrot or two, and sometimes rice or a chopped potato. Sounds awfully hearty for the tropics, doesn't it! Yesterday I read through Mrs. Rombauer's recipes using bananas, and they certainly sound good. Of course, I have to wait for the barrels to come so I can beat, sift, measure, etc.

Howard asks if you can please obtain the name and address of some member of the Tacoma Stamp Club, through the Chamber of Commerce perhaps, for trading purposes.

Elizabeth is still exploring on the floor. She has discovered the baseboards and is intrigued by the dark baseboard against the light wall. She also seems to think that getting off the quilt is a great game: reaching the floor is a challenge. Another interruption: we just finished a whole reel of film, pictures of Elizabeth and each of us, on the quilt. The five I took are the first pictures I've taken with H.'s camera, so heaven only knows how they'll turn out.

I have re-assumed enough of the housework here so that my mornings are completely filled from the time E. gets up at 6 until we have lunch at noon. It sounds awfully trivial, but I must say I'm much happier with even that full a day! I get dressed, feed Elizabeth, and fix breakfast for us. We eat at about 7 except on Sundays, and Monday and Tuesday when H. has those early hours. After breakfast I put away the melting butter and the jam and bread, for the flies do collect if things are left around for long. I scrape the dishes and leave them for Evelyn. Then I tear the sheets off our bed and throw them over the windowsill if it's sunny, so they can dry out a bit (really!); next I change E.'s bed and get her set for a nap. Then the game of heat-the-water-for-bottles-and-everything-else starts. With hot water in one pan, I fill another to heat while I wash out the bottles. They go into pan #1 to boil while pan #2 is refilled with water and put on the slow burner (there is only one fast burner) to boil. While they boil I make our bed, much to Evelyn's bewilderment—she's probably never seen a white woman make a bed, but I just like to make beds! The leftover hot water and that in which the bottles boiled is put in the washtub and I wash out our underwear, H.'s sport shirts, and a dress of mine. After the washing is hung out, I generally have about ten minutes to sit in the breeze before E. wakes up at 9 or 9:30. After her bath, I do as much cooking for our dinner as I can as the kitchen gets the sun in the afternoons and is rather warm then. Howard gets home for lunch at 11:30, just about the time Elizabeth wants her lunch, but there is no mealtime conflict as there was four months ago since I fix our lunch early and we eat as soon as the child is through. Generally by the time we sit down to lunch I am soaking wet and have been since about 8:30! So after lunch I take a shower and change my clothes. The last few days I've been running off to the Ramsarans' sewing machine, but otherwise I read or sew.

It isn't exactly a fast pace, but now that we have our books, pictures, rugs, silver, and a few curtains, we feel as if we really live here. We have one pair of the brown draperies up in the living room, and they look just lovely. I'd say that they make the room look "warmer" when they're drawn—not in the sense of heat, but of personality. We have all five rugs in the living room, and I confess that I feel smug every time I think how nice everything looks together! We are using your lavender bedspread. One of these days we may need a blanket, but not yet. One of the masters' wives who has been here five or six years bought slacks on their last leave in England, because she got so cold here in January and February that she had to go to bed every night at 8 just to get under the covers! I don't know how long it takes to reach that stage, but it must be quite a ways off.

Well, kiddies, I must put hems in the living room draperies so I can use the pins therein for another pair. It's such fun to have the typewriter so that I can just ramble on and on!

Much love to both of you,

Marian

Monday—10:30 a.m.

Dear Mother—

Just finished reading your three letters that arrived in this morning's mail, and since I always finish reading them feeling as if I'd just had a nice chat with you, I feel I should answer!

About this two-year business, I must have forgotten to mention that the school here seems to take it for granted that Howard will stay the two years as he is desperately needed for that length of time. He had to sign the paper saying he would be available for both years, you remember, and it seems the U.S. Educational Commission in London can only make the actual appointment for one year at a time but everyone assumes we will stay the second year, barring complete inadequacy (which isn't likely!) or illness, utter inability to adjust to the climate, or the like.

I am in the midst of basting drapes to go here in our study, the room right off our living room. The outside stairs to the third floor go right by the window in here, and we are really sick of everyone peering in on their way up.

I, too, wish we had taken all our insurance out here! How stupid of us. We plan to do about the theft insurance, by the way. Did I tell you that I keep our silver locked in our buffet, and that I carry the keys with me all the time?

Again, love to you both,

M.

November 2:

Howard took the long-awaited boots [that arrived in the trunks] this morning and drove out to the sea wall. Returning, he said the mud there is atrocious—it clings and sticks, making walking all but impossible. He found several strange-looking plants but is still rather helpless without a manual.

Yesterday Howard bought a nice-looking piece of pork. I roasted it for two hours and it came out like leather, so tough we couldn't eat it.

It seems odd to us that people here complain of the high price of meat. They look utterly uncomprehending when we say we just couldn't afford to eat meat at home!

November 3:

Evelyn arrived at 9 this morning, saying she'd forgotten to buy something in town and had had to return for it. Enough of that nonsense. I told her she'd better plan to buy things on her way home. At 11 she said she felt feverish and had a headache because she was "bilious." So—I told her to go home.

November 4:

This morning Evelyn arrived on time, but I got peeved when I found a dish she'd used and put back unwashed. So I tore into her, telling her that lateness would no longer be tolerated ("But I have no way of telling the time," she said. Nuts—how do all the other girls get to work on time!); that she must wash dishes carefully after using them; that she must sweep *all* the rooms (yesterday she skipped Elizabeth's room, and denied it when I mentioned it; unfortunately, Howard had planted some cigarette ashes under the crib!).

Today is Election Day at home. We tried to get a U.S. station on our radio this evening but couldn't. The woman next door had her radio up so loud that we could, however, hear the BBC news broadcasts clearly. When we went to bed, Ike was leading.

November 5:

The BBC carried the news of Eisenhower's victory this morning. We heard it while we ate breakfast. We're awfully pleased but sorry to be so far away from all the excitement.

I cleaned up this morning, again enjoying the feeling of being alone in my house. When Mabel arrived at noon, she was shocked to think that

Evelyn hadn't been here. Half-day help is never given a holiday for a mere birthday, she told me. Besides, Evelyn usually takes fish home for Mabel's cat and she hadn't told Mabel not to count on her today. I felt sorry for poor Molly, the innocent victim, and asked Howard to run Mabel home so she could leave Molly's fish. I guess I shall have to face facts and toughen up: it is distasteful to harp at anyone about such things, but I shall.

Thursday, November 6, 1952

Dear All:

This is No. 1 in my series of carbon copy letters to you.[17] It is 10:30 a.m. and I just finished reading today's mail. To the Irwins: I can't understand why you haven't heard from us oftener, as Howard writes quite frequently, except that we have only heard from you once every ten days or two weeks.

Elizabeth is usually bright-eyed at this time of day, but she only slept for half an hour before her bath, so she is cranky and sleepy now. We borrowed a playpen from the Ramsarans as their Susan no longer needs it, and we put the quilt the Orrs gave us in it as a pad. Elizabeth is very happy there and only mildly resents being fenced in. Sometimes she lies there for ten or fifteen minutes (a long time for her) curling her toes around the bars. She still tries her best to creep but doesn't get too far. Her little knees and hands get so red—but she's getting tougher all the time, and when she does reach the crawling stage I don't think the floors will seem too hard.

Having servants is an education. About two weeks ago Evelyn asked if she could have November 5 off, as is was her birthday. Howard, whom she asked (I have refused her so many times), said yes, so yesterday she didn't come. Mabel informed me that that is *not* done, since she works only in the mornings. We decided that I should get "tougher" with her, and now I am determined to be at least a bit more firm. After I said "no" half a dozen times to her requests for cheese, butter, jam, tangerines, etc. she ceased to ask for anything, so perhaps there's hope.

Question: Would people rather see Elizabeth on a Christmas card, or a palm tree? Of course we'll have to decide before you can answer, since we must get our cards out quite soon; we'd go broke in a hurry if we sent them all airmail!

Bee: Evelyn must have thought I'd lost my senses as I sat in the living room reading the part of your letter about duty charged in the U.S. on goods from B.G. Good Lord—why would anyone want to export worm gut, whalebone (where would that come from down here?), lifeboats, ice, or leeches! I suppose for free items the government would just naturally pick those of interest to no one. You say, "Books, printed more than 20 years at the time of importation." Does that mean a new edition of a 20-year-old book would be dutiable? We could always send you antique volumes, but probably the only ones available are in the public library, with pages missing! I haven't read a thing since I started on the drapery business, but *Dr. Faust* is still on my list. We love the *Saturday Review*. So far, it is the only magazine we have received—all four issues of it!—and we devour every word.

We were tickled with the results of the election. The BBC covered it all very thoroughly, giving the returns pretty much as they came in Tuesday night. Howard said that he was asked to explain the working of the electoral college five times at school yesterday.

Today we received a letter from Port of Spain saying that our barrels were due to arrive here yesterday. I hope H. will have time to see about it this afternoon: no doubt what the letter really means is that our barrels will come in another two or three weeks. If they are really here I shall be overjoyed!

We hope to have a turkey for Thanksgiving. Howard says all the ones he's seen are so scrawny that we can probably get one small enough for us. By the way, Mother, how do you make dressing?

We heard yesterday that the U.S. consulate is being closed—not enough reason to have one here, I guess. So Wesley Jorgensen with wife and child will be leaving at the end of the month, and glad to go from what they've said. We're sorry to see them go, since he is an American and knows the State of Washington at that. From now on our official business will go through the consul at Port of Spain. We know no other Americans here, but one of the masters mentioned a family he knows, and another American who works for the BWI Airline.

Father asked for the names of the Q.C. masters we mention often. Archie's real name is Archibald G. Larthe de Langladure, but they let it go at "Larthe" for convenience sake. He and Ken Maudsley, who teaches history, and Howard are the only white (European) masters. John Ramsaran is Trinidadian, and Mr. Hetram is, I guess, East Indian [Guianese]. They are the only ones, besides Mr. H.A.M. Beckles, whom I've met.

We had hysterics last night listening to the news. Every time the announcer (female) mentioned the acting governor it was "His Excellency the Officer Administering the Government, the Honorable John A. Gutch,

QBE." It does sound funny when repeated two or three times in the space of a few sentences. I guess we're just too used to hearing our dignitaries referred to as "Truman," "Ike," etc.

Next Monday is another of those holidays, and Howard wants to go out to Atkinson Field to survey the plant situation. I think he's going to go fishing Sunday, too.

Elizabeth is healthy and happy, as H. and I are. It's strange to think of Christmas being so near—we miss you all and would so love to see you.

It's just about time for lunch, and Elizabeth has finally fallen asleep! Must hie myself to the scullery—

Love,
Marian

November 6:
Now we do feel at home: our three precious barrels were delivered this afternoon. We spent a very dirty and dusty hour unwrapping our dishes and pans, and I put them away.

Evelyn worked this morning, by George, from 8 until noon. She came in at about 10:30 to say she was going, but I surprised her and told her to clean the baseboards.

Thomas informed me today that he waxes the floors once a month for the $3.50, and that the middle-of-the-month polishing job is done out of the goodness of his heart, "for nothing." So we have no complaint against his failure to polish the floors last week. Such wonderful reasoning.

November 7:
The little flower man came again today [Editor's note: No previous occasion is mentioned.] with his customary bowing and scraping. He asked if I knew how to peel back the petals of the pink water lilies, and when I said yes he bowed even more. All for twelve cents!

November 8:
Howard left at 7:30 to do the marketing, hoping to beat the crowds at the government produce market. Fruits are so much cheaper there that it's worth waiting a little longer for service, but not the hours it takes if he goes shopping later in the morning. As it was, he got home about 10:30. Bought some sapodillas—a fruit that outwardly resembles little new potatoes, and whose flavor reminds me of root beer.

November 9:

This morning we watched a grand parade assemble on the Parade Grounds and then march off with bands playing loudly. The occasion was the cornerstone laying for a new Seventh Day Adventist hospital. First came a police guard consisting of two handsome policemen wearing their dark tunics, dark trousers with the red stripe up the side of the leg, and white gloves, mounted on their equally handsome horses. Next came a dignitary of some sort, all dressed up in a tricorn hat and carrying a sword. Then some policemen and the police band, whose members wore white tunics. Following them came a group of militia men followed by their band, and then the Cadets from Queen's, who unfortunately lacked the polish of the professionals. A few nurses, out of step, and Red Cross ambulance drivers came next, and then some straggling civilians who were probably church dignitaries. And then bicycles, dogs, and a bakery truck.

I baked date bread for our picnic. It tastes good but is not the date bread of the U.S.A. Brown sugar here is very damp and very molasses-ish,[18] and my date bread turned out like "health bread," with a strong molasses flavor.

The laundress, whom Mabel says is Evelyn's mother, came by this evening to say that $8 is not enough for so much laundry. I told her it was the amount we agreed on, and she said we couldn't get it done anywhere for that. She actually called me "my dear"—and that did it. I told her I had another woman who could do it, and asked to have Evelyn bring back the dirty clothes. Nuts to her! She ironed too many handkerchiefs wrong side out, anyway.

November 10:

Last night it really rained: we had puddles all over the gallery floor this morning. The rain kept on, so we canceled the picnic plans. It was beautifully cool, though, and we both felt refreshed. Put a shirt on Elizabeth for the first time since we've been here.

Evelyn and I finally had it out this morning, with the result that she no longer works for us. She spent a good hour downstairs with the maid, and I had had enough. When she came upstairs I paid her $4 and told her I was through being patient, that she hadn't dusted the banister, that she'd left cleaning rags in the washbasin, the rug in the hall was left hanging out the window, etc. She thanked me for the money and left, and I thought that was that. A few hours later the laundress came, asking why I had fired Evelyn. I explained that her work wasn't thorough and that she spent too much time downstairs, and the mother-laundress seemed to agree. But about 4 o'clock, just as we were leaving for a drive, Evelyn and her brother came. First she said I should have given her $4.50 instead of $4, but refused to explain why. Then she said I'd have to pay her a month's wages in advance. And then she said the union ruled that two months' pay was due a servant fired without notice!

We found that hard to believe, so Howard told them we'd be happy to pay if they could produce proof from the union that Evelyn was entitled to the money. They glowered, Evelyn muttered, and they left. During this last interview Howard and I were both very pleasant, and Evelyn sneered the best sneers I have ever witnessed. She was quite rude. And they haven't been back since. Mabel informs me that the "brother" is Evelyn's stepfather, that she can't claim two months' wages because she didn't get the job through the union, and that "Evelyn is like all those young girls who wants work but won't do the job."

November 11:

Winifred, the woman who brings our eggs,[19] asked this morning if I knew anyone who needed half-day help. I thought quickly and asked if she would want to come here once a week to scrub the kitchen floor, the shower, lavatory, and back stairs. Somehow I don't enjoy those little chores and would just love to leave them for someone else. We settled on $1.50 a month, but it certainly doesn't seem like much.

Went to the Ramsarans' for curtain work after lunch, but did little sewing. I was interested to learn from Margaret that refrigerators are considered not even a luxury but an extravagance in England—only two people they knew had them! It is cool enough the year round so that on one or two days only in the summer will milk sour, and their bacon was firmer there than it is here in the refrigerator. We talked about frozen foods and the relative prices of chicken, lamb, and ham. During the war and afterward, they bought a chicken about once a month, although meat was very scarce. They couldn't afford chicken any more often than that.

November 11, 1952

Dear folks,

The rains have begun. At first the torrential downpours were a bit frightening, but now we're little more than annoyed by them. They are intermittent (thank the Lord!) but I don't see how any more could fall at one time without the rain entirely displacing the atmosphere. The sound is not unlike that of a waterfall—a sort of a roar that makes it necessary for us to shout in order to be heard by another person in the same room. At such time we just shut off the radio and cease talking—almost. For the last week or so it has rained about two or three times a day for 20 to 30 minutes each time. Each rain ends as abruptly as it started, the sun usually comes out within a few minutes, and as soon as the water in the street, on grass, etc. has evaporated, it's as warm as ever. In other words, rain here does not coincide with the passage of a weather "front" as in temperate climes, but rather simply represents a condition of humidity saturation in the atmosphere above. The heavy rains relieve the humidity for a time but the evaporation plus the introduction of moist air from the ocean spells another shower in a relatively short time. Needless to say, the humidity is higher now than when we came but it has increased so gradually that we're hardly aware of the change. Yesterday the temperature dropped to the low 70s and we really felt cool—almost uncomfortably so. Ordinarily it's between 85 and 95. Even at night it seldom gets below 75. No complaint whatever from either of us—we've gotten completely adjusted to it and now really like the uniformity. It certainly makes enjoyment of the outdoors easier and dressing is a relatively simple matter. It's hard now for us to picture Seattle in the cold rains with more than a hint of winter in the air at night. It's probably as difficult for you folks to visualize us sitting here in our "gallery" with the windows wide open sipping rum-and-lime. We're dressed in clothes we'd wear only in July and August at home and yet it's almost the middle of November!

We've had to dismiss our maid, Evelyn, for a number of legitimate reasons. By taking her time, Marian is able to do most everything in a morning and without getting overheated. We remember the book written by a doctor on the physiological aspects of tropical living in which it was said that it is better for a white woman to maintain her usual household activities than to cede them to someone else. It's not only good for the body but for the mind as well.

I'm glad news such as that contained in the clippings you enclosed in your last letter (about Van Fleet's letter[20]) does not reach the local press for it would indeed be the cause of some embarrassment. Most people here find it difficult to conceive of an America split apart by political coniverings. America is to them a single entity, and any incident such as that one reflects on the country as a whole, not on the Democratic party alone. An interesting sidelight concerns the British influence here. It is almost traditionally resented by the population of the lower class (even to the extent that they refuse to stand during the playing of "God Save the Queen"). These people, believing America as it's portrayed by MGM, openly favor U.S. annexation of British Guiana. They have far greater faith and hope in our country than in their Mother Protector.

Love to you all,

Howard

November 12:
Big news from the college today: a new principal will arrive about the first of December, a man named Sanger-Davies, from Bathurst Technical School in Bathurst, Gambia, West Africa. Some masters suspect the fine hand of Captain Nobbs, the former principal, for Mr. Sanger-Davies is a chemistry man, as Nobbs himself was. Several of the masters, contented with Mr. Beckles's none-too-strict regime, are fearful that the new man may demand more of them.

Our first issue of *Time* arrived today with all the election results. What a wonderful tie with home! I sat right down and read most of it while Howard had his first session with a Mr. Stuart, who is receiving private tutoring.

November 13:
Anticipating the Ramsarans' arrival for tea this afternoon, I made orange bread and cookies. Also cleaned, washed diapers, and did a little ironing before I took a quick shower and cleaned up. Winifred came this morning and really scrubbed. She goes over the floor with soapy water and a metal scraper, thoroughly cleaning it, and then rinses it just as carefully. In comparison, Evelyn merely swished the cloth over the floor.

The Ramsarans remarked on the mugginess of the day. About 5 it began to rain and the air cleared rapidly, but we couldn't hear each other because of the rain on the roofs.

I showed Margaret around the flat. She admired the copper chafing dish but had to ask what it was.

Friday, November 14, 1952

Dear All—

No doubt you are all peeved at my lack of correspondence these last few days—I can truly say I've been busy! Our barrels arrived a week ago last Thursday, and we were notified of that fact promptly. Nothing was broken: the worst damage consisted of a broken plastic foot on the waffle iron (the boob who packed that particular barrel put the waffle iron and toaster in the very bottom of the barrel with only a thin layer of newspaper as cushion), a few little dents in the chafing dish (which I could have sworn I'd left at home), and some chips in the enamel on my dish pan. The dishes and glassware were packed beautifully and absolutely nothing among them was damaged. So we really do feel settled now, and it is just wonderful to have everything here. Are the two Czech glass dishes around? Also the cookie press? Nuts—I wish they were here!

The big news from Queen's is that a new principal will arrive the first of December to take over from Mr. Beckles, who has been acting-principal since last spring. There was quite a hubbub about it all, as Mr. B. has been quite an easy man under whom to work, and some of the masters don't want to have to put themselves out for a more efficient person! Although H. doesn't know the situation too well in his short time at the school, from a few personal experiences he feels things could improve, and is not sorry to hear of the new man's coming. His name is Sanger-Davies; he is 44 and has a wife and young son [who attends school in England]. Archie is sorry about it all because if Mr. B. had been made principal, he himself would probably have been appointed vice-principal.

The big news on the domestic front is that Evelyn's questionable services are ours no longer, thank heavens. I am now doing the housework myself, and enjoying it. As I told Howard, it is old stuff, and its very familiarity makes it welcome in these strange surroundings. And good Lord—I was getting nastier by the day with nothing to do but sit! A little work is good for the soul, and I get almost everything done by noon. My afternoons are as free as I want to make them, if I want to take a nap or go out. It just isn't so hot here that activity is impossible: I find that I don't give the heat or humidity a thought when I'm busy. Margaret Ramsaran has done her housework for the six months they've been here and is just now getting a girl to come in the mornings because she is all tired out. If I get in a similar state I shall certainly welcome someone to help, but at the present it is just good exercise.

Margaret, John, and Susan came over for tea yesterday. I have passed on our four issues of *Saturday Review* to them, and yesterday they took home the *National Geographic* with the article and pictures on the Columbia River, also the Indoor Bird Watchers' Manual. I do enjoy them so much—the last time I was there curtain-making (ostensibly—I only finished one) we thoroughly discussed frozen foods, practically tasting frozen peas, strawberries, etc. They are new enough here, too, so that they look back on London as I do on the States, with a certain amount of longing for fresh celery, no mildew problem, and a needed fire in the fireplace. None of us has said we wish we were home: I don't, and I don't think Margaret does although her mother probably would prefer it. We compared grocery stores and food prices, and they say living here is much more expensive than in London. But their food in London is still so severely rationed—it sounds quite grim to me.

I solved one problem last week, long after I should have. Hair washing is no joy here, with no running hot water. I do it in the shower because that is the easiest way, but until last week, when I used a vinegar rinse, it felt awfully sticky. Good old vinegar.

Bee, I know what you can send me for Christmas: a plastic cover for the toaster! Everything gets so darned dusty that I now keep it covered with a piece of waxed paper and a rubber band, but the rubber band is forever popping off.

I made orange bread yesterday to have with our tea—came out beautifully. Also some cookies, in which I substituted 3 tablespoons brown sugar and 9 white for 6 tablespoons of each. Tasted good—about the same flavor that brown sugar at home would give it. Our sugar is very coarse and rather dirty looking. I made some grapefruit gelatine a week or so ago, and the color was hideous—a dirtyish yellow green!

To the showers. Oh yes: if you parents really want to give something to Elizabeth for Christmas, I think she has just about reached the car-seat stage. Last week we went for a ride and I could scarcely hold her, she wiggled so. They are available here, but I don't know how much they cost. Shall find out.

Love to you all—

Marian

I have solved the Clorox problem, thanks to the Ramsarans. An English product called Milton.

November 14:

Thomas brought vegetables this morning. For 44 cents I got lettuce, spinach, beans, string beans, a little papaw.

Miss Osborn came by today to scold a workman for a bad job of screening our kitchen jalousies [louvers]. I asked her in to show her the still-leaking spots in the gallery. For a woman who can be perfectly bitchy, she surprised me by being quite pleasant.

Saturday, November 15, 1952

Dear Parents:

We are in the midst of Christmas card making, so this will be brief. *Time* is coming hot and heavy now—we got our second copy today. Still no *New Yorker*.

I forgot to tell you in the last letter that Winifred, who brings our eggs twice a week, is going to come every Thursday morning and scrub the kitchen floor, shower, w.c., and back stairs. All chores I can do without! She has ten children and her husband is badly crippled, and I shall probably end up by paying her more than the $1.50 (monthly) that I told her I would.

Howard says if you can get hold of anyone who would like a set of B.G. stamps, he will send them and the person can pay you—thus depositing a wee bit of money in our Central Bank account. Since the present issue will be running out with the new Queen Elizabeth issue next spring, it is a good opportunity for an avid collector to get them. Did you ever get the name of a Tacoma Stamp Club member?

Elizabeth is back on orange juice and egg yolks now in addition to her bananas and cereal. She is all well again, bless her heart. Mrs. Orr's quilt came back from the laundry today, looking almost like new. The laundry here won't take sheets, towels, etc.—just clothes. H. really had to talk them into doing the quilt. We are in a bad way because of the laundress's returning our last week's laundry, and our new laundress hasn't appeared yet.

I had better quit. My typing is all geshot!

Much love,

Marian

November 16, 1952

Dear folks,

Marian made a discovery in one of the secret crevices of her wallet last week—$60.00. How we could have used it a couple of months ago! But now that finances are satisfactory, we sent the sixty bucks home to join the very few bucks left in our Central Bank account. As yet the Smith-Mundt money [Fulbright grant from London] has not been deposited, at least not as of ten days ago. Needless to say, we're not in the least surprised.

After perusing the local offerings, at sixpence per, Marian and I decided to make our own Christmas cards. We got some heavy cardboard and I cut 20 cards from each sheet. After folding each card in half, I inked on a palm tree and a banana plant between which we printed "Merry Christmas" and "Happy New Year." On the inner half are our names next to a photo of Elizabeth. We hope to have them in the mail by Friday. With sixty or so cards to send, they'll go by regular mail. Let us know when you get yours?

Marian and I came to the conclusion last night that we're eating better here than we did in Tacoma. We have at least a meal a day with a meat course, sometimes two. And we're certainly eating more fresh fruits and vegetables than we did. We do miss the variety we had in the States though. As yet we're not complaining about having a leg of lamb and lamb chops each week! I bought a chicken yesterday, our first since we've been here.

Do you have any philatelic friends, Dad? If so, see if you can interest them in a set of B.G. stamps. All I'm trying to do is legitimately transfer funds from B.G. to our Central Bank account in Tacoma. Doc Alcorn has been my only customer thus far. For the collector it's a good investment because of the necessary cessation of the current issue in June with the coronation of the queen. That event assures two more issues in the next year or so: a Coronation Commemorative set followed by a new regular issue. As a sales angle, you might mention that the previous (George V) issue now catalogues at a figure in excess of $26.00 U.S.

It's still hard for us to believe that November is half passed. Thus far I've noticed a few trees lose their leaves, only to replace them within two weeks. Most trees are more or less dormant, but this seems to be the result of the prolonged dry spell that preceded the rains that have just begun. An armchair ecologist might conclude that plants without the challenge of a vigorous climatic cycle must certainly be degenerate. Such a statement would be true but for this fact. The very conditions that have eliminated competition with the inorganic environment have brought about another form of competition: one among the plants themselves. You can't imagine the number of species of plants crammed into an acre. True, the coniferous forests of western Washington are dense, but the number of species in an acre is small, usually no more than a couple of dozen and, if undergrowth is completely choked out, as few as one or two. Forested areas here never present that picture. They are even denser than the densest I've seen in Washington or anywhere else. And undergrowth is always present. One observer says that if one species is represented by two specimens within an acre it may be considered abundant. Such distribution in a temperate flora is usually termed "intermittent."

I must close for dinner is nearly ready.

Love to you all,

Howard

November 16:

Poor Mabel had a bad afternoon today. We don't know just what happened, but she didn't eat her lunch and at 3:30 when I went to the kitchen to fix Elizabeth's orange juice, she looked quite ill and said she was dizzy. Howard took her home shortly after that and said she could scarcely walk.

November 17:

Mabel said today that she feels better, but that Mr. Beckles is going to make an appointment for her to see Dr. Kerry. She has high blood pressure, she says, but she also hasn't been to a doctor in five years. She takes pills for her blood pressure, but they don't mean much. The patent medicine racket here makes me so mad. The papers are liberally spotted with ads for cure-alls, and a few days ago I heard over the radio an ad for "Magic Healing oil— good for man or beast." It supposedly cures any ailment, internal or external, for man, donkey, or chickens. There are many such products advertised, so they are presumably popular; yet the children look so undernourished it is a shame their parents don't spend the money on food instead. We've noticed various bottles of junk in both the Beckleses' and the Larthes' homes, too, and certainly they should know better.

Howard told me that Margaret had invited Miss [Lynette] Dolphin to tea so that I could meet her. Although I had decided not to leave Mabel alone with Elizabeth, I changed my mind and went since Mabel seemed to feel well. Miss Dolphin is the prep form mistress and also teaches singing at Queen's.

We guess her to be in her early thirties, and she dresses beautifully, is very well groomed, and has a grand personality. She has recently returned from England, where she was doing advanced work in music.

Her sister Celeste arrived about 5. She is younger and very animated—used the word "super" in every sentence. She has been back from her leave about three weeks, and the trip to England was "super," the food "super," etc.

This afternoon I discovered mold on my brown shoes both inside and out, and on the soles of my blue shoes. Mrs. McLaren said we could expect to find it on anything, from now on—but Miss Dolphin just smiled and said she'd not had that much trouble with it except on woolens and leather goods.

November 18:

One of those quiet days.

Mabel went to the doctor at 5. Poor woman, I do believe she was frightened at the prospect.

I made a cake this afternoon which turned out looking, as Howard aptly said, like a pancake. There are plenty of things that could do it: no vegetable shortening available, so I used cooking butter; baking powder doesn't stay fresh here so we should use twice as much, I am told; the flour imported from Canada is stuff that the Canadians wouldn't keep for themselves; and the local sugar is very damp and coarse. At least my cake was edible!

Mr. Rodway[21] has proposed a trip up the Demerara River for this weekend. Nothing definite, since he's trying to get in touch with Herbert Allsopp. Howard hopes it will work out, since he hasn't been up that way yet.

Thursday, November 19, 1952

Dear All—

I was most thankful to receive a total of four letters from you today—I need a cheering word. Woke up at 5 this morning with a violent case of diarrhea and for a while thought I just might fade away. It's 10 now, and I am feeling only slightly repulsive. I am taking some of E.'s medicine.

Bee, I'm sure Elizabeth would be most grateful if you could find one of the plastic shield things to put on a baby for shampooing. She is quite good-natured about the soapy water dripping over her face, but I do think she'd be happier without it.

To answer Bee's questions on clothes: I certainly do wear the clothes you and Mother picked out! The only one I haven't worn is the brown sheer, which I am saving for next spring. Yes, darn it, some idiots here observe the seasons in their clothing. Women wear black, clingy crepe dresses with sleeves, woolen jackets, etc. I wear my two striped cottons, the old brown plaid and the new two-piece in the morning (no more than two mornings and then they are washed); and change after lunch to my brown-and-white checked, the good old lavender and gray dresses, or that rayon print with the splashy colors. They are all washable, and I prefer to feed Elizabeth and cook our dinner in something that can be washed. Both jerseys are very comfortable, and I enjoy wearing them if we go downtown or out for a ride. White shorts are worn for tennis, and I think that's all. Jeans would be too warm. I've worn pedal pushers a few times when it's been cool but have never seen anyone on the street in such attire. Howard loves his cool shirts.

Much love to each,

Marian

November 20:
I decided to make a good old cornstarch pudding for dinner since Howard had purchased some cornstarch for me. According to Margaret, what we call cornstarch is corn flour to the English, but Howard brought home what I would call corn meal! Anyway, we had pudding for dessert and it tasted good, even if Howard did insist on calling it "cereal pudding."

Laughed to myself this morning when I heard a colored girl, walking down the lane beside the house, singing "White Christmas" to the radio's accompaniment. I wonder what she'd think of a real white Christmas.

November 21:
The on-again, off-again trip up the Demerara is definitely on. It sounds more like a social call than Howard's U.S.-variety field trip: a chauffeur-driven car will pick them up and take them to the boat; they are to take suits so that they can attend church on Sunday; they will take no food or bedding as that will all be furnished!

November 22:
Howard left this morning in a "huge" black Chevrolet, complete with chauffeur.

A little girl came to the back door today selling bedroom slippers for $2 a pair. I still don't know if she was truly pathetic or just a good saleswoman: she said her mother was ill and she had to have the money, all in a voice that threatened tears. All I had was $1, so I offered it. She took it, left a pair of slippers, and said she'd be back on Monday.

Frances, the new laundress recommended by Margaret, brought the first batch back today. She is undoubtedly an artist at her work, and her white, starched sheets and dishtowels are a vast improvement over Evelyn's mother's work.

November 23:
I had to go to bed early last night in self-defense: the mosquitoes seem bigger every day. The rain started at about 1:30 a.m., and after checking for puddles I was wide awake and read for a while.

Howard got home about 6:15. I was beginning to worry, since he'd said he'd be back at 3. I should know better by now. This mission was well set up with a good catechist in charge. Between rainy spells Howard did some collecting, helped by a young native who suddenly appeared with a handful of specimens. Saturday night, visitors came to talk to the strangers. Howard was startled to find how intelligent the natives are, despite their lack of formal education. One who had read a book on fishes carried on a detailed discussion with Howard on ichthyology.

The Lutheran minister, Mr. Bowen, who was host to Howard and Mr. Rodway, has suggested that Howard might be able to obtain a building or room at Atkinson Field to use as headquarters for his fieldwork. We hope so.

Monday, November 24, 1952

Dear Bee, Father, and Mother:
We get our *Time* on Saturdays, and I read it from cover to cover at the first opportunity, skipping lightly over the sports. The advertising is interesting, concerned mainly with shipping, ports, machinery, equipment, etc. It is actually our only news—we get a Sunday paper occasionally, but the papers here are uniformly uninformative.

I have seen a little mildew on a few dresses. I guess the test is yet to come. We have still had quite a bit of sunny weather, but the solid rain is supposed to start any day. It does present problems. Yesterday's diapers, hung up about one o'clock, weren't dry this morning so I hung them out in the little sun and breeze there was. Thank heavens we didn't get flannel diapers! And damn it all, I hemmed four more of our living room draperies on Saturday (slow but sure is my progress), and then all day yesterday it rained. The material absorbed so much dampness that the curtains sag in the middle, are an inch longer than they were Saturday, and look "pulled" along the side seams. Grrrr. I shall ignore the side seams after pressing—that may help. I shall eventually re-hem them. At least I now know what happened to the dining room curtains, which now touch the floor—I didn't think I'd left them quite so long!

I just finished sealing Christmas cards—it doesn't seem possible that it is just a month away! I bought a present for you, Bee, on Saturday. We have decided to buy things as they appeal to us and then try to get them home without paying duty (we still haven't checked to find out if more than one year's residence out of the U.S. lets us take everything back home sans duty) as they really wouldn't be worth your paying anything. We would send you duty-free gifts, but they aren't worth it. Anything such as the cotton scarves you mentioned, Bee, is just not up to U.S. standards. Coins would make lovely bracelets (thanks for the idea!) but we can't see sending just the coins and making you bear the expense of the conversion to jewelry.

I would love to know what, if any, is the standard of taste here. "Taste" as we think of it is completely lacking in any of the homes we've been in, excepting the consul's. People still hang their pictures way up high on the wall suspended by inverted V wires a foot long. The good china in the stores would make that at Woolworth's at home look wonderful—really! And it isn't cheap. Even my pots and pans look like artistic creations compared with the British stuff sold here: it is heavy, has straight sides, is made out of enamel or heavy metal but not aluminum, and isn't stackable. Glassware is ordinary. Towels are ugly. And the furniture! Granted there are some good-looking modern pieces, all made in one style—our Morris chairs represent that. But the "traditional" furniture is heavy and ponderous. Dressing tables with the two hinged mirrors on the large one. Gorpy stuff that reminds me of cedar chests at their worst, if you get the point. Goodness—how I do stray from one subject to another! Bowl covers are unknown. Ditto beanbag ashtrays. And to the English a waffle iron is an iron grid that is dipped into hot fat, then into batter, and then into the deep fat again!

Howard had another adventurous weekend. Saturday morning he and another master, Mr. Rodway, accompanied a Lutheran pastor to a mission several hours up the Demerara River. I won't say more because I hope he will write you about it himself. I am busy developing a pooh-pooh philosophy about snakes, river, tiger, etc.

E.'s favorite song is now "My Grandfather's Clock," which will evoke a giggle almost any time I start it. Unfortunately, I can't remember all the words (help, Mother!), but Elizabeth is most charitable about such lapses. She loves to play "mosquito" (you know—zzzz, zzzz, zzzz, gitchy gitchy gitchy!) and she loves to aim at Howard's glasses when he's on the floor playing with her. In case I haven't mentioned it, Mother, the two little knit cotton dresses are ideal for the coolish days when it looks like rain but doesn't get that far. Mabel, the optimist, puts the little panties on Elizabeth without a diaper. Looks cute but doesn't last long. I finished a dress for E. last week. It is a six-month size and she should be able to wear it by January. Or have I written you that before?

Must close now as Howard wants to add a P.S. to the parents. But first: I roasted my first chicken last week! It was just lovely except I failed to heed Mrs. Rombauer's warning to stuff it just three-fourths full. The poor chicken looked a bit messy but tasted fine.

Much love to you all and a happy Thanksgiving,

Marian

Maybe I'm silly but I'm afraid that if we did arrange to talk with you all [via ham radio] I would become soppy-maudlin. And this is a bad time of the year to be homesick.

Howdy—

This trip was made about 35 miles up the Demerara River and was more enjoyable than the one I made up Mahaica Creek a few weeks ago, simply because things went a little more smoothly. The missionary, Aubrey Bowen, is very liberal for a man of the cloth. I suppose missionaries must be or they would lose their sanity. He built the mission (and several others) almost single-handedly since the close of the war. A very likable chap, he has the type of personality that neutralizes all bitterness, and there was much bitterness to neutralize when it came to the ownership of the land he chose as the mission site. A number of squatters in the neighborhood made individual claims to the hill, but Bowen went to each of them, fished, hunted, ate, and drank with them, and in each case erased the hatred that had been engendered by an outsider making claim to their land. This in my mind exemplifies the very situation faced by many homesteaders in the [American] West during the 1860s and '70s and shows what a valuable asset amiability is. His catechist is seemingly very able (far more so than the fellow at St. Cuthbert's) for the spirit behind their Harvest Day activities (part of which I witnessed) was tremendous, despite rain. One thing has been made very clear: the aborigines I have seen are not stupid but simply have not had the opportunity for advancement. The greatest service rendered by the mission is the training that terminates in their being able to read. Most of these people are keenly aware of the goings-on abroad and they have a fair picture of their status in the international scheme of things.

We left Georgetown Saturday morning on the Demerara River day steamer (recently converted to diesel) and arrived at a landing near the mission at noon. The boat and all other public conveyances are very British in the matter of accommodation; second class is nonexistent. You either go first class or third and the latter is usually pretty poor—in this case passengers had various freight items for seats, and these were near the engine. First-class accommodations were on the top deck and were really quite pleasant. At the landing we were ushered into small launches and were ferried to the mission landing, some 3,000 feet downstream.

The Lutherans seem to do a much more thorough job of establishing a mission than do the Anglicans. According to Mr. Bowen, money makes the difference. The church was a white shingle affair carefully built without the slightest suggestion of rusticism. The catechist's home, though a bit worn, showed the same neat work. Incidentally, Mr. Bowen lives in Georgetown and owns a 1952 Chevrolet, chauffer driven; he says the missionary for Berbice and that for Essequibo each have 1952 Chevrolets, chauffer driven, but he confesses there is hardly enough road in those two districts to merit them. The cars are the gifts of the U.S. Lutheran churches, both Orthodox and Evangelical (the latter faction being more instrumental in fostering the B.G. missions).

Unfortunately, it rained shortly after we landed, but that's to be expected at this time of year. After the shower, I went collecting specimens and was given many of the local common names by a wide-eyed boy who accompanied me. The pickings are few now as not many plants are flowering—according to manuals, they should resume in late December and January. Rodway, an English master at Queen's and a lifelong resident of B.G., was very helpful in his explanations of local phenomena, traditions, terminology, etc. He's an avid fisherman, but since the river at this level was brackish, he had no success.

We had supper, which was of the same fare as the preceding lunch and the subsequent day's meals: curried chicken, plantains, cassava, and rice. This was prepared by the catechist's wife and seemed (according to Bowen and Rodway) very typical. Very tasty but on a long-term basis miserably unbalanced—no fats, little protein, nearly all starch. After supper, numerous inhabitants of the vicinity dropped in to chat, so we ended up having an old-fashioned bull session. I was amazed at that point that I could be sitting in the wilderness of British Guiana and conversing freely with an East Indian, two Negroes, two Arawaks, a missionary, and a fellow teacher.

On Sunday morning we attended the service, and it was very interesting to make a comparison between it and the services I am accustomed to. Part of the difference was that lying between Presbyterianism and Lutheranism, and part was due to the missionary approach. Essentially, there was much singing (five hymns and a chanted service) and little talking (announcements and a short, snappy hellfire-and-brimstone sermon by Mr. Bowen). The service was in observance of Harvest Day, a mission-initiated day of thankfulness, corresponding to our Thanksgiving. The church was bedecked with offerings and, strangely enough, these items were auctioned off afterward. The auction was held after lunch and was conducted by the most impressive man in the area, generally acknowledged to be physically superior; his name, appropriate enough, was Sparta Benjamin. If you were to see a silent movie of the auction you might think it was something staged by Hollywood. But if you were to hear the conversation in this auction, you would be amazed by the power of speech possessed by most of these people.

Among other things of interest, I noted two graves whose epitaphs made clear that two Englishmen and the wife of one had been buried with great pomp in 1812, 1816, and 1824, respectively. Surrounding the graves had been an elaborate wrought-iron fence. Now lying in the forest, the rungs of the fence had been knocked out by the natives, who used them for grates over their fires. The story behind this seems lost, according to Mr. Bowen.

It's nearly time for me to be off to school, so this will have to do for now.
Howard

November 24:

I spent a good hour unsticking and regluing the envelopes for our Christmas cards. All our envelopes have sealed themselves and we shall have to steam them open before they will be usable.

The little girl came back for the rest of her money and brought another pair of slippers.

Elizabeth surprised us today by sitting up straight all by herself. She looked quite pleased and managed to hold her balance very well.

Tuesday, November 25, 1952

MERRY CHRISTMAS, HAPPY NEW YEAR
The gleam that came into her eyes when she first saw the tree ornaments! Every time that I begin to feel sorry that we aren't nearby you all for Christmas, I just thank goodness that E. is (and will be next year, too) too young to expect the full Santa Claus story. Imagine—no fireplace to put a sandwich and cocoa by—no place to properly hang a stocking. We'll just wait until we're back in the States and then Santy will really have a job to do!

We miss you both but know you will have a grand Christmas. We shall most solemnly drink to your health on Christmas Day! Love, & cheers!

Marian, Howard & Elizabeth

November 25:

After I dashed around all morning hanging clothes outside and bringing them back in when rain started, the day cleared off beautifully at about noon. Even Elizabeth's gauze diapers refuse to dry when it rains all day!

Mabel took Elizabeth down to Water Street, where the main department stores are, to see the Christmas windows. The merry-go-round at Fogarty's wasn't working but there was a Ferris wheel, and Bookers had a Santa Claus who "jumped" up and down on a spring.

We are planning to go to the Philharmonic concert Thursday evening, after eating our Thanksgiving dinner. Thanksgiving—with sunshine and cotton dresses!

November 26:

A lovely sunny day. I can easily understand why Mabel told me she prefers the hot sun to the rain, for the warmth and brightness is a real relief from that all-pervading dampness. Howard found mold on his blue suit today, and I continue to battle it on my blue shantung dress.

I went downstairs this afternoon to open the door for Mabel and Elizabeth and found a hen perched on one of my suitcases, all settled down for the night. My first thought was that it was some stuffed bird that Howard had brought home. I didn't know what to do with it, so Howard put it outside. How it found its way to our entry I don't know.

November 27:
Thanksgiving Day, and a very bad day for me. It started badly when I discovered ants by the score in the cake I made yesterday. After breakfast I happened to look in my flour tin (the cake was also in a tin box) and I found ants were in that, too. That meant throwing away about three-fourths of a good cake, and then spending half an hour sifting several pounds of flour and fishing out the little devils.

As I was cleaning the living room I heard *Lunchtime with Lillian* [radio program] and Lillian discussed Thanksgiving at length, calling it the most American of holidays. She played "Come Ye Thankful People, Come," "We Gather Together," and "My Country, 'Tis of Thee." The words to the last one sounded utterly beautiful to me—"thy woods and templed hills" seemed to be a long way off, and I stood broom in hand and tear in eye.

Mrs. Patoir from downstairs offered to bake a lemon meringue pie for us since it was a holiday. The thought of five eggs going into a pie seemed rash, but it was awfully nice of her. A good pie, too. Mrs. Patoir prides herself on her ability to make "all the American dishes" because she had an American grandfather.

After lunch I went downtown to do a little Christmas shopping and discovered that size 13 socks for Howard just aren't available, and even size 12s are few and ugly. Christmas tree ornaments at Bookers were of poor quality and expensive at 48 cents and 60 cents each, not even as pretty as those at Woolworth's.

We couldn't have our Thanksgiving chicken for dinner because we'd bought a frozen one and it just wouldn't thaw out. So we had leftover leg-of-lamb soup and the pie.

The B.G. Militia Band concert to benefit the St. George's Cathedral restoration fund finished the day. We walked over to the college, where it was presented, and found men wearing tuxedos and dinner jackets, and women in everything from strapless velvet formals on up and down—flimsy sheers, dark crepes. I wore my old blue shantung, H. his blue suit—always conservative, you know. The band is much more impressive when marching. They smothered Miss Dolphin's piano, and it is just difficult to enjoy orchestral music played by a band! There were also a bosomy British soprano, a slightly effeminate basso, and a saxophonist who played three pieces "accompanied by the composer"; all three pieces sounded identical, but Mr. Martin-Sperry[22] is a generous patron of most musical functions here, we are told. I don't mean to sound really uppityish because we did enjoy it, for the local color if not the music. The archbishop was there, dressed as I have never seen anyone dressed before, in long stockings and frock coat. Shades of Dickens!

We don't mean to be critical, but it irks us to think of rising when His Excellency, the Officer Administering the Government, the Honourable John Gutch, CMG, OBE, and party make their grand entrance (late), and then rising and waiting for them to leave at the concert's end. So much pomp for a mere representative of the government—and such a dull-looking man, too. But as Howard says, the OAG is in a sense B.G.'s president, so perhaps there is something to it. Annoying, nonetheless.

November 28:

Shortly after Howard left to go to a Science Club meeting, while I was in the midst of the dishes, Mr. Rodway and Rev. Bowen stopped by to see if we were going to a native wedding tomorrow at Buxton. Howard hadn't mentioned it to me; sounds interesting but I don't know about taking Elizabeth. Mr. Bowen most definitely does not fit the stereotype of a Lutheran missionary, and I can see now why Howard thought he was good company.

Thomas polished the floors today, and until it rains again they will look beautiful.

Had a nice chat with Mrs. Patoir this afternoon. She does so want to be friendly; perhaps I shall have to overlook the state of her dresses, kitchen, maid, and dishtowels.

November 29:

We decided not to attend the wedding, and Howard dropped by Mr. Rodway's house to tell him. He ended up staying all morning, discussing everything from fish and government to personalities in Georgetown and the college. Mrs. Rodway, he says, is "racially indistinct." So many people are here.

The speaker at the Science Club meeting last night was a government economist who discussed, inadequately in Howard's opinion, B.G.'s economic future, all things considered. The whole issue seems to center on the advisability of industrialization or the further intensification of agriculture. There is fairly widespread agreement, though, that local problems won't be solved with present conditions as they are.

November 30:
Howard finally put up the rods for the curtain valences. I think he bent more nails than he used, for the wood here is so hard that thumbtacks are useless, a handsaw dulls in short order, and all but the best nails are bent like spaghetti.

December 1, 1952

Dear folks,

Busy, busy, busy! We're in the usual rush of work at school just preceding Christmas vacation.

I went to a meeting of the B.G. Science Club last Friday night per Herbert Allsopp's invitation of some weeks ago. Although the issue presented was not very adequately covered, the response of contributory remarks and general questions made it a very profitable evening indeed. It had to do with the economic considerations in B.G.'s development. We've been here three months now, so that most of the glamour has worn off, leaving B.G. in her true light open for comment. Agriculture versus industry is the issue. Has B.G. reached its agricultural peak and readied itself for industrialization, or is a more intensive approach to agricultural economy the answer? Proponents of industry have "Trinidad fever" and feel that the same could happen here if only there were enough money. We have manganese-rich columbite, very productive bauxite, and a number of hard timbers endemic in Guiana. But to market these in their more needed form would necessitate a tremendous investment in refining plants. Both columbite reduction to manganese and bauxite reduction to aluminum require abundant, cheap electric power of which there is none here. What of the falls? To restate what one observer said, "British Guiana has expertitis." It seems that from time to time experts on hydrography from the U.S., U.K., and Canada have come down, investigated, and published all kinds of conflicting reports on the practicality of installing hydroelectric plants—resulting in no action. The timber problem is this in a nutshell: No road in the colony penetrates more than 35 miles into the interior, and since most of the hardwoods are as heavy or heavier than an equal volume of water, river flotation is out of the question. (There are virtually no softwoods.) And with the land below, on a level with, or just slightly elevated above the rivers for a considerable distance inland, roads are risky, particularly in view of the frequent flooding. So timber exports are slight when compared with what they might be. Yet, many (probably most) people here talk as if there will come a fairy godfather with unlimited dollar benevolence to industrialize the colony. Most people forget that without secondary industries, conversion from agriculture to primary industry puts people out of work. The more astute are fully aware that when a potential investor seeks guidance from the U.K. on a good bet, he usually ends up in the U.K. or else on an island where overpopulation is a general problem (.95 people per square mile in B.G.; 420 in Barbados, for example).

Agriculture seems to be the answer, although it's not that simple. Rice is not in universal demand for the dollar-rich countries, so it merely feeds local mouths. Cane sugar is gradually being supplanted by beet sugar in temperate climes and so it, too, is gradually becoming more of a local product. The interior of the colony is reportedly very suitable for cattle rearing but, as above, transportation is the obstacle, what with no roads, and rivers navigable for only a hundred or so miles.

Conclusion: There is no simple answer to British Guiana's economic ills. Any ideas?

Once again, it's late and I'm pooped.

Love to all,

Howard

Monday, Dec. 1, 1952

Dear Everyone—

Happy December to you all! I guess this month we really will get rained upon. Everyone said we could expect rain in November, but there wasn't enough to amount to anything. We hear Christmas carols on the radio all the time and we're gradually getting used to the idea of Christmas being possible in such a summery place.

Downtown at Bookers I saw tree ornaments, again à la Woolworth's worst. They had the same plain balls and fancier doodads, but none of them had the good detailing that U.S. dime store products have. The ornaments we shipped here are all intact, except for the candy canes, which had been attacked by ants. I also saw some Christmas cards with local photographs on the cover, sickly sentiments poorly printed inside, for 18 cents. I bought "When We Were Very Young" for Elizabeth, also some other cute children's books that I will probably just put away for now. And I bought some cheap cotton material to make E.'s scrapbook. Also 12 toothpicks for 12 cents. Could you send a few? I do prefer them to broom straws for cake testing.

Thought you might be interested in the dollar bills. The same design is on all bills, but the $2 is blue, $5 is green, $10 is brown, $20 purple, and $100—I can't remember. The paper is very poor. They haven't been in circulation more than a few years and yet some of the bills look just ancient.

Elizabeth has had another touch of diarrhea, but we had some of the medicine on hand and she is doing quite well now. I can't figure out how she gets it, but with so many little flies and ants around I guess it is inevitable.

Frances, our new laundress, does the most artistic job of ironing sheets and dishtowels! She starches everything enough so that it looks like new. Alas, I'm afraid she uses the sun as bleach, which is fine for the white things but a bit rough on our towels. I now have one very pale yellow hand towel.

We are still collecting coins for you. Trying to find nice new ones. Mother, if you want some, do let us know. How would they be on buttons: you know the button-making kits that are sold in dime stores? Could the coins be glued onto the button backs?

Must clean up and get to work on my curtains. Since my Thanksgiving goal didn't pan out, I now have my sights set on Christmas. Shall be utterly humiliated if all is not done by then.

Much love to each of you,

Marian

We received a gift card for The New Yorker *last week, so we expect to receive the magazine itself shortly. Many thanks—our magazines mean so much here!*

December 1:

We had our first beefsteak tonight. Simply lovely! Especially at 65 cents a pound. Lamb is 87 cents, mutton 76 cents. It's hard to believe.

December 2:

Howard's stamp albums are getting awfully moldy. Only the covers are affected, but what a smell! I had one in the sun all morning and that seemed to help, but as soon as it is put back in the dark it will start again. Ugh.

I found a butterfly in the kitchen this morning. It had laid its eggs on one of the windows. Howard scooped up the eggs, which were a pretty bright yellow, to take to school.

I also found a dead lizard in the hall. By the time I got around to sweeping it up, it was covered by ants. This place is a walking laboratory.

December 3:

Went to town today for more Christmas presents. Howard dropped me off at Psaila Bros. ten-cent store. It compares to Woolworth's as Yong Hing's does to the Big Bear—not very favorably. The store is small and dark, and most of their wares look awfully cheap. They have the usual dime store variety of candy and glassware, toys and stationery.

Toys are disappointing. Dolls have such ugly faces and nearly everything looks cheap, even dolls costing $5 and more. I found a few things for Howard, but on the whole it is hard work. The majority of the available merchandise is serviceable, but it does so lack character!

Saw two tiny East Indian babies, much smaller than Elizabeth, with pierced ears. One had gold earrings, the other pearls.

December 4:

Worked like mad today, baking cookies and date bread in the morning before Winifred arrived to do the kitchen. Just brought the clothes in before we had a quickie shower that came in through the closed windows.

Miss Graham, the biology teacher at Bishops' High School, came to tea. She is a strange creature. Howard says she tries her best to be masculine, and she does everything short of shingle her hair. She sails a boat for a hobby, hikes, etc. Unfortunately she doesn't look very clean— her dress was filthy, hair greasy, face questionable. She speaks so poorly that it is very hard to understand her; her words are sputtered out and her enunciation nil. Howard was most provoked with her, for she returned some slides belonging to Queen's that she had been using all fall, and which Howard has needed. At 5 I decided to feed Elizabeth, and Miss Graham decided to go.

December 5:

Howard did our shopping and brought home a five-pound roast of beef that cost $3.14, hard as it is to believe.

Now it really seems like Christmas. After dinner I took out some sequins, beads, and clear nail polish and made some tree ornaments out of cigarette box tinfoil. Just stars and crescents, but they look pretty with the glitter on them.

December 8:

I think my shopping is all done! The clerks here amaze me. The man at Fogarty's asked me with no prompting how we liked our "Jackson Cooker." Still more surprising was a woman at Bookers who knew our address; we don't have a charge account there and seldom even go in.

Out of the welter of junk such as cheap pottery figurines and teapots, I have found a few lovely pieces of china and glassware. Unfortunately, they are fearfully expensive (a crystal vase with leaf patterns in brown was $25, a similar bowl $15, and a lovely tea set for eight was $72).

Tuesday, December 9, 1952, 7 a.m.

Dear Mother and Daddy—

I certainly hope this arrives before you leave [to spend Christmas in Los Angeles with Bee]. I'd have written sooner but Sat. I got a cold and felt punk. H. bought some antihist. stuff that really seemed to help. Feel fine now.

I'm just about finished with Christmas shopping. Bought E.'s car seat yesterday—I wish it were prettier but it was the only kind available. Ivory metal with brown canvas seat and back. It cost $11 here, so about $6 or $7 U.S. would be right, I guess. Why don't you put it into the Central Bank account.

Thanks so much for the address labels. My writing gets worse and worse as I do less of it. I was embarrassed last month when the check I wrote for the car payment came back with a note saying they didn't know what account it was for—the note was addressed to Mrs. Drwin.

Our chief present for E. was to be a high chair, but I bought a "low chair" instead. The seat is about a foot from the floor, and when she's through the tray stage H. can remove that and she'll have a cute little ivory chair. There were two high chairs here—one locally made was $26.25, the other from England was $34. This low chair was $15 and matches the little crib. I'm making another dress for her—scrap enclosed. Also finished a cloth scrapbook, which is cute. We bought an icky, faded yellow rubber ball (no bright and shiny red ones!) for 40 cents, a set of plastic teething beads, the Milne book. No dolls—we received a package from Helen Sterne [Marian's aunt] last week, labeled "one stuffed toy—value $4.95." I had to pay $3.04 duty on it. It was certainly sweet of her to send it, but the duty is awful.

I've purchased a record for H.—Brahms's Second Symphony played by Furtwangler and the London Philharmonic, a 12-inch LP, $8.50. But choice is very limited, the LP's are so new here and way too expensive for most people.

Men's clothing is repulsive—ties are hideous, no large-enough socks, etc. H. needs more slacks and is going to have two pairs made this month—none ready-made! He is due home from gardening any minute—breakfast is almost ready.

There's so much junk around. I found a cute children's tablecloth and bought it for either future use or a gift to take home. Also some wonderful children's books in color photography. Of all the things I see downtown, the only ones I care for are a costly tea set, two lovely small glass vases, and the silver, Wedgwood, and Doulton at Bookers. There are counters full of heavy, cheap doodads.

H.'s vacation starts the 19th and he really needs it—he's been going strong, per usual.

Aha—breakfast now over, and H. is in a hurry to go to school so I must finish this.

Miss you both—wish we could spend Christmas with you. Bon voyage!
Much love,
Marian

December 9:

Before I bathed Elizabeth this morning, we went downstairs to thank Mrs. Patoir for sending up two coconuts. I took my *Good Housekeeping* issue with the cake recipe, and she seemed pleased. Said she certainly admired me for doing my own housework, that no other English, American, or Scotch woman she knows would do it. She goes barefoot during the day, wears filthy dresses, and has bad teeth, beautiful blue eyes, and a very generous heart. I have decided to overlook certain details. She offered to sit with Elizabeth any night we want to go out, saying it is a relief to get away from her noisy family.

Our rum distributor, D'Aguiar Bros., Ltd., presented us with a bottle of five-year-old rum, two glasses, five balloons, and best wishes for the holidays. Also the hope that they can continue to serve us next year. I was most impressed!

December 10, 1952

Dear folks,

With the end of the term just a few days off, there is the usual rush to finish the work set out. In most of my forms we're near schedule.

The stores here are just like those at home at this season. We even have a couple of Santas, or "Father Christmases" as they're called, one of them with a red (painted) face! But catch this mercenary angle: The kids have to pay to see him. (He's on the radio each day, too, limey accent and all.) But we find it difficult to feel Christmasy when it's 88° to 92° outside, virtually the same as when we came. In other words, we have to work at it somewhat.

In respect to my research project, I've had some luck getting a place to use as a headquarters out at Atkinson Field. It seems that the B.G. government gave the U.S. a 99-year lease on the site but since we have no use for the base at the present time, we have allowed local commercial airlines and other business endeavors to utilize the installation. Among others, one Louis Chung has rented what was the main terminal building and uses it as a shipping point for exporting fish and animals to zoos in North America and Europe. He has more room in the building than he needs, so I've asked him for a corner, nook, cubicle, or whatever in order that I may work in that region without having to carry my presses and other equipment each time I go out.

My poor stamp collection is in the process of being salvaged from near destruction. When we first came I simply set the albums on the shelf and forgot about them. But a couple of weeks ago I discovered to my horror that the unused stamps with glue on their backs were starting to stick to the pages. So I've bought some cellophane and am now enveloping all unused items. What price humidity!

Yesterday two annoying incidents occurred: The right arm of my glasses snapped, and the electric razor quit. I took the latter apart and found that the motor bearings are so badly worn that the armature is (and has been for some time) rubbing on the fields. This seems poor in view of the fact that the razor is not yet a year old! I can't get it repaired here, so it'll be on its way to you soon. The glasses can be fixed here, thank goodness. Incidentally, I've since learned that the optician I went to is a devout Communist—not uncommon here.

I went to a Literary and Debating Society (school function) debate a week ago and was disappointed to see that it was nothing but an elocution exercise in which the boys were bombastically smearing each other under the guise of parliamentary repartee. It struck me as a challenge, and I've since become ex-officio adviser. Have already initiated some reforms.

Three events in the near future have our interest. Queen's College's Speech Day is on the 12th, at which time last year's valedictorian, salutatorian, and others will give short speeches. His Excellency, the Officer Administering the Government, the Honourable John Gutch, CMG, OBE, will deliver the principal address and present the prizes. (How do you like his title?) On the 15th the Georgetown Philharmonic, with a local piano soloist, will present, among other things, Grieg's Concerto. And Miss Graham of the Bishops' High School biology department (whom we had for tea last week) has invited us to their Speech Day on the 17th. So you see, we're kept pretty busy.

Have you received our Christmas card yet?

Time to turn in.

Love to all,

Howard

December 11:

We are renting a casuarina tree, potted, from the Botanical Gardens, which will be delivered the Monday before Christmas. It is the closest thing to a fir available: has no leaves, but feathery branches.

Howard's two private students came at 4 this afternoon for their lab work and stayed until 8, talking about the States, schools, and so on. Howard says they are naively curious about us—what we do, think, read. Their questions are interesting and show a lack of knowledge concerning the functioning of an independent country. They desire all sorts of information and lap it all up.

December 12:

The Ramsarans are moving. The Camerons, from whom they were renting their house, sent word to Mr. Beckles today from Trinidad that they will arrive here tomorrow. And they were supposed to leave England on the 19th and get here the first of January! Such complete thoughtlessness burns us. Margaret is in a stew, but at least the local government-housing people have lined up a place for them to move into: the story above the old Technical Institute (a trade school). They will come here tomorrow for lunch, and Howard is going to help with the car.

December 12, 1952

Dear folks,

On our dining room table is one of the hugest and most beautiful flowers we've seen. A man, very gallant in manner, brings us lotus lilies (pink water lilies with long stems) once a week at the rate of ten for 12 cents. They're big enough; about six inches across. But this one is cream, and about 15 inches in diameter—the famous Victoria water lily—costing all of 14 cents! It completely fills one of our copper bowls. Looks like an ordinary water lily but for the extreme size and the very spiny sepals (bud covers).

You ask about school. I don't discuss it at much length because, like any job, we like to more or less forget about it when at home. As for the new principal, Mr. Sanger-Davies (who's due to arrive in a day or two), I didn't intend to convey any hostility felt by me about his coming but rather to give you the general impression of the staff. I'm not as yet in much of a position to evaluate the situation since I've yet to meet Captain Nobbs, and it is with his reign that Mr. S-D's will be compared. Mr. Beckles, in his true light, is a very cordial gentleman, extremely friendly, but has the annoying habit of never taking sides in any issue of controversy—hardly the person for headmaster. Many staff members (the more phlegmatic ones) feel that Beckles's interim trick has been good for it has given them more freedom of action, etc. But most of us note the increase of academic and disciplinary laxity—sufficient cause for a man of some firmness and true administrative power.

Detention is an institution of punishment in British schools. Actually, the name denotes the cause rather than the cure. Each form has a Detention Book, which it carries from room to room, in which disciplinary and other offenses (here spelled "offences") are recorded. Then, at the end of the day, all boys recorded in the various books must go to the detention room and remain for an hour and complete the special tasks given them. It should carry an air of disgrace with it, but, unfortunately, many boys go day after day showing no repentance or remorse. Under Captain Nobbs's regime, a boy who went to detention three times in a week would be summoned to his office for a caning. But Mr. Beckles hasn't maintained the practice, resulting in some boys being assigned detention five and even more times a week. As a result, some of us have been giving out two, three, and more hours for each offence.

A series of staff meetings will be held next week to review the boys' progress during the term and then to make recommendations for improvements—one of them will most certainly concern detention. It may seem like a small matter, but the success of this type of school seems to lie in keeping the boys carefully subjugated and aware of responsibilities. Of course, our (U.S.) public school system has as a major premise the gaining of an awareness of the problems of democracy, to be achieved through participation in electoral processes leading to student body president and so on. But in this type of school (said to be more "British" than most schools in Britain) such experience is not afforded. This seems strange to me in view of the hue and cry for B.G.'s independence.

Everyone seems most impatient to have B.G. freed of Britain, but on the other hand few profess to know the responsibilities of democracy, to say nothing of its operation. Such naiveté could be serious here amid the unstable South American republics. Most people here ignore the fact that B.G. physically lies in and is very much a portion of South America, and not an island in the Caribbean. They forget that B.G.'s problems, economic and otherwise, are not those of the insular colonies.

There is in the current *Time* an article that burns the eyes of the Guianese. It relates how U.K. has invested $400 million in bauxite operations in Gold Coast, Africa [the future Ghana]—just after having made it plain to the B.G. government that they simply did not have the capital to develop the workings here. Such conflict in reasoning (ostensibly) causes street scenes and general unrest. Of course, U.K. hopes either or both U.S. and Canada will step in and work the B.G. deposits, but Alcoa just closed its operations on the Corentyne River (throwing 5,000 out of work) because the British were taking too much of the profit in the form of sterling and taxes. Yes, there's a good deal of unrest here, and recent events in India, Ceylon, Jamaica, and Kenya don't serve as sedatives.

December 13: We went to the Speech Day ceremonies and learned that in reality it was a delayed graduation exercise minus the graduates! All of the ceremony, pomp, etc. centered on the principal's report of the previous year's activities (in which my being secured was discussed at some length) and the comments of His Excellency the OAG, which made it clear that the solution to B.G.'s short staffing at Queen's was not met by securing temporary personnel from outside (true enough but rather crudely put) but rather by initiating foreign-study scholarships for the most promising.

Aside from that, it was a very enjoyable affair. Included on the program were the awarding of prizes (mostly in academic achievements), the presentation of two short plays, one in French, and singing by the youngest boys.

I'll be very glad when at last our coming here will be taken as a matter of fact and not be the cause of much official note (as here) or of the bowing and scraping that we've endured at the downtown stores. We appreciated it at first, but now it's a bit bothersome—I almost prefer going to a store where I'm not known.

Love to all,
Howard

December 13:
Lordy, what a day. The Camerons arrived at the college at noon and told the Ramsarans not to hurry their moving. John said they'd be out by 6 p.m., and Mr. Cameron said, "Make it by 5." I scurried around here all morning fixing a real dinner for noon, and after lunch I went over to the Queen's compound with them and helped pack china and sweep while Howard continued the box shuttle back and forth; he made a total of 13 trips. The big pieces were carried by donkey cart. By 5:10 everything was out, and the Camerons' house was reasonably clean, quite neat, and littered with the artificial flowers and ball-fringe tablemats that the R.'s had hidden when they moved in. We were all exhausted and thoroughly enjoyed the tea that Beryl Maudsley provided. The Camerons drove up about 5:30. Mrs. McLaren told me they [the Ramsarans] had had animal life in their beds for over a month after moving in. Howard and I are curious to meet the Camerons—just to see what manner of people they are.

December 14:
Margaret brought a chicken over this morning, which was boiled on our stove. They have a one-burner electric plate, a kerosene stove that they don't know how to operate, and no shelving at all. The john is practically in their living room. The whole w.c. is just enclosed in louvers. Smack in their bedroom is a stairway to the attic. It sounds pretty grim to me, and I'm glad we're not government servants compelled to live in government-furnished quarters—at a cheap rent, granted, but under such conditions!

Monday, December 15, 1952

Dear Mother—

It's 2:30 and our mail, unusually late, just arrived. I should be taking my shower but couldn't resist writing!

The weekend was truly hectic. Friday was Speech Day. The OAG gave a brief speech before presenting the prizes. He was obviously bored by the goings-on and didn't so much as smile at the boys when he shook their hands. Still, it was fun to see how they do it.

As a result of Saturday's exertion I have prickly heat—the worst yet! All over my front, back, and "sit-upon"—and I can see why babies complain.

Tonight we hear the Philharmonic concert. H. has been approached about playing string bass in the orchestra—he's more or less reserving judgment!

Damn it all—I guess I will end up by lining all the brown draperies. One pair has faded a lot already, on the back, and I can't let that go on! Have I ever said that there are Singer Sewing Centers here? We are considering a secondhand machine (vintage like yours) for a Christmas present, as I know I'd use it a lot here for E.'s clothes and mine, too.

The Larthes have invited us to eat Christmas dinner with them—we accepted gladly since it will be fun. If Elizabeth were more aware of the occasion we'd stay here, of course.

Well, I do need a shower and some prickly heat powder, so that's all for now.

Much love,

Marian

My cold is gone, and E.'s is almost gone. Mabel asked me yesterday if E. shouldn't wear a cap outside, because the sun was still bright and wouldn't be good, maybe, for her cold!

December 15:

I'm afraid we were disappointed today by Georgetown's Philharmonic. It was quite pathetic. In attendance were the OAG and wife and all the other local personages desirous of being seen at the correct functions, dressed to the teeth in clothes ranging from velvet formals to fluffy prints. We sat next to Dorothy and Archie, and when a soloist came out and stood by the piano, Dorothy whispered to me, "What's he standing there for?"

The music was frankly awful. Margaret said the six first violinists could have been playing six different compositions, for their bowing was so far from being in unison. A young man with a forced artificial voice sang "The Prize Song" from *Die Meistersinger* and "La donna è mobile"—both broke my heart. At intermission no one discussed the music, which was lucky as we would have been embarrassed.

Howard met Mr. Cameron today. He is very anti-white, according to Mrs. McLaren.

December 16:
Things really do pick up at Christmas. We find we'll have to skip Bishops' Speech Day so that Howard can attend the "feeds" of the houses at Queen's on Thursday, although his house feed is scheduled for Friday and we will both go to that. These feeds are, we understand, just what the name implies. The boys collect money from their houses all during the fall term and bring more money from home in order to have a whopping big eating party at the end of the term.[23]

Wednesday, December 17, 1952

Dear Mother and Daddy—

Christmas is almost upon us, and I'd give almost anything to be able to send you something more than just this letter. It seems positively strange—I'm thwarted! But consider this letter a little giftie, and I shall get more personal and sentimental than usual, because Christmas is the best time I know for those honest emotions.

We both feel we're learning so much here—in different ways, of course. The wonders of American life (as I knew it) return again and again to me, and I think of the little conveniences that I had never consciously appreciated before, and the spirit that is the essence of a confident and well-fed population. (Did I ever tell you that the motley crowd at La Guardia really floored me—they all looked and sounded like refugees. And there I saw my first billy-club-swinging policeman. I would probably have to live in that atmosphere awhile to properly appreciate the West Coast!) Some of the people we talk to (H.'s two private students, for example) think that just to go to America would solve their problems. Guianese who do go write glowing letters—I can't help but wonder if they don't build them up some, for the change must be terribly hard for them to meet.

Howard is at school trying to finish his end-of-term markings. I've seen him briefly today at meals, and that's all. Tomorrow and Friday there are meetings of all masters to discuss all the boys—sounds arduous, doesn't it.

I can't imagine anyone being happier with domestic routine than I am! There isn't time for me to dust our jalousies and wash all our windows, so I just ignore them—otherwise we are clean and well fed and contented. The very pattern of housework is interesting to me—and I am able to fit my morning jobs together very neatly now. After lunch I putter—read, sew, think about dinner, bake cookies, etc. Some days seem like a three-ring circus, and I finish the dishes after diner and feel I've had enough. But it is such a satisfying tiredness.

Every morning near 6 a.m. I stagger from bed, get dressed, comb my hair, and go to Elizabeth. Sometimes she is sitting up waiting for me, and sometimes when she hears me she flops on her stomach and kicks her legs violently like a swimmer—she invariably wakes me up and is so cute I laugh with her and talk to her while I get her ready to eat breakfast. If Howard is awake I take E. in to our bed, where she kicks H. and plays with our alarm clock. Otherwise she goes back into her own bed and plays very well by herself considering that she's frightfully hungry. I feed her breakfast and lunch in her little chair, and she sits there with her mouth open like a baby bird's—so eager for food. She loves cereal and carrots and string beans and apricots impartially—she's just plain hungry. I give her an egg yolk and fruit at lunch and half a can of vegetables and either another vegetable, a fruit, or custard for dinner. Not up to Dr. Hellyer's quantities, but sufficient.

Elizabeth crawled today! Something suddenly clicked, and she scooted halfway down the living room floor. And then she sat in front of the radio, which was on, and looked at it so intently that I couldn't help but think of "his master's voice"!

Well, dears, I'm going to write a little note to Bee and then go to bed. Merry Christmas to you both, the dearest parents anyone could have.

Much love,

Marian

Wednesday, December 17, 1952

Dear Bee—

Here I am in my old lavender dress. Outside the night is perfectly lovely with the stars so bright that the Little Dipper looks like a bracelet charm. Our tree will be delivered next Monday and I can't wait to see it. H. told me it would be potted, and I had in mind a small table-size tree—but he said it might be six or eight feet tall! If it is that high, we still won't need to worry about enough decorations since these casuarinas have fewer branches than firs and just wouldn't hold the profusion we're used to. I love our homemade decorations, and I think we should establish the tradition of making at least a few new ones each year.

The enclosed program is from Monday night's concert, which was attended by Georgetown society, all dressed up in its velvet formals and tuxedos. We thought the quality of the music was quite poor, aside from the clarinet soloist; he is the conductor's son, just fourteen years old, and the best of the evening. A Mrs. Taitt has been doing her persistent best to rope H. into playing double bass in the orchestra, but he's afraid he wouldn't be able to take it. We hear she bosses the conductor and has on occasion seen fit to reseat the orchestra, interrupt rehearsals, etc.

I can't wait to see Elizabeth's reaction to our tree. I think she'll love it. She takes such an interest in bright objects and moving forms—she still loves her afternoon walks and is intrigued by every dog, car, and person they see. Mabel says she sometimes turns around and looks back to get a better look.

I'm running out of ink, and it's 10:15 and H. still isn't home! Well, to bed. We wish you were here in person, Bee. The things you've sent are sweet substitutes, but we would love to have you yourself.

Much love and Merry Christmas,
Marian

December 18, 1952

Dear Dad,

This to you separately because of the contents that I hope to get through: The white one is for Mother, the blue one for Carrie [Howard's grandmother]. I'll entrust you with the wrapping, etc. I feel badly that there's nothing for you, but I trust you understand that there is really nothing very suitable that can be sent in a letter.

Today or tomorrow should mark the end of our staff meetings (to consider each boy's progress in the past term) and thus bring the term to an end—and, very frankly, I'm really tired, though pleasantly so. It is fatiguing to remain fixedly concentrated on the futures of others for days at a time. Sometimes I wonder if my comments do justice to a boy's progress, and at other times I think I've been too lenient—all this, and I still haven't done any Christmas shopping.

We'll miss you at Christmastime. I'll take some more pictures soon and send them along.

Howard

December 18:
Howard left at 4:15 for the house party at the college and said he'd be back about 5. Ha! At 7:30 I went ahead with my solitary dinner, and he finally arrived at 8:30. Three different house feeds rolled into one afternoon, and poor Howard, to be polite, ate cake, meat patties, cookies, apples, ice cream, and pop at each. Felt rather green by the time he reached home.

We cracked almonds for my Christmas pudding, which I hope to make tomorrow.

December 19:
Howard collapsed after eating very little lunch and slept most of the afternoon. Indigestion.

At 4:30 we went to Howard's house feed. I met several masters and a few more wives. We ate meat patties, fruitcakes, chocolate cake (heavy as lead), apples, walnuts, ice cream, and pop. Archie was in charge, and he began by proposing a toast to the Queen. After everyone was stuffed we went to the main hall, where boys from two other houses were assembled. The entertainment went on and on and on. Miss Dolphin, an invited guest, was asked to play for group singing, and the singing turned the boys into a mob. They shouted out Christmas carols with gusto, oblivious of any sacred character attached to the carols. After the singing was over, Ken Maudsley got up to start some silly games. We had had enough, but things went on for another half hour. We were glad to get home at 8.

December 21:
Learning the hard way is discouraging business. I spent the whole day baking Christmas cookies, four kinds, and by the time the last ones were out of the oven, the others were soggy from the dampness of the day. Damn. I guess I shall heat these up tomorrow before packing them.

December 22:
I packed the cookies in cute little baskets, tied them with red ribbon, and we delivered them to Mrs. Patoir and then went to the Beckleses'. There, we heard more of Mrs. Beckles's ailments and complaints. We discussed Christmas record buying briefly, and she told me there was a nice record out called "Mom and Dad." I nearly flipped—it is a perfectly horrible pseudo-western-type schmaltzy music, utterly awful.

Our tree was delivered before lunch. It is tall, spindly, and a bit crooked. We will decorate it after dinner.

December 23:
Winifred thanked me today for the $3 we gave as a Christmas gift. I wonder how far that little bit goes for a family of twelve! We talked a bit about Elizabeth, and she said it is unusual for a child Elizabeth's age to sleep clear through the night! Mercy. Of course, people here don't give babies solid food until they're nearly a year old, so I suppose the poor little creatures wake up hungry two or three times during the night. So many babies we see look just tiny and peaked.

December 24:
Howard became disgusted with the mess in our courtyard and cleared out many of the dead branches of the traveler's palm. He said mosquito wrigglers were having a grand time in the water-filled branches, and the garbage dumped under the tree was appalling. It looks beautifully neat and respectable now.

While he was doing that I chatted with Mrs. Patoir. She cited instances of English workers being given preference over natives when the latter were clearly eligible: her husband has been passed over for promotion to paymaster, and a white man whom she said is "illiterate" given the job instead. Mr. Patoir is half Arawak Indian and has some Negro blood. One of her daughters, she said, has turned toward Communism, thinking that might help here. She said, "If only the Americans would take over B.G., what a change there would be. Why, just look at what they did at Atkinson—the lovely buildings, the pool, the good roads." According to her, resentment against Britain runs high among natives.

We ate our Christmas dinner of roast chicken, dressing, mashed potatoes, corn, and Christmas pudding and then settled down to wait for the police choir. They arrived at the Patoirs' about 10:30 and sang several carols, and included "Going Home." Their voices were good and strong, but we were sorry they chose to sing inside the Patoirs' small flat and not outside.

Christmas Day, 3:30

Dear everyone—

We shall never forget this day, for Christmas in Guiana is an enriching experience. Mrs. Patoir told me yesterday that people in England and the States may "spend" Christmas, but people here "keep" Christmas: this makes a great difference in the spirit of the day. Without snow, chimneys, fireplaces, and firs, Christmas is pared down to its essence, and everyone here helps by being considerate, friendly, and cordial. Last night the police choir (25 voices and very good) serenaded the Patoirs, for Mr. P. is assistant paymaster. The P.'s requested them to sing "Going Home" for us, thinking we must be very homesick. We were homesick, but the genuine spirit we find so in evidence here is wonderful.

We returned a few minutes ago from the Larthes', where we ate home-cured ham and roast duck, with dressing, applesauce, mashed potatoes, and peas. For dessert we had plum pudding and "mince pies," which to the English means little mince tarts about two inches across. All very good. E. missed her nap altogether and H. said he ate too much, so they are both sound asleep. We were proud of Elizabeth—she kept her poise completely when plunged into the Larthes' living room crowded with five children, four adults, an electric train, two cap pistols, balloons, and a large dog! She blinked at the cap pistol shots, but that was all. We took pictures of her this morning, with shampoo shade on, having lunch in her chair, and playing with her new toys. We bought (with a check from the Irwins) an abacus that is on an easel-like frame, which she seems to enjoy. Also a miniature "hammer strike" such as carnivals offer, and she does enjoy hearing the gong. Mrs. Ogle, upstairs tenant, gave her a little rubber doll, and the Beckleses stopped in with a rubber ball for her. We haven't tried the car seat out yet—she hadn't been in the car for nearly a month (papa too busy for drives!) and was afraid of it—so mommy held her.

We have had a "record" Christmas. I gave H. Brahms's Symphony No. 2 in D Major; he gave me Schubert's Symphony No. 3/Bach Sinfonia. Beethoven's Eighth and Don Juan/"1812" we bought with other gift money—also a large mirror for our washbasin (H. had been shaving by touch). H. bought a pinup light to put over my dark kitchen sink (I couldn't tell if dinner dishes were clean or not!) and I installed it this morning. He also gave me the cookbook of *West Indian Cookery*, which should be fun, and a good big book for me to transcribe (type) my journal into. I gave him a big thermos for "safaris" and we gave each other a total of three photograph albums. H. was tickled with the pretty socks, and we love the handkerchiefs from "Santa." H.'s Santa also gave him a mechanical pencil, and he is very pleased with the stamp books. The package for Elizabeth from Bee has not arrived yet. Christmas cards meant so much this year, and we devoured notes from friends.

We had our own Christmas dinner last evening—roast chicken and dressing, mashed potatoes, corn, cucumbers, and my Christmas pudding, which was good. (Don't quite know if H. and I will be able to finish it, but it will keep well.)

Our tree is eight feet tall, *very* spindly. But we put our three light strings on it and all our ornaments, and it looks beautiful. Imagination is needed here to enjoy Christmas, but with love and happiness in our hearts we have had a lovely day.

Daddy—your wire was delivered this morning. Bless your hearts! We're off to the Ramsarans' soon, and I must feed E. in a few minutes. We hope your Christmas was as lovely as ours—our thoughts are with you all. Happy New Year!

Much love,
Marian

December 25:
At about 11:30 we left for the Larthes'. The dinner was lovely—afterward we just sat for a while, but conversation was difficult. We were all too full. We left at about 3 to come home and nap.

The family came to life around 4:30. Then we left again, this time for the Ramsarans'. Had tea—bread, butter and jam, sponge cake, and Christmas cake, which is a white fruitcake iced with almond icing and white powdered sugar icing over that. Very good, if you ignore past experience with plain fruitcake! (Mrs. Patoir sent up two pieces of black fruitcake, iced the same way. Standard English practice, I guess.) Elizabeth was as good as gold. She went to bed in Susan's crib with a bare minimum of fussing and no real crying. We had such an enjoyable evening with them, talking about many things but concentrating on race problems. Margaret said they had a few friends who stopped calling after her marriage to John. She says that in England, a colored student in a college is treated as a special pet, and in the army, too, not ignored as they have been in my experience [in the U.S.]. John said he was given extras frequently. But still, we find some of the English people here to be frightfully race conscious and confident of white supremacy.

At about 10 we ate again—leftover turkey, dressing, salad, and several kinds of little pastry things that Margaret had made. Their new home is really weird, but they were at least organized enough to enjoy Christmas.

December 26:

This is Boxing Day. Howard and I thought it must have something to do with the pugilistic sport, but yesterday we learned that it stems from many years ago when Christmas Day was kept a religious holiday, and the day following it was set aside for the giving of presents and gift boxes—hence the name.

Mabel had the day off, so I washed diapers. After lunch we took a drive. Boxing Day is by tradition a day for celebrating, and many of the drivers on the road had evidently been doing their best to keep tradition alive. After several close calls we came home to take a nap.

We had quite an evening at the Larthes' party, not especially enjoyable. Again we put Elizabeth to bed in a strange crib, and again she was a model child. There were ten of us in all. One couple is Canadian, forty-five-ish, just returned from a six-month leave in Canada. Also, the Maudsleys from next door. The third couple arrived absolutely potted from another party (he came up the back steps and could barely make them at that; didn't say a word all evening. She is unfortunately the dramatic type, a show-off, loved doing charades, etc. Also baited her husband into doing things he was far too gone to do), and H. and I both wished they'd just stayed at the first party. Dorothy and Archie are fun in themselves, but we don't like their kind of entertainment, many drinks and games. (As a forfeit for one game, Howard, who was decreeing the penalties, unknowingly assigned a forfeit to me to go sing a carol in front of the Camerons' house. I sang "Silent Night," silently.) We left at about 11:30 and the others were just going strong—jokes we didn't understand, etc. Ugh.

December 27:
The garbage man came to the study window this morning and asked for his envelope. This envelope racket is completely new to us: the bread deliverer, postman, laundry deliverer, and "cart man" (garbage man) all left little envelopes about an inch and a half square, in the two weeks before Christmas. These little envelopes all had printed on them similar greetings: "With his usual courtesy, your district cart man wishes you the Season's Greetings" (in fairly large type), "and humbly solicits a donation" (in little tiny type). Mabel said a shoe repair man left an envelope at the Beckleses', and the garbage man in her district left one with her, which she told him she wouldn't fill as she had no money to do so! We gave them a shilling each, except for the postman, who got a dollar since he delivers so many magazines for us.

December 29, 1952

Dear folks,
The day after Christmas, the 26th, was Boxing Day, and the day following that, the 27th, Eze Day. We've learned that Boxing Day still remains a legal holiday in England and Wales (not in Ireland and Scotland), and so here. B.G. takes advantage of every holiday opportunity: to wit, Eze Day. Eze is the name of a tribal chieftain of Nigeria (S.W. Africa) who visited B.G. in 1949 on his way to N.Y.C., where he recently took a master's degree with honors in political science at Columbia. As for the cause of that initiating a bank holiday, well, we still don't know![24]

We were saddened with the news of the Globemaster crash at Moses Lake. As disastrous an event as it was, it served something of a useful purpose here in that our home city and state were more closely identified to those we know here, many of whom still cannot separate Washington, D.C., from Washington State. A recent *National Geographic* article (November) on the Columbia Valley aided this as well.

Incidentally, one fact that really calls for little discussion and which I may have mentioned already: Our staying here for the full two years is a certainty. In fact, I've already been approached by the principal, Mr. Sanger-Davies, about an additional year or two-year contract, but as it's awfully early to think about that, we've carried the matter to no definite resolution.

School reconvenes on the 14th, at which time I'm going to reorganize the long-defunct Q.C. Philatelic Society. There is considerable interest (several private collectors) among the boys in the higher forms, which is just where I hoped it would lie (less discipline to worry about, more sincerity, greater responsibility, etc.). I've discussed the matter at some length with Mr. S-D, who seems pleased and satisfied with the proposal.

On the 25th I'm to review two books (*A Dictionary of Biology* and *Recent Biological Discoveries*) over Radio Demerara for the British Council. The council's purpose is to disseminate British culture among subject peoples in particular, less particularly those not in the Commonwealth (there's an office in N.Y.C.). The U.K. subsidizes it quite substantially, but the selected media are of questionable merit here. Book reviews are certainly not of interest to the masses at this stage, nor are concert programs—these being the council's two major endeavors on the radio. Considering their dedication toward the removal of U.S. influence here, it seems a bit strange that they're interested in me for reviews. I've often been mistaken for a Canadian—maybe that's it!

Happy New Year to all—

Howard

December 29:

Howard and I went downtown today, hoping to buy some gifts for ourselves with money we received as Christmas presents. We didn't have too much luck. I had seen a good-looking saltcellar, pepper, and sugar set at Fogarty's before Christmas, but it was gone today. Nothing like it at Bookers either. However, we did find two lampshades at Sandbach Parker, one for our bedroom and one for the dining room. They are of plastic, and cost $3.00 and $2.14! Mercy. We also bought a new bathtub for Elizabeth. This one is oval, white enamel, and almost three feet long.

We stopped in at the Caribbean Novelty and Gift Store, a little shop that has intrigued me since we've been here. Unhappily, we were both disappointed with most of the merchandise. We had a lucky break and found a tray, of locust wood, a good size and shape, large enough to hold teapot, cream, sugar, etc. When people serve tea here, they do it in the living room with trays—but the only trays available in the department stores are absolutely hideous, so this was really a find. But the other wares were not well made or were not pretty. Basketwork was frightfully expensive.

We got home in time for Howard to meet with his two students, but in the midst of the lecture a shower surprised us. So Howard tore out to the car and drove up to the sea wall in search of Mabel and Elizabeth. After going past the house where they stood protected under a porch, he saw them and "rescued" them. Mabel said Elizabeth was amused by their dash for cover and squealed and giggled!

December 30:

The mailman left several magazines for us at the Beckleses', since they were addressed to the college and the college was officially not open. So Mabel brought us a *Saturday Review* and our first three *New Yorkers*. What a treat!

We had invited the Ramsarans to come over tomorrow to ring in the New Year with us. Howard stopped by there today and found John suffering with his old complaint, dysentery, Susan in the process of getting a cold, and Mrs. McLaren laid low with what appears to be food poisoning. So the party has been called off, and we hope they all get well quickly.

January 1, 1953:

We stayed up just long enough last night to greet the New Year, with the help of a pot of coffee. At midnight we heard a few automobile horns but very little hilarity other than that.

Just before we turned out our bed lamp I noticed a huge spider on the dining room ceiling. It must have been five inches across!

Thursday, January 1, 1953

Dear Mother and Daddy—

I thought you should have at least one letter waiting for you when you get home from Los Angeles! I have been awfully lax about writing anyone since Christmas, for I've spent all my sitting-down time typing up the journal, which, it appears, may be quite a lengthy volume.

Our first three *New Yorkers* arrived last Tuesday—big fat ones with all the wonderful Christmas ads in them. I can't say I'm enthused about cashmere cardigans with fur collars and cuffs and sequin doodads, but it's great sport reading about them. And we do so love getting *Time*. Thank you for everything!

We are now in the study drinking coffee and eating the Lady Baltimore cake I made yesterday. (I spent nearly two hours before making it, trying to decide how to use up 3/4 cup of egg whites.)

We "celebrated" New Year's Eve in our own sweet way, Howard working on the stamps for the Q.C. Philatelic Society, which he is trying to rejuvenate next term, and I typing more journal notes and reading *The New Yorker*. It was a noisy night outside, and we could hear people whooping it up. We did open our bottle of five-year-old rum before dinner, but unfortunately I couldn't tell much difference between that and the two-year-old that had been in our first drink!

Mother, do you suppose you might be able to send my chafing dish cookbook before our six-month duty-free period ends? I do wish I had it. We certainly have learned our lesson on this surface-mail routing. So far, the only person who has received our Christmas card is H.'s aunt Florence, and we sent one to her by airmail because it was delayed for lack of her California address. Next year we will send them out by the first of November. At this writing, we still have received no package from Bee.

Must write a few notes and then wash dishes. Hope your trip home was as pleasant as the one down.

Much love from all of us—

Marian

Did we tell you E. is getting an upper tooth—possibly two? Next week we will buy a sirloin steak for her!

(We assume you sent the records by surface mail. Correct?)

January 1, 1953

Dear folks,

Sorry our cards haven't arrived—hope the fifty-odd people to whom they were sent will understand! . . . The G.P.O. here said in October that if we mailed them by December 1 they should reach various points in the U.S. by Christmas. Next year we'll get them out by November 1.

We spent New Year's Eve (Old Year's Night here) enjoying ourselves with our usual after-dinner pastimes. At 11:30 we began to get expectant, and finally just before midnight we went to the window—but nothing happened. The hour was announced on the radio with much ringing of bells, but Georgetown was quiet. An occasional car horn was heard and some voices in the adjoining alley, but, as usual, the crickets and frogs had command of the ether. And so 1953 was upon us.

Elizabeth seems confused on Thursdays (Mabel's day off). When 4 o'clock rolls around she gets restless, wants to go out.

We've been having a good deal of rain since Christmas, but the showers are not as regular as we had expected. Sometimes we have one or two a day and sometimes five or six. It's seldom very hard to see them coming what with the big black clouds that roll in from the east. The rain usually pelts down for ten, fifteen, or twenty minutes and then stops, the clouds part, and the sun comes out. Our gallery ceiling still leaks in three or four places, and when the wind blows gustily, as it often does during a shower, the air inside seems very damp, almost misty, because of the multitude of slats (jalousies, as they're called locally) through which the damp air and droplets stream in. It seemed so strange to have our Christmas tree rocking and swaying in the breeze.

Now is probably as good a time as any to tell you about local varmints—particularly the types that invade homes. No. 1 on the list is the cockroach, which ventures forth only at night, usually solitary, and has done us no particular damage. Our offensive has paid off—we seldom see them. Ants are most pestiferous here. Not a single sugary thing can be left out without it being simply swarming with ants in an hour. Pesky things, they have even made their way into cookie tins, jars, etc.—even in the refrigerator! Water is the only thing that will stop them (DDT doesn't seem to bother them too much). So when Marian bakes a cake or whatever, she puts it in a tin and places that on a rack from the oven, the rack's four feet standing in water-filled jar lids. Then we have the marabunta, seldom of much consequence indoors (one gets in every now and then but usually makes its way out as well). It is a rather large brown wasp, the maid or polter type. I cannot yet give a firsthand account of its ravage, but those who can say that it never fails to raise an egg-size welt, and there's also the reputedly true story of a motorcyclist who was stung and who, in consequence, fainted before he could stop driving. The hardback is a black beetle, up to one inch in length, which when in season flocks to bright lights at night. Archie tells us of coming into his kitchen and finding the floor absolutely black with them—crunch, crunch! Every once in a while they come in here, but they simply dart at the lights, eventually hit the bulb or wire, and then clumsily fall to the floor. Among the other creatures frequently encountered are bats (we've been visited several times), lizards (beneficial—help keep insects down), frogs (get into toilet tanks), and scorpions (encountered one in the shower yesterday, three to four inches long and fierce). Spiders are here in great force and size. Two of the big ones are web spinners, most hunting their prey and that usually by night. Two nights ago we cringed at the sight of a monster with a six-inch leg spread on the ceiling—next morning it was on one of my shoes but skittered away as soon as we stirred—makes a papery rustling noise when walking. Last on the list are the termites, which are all but impossible to control. We have them in our john—many little holes in the wall, from each a stream of reddish sawdust falls. We even have one party in our radio cabinet! Well, they all contribute to the difference in life here from what it was at home.

Many thanks for the stamps. Would also appreciate your sending (a few at a time) those you've clipped from my letters as they're needed for trading. I've just recently established a contact in Kenya, East Africa.

Love to all,
Howard

Sunday, January 4, 1953

Dear Tom—

I don't think we ever decided on the extent of the B.G. sets wanted by your stamp-collecting friends, but, hoping they'll want them complete, I've enclosed four sets, 1 cent to $3.00, U.S. value about $5.00.

If the two highest values are not wanted (actually they are the most valuable to a collector) just pull 'em out and enclose them in a future letter—they can be exchanged.

Thanks for the "business."
Howard

January 5:

Howard has hired a man to wash the car twice a month and polish it once a month, for $6 a month. He came by this morning and went to work on it. It seemed like an unnecessary expense until we realized that Howard simply doesn't have time to do it so often, and that the car really needs cleaning that frequently. Howard says there is a little rust already in some places.

January 6:

John came by this morning to return some magazines. He said his family is recovered, although Mrs. McLaren's bout was quite serious. They're going to come to tea on Friday.

January 7:

The rain really came down, and in, today. Miss Osborn stopped by to see if our leaking roof had been repaired and saw by our cake pans and blotters on the floor that it hadn't been done. She then went out to find the carpenter who'd said he repaired it, and brought him in to see. They gesticulated and jabbered away at each other for several minutes, Miss Osborn maligning his work and the carpenter defending it ("I am not a tinsmith. I am a carpenter, and a good one," he said lifting his head proudly). We wished we had a tape recorder.

Thursday, January 8, 1953

Dear Parents—

By now you are all back in your routines, I suppose. Queen's starts next Wednesday, so Howard still isn't in his regular working schedule.

Yesterday he finished building our bookcase—five feet long, two shelves, of cedar. Last night I started to stain it with our dark floor wax, and tonight I hope to finish it. I've done the sanding, too. It won't have a high gloss but will be a pretty deep brown. H. has put it together with bolts so we can bring it home easily. Our radio-phonograph cabinet will be similarly built—we hope to get it done next week.

Tuesday we bought a nest of three tables, a Christmas present using several checks. The two smaller tables needed some work done on their tops, but the salesman guaranteed it would be done. They were delivered today, and I guess we'll have to send them back. The tops were beautifully finished, except they used a lighter stain to redo the repaired areas. Looks funny.

Howard learns tomorrow whether he gets the use of a two-room bungalow at Atkinson Field. He talked to some government man Tuesday and is to phone him back tomorrow. We're hoping he does get it—it would be an ideal place to leave all his presses.

The [unidentified] clipping has caused us to wonder just what most people at home think of the McCarran Act. There is a good deal of discussion about it here, and *Time* hasn't said too much as yet. We suppose this editorial is quite biased, as it completely overlooks the aspect of the bill designed to keep out Communists.[25]

The Ramsarans are coming to tea tomorrow. I have refrigerator cookies ready to bake and will probably make some orange bread tomorrow. Today has been a busy, busy day—I find I have as much laundry to iron here after two days as I did at home for a week, except sheets and linens of course. I ironed this afternoon after doing diapers and mixed up cookie dough almost at the same time, if you know what I mean!

I hope Tacoma doesn't seem too lonely now!

Much love from all of us—

Marian

January 9:

After lunch Howard drove over to pick up the Ramsarans, thinking the long walk might not be too good for Mrs. McLaren. She does look awfully thin and even more frail than before. The orange bread was good, and I enjoyed using my new tray for tea.

Richard Allsopp stopped by to invite us to have tea with them on Sunday.

January 10:

We are intrigued by the obituaries that are read over the radio several times a day. Appropriate organ music is played and an announcer says: "We have been asked to announce the death of Mrs. Iris Mac Campbell, known as Moth Mac, which took place at the late residence at noon today. Services will be held at the B.G. Funeral Parlour tomorrow morning at 10 o'clock, and relatives and friends are asked to accept this intimation." Oh yes—I left out the list of relatives. They announce the person's name, "better know as Aunt Hattie, mother of John, police sergeant; Arthur of the post office; Mary of the United States; and aunt of George, bookkeeper of Bookers Drug Stores." As often as not, when the surnames of the offspring are given, they differ from that of the parents.

Even more alarming are the announcements that are given over the radio for the benefit of those living in the bush, where no telephones are available. They follow this pattern: "We have a message for Mr. W. X. Fuller, Rupununi settlement. Calling Mr. W. X. Fuller, Rupununi settlement. Here is your message: 'Your mother is dead, funeral tomorrow.' We repeat that message. 'Your mother is dead, funeral tomorrow.' The message is signed, 'your sister.' This message is signed, 'your sister.' Will anyone living in the Rupununi settlement and in a position to do so, kindly give this message to Mr. W. X. Fuller."

Of course, both grisly announcements are necessary here. Burial must take place the day of a death or on the following day, due to the speed of decomposition here, and that doesn't give enough time for newspaper obituaries. The second type, the radio message, is used frequently for other urgent news: "Arriving Tuesday at 4:15, please meet," or "Missed boat due to flooded creek," or "Party of five arriving from U.S. next week." We do feel sorry for those receiving bad news in such a manner—think of the shock it must be.

January 11, 1953

Dear folks,

My vacation ends Wednesday, at which time I return to an altered schedule and a new principal. I complained about the comparatively heavy program I carried last term—a succession of 40-minute periods, no labs, etc.—and he made some rectification. I now have eight free periods a week (four last term) and three 80-minute labs (I asked for five).

This year's schedule includes for the Guianese many important events. At the end of this month the Indian cricket team (from India) arrives to challenge our Indian contingent. Cricket means everything here (as in England, I suppose)—business stops, radios blare, schools close, streets are deserted—far "worse" than the World Series.

In April B.G.'s first general elections will be held in which suffrage will be universal (illiterates and all)[26] and whose outcome will be a bicameral legislature with extended powers. All of this is according to an approved constitution and will result in less power for the present governor.

The constitutional government is a plan set forth by the Caribbean Commission (U.S., U.K., Netherlands, and France supervisory body on Caribbean Affairs), which supposedly will help the economic stalemate existing here at the moment. The local wealth is largely based on agrarian produce and is currently augmented by bauxite exports (market is falling, however), but agriculture, while vital, is not the key to national wealth today. B.G. is full of industrial potential, but nothing more. There are 200 waterfalls to choose from for a cheap power source. Then aluminum may be produced here (instead of shipping the ore, nearly 65 percent of which is waste). Roads are needed, both coastal and interior. The interior affords cattle-raising areas and endless tracts of forest, to say nothing of exotic scenery, a tourist magnet. Should these or even part of these and other potentials be realized, a host of secondary industries will follow. Such is the prospectus. Of course the one thing needed is capital, and since there is none here, it will have to come from outside. Foreign capital investment, outside of the Canadian-backed Demerara Bauxite Co., is scarce here because of U.K. taxation. U.S. industrial observers and analyzers are coming and going all the time, but nothing comes of their efforts. (Despite the unfavorable impression left here in the wake of the military at Atkinson Field,[27] the man-on-the-street feeling is that this place would do much better under U.S. supervision.) Stable, self-maintained government is being offered as an attraction—in time, of course, U.K. controls will be relaxed.

B.G. turned down the earlier proposal to join the Caribbean Dominion, which is due for action in London next month. At present the dominion will embrace all of the British Caribbean Islands, British Honduras (south of Mexico) having turned down the offer as well. B.G.'s action was statutorily based on the feeling of there being a "continental destiny" here—yet no one talks of encouraging economic ties with neighbors Venezuela and Brazil. (The real answer lay in the fact that under the proposed dominion, B.G. would serve as host to the excess insular population; very excessive in some cases: nearly 200,000 on 166 square miles in Barbados.)

These are the things in the minds of the hopeful, and one feels that any coronation celebration will simply be by and for the Europeans—for the local people have little mental allegiance to any overseas monarch.

Love to all,
Howard

January 11:

We did enjoy our afternoon and evening with the Allsopps today. In the first place, they are about our ages and have similar interests. We were both intrigued with the stacks of records and piles of books that are crowded into their living room.

We stayed until nearly 7, and only left then because Mabel was here and anxious to get home. The Allsopps live in a tiny house in a district called Subryanville, a little village outside of Georgetown proper, where there is no city water system, and they have a man come each day to pump water. There are many open canals and waterways, and the mosquitoes were awful.

Monday, January 12, 1953

Dear Family,

My goodness, what a lot of mail we got today! Three letters from Mother, one of which was written December 20! and one each from Bee, four friends, Howard's mother, and a stamp man with whom H. is doing business. And *Time*.

At this minute, Elizabeth is lying on her back on the living room floor, staring into space, and muttering things like ga-ga and ah-da and yahhh. Before I started this, I was lying down beside her, and she seemed quite amused by that! I have quit using strained food for her (only beets, carrots, spinach, and beans were available) and am now mashing everything with a fork. She seems to love just about everything except some fresh spinach, chopped, which I tried yesterday and which caused her to gag. She is still crawling like mad around the flat, and heads regularly for the stairs when it occurs to her. She spends long periods in the playpen.

Howard is still at school working on our radio/phonograph cabinet. It has taken him longer than he thought it would because everything possible has gone wrong: the wood sticks in the saw, much sanding needed, etc. Of course, I will do the final sanding and staining once he brings it home. I just love to do it—I'm so proud of our efforts with the bookcase, and now that it has been polished it looks really good.

I think I mentioned once that we were considering buying a sewing machine. Howard priced them a few days ago and got a shock. It seems that treadle machines are still being made for places like this where electricity is so damned high. (They may still be made at home, but I've never seen any new ones.) And these new treadle machines, used, cost from $90 to $200! Brand-new they are about $300. We will keep our eyes open for an old one, but we see no point in spending that much money. Aren't the treadle ones really cheap in the States?

We had eggplant Saturday night, and I just love it. Eggplant is called melongene here and is long rather than round, but otherwise just the same. Thomas has also brought us okra, here called ochroes, and we had it once with tomatoes and corn and liked it. Last week I cooked it just with corn, and it turned dark and was so terribly glutinous that we couldn't eat it. Saturday I learned from Margaret that the darned stuff has to be put into boiling water practically the second it is cut, in order to avoid the slime. I told Thomas we didn't want any more, for a while at least. I put some in chicken broth a few weeks ago, with tomatoes and corn, and that was tasty, I must say.

Yesterday afternoon we had tea with Richard and Joy Allsopp. He is a French master at Q.C. and brother of the Allsopp who took H. up to Mahaica Creek. Richard is in his twenties, and they've been married about as long as we have, which is pleasant—company our ages seems to be scarce! We are quite sure that many here wouldn't approve of our having gone to their home or of our intention to have them here soon, for they are both Guianese of African descent. Joy is very pretty, with dark skin and long wavy black hair indicating some East Indian or perhaps white blood. Richard is definitely African, very good-looking. He is a mimic, a punster, and to some extent a ham. He mimicked Mr. Beckles and Mr. Sanger-Davies, both funny and easily recognizable. Richie is of a rather dramatic bent and gets a huge kick out of everything. He is also very intelligent—was educated in England with the help of a British Council scholarship and has an English accent. Joy hasn't been out of the colony and isn't looking forward with much enthusiasm to their coming leave in England. Like others who have lived here a long time, she even feels cold here! I think she works downtown somewhere—H. says he thinks he has seen her. The brother, Herbert (I was glad to find out he has a nickname—"Bertie"), and another pretty, young Guianese girl were also there. Every time I looked at Howard I thought, My—how pale he is! He said he thought the same of me. We had an awfully nice time and enjoyed them very much.

Richard says that there is generally friction when a man from South Africa comes to the West Indies. We were speaking in connection with Sanger-Davies, who has already embarrassed Howard by referring to white–black difference in the presence of some Negro staff members; he said the "set" of the British in Africa is that the natives are just plain lower than low, and that any white is better than the best black. Here it just isn't that way. Richard told an amusing story of an Englishman who came here from South Africa a few years ago, with orders to bring the Transport and Harbor Department back up to par. Trains were running way off schedule, and things in the department were in a mess. This man arrived, and almost before he said how-de-do he was reading the riot act to all the members of his staff. He issued orders right and left and made some strides toward efficiency, but the T. & H. Department couldn't take it. Everyone went on strike: the colony was without railroad transportation, bus service, or freight service, and the nurses threatened to strike in sympathy. So the man was asked to retire, not because he wasn't doing his job, but because he was antagonizing everyone so terribly![28]

Howard just staggered home with the cabinet. It needs some plastic wood here and there, but I will start to sand it anyway. Poor Howard doesn't feel too well. He had a wretched cold last week and it hasn't left him yet.

My typing is getting worse and worse so I'd better quit.

Much love to each and every one,

Marian

January 14:

School started today, and Howard says Mr. Sanger-Davies has really taken charge. He announced that *Twelfth Night* will be given, and Howard said we'd help with costumes. The masters don't know just when they will have time to produce a play, what with a track meet, swimming meet, Indian cricket matches, and so on during the term, but Mr. Sanger-Davies seems to think it will be a snap.

A Chinese fellow came to the door yesterday, saying he was an American, was in desperate need of money, and had seen Howard's picture in the paper. He came back today and repaid $2 of a $3 loan that Howard gave him. Mrs. Patoir sent up one of her little girls to tell us not to give anything to the man, that he is known around town as a thief! Mercy. The fact that he brought back part of Howard's money must prove something, though.

January 15:

I rushed like fury to get the diapers done and to feed Elizabeth, and Howard delivered us at the Ramsarans' door on his way back to school. It is a relief to have someplace to go—I find myself feeling quite stifled here with so few contacts.

January 16:

Poor Thomas arrived this morning, with a basket full of slightly wilted vegetables, in a mood of great indignation. He was walking up the street from his little garden near the railway station, when a policeman stopped him to ask where he got the vegetables. He told him that some he had bought and the others he had grown. The policeman didn't believe him and thought Thomas had stolen them. He wanted to take him to the police station, but Thomas said he couldn't do that because he had no proof. The officer grabbed hold of Thomas, and I guess there would have been a scuffle, but a corporal came up to them and asked what was going on. Thomas explained, and the corporal said to forget about it. Thomas was really mad and said, "Madam, I don't know what this country is coming to, grabbing a man on the street like that."[29] He has worked in this neighborhood for ten years and is now working for the attorney of a large hardware store here.

January 17:

In a British magazine, I read yesterday that Mamie Eisenhower is from "what British people call a lower middle-class family." Today in *Time* I read that she is from a "well-to-do family in Denver." The *Time* article said that her father was a meat packer—possibly the British identify such a trade with the lower middle class.

January 18:

After I gave Elizabeth her lunch I thought she was awfully warm, took her temperature, and found it to be 104.5. Howard went upstairs [to borrow the neighbors' phone] to call a doctor, but he couldn't get hold of Dr. Kerry. He called a Dr. Bissessar instead, recommended by the woman whose phone he was using, as a children's specialist. He came about 3:30, couldn't find anything wrong with Elizabeth, but said she might have had a chill. He left a prescription for her, also one for Howard who is suffering again with diarrhea. I liked his manner with Elizabeth: he sat down and began talking to her and seemed to be in no hurry at all. He let her play with his little light and stethoscope, partly to please her and partly, I think, to watch her pick them up.

January 19:

It rained, and rained, and rained today.

Dr. Bissessar dropped by while I was feeding Elizabeth, just to check on her. Obviously she was fine, but he stayed for several minutes while Howard asked him some questions about health and sanitary conditions here. He said we needn't worry at all about filaria (elephantiasis), that there is a class of people who get it, but that they generally go around barefooted in muddy yards. Also, he said our canned milk is fine—even though the consul's letter had said it wasn't up to the U.S. standard.

January 20, 1953

Dear folks,

The new term has begun—wham, bang, zowie! How can two men be so completely different? From the monastic air of last term, Q.C. has now adopted the earmarks of a beehive, minus drones. The "king" bee has, among other things, injected a bit of militarism and activity in the affairs of state.

I think I told you about the mixed reaction concerning his coming. Well, now that he's here and operating, Mr. Sanger-Davies has already proved himself a man of ambition and determination, has gone a bit overboard in fact. Among the items on our prospectus for this term (ends April 1) are: initiation of Philatelic Society (by yours truly), full-length production of Shakespeare's *Twelfth Night*, participation in all-city athletic events (annual Georgetown affair but previously minus Queen's participation), raising of standards (much needed) in the literary and debating society, all this to be followed by the usual end-of-term exams.[30] An ambitious program, considering the general run of academic doings is quite a bit more rigorous than at most U.S. high schools. If it's successfully completed, I'm afraid my hat will be off to this system, despite the accusation that Queen's is more "British" than most British secondary schools. No particular love for things British implied, just for the system irrespective of its source.

There are some things about Mr. S-D that do bother us, however. Such possible affectations are wearing the cap and gown throughout the school day (our biggest reason for abstaining from that practice is the factor of stewing in one's juice, to say nothing of its being passé, even in B.G.), obvious second-ranking of blacks and coloreds to whites (seems strange considering his missionary background but not so strange considering his last post was in Africa, where it appears the blacks are considered scum and the whites are pedestalized), and a generally pompous attitude toward the boys. Small points really, or rather, small prices to pay, considering the future of the school under Mr. Beckles's all-too-kind hand. Beckles is now, as before, assistant principal and seems more at home as such.

As I write, I'm watching one of our little friends, a hunting spider, on the typewriter. They're quite unlike the spiders we know, spin no webs but stalk their prey. They walk very jerkily and when confronted with an obstacle, they jump! Their legs are short, stout, and hairy. Interesting things to watch, particularly when their eight eyes simultaneously reflect light in a sort of iridescent glow.

It rained hard nearly all day—something we've experienced very little of. The city gets pretty sodden, what with our being below high tide level. The water just accumulates until the tide is low enough for the ditch locks (called kokers) to be opened. When the rain is infrequent, sometimes we forget how we are very much at the mercy of the water in Georgetown. The Dutch carefully laid out a system of irrigation and drainage ditches, the two systems quite separate. The irrigation ditches lead from the interior and are about four feet higher than those that drain the land. The inflow of water via the irrigation channels is carefully regulated, and the outflow via the drainage canals, though active only a few hours a day, is apparently sufficient to keep us from being flooded. It's no less amazing, however.

Sorry about the return of the loose-leaf binders you tried to send, but we're not too surprised. People here regard the U.S. Customs as the worst (toughest) anywhere—they call it "security fever."

On Saturday, Herbert Allsopp and I are going to drive out to Atkinson Field to settle the possibility of a place for me to use as a base of operations for my fieldwork. As I've written before, Allsopp suggested Louis Chung, the animal exporter, as a prospect, and that seemed O.K. except that nothing came of Louis's promise to let me know what his boss in the U.S. thought of the idea. Then I took Mr. Beckles's suggestion and went to the Colonial Secretariat and attempted to use official channels, but it soon became apparent that U.S. government red tape is child's play as compared with the British Colonial version. The routine I got (after making three visits) was the I'd have to go to the base, select a building, get the base supervisor's approval of my choice, make a formal written application to the Atkinson Field Board of Control, and then await their decision as regards approval and rental. All this for such a little thing seemed absurdly complicated, so I asked Allsopp (a Fisheries officer, so well acquainted with government idiosyncrasies) for some simple, quick alternative. It sounds as if the B.G. government has a uniform method of handling such matters, whether peanuts or millions are concerned. I hope our Saturday venture will clear the matter up once and for all.

Love to you all,
Howard

January 20:
More rain. It has been windy and really nasty today. I think I am coming down with flu or something—I've been really cold today and I ache. Elizabeth seems to be fine.

January 21:
I haven't done a thing today except work on a curtain. Feel better but my throat is sore. It is still rainy!

Thursday, January 22, 1953

Dearest Dearies—

Oh dear, I do feel maligned today—everybody is scolding me for not writing. Do you kiddies realize that we are flooded with answers to Christmas cards, all of which have to be answered in some detail since many are from people we haven't written at all. To make it easier for myself, I have written out a semi-form letter, which I use for all the details about Georgetown and our way of life. But still, typing is typing, and I don't have much time for it—that sounds ridiculous, I know, because I have hours and hours with nothing of importance to do—but today, for instance, I must have spent a good hour running up and down the stairs hanging, unhanging, and rehanging clothes according to the whim of the weather. I was optimistic today—we had about ten minutes of sunshine in which I hung the diapers outside. Ten minutes later, they came in!

Now that I have started out as No Letter Should Be Written, with an apologia, I shall go on to say that I hold long, silent conversations with you all over the dishpan, the broom, the ironing, etc. Just yesterday I was thinking about all the lovely hamburgers Bee and I consumed at the Winthrop last year—and the potato chips. I can just see a potato chip here, after about five minutes' exposure. Ah well. And do you know, Mother, I actually miss our long, long, long telephone conversations, even though my feet used to go to sleep as I sat on the floor smothered in that curtain? Such fun!

We have just finished dinner and are now drinking the dregs of the coffee. Our first issue of *Life* arrived today, and I hope you realize that I chose a letter to you all over reading it! But then, typing in bed isn't quite up to reading in bed, is it. Oh—I *am* in a silly mood tonight. We had poached eggs on spinach à la chafing dish for dinner, with corn pones baked on the griddle. Since eating out is impossible here and there aren't even any drive-ins for take-home orders, I find cooking at the table a pleasant change. For the past few weeks I've been using either the griddle or the chafing dish on Thursday nights—the week seems a bit monotonous by then and the change is fun. We also had baked custard.

Winter is here. It is so dark at 6 or 6:15 when I get up that I have to have a light on to comb my hair. We eat breakfast with a light on. And is it wet! Can you imagine rain, heavy, noisy rain, coming at intervals varying between a few minutes and a few hours, for several days? We had a man come to fix the roof a few days ago, and I'll swear the leaks are worse now than ever before. He must have jarred loose some of the chinks. My cake pans are all getting rusty from being used to catch rain in the living room. I washed my blue shantung dress today, trying to rid it of that awful moldy smell. The dry cleaners couldn't faze it, and the mold came right back. The washing seems to have helped, but when I ironed it, it got all shiny the way rayon unfortunately does.

I had two crises today. One concerned ants. Winifred left her basket on one of the kitchen counters while she was scrubbing. She moved it; I glanced at the counter and saw that it was covered with ants where the basket had been placed—there must have been hundreds! I grabbed the flit gun and blasted them and then washed them up. She had some raw meat in the basket, and I find the damned things go for meat, raw or cooked, before anything else. Later on I found some in my tin of bread crumbs. A few days ago they were in my powdered sugar, cornmeal, rice, cereal, etc., which are all kept in our "meat safe." Have I told you about the meat safe? It is just a little cabinet with screened doors and panels, and I suppose they call it a meat safe because in England you would be able to keep meat inside safely. But here, aside from spoiling, meat would be enjoyed by our little friends in no time at all in such a cabinet!

My second crisis occurred when I took my turquoise dress with the pleated skirt out of the closet in Elizabeth's room, where I keep all my clothes, and found strange spots that look like a high water mark on it. I took out my yellow two-piece dress, and it was really soaked through! A leak in the – – – wall! The poor yellow dress is all moldy and a mess. I shall try to have it cleaned—both of them, for that matter. I was upset and mad for a while but consoled myself with the thought that the blue one cost little even when new, has seen many good days and is a bit faded, also is really too warm to wear here. I shall be crushed if the yellow one is beyond help, since it has years of wear left in it—didn't we get that in 1947? And some here have the gall to say, "Mold—why I've *never* had any trouble with mold here, unless on woolen things which I don't wear here." Grrr.

Bee, we were delighted to receive a card from the *Saturday Review* people yesterday, telling us that our subscription is renewed. The card was mailed more than a month ago—another slow boat, I guess. Howard says the *Saturday Review* is a great comfort to him when he gets mad at himself for not being able to find words he wants. He even reads it first thing in the morning, while he's still in bed, when I can't even get my eyes open.

Have I written that Margaret is going to have another baby? We're going there for dinner tomorrow night.

Tuesday I thought I was getting a cold—had to wear a sweater, shivered all day, and ached like a 90-year-old. Yesterday I did little, and today I feel fine. Howard, too, thought he was getting another cold and even had some swollen glands and a sore throat, but today he feels fine, too. Such a healthful climate!

Mr. Sanger-Davies wears his cap and gown all day and is trying to get all the masters to at least wear them for the Wednesday assemblies. H. refuses. S-D has said that *Twelfth Night* will be given this term, along with a militia band concert that includes the Q.C. choir, city-wide sports day, Q.C. track events, and the Indian cricket tour. All told, this accounts for fifteen half-holidays, and the term ends the first of April. Exams fall during the last week, but the masters think no one will be in shape for them by then! It sounds like a mad rush, just the opposite from Mr. B.'s slow-moving ways. Howard is involved with the Philatelic Society, too, which he enjoys tremendously, of course. He has twelve boys lined up and their first meeting will be next Friday.

Father, H. says the high limit on the B.G. stamps is $3, no $5's.

H. just informed me that we have had five inches of rain in the past two days. Beat that!

My goodness, it is after 9 p.m. and my dinner dishes are waiting. I miss you all dreadfully—why don't you buy a raft and float on down! Elizabeth sends a great big hug—she almost puts her arms around my neck now—she is so precious! And we all send our love—

Marian

Oh boy, parents—am I learning thought control! I think I will really have character when we leave Georgetown—and I bless you both for endowing me with a sense of humor! It certainly helps.

I feel awful about not writing oftener—H. and I almost believe that this place fosters timelessness, for we're scarcely aware of the weeks going by.

January 22:
This weather is ghastly. It has rained all day long. The mail didn't come until 5, when the rain let up some, and our bread delivery was at 7:30 instead of the usual 4:30. Here, everyone just waits until the rain lets up to go about his business—the streets are bare while it is raining, but the minute it stops, out come the bicycles.

This afternoon I discovered a leak in my closet. I don't know how long water has been coming in, but two of my dresses were wet and moldy. Howard was so mad when I told him about it that he went right over to Miss Osborn's, interrupting a class, and told her that this place isn't worth $100 a month and that she'd better get the leaks fixed once and for all. He walked out, leaving her sputtering behind.

Each night when Radio Demerara goes off the air, "God Save the Queen" is played. Howard and I sing "My Country, 'Tis of Thee" to the music—we block the urge when in public, but at home we enjoy it as the American hymn.

January 23:
Miss Osborn came by and took in the closet leak with unusual silence.

The Ramsarans have wanted us to meet Lloyd and Doreen Luckhoo for some time, so tonight they had all of us to dinner. The Luckhoo family here is evidently an old one, and influential. Lloyd has two brothers (all three are lawyers) and a sister who is a solicitor. One of the brothers is more or less in politics here.[31] Lloyd, besides having a good law practice, is co-owner with one of the brothers of the Carib nightclub, and he and Doreen have two little boys. Margaret tells me their house is enormous and that they own four cars and several horses: Lloyd is a director of the Georgetown Turf Club and has been invited to represent the club at this year's Kentucky Derby. They are both charming, and Doreen is pretty, sweet, and so natural. She and John grew up together in Trinidad.

January 24:
Howard went out to Atkinson Field today with Herbert Allsopp to talk to a man about quarters. They found a building that will do beautifully, and Howard will use a room in it [as a base for his plant collecting]. It has two toilets and running water!

They took a complete tour of the airbase and spent some time talking to an American who has been running the hydroponic gardens there. Howard said he got a kick out of hearing American slang and swearing! The hydroponic gardens were built by the Army to provide vegetables familiar to the GI's stationed there during the war. It must have cost a great deal, but evidently it wasn't done on a permanent basis, and some of the beds need overhauling now. This man has been running it for the Demerara Bauxite Company, but just a fraction of the available gardens is being used. The bauxite workers would rather eat plantains and eddoes and cassava than beets, carrots, and tomatoes, and it just doesn't pay to grow the temperate climate vegetables for them.

Howard brought a huge tortoise home—it is at least a foot long and about seven inches high. Such a funny-looking thing—the shell is so very heavy, and its head is covered with white spots while its legs have orange spots on the leathery skin. I think he intends to take it to school.

January 25:
Testudo, the tortoise, spent a quiet day behind the curtains in a corner of the living room. Howard says they don't need much to eat, and that we should give him a little time to get adjusted to his new surroundings. His name is that of a species of tortoise.

Howard gave a book review over Radio Demerara this evening, and it went quite well. His voice sounded very natural, just a bit deeper than it does ordinarily. There was one pause between pages; he said later that the announcer had mixed the pages up when she read through the review beforehand. The radio station is housed in an old dwelling, not at all suitable for the purpose. The studio had large French doors opening onto the street, battered carpets on the floor but no wall-hanging to absorb sounds. He said the floor was littered with cigarette butts, and the announcer, Olga Lopes-Seale, was attired in slacks.

John, Margaret, Mrs. McLaren, and Susan came by here to listen, saying their radio gave out yesterday.

Monday, January 26, 1953

Dearest Mother—

We have just finished lunch, Howard has gone back to school, and Elizabeth is in bed for a nap. Thank the Lord, we have had sun the last three days—today is beautifully clear, but there isn't too much breeze.

I received two letters from you this morning and was glad you enclosed the *Trib* with the inauguration story. Starting in February, we will only have one mail in and out of Georgetown a week—this was announced in the paper yesterday by Pan American Airways. Too few people coming here, the article said!

I have been thinking about what you wrote—that you miss young people around. Isn't it too bad that you don't know someone like Miss Forbes at CPS [the College of Puget Sound]—someone who would know of a few students who would enjoy a few hours in a home. If Mrs. Drushel is still dean, she wouldn't do much good—Howard and I were talking just last night about the change in attitude we have had concerning "foreigners." Now that we belong to such a category and know how it feels, we can appreciate how lonely some of the foreign students must be in a strange country, and how grateful they must be (as we are here) for friendship and hospitality. When we get back to the States, we hope that if we do live near a college or university, we can make a point of inviting such students to our home as much as possible. Did you read the article in *Time* about the woman in some little Midwestern town [who has been hosting] Nigerian students? It was a good one! You and Daddy might not want to do it, but I know you would get a kick out of it, and I don't know of any two people who could better entertain college students—even if they didn't speak much English.

You wrote a week or so ago about what a good baby Elizabeth is. She is really the easiest child to be bringing up—I suppose there are times when I am as anxious as only a mother-with-the-first can be, but most of the time things go along so very easily and smoothly. Of course, I believe firmly that her wonderful good nature, appetite, disposition, etc. are as much part of her "pre-destined" being as are her little hands: I think she was created so happy and sunny and cute just so that her parents wouldn't have to worry about wrong diets, allergies, and crankiness. It is so easy to love her—of course, I can't think of any baby I wouldn't love, but Elizabeth is just completely lovable!

The cuts of meat that are available at Bookers are roasts, chops, steaks—occasionally there are others, but not often. Last week I got hungry for meat loaf, so I ground up a lovely bit of beef for it. Thank heavens I have the grinder—everyone here has one, of course. We have had Swiss steak, Swiss steak with tomatoes, with onions, with both—I do love it, but enough is enough. Tonight we're going to have spaghetti. Oh yes—last week I cut up two mutton steaks and made a stew. And for the past two Sunday mornings, I have made cinnamon rolls since I do love them and there is no bakery here that turns them out. I am gradually getting into pies, too. I take the easiest possible way, I admit—which is a crust using dried bread crumbs (with cinnamon, powdered sugar and melted butter—we think it's good) and a package of butterscotch pudding. Canned cherries are available, so one of these days I shall work up to a cherry pie. With a legitimate crust!

Friday night we had dinner with John and Margaret and another couple, Lloyd and Doreen Luckhoo, whom they have wanted us to meet. They are both intelligent, friendly, have no airs—we enjoyed them tremendously. Margaret's dinner was interesting, and if typical, I'm afraid I can see the truth in the "awful English cooking" business. We had roast beef, which was very nice; Yorkshire pudding that was entirely different from yours—not as light nor as crisp; roast potatoes; boiled potatoes; rice; cabbage; corn; a rather strange East Indian bread-like thing, starchy too. Mint sauce and gravy. For dessert, vanilla ice cream with canned pears and strawberries—a nice combination. But so much starch, and so few vitamins—we think it strange.

Well, I am going to write a note to Bee and then take a bath and change my clothes.

All our love to both you and Daddy—

Marian

Monday, January 26

Dear Bee—

Christmas just a month past—it seems impossible! After all our rain, we have at last had some sunny days. It is such a relief after the dark and dismal days—true, it is pleasantly cool, but so gloomy and wet.

Limelight is here—we do want to see it but I don't know just what can be worked out. Have you seen it?

Mrs. Sanger-Davies arrived yesterday, according to Mabel. I don't know what she's like, but her husband isn't particularly well loved here. For instance, he preaches efficiency, but H. says he overstays the class period by ten or fifteen minutes (forty-minute periods here) when he uses H.'s lab for a class.

I am sticky and itchy from prickly heat—shall take a shower and be a lady for a while!

All our love to you,

Marian

January 26:
Howard came home this morning after his gardening session, with his yachting boots sopping with mud. He is disgusted with the whole situation, as the "garden" is so sodden that the boys haven't even been able to plant anything. Mr. Sanger-Davies says that next year there will be no garden—the course will just be ignored when the schedule is made out.

January 26, 1953, 8 P.M.

Dear folks,

We feel as though we're back in the "school rut." Although Mr. S-D's presence is more or less taken for granted now, there still exists enough negative spirit among the faculty to constitute subversion, but I'm sure he doesn't know (or if he does, he doesn't care). It's interesting to study the faculty and to trace the sources of complaint. The five or six temporary appointees naturally have little to say, the old-timers near retirement are equally mum, but the in-betweeners are particularly vociferous.

The rain is pouring as per usual—sometime or other most every evening—and is so loud on our roof that we can't hear the radio. It seems so strange to have the windows all shut and still have a breeze blowing through the place.

I gave my first radio review yesterday afternoon—not very eventful except that one of the regular announcers in looking over my script got the pages out of order, a discovery I didn't make until I was on the air. I almost said, "Oh, hell!" The station is haphazardly arranged in an old, sagging residence, so rickety that people must walk on tiptoe to keep from causing the pick-up arm to jump grooves in the recordings. I wonder how many people heard me. The Ramsarans and Marian listened here in our living room, said it came over very well.

My Philatelic Society now embodies about 15 more or less handpicked members—our first meeting is this Friday night. Should be great fun. Most all of the kiddies collect stamps, but, of course, this group will involve only boys who are seriously interested.

Herbert Allsopp and I went to Atkinson Field Saturday to try to settle my securing a base of operations. We saw a very suitable office but red tape can't be avoided. I'll have to get clearance from the Atkinson Field Board of Control. The board meets on the 3rd of February. If my application is refused, I guess I'll have to pitch a tent and risk bushmasters and jaguars!

While out there we scouted around a bit. The field is so reflective of an American military installation: sterile barracks and offices, but such little things as electric and plumbing fixtures looked like old friends. Unfortunately, the buildings are fast deteriorating because of their being constructed of pine, which doesn't stand up to the high humidity here. Among the civilian concessions are a guesthouse and restaurant. The fellow who runs the hydroponic gardens was refreshingly American but unfortunately a military "2-2" boy—absorbed, disgustingly absorbed, in his doings and thoughts. Such a pity. His wife is from Japan; they met during the war. We also stopped at Louis Chung's fish place. Louis sheepishly said he hadn't looked into our proposition. He's really got a paying business— buys fish for 1.3 cents U.S. and sells them for 10 cents U.S. per. Not bad considering he shipped out 250,000 of the wigglers last year.

Love to all,

Howard

Tuesday, January 27, 1953

Dear Mother—

Good news: the records arrived today! We have played the David Rose–Gershwin record and love it—I don't think we ever thanked you and Daddy for sending it and Victor Young, but we are certainly glad to have them. We haven't played *April in Paris* yet, but the selection sounds excellent.

Elizabeth has just gone for a walk wearing the little pink Carter's dress. Those two are the only dresses we brought that she can still wear—and Ruth's pink one, too. The Carter's will last a long time—there's still a lot of room to grow in.

Getting back to the records, what happened to Beethoven's Ninth? We can live without it but we just wonder if you forgot it. I trust it is there somewhere.

We have a new pet. His (her, possibly) name is Testudo (a species name, says H.) and he is a tortoise about 14 inches long and 7 inches high. H. brought him home from the airbase Sunday and he spends most of the time hiding behind my curtains. He comes out quite often, though, and this noon he had his first meal—a tangerine. I wouldn't call him completely housebroken, but he's very neat. Several people here have them as pets, and John says he knows of quite a few in Trinidad, none as big as Testudo, however. We keep him segregated in the little tower enclosure where H.'s students do their lab work—also housed there are a few old stuffed birds and a rabbit skeleton!

We are drinking tea—no goodies, just tea. Thursday afternoon I shall spend with Margaret and Mrs. McLaren—I'll dash over after lunch with E. and have a good chat. I plan to bake some orange bread to take—Margaret liked it so much. Also some magazines—they love our *Saturday Reviews* and *New Yorkers*, and we have a large stack of some English ones I borrowed from them.

My spaghetti last night was delicious—I made a whole pot (Dutch oven) of it and H. and I ate way over half. A nice change. I've started using serving bowls at the table—it's really nicer than fixing plates in the kitchen all the time—and the bowls are all so pretty.

Much love,
Marian

January 27:

At long last, the records have arrived. We were worried a bit: the customs notification said we had "One Box, Burst" and we didn't know just what to expect. But the box was scarcely damaged at all, and the records are all in fine shape. No duty to pay, either.

Howard peeled part of a tangerine today, and we put it on the floor in front of Testudo, who just looked at it for several moments. Then he cautiously took hold of it and proceeded to eat it, skin and all. He grabbed it, shook until a piece broke off, swallowed, and grabbed again. His head jerks forward in a darting motion to get the fruit into his mouth. After he finished, he wandered around for about fifteen minutes and then went back to the shelter of the curtained corner.

January 29:

Howard went to a meeting of the Literary and Debating Society after dinner. I had quite a shock while I was washing dishes. I looked up, and through the jalousie I saw a man standing on the porch. He said, "Good evening," so I said, "Good evening," too. He stood there as if waiting for me to open the door, but as I had no intention of doing that I asked what I could do for him. He crouched down so that I could see his face through the louvers and said that he was going to a party, and there were some girls going to this party, and could he have the master's car to take the girls to the party! I was taken aback but said very truthfully that my husband was out for the evening. He thanked me and left, but the fragrance of his hair goo or brilliantine lingered for some time. What a crazy request, yet it is typical of a habit people here have of asking for anything, just to see if perhaps they might get it.

January 30:

Last night I had a most revolting experience. After Howard came home from his meeting I went to the kitchen to rinse out a coffee cup. As I turned on the light a rat jumped off the counter and ran around the side of the room all the way to the sink and slithered through the jalousie. Being the clear-headed, collected type, I screeched for Howard, who came in time to watch it disappear. It was just a small one—anything very large would have been unable to get through the jalousie and wire mesh covering the window over the sink. But the thought of a rat just gives me the shivers.

This afternoon, after washing my hair, I sat in the living room and played *Kiss Me, Kate*, our Fred Waring record of Rogers and Hammerstein songs, and the new *April in Paris* record. The ideal time of day to play records is between 1:30 and 4, when Radio Demerara is off the air.

January 31:

Howard cut a hole in a large wooden box so Testudo can now turn around in his little house. We did have a cardboard box for him, but once he got in he couldn't get out. He ate a banana today, but only after Howard placed him right smack in front of it. He's a timid creature. As a pet he certainly is no trouble.

Just now, on the *Ovaltine Talent Program*, we heard a steel band playing "Jesu, Joy of Man's Desiring." The effect of the steel band is not far from that of a xylophone and quite like that of a marimba. What next!

Sunday, February 1, 1953

Dear Family—

Four o'clock on a Sunday afternoon, and Testudo and I have been deserted by the rest of the family. Elizabeth and Mabel have just gone for a walk, and Howard left about an hour ago for an Indian wedding. There will undoubtedly be a good deal to tell after said wedding; at this point, all I know is that today's ceremony is merely a part, and the rest will take place next Saturday. However, John is going, too, on Saturday, and

Margaret asked me to have lunch with them. She said they went to an Indian Thanksgiving service and found it dull. The women sit on one side of the room, the men on the other. The entire service is in Hindi, which John understands, but of course he wasn't by their sides to whisper. Shoes are left at the door. The bride today is a niece of Mr. Hetram, one of the Queen's masters.

Elizabeth has, almost, six teeth. Number six has been giving her a bit of trouble lately but is almost through now. Friday I took off the yellow harness that we had been using in the Taylor Tot [stroller] to hold her in: Mabel reports that she sits up with no help now. Her little feet nearly touch the "floor" of the stroller. And her hair is growing. It has a slight tendency to wave a bit in back (common sense compels me to add it must be because of the heat when she lies on her back), but the front and top are absolutely straight. She is so sweet! Some of her bah-bah and gah-gah sounds are delivered so emphatically now that we expect sensible words daily—I do, that is—I'm sure that one of these days she'll look at me and say ma-ma instead of gah-gah!

Howard's first meeting with his stamp club was last Friday, and he was quite tickled with the response. Eight boys attended, which he said is a good number since everything is conducted on honor basis, and too many boys might lead to difficulty. There are three or four older boys who are interested in America, why H. is here, what his research involves, etc., and Howard told them he'd take them out to Atkinson Field when his shelter there is confirmed, and they can spend a weekend. One of the boys hasn't been outside of Georgetown in three years! They are also keenly interested in the stamps and want H. to give them a series of talks on water marks, perforations, secret marks, etc. I'm so pleased for Howard—to me (to him, too) such contacts outside of class are so very important to a teacher, especially in this situation where he can impart so much more than just biology.

Mr. Sanger-Davies has again mentioned to Howard how much he wants H. to stay for a third year. This may be another of his rash statements (like telling H. not to worry about getting a dozen new microscopes, on the first day of his arrival here. Ha) but, on the other hand, the college really will need him. It's too early to make plans, of course.

Howard's mother informs us that her sister is planning a voyage to South America with another couple, including a stopover at Georgetown. It is being planned for next fall, and we certainly hope it works out. My homesick twinges are on the wane, as well they should be by now. It is silly, but it helps tremendously to hear Margaret say that she would leave tomorrow if it were possible, and that she's felt dragged out since the first month they arrived—for I certainly don't feel that desperate at all. Neither Howard nor I have been affected with the lassitude that seems so general here. Some of the men at school have told Howard that he's doing too much—that he will ruin his health, etc., and he just laughs and says it is about half as much as he did at home. Which it is! My goodness—last year at this time he was holding down two jobs as well as school. I think so much of it is state of mind. Margaret told me once that she and John went to the theater about once a week in London—I know that she misses "something to do" as much as anything. And Howard and I are both pretty good at keeping busy. Right now I'm trying to find time to get to town to purchase terrycloth for bibs (the little ones are falling apart) and material for petticoats. All my slips are ripping along the back—I think it must be due in part to so much perspiration. I prefer the petticoats anyway. Also, I want to knit some dishcloths if I can find the cotton yarn here. The other night I straightened out my sewing basket, and the sight of the pretty trimmings I brought for E.'s dresses made me want to sew up a dress for her, too.

If you have a chance, look at the pictures of Trinidad and Tobago in the January issue of *National Geographic*. There are a great many similarities to B.G.: the people look much the same in their bright cottons, saris, and straw hats; anything is carried on the head in preference to in the arms (I don't think I told you that we once saw a woman with a basket on her head, and in the basket were two white ducks and a chicken); the pretty orange blossoms and seed pods we see everywhere—right outside our dining room window, too. Unhappily there is no blue surf or white beach here—it would be wonderful if there were.

I am going to mix up some pudding for Elizabeth's supper. The little monkey is still ignoring her milk—do you suppose it could be the tooth that is troubling her?

Again, love to you all,

Marian

H. wonders if you would please enclose a few used B.G. stamps in each letter. Just tear off the envelope corner. (How I drooled over the sewing machine ads! Heavens—we certainly won't invest in one here if they're that reasonable at home.)

February 1:

Howard returned late this evening from the first part of a Hindu wedding. Mr. Hetram's niece is the bride, so Hetram invited Howard and some of the other masters to attend. This ceremony, known as the telak, consisted of the pundit of the boy's family absolving the boy from the effects of evil spirits in his marriage and in his future. The ceremony took place at Cane Grove, an old plantation about four miles west of Mahaica and one mile south of the highway. There was feasting, of course, and Howard and Hetram and Ram, Hetram's brother, were urged to eat with knife, fork, and spoon from plates. They insisted, however, on eating as the others did, with fingers from leaf plates. The food consisted of curried rice, curried pumpkin, and coconut water. They gave Howard a package of food to bring home that included mustard greens, tomatoes (little tiny fellows, about the size of strawberries), poori or large, flat cakes made of cassava flour, and some sweets about the size of our little fingers made of a dough and fried in deep fat—I think! We don't know their name, but I thought they were very good.

February 2:

It is raining today. Howard got up at 6:30 to go to his gardening class but came back in a few minutes, quite disgusted. The garden plots are just a muddy mess, much too wet for planting.

I went to town this afternoon, to buy some material for new bibs for Elizabeth. After diligent looking, I succeeded in finding some rather pallid blue and white terrycloth, and more lively colored binding tape. I had fun purchasing some incidentals like pins, elastic, and table pads and became so burdened that I spent $1.50 on a pretty woven straw shopping bag from Italy.

After Howard picked me up we went to the Midget Book Store in search of decent valentines to send out. The ones I'd seen downtown were awful, and unfortunately those at the Midget were just the same. Tonight after dinner I made some out of red ribbon and dime store lace edging—we decided to send them out "from Elizabeth." So they will go into the mail tomorrow.

February 2, 1953

Dear folks,

I'm writing from our desk in the "study," having just finished a lunch of peanut butter and lettuce sandwiches, Klim, and a mango and banana, and am now watching Testudo finish off the banana peel and peck away at the stringy mango seed. He's turned out to be a pet of a sort—not demonstrative but rather dignified in his suit of armor, shy but not so completely elusive as at first. He has for a house an overturned milk-can carton with one end cut out just enough to admit his shell. He remains inside most all morning, comes out to eat at noon, wanders around awhile, then returns for the rest of the afternoon and night. Rather neat in his habits, too.

This past weekend was for me both dull and interesting. Contributing to the dull side were 120 exercise books to be corrected. I hate to take my own time in working on them but if I let them, there would be a mad eleventh-hour scramble to finish them before the respective classes next week. So most of Saturday and Sunday were thus consumed.

Later (5:00 p.m.): By prearrangement, Doodnauth Hetram, Latin master at Queen's, stopped by for me Sunday afternoon, and we went some 20 miles down the East Coast Road to his old stomping grounds to witness part of an East Indian wedding ceremony. Hetram and his relatives are all of the highest, or Brahman, caste and, like all good Brahmans, they adhere very closely to tradition. The wedding in Indian custom is a much more complicated thing than we have. The father of a girl of marriageable age seeks for her a husband, this done by him because he supposedly knows his daughter best and also knows men well enough to select an apt mate. The next step is for the young man to be presented to the girl and the rest of her family. Step three is the visitation of the prospective groom's home by the prospective bride's family (with gifts), minus the bride herself. At this time a pundit, or officiating priest, clears from the boy's future all possibility of encounter with evil spirits (Indian version of "They shall live happily ever after"). It was this ceremony that we witnessed. The fourth step, which we shall see next Sunday, is the wedding itself, to be performed at the bride's home, at Suddie, across the Demerara River. After the wedding, the couple spend one day together, after which they return to their respective homes for a fortnight. Then they are free to live together thereafter.

All this is Hindu custom, which is tenaciously perpetuated generation after generation. The great degree of illegitimacy of children we read about before coming here is in part explained by this fact: the British do not recognize a man and woman united by the above means as being officially married. The time at which two may be married is astrologically determined, and in result, many marriages occur simultaneously.

The interesting thing about this is that Hetram, while being a Brahman Hindu, is at the same time thoroughly westernized (has a B.A. honors degree from London University) and so is a very competent interpreter of these affairs.

The people involved are what may well be considered the "backbone of B.G." They are the hard workers, the down-to-earth folks whose dependency is on the soil alone. They all strive to own land, to till it, beget children, and then to increase their holdings as means permit. All of this is enriched with tradition and ceremony of a very Oriental flavor. The East Indians as a group are so much more distinctive because of the culture they brought with them. In contrast, the Negroes have none—they largely copy as best they can the British example.

Despite protests, I ate in true Indian style at this gathering—cross-legged and all. The food was entirely vegetable (the godliness of animals makes consumption of flesh prohibited) and highly seasoned with curry (which I really like!). One eats from a lotus leaf and takes the food to his mouth with a piece of poony (thinly rolled cassava dough), which is also eaten. The table beverage is coconut water (local ditch water is risky unless one has used it constantly and has thus developed an immunity to the hordes of pathogens) and for dessert, mangoes and bananas.

Today I had an opportunity to witness the extreme inefficiency of the local "gendarmes." I had been told of such but had not had firsthand experience. While I was passing a few minutes in the staff room at Queen's before the commencement of the afternoon session, Richard Allsopp, French master, rushed up to me and asked me to grab my coat and take him in my car back to the sea wall, where he had just come from in a downpour. Sensing emergency, I ran with him to the car, climbed in, got under way, and then asked questions. Hetram, it seemed, had hit a donkey and was awaiting the police. That was about all Allsopp could say—he was in a terrible state. Upon arriving at the scene, I saw Hetram's little Renault rather badly battered and the poor donkey standing on three legs, the fourth obviously broken in several places, and his hide was deeply lacerated. Hetram had a few little cuts but nothing else—it's a wonder, for the donkey's tail had completely shattered the windshield. But we waited, waited, waited—for 25 minutes, and finally the police cruised down the road in a jeep (they'd been phoned). Two cops came over, casually asked Hetram what had happened, and then asked the same of the boy who had been leading the unfortunate animal. The stories conflicted but that didn't matter. The cops tried Hetram's brakes, found them O.K., took his statement and the boy's in writing, and then left. Fortunately Hetram could navigate his car to a garage. There we called a vet to shoot the donkey, and there Hetram, Allsopp, and E. Archer (both passengers and witnesses) gave statements to an insurance man. What was most annoying was the blasé, lackadaisical "what the hell" attitude of the police—almost as if the handling of this matter was quite beneath their dignity. They seemed to resent getting involved. And to take 25 minutes to get to the scene of an accident that occurred in the city seems inexcusable.

Many thanks for attending to the razor and, of course, your suggestions will be followed. While living in this humidity we forget its effects on inanimate things. And the customs declaration you returned should save a lot of all-too-prevalent red tape. Local customs are pretty much of a snap providing you catch the boys in a good mood. (Our records came through duty-free.)

Love to all,
Howard

February 3:

Reflecting on the purchases I made yesterday, I discovered at least one article that can be bought here for much less than at home—a lowly spool of thread. I bought spools containing 50 yards for five cents at Woodworth's at home; here I can buy 400 yards for eleven cents, which would come to about six cents in American money.

Testudo loves mangoes, we are finding. I peel one or two for our lunch, and we give the seeds to Testudo. Naturally I leave as much fruit on the seed as I can, and he gnaws it off in no time at all.

Still too wet for gardening. Howard announced to the boys who did show up this morning that from next week on, the class will be held indoors as an experimental botany course. Some are pleased, and others who enjoyed leaning on their shovels are not too happy!

Wednesday, Feb. 4, 1953

Dearest Mother—

At times our household is so peaceful—this is one of them. It's 2 p.m. and Elizabeth is sleeping soundly. I just showered and feel quite respectable again. Mabel is washing lunch dishes, and Testudo is exploring. He, by the way, is rapidly losing his shyness—he lets us pick him up without ducking into his shell now.

It poured from 7 to 9 this morning. There were no first period classes, H. said, and many boys never did arrive. Our roof leaked furiously—every time it is fixed, we get a new leak. About my dresses—it just may be that none are total losses. My yellow came back from the cleaners minus mold but still a bit smelly. I shall wash it one of these days. I'm not worrying about the aqua with pleats—I shall have it dyed navy, perhaps, when we get home, if I think it's worth it. My brown faille suit is really a hell of a mess. It's worthless as it is, so I might just as well try washing it, I guess.

They have put lovely flowered curtains up in the Red Cross Home across the street, for the visit of the Princess Royal this month. If, after she leaves, the curtains are removed I shall be most put out.

Yesterday morning Mrs. Patoir asked me if I'd care to watch a Hoover washing machine demonstration—she is going to buy one. The man washed a playpen sheet (filthy!) for me, and it seemed to work well. We're mulling over the idea. The machine is tiny, about 30 inches high; it holds three pounds of clothes and has a hand wringer. Holds six gallons of water. It costs $169—$35 down and $11 a month. We pay Frances $9 plus 60 cents a week for soap and starch, so financially it would pay. It could also keep our colored towels from fading. It would mean more work for me, ironing shirts and sheets, but would make the washing of dresses and underwear much easier—and cleaner. Of course, then we'd be paying Mabel for little more than doing dishes and taking E. out—and I don't know if it's worth it. Maybe she could iron sheets and towels.

Monday I bought uninspired toweling (white loops on pale blue—the only terrycloth available! And all the lovely colors at home!) and cute candy-stripe bias tape (blue and white), also plain red, to make bibs. Also some cotton to knit dishcloths, but it is so thick I'm splitting it.

Each time I'm downtown I try to think of things you all would like to have—it's very difficult! There are nice embroidered tray cloths and napkins—they'd be lovely if we knew an invalid who ate from a tray all the time. Or to have on hand for flu victims. Everyone here uses them for serving tea—they're all from England, of course. Purely local stuff is uninspired. We're going to purchase a rather crude, hand-carved replica of the colony's seal—about 1 foot in diameter—but who else would want it! Local basketry isn't too artistic or sturdy. There's no native pottery or weaving—I keep thinking of the lovely things Bee brought back from Mexico. There's no comparison at all. How about an insect collection!

Friday evening we're supposed to go to the Beckleses' for a drink—to meet Mr. and Mrs. S-D. Of course, the B.'s want Mabel to help, so I shall have to see if Mrs. Patoir can sit with Elizabeth.

Back to gifts—Monday I saw lovely little two-inch pans, cute shapes and sizes, for cakes or Jell-O—they're English and unlike anything I've seen at home. I almost bought some for myself but said "next time I'm downtown—" They would make cute teacakes.

Elizabeth is such a little girl now. She is so bright and alert and knows pretty well what "no-no" means. If you were here we would sit for hours watching her and saying, "Oh, isn't she cute!" Because I do all by myself, and if you were here to encourage me I'd never get the floors swept! I waste no time worrying about her future—but I do think a lot about it in terms of how we can help her to do things for herself—and I miss talking such things over with you. But thought waves do come in handy, don't they.

I dislike many minor aspects of our life—mold and bugs, chiefly—but I'm nonetheless overawed with our good fortune in being here. It is fascinating to be outside of our own country for a while—so many of our set ideas are changing. And we three have fun together here as we would have anywhere—we're a very happy family!

Love and kisses to you and Daddy,

Marian

Thank you for the address labels and rubber bands!

February 4:

Had a bit of a shock this morning when I noticed Testudo under Elizabeth's crib! He really gets around now—seems to enjoy a walk around the flat in the morning, and then he retires to his little home after his lunch.

February 6:

Howard and I met Mrs. Sanger-Davies today to discuss the business of costumes for *Twelfth Night*. She is very plain, unpretentious, and quite pleasant. She has the enthusiasm of a missionary, especially regarding the costuming job—an enthusiasm I find it hard to share! Sometime this weekend I am to see the costumes that the college already has, and then on Tuesday we shall go to town to look for suitable materials.

Tonight we go to a cocktail party at the Beckleses'. Mabel, worried, asked me this afternoon what would become of Elizabeth! We have arranged to leave her with Mrs. McLaren and will pick up John and Margaret and drive them over. Mrs. Beckles told Howard to arrive at 6:30, but when I told Mabel that was the time we were planning to leave, she said, "But Madam, I'm not going until then—here, when someone says 6:30 they wants you to come at 7." Doesn't it seem silly—at the same time, it explains why we've found people still taking baths when we've arrived at different places "on time."

February 7:

I guess I should say we had a good time last night—if a bit strange at times. Howard spent much of the evening listening to Archie discourse on the roads of Nigeria, and from what I overheard he covered them mile by mile. I had a lovely time nibbling on the goodies; as for drinks, Mr. Beckles asked Howard what he wanted but just brought a tray around for me to select from. I chose a highball but didn't care for it. A little later he brought me a pallid cocktail.

Mrs. Sanger-Davies is a bit gauche. She asked Margaret how long one was supposed to remain at such a function, and Margaret, although taken aback by the question, replied about two hours. Promptly at 8:30, Mrs. S-D turned to Mr. Beckles and said, "Well, I suppose we'd better be moving on, hadn't we." Poor Mr. Beckles! They moved on, and we left about 9.

The final ceremonies of the Indian wedding took place tonight, and Howard should have been there. He and John drove back to the groom's house this morning, returning after more feasting at about 1:30. According to plans, Howard was then supposed to pick up Mr. Rodway and take him across the river to the bride's home and the festivities, which were to last all night. But Howard found that Mrs. Rodway was ill, and after taking the Rodways to a doctor, he had missed the only available ferry.

Thinking I was to be all alone for the day and evening, I had left Elizabeth with Mabel and gone to the Ramsarans' for lunch. We had a lovely afternoon, and I was most surprised to see Howard walk in the door after I'd been home half an hour.

February 8, 1953

Dear folks,

It's as human a trait as any to have a complaint about any situation. At the moment, we feel quite starved for a young American couple with interests more or less akin to our own—someone for Marian to discuss baby problems with and a fellow who would dig at the British with me. This place is not at all devoid of America; we see and hear it every day, but we do miss talking with Americans about American ideas and American gripes—old homespun stuff, you know. Now that Wesley Jorgensen has left (the U.S. consulate is closed), we're probably the only Americans in Georgetown, and that fact gives us a strange feeling. As I walk down Water Street, the loitering and passing blacks look, and you can almost read the expression on their faces—another Englishman! But then in a shop I speak up all hearty and hale and ask for this and that—at once the clerks know that I'm not British but in all probability Canadian. If I intend to do business there very often, I let them know through the idle chatter that occurs in all stores that I'm from the U.S., and then you see faces light up. The British are regarded by the average Guianese as an occupying force, not citizens of a mother country. But Americans are friends—"If only there were more of you here," I hear so often.

I suppose this is a state reached by all real Americans in foreign lands, this state of proud loneliness. We're liked most of all for our intelligent progressive spirit—if we want to see something done, we do it, and do it ourselves. I can imagine how refreshing that must be to some who are long accustomed to official inertia and acts accomplished for one faction by another under compulsion.

The paper today sheepishly explained the noticeable upsurge in the fly population—inability of the Sanitation Department to deal with the abnormally high volume of holiday refuse. They just piled it up in an uncovered place, applied a decomposition agent that was quickly neutralized by the rain—and the result: flies. Better than mosquitoes, but annoying nonetheless.

My plans to attend the Indian wedding did not come off per schedule. Hetram, John Ramsaran, and I went to the groom's parents' house again yesterday to partake of another ceremony; John, being bilingual, clearly understood the pundit and was a bit dismayed by his inclusion of English and Creole expressions—"broken Hindi," John termed it. It was our plan to return, dress, and then cross the Demerara by ferry to proceed to the bride's home for the actual ceremony, which took place last night. John couldn't go, and in his place I was taking Mr. Rodway. After dressing, I stopped for Rodway, and at first sight it was apparent the man was distressed. He said his wife was ill and that I'd better go on alone. His painful look made me ask the nature of her trouble, and he said she'd just had a "nervous seizure" but since they had no transportation, they couldn't get to a doctor and were trying to "sit it out." To this I said nonsense, helped him get his wife into the car, and went to Dr. Kerry, who said he'd see them home. By this time I'd missed my ferry but went to the stelling [dock] to see if I could take the next one—no good; in fact, the next three trips were booked full, and so I wouldn't be able to cross until 7:15. Since my chances of finding the place in the dark were all but nil, I decided the hell with it. It was going to be an all-night affair and that didn't particularly appeal to me anyhow.

When Mr. Sanger-Davies made it very clear that *Twelfth Night* is to be produced this term, we all cringed and hoped that with the 1,001 other extracurricular doings scheduled before his coming, he might see that Shakespeare would be not too welcome. But he has made it plain that we'll not only have *Twelfth Night* this term but *Trial by Jury* next term!

I'm a tired boy, so good night.

Love to all,

Howard

Sunday night, Feb. 8, 1953

My dears—

It is *late*—all of 9:45, and I don't promise to be coherent! This business of getting up at 6:30 every single morning isn't bad, but it doesn't lead to night-owlishness.

We have had a busy weekend. Friday night we attended a cocktail party at the Beckleses', to meet the Sanger-Davies. Howard was more or less stuck with Archie all evening. I didn't care for the drinks at all—had a highball, cheese-glass size, that didn't taste like much of anything, and then two cocktails that really didn't have any taste. The goodies were lovely: eggs stuffed with minced ham; tiny pastries filled with curry; onions and cheese on a toothpick; guava jelly and cheese tarts, too sweet to suit me with a drink, but good anyway! I ate and ate and ate. As far as I was concerned, the high point of the evening came when Mrs. Beckles put some records on the gramophone, one of which was Patty Paige's "I Went to Your Wedding." It is all the rage here and evidently one of Mrs. B.'s pets, for she said, "I think this is so sweet." Margaret didn't hear the remark, but when she heard the music we looked at each other and just about exploded, thinking of Mrs. B.'s frightful taste in music (her remark that the "Mom and Dad Waltz" was a pretty tune is now a classic).

The party broke up about 8:30, and we went to the Ramsarans' and had coffee. Stayed until about 11. Dear Elizabeth was asleep at 6:30 when we took her to the Ramsarans' but went back to sleep shortly after we tucked her into Susan's crib. And then we had to wake her up again to bring her home, but she went back to sleep immediately here, too. Such a good child!

We are still swimming in rain now and then, but that's not all. This damned *Twelfth Night*! Mrs. S-D, Howard, and I had a little conference about costumes Friday afternoon. We don't have time to send to England for patterns, so, she says, we can just whip up the little Elizabethan numbers freehand. Ha. She may, I say, but I have to follow directions like mad for one of Elizabeth's dresses—let alone doublets.

The S-Ds are quite a pair. They have the true missionary zeal—sort of a "damn the details and full speed ahead" attitude. She and I are going to town to look at materials on Tuesday. She isn't much to look at. Her hairdo is quite laissez-faire—she just pulls it back in a mousy knot and has a quaint ribbon around her head and under the knot. She seems pleasant, aside from the *Twelfth Night* business. They have a teenage son at school in England.

We wrote Wesley Jorgensen, who is now in Port of Spain, asking about duties and such when we leave. We can each take out $500 U.S. in merchandise—curios, household goods, etc. This could apply to the car. We can take back household effects duty free, if they have been in use over a year—this excludes "automobiles, horses, carriages, sleighs, boats and similar articles, and provisions and other consumable supplies—" so we plan to leave our sleigh here!

Do you remember my writing that someone here said that ladies just don't work in offices or other jobs when pregnant? Margaret and her mother both scoffed loudly at that and said that many people here who speak of English ways with authority really don't know what they are talking about. Of course everyone has his own opinion. I am still amused by Archie's remark that no true Londoner would want to be in London for the coronation in June—I think he even said that a genuine Londoner would leave town for the event. Margaret and her mother would give anything they own to be there for the coronation. Margaret especially is steeped in the history and traditions of the royalty and loves it all deeply.

Well, I am sleepy. Elizabeth's sixth tooth, the one that was troubling her, is through now, so we're all happy. I'm going to try giving her Klim in her cup instead of the canned milk. Associations, you know.

Much, much, much love from all of us,

Marian

February 9:

Had my first session with the dentist today. He is Dr. John Ho-A-Shoo, recommended by the Larthes. We noticed that he graduated from Northwestern in 1947. I hope his work is good. His office is a far cry from the white sterility we're used to at home, but it seemed clean. Archie and Dorothy said he's expensive—$2.50 for a small filling, $3.50 for a large one! I had four cavities and go back Friday. Howard thinks he will have his wisdom teeth out during the next holidays—they're in pretty sad shape.

February 10:

Dutifully, I went over to see Mrs. S-D about materials for costumes this afternoon. I rang several times and waited and waited, but got no answer. Came home, put some records on the phonograph, and proceeded to cut out a little sacque for Elizabeth. She is growing so darned fast that her little shirts no longer fit.

Wednesday, Feb. 11, 1953

Dear Mother—

First, while I'm thinking of it, will you write down your recipe for sugar cookies and send it? They're so good. We love the English biscuits, but they are expensive and, you know me, I think cookie baking is one of the chief joys in life!

It is 10:15 and I am heating water for E.'s bath. She just had her orange juice and is in the playpen.

Going back to cookies—I've found your refrigerator cookies to be the only ones I've made that stay crisp. And I can't get cake icing to firm up. Grrr. We expect a short dry season in the next few weeks—the next rainy season starts in April.

Bath time—more later.

Lunch is over; Elizabeth is rocking her crib along the floor and probably won't go back to sleep. I put her to bed from 12 to 2 every day now, and she always sleeps some of that time.

Tomorrow I shall take E. to Margaret's—I'm trying to think of something to bake and take. I hate to go so often, empty-handed! And Sunday we will have the Allsopps to tea. I have discovered a good cake recipe using egg whites—Mrs. Rombauer's angel cupcakes, only baked in a square pan. It's the first cake I've made in ages that raised properly. Anyway, I shall probably make that and orange bread and grilled sandwiches of some sort. People here *really* eat with their tea!

I should take a shower. Must go to the school compound, meet Mrs. S-D, and watch the *Twelfth Night* rehearsal. H. is doing about background music for it—quite a job. Wish I could work up some enthusiasm over the costumes. Rehearsals are also under way for *Trial by Jury*, which will be given next term. Never a dull moment!

Has Daddy had his picture taken yet? If not, *shame!*

Much love to you both,

Marian

February 11:

Learned at noon that Howard and I were supposed to join Mrs. S-D at the college to take measurements, peruse the costume situation, etc. As far as I was concerned, it was a rather grim afternoon. She isn't the soul of tact, but her enthusiasm is apparently unbounded. We tried all the available costumes on the proper boys and took measurements for the missing parts. I don't know who was more embarrassed about the measuring business—the boys or me!

Howard is now involved with the incidental music for the play. We are just hoping that it will turn out well enough so that the school won't be a laughingstock. John [who will direct] says the boys just don't know how to act. They don't know the difference between speaking loudly and shouting, and their speech is so quick as to be unintelligible. Their movements are wooden, their voices don't carry, the amplification setup is bad—and on and on.

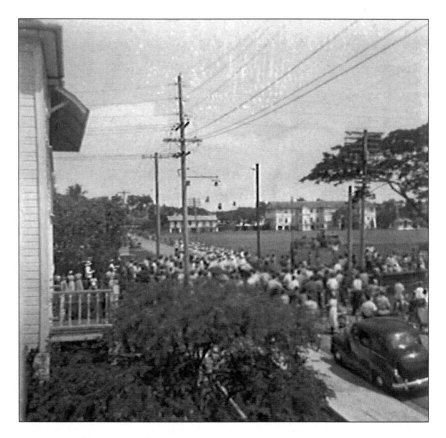

Glimpsed from the second-floor windows, the Militia Band is followed by a crowd, February 14, 1953.

February 12:

I waited until Elizabeth woke up after her nap, at about 1:30, then bundled her into the Taylor Tot and off we went to the Ramsarans'. Good Lord—the rough road! The poor child was nearly shaken to bits but seemed to be quite unconcerned by it. Once we arrived she spent the entire afternoon chewing contentedly on scraps of material.

John and Howard arrived at 4, with horrible tales of books missing from the school library. It seems that the new Head, anxious to prove that the boys are honest, has been leaving the library open and unattended—with the result that many reference books have just disappeared. Howard says six or seven biology reference books are gone, and they are next to impossible to replace here. Mr. Beckles took it rather lightly, merely saying that the school could expect to lose one or two hundred books before

A crowd gathers to watch the Princess Royal plant a tree, February 15, 1953.

the boys learned that honesty paid—and the entire library contains all of one or two thousand books! On days like this, the school seems to have gone wild.

February 13:

More and more rain. If it rains tomorrow, the parade honoring the Princess Royal will be held at Queen's. I can't quite imagine what it would look like, but the likelihood of good weather seems small.

I am disappointed—I had hoped that Dr. Ho-A-Shoo would finish with me today, but I'm to return on Tuesday.

Howard has gone to his Philatelic Society meeting, and I have to force myself to sew on a costume when I'd much rather be in bed, reading.

February 14:
We got to the Sanger-Davieses' house at 9:30 this morning, fifteen minutes late, but I'd rushed like mad to get there even then. Once there, we waited while Mrs. S-D ran around collecting her things. Finally, we got downtown about 10. She is awful to go shopping with—at least five times she put both her purse and shopping bag down on the floor and walked away. I kept my eye on them but grrred mentally when at one point, as she went striding off across the store, she called back asking me to "guard her bags." Ah well. We bought yards and yards of material at Fogarty's, then went zooming down the street to Bookers for meat, and further on down to Stabroek. She doesn't merely walk, she gallops. It was warm and muggy, and even with my long strides I had to work to keep up with her.

Howard picked us up at 11:30, just as the crowds were gathering to welcome the Princess Royal. All this was right in the midst of a brief but fierce shower, and the crowds scattered like mad. We watched part of the parade from our windows. . . .

Sunday, February 15, 1953

Dear All—

First of all, the paper is cut in half because Howard cut all our carbon paper in half to type out many copies of a test. He gave objective tests to all his classes last week, and my but how the boys did howl about them.

We got a huge batch of mail yesterday. What a long week it is with just the one delivery! I was about to give you up, Mother, but the postman brought a second batch around 5 with *Time* and the Scott's [stamp] catalogue with your long letter enclosed. We love Elizabeth's valentine. It is on her dresser now—I held it up to her yesterday and pulled it open and shut, and she giggled.

Well, Testudo is quite a character. He started out rather reserved, but we feel his adjustment to our comparably high degree of civilization has been good. You ask, Mother, how he spends his day. Well, he sleeps well at night, like Elizabeth. Generally he comes out of his little house at about 9:30 and takes a stroll into the kitchen or into our bedroom if it is sunny. He *loves* the w.c.—just why we don't know, but Elizabeth does, too, so we keep that door closed now. Anyway, some days he wanders around until noon, and other days he goes back to his little house after brief exercise. At noon he gets relatively excited in anticipation of his mango seed. This is served on a newspaper, and he delicately bites off the fruit, leaving the seed clean. Today, for instance, he was obviously not satisfied with the mango seed, so Howard gave him the mango peel and two banana peels. He was pleased with the mango peel but ignored the bananas. After lunch he generally goes back to his little house and stays there until next morning. The first few days we had him, he wasn't very well trained. Lately, however, he has been no trouble at all. Howard washed his shell off this morning, and minus dust he's very handsome. And Bee, he is a tortoise, if you please, not a turtle. The former prefer dry land, the latter water. We took a picture of him, but I'm afraid we had to ruin it to untangle a mess of film that jammed in the camera. But he won't run away.

It is about 10 p.m. now, and we just finished a lamb chop, salad, orange bread, and coffee. Joy and Richard Allsopp came over to tea, and we had quite an afternoon. The Princess Royal (Mary, an older sister of the late king) visited the Red Cross Convalescent Home across the street at 4:30 and planted two trees. Mrs. Patoir asked, before the Allsopps came, if she could watch from our windows. I said yes, of course. And then Mrs. McLaren appeared and asked if she could watch from our windows. Naturally I said yes. So when Howard picked up the Allsopps and brought them, we were quite cozy. Mrs. Patoir got all embarrassed and refused tea, and Mrs. McLaren had already had some. So we drank and ate and watched HRH the PR plant the trees. During all this, Richard, who is definitely anti-British, was making quips about the ceremony, not offensive but not too respectful. Poor Mrs. McLaren was undoubtedly offended, but we were more or less powerless. Finally, Richard said something about the Queen, and Mrs. McL. popped up with the correct date and proceeded to tell us the dates of all previous Royal visits to B.G. She and Margaret are really up on their Royal history—it is wonderful, and I admire them for it. Richard got the point and subsided a bit after that.

I am going to do some costume sewing with Joy. We sent them off with a large stack of magazines—New Yorkers and Saturday Reviews, a few Times and a Good Housekeeping. My goodness, but they will really be well-read magazines by the time they fall apart!

We hear now that Howard's aunt isn't going to go on the cruise—she is going to buy a house in San Clemente instead. So she won't be coming. And Bee, you're going to Mexico? Will no one come to see us? Really, Georgetown is quite a decent place despite the mildew!

Oh my, I do feel flippant. Howard and I had a drink at 9, and it tasted good. We are now drinking coffee. Nescafe, that is. We've had it at the Ramsarans', and I just love it for after-dinner coffee. I wouldn't want it for breakfast, but it's lovely at times like this.

Elizabeth is dearer every day. Every once in a while when I tell her to say "mama," she does and it thrills us all to pieces. Generally, I admit, she just giggles or says "ah-da." She is back on her milk again, lapping it up from both cup and bottle. I certainly wish you all could see her—she is the happiest child you can imagine. And so responsive—I just can't let myself feel grouchy around her, because she looks so puzzled when I don't smile at her.

I am dying for sleep. This is ridiculous, though, writing on a Sunday evening. I am going to revise my schedule and start writing on Saturday afternoons. Then our letters can catch the Sunday plane.

Dearies, we miss you all but want you to know that we're having a lovely, happy time here. When I think of the wonderful tales we can tell about B.G., it sounds fantastic! The journal is being kept up to date, and sometimes I even refrain from writing an interesting tidbit in letters so that you will be interested in reading the journal. Isn't that nasty of me.

Must go to the kitchen and face my two plates and greasy skillet.

Love and kisses to you all,

Marian

February 15:

Howard went to pick up the Allsopps a few minutes before 4. While he was gone Mrs. Patoir tapped on a window and asked if she could come in to watch the Royal proceedings at the Convalescents' Home across the street. She said that Mrs. Ogle hadn't been very cordial and in fact had suggested that she would be able to see more from our flat! Of course I told her to come in. She and I were looking out the front windows, and who walked up to the gate but Mrs. McLaren, also asking if she could watch from our windows. So when Howard returned with Joy and Richard, we had quite a houseful. Mrs. Patoir stayed by herself in the little tower and seemed awfully embarrassed but pleased when I asked her if she'd like some tea. She refused, flustered. Mrs. McLaren had had tea already, so we four went ahead.

Richard told Howard later that he hadn't realized at first who Mrs. McLaren was, and he made many quips about the folderol to do with royalty. Howard says he is passionately anti-British. Anyway, he was puzzling aloud about some date, and Mrs. McLaren snapped around and told him, and then went on to tell us the dates of all previous Royal visits to B.G. Richard, hearing her British accent, decided to quiet down—thank heavens! I'm sorry if she was offended, but Howard and I find a bit of the light touch toward the Royal family refreshing now and then.

The Allsopps want to come some evening to listen to our records. I hope it can be soon; they are such nice people. Howard and I feel the importance of getting to know some of the local people as well as the English. The more we experience the ease with which people of different colored skin get along together here, the less defensible seems the situation in America. And how embarrassing it is to be asked to explain it!

February 15, 1953

Dear folks,

Sanger-Davies has committed a faux-pas. Idealistically, he ordered the library to be left open (and unattended) during school hours. The result: a noticeable deficit in reference books (ten missing from the biology section was enough for me—I removed all the remaining volumes into the lab). He pooh-poohed warnings from staff, and not until Friday was the evidence clear enough—with cows out, he locked the barn door. An open library to boys who have had all temptation barred from them heretofore is obviously too much—particularly here where books have ten times the value (not monetary) they do at home.

We had our first glimpse of British royalty this weekend when Her Royal Highness, the Princess Royal—doesn't that sound silly; she's Mary, an older sister of the late king—deigned to soil her shoes in Guianese mud to visit the local Red Cross establishments, of which organization she takes charge throughout the Commonwealth. One such establishment is the Red Cross Home for Convalescent Children across the street. About 3:30 people began to line the sidewalk opposite the home, and cops kept them off the street (and made me move the car into the driveway). The good Princess arrived tastefully late with His Excellency, the O.A.G., the Honorable John Gutch, O.B.E., C.M.G. (whom Mr. S-D fondly calls "dear John"). After spending some time in the home, she emerged to "plant" two saplings, and then the party drove off, sans any whit of an indication of cheer, vocal or otherwise.

In all probability we don't realize the busy lives these nobles lead (after having read about their overfull routines, I don't envy them), but still, there is just enough American blood coursing through our veins to cause us to object to this principle of recognizing in some mortals semi-divinity—His Excellency, Her Royal Highness, and His Worship just don't click.

Love to all,
Howard

February 18:

Howard was up several times last night with diarrhea. He felt so awful this morning that he decided to stay in bed. Queen's wasn't built for such an emergency anyway—the john nearest his lab is about three city blocks away. I hoped to use the phone upstairs, but Mrs. Ogle didn't answer the door. So I stood in the street for a few minutes and finally stopped a small boy on his way to school and asked him to give Mr. Sanger-Davies the message.

I wasn't in the mood at all to enjoy sewing on costumes, but Mrs. S-D was expecting me so I went over. We cut out several pairs of breeches and I brought them home. Tomorrow I shall sew them up at Margaret's. Evidently Mrs. S-D has had considerable experience with such work, for the few bits she's done already look quite splendid. She seems to have the knack of visualizing a costume and the ability to create it as well.

Thursday, Feb. 19, 1953

Dear Mother—

Howard is busy typing out #3 stencil, for the constitution of the Education Society, which he hopes to get out of—or have I mentioned it at all? It is just being organized by Cameron, and H. is temporary secretary. The job is really too much what with the Philatelic Society, Literary and Dramatic Society, etc.

After looking at the calendar, I took some pictures of Elizabeth on Tuesday to send you. Unfortunately, H. was feeling below par yesterday, so the pictures may not be developed in time to arrive on your birthday. But we shall send them sooner or later. I was in such a hurry to get them, I didn't even wait until afternoon when E. would have been dressed—she is clad only in pants, as she usually is!

We have had four solid days without rain—thank the Lord. This is our short dry season, I guess. It seems awfully hot after the cool dampness, but drying clothes outside is a grand luxury!

Elizabeth and I walked over to the Ramsarans' at 1:30 this afternoon. I suppose it's the hottest part of the day, but I didn't want to wait until 4 when it cools off. The road is frightfully bumpy but E. doesn't seem to care. We took the little clown, a box of cookies, three costumes to sew up, and a torn sheet to mend—in the pocket of the Taylor Tot. The few people we passed on the street must have thought I was crazy—no one goes out in the sun if he can help it, let alone takes a baby in it. But then, most people seem to think a little sunshine would kill a child—I disagree! We were both warm after the walk, but when we arrived I took E.'s dress off and gave her a good big drink of water, and she was just fine.

I do hope she stays so friendly and at ease away from home—right now she's a joy to take out because she's so good. Granted, she searches for a scrap of paper or a thread on the floor and puts it in her mouth, and she crawls so quickly that we all spent a good deal of time chasing her—but she's so happy, doesn't fuss, and seems to enjoy exploring strange ground.

We are deep in costumes for *Twelfth Night*, and H. is doing his best to dig up appropriate incidental music. I think everyone but the S-Ds wishes the play would go hang, but who are we anyway!

Oh yes—I meant to say in connection with H.'s not feeling well that I'm now boiling our drinking water—that may be the cause of it all.

I've tried a few good recipes in my West Indian cookbook. One is baked, stuffed melongene—eggplant to you—very good. I shall have to send it to you. Doesn't melongene sound more exotic than eggplant!

I'm sleepy—love and kisses to you and Daddy,
Marian

February 19:

An East Indian girl appeared this morning while I was bathing Elizabeth and asked for work. She said she'd been working at the Brown Betty[32] but the work there was killing her, and did I know of anyone who needed help. She wasn't particularly appealing to look at: a rather attractive face, but she'd covered it with that lavender-colored powder which is used here.

Elizabeth and I strolled over to the Ramsarans' this afternoon. We were both sweltering when we arrived. These damn breeches. They look so darned simple, but I sewed the first one up all wrong before I caught on. I did two white ones, a lavender pair, and one gray and left the second gray with Margaret to do. Both she and Mrs. McLaren were sewing, and there were scraps of material on the floor that fascinated Elizabeth.

When it was time to come home, Mrs. McLaren said she'd walk part way with us. She poured out some of her unhappiness to me, adding that she may have to go back to England if she can't snap out of this depression. Also, she is feeling the frustration of being without her own home for the first time. It is certainly understandable: here, with so few outside interests available, we are all thrown on our own resources, and a woman can't go out alone after dark even for a walk. Such things as classes, lectures, concerts, etc. are mighty few and far between. My heart goes out to her. She just hasn't enough to do here.

Friday, Feb. 20, 1953

Dear Mother—

Greetings on (or about) your birthday! I would have polished up the coins for you [seven coins pasted to card], but I personally prefer the antique look.

Elizabeth is entering the "play in her own room" phase. So far today she's knocked the playpen gate down once and pushed through it twice. Too smart for us!

Oh boy—it seems awfully warm today. I just made some cookie dough—part plain, part with orange rind, and part with dates. H. has a Philatelic Society meeting tonight so I shall probably bake them after dinner. Cooler then, too.

I must take a shower and be off to Mrs. S-D's. The play comes off March 20—we'll all be so glad!

Love and kisses—I wish I were nearer and could bake a cake for you!

Marian

February 20:
Went back this afternoon to the Sanger-Davieses', returning the pants. She gave me the leg measurements, and now I'm to put the leg bands on them. It's absolutely shocking to think that the play goes on in less than a month!

February 21:
The Chafing Dish Cookbook arrived from Mother today, and Howard picked it up at the parcel office for me. Each of the recipes looks so enticing, but the list of suggested items to keep on the cupboard shelf amuses me. Nice little cans of fish and crab are frightfully expensive here, tuna fish is

something we don't even see, and canned meats like Vienna sausage are over $1 per small tin.

February 22:
Since the disappearance of those library reference books, several of the masters have decided that they would prefer to keep the remaining volumes close at hand. Howard brought a few home—they are wormy, moldy, and the pages are all brittle. I do hate to think of our books suffering such a fate.

Monday, Feb. 23, 1953

Dearest Parents—

Five o'clock. Howard is at school—he had "games duty" today from 4:30 to 6. Elizabeth is out, as the afternoon has been good and clear. H. left me with Margaret after lunch, and I sewed up two more pairs of britches (phonetic!) for the play. We had a quick cup of tea, and then H. picked me up at 3 to go to the dentist. As far as that dentist is concerned, I'm through—in a few months I shall try another man. Dr. Ho-A-Shoo just doesn't seem thorough enough to suit me—or my poor old teeth.

Elizabeth is almost standing up by herself now. She crawls up to us, puts her arms around our legs, and gets up on her knees; then, if we take hold of her arms, she can stand. I was watching her try it this morning—she braces her arms against the rails of the playpen and tries that way. Her arm muscles are so strong that, when her legs are just a bit stronger, she'll have no trouble at all balancing herself.

Glad you liked the valentines. They're fun to make. H. and I are considering making all future Christmas cards and such like—make it our "family trademark." Your cards arrived today for H. and me, and E.'s came Saturday. Slow sorting, I guess. The cookbook also arrived Saturday, and after I read through it we had a chafing dish supper last night—with "lamburgers" from the *200 Dishes for Men to Cook* book!

Goodness, Mother, I don't know what to say about dresses for E. They are a perfect weight for the "cold," windy, wet days, and they look so cute on her. The size 2 will fit her for quite some time. My only reservation is that the skirts get in her way when she crawls—but if she's starting to stand now, she'll be walking soon, won't she. I think yellow posies would be awfully cute—or blue. I'm going to buy her some shoes tomorrow if I get downtown. She really needs them now, she looks so cute and like such a big girl.

For Howard's birthday—I asked him if there was a book he'd like to have, thinking to myself of Rachel Carson's first book, but he mentioned one on "the grasses of B.G.," by Hitchcock, available through the U.S. Department of Agriculture. I know what I think he would love—a world globe—but that, of course, would have to be a stay-at-home gift, wouldn't it! I shall make further enquiries.

Could you write to *Good Housekeeping* and get reprints for me of their cake and cookie books? Both my January and February issues are "out," but in one there is a notice about the pamphlets' availability. Nuts—better wait till I can check because I think there is another I want, too. They cost 25 cents or 55 cents, which is why I thought you could send for them better than I.

Well, now we've eaten. I have in front of me coffee and cookies, two coconuts to grate, and a pair of lavender breeches to finish. Mrs. S-D stopped by about 6—she'd just finished a tennis game. She looked frightfully like an American cartoonist's version of an Englishwoman, age 55, stockily built, who has just finished a game of tennis! Drippy, red-faced, puffing—and just too pudgy to look decent in tennis shorts.

The cookies with dates are delicious—so are those with orange peel. You should try them!

Well, on to the coconut. You should be here, Daddy—coconuts are four for 24 cents B.G. You could grate them for me, too.

Much love from
Marian

February 23:
Mrs. Sanger-Davies stopped by to tell me she has arranged for me to borrow a sewing machine from a Mrs. Wieting. Howard is to pick it up tomorrow.

February 24:
Mrs. Wieting's maid brought the sewing machine by this morning. I was in the kitchen and didn't hear the door, but when I went downstairs for the mail Mrs. Patoir said she'd taken it in. The machine is a Singer electric portable and a real joy to use.

Finally, Howard has received the go-ahead signal to proceed with his activities at Atkinson Field. He is to pick up his pass Saturday morning and is planning to go on out to the Field to spend the afternoon.

February 25:

Trekked through the Military Road this afternoon to the Sanger-Davieses'. I cut out more breeches—I scarcely need the pattern now. These are black silk for the stagehands, also a pair of black satin for the Duke and bright green ones for Viola and Sebastian.

I had tea with Mr. and Mrs. Sanger-Davies after we finished the sewing and cutting for the afternoon. Mrs. S-D thinks it would be only proper for the boys to wear evening dress to the concert Friday. Little does she know. Just before I left, Mr. S-D crumpled an envelope and threw it over the side of their porch. "Why, Joe," said his wife, "you dirty little pig." "Never mind," he replied, "it will blow away."

February 26, 1953

Dear folks,

Well, the madhouse continues—and gets progressively madder. Nothing like trying to conduct a vigorous academic program (in preparation for state examinations) while being pushed into a play production that taxes boys and staff beyond capacity.

Marian spends most every evening making breeches. We finally got the loan of a sewing machine (thanks to Mrs. S-D's higher-echelon contacts) but have long since recognized the error in not bringing yours.

I've just about completed selecting inter-scene and inter-act music, and tomorrow will start the touchy task of integrating the various tidbits with stage action.

I feel awfully sorry for John Ramsaran, not only because the production of any Shakespeare is a great task but also because there are too many assistant Indian Chiefs. At least two other staff members are aspiring dramatic coaches, and instead of helping John they seem only to slow things up. You know, John tells a boy to gesture like so, and on another occasion, one of the other men tells the boy to do it differently, and if so done before John, the boy is told to gesture as he was shown in the first instance. And so it goes, day by day. At this point, we wish that March 20 were next week so that we could be through with *Twelfth Night* once and for all.

At long last, I've got a place to work from at Atkinson Field. Mr. Roatgever, chairman of the A.F. Board of Control, seemed convinced there's nothing subversive in my intent—so, at great length, my research can get under way. Until the end of the term, I'll devote every Saturday to my work and, during the vacation, most all of the time. Needless to say, I'm very impatient.

The people of Georgetown are all excited about the arrival of the Indian cricket team, which arrived today after spending a week in Barbados and a couple in Trinidad. They're slated to be here for about three weeks. It's about as exciting to these folks as the World Series is to our ardent baseball fans. To date I've supervised only a couple of school cricket matches, and although I still don't quite understand the game, my impression is that it would be too slow for most U.S. grandstanders.

The radio is on and the local announcer has just introduced the SHEP Fields show. Likewise, we're treated to PATTY Paige, JOHNNY Ray, but, strangely reversed, we also get the Mills BROTHERS, harmonIZing. Advertised are gents' moc-ASS-ins. We recently heard Bee-THOV-en's Andante CantaBILE and Brahms's Symphony in a flat (not in A flat, but just any old flat). All radio programs are carefully SHED-uled (complete with copious spray of saliva). Some of this shifted emphasis is British, but most of it is local.

Yes, I miss my double bass as much as you do your piano, Mom, but vicious politics make me hesitate to join the Georgetown Philharmonic. Most everyone has advised me against the move.

I'm tired and it's late.

Love to all,

Howard

February 27:

Thomas had a set-to with Mrs. Ogle this morning when he brought our vegetables. It seems he came in the gate to the driveway and parked his bicycle against the garage. Mrs. Ogle called down and said he should have gone around the back way, that the gate and driveway were "private." He answered that it was too muddy the other way. He muttered all the way up the stairs and told me that "these native people are worse than anyone." He said, "In America, you are either white or black. Madam, she is black." He sputtered for a while, quite disturbed. Among the vegetables were three lovely, large tomatoes—for which I paid 62 cents. We ate one tonight with dinner and were just a bit disappointed with it—not too much flavor.

We must leave in a little while for the Militia Band Concert. Neither of us is in the mood. It is windy out and fairly cool, with showers. I'd love to go to bed and read. Ah well—art of any sort is An Occasion here.

Saturday, February 28, 1953

Dearest Everyone—

Last night was one of those precious times that make every little discomfort more than worthwhile. It also made me think seriously about this place's book possibilities. We attended a B.G. Militia Band Concert, a benefit performance for the Q.C. Stage Equipment Fund. We picked up Margaret and Mrs. McLaren, leaving John at home with Susan and *Twelfth Night*. H. and I were in a bad mood to go out—it was rainy and we both thought longingly of reading in bed. But heaven knows, it was worth it. We wore rather casual clothes—H. his beige suit, and I the green jersey and spectators, just the things for a band concert at home. We were greeted as we entered the hall by Archie and Dorothy, who were decked out in formal attire, and told that all staff members and wives were supposed to sit in the balcony with the governor's party. Ha! we thought—how out of place can we be! But HH the OAG was kept in the Legislative Council with a filibuster, so at least *he* didn't come. The S-Ds, Beckleses, Camerons, et al. wore formals and white dinner jackets.

Guest soloists were Miss Dolphin of the college, who wore a gorgeous yellow gown, looked stunning, and played beautifully. At least she played one solo and we could hear the piano then; when she played with the band, too much was lost. Another guest artiste was one Kathleen Howe, onetime singer at the Covent Garden opera house, according to Mrs. McLaren. She is awfully large. Her gesturing is absurd, she sharped her high notes and flatted the low ones, and sang "Ave Maria" from *Cavalliera Rusticana*, "Vilia" from *The Merry Widow* (oh dear—she wasn't the type), and another selection I didn't know. The Q.C. Junior Choir sang several folk songs—Welsh, English, etc.

The band played *Les Preludes*, incidental music from *A Midsummer Night's Dream*, Quilter's "Children's Overture," and a hodgepodge of Tchaikovsky—"Reminiscence of—". Howard says that the band produced some lovely effects, and that as a band they are good—no denying that. But oh dear me. During *A Midsummer Night's Dream*, Margaret muttered in my ear, "If these are fairies, they're fairies of your and my size!" It was a bit clompy and sounded as ethereal as a fire alarm. And the "Reminiscence" business was a panic. There were three logical endings, and each time, as the band stopped, one or two people began to applaud, only to have the band burst into *Romeo and Juliet* or something else. The final touch was the end, the *1812*. The band wasn't content with a mere touch of the chimes at the end, but the man banged away on them note by note to the bitter end.

Mrs. Sanger-Davies told us to come over to their home for a few minutes after the concert, so we went. She, by the way, looked just utterly grim in a black sheer blouse that showed her none-too-attractive undergarments and a black taffeta skirt that had horizontal packing wrinkles in it. And her hair was as untidy as ever. And I must add that throughout the concert, her husband wiggled, twisted around, got up to peer over the balcony, and spent much of the time wandering around the hall. Mrs. S-D, Mr. Beckles, and Mrs. B. also got up and bent over the balcony railing—such a lovely view we had of them! H. and I were absolutely delighted when, hearing a rustling behind us, we all turned around and found the night watchman, dressed in his ragged working clothes, plodding through the balcony to punch his time clock.

We dutifully trotted over to the S-Ds', hoping to stay about fifteen minutes. No such luck. Others appeared—the Larthes, Beckleses, Mrs. Howe, a man named Martin-Sperry who is something of a patron of the arts here (he composes music for the trombone). Mrs. S-D brought a trayful of empty glasses into the living room, produced bottles of rum and whiskey, and asked each of us several times what we wanted. Finally, with bottle caps all over the floor, we were served our drinks (sans ice—repulsive). She trips around with the social grace of a little donkey—very good-natured, hearty, and doing her best.

And I made a conquest. A late arriver was the Major S. W. Henwood, who conducts the band. He talked to Mrs. Beckles for a while and then was introduced to us. He told H. to go talk to Mrs. B., saying he would talk to me. He told me what a grand performance his band had given, that their best number was *Les Preludes* ("beautiful," he said—we all thought it was quite dreadful). Second best, he said, was the "Children's Overture," which had Margaret and her mother simply writhing. He is a short man, fifty years old, has been with the band for thirty years, and has conducted it for eighteen. He had had a little drink with the men in the band and just didn't care about anything! His face was rosy, he has a little mustache, and he makes rather grandiose flourishes with his cigarettes. He is frightfully conscious of his importance here and was garrulous and as pompous a person as I've ever met. "Now Mrs. Howe, Lynette Dolphin, and I understand each other," he said. "They're artists. I can't sing and Mrs. Howe can't conduct; Lynette can't conduct and I can't play the piano. We go over the scores and mark them carefully—mind you, it's hard work—but we can understand each other." He also told me that he selects the band's programs. "I have a good government here. They say it's Major Henwood's band, and they let Major Henwood run it." By this time I was entirely enthralled and leading him on. He has men of sixty and boys of fourteen in the group and said he wants men with no formal training in music—"If they've had training, I have to break it all down." He asked what my name was, I said "Irwin," and he said, "What does your husband call you?" I told him and he said he'd remember that, and that his drink was rum and water ("I drink rum and soda only under protest") and he thought it would be very nice if we'd have him up some evening, "not for very long, just a half hour or so—just a little cocktail party." Gad—. According to Miss Dolphin, it is hard to find the gentleman in a truly sober moment. I believe it! About this time, Mrs. S-D carried Mrs. McLaren and me off to see the costumes, and when we came back to the living room the party was breaking up. H. told me later that the Major had been impressed with me, or some such. He's just a show-off—he's the one who so carefully shows his profile when conducting.

We got home at midnight and giggled for an hour or so. The whole idea of people getting all gussied up to go to a school auditorium to hear a band play just tickles us to pieces. It seems so ridiculous. And you should have heard the congratulating that went on at the S-Ds'. Everyone told the Major what a splendid performance it had been, they told Mrs. Howe that she had sung beautifully, etc. Mrs. McLaren asked Mr. Beckles if he thought the music sounded better in the balcony (we had already decided that it did, in the sense that the flaws were more clearly audible!) and he said, yes, he thought the blending was lovely. It is all taken so seriously—art with the capital "A." Of course, the Ramsarans are used to Sir Malcolm Sargent and "the best in the world," at frequent intervals. This must seem even more caricatured to them.

Mrs. McLaren and I are going to the S-Ds' this afternoon to do some more sewing. The breeches are coming along beautifully, but there are all sorts of little tapes and snaps ("press-studs") to be put on, and those details take such a long time. We have about two weeks in which to finish them up. Howard tried the records yesterday at Queen's, and luckily the Head was there to hear for himself the miserable loudspeaker system, which H. has told him about several times and which he didn't seem to think needed any repairing. Howard says the music will do beautifully if the phonograph hookup can just be fixed.

Elizabeth now says "mama" whenever we ask her to! It just about thrills me to pieces to hear her. I ask her to say "da-da," and sometimes it almost sounds like that, but other times it is "ba-ba" or "ga-ga." And she does so want to stand up. Any time we take hold of her arms, she pulls herself up; it is the business of gripping something that keeps her from standing all by herself, we think. Thursday at the Ramsarans' we had quite a time. First she found a little blob of dark floor wax under a chair and proceeded to have a lovely time with that. Then I knocked my pin box off the chair arm, and we had to find all of them. Next I lost my needle and we were afraid E. would find it first. In between of course we had to jump up to get Elizabeth away from the brooms, the stairs, the magazines, etc. She is so happy playing on the floor, exploring table legs and chairs—I think she's awfully good, really, it is just the inevitable things like stairs and pins that cause trouble. Susan was so cute. She wanted to help clean the wax off E.'s hands, and very gently washed one while Margaret did the other—I was holding her. Later on, Elizabeth headed for the stairs, and Susan dashed over to her and carefully held onto the top of E.'s head while I came. She is a dear, bright little girl.

Howard is spending the day at Atkinson Field, finally. He got the run-around from all sorts of people, and we had just about decided his activities had been suspected of being subversive, but it's all straightened out now. Thank heavens.

Well, dears, I must gather together my pins, breeches, scissors, and such and prepare to prepare. I'm glad we aren't getting newspapers regularly, because it really tore my heart to see the lovely ads!

Love and kisses to you all—

Marian

Thank you for the rubber hands. It is hard to remember that such insignificant little doodads can be so bright and cute. Utilitarian things here aren't the least bit gay or cute.

February 28:

Mrs. McLaren came by at 2:30 and we went to Mrs. Sanger-Davies's. She sewed some little rosettes to put on the finished breeches, and I cut out more of the same, this time in black silk, also the yellow and pink longies for the Fool. About 4:30 Mrs. S-D said that the head of the Department of Education, Mr. A. A. Bannister, and his wife were coming to tea. We said we should leave, but she urged us to stay. Mr. Bannister, the first Negro to hold his job, seems quite pleasant, but his wife was very, very silent and didn't seem to be very happy about anything. Richard Allsopp stopped by to see about a tennis game, and he too had a cup of tea. Finally at 6 Mr. S-D reminded his wife that they were due at Government House at 6:30, so our little party broke up quickly.

Howard returned from Atkinson Field a few minutes after I got home. He has a room in an old office building, and it has electricity and adequate plumbing and screened windows on three sides. Not until after dinner did he break down and tell me, somewhat sheepishly, that he'd brought back another tortoise, which he'd found near the spot where he picked up Testudo. Testudo was already asleep for the night, so we won't be able to see how they get along until tomorrow.

Mr. P. H. Mangal, science teacher at Berbice High School for whom Howard fixed an antique microscope a few weeks ago, stopped in this evening. He teaches biology, chemistry, and physics and I gather he is just one jump ahead of his students in all his subjects. He will be coming to Georgetown each weekend to take a class from Miss Graham at Bishops' each Saturday.

March 1953:

Lionel Luckhoo's "Dunce Motion" is passed into law. The lone protester against the Undesirable Publications Act in the colony's Legislative Council had been Cheddi Jagan, who upon his election in 1947 was, at twenty-nine, the council's youngest member, and who in 1950 had been a founder of the People's Progressive Party. As Jagan later recalled, the Legislative Council "hastily rushed through a Bill giving the Governor power to decide what books, films and gramophone records should be allowed to enter the country. A few months before that the Governor had confiscated several bundles of books imported from the United Kingdom and destroyed them by burning." The law further held that distributors of banned materials were subject to a stiff fine or a year in prison, and that anyone in possession of the works who failed to turn them in to the police was subject to a $250 fine and imprisonment for six months. The notoriety of the Undesirable Publications Act made censorship a central issue during the last weeks of the election campaign.

March 1:

The tortoises have spent much of the day becoming acquainted with each other. The new one, formally named Tabulata but called Junior, has followed Testudo around the flat quite a bit, and they spent several minutes at a time with heads lowered, touching noses.

March 2:

I went downtown after lunch. My chief purchase was socks and shoes for Elizabeth, no easy buy here, it seems. At Bookers they had one style in her size but the sole was too stiff. At Fogarty's the man showed me a cute pair of sandals that would have fit her, but they would have been more appropriate for a three-year-old. The only soft-soled shoes he could find at first were little tiny ones, for a new baby. But he looked some more and finally came out with a pair of white high shoes, called "boots" here, with two little buttons instead of laces. I tried them on her this afternoon and they're much too big, but she'll grow into them quickly, I imagine.

Socks are hard to find, too. I got one pair of white socks, five inches long, at Fogarty's, which have a red and blue cuff in a "Coronation design," according to the tag. Bookers has blue and pink socks, six and a half inches long. And that's all!

Howard has gone to a rehearsal at school, and I'm about to go back to my costumes. His music selections are fine, everyone agrees, but he has to go back to the British Council to get some more records. Seems they want a prologue now, after all.

March 3, 1953

Dear folks,

I know this is long overdue, but your son is a bit snowed with various and sundry obligations. The snowball of activities (we all knew it was coming) has begun to roll and tempers are shortening, nerves are frazzling—the term's end will be welcomed with open arms. And how!

Twelfth Night is due to come off on the 17th, yet the boys seem barely familiar with Acts IV and V—to say nothing of having learned their lines and interpreting them meaningfully. That usual last-week miracle is bound to occur here as everywhere, but it's still hellish trying to meet this deadline. Marian has been devoting every spare minute to costumes, and I've been attending all rehearsals to integrate the musical interludes with the action—very hard to do when there are three directors, and no two agreeing! At times it's laughable, at others infuriating, like having an orchestra with three conductors. Anyone having a part in the production has had to all but drop academic endeavor—very difficult for me to do with a clear conscience considering my mission, but that's what the principal wants. Q.E.D. (Latin = quod erat demonstrandum, or "that which has been shown"; B.G. = quite easily done.)

Speaking of the principal, he proved himself once and for all an ass last Friday night, the evening of the band concert. He demanded the house lights be left on throughout the program and that the footlights be left off. Miss Dolphin, piano soloist, and Mrs. Howe, soprano soloist, asked for the very logical reverse conditions, at least during their respective phases of the program, and the electrician did as they wished. Fuming like a geyser, Mr. S-D told Miss Dolphin (a staff member) the next day that he would never be "crossed again like that" and mumbled the afterthought that "natives here don't know their place." He forgets that this is not Africa but B.G., where all peoples get along beautifully on a basis of equanimity.

Alarmed at social mixture in schools here, Mrs. S-D has uttered too often the words, "It's a pity the European children cannot be in a separate school." Needless to say, the principal and his wife, via their blunt, unmeasured statements, are fast approaching infamy. At times some of the things they blurt out are hard to believe as products of their supposedly elevated minds. Truly, we all hate to admit this for we had such great hopes with the change of administration.

My shipment of *The Flora of Surinam* from Amsterdam finally came today. It, with *The Flora of Trinidad and Tobago*, which I got some time ago, makes possible the progress of my research project. I went out to my quarters at Atkinson Field last weekend and began surveying the environs—I can't wait for April (vacation month); I'll practically live out there then.

You asked about our seafood—well, what seafood? It's the old bugaboo again—the same thing that makes swimming unheard-of: mud. There's so much mud suspended in the coastal and estuary waters that few fish are found to exist. Fish are caught upriver and some 50 miles out at sea, but shipment to Georgetown makes their price a bit too high for most. No edible crabs, lobsters, clams, oysters, etc. for the same reason. We've had fish only twice, aside from the few I caught in the local trenches.

Love to all,
Howard

March 4:

Came back from Mrs. Sanger-Davies's today with a new project—a jacket which needs a frill on the cuffs and snaps up the front. The jacket is pale green with magenta collar and frills, and I think the pants to go with it are magenta. Giddy!

Both of the S-Ds are quite pleased because the gardening venture, which Howard abandoned with Mr. S-D's approval,[33] has turned into a successful project on a free, unsupervised basis. Mr. S-D has allotted plots to any boy who wants one and is offering a prize for the best Coronation garden. Of course, as H. points out, he is not supervising the use of tools, and over half of them have now disappeared. We're betting that enthusiasm will die down, too, once the fun of growing something other than the prescribed beans wears off.

Thursday, March 5, 1953

Dearest Parents—

It is twenty to 11, and at 11 I must start Elizabeth's lunch. But Winifred is in the kitchen doing the floor, the clothes aren't dry enough to iron, and Elizabeth is playing happily in the playpen, so I shall write a short note.

We had the typewriter fixed, thank heavens. It cost $9.50, and considering what typewriter repairs cost at home, I don't think that's bad although we did shudder a bit.

Let's see—I don't think I've told you that we have a little playmate for Testudo now. Howard found him last Saturday when he was out at the Field, and couldn't resist. They wander about quite a bit during the morning and afternoon. Under our bed is a favorite haunt. Howard keeps his shoes there, and the new tortoise (we call him Junior) seems to enjoy crawling on the shoes. Have you any clues on the housebreaking of tortoises? They are fairly neat, but I would like to confine their contributions to a single part of the flat. Ah well—otherwise they are a cinch to have around.

Howard's copy of *The Flora of Surinam* arrived from the Netherlands the first of the week. He says it looks more complete than the one for Trinidad and Tobago, and is anxious to get to work. The cricket team from India is here, and if our good weather holds they will be playing all this week and next, which means that H. will have afternoons free. He wants to go out to the Field tomorrow after lunch, stay the night, and return on Saturday. Imagine—it is just about 30 miles, but such a tiring and arduous drive that he says it isn't worth going and coming on the same day! His space there is a room in an otherwise empty building, with plumbing, electricity, and a water faucet outside. When the present term is over at the end of the month, he wants to spend several days at a time there. Mrs. McLaren has offered to come over anytime, to spend the afternoon, the day, or the night, which I thought was awfully nice of her. I don't mind being alone, but it just gets mighty boring after a while.

Monday I went downtown and bought some shoes and socks for Elizabeth. I took an outline of her foot and asked for soft-soled shoes. The clerks all looked utterly astounded—"That large, and she isn't walking?" The ones I bought are too big, but since she isn't walking I don't think it can hurt her. They were the only thing available; the other high shoes were too small. Children's shoes are available, made by a name Margaret recommends, but baby shoes are a bit scarce.

I have made the little sundress for E. in the red-and-white check material we brought. And I've cut out the blue sheer with the little white flowers that you bought—it will have white organdy collar, cuffs, and pocket edges. They are both one-year size and too big still, but she's growing rapidly!

Later—Elizabeth has been fed and is sound asleep. She gets so sleepy in the morning but just can't seem to take a nap. Consequently, I feed her at 11:30 and put her right into bed, and she didn't even peep before she went to sleep! She still isn't standing by herself but gets a big kick out of pulling herself up with someone's help. Mother, the pictures I took for your birthday didn't turn out at all well. It seems I was heading the camera into the sun, or something. But now that we are wearing shoes and socks, we shall have to take a picture of *that* for you. Someday I'm just going to pop with pleasure when I smile at her and she smiles back! Often when we are in the kitchen and she heads for parts unknown (generally the bookcase), I just laugh and call her name, and she answers with a little giggle, turns around, sits down, and then comes back to the kitchen. Of course there are times when she giggles and keeps on going, too. But she is so beautifully happy that I just love to hear her laugh. And I'm sure it's contagious—if she's bumped her head or is fussy, and I talk and laugh with her, she'll respond—just as I do to her when I'm tired. The power she has in her arms is tremendous. I wear my hair pulled back and tied with a ribbon, and just lately she's discovered the pretty bright ribbon. Already she's poked me in the eye several times today, trying to turn my head around so she can pull at the ribbon. There are moments when I'm quite overawed: being Elizabeth's mother is one of the nicest things that's ever happened to me!

We just don't know what to make of the S-Ds. Right at the moment, if I were to characterize them briefly, I would say they are bold as brass, a bit dense, conceited, and none too clean. They seem absolutely insensible to local customs and feelings, and, as H. says, give Mr. S-D time and he will insult everyone on the faculty. The other night at the concert, he told Miss Dolphin and Mrs. Howe that the houselights would be on during the entire program because he wanted to see as well as hear. They protested; he stood firm. So they asked the electrician to dim the lights during their numbers. Afterward, he told Miss Dolphin that that sort of thing would never happen again, and as he left, said in a tone which she could well hear that "These native people don't know their place." We seethe at that. Miss Dolphin is as lovely a person as you could find anywhere, enjoyable and personable as well as very talented.

I must go wash lunch dishes, finish washing the diapers, do a bit of ironing, and take a bath. Howard says John invited him to go over to their house, too—he had intended to mark some books, but we'll all go now. So I shall have to take more cookies!

Love and kisses to each of you,

Marian

March 5:

Howard had the afternoon free because of the Indian cricket team match here, so we all went over to the Ramsarans'. It was awfully hot today, and none of us felt particularly gay. Howard and I both came home with slight headaches. I met Mr. October, the school's secretary who is in change of the groundsmen, donkeys, and supplies, among other duties. Mrs. McLaren announced dolefully that weather such as we have had today is standard for the months of May and June.

Saturday, March 7

Dear Mother and Daddy—

Well, Howard did go out to the Field yesterday, laden with hammock, pillow, two cotton blankets, baskets with equipment, etc. Also a basket of food—he said it was way too much, but I always have visions of him starving to death. He bought two more thermos bottles, and I carefully filled one with milk, one with fruit juice, and one with hot water so he could make Nescafe this morning: remembered an hour after he'd gone that I forgot to put the Nescafe in the basket. Luckily, he can live without coffee in the morning!

Mother, your package [for Marian's birthday] arrived last week—Tuesday, I think it was. I haven't opened it, although the temptation has been mighty strong. Was quite pleased to find out the duty was only 35 cents—the man disregarded the earring declaration and called it all underwear! The customs men here are just awful. The one who checked the package Tuesday flung two large boxes off his table onto the floor—just brushed them off to make room for another. Howard has seen one man walk on some packages that were on the floor, and another time he watched as one man casually dropped a box, listened to the sound of breaking glass, and went on about his duties without paying any more attention. So don't send us anything at all breakable!

You asked about books we might like to have. I find cookbooks as fascinating as Daddy does—half the fun of cooking something new is spending an hour or so beforehand deciding what it will be. I once had a glimpse of a book at the Singer store, which gave clues on how to sew anything and everything. Didn't look at it thoroughly, but something of the sort would come in awfully handy. And I would love to have the book that was given partially in the *Journal*—was the name of it *Karen*?—about the little girl with cerebral palsy.

Howard's mother sent me a birthday check, and Monday afternoon I'm going straight to Fogarty's to see if the pretty glass bowls are still there. At Christmastime I saw several lovely things in the stores—all too expensive to buy just for the fun of it. But this may be my opportunity. The bowls look rather Swedish—one is low, wide-mouthed, and has brown lines in a pretty design at the bottom. The other is narrower and higher and has a leaf design in yellow and brown that reminds me of our Tacoma living room draperies.

I'm glad you wrote what you did to H. about doing too much! We both feel an obligation to participate in more here than we normally would at home, just because we don't want people to say, "Look at that American who just earns a salary second to the headmaster and who sits around doing nothing—"; you know what we mean. Poor H. was all wound up last week, and if next week is the same I shall rummage around for my little bottle of phenobarb. I'm so glad he can get out to the Field now. It's good for him to get away from school and turn to the work at the Field itself, which is so important to our future.

My goodness, Mother, but isn't mental control wonderful? In the last few weeks I've been feeling much more settled than before here. I told H. a few nights ago that I'm really going to be proud of us when we get back home. In Tacoma it sounded pretty damned glamorous to say that we were coming here for a year or two. Now that we're here, I find it almost anything but glamorous; certainly the life we lead isn't the gin-and-tonic-on-the-veranda life that many associate with the tropics. But we're sure having fun! We both are glad that we aren't here for just one year (we assume we're here for another) because now half that year is gone, and I'm just beginning to feel at home. I look at the cobwebs on the ceiling and think that it's worth it having them there: I'd rather have cobwebs on the ceiling until I'm ready to get them off, than have a girl here in my way all the time.

I don't think this paragraph makes sense—but maybe you'll understand!

We shall have to concentrate on the coins for Daddy's friend. They are, I think I'm right, the four-pence pieces that are local B.G. coins and that will be called in when the Elizabethan coins are issued. Ah yes, I found the one that I shall send, if H. says I'm on the right track.

Must write to Bee and H.'s family. We are out of the regular stamps, so I'm going to open the envelope I used for a previous letter and insert this, then use a 48-cent stamp. The deadline for mail to the States is Sunday at 10 a.m. Daddy, I do wish you'd get around to having your picture taken. We really do miss your sweet face!

Love to you both, and a kiss from Elizabeth—
Marian

March 7:

Howard returned at about 4 and said the drive back was hellish. He spent most of Friday afternoon waiting for an electrician to come turn on the lights and then for a plumber to come do about the water. By the time they had come, found out the trouble, gone back to their shops for parts, and finally fixed the things, it was dark, so he ate his supper. He collected about a dozen specimens this morning, and says his chief task for a while will be to compile a key to the different families, for without that key it takes him an hour or two to identify each specimen.

March 8:

This afternoon I attacked some more costumes: two yellow tunics for the stagehands to wear, two light blue ones for sailors, and two dark blue ones for sea captains. Mrs. S-D had failed to cut a two-inch bit on the front of each yellow top; I am sure she meant to cut it, but who am I to meddle with her precious costumes? I sewed it up as cut.

It started to rain while I was sewing, and Howard said he'd go pick up Elizabeth and Mabel. He came back, said he couldn't find them, and set out again a little later. While he was gone, Mabel dashed down the street to say that she and Elizabeth were sheltering in a Colonel Haywood's garden and to please tell Mr. Irwin that's where they were. Elizabeth thought the excitement of running from the car to the door in a downpour was great fun and giggled and kicked as Mabel scooted in.

March 9:

Mrs. Sanger-Davies stopped in this morning, about a minute after I'd finished cleaning the front part of the house. She brought a monk's robe and hood for me to stitch, also a pair of blue breeches that had somehow become buried. Mrs. McLaren and I went over at 3 and sewed on some frills and snaps. I tried to cut out some skirts, and succeeded finally, but only after Mrs. S-D had jumped and skittered around in her customary disorganized fashion. Oh dear!

March 10:

Gads—will we be glad when this wretched play is over and done with. Poor Howard has been out so many evenings to rehearsals, and all the bickering that has gone on between various staff members and wives just isn't worth it.

I strolled over to Mrs. S-D's house this afternoon to see if there was anything to do, and she said, "Oh heavens, yes." Luckily, just a few minutes after I arrived, another caller came. So I picked up a few odds and ends and came home!

Tuesday, March 10, 1953, 8:45 p.m.

Dearest Mother—

What a rat race. Howard is at school, doing about the music for a rehearsal, although I expect him home soon. Mrs. McLaren came by this afternoon and we chatted awhile here, then went over to Mrs. S-D's, where Mrs. McL. sewed little rosettes onto breeches and I cut out a black satin skirt.

Mrs. S-D is so disorganized. Of course part of it is due to the fact that her house interior is being painted, and naturally she is a bit concerned about getting the costumes done. But still, it doesn't make for a very peaceful afternoon! At any rate, I couldn't see a clock anywhere, and by the time I got home it was a few minutes after 6 and Howard was feeding Elizabeth! He had to be back at school at 7, so we ate in a bit of a rush.

The bowl I bought with the money from the Irwins is so pretty. It is Czech glass, very simple in design, and it just cries out for gold chrysanthemums or big purple grapes—the band of brown around the bottom I mentioned before is very reddish and looks almost maroon in artificial light.

We got two *Saturday Reviews* today, and in one I opened right to the article on cookbooks. Don't some of them sound wonderful! I didn't tell you that the last time I was killing time downtown waiting for H. I browsed through some books at Fogarty's and came across a cookbook (can't remember the name now) that was illustrated with the same lovely photographs that are in the Carnation cookbook you have—the gorgeous petit fours were used as facings for the cover.

Well, it's about 2:30 Wednesday now! H. wanted to use the typewriter at school this afternoon, so here I am— [handwritten]. Mother, I *love* the earrings, and the slip! The earrings look so cool and fresh, I'm sure they lower my temperature a few degrees. I'm going to keep the slip to wear with my sheer dresses and blouse—my other slips I've ruined (they stick to my back when I get damp, and then rip when I reach out or up for something), but I'm in the process of converting them to half-slips. *And* a knife and fork in our pattern—my goodness, aren't you and Daddy sweet!

Bee sent three precious cards, two containing sequins and a book on gift wrapping that makes me wish Christmas were nearer. It has some good ideas that I'm awfully eager to try.

Howard gave me an essential item that we've done without for six months—a little salt dish. I've sworn countless times at our saltshaker, for the salt won't come out of it, or even out of the big box very easily. This salt dish is silver plate, with a little top, spoon, and a peppershaker and a little sugar shaker—the last two are about two inches high. H. tried to get a set at Christmas but they'd all been sold.

My only real problem at present is obtaining a toilet seat or what have you for Elizabeth. Potties available: (1) plastic, (2) ceramic. Period. I'm sure that being trained on a potty wouldn't warp Elizabeth's personality, but the darned things look so uncomfortable. H. says he can cut down a chair and cut a hole in the seat, so that's what we'll do—the only question is time in which to do it.

Your precious granddaughter is sitting at my feet playing with an old adhesive-tape roll. I've been giving her bread and butter lately—she *loves* it. I break off a little bit, which she picks up and pops into her mouth very handily.

I'm just about to go make a cake—marble, I think—I've never made one but I've always loved them. Living here where bakeries offer bread only (a few cakes, but they aren't good) is the loveliest excuse for baking all the cookies and cakes I want to! But I would love to have a package of brown-and-serve rolls handy, or a dozen cinnamon rolls from MacDickens, now and then.

Many thanks again for the gifties. I think you and Daddy are the dearest, sweetest parents in the world, and for each of you today a special birthday hug and kiss.

Much, much love,
Marian

March 12:

Howard and John went downtown to see about borrowing a loudspeaker system for the music. A man at Bookers had promised it, and they were just checking. They arrived at Bookers to find that the set had already been sent up to Queen's; and as they arrived there, Mr. Sanger-Davies was just telling the men how to set it up—not to Howard's liking, it turned out, so they got it straightened around and set for tonight's rehearsal.

The Ramsarans have a new blow—they must move by the end of April. It certainly doesn't seem fair, when they were promised that they could remain in that barn until fall if they desired. As Margaret says, they hated it but had planned on remaining until June, when they can (they fervently hope) move into the Larthes' house in the compound. They already have a place lined up for the six weeks—a house that is too small, they say. As yet they don't know just how much furniture will be included, and as they have a houseful of Margaret's friend's furniture, we have offered to fill our flat up with whatever we can, until they can get into the Larthes'. Such a mess. Margaret says they'd go back to England in a jiffy, except that John would be out a job, they would have no place to live, and they'd have to pay their own passage back. Worst of all, we suspect that if John were English they'd have been better taken care of.

And the S-Ds are of no help at all on that score. Mrs. S-D has said to Mrs. McLaren that "you have to handle these native people"—meaning the masters—"with an iron glove." And she told Mrs. McLaren that "the Allsopps are West African, you know." The reply to that gem was, "No—they are Guianese." That would be a first-class insult to the Guianese here, who would be as much at home in Africa as I! Mrs. S-D also asks questions like "Is she nice?" and "What color is she?" about all sorts of people. It's almost too much to bear.

March 13:
Mrs. McLaren and I sewed on more snaps and more rosettes this afternoon from 3 until 5, then had a cup of tea. Just odds and ends left to do now.

March 14:
This afternoon I became bogged in that horrible "How can I stand this place for 18 or 30 more months?" mood, which is silly, so I baked a cake and hot cross buns. Took one pan of the buns to Mrs. Patoir, who sent the empty pan up shortly with a dish of coconut ice cream that was truly delicious.

Saturday night, March 14, 1953

Dear Bee—
I'm in a truly repulsive state—didn't get around to a shower this afternoon because I was engrossed in some baking, and before I knew it I had to scurry to fix H.'s dinner at 5. I just finished painting all our books' inside covers with a poison that supposedly will discourage bugs from devouring them. We were starting to find little bugs in some. I didn't do cookbooks or Elizabeth's books—we will just keep an eye on those. There are books spread all over the floor, and the smell alone is enough to discourage the pests. At any rate, I have fumes up my nose and feel itchy all over. Lovely! It's 10:30 and I'm consuming a cup of coffee and a hot cross bun (product of this afternoon's labor) and trying to stay up till H. comes home.

He is at a rehearsal. Tonight they were going to go straight through the play, and it is so *long*. H. expected to be home by midnight. Few of the boys know their lines completely, and yet the play goes on Tuesday night! At least the costumes are all done. The S-Ds have made numerous, if passive, enemies over this darned play. One teacher's wife, an elderly lady who helped with a previous production of *Twelfth Night*, went so far as to say she thought the men should "sabotage" the play—do their worst, so S-D would get the point and try no more productions.

I love the book on gift wrapping. I read through it Wednesday afternoon completely fascinated by the ideas. And the sequins came through without question, so I shall use them on cards and presents and have great sport. Thank you, Bee!

This is a miserable excuse for a letter. I shall type a long one soon—after the play.

With love from we three,
Marian

March 15:
The rehearsal lasted until midnight, all right! Howard said it went quite well, and that the makeup and costumes helped. He was irked that Mr. S-D kept all the boys for 45 minutes after the rehearsal was over at 11:30 so that he could take pictures. He says the boys are all exhausted.

March 16:
Second dress rehearsal tonight. It's hard to believe that after Wednesday night the play will be over; it's been in our minds for only two months, but it seems like ages.

Howard talked to a man in the Finance Office about our income tax and was told that we do pay B.G. tax on our earnings here, but that a directive has to be sent out to someone to confirm it before we can actually do so!

March 17:
Busy day. Howard came home at noon and conveyed a message asking if I could help iron costumes after lunch; he said Mrs. McLaren would stop by for me around 2 and we'd walk over together. As soon as we'd finished eating I tackled my old faithful brown faille suit, in which I arrived in this colony, and which has suffered from various degrees of mold ever since. However, after washing it a few days ago, the mold seems to have vanished, and all it needed was steaming and ironing. This took over an hour, but the results were good.

We ironed until nearly 4:30, then came back here for a cup of tea. I don't know just why I felt so leisurely, but I did—we lingered over our tea for an hour, and then the real rush began.

Howard came home to feed Elizabeth and said that Dorothy Larthe was in a state of despair over the makeup and could I please help her. So after eating a hurried dinner, we're off in about five minutes as soon as Howard finishes changing his clothes. I feel as nervous as if I were actually in the damned play!

Wednesday, March 18, 1953

Dear Family—

Well, kiddies, we've had it! It is 9:15, and here I sit comfortably in my robe while Howard slaves away on the last few minutes of *Twelfth Night*, for tonight's performance started at 6 p.m. (making it a matinee) so he should be home in another hour or so. Our few days of dry weather seem to have left us—it is pouring now as it has much of today, and I have the floor dotted here and there with cake pans, blotters, and a baking powder can: it makes a lovely noise— plink, plink—plank!

I had planned on going to the play last night with Margaret: she was going to get a cab and pick me up. Mrs. McLaren and I did some costume ironing yesterday afternoon and came back here for a cup of tea. At 5:30 Howard came back, said Dorothy (who had volunteered to help with makeup) was apparently expected to do it all herself and was frantic and could I help. I had already told Mrs. S-D that I couldn't help dress the boys because Margaret was coming by for me, but since Dorothy was really desperate I was glad to help her. But—when I got there, I found Joy Allsopp helping with the makeup, and was asked to please help the boys with safety pins, their neck ruffs, snaps, etc. The trouble was chiefly revolving around the fact that Mrs. S-D, in charge of costumes from the word go, was having a dinner party and so couldn't be there to help! I hadn't been to one rehearsal and hadn't seen a single boy in his costume. Well, Malvolio came up with a roll of black material, asked where Mrs. S-D was, and then said she was supposed to make a belt for him out of this material. It was about 7:30 then, the show scheduled for 8. As far as I was concerned, a belt was a belt so I measured off a piece of material, cut it, folded it and pinned it around his middle. At approximately 7:50 the dear lady walked in to check on the boys' costumes, saw the belt, and cried in a truly horrendous voice, "Who cut this?" "Mrs. Irwin did," the poor boy said. Then she bellowed at me, "Did you cut this?" I said yes, and she informed me it was her husband's cummerbund, which she wanted to use to hold Malvolio's pants up! I said I was sorry, but no more. And I'm afraid I really wasn't sorry, for she should have been there in the first place.

QUEEN'S COLLEGE

Presents

William Shakespeare's

"TWELFTH NIGHT"

on

Tuesday, 17th March, 1953, at 8.00 p.m.

AND

Wednesday, 18th March, 1953, at 6.00 p.m.

The play went very well, I thought, and Howard did nobly from the first "God Save the Queen" when the OAG walked in, until the last "GS the Q" at the end. He said there was great pandemonium backstage, for all the boys wanted to stand in the wings and watch all the time, but from the audience it looked fine. The best they've ever done, Howard said, and I can believe it. Really, it was quite a thrill watching the play, with a Chinese boy as Olivia, two little East Indians as Viola and Sebastian, a light-skinned Negro as the Duke, little Patrick Maudsley looking almost anemically white as the page, and the other characters ranging from white to black. Just think—probably not one of those boys has ever seen a professional stage performance.

The masters who've worked on the play are just dead. Mr. Barker, the stage manager, built all the flats [sets], did about curtains and such, and says he hasn't taught a class in three weeks. John is scarcely his old congenial self; he has become very curt. H. said this noon that the masters have all agreed to a proposal: Mr. Beckles is going to read an announcement to S-D at a coming staff meeting, to the effect that, since dramatics is not a curriculum subject, the masters would like to be consulted for their approval before further dramatic endeavors are undertaken. They hope that S-D will add a drama teacher to the faculty—that would be fine!

After the play was over we stood around for a few minutes chatting with Mrs. S-D, and I met the Camerons. You would have thought he'd run the whole show, and all he did was send the newspapers a notice and give an announcement to the radio station.

I'm having fun with my new cookbook. Sunday I concocted a dessert called "Peasant Girl with a Veil"; isn't that *awful*—Howard nearly died! But it sounded good, and was: a mixture of dry bread crumbs and jam, molded and chilled, served with whipped cream. Well, I whipped canned milk, only it wouldn't get stiff, so I added a bit of rum for flavor and the runniness didn't matter. Tonight I baked some fig bars, only I substituted dates for figs. They are delicious—have pineapple in them. Oh yes, I had to use some brown sugar instead of all white, but they still taste darned good. I suppose it is a horrible habit, but I seem to use cookbooks as idea sources and then make my own variations as time and supplies dictate.

I just saw the car go by, so Howard must be taking the Ramsarans home. Margaret was going to take Susan for a while tonight: she saw part of a dress rehearsal and was simply enthralled, and was so quiet and good that M. thought it would be all right tonight.

Mother, in case you're wondering about the check you sent H. to reimburse us for duty, we haven't cashed it yet. The bank is only open until noon and H. just hasn't had a minute to get there in a morning. Bank by mail? Ha! We write out our own deposit slips, in duplicate, and then after the teller counts our money he signs the slip—the machine age hasn't hit B.G. yet.

Our Elizabeth will stand by herself any day now—she loves for one of us to take hold of her hands, so that she can pull herself up. Today she was having her afternoon cup of milk in the kitchen with Mabel, and as I walked by to the shower I looked in and said hello. By George, she said "mama." Such a happy coincidence! She is precious.

Here's Howard, home from the wars. Love and kisses to you all,
Marian

March 18:
I really did enjoy the play, except that it lasted an awfully long time and I got tired of sitting. The boys did very well, and Howard said they required the least prompting last night of any night's rehearsals. We couldn't hear

any prompting at all, and I only caught one long, awkward pause, so I think that was a good score considering the short time the boys had in which to memorize their lines. The costumes looked bright, gay, and elegant—the time was well spent in making them, I guess, if someone will just take good care of them once tomorrow night is over.

Howard said at noon that Mrs. S-D had charged into his lab today while he had a class and asked if I could help this evening. The matinee started at 6 this evening, so we went over at 4:30. I made two pairs of garters and gathered a ruff or two. Mrs. S-D flew in for a while but at 5:15 donned her raincoat and said she had to go to a meeting. I told her I'd have to leave at 5:30, but she didn't seem perturbed. Before she left, she asked me if I'd seen the play last night, and if so, what did I think of it! Talk about a scatterbrain. At any rate, by the time we left to rescue Elizabeth and Mabel from the rain, Miss Dolphin had arrived and asked for something to do.

Margaret and I sat together last night, and I don't know when I've seen anyone as nervous. She practically ruined her program, and rolled and fidgeted with her handkerchief all through the play. I think John did beautifully [as director], considering the limitations and hindrances that he had to battle.

March 19:
Today it is raining as if our few days of sunshine had never existed. Our puddles are larger than ever in the living room, and the tortoises seem to know instinctively when I put a pan on the floor to catch rain water: they go right to it, tip it over, and there we are again!

Margaret, her mother, and I rehashed the play, agreeing wholeheartedly that we are thankful it's over with. Nice to have the men home again.

March 20:
We scurried this morning to get Howard ready for an expedition to the Field; he left after school, at about 3:30, and took baskets and boxes and all sorts of bundles. Much of it he can leave there—the hammock, blankets, hot plate, and such. I bought an electric plate for him, and a broom, and made some rather ugly gray curtains (he said not to make them attractive—they might lure someone in if too good-looking).

So tonight I am on my own—think I shall take an old *New Yorker* and go to bed.

March 21:

All sorts of mail came this morning: first, three magazines; a little later our regular mailman came with a stack of letters and *Time*; and still later another man brought a package of Pocket Books that Mother had sent. He started to explain the sorry looks of the package, which was torn open and bedraggled, and seemed surprised when I said it didn't matter, as there was nothing breakable.

Howard drove up just after I tucked Elizabeth into bed. He had to eat cold pork and beans Friday night, because with three electrical outlets in his room, he hadn't checked before to see if they worked—and they didn't. He had to bring all his gear back to town, since he doesn't trust the simple screens on the windows. Much too easy for someone to break in, if there is anything left that looks attractive. He also brought a large squash, rather like a summer squash.

March 22:

Today is beautifully clear, bright, sunny—warm, of course, but it is a treat compared with the dankness of a rainy day here. I washed our mosquito net this morning and it was dry by afternoon. Since we are scheduled to have rain during the month of April and on and on until August, I feel I should wash and dry as many "extra" items as I can.

March 23:

Howard just left to attend a meeting—this time it is a professional association for teachers, or something. He wasn't too eager, but Ken Maudsley is secretary and told Howard that he is considered a curiosity, so he thought he should be polite at least once and go.

March 24:

The meeting last night was of senior civil servants, and when Howard came in he said that he'd certainly felt out of place. The category "senior" is based on pay, and he said that all the other men there were in their forties and on up to 65. One forthright gentleman asked Howard just what were his qualifications and said that he was certainly young to be in such a position!

Marian and Elizabeth, March 1953

Wednesday, March 25, 1953

Dear Bee—

Just a shortie to wrap around the pictures. Doesn't E. look grown up when she's dressed? So seldom do we see her with a dress on!

I'm going to try to make some orange rolls like the luscious ones we used to get at school. Don't know just how to make the gooey part, but there's nothing like experimentation.

H. is correcting tests. We are also listening to Churchill talk on Queen Mary—the radio went off the air early last night after playing solemn music for an hour or so.[34]

We are also having a drink, and I should set the table. This is a silly little note, but enjoy the pictures!

Much love to you,

Marian

Wednesday, March 25, 1953

Dear Mother and Daddy—

Mother, your package arrived today. *Many* thanks for the bracelet and necklace. I do love white jewelry! I'm wearing the bracelet now. We will take one puzzle to Susan tomorrow—instead of cookies, maybe. I think I'll take the growth charts, too—they should help Margaret with her "Susan is a *big* girl now" campaign. Did you really pay just 20 cents each for the bibs? They're darling—I'm almost tempted to save them. The duty came to only $1.16.

H. is correcting exams now. We'll celebrate his birthday on Sunday, as he's going to the airbase Friday.

I bought a record for him—LP—Rossini overtures, and a plain, conservative white sports shirt that he'd mentioned. Also found a cute lamb for E.'s birthday—chenille, white with brown legs, brown eyes. Really cute. Couldn't find white dollar-sized buttons *anywhere*, though—isn't that strange!

Love and kisses,

Marian

March 26:

Margaret showed me a wonderful little alligator, quite dead and preserved, which she bought at the Self-Help Gift Shop on Water Street. I've seen the sign but never ventured in—there's something about second-story shops that unnerves me. But according to Margaret they have, at times, a good selection of local novelties and curios.

Friday night, March 27, 1953

Mother dear—

Howard is at the airbase and will be back tomorrow for dinner. Because of rain, the games scheduled for today were cancelled and therefore the holiday Monday is called off. But after next week H. will have plenty of time for a month, to be at the Field. I'm sorry you're confused about his endeavors. On some points I myself am none too clear, but here's the scoop: The sandy strip on which H. wants to concentrate runs through the Field and is easily accessible to his quarters there (I'm not sure if it's within walking distance, but there are roads if it isn't). The bush itself is really impenetrable without a knife to hack at the vegetation. And there are snakes and bad bugs there, which [because they're so small] you just can't see. So H. feels that the sandy region is better because the vegetation isn't nearly as dense. Also, it is a natural limitation, which makes his collecting easier.

Today we had a letter from you, and we don't know just why it arrived today; last Friday we had some, too. The plane is supposed to land late on Friday, and our mail should be delivered on Saturday. Can't decide if some mail arrives on another plane, or if carrier pigeons enter into the picture somewhere!

I do so enjoy your letters: so often you write just the things I need to hear; that is confused, but I think both of us write quite a bit the same as we talk (slightly garbled, if this is an example); at any rate, your letters sound just like you. Howard and I feel we're doing right by Elizabeth, but I'm sure you can imagine how I sometimes yearn for the lovely and lengthy conversations you and I have enjoyed, about child-raising in general and Elizabeth-raising in particular. If I hadn't always felt that I'd make a good mother, I think now I might have some doubts: but rest assured, I certainly feel confident on that score. Confidence and all, however, I still miss talking about it sometimes. If there is anything we want to avoid with E., it's being overprotective. To be sure, we comfort her when she falls down, and we do all we can to keep her from serious injury, but we try not to overdo it. If she does fall down or if something frightens her, we pick her up and comfort her, and after about two minutes she's calm and giggling over something else—and back down to the floor or playpen she goes.

Daddy, have you read reviews about *A Brighter Sun*? The author [Samuel Selvon] is a Trinidadian, former pupil of John's. He's quite proud!

Love and kisses to you both—

Marian

Saturday—the Pocket Books arrived today—Goody! Brave Bulls *is the only one I've read and I shall pass it along to someone, no doubt—H. hasn't read it, though. Bee's book on doll making arrived—"How to" books are a godsend to have, and such fun. Many thanks for the books.*

March 27:

Howard is at Atkinson Field tonight, but he'll be back tomorrow, so I shouldn't feel as lost as I do. Ah well, to bed I go, with one of the mysteries Mother sent.

Saturday, March 28, 1953

Dear Family—

I shall do well not to fall asleep—it is warm and I feel drowsy but shall persevere. Bee, about the patterns—thank you so much for finding them! I have no idea about duty, but why don't you just put them in an envelope, mark it "printed matter" in big letters and "dress patterns" in little ones, and try it. We don't know just how wide an interpretation there is on the printed matter level, but I shall be only too happy to pay any duty, as it couldn't be much on such a purchase. The patterns sound cute, and each time I go to town I see some material I'd like. I shall send you bits of whatever I get. On materials, Mother, I'm awfully glad I brought the pieces that you bought for Elizabeth, because, oddly enough, there are very few patterns that are small and dainty, and not much in the way of thin materials. Much of it is regular-weight cotton but in bright, splashy colors and prints.

For Elizabeth's birthday I really don't know what to suggest. A picture would be lovely, Bee—so far, I haven't noticed mold attacking ours. And Elizabeth's own room could be a bit more colorful. I have the two cherub pictures hanging over her crib and have been considering lately the purchase of a cork bathmat that I saw downtown, to use as a pin-up board for all sorts of little pictures.

Mother, I too was just sure that there would be nursery chairs here. But no. I have seen pink plastic potties, blue plastic potties, and white enamel potties. Punkt. Margaret mentioned once that toilet chairs and seats for babies are quite new in England. And as for training little ones here, well, it's simple. I guess babies wear diapers, but toddlers generally (this is not true of the European children but of the native population) wear a little shirt or smock that may reach the knees or stop short at the waist, and that's all! For instance, the five little boys who live behind us appear very neatly dressed when they go to school or downtown, but when they play around outside, they wear these tattered and patched little shirts. We see boys of eight or nine similarly garbed—for some reason, little girls seem to wear dresses with quite modest skirts. But back to the toilet training—I don't think there is any. The nearest drainage ditch or the curb or the sidewalk all serve the purpose. Grown men use the sidewalk with no qualms, and little boys make quite a game of it sometimes. I guess sooner or later they learn the whys and wherefores of toilets and plumbing, but probably there are precious few who have ever seen, much less used, even a blue or pink plastic potty. Yes, Mother, I would love to have you send a little seat. Each time I look at the cute little rocker, I think what a shame it would be to cut it up. (It cost a magnificent $7 B.G., but still it is cute.) And Howard has too little time as it is. I have thought that anytime now we can start on this great training project, but the books both say that 15 months is a good time, and E. is just reaching the stage where she remains dry for two hours at a stretch, several times a day. I'm sure it won't take long, once we start.

Father, about your question concerning restaurants, theaters, etc. Well, kiddo, there isn't much! I don't know of any restaurants downtown. There is the Brown Betty, where one may obtain ice cream, sodas, hamburgers, etc., but it always looks pretty dirty to us. The hotels are available, but from what we've heard the food isn't too sharp. Bookers has a soda bar. The Carib serves meals, but that means a drive of several miles, and after-dark driving is hellish here. There are a good many movie theaters, and some good movies do come. *Five Fingers* was here two weeks ago but was only shown on Wednesday night, when H. had to do about *Twelfth Night*, and Thursday night, when he had students here. We haven't seen a movie since January because Howard has been out so many nights with one thing or another. There are precious few live plays given here; Bishops' High is known for theirs, but this *Twelfth Night* is the first one Queen's has done in several years. There's nothing like little theater or such.

Howard's vacations will be spent, mostly, at the Field. He has the month of April off, and the next one is six weeks in July and August. Heavens, we have no plans! I really think Howard should try to get into a party going to Kaieteur Falls: it sounds awfully rugged, takes ten days to two weeks and a party of sixteen or so. I might be tempted but wouldn't consider leaving Elizabeth for that length of time. It is possible to see the falls by plane, but that is expensive, and everyone who has gone the overland route says that it is the only way to really see them. Sounds like Howard's meat!

Mother, the *Good Housekeeping* booklets are *Cookie, Cake, Cake Decorating*, and *Pie*. I still don't have any issues around—they are really enjoyed here!—so maybe you can look one up to see about the price. Twenty-five cents each, I think, but I'm not sure. And I've seen both cookie press and cake decorator here; it just remains for me to decide whether I want them badly enough to buy them.

Thursday I took a puzzle to Susan's mother, and she was very pleased. Also took the charts to Margaret and the doll-making book to Mrs. McLaren. Poor Mrs. McLaren is such a good, quick seamstress that she makes things too quickly for her own entertainment! She was quite intrigued with the book and will probably make a doll for Susan before I even get started with Elizabeth's birthday doll. Must get to the kitchen and bake a birthday cake for the lord and master!

Love and kisses to you all,
Marian

March 28:
I was in the process of icing Howard's birthday cake when he returned from the Field, earlier than I'd expected. Once again, he ate cold pork and beans; this time he'd taken an extension wire to enable him to use the hot plate, but used it to rewire the old lamp! It showered some this morning, and he said that at one point he sat in the car for an hour waiting for the rain to stop. It must have been fascinating to watch the insects scurrying around to seek shelter and to hear all the birds as they came out for a bath.

Howard had a shower and put on his new white shirt, and we had a drink before dinner, which ended with ice cream and cake.

March 29:
Howard is buried in the last of his exams, trying to finish correcting them. I have helped him with one set, and although it is horrible to find such big holes in the boys' knowledge, we couldn't help laughing as we read "the gonads are located" variously in the head, the neck, behind the heart, etc.

March 30:
Mrs. Patoir came up this morning with some magazines and asked if, when I go through Elizabeth's outgrown clothes, I might find something for the little baby who lives behind us—the last of six little boys there. The child, Noel, was born December 22 and, according to Mrs. Patoir, still can't hold his head up. She and her daughters take care of the baby nearly every afternoon, bathe and powder him, take him out, and so forth. She said today that one daughter has made two little rompers for the baby, because his mother just didn't have any clothes for him. They've also bought cod liver oil and two nursing bottles, after finding out that all his mother had for him was an old soft-drink bottle. And they bought a can of "patent barley" after learning that the child has been fed on "ground tea," or tea made from any old leaves found in their yard! I can't understand how the child lives at all. At any rate, I gave her Elizabeth's little blue shirt and some tattered and

stained bibs that I was ready to throw out, and said I'd buy some vitamins for the baby. Oh yes—she said the family is too proud to accept free food or medicine from the crèche [day nursery]!

The day was lovely, and at last the Queen's College sports event could take place. Dorothy picked me up at a little past 2, and after stopping by for the Archbishop's brother and sister-in-law, we proceeded to the Georgetown Cricket Club grounds, where the event was held. Staff members and families had seats in a "pavilion," or tent, in the middle of the field, so we could see nearly everything that went on. Although I've seen few track events at home and know very little about the fine points, it seemed to me that only a few boys had anything that could be termed style or finesse in running, jumping, or taking hurdles. Howard concurred and said he thought there was only one boy who showed any real promise at all. Howard was really sunburned afterward, for as a field judge he was smack in the sunshine from 12:30 until 6. At 3:30 tea was served to all of us in the pavilion, although something cold would have been more suitable as far as we were concerned. Miss Dolphin was in charge of that, and she'd done very well—we had meat patties, little cakes, sausage rolls, guava tarts, bread and butter, and other little goodies.

April 1:
Howard has gone to one of those horrible end-of-term staff meetings. He said at lunch that scarcely anyone has finished his reports, but the meeting still stood. Tonight he is going to give a talk before the Georgetown Science Club—his impressions of B.G., why he's here, the Fulbright scheme, etc. etc.

April 3:
Good Friday. Here, as in England, hot cross buns are baked only for this day; we left an order with our baker for six. They were delivered yesterday, and I'm afraid we're a bit disappointed. They are just little round loaves of bread dough containing a few raisins, with a cross of dough placed on the top. Rather hard but filling: we could only eat two each, a mere beginning with buns as we used to know them. H. and I agree that the ones I made a few weeks ago were much more to our taste.

All the regular radio programs have been replaced with somber religious music today. We have had chorales and masses since breakfast, with only the BBC news as interruptions. The number of radios audible was diminished: evidently the people downstairs, next door, and behind us prefer their music a bit more secular.

Friday, April 3, 1953

Dear All—

I can't believe this is Friday. In fact I'm utterly confused: here, yesterday was Holy Thursday and a holiday all afternoon. Everything is closed today, and will be tomorrow and Easter Monday as well. I was unconscious of the holiday approaching, so Howard did no weekend grocery shopping in advance, and now I'm holding my breath that our stores will last until Tuesday!

Just as I thought, we received package notices last Monday, and Howard picked up both parcels at noon. H. says he'll write you this weekend. Bee, we both love the record—it's so pretty! It arrived in perfect shape, too. And Mother, the socks are grand—I love the plain cotton ones with the clocks! Yesterday Elizabeth wore her new red ones when we went to Margaret's and, naturally, everyone commented on how lovely they are. She was quite intrigued, too. How I love to see the pretty cards and ribbons and papers. I have started to reuse both ribbons and paper, and it really does iron out as we are always told by the magazines. I took some sugar cookies and Easter bunny cookies yesterday in a box that I'd covered with some of your pink paper, Bee. Looked quite fetching.

Did I tell you that last Sunday I made an Easter egg for Elizabeth? Lavender cotton, stuffed, trimmed with pink, blue, and chartreuse rickrack. It's really cute, and I think she'll enjoy chewing on it. And just last evening I finished a doll for her. She has blonde hair, blue eyes (no chin—the only thing about that pattern which I don't like, but next time I'll remedy that), a red-and-white check dress and brown shoes. Bee, don't ever think I'm too busy for "handcrafts." There's nothing I enjoy more! You'd laugh to see the scraps of paper, tinfoil, etc. that I'm now saving for gift wrapping.

School is all over now. Yesterday the staff had its last meeting with S-D, and it appears that that gentleman has calmed down a great deal. Of course it remains to be seen if his actions will follow his words. He won't say definitely whether *Trial by Jury* is going to come off next term; Miss Dolphin is planning to have rehearsals during the vacation, so you'd think he'd have to make up his mind pretty soon.

Elizabeth succeeded a few days ago in opening one of my kitchen cupboards; now she makes a beeline for it every time she's in the kitchen. She pounds on the top of the Dutch oven, leans over it and reaches for an old Klim can, and then plays contentedly with the Klim can top for quite a while. As soon as I close the door, though, back she goes to open it again. And just yesterday morning, I put her in her own room for a while as I always do. She yowled for a few minutes, and then after a pause I heard her padding down the hall. I suppose it sounds strange to speak of a triumphant tone in the sound of knees and hands hitting the floor; but hers was a triumphant crawl if ever there was one! Now we slam the door and shut it tight—and does she resent it.

Warm today—now for a shower. Love to you all—

Marian

April 4:

This morning at 2:45 I was awakened by noises outside, and glancing out our bedroom window I saw great clouds of red smoke. I woke Howard, and we both got out of bed to peer out the window. Luckily the wind was blowing in the other direction. We learned this morning that the house that burned is just a few blocks away. I was surprised at the number of people who went dashing down the street to watch. Bicycles and cars went by in large numbers. Everyone was excited, and from upstairs we heard Mrs. Ogle cry, "Oh my God, what a terrible fire." Actually the fire was pretty bad: it ruined the house, leaving only a shell of the main floor and completely demolishing the top two floors. No one was hurt in it, however.

April 5:

Easter Sunday, and it seems as if our long, long wet season is about to begin. Off and on all day we had sudden, hard showers.

After lunch I baked cookies, a cake, and both cinnamon and plain rolls for Howard to take with him tomorrow. Yesterday the bread boy brought bread to last until Tuesday evening, and I know it will be too stale to be enjoyable. So—rolls.

Mabel had the day off, so we three went for the first ride we've had together in a long time. The weather wasn't too good but Elizabeth didn't seem to care. We drove almost to Mahaica, which was farther than I'd been before. It is such a strange country: monotonous in that it is the same everywhere, yet arresting in the way the lush but flat, green land is broken at intervals by the spindly palms and the flat-topped, windblown trees that we saw in a few places. And the vivid hibiscus, magenta and scarlet, is magnificent among all the green vines and leaves.

April 5, 1953

Dear folks—

The term ended peacefully for which we are all glad. S-D saw the light at last and pressed no further. The only tension of the staff meetings arose when John Ramsaran announced rather bluntly that he would not direct *Merchant of Venice*, which S-D has asked for next year. No one volunteered, so time will tell. Miss Dolphin, the music mistress, is trying to press me into service on the next production, Gilbert and Sullivan's *Trial by Jury*, but until the producer-director is selected, it's strictly hands off (a job I know I could have but I definitely will not take—I'm already two weeks behind in all my forms).

Enclosed is the program for the annual track heats (here called Athletic Sports), which were held at the Georgetown Cricket Club grounds, not on March 20 but on the 30th. As a judge I had a fairly easy but interesting time. Although only one record was broken, the boys did fairly well. The "Late for School" race was interesting but ended in near disaster for one boy. The boys place at specified locations on the track their shoes, their shirts, their ties, and their bicycles. All articles in each pile are thoroughly mixed. They are started, run to the first pile, select their shoes, then on to the second for their shirts, then to their ties, and finally their bikes. The object is to reach the finish line as soon as possible "properly dressed." The first boy over the line was disqualified—shirt tail out. So was the second—his tie was loose. But the next fellow was O.K. and won. So jubilant was he that he looked around while his bike was still going at a good clip, and before he looked back he had run slam-bang into a post, which hurled him and the bike up into the air. When he came down (on his head) the bike was on top of him, pedals and sprocket in his ribs. But for a torn shirt and temporary absence of breath, he was all right, thank the Lord. Tragedy for him was the condition of the bike, which he had borrowed for the occasion.

The conduct of the crowd was something new to me. While most everyone is nice and well behaved individually, the crowds seem to bring out the worst behavior. The guardrails in front of the stands were torn down, the broadcasting booth (not in use on this day) was damaged, and when the prizes were awarded (not by Gutch, as on the ticket, but by the Archbishop of the West Indies), the mob all but snapped the two-inch ropes used to restrict onlookers. More than once the police had to flail individuals for blatant disregard of common-sense regulations. (They have short sticks with braided leather thongs extending for two inches or so.)

On the program you'll notice the division of the school into six "houses" (each named for a former principal), which are somewhat like clubs or fraternities, each including a few boys from all levels and each most functional in athletic competition—our house, Weston, won this contest.

Tomorrow I go to the airbase for four days, per my weekly plan during this vacation. Next Sunday we go to the Allsopps' for a sort of record soirée, and the following Sunday Mabel will be here all day so that Marian and I can go to the base for the day (a nice change for her).

I gave my talk to the B.G. Science Club last Wednesday. I really wasn't in the mood, but everyone seemed to enjoy listening to an American, even though they weren't too sure of what he was trying to tell them. Unfortunately, the reply (British custom at all such meetings) was given by an American criticizer: claimed most Americans came here for what they could get, leaving nothing; hoped I wouldn't be placed in that "lengthy column of infamy" when I leave. Oh well.

Love to all,

Howard

April 6:

Howard succeeded in leaving at shortly after 8 this morning, which I considered remarkable in light of all the paraphernalia that had to go along. He said he'd probably spend today and tomorrow working on his keys and begin his collecting Wednesday. I can't help but have visions of him without enough food; the only thing I forgot to include was a package of dates.

Before he left, we looked from the kitchen into the living room and saw Elizabeth standing in the playpen, all by herself! My, but we're proud! We went in to her, and after a few minutes I helped her sit down; she looked a bit unsure of herself, as if the floor might be a long ways off.

April 7:

Mrs. McLaren came over at 4 to have tea with me, and we had a lovely time. At 6 Elizabeth came home, so I fed her, and then invited Mrs. McLaren to have supper with me. She had a choir practice at 7:30, and I saw no point in her going home. So we had scrambled eggs and sausages and talked awhile longer, and it was 8 before we even thought to look at the clock. She's going to teach me to crochet—here, at least, there is no excuse for lack of time. She worked in an art needlework shop for a time and while there learned all sorts of fancy embroidery. This is my chance! She told me that John is growing increasingly unhappy about his treatment at Q.C. Mr. S-D has on at least one occasion lumped him in with the local masters, who've had very little training and earned no degrees, instead of with the white men. It is infuriating, for what they really need here are natives who can win the respect of the local people; and too many of the white men just don't give a damn about that. John has all sorts of qualifications and degrees—including one in theology that I hadn't known about.

Wednesday, April 8, 1953

Dear All—

Sunday we're going to the Allsopps' for the afternoon and will take some records with us. Richard is a bit strenuous and dramatic, but if everyone else keeps calm, it's fine.

And the following Sunday we had vaguely planned on leaving Mabel here with Elizabeth and going to Atkinson Field for the day. But darn it all, I just don't know. Just lately, Elizabeth has shown signs of wanting definitely to be where I am, and I don't know that I want to leave her for a whole day. Of course, she does see Mabel every day and I'm sure she loves her, but it wouldn't be the same. This afternoon, for instance, she was in the kitchen with Mabel while I was reading in the bedroom. I got up and opened the squeaky closet door, and I could hear her give her little cry or mutter of pleasure, and in a few minutes her little face peeked through the doorway. And twice in the last few days when I've gone downstairs to answer the door, she has been very worried, and just as relieved when I reappear. We may decide to take her along with us.

Goodness but I'm uninspired. I think I have drugged my mind with mysteries, as I've been reading furiously these last few days. I shall write again, though, in time to catch the weekend mail.

Love and kisses,
Marian

April 8:

This is the sort of weather I really loathe: muggy and hot, with no breeze to speak of. I felt uncomfortably hot and wet this morning by the time I'd finished feeding Elizabeth her breakfast, about half an hour after I'd gotten up! And after I'd done the dishes and cleaned I was really a wreck.

April 9:
Unfortunately, today has been just as warm and still as yesterday.

Howard came home about 6, tired and unnerved from a typical close call that occurred on the way home. He said he and another man just barely managed to stop their cars at a right-angle bend on a bridge; the other man was going much too fast on that road.

The food held out fairly well, considering the lack of refrigeration. The rolls were a bit moldy today, Howard said, but not bad. He's decided to buy a cot: the hammock is fine for short naps, but Howard says he woke up about 3 and couldn't get back to sleep. Tried the floor, and despite a few sore bones, woke up after a good sound sleep. He's collected 75 specimens now, which I think is very good in the little time he's been working on it.

Howard is going to take me out to the Field a week from Sunday. He says there is scarcely a square foot of ground without ants on it. Insects are bad, but he keeps them away by chain-smoking. Three-foot lizards are around, too. These I must see!

April 10:
Oh Lordy. Today was another hot and sticky one. Decided I was silly not to wear shorts in such weather, despite convention. Howard encouraged me, and I was much more comfortable. There is something about slip and skirt sticking to legs that is annoying, especially when topped by a blouse plastered to the back!

April 11:
Not long ago I asked the Ramsarans about shoe repairing here, and they said the only place they knew about was the Bata shoe store and that its work was no good at all. So today I asked Mabel where Mrs. Beckles has her shoes repaired and learned that she has a shoemaker who comes around. Mabel said she'd tell the Beckleses' cook, and that the cook would get in touch with the man.

It is pouring—maybe all the muggy weather was just leading up to this, and the weather will be better when it stops. No walk for Elizabeth, though. The sky is very dark, and I have the light on even though it's just about 4.

Mrs. Patoir is coming up later on, and Howard and I are going to a movie. Hope the rain lets up a bit or we'll never hear the sound track!

April 12:
The less said about last night's movie, the better. It was ghastly—Mario Lanza at his best, I guess. We were both embarrassed at the Hollywood portrayal of the U.S. Army as a bunch of nitwits.

We had a lovely afternoon with Joy and Richard. We went to their house right after lunch and played records. Everybody seemed to enjoy the music up loud, so conversation was carried on at the shouting level.

Joy and I got involved in a discussion of handicrafts, and I asked her about buying local wares. She gave me some good advice: Don't buy at the department stores, for their stuff is just second grade. The Allsopps know a man who does almost anything with wood—trays, coasters, ashtrays, etc.—and Joy will take us there whenever we want to go. She also knows a parole officer at the prison who will be able to get some of the lovely inlay work that the prisoners do with wood.

We had such a grand time that we were nearly an hour late in getting home! But Mabel had gone ahead and fixed Elizabeth's dinner and was feeding her when we arrived. Such a blessing, not having to worry about Elizabeth.

April 13:
More rain today. Howard splashed around doing some errands, then left for Atkinson Field at 9. My own day has been quiet and uneventful, broken by the return of my white linen shoes. The man picked them up yesterday morning, and for 36 cents I now have new heel lifts. I'm frightfully impressed by the service and the price—just hope they wear well.

Tuesday, April 14, 1953

Howdy!
My, it certainly is amazing how a slightly different weekend can bring one out of ye olde rut. Howard returned Thursday evening with a reddish-brown face and another addition to our rapidly growing household establishment. This one is a baby tortoise—not really a baby since we guess it is about two years old, but he's only about four inches long. And how he scoots across the floor—looks like a mechanical toy. Our only problem concerning Number Three is that he'd be awfully easy to step on, and there is also danger of him falling through the banister railings and landing on his noggin downstairs. He's really cute. Howard couldn't resist bringing him

home, and now I can't resist letting him stay! I say "him," but we don't know just what he actually is. His shell is still a bit soft and there is no depression in the bottom at all.

Well, I have taken the downward path and have succumbed to wearing shorts in the morning. A few days last week seemed so damned hot that I nearly perished, and Howard told me what the hell, this *is* our private home. According to this morning's paper, the temperature Sunday and yesterday at 8 a.m. was 77.8° and 76.8° respectively, and at 2 p.m. they were 85.1° and 84.0°. Maximum yesterday was 86.9°. Not what I'd call cool. Elizabeth is the only one who is truly sensibly dressed.

Bee, we received Lynn's letter [a college friend's request for general information about B.G. to share with her classroom students], and I'm going to answer it this week. H. is working on some of the background material for me—took some books and stuff with him to the Field. I'm sending to you a booklet called *Children of Guiana*, which we thought very interesting, and wanted to buy copies for you all. However, we got two and then discovered that the stock was gone. So—after you go through it, would you see that Lynn gets it for as long as her class wants it, with the understanding that it eventually gets back to you so that you can relay it to the parents. It gives a lot of information in a simple style and will, we think, be ideal for Lynn.

Saturday night we saw Mario Lanza in *Because You're Mine*. We were acutely nauseated, disgusted, and embarrassed. I hope none of you saw it, but if you did you know why I say "embarrassed": if the dopes in Hollywood knew the impression such films leave in foreign countries—well, maybe they do. This one was about the Army, the typical Technicolored Army with Spring Byington making a fool of the commanding general, who was her husband. Ah well.

Mother, next time you're downtown, will you please check to see if the Turkknit people sell washcloths separately? I don't know what's happened to E.'s little washcloths, but the white ones are gray and the pink ones are just about the same. The towels are in splendid shape, but if you can find white ones with pink and green binding, and plain pink ones, I'd appreciate your just getting them and keeping them for me. These will do all right as long as we're here, and new ones might get just as bad—but they really do look repulsive.

We've decided to go to Atkinson Field next Sunday, and Howard says it is definitely no place for Elizabeth. Too many insects, too hot, no place for a good nap, etc. Since I hated to disturb her routine to the extent of having

Mabel do things I usually do for Elizabeth, we're not going to go until about 10, after orange juice and bath. After that, E. just plays until lunch, and since Mabel has fed her several times I have no doubts about that. We'll be home in time for dinner. H. says it's high time I had a change of scenery!

Last Sunday we had such a good time. Right after lunch we went to the Allsopps' and proceeded to play records (loudly) until after 6, with just a break for tea. I nearly went mad, because we had to shout to talk, but I had taken some sewing (E.'s birthday dress) so took refuge in that. Howard, Richie, and Joy had great fun comparing three different versions of Rossini, plus many other old favorites. Howard had his first good, meaty discussion of the technical side of music in months, and everyone was pleased as punch because we four seem to be at about the same stage of appreciation and enjoyment.

Clifford and Betty Evans are giving a talk and demonstration on archaeology at the B.G. Science Club meeting this Friday, and both of us have been invited to attend. I'd like to hear them.

Elizabeth loves to stand up—holding onto playpen, chairs, beds, anything at all. Sitting down is still something of a challenge, and she always waits until the last possible moment and then just plops down, looking quite startled. She loves to be sung to, and since I heard a record of "Mr. Grandfather's Clock" not too long ago, I can sing that to her now. She loves it, and I'm eagerly waiting for the day when she can do the "tick tock."

I must go do about dinner. Not that there's much to do about when H. isn't home, but I hate to keep E. waiting.

Much love and a kiss to each of you—

Marian

The election is the topic here now—we expect some excitement on the 27th— Election Day!

[Enclosed with the letter was an undated clipping from an unidentified newspaper:]

GENERAL ELECTION EQUIPMENT SENT TO NORTH WEST

Work at the BPI and Registration Headquarters reached a new peak yesterday as the full staff joined in the sending out of General Election equipment to the Returning Officer for the North West District.

There was only one hitch—the late arrival of the essential "small things" which had to be prepared and processed outside the office.

This hitch was another of the contributory factors to the Tarpon leaving Port Georgetown more than half an hour behind schedule.

The Tarpon steamed away with five packing cases of election material, estimated at around 250 lbs. The cases contained 134 ballot boxes for the four candidates in the area. Each of the 28 polling stations will have a box for each candidate.

Then there were things such as blue denim screens, spring rods, posters, screw hooks, rubber bands, clips and even pins, all of which are necessary for the election. There were also such things as sealing-wax, matches, candles, and the like.

It was emphasized that for the want of one of these things a whole election might be lost, and perhaps the colony put to thousands of dollars expense.

Election Office is going all out to leave as little as possible for the Returning Officer to do.

The five packing cases should be in the hands of the Returning Officer, North West District, by Wednesday morning. Arrangements have been concluded for all the presiding officers to meet him in the afternoon and discuss their plan of operation. In some cases that day would be the first and the last that they would be meeting the Returning Officer before polling day. In others it takes more than a week to cover the distance between the outpost and the Mabaruma headquarters.

The 134 ballot boxes sent are all of uniform size. They are eight inches by five by five. On the face of each of them there has been mounted the name of [one] of the four candidates, a recent photograph of him, the symbol he has drawn, as well as the colour. These four different kinds of mounts are necessary to guide candidates who cannot read and write. And there are many in the North West District.

In between the day's hectic preparations, the office had to attend to details affecting candidates and voters in the different constituencies.

A check-up has disclosed that the radio-telephone services between the City and the "bush" are also at a new high. Most of these are calls to and from Returning Officers who want small and large points cleared up.

April 15:

Life seems awfully simplified when Howard isn't home. Somehow I find time to do all sorts of extras—silver and copper polishing mainly. Today I went through my closet and washed a dress (brand new—I've never worn it) that had that awful moldy smell in it, also a blouse. After lunch I went through the trunk in our bedroom and checked on all our linens and blankets. They're doing fine—no casualty in the lot, except the beautiful quilt that Howard's grandmother made, which has a slight odor about it. When Elizabeth woke up I went through the trunk in her room. I found a couple of white shirts of Howard's and blouses of mine that were in an awful state—they'd turned yellow every place, apparently, where they'd been subjected to perspiration when worn. They'd been put away clean, but that doesn't seem to make much difference.

April 16:

My, but it was good to see Howard this evening! Margaret, Susan, Elizabeth, and I were standing by the Parade Grounds watching a practice parade (the Queen's birthday is next Tuesday, and there will be a big whoop-de-do), and we spotted the car as Howard turned the corner into Parade Street. He certainly is getting tanned.

April 17:

We had received an invitation a few days ago to attend the Evanses' lecture on archaeology at the B.G. Science Club meeting tonight, and I was looking forward to it. But Howard had a stamp club meeting, so I stayed home and finished a Perry Mason thriller.

Friday, 17th April 1953

Dear Sister-in-law,

This is the slacker writing, conscience-stricken that he has received and not acknowledged [birthday gifts]. (Incidentally, he's having a rum-and-lime, so he's not fully responsible for the following—his wife mixed the drink.) Respighi did nobly with "The Pines of Rome" and "The Fountains" thereof—in fact my receipt of the record inspired an interesting conversation over the customs counter in the P.O. It seems the clerk (locally "clark") is something of an armchair musician himself, radio-wise at least, and it further seems that Radio Demerara has passed up Respighi as good listening fare and in consequence, our friend had never heard of the gent from Italy. He read the comment on the back of the envelope while I drummed a few fingers on his polished counter, and then he told me of a collection of 600 78's for sale at a dollar each—I told him my pockets are lined with cotton, not gold, or even silver. Thanks anyhow.

Ah, life in Georgetown. As you walk in (preposition is "in," not "down" or "on" as in U.S.) Water Street, the loitering fellows with the darker skin leer, some in hopes of a handout, others in disgust, still others in despair. For B.G.'s population is growing, thanks to DDT, but job opportunities are not. So they wait for the next ship to pull up the muddy Demerara and scramble to her side hoping to be called aboard as stevedores.

Shall we go the rounds? Let's pretend this is Friday morning and we're going to shop for the week. We drive down Main Street and do our damnedest to avoid the cyclists, some riding three abreast (two abreast is the legal limit). At the Post Office we drop our wife's latest letter through the shiny aluminum slot and pick a few stamps. The counterman, locked in a little cage, squints over his glasses and is sometimes puzzled with our accent. But, since all is basically English, we finally get our stamps and make our way to Stabroek Market (see 12-cent stamp on envelope). Stabroek is something of a pageant, reflective of the "Old" Georgetown, as we have been told so often. As we walk in we quickly become aware that it is dark, dank, and in fact doesn't smell very good. In the back are the fruit merchants, their produce spread all over the concrete floor. They say nothing but glance disapprovingly if you walk by. They all have the same things—it's awfully hard to decide who to deal with. But we have our favorite fellow, who does a little more than you expect—gives you an extra sapodilla or tells you in (much?) confidence that his grapefruit are no good this week, go to Ramcharry, his are better. Then there's the black woman whose garb evokes Aunt Jemima—you pick out a bunch of her bananas and she grunts, "Two shillin'," you pay, and that's that. On to Bookers.

Bookers Amalgamated Groceries has the clubby air that British shops are reputed to have. In contrast to American groceries, we find the place swarming with clerks—yet you must expect to wait quite awhile here. We find that's all because of the division of labor imposed on the staff as a sort of security measure. One girl fills our order and makes out a slip; then she calls out, "Sign de bill!" At length a gentleman of some portliness appears and says, "Good mahning. How you keeping?" He affixes his initials and leaves. Then the clerk calls, "Cash, cash boy!" An emaciated little fellow with slicked hair takes our money and then manages to get back with our change. Over at the meat counter there's nothing but lamb and mutton, very rarely beef and liver. We're surprised to see they have an electric band saw to cut bones, something that many of our markets at home didn't have.

Over on Camp Street is Yong Hing's Self-Service market, the only one of its kind in this city. As we walk in we are scrutinized by a girl who asks us to leave any shopping bags or other vessels at her table until we've paid for our purchases. The goods are laid out in neat rows. In the back are three old refrigerators, a Kelvinator, a G.E., and a Frigidaire, in which we find butter (from New Zealand), margarine (from Trinidad), and local eggs and bacon. The labels on the cans are a study in international advertising, some with as many as three languages. Finally we wheel our carriage to the counter, pay, and head for home.

Well, it's time to eat, so down goes the pen.

Love,

Howard

Hi!

After reading H.'s letter to you, I wonder just how strong I made that drink! We do like "The Pines" so much. We hope to take it to the Allsopps' before long so we can hear it on a console model—makes a great difference.

The patterns arrived today—they're both just right. I won't be able to sew for a few weeks—the Ramsarans are moving next week—but maybe I can get the material and cut them out. Doing E.'s little dresses is good practice for me in following patterns. I need it: just yesterday I discovered that the first two dresses I made for her close "boy fashion" in back—wrong side lapped over!

Dinner dishes are calling.

Love,

Marian

April 18:

I fully intended to write some letters after lunch, but it was so still and muggy that I just sat, read, and fanned myself. Howard was at school all afternoon with his pupils, and around 4 I got up pep enough to do some baking.

April 20:

A day like yesterday is so very refreshing. Howard and I left here at 10, leaving Elizabeth with Mabel, with few qualms. We arrived at Atkinson at 11 after a drive that Howard said was much calmer than usual during the week. We walked through the building where he has his room, and I was really taken with the American plumbing and hardware. The building is a mess; upstairs there are all sorts of papers that are just blown around on the floor, and downstairs there's a supply room that never was completely emptied. Behind boxes of stencils and photographic papers and blueprint paper, we found three empty beer bottles. Then we had our lunch and went out to see the Field. We drove on old runways and got out to investigate an old wrecked plane, which made us both feel sad. We also stopped to take pictures beside an old clump of bamboo that made the weirdest wailing and creaking noises. Then we followed another road, which led to the Madewini Creek, finally getting out to walk the last few yards to the creek since Howard didn't trust the sandy road. It's a pretty little creek, with water the color of very strong tea, and when the sun shone on a shallow bit we could see that the sand in the bottom was truly white. The huge leaves and tangled vines practically grew into the water—there was very little bank.

We walked up the road on the other side of the creek, but it was awfully hot and as far as I was concerned, each step took an effort. Since we both felt sleepy, we drove back to Howard's office, and I stretched out in the hammock and Howard took the cot—and we slept until 4! It was quiet (not even yowling kiddies, which H. said is most unusual) and cool, and our nap was really refreshing. We drove around the Field a little more and then headed for home.

The dirty children and scrawny dogs one sees along the road into town still depress me. Though everyone seemed dressed in Sunday best, there were still those awful shacks that are all askew and from which the palm thatch roofs always seem to be sliding off.

We got home just as Mabel was feeding Elizabeth her supper. Mabel said E. didn't cry at all but did look around for us when they came in from their walk.

At 8:30 Howard picked up the Evanses from the Woodbine Hotel and brought them over for the evening. They were to leave this morning on the 6 a.m. plane, and their thoughts were largely taken up with the 50-odd crates they've been packing and getting off. I felt as if a breath of fresh air had been wafted about after they left. So many of the people we know here think of B.G. as a hellhole, or "hardship duty," as Jorgensen called it. I know Howard doesn't need the encouragement, but it certainly does me good to hear fellow Americans talk about the wonderful opportunities available here for research. Then, too, they said that they've been in cities in Brazil twice the size of Georgetown that had only uncertain electricity and water supplies. They think that Georgetown is quite a decent city—but they also said it seemed to be warmer here than any other place they've been in the colony.

April 20:
I think our little girl has finally learned the secret of sitting down. This afternoon, as I was drying my hair in the living room, I watched her stand up and then sit down by falling first to her knees.

Howard left for Atkinson at 10. Forgot his toothbrush.

Tuesday, April 21, 1953

Dear All—

Howard has just a week left of his vacation and is taking advantage of it—he went to the Field yesterday and will come back Thursday. Sunday he will take three of his 6th Form boys out to spend the night—Ramphal, Phillips, and Mekdeci. Eventually, he will take all the 6th Formers out who want to go: we're continually amazed at the number of people who've never even been that far from home.

I certainly enjoyed going last Sunday. We left at 10, just as soon as I'd finished bathing Elizabeth. The drive out was much easier than usual, according to Howard, as there were comparatively few vehicles, humans, and animals on the road. Also, it hadn't rained hard in days so the road wasn't boggy as it sometimes is. H. showed me through the building where his room is. It's just like thousands of other U.S. Army buildings, except that there are no windows at all—just screens. Upstairs, the building was equally divided between two large offices, with darkroom and john in between. Downstairs, the building is chopped into smaller offices, and H.'s is one of those at an end. His own john is just through two other rooms; unfortunately, he has to go upstairs (no lights up there) in order to wash his hands since the basins downstairs were removed. After we ate, we drove all over the base, and then to Madewini Creek. The huge, three-foot leaves of some plants and tangled vines practically grow into the water. We walked around a little, but the air was heavy and hot. All around the Field are little dirt roads leading to clearings, some with cement foundations still standing. Others have been jackhammered and taken away for rubble. It has the appearance of a ghost town, despite the fact that the Field is very much in use.

The Doctors Evans came Sunday evening and we certainly did enjoy talking to them. They were to leave Monday morning for New York and have been frantically trying to get their 50-odd cases of specimens packed and ready for shipment. What I appreciated most of all was hearing affirmation from Americans of the almost unlimited opportunities here for research. Lord knows Howard believes in it firmly, but I don't know of anyone else we know here who takes that attitude. Every once in a while I lose sight of the real reason we're here, and get bogged down in the petty routine of tropical housekeeping. And then we talk to people like the Evanses, and by George I know it's grand that we're here, and it takes the curse off the ants and the mildew.

Our Elizabeth is certainly growing up. She's discovered the "sh" sound and uses it a lot in long conversations which I'm sure have some meaning, but just what that meaning is I'm afraid I don't know! Her bath time is as good as a circus now. In the last few days, she's learned to slide way down on her back, letting the water get into her ears and almost onto her face. The only trouble is that washing her becomes a bit messy as I try to hold her up and she just relaxes into the water! Of course, when I want to rinse off her hair, she decides to sit up and just won't go back, thank you.

The Ramsarans are moving on Friday, and Thursday afternoon I will help to pack china and books. I hope Elizabeth behaves herself. We're going to keep their piano and huge, uncollapsible baby buggy downstairs. The piano has deteriorated some and Margaret feels all the moving around doesn't help any; after they move into the Larthes' house in June (they hope), they will have it repaired. And then we will move the table that's here in our study out into the tortoises' quarters, where it really is cooler and breezier, and put in the study the furniture that Margaret's friend Joan left with her when they went on leave to England. There are two chairs, a settee, a bookcase, and some little tables that I know of. Complicated, isn't it?

We sent a huge envelope of stuff about the colony off to Lynn Langtry the other day [for use with her grade school students]. It was fun doing it, and we ended by enclosing a newspaper, a dollar bill, some coins and stamps, and many pictures.

It's muggy and maybe will rain soon. Think I shall get a glass of cold water and relax.

Love to you all,

Marian

Daddy—H. is still waiting to hear from the local government about his tax. The Legislative Council has to pass a bill or something.

April 21:

Today has been pleasantly disorganized. Soon after breakfast I noticed great hip-hurrah going on in the Parade Grounds—bands, police, militia, horses, and all. I had just (luckily) cleaned up the tortoises' tower when Margaret, Mrs. McLaren, and Susan came by at about quarter to 9, asking if they could watch from our windows: Today is the Queen's birthday, and in her honor a rather elaborate parade was held. There was a large crowd that filled Parade Street up near Mercy Hospital. We had a good vantage point and could see all the men and horses as they marched down the field. The Governor (we have a new one, Sir Alfred Savage from Barbados, who arrived a week ago) was there in his blue uniform and hat with the tall white ostrich plumes; he and his wife arrived, and left, in his big Buick with a mounted escort carrying lances. In front of the car rode four men, plus a fifth on a lovely white horse. This one was the bugler, and he really blew flourishes!

After the Governor had reviewed the troops, the National Anthem was played. Then the Union Jack was lowered and the Queen's Colours were run up and the National Anthem played again. Then the Union Jack was returned, and of course was saluted again with the National Anthem. After that, His Excellency left and the parade was over. Generally there is a reception at Government House following a Birthday Parade, but because the court is in mourning for Queen Mary, there is no such function this year. As we watched the people stroll by, it seemed that standard dress for those on the dais had been black and white dresses for the ladies and gray suits for the men. We all clucked at one woman who wore a red belt.

April 22:

After yesterday's beautiful weather, today it has poured. I had to spread out all the old blotters and cake pans again, and even discovered that the sleeves of two jersey dresses were soaked again from the leak in my closet. My lunch was interrupted by Miss Osborn's arrival, and I must say she was remarkably silent after seeing the puddles and the sopping sleeves. The carpenter came in with her, and he thinks he knows what the trouble is in the closet. I hope so—I'm sick and tired of wet clothes.

April 23:
Elizabeth and I walked over to the Ramsarans'. They all looked tired—it's frightfully hot weather in which to be moving. I was prepared to help pack dishes and books but found that nearly everything had already been taken out. The minister of John's church had lent him a car, and using that they'd managed to move out nearly all the small things.

April 24:
Scurried around this morning to get lunch ready for the Ramsarans at noon. Howard came home from the marketing with a sad tale: no meat and no oranges. Evidently the ship from Trinidad didn't arrive on time! Anyway, he bought a small chicken (we discovered again that its crop was full of rice; Howard was provoked and took it back to Yong Hing's to get some money refunded), and I made chicken pies.

Even though this move is fairly well organized, the Ramsarans all looked tired. Mrs. McLaren helped me with the dishes while Margaret relaxed a bit, and the men chased around trying to find a lorry or dray to finish their moving. Finally they got hold of a good strong dray and went back to work. At about 4:30 it came here with the piano, a wardrobe, desk, Berbice chair, two rockers, and four wicker chairs—all of which we fitted in inconspicuous places. The piano stays downstairs, covered with an old bedspread. They never would have managed to get it up our narrow stairs!

I was feeding Elizabeth and Mabel was fixing her bed when I heard a light knock on the door. I asked Mabel to go, but before she could get past the study I heard her say good evening to Mr. Cameron! The nerve of the man, to just walk in. Serves us right, I suppose, for leaving the door open. He chatted with me until Howard came, then consulted with him on some AMM[35] business.

April 25:
Howard spent the morning taking John and Margaret around to change their address with the baker, newspaper, etc. They will really miss having a telephone, as they will now have no handy way of calling in grocery orders and the like.

April 26:

We stopped by the Allsopps' this afternoon with some magazines for the fair that Joy is working on. Richard is to be a presiding officer in the election tomorrow, and we looked over some of the paraphernalia that the job requires—everything from sealing wax to pins, plus envelopes of all sizes filled with tags, ballots, and tickets. All of it is stuffed into burlap bags, and part of his job is to see that it is all there, for any deficiency would invalidate all the votes in his district.

April 27:

After lunch we drove out to the airbase so Howard could collect some specimen plants for use at school. On the way we saw Mr. Barker, chemistry master at Queen's, in a little shack—Howard stopped, and we learned that he was acting as a presiding officer there.

We saw no Election Day violence on the way, but there were groups of men standing along the road at all the villages, and obviously they were talking politics. Got home around 5.

April 29, 1953

Dear folks,

School started today. Nothing very exciting—except for the addition of a Mr. R. W. Batchelor, new art teacher. He's an old Queen's boy who got his higher training in Aberdeen, Scotland. Nice fellow, too. About my age. (Not so "old" at that!)

The news of the hour is something I hadn't mentioned previously because it never seemed like enough of a certainty to merit your concern. B.G.'s first general election has just been concluded, and in 18 of the 24 electoral districts, Communist representatives have won seats in the new House of Assembly.[36] So, in brief, starting May 1, we will be governed by a Communist regime. It's not as bad as it sounds for these reasons: (1) The governor still has the power of veto on any and all issues that originate in the House of Assembly. One of the initial duties of the House is to appoint from its membership five ministers to fill posts formerly held by Colonial Secretaries, and in all probability these too will be Communists, but the Governor has the final say on any critical items occurring in any of the ministries. (2) Strangely enough, these Communists are by and large successful professionals and businessmen[37] and, should pure Communism be advocated, would stand to suffer more than most.

But still, the fact cannot be denied that it is something we never anticipated when we came—another factor we'll no doubt reflect upon the rest of our lives. And such a peaceful transition: Election Day was like Palm Sunday until the returns started coming in. In many districts it was a landslide such as our country hasn't known—as high as 85 percent voting for the Commie candidate, but no violence. Of the total number of registered voters (about 210,000), 75 percent turned up at the polls. It all points up the general dissatisfaction of the people with the status quo, poverty-poor lives they lead, and to that extent I'm sympathetic. But there's little doubt in my mind that they do not realize what they have done. Mrs. Janet Jagan, one of the wheels in this new machine, is reputedly née Rosenberg, sister of Julius.[38] Most of them freely admit membership in pro-Communist organizations in the U.S. and U.K. Most of them have, as a result, been denied visas to any British territory because B.G.'s new and dubious claim to fame is that it's the only Communist-ruled territory in the Colonial Empire (wouldn't you know we'd have chosen it!). No regrets; nothing has happened yet, and most of those with whom I've discussed the matter say nothing of a violent nature is anticipated—so we're still far better off than the poor devils in Kenya.[39]

Do remember that the trouble this reflects has nothing to do with race (the elected include Negroes, East Indians, mulattos, an Amerindian, and a U.S.-born Jew) but simply a *general unrest* over conditions and the failure of the British to do anything significant (in the eyes of Joe Guiana) toward improvement. The People's Progressive Party was the only party that suggested finite improvement in terms the uneducated could understand—so Guiana voted PPP, probably not realizing that Communism is more than a word that was thrown at them. They are in a mood to try anything, so we'll see. I wonder if we'll be investigated when we return.

Local reaction:

"Nothing much will happen" (staff member at Q.C.);

"We'll still have donkey carts ten years from now" (another Q.C. teacher);

"The people have got just what they wanted: popular government. Now let's see what kind of a mess they make of it. One thing is certain. If I don't like it, I'll not stay; I've already applied for transfer to Freetown [capital of Sierra Leone, W.A.F.]" (Sanger-Davies, Q.C. principal);

"Mon, now things are goin' to happen" (overheard downtown);

"Did you vote PPP?" (clerk at Bookers, asked hopefully with three fingers extended).

The ensuing months will be valuable and interesting to us—the understatement of the year.

Love to all,

Howard

Thursday, April 30, 1953

Dear Mother and Daddy—

We're glad E. is too small to count on birthday parties, because even the small celebration I'd planned for yesterday (having the Ramsarans come to tea) fell through. Tuesday morning I felt grim—chills, fever, backache, etc.— and took to my bed, letting H. feed E. It didn't last long, but H. stopped at John's and explained the situation. H. went downtown and bought a cute little toy for Elizabeth—a bright red, green, and blue doodad that makes a clattering noise when pulled. That was from his parents—tomorrow I hope to get downtown to buy a bookcase or toy chest for her room, with the rest of the money they sent.

Anyway, yesterday morning we three sat down on the floor to open the gifts. The Ramsarans gave her a set of blocks and a ball decorated in a Coronation motif (natch!). Mother, we love the playsuits. E. wore the pink one yesterday and the other today, and does she look cute! So much cuter than just diapers. And the sweater is lovely, too. Cotton is just right here— wool is much too sticky, but the breeze at the sea wall is cool enough to call for some arm covering. I'm sure silly—I'd rejected the idea of plastic bibs before on the grounds that they'd be too hot—forgetting entirely the awful time we have drying bibs here when the weather "gets heavy," as the local people say. It takes two days or so, and no matter how carefully they're washed, the bibs end up smelling sour. These will be a lifesaver, and E. is so intrigued with the ruffles—they're good to chew on, she thinks.

We gave her the doll, [toy] lamb, and dress—all mentioned before. Bee probably wrote that she sent a picture—very modern, but it has lovely colors—and a silver medallion on a chain that really looks sweet when she's all dressed up. Donna [college friend sharing an apartment with Bee] sent her *A Tale of Peter Rabbit* and a real cutie called *Pat the Bunny*. It's *very* simple, has sentences like "Paul and Judy can pat the bunny. Now you pat the bunny." And the bunny is right there to pat—a white flannel inset bunny! There is also a "mirror," and a patch of sandpaper on "daddy's scratchy face." Very cute—and E. already enjoys it. I didn't feel up to cake baking but H.

bought some ice cream and we gave E. her first taste. It surprised her at first, of course, but after that she thought it great.

I suppose by now you've heard about the election results here—18 out of 24 seats in the new House of Assembly were won by members of the People's Progressive Party, the local Communist organization. Of the 210,000 qualified voters, about 75 percent voted. H. says no one at school seems worried about sudden changes, since the Governor can veto anything. All agree that one thing is clearly indicated: the people desire a change. Lord knows they need some help—and only time will show whether Communism will provide that help. The voting was quiet; we drove out to Atkinson Field on Monday, polling day, and saw no excitement. People were gathered in little groups, and everyone seemed eager and interested, but there was no violence.

I took Elizabeth for a little walk this afternoon. She loves to touch the vines and shrubs that we pass—practically falls out of the Taylor Tot to reach them. We strolled through the Promenade Gardens—pretty flowers. Unfortunately, we can't sit on the grass in this country for there is a bug of some sort that lurks there, and when it bites it causes considerable itchy discomfort. It's too bad, because E. is at the age where she'd love a garden.

Question: Is E. too young for a sandbox? There is a lot of nice white sand available, and H. is perfectly willing to build a box. We'd put it in our little courtyard. But H. thinks E. would eat too much of it!

All of a sudden I'm sleepy. It's raining outside now and is cool, so bed will feel good.

Love to you both,
Marian

Friday, 7:30 p.m.

Hi, dears!

Howard has just gone to the stamp club meeting—I'm at the table, staring at dinner dishes. It poured all day until about 5; the postman came just before we sat down to dinner.

Made a steamed chocolate pudding today—very nice. Always imagined it would be too much trouble till I thought of using the double boiler.

Don't bother to send the washcloths—I just want to have them on reserve. Some of our colored ones look strange, too—the only thing I can think that would do it is the continual dampness.

I'm glad you mentioned Ted and the telephone business [possibility of talking to Marian's parents over ham radio]. Yes, frankly, homesickness would have laid me low had we talked together—up to about a month ago. Isn't it silly! And we thought that by now he might have lost interest. H. tells me now to hunt up your letter with the local men's names, and we'll get started. Whee!

Well—since beginning this, I've read through all the stories and articles you sent. I do love the ones dealing with children's fears, etc. We give E. all the love and vitamins we can, and yet sometimes I wonder if we're leaving anything out. She is so precious to us! This afternoon she wore the rosebud dress; she and Mabel went out for a walk but ran home (much to E.'s joy) when a shower caught them. I told Mabel to go on home, and we three played on the floor for a while. E. crawled all over H., almost poked his eyes out a few times, and chewed on his shirt buttons. Somewhere along the line we've confused her, and now when we tell her to say "daddy" she always says "mama"! So we're concentrating on "papa" now, which works well up to a point—she gets the "p" sound, but says "papa" with lips only and no real sound. Poor H. is home so little when she's awake, but I suppose most daddies have that problem.

I must do my dishes. Ants are bad when it's so rainy. Don't mind the bugs so much now—our foodstuff is pretty well ant-proofed (it takes time to learn how to do that!); we haven't had a roach in weeks; we have a good mosquito repellent; and our little mouse seems to have given up. Last week, though, in one night H. got about 40 bites—a flea, I guess. Anybody care to come visit?

Mother, we don't use our good bedspread at all. The bed is too low—it would drag on the floor. Your lavender one is taking a beating, but I'm thankful we brought it.

We'll be talking to you soon—

Love,

Marian

April 30:

Thomas came to do the floors this morning, so now we're all shiny and polished again. I remembered this morning to give him money to buy some fish for us: two weeks ago Mabel told me that, given the money, Thomas will check the ice house on Wednesday and Friday to get frozen fish as it is brought in. It will be a nice change since we're still short of meat.

May 2:

The Patoirs' daughter Hazel was married this afternoon at 5, so we had quite a show to watch all day long. After lunch, Howard brought the car into the court to wash it, and I went along with him, ostensibly to write a letter. From the Patoirs' part of the house we could hear intermittent swearing, screaming, and other outbursts of the Guianese temperament. I was invited over to inspect the cake, which Howard had previously picked up from the decorator's house. He had quite a time: the woman who decorated it flatly disputed that our car was large enough to contain the cake, even after Howard borrowed a measuring tape and measured it! At last they got the cake back with one of the Patoir daughters sitting in the back of the car, steadying it. It was very large, two-tiered, iced in white with pastel-colored roses. It was placed on a small table in the center of the room, flanked with vases of lovely blue hydrangeas that Mrs. Patoir's brother had flown in from the Interior. All through the rooms there were vases of more hydrangeas, some with gold marigolds.

Later on, Mrs. Patoir asked me to come look at the wedding gifts. There were several sets of tray cloths and napkins, many sets of teaspoons and forks, a few nice silver dishes, and a few ghastly glass bowls. Several items were hand-embroidered, and one lovely hand-crocheted tablecloth was being used on the table that held the cake.

I think they dressed little Gillian, who is about eight, the earliest of all—around 3 o'clock; and from then on the poor child was screamed at to not sit down because it would muss her dress, and then someone else would say, "For heaven's sake, sit down and quit running about." The oldest daughter, Dorothy, was bridesmaid, and her dress was yellow. Heather, younger than Hazel, wore a short white net strapless dress with green shoes and gloves. Mrs. Patoir wore purple crepe with a little pink plastic purse, pink gloves, and a pink corsage. It wasn't very becoming, although she certainly looked grand in comparison with the dresses she generally wears. Mr. Patoir wore what looked like a new gray suit, as did son Brian. Son Basil was told in advance that he'd have to stay home to guard the wedding gifts, so he didn't buy a new shirt; if we'd known earlier, we would have been glad to act as guards. Little Clifford evidently had a new white shirt, but he didn't go to the church. Gillian's bridesmaid's dress was lavender and quite pretty, but Beverley looked awkward in a short blue organdy dress with a frightful straw hat. I don't suppose she's at the best age now for party clothes—she's about 11 or 12, I guess. The bride looked lovely in a gown that had a white satin skirt and a top of heavy lace, with long sleeves and a Peter Pan collar. The two things that I thought were overdone were makeup and busts! All the girls had on heavy makeup, including the bride.

Hire cars came for the wedding party at about 5, and by 5:30 they were returning. The parents looked relaxed, and the bride and groom infinitely happier than before. As they walked in the door, Mendelssohn's wedding march was put on the gramophone and turned up loud. The celebrating went on until 11:30—the music sounded so loud from up here that we didn't see how people were standing it downstairs. At 11:30 "God Save the Queen" was put on, and at that unquestionable signal, the party broke up.

May 4:
Big crash outside. The donkey cart that came for the folding chairs, plates, and glassware used by the Patoirs was just finished being loaded. The driver started to lead the donkey up the slight incline out into the street, and all the chairs, plates, and glassware slid off. What a mess. Mrs. P. is saying that she is not responsible because they broke outside her house; the cartman is saying, "Madam, don't fret."

May 5:
Howard took me to town this noon, and we planned that he'd pick me up at a little after 3. I did my shopping and looking and then began waiting. Couldn't imagine what had held him up, but at 4 I started to walk home. It is a rather interesting walk, up Main Street, for there are many old, large houses that really look intriguing. Many are three-storied and imposing, with many louvered windows running all the way across the width of the house. These old houses are built way back from the street, and many have lovely gardens and trees.

It took me about twenty minutes to walk home, and when I arrived I found that Mabel had already taken Elizabeth out and locked the door. Had to go over to the college to get the key from Howard. We're so stupid not to get a duplicate key made; we just never think of it at the right time.

May 6:
This morning I took Mother's letter with the names of the radio hams and asked Mrs. Patoir if she knows any of them. Her family knows three of the six well, and a fourth she knows. But then she said she wanted us to meet a Mr. and Mrs. Adamson; he is head of telecommunications here and has

something to do with Radio Demerara, too. She seems to think he will be able to tell us all that we want to know about arranging the phone conversation with Mother and Daddy. We were going to see the Adamsons this evening, but Howard was asked to attend a rehearsal of the orchestra that's going to play "The Water Music" at some big Coronation celebration.

May 8:
Howard's rehearsal was an experience. It was held at St. George's Cathedral.[40] He noticed, at one point, a shadow on his sheet music; minutes later he saw a bat flying low overhead. Then he noticed the church had many bats flying around. He says he pities the conductor, who is apparently trying his hardest against heavy odds. The men from the Militia Band think they know everything, but according to Howard they missed cues and don't know many of the technical aspects of musicianship. Howard's feeling was that the conductor didn't dare criticize anyone for fear the offender would be insulted and walk out!

Saturday, 9 May 1953

Dear Tom and Anna,

Marian is swamped with letters to write, so I'll give you the family and local news this week.

Elizabeth has been progressing to her presumably soon-to-come toddling days, even to the extent of standing without support for brief periods—quickly reaching for the playpen rail or settling to the floor as soon as she becomes aware of her independence. It won't be long now! Poor little girl had tummy trouble this week, diagnosed by Dr. Bissessar as a "gastric upset," and for which he prescribed magnesium citrate, well mashed with a sugary syrup. Her temperature was alarmingly high for a short time Tuesday but quickly dropped as she was rid of whatever caused the upset. She's still off her feed but is gradually getting back to it all.

People here have been unwittingly offending us with their terming the teething process "pegging," the individual teeth called "pegs," and with the insistence that any temperature rise or other upset is caused by the "pegs." Another favorite comment is "My, she's getting fat!" Judging from her pictures, do you think so? Compared with some of the wispy local infants, perhaps their observations are understandable, but we do cock an ear when Mrs. McLaren plays the same tune.

Speaking of Mrs. McLaren and her residence with the Ramsarans, we really don't know but suspect financial expedience. We had them in for tea on Friday—their living so far from us now has lessened the number of teatimes we've spent with them. The poor people seem to thrive on complaint—"you've just got to grouse." John has said to me he *doesn't* agree that complaining helps span the time. Even little Susan says they'll be "going home to London when the ship comes in." How wrong (to our minds) that a child should be anticipating the unlikely. John must remain here until April '55 or relinquish membership in the Colonial Service. He is hoping in time to be transferred to his native Trinidad, but all Margaret, her mother, and Susan can think of is London. Sounds difficult!

Last Saturday we witnessed the preparations leading up to and the reception following a local Christian wedding. The Patoirs' (downstairs neighbors') eldest daughter and one Cyril Figueira were the subjects of all the to-do. Reviewing the whole thing, we were most impressed with the excessive makeup and the overdressed parents. There was much commotion that day, frequently punctuated with rather coarse profanity. I helped out a little by taking one daughter to the baker's and bringing home the monstrous cake—24 inches in diameter and two detached layers high—and every comment from her was introduced or followed by "Oh, Lawd!" or "Oh, Gawd!" or "Oh, hell!" Such a fever pitch! At 5 two Bookers cabs rolled up, and out to one went Father and the bride. I was asked to take photos before they departed, and in doing so saw her face was layered in heavy makeup. After cab #1 left, Mama appeared in purple crepe with pink accessories and scarcely less than a pound of makeup. Within a half hour they were back, and the first of their 60-odd guests had arrived. The bride and groom entered to the strains of canned Mendelssohn. The rest of the party was as you'd expect—a crescendo of hilarity, aided by a blaring jukebox—and Elizabeth slept through it all!

B.G. made *Time* at last—but the news isn't so good.[41] We were concerned at first, largely because we were surprised. Before the election I heard only one person prophesy he "wouldn't be surprised to see them"—PPP—"get in." Next event on the agenda is the convention of the Assembly (within the coming two weeks) whose representatives will name five ministers. An interesting split has already occurred in the PPP ranks over the degree of initial reform. Extreme leftist Cheddi Jagan and his wife, Janet, advocate quick withdrawal from all British ties and the formation of a republic. L.F.S. Burnham, less hasty, feels B.G.'s best hope at present is to join the West Indian Federation and become a dominion province. Still others feel B.G. should become a dominion by itself. Another crisis has arisen over the failure of three key party wheels (including Burnham) to accept nominations for the ministerial posts. Politically, as otherwise, these are interesting days.

Our love to you both,

Howard

Now you have all the news! I've written two letters—have about six to go. Time for bed. Love, M.

May 9, 1953

Dear folks,

Now that school has reopened, the boys facing British exams in a couple of months are getting a little feverish. The fever is particularly heavy in my subject because of the '49–'52 gap in their biological studies (no instructor) and my attempt to bring them up to exam standards. Most will be ready, but I fear one-quarter to one-third failure. In an effort to help some, I've agreed to take two to Atkinson each weekend and fortify them with the exemplary information so often called for in the exams. Good opportunity to get to know them better, too.

Sort of think I'll break down and play in the Georgetown Philharmonic in the forthcoming concert on June 2—Lord knows I've been hounded enough! Everything is provided: bass, bow, stand, music.

S-D called Barker (chemistry instructor), Drayton (physics), and me in for a conference on Friday to discuss plans for establishing a rural science school and for expanding our own Q.C. science facilities to meet the expansion of the school to 700 (now 500 attend). According to plan, I will have higher-school biology while Mr. Niles, who will be returning from England in September, will take lower-school biology as well as some overflow physics and chemistry. All this is much to my liking, for while I do enjoy the antics and innocent queries of the little boys, I feel the more intensive material necessary in the higher school is, by way of review, more in keeping with my own plans. There's nothing like teaching to firmly impress factual information in one's memory and to unveil previously hidden principles—far more valuable than formal instruction.

I hope my last letter didn't alarm you too much re Communism. The next event is the convening of the Assembly and the election of four ministers by its representatives a week or two hence. An interesting split has already occurred in the PPP ranks over the degree of immediate reform to be undertaken. Cheddi Jagan and his wife, Janet, both party officers and ministerial likelies, are rather extreme in their proposals (complete break from Britain now). Others, including L.F.S. Burnham, a smart young Negro lawyer, feel affiliation with the proposed West Indian Federation is a better solution to immediate problems. Ordinarily, we might be a little hopeful when dissention tears at a winning party's ranks, but the PPP holds 18 of 24 Assembly seats—of the six remaining, two are of one party, the rest independent. So the dissention would have to be extreme before the party became materially weak. These are interesting days, needless to say.

Love to all,
Howard

May 10:
Howard took one of his 6th Formers, a boy named [Premnauth] Ramphal, out to the airbase today. They returned about 5 o'clock, hot and dusty, but apparently their day was pleasant. Howard says they walked miles.

May 11:
Elizabeth has a rather bad diaper rash. Dr. Bissessar came out this evening and prescribed some penicillin ointment for her as well as another medicine to calm her down. Neither Howard nor I could help her much today by rocking or holding her. It's too warm for anyone to enjoy being held for long, and each time I tried, she was just about as unhappy as when in bed. There are times when Georgetown seem frightfully uncivilized to me, but I'm thankful that at least we have modern medicine available.

May 14:
Before dinner this evening, we noticed that an ambulance had drawn up across the street, letting out two men who took a stretcher and walked back to a house at the very end of the muddy lane that parallels the side of our house. A few minutes later a jeep drove up with three policemen, and two of them marched down the path swinging their long nightsticks. A crowd gathered—nannies and babies, ragged little boys, and curious men and women with nothing else to do. After a while the stretcher-bearers came back carrying a woman who seemed to be unconscious, although to us she didn't look hurt. Still later the policemen came out with a man,

who was bundled into the jeep. Ambulance left; jeep left; crowd left. Mrs. Patoir told us that the man had been in court, and the woman had been testifying against him. He had beaten her up in revenge, and had also beaten the neighbor to whom the woman had run for help. Howard and I are often amazed at the complete information Mrs. Patoir has on all the local happenings!

May 15:
At quarter to 5, Howard and I went with Mrs. Patoir to meet the Adamsons in order to learn how to go about the business of the radio–short wave conversation we hope to have with Mother and Daddy. Since Mr. Adamson hadn't arrived, his wife showed us around the flats that they are at present remodeling. Heavens—they charge $120, yet their flats are completely furnished with stove, refrigerator, electric iron, and toaster as well as with good furniture and all the accessories.

Mr. Adamson arrived finally, a very charming gentleman. We can't decide whether he's Canadian or English (his wife is Guianese), but at any rate he was certainly cordial. He called his good friend Louis Fonseca and gave him all the information about Ted Caesar's call numbers [in Washington State], and we left with the agreement that Fonseca will get in touch with him, and he in turn will get hold of us when a date has been made.

May 16:
We don't know quite what to make of last night's dinner party at the Sanger-Davieses'. The S-Ds have a three-month-old puppy named Pluto, and I'm sure I'd love him under most circumstances. However, last night I wore my brown lace dress and stockings, and Howard had on his good white dinner jacket. I can't understand why Mrs. S-D didn't see we were uncomfortable having to fight off the puppy, who was typically friendly and eager to climb up and bite our hands; but she paid little attention except to attach a leash to Pluto's collar which Howard held, thus keeping the dog off my skirts. Mrs. S-D said she did hope that Howard's trousers weren't something that could be harmed by the dog's claws—but didn't call off the dog! Finally, after Pluto drew blood from Mr. S-D's hand, he (S-D) tied the leash to a chair on the veranda. Somehow the dog got loose and joined us at the dinner table, or rather under it.

Other guests were a parson and his wife, from the village of Penitence. They seemed pleasant if a bit insipid. Joke of the evening was a play on words that tickled the S-Ds immensely: Talk centered around the Association of Masters and Mistresses, and Associate membership therein, and the obvious abbreviation was "ass." The dinner was good: roast mutton, peas, potatoes, and trifle for dessert; but poor Howard said he didn't get enough. Tiny servings.

We raced through after-dinner coffee (with gritty grounds in abundance) in order to get to the concert in time. Howard and I just don't care for Kathleen Howe—she is awful to watch. She holds her arms outstretched in a dramatic gesture that only partially conceals a notebook cupped in her hands. Her face becomes quite distorted when she sings—if I didn't know she was singing, I might think she was in agony. At any rate, the concert didn't last long, and we were home shortly after 10.

Had our first glimpse of the new governor and his wife. He looks the part, rather distinguished and dignified. She is tall, thin, and wears her dark hair à la gym teacher style, which always throws me for a loss. Looks a bit grim.

May 16, 1953

Dear folks,

Afraid we can't sympathize with your 89° weather (news of which came via four sources, so it must have been impressive)—it's an everyday event here. We don't write much about the heat anymore because we don't think about it, although now and then we hanker for a frosty morning. The past few weeks have been relatively dry and, per reputation, accompanied by slightly higher temperatures. Shade temp. ("grass temp.") has yet to exceed 93°, but in the sun (particularly on pavement) it's withering—up to 140°!

No emergency situation exists here yet. Admittedly, no one would propose that as a guarantee, for, in fact, no one really knows. The new legislature has yet to meet, and until it does, life goes on. No repercussions have made themselves felt as yet, and only one ship has changed its course; an Australian freighter is going to dock in Port of Spain, Trinidad, instead of in Georgetown. No consulates have closed (actually, only a couple are here), and no exodus has occurred. One thing has happened which most everyone here resents, Commie or not, and that is the U.S. has turned a cold shoulder on the place (to us, this is very understandable, but to the average Guianese, it is an act of hostility). Passage to the U.S. and Canada have become difficult, what with reluctant visa-ing officials in Trinidad, and Ellis Island as a prospect in N.Y. We anticipated that sort of thing during the later stages of the campaign (when PPP revealed its strength) and even mentioned it to several people. At the moment, there is considerable concern over the loss of U.S. investment capital (two bauxite mining operations) and nipping of prospects that, up to election time, seemed to be brightening. This sort of thing means nothing to the uninformed, who are dictated by prejudice, emotion, and immediate problems. Most important to you is this: if you were here, you would sense no crisis. Election excitement has died away. The beggars are back on the streets, donkey carts ply their way, and Stabroek Market still bubbles with humanity. A few have carried the thing too far, challenging authority by staging wildcat, banner-displaying (Stalin) parades, and some loiterers grumble "PPP rub you out" to passing whites. In summary, there's a little smoke but, as yet, no fire. We're eager to see what happens when the two legislative bodies meet.

Ever since we took this flat we suspected our rent bill ($100 B.W.I./ month) was a bit high but felt the convenience to the college would compensate. But as time has passed we've become firmly convinced that we were taken for a ride. Mr. Beckles had told us it was "quite fair," and on the strength of that recommendation we were satisfied. Thus, another principle is born: never believe one person in a strange place. He has since said it is too much (forgetting the initial endorsement?), but not before I suggested that fact to him. To cut what could be a disgusting, long tale, it's 30–40 percent too much, and we intend to do something about it. Next week I'm seeing A. G. King, a lawyer (who owns no property himself) with a good reputation (recommended by a police official who lives downstairs and who has a similar gripe) to see if I have a case. If so, we need only get a statement from the former tenant as to the extent of his rent when he lived here (reputedly $65/month) and take it to court. Miss Osborn, the owner, will be asked for a statement of the cost of repairs and improvements between the two tenancies. After appraisal of the flat as it stands, our statement regarding monthly bills (installments) for stove and refrigerator—furnished in all other $100 flats—plus a couple of other good complaints (leaking roof that she will not have fixed properly; her refusal to permit me to wash the car in the driveway—this I've ignored, and today she came around to order me to take the car out of the drive, which I refused to do. She stormed off, sputtering she would get the police to "get" me for trespassing. An hour later, while I was downtown, a cop appeared and asked Mrs. Patoir what was going on. Mrs. Patoir's resourceful reply: "Nothing criminal has happened here." Finis) will be reviewed—if in our favor, we get a rebate on the total difference.

The first reply to my queries concerning the use of my research work toward a Ph.D. came back from Washington State—no good. The reasoning: "Typically and preferably thesis research by a student is done in an area and field in which the adviser is very familiar and most capable." This we interpret to mean that Washington State has no one "familiar and capable" with tropical ecology. Next inquiry goes to Oregon State, and if that doesn't pan out, we'll try some Southern schools. University of Miami (note *Time*, May 18) sounds like a good bet. In these matters I've always respected Doc Alcorn's judgment, and since he thinks it's a sane idea, I'm bound to exploit it.

Yes, I suppose it was silly of me to resist the urge to join an orchestra, but at this stage it's not entirely pleasurable. I'm as rusty as a hobnail, and the instrument is a bulky, full-size affair that weighs a good many pounds more than anything I've handled before. The bow is a Butler; that's why I wired for mine. So far, Mrs. [Dorothy] Taitt (the organizer) and I haven't drawn swords, but everyone who has had anything to do with her says a showdown is inevitable—I hope not. (Program: "Water Music," "Royal Fireworks Music," etc.)

Last night we had a weird time. The S-Ds invited us to dinner together with a parson and his wife. Didn't know whether to expect drinks, but, sure enough, in true S-D style, there were the rum bottles right on the coffee table. The parson smoked and took a couple of rum-and-gingers, so there was no tension over that. But the S-Ds have a three-month-old dog that persisted in puncturing our fingers (in preference to our clothes) with his needle-like teeth. Finally, after one nip drew blood from S-D's thumb, he took the animal out on the veranda and tied him to a chair. Back came Pluto with chair trailing behind—up to the French door. S-D winced when it appeared the glass would give way.

At the dining table we writhed in chairs whose sagging cane seats all but embarrassed us, what with broken rods stabbing us here and there. The conversation, dominated by bantering host and hostess, got, somehow or other, to the Association of Masters and Mistresses (teacher's association just organized by Mr. Cameron). S-D harped on the ASSociate membership qualifications necessary in the ASSociation, this soon abbreviated to ASS. At length (the parson was forced to titter) S-D opened a champagne bottle, which popped and sprayed. Mrs. S-D's comment: "Joe, you ASS!" They had to receive the Governor's party at the college hall, so we followed them over and sat with the parson and wife. The subject of this occasion was Mrs. Kathleen Howe, who was giving her farewell concert. Mrs. Howe, revered by most Georgetown concertgoers, no doubt represents (or has represented) the pinnacle of operatic interpretation here but, like many others, is in reality pretty much a has-been. She is hard to watch and hear alike. Fortunately, her performance lasted just a little over an hour, so it wasn't painful. Sideline on the affair: Mr. Cameron, organizer of the concert, when asked beforehand if he would say a few words of thanks at the conclusion of the music, muttered, "Well—I can't very well thank myself!" The Archdeacon of Guiana did the favors instead.

Tomorrow I give another book review on the radio. Always something.

Love to all,

Howard

Dad, there is a local military force but it's all-Guianese, so while it stands as a potential defender of peace, there's not much you can do when a large portion of its men sympathize with the agitating body. —H.

Sunday, May 17, 1953

Dearest Mother and Daddy,

Just a short note. We're having copies made of the picture of E. and me. The enclosed were taken the day Howard and I went out to the airbase, except for the one of Elizabeth, which was taken on her birthday. Howard's parents sent us some money for E., and I tried to find a low bookcase or toy chest for her, but was told at Bookers that they only order children's furniture once a year, before Christmas, and that they have nothing now. Fogarty's had one hideous blue wardrobe and some little rocking chairs. So we're going to have one made. A carpenter did some work for Howard at school, and H. thought his work was very good. I guess we'll have him frame the picture Bee sent, too.

Howard has just written a short note to the State Department asking for their opinion on the situation here in regard to our return to the States. So far, everything here is as calm as can be, except that many people are upset to find that there are Communists in the PPP.

H. is giving a book review on the radio this evening. It was a chore, since the book was dull—about Sir John Hawkins.[42] I splurged and bought *The Caine Mutiny* and *The Old Man and the Sea*. Very inexpensive, hardcover editions but of good quality. Loved *The Caine Mutiny*. Have you read it? Also bought a paperback copy of *Prester John* by John Buchan, whom I hadn't discovered before I read *Greenmantle*. Am going to get *The Thirty-nine Steps* when I see it.

H. wrote Washington State College[43] not long ago, asking the head of the botany department if the research work he's doing here would apply toward a Ph.D. thesis. The reply said in part "that typically and preferably thesis research by a student is done in an area and field in which the adviser is very familiar and most capable." We were rather surprised at the reasons for the rejection—and we can't believe it is that way with all schools, or else how would any progress be made at all? Howard is writing Oregon State now and is mulling over the idea of writing to Miami University after reading the article on it in yesterday's *Time*.

Elizabeth is fine now, but I think she must be getting some new teeth. Isn't interested in lunch but wants her milk. She's hungry for breakfast and supper, so she won't waste away!

I'm so glad you're going to subscribe to the National Society for Crippled Children and Adults magazine. I know I shall enjoy it.

We'd love a wading pool! I'd never thought of the sandbox idea in terms of sand sticking to Elizabeth; and H. says the sand might get too warm sitting in the sun, too. But the wading pool sounds great. Do they make any large, adult-size ones?

Mother, I really don't need any more shoes. My red ones are awfully comfortable. I wear them nearly every day, but they're holding up beautifully. I've washed them several times and H.'s once, and they come out looking almost as good as new. Since you underlined the "answer," the size is 9 Narrow. But, again, I don't need any. You're cute!

Bless your hearts, don't expect to hear Elizabeth's little voice for quite some time! She gets coy even when we ask her to say something and just smiles at us or says "mamamam" or something else that is completely unintelligible. Patience!

Much love to you both,
Marian

May 17:

Last evening Howard and I sat on our door stoop for an hour or so, listening to the neighborhood children play, watching the progress of a drunk, and finally, after most of the street's lights went out at 10, we just watched the light from our own windows as it played on the traveler's palm. Noisy as it sometimes is, the tree can look quite beautiful.

May 18:

Rain. Steady rain. It was cool enough so that when I took a nap after lunch I tucked Howard's bathrobe around my feet; otherwise, it is still steamy and wet.

May 19:

I rescued yesterday's diapers and other washing this morning and put them in the sun. They were just about as wet as when Mabel hung them up yesterday. So nice to have the sun out, but there's little breeze.

Wednesday night, May 20, 1953

Dearest Parents—

I am truly tickled pink. I don't think I wrote you about two weeks ago when Elizabeth picked up her spoon so that she could have given herself a bite had she wanted to. Well, tonight she fed herself four whole mouthfuls! I just barely guided the spoon the first three times; the fourth I said to myself, "Let her do it all by herself," and sure enough, after dunking her nightie sleeve in the beets, she got the spoon in her mouth. Bless her heart.

We may be moving! Things have come to a crisis with Miss Osborn, and we finally felt we could take it no longer. Howard has a man who washes the car each Sunday; a few weeks ago, this chap brought another man's car here so that he could use our hose to wash it. The only place here where there is a faucet to attach the hose (or any faucet at all) is in the plot of ground that serves as a driveway to the garage as well as the entrance to the third-story flat. Well, the ladies upstairs complained to Miss Osborn when the stranger's car was washed in what they call their entranceway. We didn't exactly blame them, and we certainly didn't tell the washer he could use the hose for any car other than ours; he just did. Well, Miss O. sent a truly nasty note saying that no cars could be washed in that court. We thought that unreasonable in view of our high rental and the fact that there was no other place, and so last Saturday H. told our man to go ahead and wash the car per usual. In a little while Miss O. came storming up the street and told H. to move the car. H. refused. She said she'd call the police; H. told her to go ahead. Well—evidently the policeman came, but this was after the car had been washed and H. had gone to the post office. The officer asked Mrs. Patoir what the trouble was, and she said, "There's nothing criminal going on," and he left. Next day a huge chain and padlock appeared on the gate; a great inconvenience to the tenants of the third floor because the postman, their friends, etc. can't get to their flat. But Miss O. insists that the gate remain locked. What a horror she is! Anyway, Mrs. Patoir convinced us that our rent is ridiculously high and said we had a legal case—she also recommended a lawyer. H. saw this man today, and the lawyer, who knows both Miss Osborn and the flat, said that he would issue an ultimatum: either the rent is reduced to that which the former tenant paid (we think that was $65) or else the contract be considered broken. If she refuses, the case will be taken to the assessment court; and the lawyer told H. he doubted very much if she'd want that, since the court would undoubtedly force the rental way down. We hope she'll break the contract in the hope of securing another gullible soul. She's planning to go to England next Monday; no doubt she'll be fit to burn when she gets the lawyer's letter. We're tired of being suckers—granted, we took the Beckleses' word that the place and price were fair, but now that we know a bit more, we just can't sit and take it without a fight. Our straw mattress is getting frightfully lumpy, anyway. Mrs. Patoir was truly shocked when we told her that it was straw; but the ones at the guesthouse were straw, and how were we to know that such things as inner spring mattresses were available! Nothing like learning by doing, as the educators say. And it is funny, in a way. We'd love to stand up to the formidable Miss Osborn; everyone here seems to take her as they do life and death—with complaints but no positive resistance.

Mrs. Patoir says she'd hate to feel that people in Canada would take advantage of her daughter and son-in-law the way we've been taken advantage of—that's why she's been so persistent in setting us straight.

Howard is at orchestra rehearsal. It doesn't seem possible that the Coronation is so near. Great doings are planned, of course, including nearly a week off for Howard, which he doesn't appreciate since he was operating on a very close schedule and resents the lost class periods!

Howard just walked in: his instrument wasn't there tonight. The person in charge of it all forgot about it. Oh well—he's waiting for his own bow to arrive, anyway.

The April 4 *New Yorker* arrived today, several days after the April 11 issue. I made Howard squirm while I read the French in that Kaiser ad—remember it?

Yesterday for dinner I made drop biscuits—your recipe, Mother, only I was too lazy to do the rolling out. Tasted good. Monday I made the plain cookie recipe in *Joy of Cooking,* only spread it in a square pan, in two layers with dates in between. *Very* good, and heaven knows simple. Sounds as if I'm getting lazy, doesn't it! We've been eating a lot of fresh pineapple lately. They cost about a shilling each now, and we get three meals from one. Very refreshing, and certainly different from the canned variety. I noticed in the paper that tangerines are back at the market—we haven't had any since last fall.

Mabel has taught Elizabeth to wave "bye-bye." At least, she sometimes will do it. She has such a delightful sense of humor: we play peek-a-boo while I dust in the mornings. She's in the playpen, and I peek out from behind chairs and tables as I dust, and then we both giggle. She just discovered today the joy of dropping her beads down the stairs; I went after them the first time, and the minute I handed them back, plop down the stairs they went again!

Much love to you both,
Marian

May 20:

This morning, while I was cleaning the living room, I watched an East Indian woman sit down on the sidewalk just a few steps away from our house and burst into tears. She sobbed: great loud wails, sighs, and groans. This went on for several minutes; finally a few women stopped and evidently tried to comfort her, but to no avail. Both the gardener and the maid from the house next door seemed to be interested, and the maid swung on the gate for about fifteen minutes watching the proceedings. Eventually, still sobbing, the woman was led away up the street by some of the others who had stopped.

Howard talked with a lawyer today about our rental situation here. The man, a Mr. A. G. King, told Howard it was a shame we'd had to sign the contract, but said he would issue an ultimatum to Miss Osborn that either she bring the rent down to the $65 that the previous tenant paid or else break our contract. He thinks she will take one of these choices rather than have the case brought to the assessment court where, Mr.

King is sure, the rent would be snapped back to a more reasonable figure. We hope to get it all settled before long—by the end of the month, if possible.

May 21:
Elizabeth and I visited the Ramsarans in their new home this afternoon. This house is some improvement over the last, but not too much. They have rats and ants galore, and the rooms are arranged with little thought to convenience or ventilation. In fact, the lack of air is the main trouble: they get scarcely any breeze at all. Today it was muggy and hot inside, yet as soon as we got out to the car we felt a nice breeze.

May 22:
I baked this afternoon for the first time in several days. I think I shall change bakers soon: yesterday, the Ramsarans had whole wheat bread as well as white, and they say that Harlequin's bakery also offers currant bread. As far as we have learned, Tang's bakes white only, and we're tired of it. So today I made orange rolls, cinnamon rolls, and a cake.

May 23:
It rained so hard this morning that I gave up all thought of cleaning and concentrated on mopping up puddles. We had several waterfalls in the living room, and the water poured in nearly all the windows in the tower. We had several cake pans out there, to catch the water, and we noticed that Testudo seemed to enjoy lapping up the water. Howard quoted the books as saying that tortoises can't drink, but Testudo was certainly doing nothing else!

May 24:
Until noon the sun shone, so I managed to get yesterday's washing pretty well dried before today's rain came. Howard left at 9:30 with three boys for the airbase—unfortunately, it rained out there, too, so their day wasn't as good as it might have been.

Since it is still raining, I told Mabel to go home early. Now, at 4:30, Elizabeth is roaming around. She just turned the volume knob of the radio up full blast; now she's in the tower peeking into the box where Junior is; turning over the wastebasket; trying to pull things off the table; and so on.

May 25:
Heavy, gusty showers most all day long. Howard says that each Monday morning there is a moldy film on all the furniture at school. I find it here, too, when I don't dust carefully enough.

Tuesday, May 26, 1953

Dear All—
This crazy climate! I'll swear it's the wettest rain anywhere. Luckily, we seem to get a few hours or a day of sunshine just often enough so that the wet clothes don't pile up too badly, but when it is raining, even a handkerchief doesn't dry in 24 hours. Ghastly! One day last week, Howard and I took a nap after lunch—it must have been last Saturday. We were both chilly, and I huddled under his bathrobe while we went under the bedspread. In the next day's paper, we saw that the minimum temperature for Saturday was 73°! Heaven help us when we return. Elizabeth never sleeps with any covers—she kicks them off whenever I try to cover her, but her legs always are warm, so I can't worry.

Everyone is excited about the Coronation. Many of the stores have colored lights and decorations up, and all along Main Street (there is a broad, tree-bordered path in the center of Main Street) there are poles on which flags and lights will be hung. If only it doesn't rain, which it probably will. All the clubs are having dances; there will be at least two concerts— Howard's group doing "The Water Music" and Mrs. McLaren's choir and the band are doing the dances from *Prince Igor* and something else. All the schools are putting on a pageant, one scene from each school.

Are strawberries really in season? Ah me. We do have something here that we certainly wouldn't be having at home, and that's meat. Last Friday, Howard bought (I just noticed the sales slip here) 3 lbs. 5 oz. of round steak, $2.12; 1 1/3 lbs. mutton chops, $1.05—that's four big chops; and 2 lbs. shoulder mutton steaks, $1.20. I suppose that would come to about $3 in your money. I've just started giving Elizabeth meat again—she's had ground beef three times now and seems to enjoy it tremendously, although it takes her ages to chew even the little tiny crumbs. Next week we'll try lamb. The baby books both say that a year-old child should like onions: I have a feeling, Mother, you didn't give them to Bee and me or else we'd have liked them more later! I love them now, and we eat them quite often. I've some leftover boiled onions that I'll try on E. tonight, just for kicks.

When she's through eating I raise the tray, take off her bib, and wash off her hands and face. Then she always holds out her arms to be picked up—I think that's one of the most delightful gestures she makes.

We haven't heard anything from the lawyer yet but trust he's not forgotten us. Miss Osborn left yesterday for England, leaving a nephew in charge of her affairs. The Patoirs think the nephew is just as obnoxious as the aunt, but Mr. Patoir feels better able to cope with him since he's a man, and comparatively young at that. Miss O. is really an old so-and-so.

Mrs. McLaren is coming over tomorrow evening to give me a crocheting lesson. Howard has rehearsals both tonight and tomorrow night, so perhaps tonight while he's gone I shall make some cookies or something.

Love to you all,

Marian

May 26:

The sun shone this morning so I got yesterday's laundry dry. I'd just about made up my mind to go downtown after lunch when clouds developed, and I decided it was safer to stay at home. A good thing, since it has been pouring off and on this afternoon.

May 27:

Finally made it to town. I bought some material for a dress for Elizabeth and some for a dress for myself. After finishing my buying, I walked home. It was lovely and sunny this afternoon, and I enjoyed my walk tremendously. The breeze is pleasant all the way up Main Street, although the two-block stretch along the railway track is a bit hot. On the way home I stopped and talked to the grandmother of the six little boys in back of us—I do wish I knew their name. She had Bruce, the one who visits me occasionally, with her. They're very grateful for the bottle of vitamins we gave them; she thanked me for the "syrup" and said it had helped "Baby" with his teething.

Friday evening, May 29, 1953

Dear All—

Oh boy—it certainly is warm! I'm all itchy and prickly, for the first time in quite a spell. Everyone is holding his breath about the weather: there are so many affairs planned for this next week, and quite a few of them require good weather, which is doubtful at this time of year.

The little toilet seat arrived yesterday, Mother, and isn't it cute! I think I'll wait until the Coronation hip-hurrah is over before we tackle that, though, because I shall be gone more than usual, and I think it would be easier for Elizabeth if she and I began that by ourselves in comparative peace.

In your last letter, Mother, you mentioned receiving some letters from us which had been opened and resealed with Scotch tape. Someone else may be doing it, but on occasion Howard and I do it ourselves. In the letter H. mailed yesterday with the enlarged snaps of E., I forgot to place the pictures until I'd already sealed the envelope, so I slit the paper and resealed it. And we just can't get too worried about the political scene: we notice no changes, and Howard said that he didn't even get any "PPP" catcalls downtown this morning. Naturally, we will keep somewhat on the alert, but the most alarming things by far have been the *Time* article and a Drew Pearson column that H.'s mother sent.[44]

Wednesday I finally got downtown. I bought some pale yellow cambric for a dress for Elizabeth and, for 60 cents a yard, some cotton for me, scrap enclosed. Bookers had lovely—(darn it, the name slips my mind, but it was a well-known American textiles company) material, but it was $1.20 a yard, and I thought it well to start on a more minor investment! I still do some silly things when I'm trying to follow a pattern.

I also got to the Self-Help Gift Shop, finally, and was surprised and pleased with some of the things they have there—some nice basketwork, wooden things, and so on. Also tarts and pastries and deviled crab in the shell—none of it refrigerated. I walked home from town, enjoying the sunshine and the pleasant breeze; in Thursday's paper I noticed that at 2 p.m. Wednesday the temperature was 85°! I am convinced that the good Lord provides rain here so that everyone will fully appreciate the sunshine.

Coronation week is upon us, almost, and what a schedule! Tomorrow we go to see the Police Gymkhana, just across the street at the Parade Grounds. Mrs. Patoir asked us if we'd like tickets, and Mr. P. obtained them for us. On Sunday evening we go to a pageant at Queen's—it consists of scenes put on by each of the secondary schools here. Monday night is Howard's concert at St. George's Cathedral. On Monday morning I am going with Mrs. McLaren to the grand opening (by His Excellency the Governor, no less) of the "Loyal Tribute" exhibit, put on by the Bookers stores, consisting of scenes, pictures, replicas of the Crown Jewels, etc. On Tuesday, Coronation Day itself, I don't know for sure but I think there will be a big parade reviewed by the governor—if so, we'll watch that from our windows here. Tuesday afternoon we will have tea with the Ramsarans. Thursday the other concert, with Mrs. McLaren's choir, will be held at Queen's. I think that's the end. Nearly all the stores and government buildings are beautifully decorated—much more elaborately than I had imagined they would be. Painted wooden medallions, crests, crowns, roses, ciphers, etc. are blossoming all over. The schoolchildren were given their medals today, and yesterday the Convalescent Home put up some bunting and a Union Jack. All the bicycles are decorated with gay little flags, and I suppose by Tuesday many houses will be decorated, too. Interesting and fun for us.

Wednesday night Mrs. McLaren came over while H. had a rehearsal, and gave me a lesson in the fine art of crocheting. She certainly is a good teacher. It seems fairly straightforward, although I can't count the stitches as easily as in knitting.

I'm sleepy. Howard is now home from his stamp club meeting, so I may go to bed. He's making a list of people to whom he will send first-day covers with the new Elizabethan stamp.

Howard said he had an awfully hard time at the post office yesterday trying to explain the toilet seat to the clerk. The man had never heard of such a device but said that there were many things in America that weren't found anyplace else. Duty was $4. By the way, please let us know how much duty you have to pay on the things we sent. We'd love to send more if it isn't exorbitant; if it is, we'll just wait and bring things home with us.

Must go to bed. Yawn!

Love to you all,

Marian

May 29:

While I was fixing Elizabeth's supper, Howard and I overheard some of a heated argument between Mrs. Ogle and Mrs. Patoir, concerning us. Mrs. Patoir took our part, and Mrs. Ogle was vehemently against us—we don't know just what it was all about. Too bad to make enemies.

May 30, 1953:

The first session of the new Legislative House of Assembly takes place. The newly elected ministers marched together from the PPP's office on Regent Street to the legislature a few blocks away. John Gutch, the colonial secretary, recalled the day: "I had to push my way through a throng of exuberant PPP supporters, some of them carrying placards and shouting 'Limey, go home!' (Limey being their slang for European) and other abuse. Then, as the rest of us watched from the verandahs, the PPP arrived led by Jagan, all clad in white sharkskin, the men with red ties and the women carrying red handbags. The public gallery at the back of the Council Chamber was always crowded with noisy PPP supporters. The Speaker, Sir Eustace Woolford, a distinguished Guianese of the old school, presided with patience and skill over our rather stormy meetings. . . . Mrs. Jagan and I shared the distinction of being the only two 'white' members of the House."

Cheddi Jagan later wrote of regretting the choice of dress that day: "The decision on attire had been made by Burnham while I was [in another district] after our election victory. If it had been left to me, I would have selected a simpler and less conspicuous outfit."

May 30:
More rain today. By afternoon the sun was shining, so Elizabeth was able to go out walking.

Howard went out to a rehearsal right after dinner; he came back a few minutes later and said that Mrs. Taitt had forgotten to let him know that tonight's practice was for the choir only. The entire orchestra rehearses tomorrow night, which means that we won't get to the Pageant as we'd planned.

May 31:
It poured this morning, then around noon the sun came out. Now, at about 2:30, we're just watching a huge black cloud as it blows over us from the south. The sky toward the sea wall is still blue, but it is beginning to shower now. Up the street we can see the steam coming from the pavement as the rain hits it. And now it's pouring again!

June 1:
(All of these Coronation festivities are being written in retrospect; life was too complicated at the time.)

At 8:30 this morning we picked up Mrs. McLaren and proceeded to the temporary building behind the Royal Agricultural and Commercial Society museum, where the "Loyal Tribute" exhibit is being held. First we sat down

Mabel and Elizabeth set out for the sea wall.

on folding chairs in a sheltered area outside to await the governor and his official opening of the exhibit. Three hundred tickets were given out for this opening; after today, anyone can see the "Loyal Tribute" while it is here in B.G. The ceremony was short and was begun with a prayer given by the Archbishop of the West Indies, Dr. Knight. Sir Alfred gave a very short and pleasant speech, and an official of Bookers told just why they had gone to the trouble of bringing the exhibit here. Then, with a bugle flourish, the exhibit was declared open.

We had to wait in line for several minutes while the governor's party trooped through. It was very hot and sultry and there was a large black cloud overhead, but fortunately the rain didn't materialize. Just inside the doors of the building stood two royal guards in their scarlet coats and bearskin hats—not busbies, according to Mrs. McLaren, for busbies are not as high as these towering hats were. Unfortunately, the guards' uniforms were mounted on store dummies, and Mrs. McLaren told me that actually the guards are all over six foot two. Inside were gorgeous huge (4 foot by 5 foot) colored and illuminated pictures of the Queen from babyhood on up, and portraits and photographs of all previous rulers. Most fascinating were the replicas of the Crown Jewels—gorgeous things that must have been costly even if they were just representatives. All the children—and grownups, too—were smitten with a miniature of the State Coach in its golden glory, accompanied by all the horse guards and the foot soldiers, in their splendid uniforms. It was all small enough so that the soldiers were about three inches high, and the procession marched round and round a pillar decorated with paintings of the London crowds.

We left the exhibit at quarter to 10, just in time to walk up the street to the Astor Theater, where the primary school children of the city were going to present a musical program. There were nearly a thousand children, accompanied by the Militia Band, and they sang patriotic and religious numbers and some folk tunes. The children sat at the front of the theater facing the stage where Sir Alfred and Lady Savage sat, so we couldn't see the children's faces. But they were arranged by school, and we could clearly see the little girls' hair ribbons—red, blue, yellow, green, and white, for whichever school they attended.

The children in the audience were wonderful to watch: they mouthed the words to nearly all the songs and stood up fascinated to watch the band as it played something called "Village Smithy," with bird whistles and horse hooves. Again it was very warm and stuffy in the theater, and the children in the audience kept up quite a buzz during the performance. Had a headache when it was all over.

After dinner we went to St. George's Cathedral for the Philharmonic Concert in which Howard played. I have no idea how old the cathedral is, but it certainly looks like a product of the Victorian Age. The vaulted ceiling is very high, and the inside walls are plain dark brown panels with white woodwork. Of course, the white is very dingy, and in places the plaster trim is crumbling away. I sat fairly close to the front of the church and was able to see the elaborate wrought-iron work that encloses the choir loft and the nave. Howard says that at close range it looks awfully rusty, but from the pews it isn't bad. The Bible at the lectern is held up by a huge, highly polished brass eagle; there is an ancient and stained Union Jack hanging to the left of the altar. Howard had mentioned a huge marble "thing" which he laughingly said looked like a birdbath; I saw it as we went out, and my word, what a strange thing to have in a church. We suppose it is used for holy water or christenings; it is a larger-than-life statue of a kneeling figure, holding a marble basin or bowl about two feet in diameter.[45]

The concert was one of many Coronation week events.

As far as the music was concerned, the violins gave us a few bad moments in "The Royal Fireworks," but generally speaking the program went quite well. The chorus sounded pretty good; Kathleen Howe was soloist and sang something from "The Messiah." Mr. S-D accompanied her on the organ and really out-blasted her with all stops out. Howard enjoyed playing but said he nearly died of the heat.

And the bats in the church—there must be hundreds. They flew around the orchestra and the choir and into the congregation, flying so low that I wondered several times if I'd scream if one flew into me. Decided I would!

After the concert we braved the traffic and drove through the downtown streets to see all the lights and decorations. Some of the stores have very elaborate lights—the Town Hall and the Victoria Law Courts were outlined in single strands of white lights, effective and simple, making them look a bit like old castles. Bookers Universal really went wild, but in a tasteful way. They had broad stripes of red and blue bunting fastened near the top of the building with large golden crowns, and drawn nearly to the ground. Really prettier in the daylight, for they played yellow spotlights on it that ruined the colors. Everyone in the streets was in holiday mood, and traffic was creeping through the bicycle and pedestrian menace.

June 2:
We were awakened at about 6 this morning when the neighbors' radio went on, loudly relaying the Coronation procession from London. The ceremonial parade that was originally scheduled to take place across the street from us had to be relocated to the militia grounds because of the boggy conditions at Eve Leary.[46] We still were able to watch the people swarm up the street—such a crowd. Howard went downtown at 8 to get the Coronation stamp issue and didn't get back until about 10. The weather was fine but for one brief shower.

We had tea with the Ramsarans this afternoon—an elaborate affair with a pretty cake decorated with a silver dragée and candied cherry crown. Elizabeth sat at the table with us, in Susan's highchair, and was really good, although I just stuffed bread and butter in her little mouth during the Queen's broadcast, for Mrs. McLaren was trying so hard to listen to it over Susan's chatter. I wore my rust-colored sheer for the first time. Evidently it shrank when I washed it not long ago: I had to let the hem out about an inch and a half, also had to move over the hook at the waist and remove the button at the throat because it just wouldn't button, and it feels a little short-waisted. But still, it's a wonderful dress. I wore it all afternoon, got hot and sticky, and held Elizabeth, and when we came home it still didn't have a wrinkle in it.

June 3:
We're tired! Today I have a cold, too.

The Sanger-Davieses are giving a cocktail party for the staff tonight. The "invitation" consisted of a notice posted on the bulletin board in the Staff Room—"All staff members and their wives are invited"—etc. We've decided not to go—complete lack of interest.

June 4:
Today there was a "decorated vehicle parade" that I hadn't even known about—with Elizabeth, I watched people flocking through the Military Road at about 3 but didn't know why. Howard watched from the Staff Room and said that a few of the companies downtown produced good-looking floats but that the majority of the "decorated vehicles" were bicycles with crepe paper. The winner was Mullard Radio, with a car that was more or less covered with a "table" on which were a Mullard radio, a vase with sunflowers in it, and an ashtray that contained a cigarette that smoked.

We left Mrs. Patoir with Elizabeth and walked over to Queen's for another concert, this time the Militia Band with another choral group. We thought the band very poor—there weren't many players, and they were off-key much of the time. The choir consisted of nearly 200 voices, and I enjoyed them . . . except for two idiots in the bass section who had on illuminating neckties—they flashed on and off quite merrily during the first few numbers, and then evidently they removed them. The program included some dancing by somebody-or-other's pupils, and the costumes worn were lovely but the dances dull. An interesting part was done by Celeste Dolphin, consisting of short songs and dances by each of the racial groups here—Amerindian, European, East Indian, Negro, Portuguese, and Chinese. The program on the whole was too long, and we were mighty stiff when we left.

June 5:

Tonight there has been wild excitement—a torchlight parade all through town. It didn't pass us, but we could see the torches up on the sea wall and then on Camp Street. People raced by here on foot and on bicycle, carrying babies and pulling toddlers along with them. It went on for about two hours with enthusiasm undiminished. Also there have been numerous spur-of-the-minute parades spearheaded by a steel band. Everyone has been in gay holiday mood, and the local people all say they've never seen anything like it before.

June 5, 1953

Dear folks,

I received a note from my old friend J. Manuel Espinosa, of the International Information Service (State Dept., D.C.), in reply to a letter of inquiry I had sent him concerning our status as U.S. citizens in a pink-tinged country and repercussions, if any, on our return. His reply was as I had thought—no real anxiety as yet, just watchfulness—and that is as it should be, all things considered.[47] In passing, he mentioned a note he had received from you, Dad, via Senator [Henry "Scoop"] Jackson, so you should have as complete an answer by now as I got.

As for our rent case, it looks as if we will be moving. Nothing definite yet, but my lawyer said Miss Osborn's attorney felt "inclined to let us go," doubted that she (holidaying in England at present) would lower the rent,

Among the buildings decorated in honour of Queen Elizabeth's coronation were the Victorian-style Town Hall (above) and bunting-draped Bookers (below).

and would move to evict us if we threatened to carry the matter into the Assessment Court. One angle that doesn't help is that her lawyer is connected with the Assessment Bureau, so that if we did stand adamant and force a reduction, we would probably not get enough of one to compensate for costs. At the same time it's all too clear we're being robbed. From the point of objectivity, we don't want to raise a stink (probably to be distributed by the news-hungry local press), for in my position it wouldn't be healthy to do so unless the matter really merited it. Nor do we want to be fleeced by our unscrupulous, exploiting landlady. Solution: move elsewhere. She has been cabled by her man, and if she agrees to our release, we'll probably be under a

new roof by the end of the month. There are several places available now (six-month deals for the most part, the owners on leave in England), some of them government offerings at 10 percent of salary.

The Coronation has come and gone—and has left a refreshing atmosphere in its wake. Concerts, parades, exhibits, competitions—we've had all, some good, others not so sharp, but all heavily patronized, and considering both what they represent as well as the outcome of recent elections, it looks as if all wounds are temporarily healed. The bow did arrive in time for the Philharmonic Concert (many thanks again), and the program went remarkably well (exception: a tuba player who showed up drunk). All of the public buildings and most of the major department stores were decorated with red-white-and-blue bunting and Union Jacks, and at night glittered with strings of lights and illuminated crowns inscribed "EIIR." Our new governor, living up to his reputation of being a "people's governor," threw open the gates of Government House and welcomed one and all. Such a mighty crowd poured in that the wrought-iron portals were torn from their very hinges. Not a few are nursing bruises, cuts, and even fractures as a result of the fracas. Marian and Mrs. McLaren attended the opening of "A Loyal Tribute," a display of replicas of the Crown Jewels, state coach, crowns, etc. put on by Bookers. Few anticipated the response that was to follow: even now there is a block-long line waiting to get into the specially built building. Steel bands[48] (composed of "steel drums," 55-gallon oil barrel heads with carefully hammered, tuned depressions radially arranged) plied the streets, beating out "Rule Britannia," accompanied by hordes of walking or cycling, calypso-loving, banner-waving fans (mostly Negro). Even the rain was kind. Although there were a few poorly timed showers, the week has been amazingly sunny for this time of year. All in all, the Coronation thoroughly took the curse off the elections, temporarily at least. In fact, locals say there has been nothing like it in B.G., with the possible exception of George V's Silver Jubilee in 1935.

Now as for this duty business, one would think that the safest thing to do would be to consult a schedule of taxation on imports, and that's what we did when we first came. We found duty rates were high on most new items that would commercially prove competitive with British manufactures. Hence, machinery, clothes, toys—in fact, most gift items—seemed unwise things to send here. But Bee and Mrs. Sterne did send a number of small things, and in getting them I found that (1) knowing the customs clerk was a big help (my man is a music enthusiast); (2) that if he was in a good mood he wouldn't convert a U.S. declaration to local currency before computing tax (thus a $1.00 U.S. item taxed at 33 1/3 percent would cost 33 cents B.W.I. instead of 58 cents ($1.00 U.S. = $1.74 B.W.I. x 33 1/3 percent); (3) that a customs declaration on the outside of a package stating name and value (slightly underrated) of contained items saved a lot of haggling with our clerks here who don't know too much about evaluation of U.S. goods; (4) that postage is deducted from content value. In conclusion, it isn't as bad as it appeared on paper, but still some items are poor imports, e.g., records, clothes, and machinery that the British turn out for much less. For instance, Beethoven's Seventh sells for $6.05 U.S. in the States and here for $8.95 B.W.I.—same company (British Decca, Ltd.), orchestra, conductor, etc. The difference is much greater in clothes—whose quality is A-1 but whose cuts are not ours. The bow got in under #2 and #4 above, so cost me $2.50 B.W.I. ($10.00 − $2.44 x 33 1/3 percent). The razor you returned was not taxed because provision is made for sending items abroad for repair that are not made locally.

Next week the Larthes leave for England with their three children (another boards in U.K.) and car to the tune of $1990 B.W.I. one way. Archie, a veteran of government service in Nigeria and Gold Coast, says that for the Colonial Service careerist, B.G. offers about the worst terms possible in the Commonwealth. Seems to be some truth in it as evidenced by the fact that besides S-D, the Larthes and Maudsleys are the only British folks with the Q.C. staff. The unfavorable terms seem to concern no provision of housing, leave only every three years (instead of every eighteen months as in West Africa), and a generally lower salary scale. Politically there is no motive, for events in West Africa seem anything but inviting at the moment. Archie says that in Africa (or at least when he was last there) all staffs are 50 to 75 percent white (S-D, from Gambia, concurs). He's going to do his best to get back to West Africa. Failing that or any other colonial prospect, he'll return to B.G.

I went to my Indian barber, Albert Massiah, for a much-needed trim and there saw a 50-ish British lady with five little boys, all being shorn. She constantly referred to them by name in a possessive manner, yet this seemed strange for one was white, one Negro, one Indian, one Chinese, and one Portuguese. After she and the boys (about seven to twelve) left, Massiah said in a proud Indian dialect, "You know, she makes me feel British Guiana is the best place in the world to live." Surprised at this, I asked why. "That lady left England when the war ended and come here because she said she was tired of having nothing to eat and of seeing what little money she had eaten by taxes. She lost her husband in the Blitz. And instead of just living here, she adopted those five boys and is bringing them up the way all Guianese children should be brought up." After a little pause, he mused, "She only regrets that they don't have a Daddy."

Love to all,

Howard

P.S. For some strange reason your letter of May 25 had been missent to Kingston, Jamaica; didn't arrive here until Tuesday last.

Saturday, June 6, 1953

Dear All—

Gads, what a week. The Police Gymkhana was canceled due to the weather; otherwise, everything went off according to schedule.

The latest on our situation is that Miss O.'s lawyer is "inclined" to let us go. She is in England and he has cabled her, but so far we've heard nothing of the result.

That's all for now—I haven't recovered yet from all the whoop-de-do!

Much love,

Marian

P.S. for you two: How about setting the last Saturday in June as a goal for a conversation with you all? The earlier in the evening (for you) the better for us, since we're some four hours later than you.

Would you please send 10 cents each to Good Housekeeping *for these patterns: GHN565, GHN490, and GHN461. They are for a crocheted dog, crocheted three bears, and a sewn Humpty Dumpty. After all, we must begin to think of Christmas!*

Howdy—

Would you enclose the Coronation stamps on this envelope in your next letter? The issue won't be current for too long, and we want to amass as many copies as possible.

Thanks,

H.

Ye olde confidential note, Mother! To put your mind at rest, Howard and I agree that so far as possible, Georgetown isn't the ideal place to have more babies. Awfully warm here to be pregnant. Besides, medical care isn't what we'd call first rate. And I'm sure that each day Elizabeth has our undivided love, in these first two or three years at least, the better foundation we are building for her. I do wish you could see her—her back hair curls up so softly and her eyes are green-and-brown now.

Glad there was no duty to speak of on the bowls. Of course we'll send more things whenever the spirit hits—and you should know that we sent them airmail just so that H. could get the stamps back!

Love and kisses,
Marian

June 6:

Although today is lovely, there has been too much rain lately for the Coronation gymkhana to take place as scheduled. The radio announcement began, "Due to the sodden condition of the ground—," an expression we hear rather often!

This afternoon, while Howard was cleaning a piece of fish, the woman who lives behind us brought her baby up. I still don't know their name, but Brian, the oldest boy, has been coming up to see me quite frequently lately. He is, or will be, eight in October. Barney will be seven in October, Bruce six in November, Martin five in November, Patrick three in December, and the baby, Noel, one in December! Brian is fascinated with our stove, which he says is "just lovely" and "the best stove he's seen in British Guiana." He also is smitten with the refrigerator. He has offered to help me by emptying the wastebasket in the kitchen every day; also, he says, he sweeps and would be glad to sweep out the kitchen for me. He calls Elizabeth "my little friend" and is most interested in her but won't let her play with him because he says he's always too dirty. So far he's covered just about every topic from original sin to his father's salary and his brother Barney who paints "just like Daddy." He's cute.

June 7:

Archie and Dorothy had tea with us this afternoon; they leave Wednesday or Thursday for six months in England. They say that if there is any place else available, they won't come back to B.G. It seems that most other colonies pay traveling expenses on leaves for the entire family, and in South Africa leaves are given every 18 months instead of every three years as they are here. They're going far into debt to get their three children home with them—if they do have to come back here, they'll be in bad straits.

312

June 8:

Mrs. Taitt appeared at the door just as we were about to begin dinner and asked if Howard could come to the cathedral at 7:30, when a tape recording of the concert was to be made. He said no—it was then 7—not until 8 o'clock, and that's where he is now.

June 9:

Howard is out again this evening, this time playing the repeat performance of last week's concert. We are amused by the fact that everything from this concert to the schoolchildren's parade is being done over a second time—and they've all been rebroadcast on the radio, too. This must be a pretty easy week for Radio Demerara.

June 10:

Every Wednesday morning at Queen's there is an assembly; this morning, Mr. L.F.S. Burnham, the new Minister of Education, was presented to the boys and made a short speech. He said that he believed the program should be broadened somewhat and the school's aim should be to prepare boys more directly for life here in Guiana. At the end of the speech, he said that when he was at Queen's it was customary after such an assembly to give the boys time to mull it over. So, he said, without forewarning the principal, he would ask if the boys could have the afternoon off in order to "think" about the assembly. S-D could, of course, do nothing but agree; the boys cheered; Burnham held up both arms and waved the three-finger PPP sign; the boys, still cheering, waved back.

June 11:

Elizabeth and I are making progress; for a week now we've been faithfully using the little green toilet seat, and today for the first time we synchronized. It certainly isn't ideal: the little cubicle that is our w.c. gets so hot that it might as well be the oven. And we almost have to leave the door open when Elizabeth is in there, because it's too small to shut the door when her little seat is on the toilet!

We were beautifully entertained this afternoon, for the repeat of the schoolchildren's parade was held at the sea wall and they all formed their ranks just outside our windows. All the uniforms looked spic and span—probably all new. Each school has a different color uniform: brown jumpers with yellow blouses, maroon with yellow, navy with light blue, navy with white, and so on. The boys generally wear the same colors in shorts and shirts, with ties. Today all the children wore clean white shoes and socks, although I've never seen them that way downtown or on their way to school. Each school group was preceded by children bearing banners giving the name of their school. Mistresses marched along, most of them looking uncomfortable and out of step. The masters were clearly in charge, calling out the cadence and such things as "Keep your chin *up*." I nearly died when one of the Catholic schools marched by, led by a young white girl with long blonde hair, dressed in a white satin gown with a Union Jack draped across her chest. She wore a golden, plumed helmet and carried a fancy banner with the school's name—evidently she was Britannia, and although there were a few other white children in that particular group, she was the only one with long hair.

June 12:
The Ramsarans began moving into the Larthes' house today, and Howard said they expected it to be much easier than before. Tomorrow he will help with the car, and I suppose they'll send a dray around for the piano.

Saturday, June 13, 1953

Dear All—

Heavens—I've just a few minutes left before Elizabeth is due home for her supper.

First off, Bee, the package with the cutie elephant and the pretty papers arrived last week. The papers are just lovely and I shall certainly be glad to have them. First occasion will probably be Margaret's new baby! Thank you, Bee. Elizabeth loves to see me squeeze the air out of the elephant when I first dunk it—you know how all the little bubbles rise to the surface. She is still just as hard to manage in the bathtub, always insisting on submerging when I want to wash her and refusing to go down when I want to rinse her off.

Later—Mother, you said you hoped we didn't have to move. Well, we hope we can. The longer we're here, the more foolish it seems to keep on paying out $100 a month for this place, nice as it is. Most government servants pay 10 percent of their salary to live in government quarters—all the houses in the college compound, which are new and roomy, rent for that percentage. Thus John will pay 10 percent of his salary for a three-bedroom house with new plumbing and just about all the new conveniences that are available here. Everyone, including Mr. Beckles now, agrees that our rent is way too high. Some friends of Archie's lived here before the building was made into three separate flats, and they paid $80 for the whole house! Our lawyer still has had no reply from Miss Osborn, so we know nothing more than what we did. We are mulling over the idea of living at Atkinson Field—that is, we would have a house there where Elizabeth and I would be all the time, with Howard coming out on weekends during the school term and living in a boarding house here in town during the week. The political situation here doesn't seem at all alarming,[49] but we think every once in a while, "What if we had to leave sooner than we plan—?" and we both get worried about H.'s research. It's practically impossible for him to get out to the Field during the school term the way things are now. If we lived out there, he could collect on weekends and leave me in charge of the interminable paper changing[50] during the week. And on his vacations he could do great quantities of work without the drive. Heaven knows it wouldn't be as much fun during the week, but there would be compensations. For Howard, it would be pure concentration on school during the week and a complete break on the weekends. For me, it would mean having a garden and a wonderful place for Elizabeth to play. I get awfully sick of our lack of privacy here—our windows are available to all the neighbors—and even more so, I loathe the filth of garbage and donkeys and people that is unavoidable here in town. Howard thinks there is a house available at the Field, which we could rent for the 10 percent. We don't know if they'd let us move out there; it may be that only employees of the Field are eligible, but our American citizenship might help. We think it's worth a try, and if it doesn't work and we still have to move, there are always places available for a few months while the owners are away on leave. And if Miss O. prefers to go through the Assessment Court and our rent is cut, well—we do have curtains up and we are comfortable and it is a good location!

Speaking of the length of our stay, barring the usual unforeseen circumstances, we will definitely be here through the next school year, until the end of July 1954. S-D has written the U.S. Ed. Com. asking if H. could stay a third year—they replied, answering some other questions he'd asked directly but ignoring that particular question. Even if the Fulbright people don't give us the added support, if the college will continue to give H. the full salary he now gets, we will stay the third year. (Thinking of the third year without subsidy is one more reason we'd like to start paying less rent so we could save a bit.) Ah well, eventually we will know. Sometimes I think, Oh no—in three years we'll be old and gray and Elizabeth will be in adolescence! But then the first year here is nearly gone, which seems impossible. We are really comfortably settled now, and even the bugs don't bother me much any more. Except a few nights ago when a large green praying mantis flew in and lit on me and I nearly died! A great place for a biologist.

We have no more paper and since I want to add P.S.s, I shall close this joint epistle. Okay?

Mother, H. and I have both read with great interest Dr. [Norman Vincent] Peale's book. I think it is fascinating, and a great help, too. His suggestion that we look around our friends and try to spend most of our time with those who have a positive approach to life brought my attention to the fact that nearly everyone we know here complains habitually about something! Please, dear, don't worry about our or my adjustment. It certainly wasn't easy at first, but Howard is understanding and sweet and such a help. I feel now as if I could live anywhere (I shouldn't tell him that or we'll end up in Greenland) and enjoy it, as I really do enjoy Georgetown now. I shall never prefer the tropics to a temperate climate, but I don't even pay much attention to the heat now—just prickly heat now and then. You and Daddy are so sweet and I do wish you could spend an evening or a day with us now and then!

Love,
Marian

June 13:

The Coronation Gymkhana was held this afternoon, but somehow Howard and I weren't interested enough to rouse ourselves and go. The weather wasn't too good and we kept expecting rain; of course it never did rain, and the huge crowd that did see the sports seemed to enjoy it all tremendously. We heard the band and the rifle shots and the motorcycles, and watched the people gather and mill around.

June 13, 1953

Dear folks,

How do you like the stamp club's stationery? It cost quite a bit, but since we have a dozen dues-paying members and since a letterhead does impart a bit of prestige (and encourages the boys to write), it was well worth the expense. The pity of it all, thinking of the whole school now, is that this is the sole regularly functioning club at Queen's College, the only possible exception being the nearly defunct Literary and Debating Society. Too few instructors take their appointments at Q.C. as commitments to youth betterment—a job-and-wages, 8-to-4 attitude is prevalent. I don't know whether this is a pan-tropic shortcoming or just another B.G. peculiarity, but it is a fact that compared with what we're used to, extracurricular activities are virtually nonexistent. It is also a fact that the boys lack the personal initiative (so well known in U.S. high schools) and the encouragement to start such organizations. Consequently, but for athletics (largely interfered with during the rainy season), school ends at 3. This is a bad situation, worse here than at home because of the lack of constructive diversions out of the school circle. To partially counteract it, heavier homework assignments are given here than at home; of course, this is not the solution. We're quite proud of our little group.

On Wednesday morning at 8:30 a black Austin pulled up on Thomas Road in front of Q.C. and out stepped two men, one a "has-been," the other a potentiary. The has-been was Mr. A. A. Bannister, director of the B.G. Education Department; the potentiary, Hon. L.F.S. Burnham, former lawyer ("barrister at law"), now PPP Minister of Education. As they strode down the path to the main entrance, flash cameras clicked and the Q.C. Cadets snapped to "present arms." Received by Captain Maudsley (alias Ken Maudlsey, history teacher), they inspected the ranks and then were received by Principal S-D and Deputy Principal Beckles. While old-timer Bannister chatted with old-timer Beckles, newcomer S-D tried to introduce the individual staff members (arranged in the traditional reception semicircle) to newcomer Burnham, but was nonplussed to find most staffers and Burnham old friends. After we had trooped upstairs and had taken our places on the stage before the amassed enrollment, S-D delivered an introduction for Burnham, terminating it with a prayer, "Let those whose hands feel power use that power for just cause."

Burnham's first chore was to present certificates to those boys who had successfully passed last year's London Exams. (It is still amazing to me that it takes nearly a full year's time from exam to certification.) With that completed, he began his unwritten address. At first it seemed to be nothing more than a "Gee, it's good to be back" talk, but gradually the odor of PPP ideology became apparent. He ridiculed the college administration for the snobbery associated with the boys—the feeling that "once you had gained admission (to Q.C.), you had arrived," and made it known that Q.C.

will become "just another agency in the secondary education field—just another cog in the machine." Further, he intends to make "certain changes in staffing and curriculum" that will make certain the results he desires.

He cleverly ended his remarks with the humorous quip, "and behind me sits Mr. Allsopp, who had the privilege of serving in detention with me for more afternoons than I care to recall." As the boys cheered, Burnham extended his right arm and gave the three-fingered PPP salute—and nearly every boy did the same! The assembly ended with the singing of "God Save the Queen" (Burnham abstaining) and the school song. Poor Mr. Bannister, the once highly respected governmental officer, sat through it all without so much as an introduction or reference. After the boys had filed back to their form rooms, those of us who had a free period chatted with Burnham in the staff room and tried to sound him out on just what plans he had for Queen's. His reply, but briefly: (1) Deletion of the first two years (the preparatory form and the first form) because there is no true competition for admission to those levels (all boys take a scholarship exam before going into form 2)—the choice being left to school officials, and therefore an opportunity for race-color discrimination. (2) Introduction of fine arts—painting, drama, music—a good suggestion which, if followed in a sensible way and if taught by a qualified faculty, will fill a gaping void in the curriculum. One of the reasons for having left fine arts out is the lack of a suitable faculty and the high cost of equipment—paints, brushes, oils, phonographs, records, pianos, stage materials, costumery, etc., but all of this is promised! Staff reactions: How can "snobbery" be avoided when Q.C. prides itself on "school spirit"—the two terms are actually synonyms but are differentiated in accordance with viewpoint. With elementary education in such a pitiful state (we're still in the hickory switch–cat of nine-tails era), the removal of Q.C. low forms would seem unfair of educational progress (and of course S-D and Beckles wholeheartedly deny the charge of discrimination, but the fact that eight of 22 boys in the prep form are white is hard to explain to critical outsiders when the whites account for just 1½ percent of the population). Most staffers view the introduction of fine arts with suspicion, particularly regarding the promised equipment and personnel. There's plenty of food for thought here.

As he was leaving, Burnham beckoned for us to join him later at the Woodbine Hotel for a pre-lunch drink. Needless to say, I didn't go, for even if I believed in the man's principles, to be caught in public with him would be a sure way to cut short our visit here in B.G. Personally, Burnham is affable, humorous, and boyish, but he can't hold back his thorough belief in the PPP brand of socialism (or communism—hard to decide which). Nonetheless, the fact that he's an old boy of Q.C. and onetime holder of the coveted Guiana Scholarship puts him in the school's popular driving seat.

With the postponed Police Gymkhana, we saw the end of the Coronation festivities today. From our vantage it seemed to be stunt riding (on horses and motorcycles), band music, and drill work and the crowd was, as usual, enormous and enthusiastic. Even had to put our car in the court to make more room on the street. We're still amazed at the expense and trouble gone to by the local merchants (and the government) to have this Coronation an unforgettable occasion, despite the unsympathetic political victory and Britain's distance (it's about as far from Georgetown to London as from Georgetown to Seattle—in fact, come to think of it, the three cities could well be the apices of an equilateral triangle).

We would be interested to know your views and impressions regarding the Korean truce, or impending truce. The local press gives such sketchy coverage of the Korean conflict that we must rely on *Time* for most all news from that sector. There are probably few places on the globe less concerned with Korea than this one. We gather that there was much rumbling between U.S. and Britain over the desire for a truce (in *Time* it was said India's Nehru actually believed U.S. didn't want peace because of U.S.'s war-geared economy!) and many accusations tossed back and forth, the most acid coming from Attlee. What is the feeling about Rhee's do-or-die position?

Last week I stopped in at the lawyer's only to find that Miss Osborn is using her distance (visiting in London) to advantage—she has not yet replied to her own lawyer's request for a decision concerning our protest. As I believe I wrote before, he (her lawyer) is inclined to break the contract and let us go rather than negotiate a rent reduction because to do so would necessitate a pro rata reduction on all her rental properties. Furthermore her lawyer's association with the Assessment Bureau might well reduce our chances of getting a truly compensating reduction in rent. Assuming we will move, the question is where to? We could bounce around from house to house every few months while respective owners are on leave in England—that's what the Ramsarans have been doing—but it's hardly as satisfactory as living in one place, particularly in view of there being no experienced, reliable movers here. Most people hire a two-wheeled donkey cart or a four-wheeled dray and move themselves between showers, more or less figuring on a certain amount of breakage and damage with each transfer. These little Austin-size cars carry next to nothing. Point two for consideration is my all-important research, which seems to come to a standstill when school is in session. By not being able to progress I find contact is lost and a certain amount of old work (refamiliarization, etc.) must be done over when I resume. Point three is the fact that Marian is stuck in the house too much. Since there is no backyard and a concrete slab for a front yard, it must be a trip downtown or a visit to someone to get her out—not that she wants to stay in, far from it. So: we've been thinking about a solution for these three items, No. 2 taking precedence. We're inclined to move to Atkinson Field, where it is rumored there is accommodation. Of course, it's too far for me to commute daily, but there would be no problem finding a room in a boarding house in town where I could stay Monday through Thursday, and then go to the field Friday afternoon, returning Monday morning. The rent there would be 10 percent of salary, and our being U.S. citizens would be in our favor. There is much to say for the idea, its main detraction being remoteness from Georgetown. All conveniences had in the city are to be had there (electricity, potable water, sewage disposal, etc.); it's cooler at night—a pleasant relief; and we can have a garden, something we've craved for a long time; there are 200 people living there so we're bound to find friends; and—most of all—it's right at the scene of my research project, where I can devote my weekends and 3½ months of vacation where they should be. So, as soon as we hear about Miss Osborn's decision, assuming a release, we'll inquire about Atkinson Field.

Love to all,
Howard

June 14:

I spent some time this afternoon copying crocheting and weaving patterns from the needlecraft book that Joy Allsopp lent me, and in looking through it my imagination got stuck at the chapter on rug making. I keep scraps of just about everything in the trunk in Elizabeth's room, and I found the yellow rug yarn that I originally bought to use for doll hair. So now I have begun a rug. It goes quickly, and tomorrow if possible I will go downtown and purchase more yarn.

June 15:

I made a trip to town for the rug yarn, or "wool" as it is called here regardless of the fact that it is made of cotton. "Cotton" to the English appears to mean sewing thread; what we call cotton is their cotton wool. I haven't the slightest idea how large a rug will result, but I don't want it too large because washing would be too hard.

Howard dropped me off at the Ramsarans' and I had a brief chat with them. They have furniture all over the place—more chairs in the living room than a furniture display window! But they relish the cool breeze, and even though the house is theirs for only six months, they can relax for that long. The Larthes left a small tan-and-white kitty, flea-ridden, but a nice pet for Susan.

June 16:

Miss Osborn, the old battle-ax, still hasn't responded to the cables from her lawyer. Howard says we should wait until the end of the month; by that time she will have had six weeks in which to answer. If we still have had no word, we will ask our lawyer just what we can do to spur her on. The Assessment Court, perhaps.

June 17:

I baked orange cookies and date bars today, planning on the Ramsaran family coming to tea tomorrow. Howard reported when he got home that Enid, their maid, has the mumps, so they can't come. Quarantine lasts ten days. Certainly hope that none of them get it.

June 19:

Mr. S-D talked to Howard after the Association of Masters and Mistresses meeting last night. He has received word from the Board of Foreign Scholarships that it may offer us another two-year stint here. A third year is out, because they base their openings on a two-year schedule. We will know by December, for at that time they make up the brochures with the available openings listed. I guess we'll plan on staying the extra two years, but four years sounds like such a long time!

Tonight Howard is attending a Literary and Debating Society meeting. Some man from the RAF (called the "Raf" here) is speaking to them.

Saturday afternoon, June 20, 1953

Dear All:

So far today we've received no letters, but maybe the postman will be around later. The box from you, Mother, with the cup, cookie cutters, and book arrived Thursday. We love the cup—I sometimes don't put the little top down securely enough, and twice when E. has knocked it on the floor there's been a little spilled milk, but each time we were nearly through so the mess was negligible. She succeeds in picking it up, but so far hasn't taken a drink while she's held it—that takes quite a bit of coordination, really. But such a relief not to have it spill with every jiggle.

We are really at work with the toilet training, and today as the last two days, Elizabeth has been dry all morning. She is so darned cute when I tell her what a good girl she is—she ducks her head and giggles and is so proud of herself. And she is just about walking on her own now—she takes one or two steps by herself, and then collapses giggling onto the floor or against a chair. She loves to have us hold her hand while she walks, staggering a little drunkenly but definitely walking, and each day she seems a little surer. It's such a wonderful stage!

By the way, may we make a request about package wrapping? The cleaners' paper bags just don't seem to be strong enough to stand the journey . . . at least I guess that's what you sometimes use. The magazines were all spilling out of the torn paper; I don't think any were lost, but some of the lamebrains in the post office could have taken one or two. Really tough paper is best.

Well, the latest news on "How long will we be here?" is interesting if indefinite (our staying next year is certain). Howard talked to S-D a few nights ago after a meeting, and according to S-D, the Board of Foreign Scholarships has rejected the idea of our staying for a third year on the grounds that it would throw their entire program out of whack. Understandable, since the program works on a two-year basis. They said that they *might* offer Howard another two-year period but that it isn't definite. We will take it if we can, and we'll have to accept sometime before next December because that's the time when the brochures will come out, and they'll have to know, naturally, whether or not this position is vacant. This of course supposes that the political situation will remain dormant. Howard has been assured by the State Department that they are keeping an eye on B.G. and wouldn't allow us to stay here if in their opinion it became unwise.

We still haven't heard from Miss Osborn, but we're waiting until the end of the month before we ask the lawyer to do something.

Mother, will you please send some pencil leads, not the fine thin ones but the heavier ones? I bought H. an Eversharp for Christmas and now that the lead has gone, we find it isn't available here "at present," as the clerks say. Also, will you send some little pink baby aspirin? I bought some at the Big Bear [supermarket in Seattle], so I presume they will have them. Elizabeth has had several bad spells, I think because of a molar (her gum is so swollen, it must be nearly ready to come through). At any rate, each time, one little aspirin helped so much that I hate to run out. Here they sell fever powders and teething powders and all sorts of junk, but I don't trust it. Thank you, dear.

Knowing absolutely nothing about cricket, I was utterly intrigued to read in this morning's paper that Brian Patoir is a "googly bowler." He is in the Windward Islands at present with the B.G. cricket team, and yesterday he took nine wickets, which evidently is good. A bowler is a pitcher, I gather, but what the word "googly" implies is beyond me.

All week I have been simply involved in crocheting a rug for Elizabeth's room, and I'm almost done now. It is yellow, green, watermelon pink, and bright blue, and providing we don't all break our necks slipping on it, it will be cute. Rug yarn, cotton, is available here in gorgeous colors for 16 cents a skein and I just fell for it. When I finish this I may braid one—it is such a temptation!

Sighted out the window: postman. They wear khaki jackets and sun helmets and they always look so awfully hot. A warm time today, too. He'll be here in a few minutes, I trust.

Postman arrived; letters read. Mother, you asked whether there's any lusterware in the stores. The only pretty luster I've seen is a cookie jar of Mrs. McLaren's, the last of a tea set that was one of her wedding presents; the rest of it was bombed.

Strictly in the family: If we do stay here another two-year hitch, we'd do our best to figure out a way for me to get home with E. to see about her hands; possibly by then we'd be anxious to have another baby—and have it born in the U.S. Anyway, we're happy here and contented, and things will work out beautifully, as they always do. I think we lead a wonderful, charmed life!

Quantities of love to both of you,
Marian

The next time you want to buy me an Xmas present, remember the lime-colored Pyrex set—oblong, square, two-quart casserole, and two round dishes. The first three I really could use. Saw them in one of the Journals *you sent. English Pyrex's plain glass and the shapes aren't, by my standards, as pretty.*

We're set for July 4 [for a ham radio exchange with Marian's parents]. The man is Louis Fonseca. We will be at his place. Ted has his numbers because you gave them to us.

June 20:

Once again last night, Howard found himself in unpleasant surroundings at the Woodbine Hotel. It sounds ghastly. He says the bar is a place where no lady belongs—there are women enough there, but no one he'd care to talk to. Drunks, prostitutes, and just plain oddballs.

A large batch of magazines arrived from Mother today. I shall read all the stories in the women's magazines, and then be so tired of the syrup that I will wait contentedly for my next *Good Housekeeping*. The ads look lovely, and I'm afraid it makes me homesick for some of the conveniences we left behind.

June 21:

We left our magazines for an hour this afternoon to go for a drive. We took the same old drive, but there was one big difference: part of the road has been resurfaced, and it can now be driven on in comparative comfort. The "New Found Out Bar" in Plaisance is up for sale; otherwise, everything is about as it always is.

June 24:

Finished the rug just a little while ago and tiptoed into Elizabeth's room to put it down. I can't wait to see how she reacts to it.

June 25:

When I went in to get Elizabeth this morning, she was standing in her crib peering down at the rug!

Howard is amused at my latest handiwork—I'm embroidering potholders in an effort to perfect some stitches. He says they're much too fancy for mere potholders. At any rate, I don't think I'll let Frances wash them. She gets things beautifully clean, but I'll bet she uses a washboard and similar rough methods. Howard's shirts look a trifle worn at the collar, and Elizabeth's washcloths are in rags.

Friday, 12:45 p.m., June 26, 1953

Dear Mother—

I just finished washing the vegetables, and my fingers look awful. Do you remember when you had that infected finger and had to soak it in that purple stuff, and the finger was stained brownish for days—weeks? Well, I think we wash vegetables in the same stuff. It always takes several scrubbings with a nailbrush to get my hands looking decent again.

Two letters from you arrived while we were eating lunch, and I decided to go ahead and start a letter to you, even though I'll probably wait for tomorrow's mail before I end it. We hope to get the letter from Daddy with his thoughts on our third-, or as it now stands, fourth-year business. The thing that popped into our minds was "politics"—well, we'll wait and see.

I think our June rainy spell has finally begun; the last few mornings have been very wet, and it looks as if it may continue this afternoon as well.

I finished the rug—and I think it looks awfully cute. I am almost inspired to do some more. Last night I was turning some scraps of mattress pad into potholders and decided to experiment with some embroidery on them. One has yellow flowers and stems in a new stitch, and the other is bound in brown with brown cross-stitching that says "Hot!" I can never get very inspired practicing new stitches, or old ones either, when I do it on any old scrap—but somehow the idea that even the experimenting is on something useful gives me incentive. Wednesday I made cookies and used some of the new cutters—no animals this time. I sprinkled sugar on some, sugar and cinnamon on others, stuck currants into some, and iced a few. I used the refrigerator cookie recipe because that is the only one I find truly reliable here—so many of the others just get soggy and crumble away. By kneading it with my hands I got it soft enough to roll out, and the cookies ended up both pretty and good.

The term ends the 29th of July, and Howard will certainly be glad to see it. Next year should be much easier for him, with the former biology master back from England and a local man added, too. Howard will be doing the upper-school classes—fifteen- to eighteen-year-olds, I think. S-D told one of the men yesterday that the Fulbright geography man is coming—so far Howard hasn't heard definitely, so it may not be confirmed. We hope so, though. *Trial by Jury* comes on the first of August, and H. is playing bass in the little orchestra that S-D conducts (with gross arm-waving, according to Howard).

I had a good idea yesterday. I think I will buy another large tray, and then on some of these evenings when our dining room is just too hot, we can eat in comfort and breezes in the living room. A good hot meal is no fun when we sit perspiring, as we often do. We've had fresh pineapple a good deal lately, and I've discovered that we both like it much better with a little sauce of some sort. It's a little dry otherwise. Last time I made some with orange juice and a little cinnamon, and it was good, we thought. Yong Hing's finally is stocking canned celery, and so last week Elizabeth had it for the first time—she just loves it. I've also been giving her sapodillas, and a few days ago she had her first mango. We don't care for them, but fresh fruit is so much cheaper than canned that I'd love to have her enjoy them. She pushes her Taylor Tot around now, and according to Mabel she doesn't want to sit still a minute. Either she's pushed, or she pushes it.

I had to have my raincoat cleaned this week. It got dusty and moldy just hanging—I don't use it very often. When it rains here, people just don't go out. Anyway, Howard asked the man at the cleaners if they did waterproofing, and the man asked, "What's that?" The coat looks lovely now, and clean, but I don't know whether or not I can trust it!

After reading an article in one of the magazines you sent, I think I'd better buy E. a new pair of shoes now that she's on her feet so much more than before. Hers have soft soles and the heels do not fit snugly, as the article said they should. Question: Will I be able to find shoes here that *do* fit? Oh well, when a baby wears shoes two hours out of the day, I don't see what terrible damage they could do.

Saturday 10:45, June 27, 1953

Dear Parents—

Fifteen minutes before I start to fix E.'s lunch. Howard left at 9 to take three boys out to the airbase for some firsthand looks at the place—exams begin in a week or so. He will be very pleased with the stamps, I know—and aren't they as unflattering as they could possibly be! The Queen doesn't look the least bit pretty.

Howard talked to Mr. King, the lawyer, yesterday, and he said that come the first of July, he'll call the Assessor and arrange to have him look this place over. Still no word from Miss Osborn, so this is the only course.

About packages, you may as well assume I mean for you to send them here by slow boat unless I say airmail or urgent. The price for airmail is too high—unless we're sending something to you and can get the stamps back, for they're valuable even after they're used.

Elizabeth is wearing pants now, but they present a new problem—how to get them dry when the weather is bad. They just don't get dry without a breeze and sun. Some days she does very well, and others—well, just what you'd expect. Fourteen months isn't a very long time, is it. She looks so cute in the sunsuits. When she outgrows them (not for quite some time), if she's walking, I think I'll make some little sundresses out of seersucker, along the lines of the skirt-and-halters you used to make for us, only one piece.

Fifteen minutes up now, so to the kitchen. H. had a stamp club meeting last evening, and I did another potholder—a red flower and an orange one, with little blue ones around. Green stems, still a bit strange looking. Good entertainment!

Love and kisses to you both,

Marian

June 27:

Howard and the last three 6th Form boys got back from the airbase in the middle of the afternoon, and H. said it was much more fun than the previous trip. These boys talked, whereas the others were too shy. It has been lovely today—blue sky and puffy white clouds and no rain at all.

I made my first genuine piecrust this afternoon. Half of it I used for banana cream tarts, and they turned out very well. The other half I had to maul a bit to make it fit the pie tin, and, as to be expected, it wasn't as nice. But my mental barrier about making piecrust exists no longer, and I have two more methods I want to try.

June 28:

Today the rains came—right on in. We just about used up all the pans in the living room; had to put Elizabeth in the playpen so she wouldn't upset them. The tortoises had a grand time drinking up the puddles. It really wasn't funny, though, for we had to move nearly all the furniture away from leaks. A chair cushion was soaked; our radio was spattered; we took up the rugs; etc. It was a mess.

June 28, 1953

Dear folks,

This week the true meaning of Guiana—land of many waters—has become ever more meaningful. Each morning we've had downpours, followed by clear afternoons. The rain we expect, in fact, according to local prognosis, it's long overdue this time, but the leaks in our gallery have taxed our patience. This morning, for example, the usual black cloud loomed up in the northeast and advanced, a brief rustle of leaves, and then the shower. Within a few minutes we had just about used up cake tins and pans and blotters catching the cascades. Funny at first for us to be scurrying and for the tortoises to be seen taking a rare drink, but maddening that we should be paying $100 a month for what amounts to a daily crisis.

I took the last batch of 6th-form boys out to Atkinson Field yesterday (and we were blessed with a nearly rain-free day) for ecological study, etc., and damned if I'm not more convinced than ever that A.F. is the place for us to live. While hardly appearing to be ideal, it appeals to us as a place where we can live as we wish and not have to worry about the small-town nosiness and prissiness and the filth characteristic of Georgetown. It is not that we dislike it here—the advantages are enormous—but it must be faced that most of the advantages are in my favor. Educational and beneficial as this venture is when viewed collectively, the fact remains that being a mother and housewife here after exposure to our country's comparatively zenith-high personal standards is a daily up-hill battle to maintain what we at home would call a "decent way of life." We can stay with it, and may have to, but if we can get out to A.F., we shall.

On Thursday we had a weak reminder of a big event that took place in the [Pacific] Northwest in April of 1949—an earthquake. Nothing more than a little noiseless side-sway this time, but nonetheless alarming when you consider that many buildings here are on stilts.

Since the new government has come into power, not much of consequence has occurred. The ministers have been making the rounds[51] in an attempt to familiarize themselves with the problems they are expected to meet—and solve. I mentioned the minister of education a letter or two ago. Last week he spoke to the private schools union (an alumni organization) and outlined the changes to come in the new scholarship awarding procedure. With money short and education so necessary, scholarships are not just academic distinctions; they're out and out necessities. Most of them are government-sponsored, so he is in a position to make any alterations he pleases. Currently the stipends are uniform; henceforth they will be graded to means. Naturally, this system will call for discretion and responsibility such as is uncommonly met with in local government. At the same meeting, the minister of lands and mines, Cheddi Jagan, put forth a suggestion which appears pink to me: instead of paying laborers (of the Public Works Department) in cash, he proposes to pay them with government-owned land on which they will reside and work. For the East Indians this is a dream come true; nothing satisfies them more than land ownership. But the Negroes, often casual and day-to-day in their approach, remain unimpressed. As you might expect, "racial discrimination" rumblings are being heard again, especially from blacks and mulattoes.

Rehearsals for Gilbert and Sullivan's *Trial by Jury* have begun in earnest with the principal running the whole show. Miss Dolphin, the prep form mistress and music mistress, never offered her services, so S-D took the directorship himself, saying he's "quite knowledgeable in these things." Originally he suggested a chamber orchestra for accompaniment, then preferred two pianos, and now we're back to the orchestra. This late switch requires orchestrations that we are having to write out ourselves since there's not time to send for them from the U.K. Fun to do, but pressure of examinations makes this a poor time to get boys interested in G&S frippery. At any rate, the bow will be put to good use once again.

Enclosed is a more or less regular column by Benny Bishop, a rather influential pen-wielder who, as you can see, is well armed with expressions so common at home—"like it or lump it," etc.—so rare here. And his context is as sensible as any we've read, particularly apt in view of Mrs. Jagan's current prolonged attendance at a world "peace conference" in Copenhagen.

Would you mind getting ten more 10-cent packages of paper (same size)? Another boy in the Stamp Club wants to use it and will repay me in stamps. If the bill is too high, well, I don't know how we'll settle it—unless you come across a stamp collector interested in B.G. (most are).

Love to all,
Howard

[From the clipping of Benny Bishop's "Down in Demerara" column, published in an unidentified newspaper on an unrecorded date:]

Guianese who have at heart the land of their birth, and who prefer to think out things for themselves must now, with deep and grave concern ask: "What next?" . . . Perhaps it is true that extremes meet; for it is indeed ironical that the arch-conservatives and the ultra-radicals should strike common ground on their policy towards American industrial entrepreneurs. Are the ultra-radical leaders in this country so irresponsible, so self-centred, so obsessed in their own credo that they cannot see the harm which they themselves are doing to their own country by going right out of their way to attack America—with gusto— at "Peace" Conferences abroad and even in the new House of Assembly.

June 29:
This afternoon I fixed some pineapple for dinner and was inspired to try making some pineapple jam. The cookbook I consulted didn't have it, so I just went ahead. Too late I noticed in another cookbook that hard fruits should be precooked. As a result, the pineapple isn't as soft as it should be, but the flavor is good. Pineapples are a shilling or a shilling and sixpence each, so the investment is a minor one.

June 30:
Tried a new cookie recipe today, substituting the local "golden syrup" for the karo that the recipe called for. We miss maple syrup, and until we came here I didn't think much about the strictly American taste for it. Golden syrup is cane syrup, and although it serves the purpose, it isn't just what we'd like. Maple flavoring isn't available.

July 2:
Margaret's baby arrived this morning at 2:30, another little girl. Howard nearly forgot to tell me this noon, the bird. So far, no name.

July 4:
A strange Fourth, with no fireworks. The radio station devoted a quarter of an hour to such tunes as "Yankee Doodle Dandy" and "The Stars and Stripes Forever" and "The Star-Spangled Banner," all of which made me homesick for a good old traditional Fourth of July celebration at home, which we probably wouldn't have had even if we were in the States!

This afternoon we let Mabel go home early, and we took Elizabeth to the Botanical Gardens for a stroll. The paths were pretty muddy, but we enjoyed the scenery and there were few people about. After making a circuit of one part, we thought the sky looked a bit like rain, so we returned to the car and drove out through Kitty.

After we came home and fed Elizabeth, Howard went to Mrs. Taitt's house to pick up two strings for the bass. She is theoretically the Organizing Secretary of the Georgetown Philharmonic, but actually it's her baby and always has been. H. was there an hour and a half, listening to her rant on the subject of her orchestra. The people who have criticized it or crossed her in her direction of it are all on her list. H. finally broke away, exhausted and disgusted. He didn't get back until nearly 8.

Sunday afternoon, July 5, 1953

Dear All—

Oh Lordy. This is bound to be uninspired—it's too darned hot for anybody's good today! Howard went over to the college this morning to put some strings on the bass, returned home briefly, and went back for a rehearsal that went on until 1:30. He's now sprawled on the bed, dozing damply.

The only big news this week is that Elizabeth is now drinking from her cup with no help needed, thank you. We use the weighted pink cup minus the top—she had too much trouble finding the little hole. I fill it about a third to a half full of milk, and she picks it up and drinks with no trouble. The spoon still intrigues her and she likes to bang it against the dish. She picks it up easily enough, but for the time being she's lost all interest in putting it in her mouth. We've had quite a time getting one point across—that she can pick up the spoon or the cup but not the dish!

Coming home yesterday after a drive, we met John and Susan on their way to the hospital and gave them a lift. The wing where Margaret is looks a lot less suspicious than I'd have imagined—modern, many windows and balconies, etc. John says M. finally feels cool again. We're going to amble up this afternoon for a little visit. The hospital is evidently very casual about visitors—anybody, it seems, can go.

Yesterday we really missed our families—American holidays here are recognized by the local radio station to the extent that a fifteen-minute program is dedicated to the day. We took Elizabeth over to the Botanical Gardens for a walk. I hadn't been there since last September! We walked and walked, and Howard found some land snail shells, which we tucked into the pocket of the stroller. Saw some pretty flowers—the large pink and white lotuses—and large white birds that fill some of the trees.

We had hamburgers (on homemade buns) and salad, and pineapple sundaes (ice cream made from a mix) for supper, which we ate in the living room for a change. One of the chief joys I get here in preparing food is the thought that someday when we're back home some old biddy will say, "My dear, you just don't know how lucky you are to have all these newfangled conveniences—why, I remember when—" etc. Ha!

Mother, the Pyrex idea was for a Christmas gift come next Christmas! And for that matter, having only seen the lime color in a magazine, I might not like it as well as plain, so if *you* don't like it, don't get it. I just thought it would be pretty with our brown-and-white dishes, but do you think the clear Pyrex is better in the long run?

We are intrigued by the enclosed ad [not extant]—Howard needs some slacks, yet hates to have them specially made, which is necessary here. His waist is 33 inches and inside leg (to end of cuff) is 34 inches on an old pair of slacks that fit well. Could you please send for a pair of the charcoal gray ones? I would give anything if we could get hold of some of the other gorgeous men's wear I see advertised, but most of it is too expensive for mail ordering. By the way, the duty on new clothes is 33 percent while that on used clothes is 4 percent. Therefore, we would be most happy to have you send things rough-dry or slightly smudged or with "sat-in" wrinkles.

And while I'm thinking of it, could you buy a belt (straw or raffia—beige or brown) and some new little buttons (brownish pearl—remember the ones on my lavender chambray?), or *any* old belt and buttons, that would look better than the present ones on the brown chambray dress, which I left, dirty, in the closet. I could really use it now that the lavender, gray, and brown-and-white checked dresses are about ready to collapse. No hurry.

Elizabeth will need new shoes and socks before long. Red, white, yellow, and blue. Could you send a pair of each sometime? Goodness, Mother, I don't know what we'd do without you. Wear things that just aren't as pretty, I guess!

We hoped to hear from Mr. Fonseca all day yesterday, but evidently it's still hard to make contact. One of the men at school who's interested in such things said that that area—Alaska, the Pacific Northwest, and northwestern Canada—is always hard to get.

Love and kisses to you and Daddy,
Marian

July 5, 1953

Dear folks,

The end of term is at hand, with all the usual rush and confusion. The General Certificate of Education Examinations (from London) usually require a good deal of time since only two subjects are given each day, and in some subjects (Biology included) two separate exams must be taken by each candidate. (Interesting exam terminology: at home a teacher makes out an exam and a student takes it; here a teacher sets the exam and the student sits it.) G.C.E. exams start Friday but only affect 5th Form (sixteen years) and 6A Form (eighteen years) boys. All others take school (internal) exams, and of course it takes time to make them out. The G.C.E. papers (locally called scripts) are sent to London for correction, whereas the school papers are corrected by the teachers who prepared them—very much like the N.Y. State Regents Board Exams system. At any rate, the "setting," "sitting," marking, and report making must be finished by the 29th. On the 29th and 30th *Trial by Jury* (dubbed by the staff *Trial by Ordeal*) will be presented—and then six weeks of freedom. Whee!

Political news of the week: the new House of Assembly threatens to stop paying wives' passage to and from England when civil servants go on vacation leave. Many House Members want to cease paying all passages. Result if the latter becomes law: exodus of all British civil servants. The exodus will probably be more gradual if the first version becomes law. Days of anxiety for many B.G. Englishmen!

Our love to you all,

Howard

July 5:

Today we went back to the Botanical Gardens, but this time we went through the Zoological Park, as the zoo is called. Didn't have enough time to really study the animals, but it was fun anyway. They've added about a third again as many cages as were there last September when we went through it with the Beckleses. Most awful sight this time: the water camoodi, or anaconda, which would have appealed to me much more had it been sectioned off into handbags or wallets or belts!

The collared peccaries are native pigs called savannah hogs—awful little animals that smelled. Howard tells me that they can be quite vicious and that trappers have to rope them securely to prevent them from tearing their captors apart.

July 6:
Finally got to the hospital to see Margaret. John, Mrs. McLaren, Susan, and I all sat in Margaret's room, and she had the baby sleeping on her lap all the time we were there! She says they are awfully casual about many things—time doesn't mean much to the nurses. We walked by the nursery on our way out, and the babies' bassinets are all open and exposed to any insects that may come in through the open and unscreened windows. Margaret's room is small, with fresh white paint on the walls and clean flowered curtains on the French doors that open onto her own little balcony. She is in a wing that is quite new and modern, and clean—a blessing. Still, she said her room hadn't been dusted in the five days she's been there, and a maid who had come in this morning to sweep had never returned after Margaret asked her to go away until Janet was out of the room. The baby is Janet Sonia—Sonia means "golden" in Hindi.

July 7:
Good news today: lawyer King called Howard this morning to say that we may leave this flat anytime. He called Miss Osborn's lawyer and said that we'd allowed enough time for her to answer; and the business of having the flat assessed would have proved embarrassing to Mr. Mayers because he is clerk of the Assessment Court as well as Miss Osborn's attorney.

I spent the afternoon downtown buying odds and ends and priced a little furniture at Fogarty's. It's awfully high—we shall try to make do with only the minimum, at least until Howard's grant arrives in September. Before Howard picked me up, he talked to a Mr. Smith who is now secretary of the Atkinson Field Board of Control, and learned that there is a three-bedroom house at the Field that we can have for 10 percent of salary! We shall go out Saturday to see it. There is also a two-bedroom house available for the same rent; and of course if we had an extra bedroom we could have guests stay overnight. It certainly is fun to think about, and we're anxious to see the house.

July 8:
We received a bill from Mr. King today—$5!

July 9:
This business of washing curtains and rugs by hand is quite something. Last night Howard took down the curtains in the tower for me, and this afternoon I washed them all in the sink. I don't imagine they're perfectly

clean, but at least there will be an improvement. Also washed the bath mat, and it dried in a matter of four hours in the good hot sun.

July 9, 1953

Dear folks,

I'm writing early this week in anticipation of little free time this weekend. Sort of a calm before the storms, one being the coming G.C.E. exams, due to start Friday.

The other little storm is our own and we're pleased as punch about it. Faced with what would be an embarrassing situation, the clerk of the Assessment Court, who is at the same time Miss Osborn's lawyer, granted us contract freedom: we can move anytime! And move we shall.

I've already received permission from the Atkinson Field Board of Control to secure a house at the Field on the basis of my botanical research and the necessity of securing specimens for my teaching at Q.C. Marian and I go to the Field Saturday to look at a three-bedroom cottage that is now available. It will rent for 10 percent of salary ($42/month) as compared with the near 25 percent we pay here. Since we already have stove and refrigerator, its unfurnished condition is not as detractive as it might be. We have managed to get a few pieces while living here but will have to purchase a bed and perhaps a couple of living room chairs. Ken Maudsley (who knows all about all things Guianese) told me of a man who owns a truck and who moves people when there's distance involved—about $35 was his guess in this case.

I've also inquired about taking a room in town for the Monday-to-Friday teaching week starting in September. Nothing definite as yet, but I think I have one with the parents of a former student. The nice thing about this is that so far, everything has dovetailed beautifully. Because of the exams, marking, reporting, etc., we won't move until the first of August. Thereafter our address will simply be: Atkinson Field, British Guiana. More about this after Saturday.

My watch stopped. I'll air-register it tomorrow so it should arrive shortly after this letter. Probably needs a good cleaning, and jewelers are not to be trusted here—substitution of jewel-bearings, etc., seems to be too commonplace.

We've been awfully remiss about pictures lately, but Marian dropped a roll off at Bookers yesterday for developing—one print each until we see how they come out, duplicates for you folks if they're decent.

One favor: Could you find me a Handy Class Record grade book? The grade books they give us here are huge, ledger-size volumes that are damned inconvenient, and, what's more, the pages fall out! That just won't do, considering the classic secrecy of contents. The Handy Class Record is a 6-by-10-inch green-covered book with sewed pages. I know Stationers Inc. of Tacoma carried them, so they should be found at any Seattle counterpart.

Love to all,

Howard

Saturday evening, July 11, 1953

Dear All—

Oh boy! This afternoon Howard and I drove out to Atkinson Field to look over the three-bedroom house that we've been offered for $42 per month. I suppose there are umpteen hundreds like it on other Army bases, though they're perhaps on the ground instead of on posts, and have windows instead of just screens. Originality isn't its chief charm, but it is well planned and has some details that endeared it to me almost immediately. To begin with, it is located in what amounts to quite a community—about two dozen houses, all well spaced, with plenty of ground around each. They're all painted a rather ugly yellow-pink paint except that in which the man in charge of the Field lives, which is a nice white. Our house looks frightfully long from the outside, but that is mostly because of the roof—there is about a six-foot overhang (eaves), and the roof slopes up to quite a peak, giving it an Oriental cast, more or less. The space underneath the house is all smooth cement with plenty of room for clotheslines sheltered from the rain. There are two huge washtubs with running water down there, too.

Upstairs, the living room is to the right—a nice-size room, which is dining room as well. The kitchen looks heavenly after the one here—compact and conveniently planned in more or less standard U.S. style. To the left of the kitchen door is a large closet with many shelves—for storing linens, I assume, and since it can be locked I'll probably keep our silver there. Next down the hall—a bathroom! With a tub! Ah me, no more bathtubs for Elizabeth for me to lug. I shall have to make a shower curtain since the tub has a shower deal, too. Next down the hall is what will be our bedroom. Luxury—it has its own washbasin and two huge closets. All the closet shelves are planked with spaces to let air circulate, and all have enough shelves so that shoes needn't stay on the floor. Elizabeth's room is next, with its own washbasin and two more closets. The third bedroom is the largest, ditto the washbasin and closets. We shall keep our trunks in it, I shall iron in it, and H. will probably use it to store his specimens. It is built with American height in mind—the kitchen sink and the clothes poles and the shelves are all a wonderful height for us. The whole place will be painted before we move in, on Saturday, August 1. We were told it could be painted any color, but we think ivory in the living room and bedrooms, and white in kitchen and bathroom (both are rather dark) are the safest since Guianese color sense and ours seem to differ. All the windows are screened—no glass, nothing to shut at all. There are louvered panels that fit over the bottom third of the windows for privacy and to keep out too much wind. The floors are good hardwood and very solid; the only thing it lacks at all is furniture, and we shall have to pick up a few things. We'll get a nice chunk of money in September, so until then we'll make do with as little as possible.

Underneath the house next door were hung little children's clothes, and there was a tricycle across the street, so I think we'll find some playmates for Elizabeth. Big news on that score: today she walked! She was standing by me as I flipped through the mail, leaning against my chair, and all of a sudden she just took out across the floor and went quite steadily toward H., who was sitting about ten feet away. I cried, "Look, look, look" about six times before H. looked—he was reading a letter—but Elizabeth made it, and she certainly looked proud. She walked around a little more this afternoon, Mabel said. Isn't she wonderful!

Once we're out there, we can buy groceries (except meat) at a store that's incorporated in some way with the Inn. Eggs are hard to get, so we'll work out something with our egg man here in town. Green vegetables are available there, which is fortunate because they'd wilt terribly if H. had to bring them from town.

Mother, the wading pool arrived Thursday and we love it! Most of the ground around the house at the Field is white sand; we'll bring in some soil for a garden, but we'll put the pool in some sand so that E. can really have fun.

As for missing our friends if we live at the Field, I'm sure we will miss them; but everyone who has a car loves to go out there to use the swimming pool. I think we'll see some of them more often than we have living here in town. Of course, the Ramsarans haven't a car, but we'll have to arrange some way of having them out. Mrs. McLaren has said she'd love to spend some time out there with me. Taxi fare is $3 per person, a little steep to do it often.

I'm just starting to wash curtains and rugs. If you think it's easy to get curtains and rugs clean when you're washing by hand, well—it is, if your standards in the matter are as low as mine! I've washed the light brown rug, and it looks as good as it ever did coming back from the laundry. Good old sun here dried it between 9 a.m. and 4 p.m., which is pretty good, isn't it!

That's all for now, dears. Oh yes—we will buy a little washing machine come September, I imagine. Can't see washing sheets and towels by hand forever!

Love to you all,

Marian

Daddy, I loved your letter. You think so clearly, and it certainly is a help! Heaven knows there are days when I feel I'd give anything to hop on a plane and come home; but we're trying our best to look ahead, and to look at this opportunity in "advance retrospect" or looking forward backwards, or some such. I wouldn't be happy if I felt that I had persuaded H. to leave B.G. on the grounds that I missed our families and friends and country; not that I'm being noble or anything like it because, after all, we're busy building our family, and that takes cooperation in every way. We're really healthy, too, except the heat makes me feel a lassitude which I feel I shouldn't feel at my advanced age, and therefore I get provoked but take a nap after lunch anyway. Darn it all, why can't you and Mother come visit us! We could put you up in the trunk-and-ironing room!

By the way, Mrs. McLaren was here last evening and spotted my newly framed pictures of you and Mother. She says Elizabeth looks like you "through the cheekbones"! You two are in handsome silvery (tarnish-proof, they say) frames and I am very proud of you!

Much love,

Marian

Dear Anna—

Many thanks for the Canadian stamps. I kept a few, distributed the rest.

H.

11 July

Dear Tom,

Many thanks for your engaging note about years three and four in B.G. This is the sort of letter young'uns should get now and then—a sort of self-inventory—and very frankly, we welcomed it. The questions brought up are legitimate and pertinent, and, as you guessed, most of them had been uppermost in our minds. The following comments do not constitute any sort of rebuttal but merely a little reassurance on some of the issues that we as residents have been pretty well able to size up.

1. Health. With regard to the ill effects of a prolonged stay in the tropics, it's useful to look at B.G. in the light of general pantropic conditions. Many people here, particularly those in the civil service, have been elsewhere in the British Commonwealth, and I have been particularly interested in their comments on climate and conditions in other tropical places because, from the day we arrived, I could scarcely believe B.G.'s weather picture to be truly torrid. Indeed, in Africa and Asia, the Colonial Office grants leave (to England) for any civil servant after just 18 months' duty—because of the trying heat and the extremely unhealthful conditions. With this in mind, it is significant that the period of service before leave in the West Indies, including B.G., is three years. As one man put it, "This isn't the tropics; it's just 365 days of Continental summer." I'm reminded of the difference of opinion voiced by old-timers and by some younger Doctors (including friends of Doc Alcorn)—who (the drs. latter) had been in tropical regions and who in chorus agreed that the human body is a little more adaptable than we had thought. There has been considerable revision of thought on this matter since the South Pacific campaigns of World War II.

Re Elizabeth's playing in the yard—that will be possible after 1 Aug. when we take up residence at Atkinson Field. Also, as Marian has mentioned, other kiddies are about at Atkinson, so she will be afforded the necessary opportunity of mingling with them—things that would be difficult under the present conditions.

2. Yes, the career item was uppermost in our minds when we first considered additional time here. But this category requires division—first part concerning teaching. I feel (as Doc Alcorn does) that an additional contract requested or offered by Q.C. is a feather in my career hat. Q.C. applied in '51 through the Fulbright Board in London for a man to help out. This time they're requesting the services of yours truly. Another man (not

Fulbright) is coming to give assistance in lower-school biology, but that is simply to enable me to offer a diversified program in the upper school and to teach night school as well (the latter separately remunerative). Since my main mission here is pedagogical, I have to give my fullest efforts to the school and catch any outside personal benefits as I can.

It is true that I'm doing more with extracurricular activities than most other staffers, but that's the way I want it—it's easy to become a slacker here because so many people do suffer from lassitude of the "Oh, what the hell" variety. I can hardly afford that to be said of me. It's no front—I feel duty-bound, particularly in view of the social vacuum existing in all schools here. The average teacher considers it a necessity to maintain an unending abyss of formality between student and himself. Rubbish! It isn't that I'm deliberately setting out to prove them wrong—it's just the normal thing to do. I'm playing in the orchestra for *Trial by Jury* because I enjoy doing so—and when it's over I know the rapport in my form rooms will be the same, perhaps better. I mingle freely with the boys at stamp club meetings because I want to know them better—another rare desire among most masters. I cannot teach effectively when my students are all strangers. What I'm trying to say is that much of this "extracurricular" activity is part of the job.

The second part of the "career" item concerns the future, and it is here that we have the most defensible cause for another year or two in B.G. I have seldom tried to explain the exact nature of my investigations to anyone outside of the biological field because, here particularly, I'm greeted with nothing but "Oh" and "I see," while I know damned well that the person involved wonders what can come of such a seemingly senseless expense of time and effort. But I trust you'll understand that whatever assemblage of facts I can compile on the untouched flora of the interior (sand reef) of B.G. will be to my future credit—if for no other reason than as a demonstration of ability in independent investigation, this being a matter of considerable importance in taxonomic botany; inherent to the subject is the capacity to work alone in regions yet unworked. Hence B.G. is a golden opportunity for me in this respect. For more gregarious beings, B.G. is stagnation in the superlative (when compared with U.S.), and it is natural that its reputation abroad lies in the hands of such people. At any rate, by being so engaged, even on this part-time basis, I'm in the most coveted professional activity in my field, not away from it. This kind of botany thrives not in the ivy-clad university hall but in the unexplored field. The U.S. as a whole is pretty well worked out taxonomically—B.G. is barely touched. Hence the droolings of envy I witnessed when I announced our plans a year ago.

If I could have a year to devote (with teaching) to this endeavor, I would be well off. But with this not in the cards, I'd like to have more time for the present part-time arrangement. By living at the Field, things will go much easier and more quickly—but it's still just part-time work. Doc Alcorn, biggest drooler of them all, fully concurs on these points.

As to the English influence (I presume you mean in school), well, I really don't know how that will fadge when readjustment to U.S. ways and means comes again. I've tried to be objective about it, and after a year's experience I can see there are things that our system at home could very well include. On the other hand, the system here has some withering defects (by our standards)—ability-segregation for one. If you mean by English influence B.G. in general, recent events in matters political should be evidence enough that this place is less pro-British than we are. Every Englishman to be met here will heavily deny any social affinities between B.G. and U.K. Most important problem: Is the time spent here going to be as valuable as if spent at home? I think so from the professional point of view. Even in scientific work of this color, there's nothing like firsthand experience, something which few taxonomists ever have the opportunity to gain.

3. The item that hits so unbusinesslike a creature as me below the belt is MONEY. If we came home after two years' time we would not have much, I grant you—just the residue (if any) of the Smith-Mundt grant and what we brought here. So we may have to float a family loan to tide over a lean period, particularly if we find ourselves not in the environs of Tacoma-Seattle. It bothers me to even have to figure on this, but with the money bar as it is, I don't know what could be done. Next year's bills will be lighter (no refrigerator, stove, or car installments and rent at half, but weekday room and board for me will be additional), and our income will be higher (night classes added). So we'll undoubtedly accumulate a surplus. A certain amount will be set aside to cover return expenses—probably $1500 BWI or more—the balance to be spent on useful goods. We'll strive to eliminate as much initial expense on our return as possible.

We've inquired about the Orthopedic Hospital through my mother and find that once we establish residence, we will be eligible for their services and help. Both Baufield and Coe were of the opinion that at three or four Elizabeth would be ready for any preliminary [surgical] correction. Both stressed the use of this period (one through three or one through four) for toughening up—and Lord knows she's "tough" and amazingly facile.

With regard to more kiddies, we've considered this plan in the event we stay the additional period: have Marian and E. go home in the summer of '55 to have E. looked at and perhaps for M. to have another baby.

Needless to say, we'll have plenty of time for decision since we don't expect the ultimatum (if it comes at all) until middle or late fall. There'll be no bitter disappointment if it doesn't materialize—at this stage it's merely a wish.

There is, however, one point you didn't mention, and I presume its absence indicates its unimportance. But we're curious just the same: Would there be any political repercussions resulting from our tarrying in a country that's reputedly going red? As is often the case, facts and reputation are miles apart, but it's the latter we must face. The official note from the State Department said in effect there's nothing to worry about—but what about the man in the street? Is B.G. still (or was it ever) a discussion subject, or has it once again been forgotten?

Many thanks again—you see the thought thus provoked. Further comments welcomed!

Sincerely,

H.

July 11:

After lunch Howard and I drove out to the airbase to see the house that we've been offered. It is one of about twenty houses, located on a hill near the administrative offices, which look alike except for size. They vary in number of bedrooms—one, two, or three. Howard talked to Mr. D'Agrella's secretary, who said that the whole place will be painted (inside) before we move in; the only thing wrong with it now is that it's a bit grimy.

We stopped at Howard's "office" on the way out, and took down the curtains and brought his boots home. The can of Klim had soured and smelled like old cheese; the cereal smelled musty; the cans of instant coffee had rusted but the coffee is still all right. Howard's boots are moldy but we were pleased to note that they were still there and untouched—it would have been an easy matter for someone to break into that room.

July 13:

Went downtown this afternoon, and came home stunned by the high price of furniture. At Fogarty's, a meat safe is $30, Morris chairs with cushions run about $80 each, and chests are $60 and up. Heavens. After mulling it over a while, Howard remembered the name of a cabinetmaker who did some good work for him at school. He's written this man and asked for estimates—we do hate to spend a lot of money on furniture that we'd never pick out at home!

I bought shelf paper (choice of two patterns, both orange and white), toilet paper, clothespins, and other stuff. Once we move, I shall have to plan carefully so that we don't run out of such items at awkward times.

July 14:
I am determined to do this pre-moving cleaning with a minimum of strain. A little each day is the only way. So this afternoon I ironed some of the brown draperies—hot work. We're beginning to feel like goldfish again, as our privacy vanishes when I remove the draperies. We're really itchy to move away from our "public."

July 15:
We went to Susan's birthday party this afternoon. Mrs. McLaren said Susan wanted only her grown-up friends to come, so, besides us, Mr. Hetram was the other guest. Elizabeth was very subdued all afternoon, and her three-hour nap should have made me suspicious. After dinner I took her temperature and, sure enough, she was unusually hot. Gave her aspirin and some of the medicine Dr. Bissessar prescribed, and now she is asleep again. Howard is at the college, attending an orchestra rehearsal for *Trial by Jury*.

A locksmith came this afternoon to open our trunk, but evidently the lock is a good one, and he said he'd have to come back tomorrow to remove it.

July 16:
Mr. [Ivan] Skeete, the cabinetmaker, came by this afternoon with his estimates. His price for a bed frame with no headboard or footboard is $14; a food safe, $18. A chest with three drawers, $38; Morris chairs with cushions, $45. Sounds more like it.

July 17:
Went back downtown today. Bought some cute plastic to cover Elizabeth's mattress, also some for a shower curtain. Not much choice in pattern—very little is what I'd call attractive. Had one hell of a time buying a piece of linoleum for our bathroom—a boy waited on me, and the idea of cutting a five-foot square of linoleum from a roll measuring six feet in

width was almost too much for him. It's a medium green flecked with darker green, $6 a yard and not too good a quality, but it seemed to be the best at Fogarty's and was certainly better looking than most of the wild patterns they sell.

Elizabeth is fine today.

July 18:

Mr. Nightingale, the locksmith, came back today with the lock that he removed yesterday. After nearly an hour he got it back on, and the key works and everything was fine. Howard asked him how much—and he said $1.50! Howard gave him $2, and we marveled about it. I remember once at school when Marilyn had to pay $5 U.S. to have a man come out and unlock a trunk—and that was one trip. Mr. Nightingale walked out to get here each time.

I've just about finished a couch cover. We're going to be so short of furniture in our new house that I felt we needed a couch. Howard's cot, padded with the quilt Mrs. Orr made for Elizabeth, and covered with a tailored (sounds better than "plain") brown slipcover made from two draperies—that is our couch. Yesterday I bought three pillows, which I will cover with some of the material that's now our dining room curtains. The couch looks pretty good and will be comfortable. We've yearned here many times for something to flop down on.

Mr. Elmo Mayers, Miss Osborn's attorney, stopped by this afternoon to inquire about our leaving. He said Miss O. is "quite upset" by our leaving. He also told Howard that he was ready to fight the case in court, but that Mr. King said if he did, it would be the last case he'd take to court. He and Howard went over the meager inventory, and he arranged with Howard to receive the key on our way out of town.

Sunday evening, July 19, 1953

Dear All—

Busy, busy. Howard is about halfway through his year-end exams and is getting awfully tired of reading little boys' papers on which beetle is spelled "bettle" and such like.

I've been busy, too. Since the house at the airbase is unfurnished, we have to supplement our meager furniture a bit. I priced beds, dressers, chairs, and a kitchen safe downtown and was flabbergasted. Howard remembered the name of a man who built some glass-doored cabinets at school for him and who did a very good job; he wrote the man and had him come to give us some estimates, which were quite reasonable. We'll have him do the bed and the safe (the screened cupboard for open packages of cereal, fruits, etc., mouse- and vermin-proof) right away, and the others we'll fill in gradually.

Howard brought a packing box home months ago, and after eyeing it all this time I decided to turn it into a toy box for Elizabeth. It is about two feet long, eighteen inches wide, and eight inches deep. We sanded it and patched it with plastic wood, and this weekend I painted it a yellow that matches the yellow in her little rug. She gets such a kick out of putting things into something now—in the kitchen, everything goes into the enamel bathtub I keep under the drainboard. In here, she puts all her toys into the wastebasket, or today, in a big cardboard carton, which Howard first used as a cart with her in it! Great sport. She sat in the box for half an hour, throwing out all her toys and then reaching out to get them and put them back in the box. Poor child, no sooner was the first molar in safely than number two starts to bother her. Good thing the aspirin arrived, Mother—we've used several already.

Tuesday night we're going to a cocktail party at the S-Ds'. Guest of honor is Mr. Martin-Sperry, whom we've met once and who writes the music that is played here on all important occasions. It sounds like finger drills. He's leaving the colony at the end of the month. His furniture is being sold on the 27th and we think it worthwhile to see if he has anything we might want. Mrs. S-D has tried her best (asking H. but not me) to get me to do some sewing for *Trial by Jury*. I would if I had a machine, but I do not want to have to sew there, and with little Janet taking up most of the Ramsarans' time, I don't feel I can ask to use their machine. The silly thing is, many of the staff members' wives have machines, but Mrs. S-D seems to want to keep it within the elite (ha) group of white women. Or so it would seem, because apparently she hasn't asked the others.

Getting back to my preparations for this great move, I've packed all of our spare dishes, washed all the rugs but the two larger braided ones, and done about half of our curtains.

I bought shelf paper the other day, for the kitchen, at Fogarty's. I needed three rolls, and they only had that many in one pattern so that's the one I got. Good thing I like orange! I had a hideous time trying to buy plastic for a shower curtain—finally settled on some that is striped in green, chartreuse, and white. We decided to buy a square of linoleum for the bathroom, to go next to the tub and under the washbasin—we couldn't see trying to fit it around the john so we're skipping that. With E. using the bathtub, linoleum will be easier to mop up than the hardwood floor. Well, I picked out a plain dark green that I liked, but it was all cracked so I turned it down even though I was offered it at $4 instead of $6 a yard. Bought some that is green flecked with darker green, at $6. Pretty thin compared with what we used to see at home, but it will help tremendously. I also found some plastic to cover Elizabeth's mattress. It has a yellow background with all sorts of cute little animals in different colors holding little cards with names like Jacqueline, Luce, Roland, Rolande, Anne, Marie, etc. It is made in Canada—Quebec, I think.

Well, dears, it's been a hot and muggy day and I'm sleepy. Good night!

Love and kisses,

Marian

Mother, I hate to do this to you, but will you please:

1. Buy a copy of Joy of Cooking *for me. Mrs. Patoir asked if I could get hold of one for her, and I'd like to give it to her when we leave the flat because she's been so sweet.*

2. Dig out the pair of brown flats—slings—that are in the buffet, or at least that's where I put them. I may as well wear them out here, and I think one of these days I may go through the toes of my Joyces.

3. Send me my beloved dish drainer and the red rubber tray that goes with it. Darn it all, I'm just plain silly to keep on drying dishes by hand, and since I can't get those things here I'd really like to have you send them. If the bill for sending these items is over a dollar or so, as I suppose it will be, please keep track and take it out of the $500 grant installment that will be coming to you in September. (I assume we have nothing in our bank account at present.) Definitely, I want to pay for Joy of Cooking.

After we move, please address any and all packages to H. at Q.C. That way will be much simpler since the customs inspection is in the city, and he will check the mail at least once a week at the college. Is that garbled! I am sleepy.

Wasn't The New Yorker's *account of the Tabasco factory interesting? How we do love our magazines here. Read them much more thoroughly than ever before.*

Love to you and Daddy—we miss you!

M.

July 19, 1953

Dear folks,

Well, a little nearer to the end of term now—and the closer we approach the more impatient we get. The impatience is not over school (although I'm a bit "saturated") as much as moving. Last Saturday we drove out to Atkinson and saw our house (to think our first would be on the Demerara River in British Guiana!). It's a three-bedroom, one-story layout with great overhanging eaves and many pane-less, screened windows. Such an improvement over what we now have. As for furniture we'll need, our want list looked pretty formidable, and a trip to the shops confirmed our suspicions. Secondhand furniture is just about out when it comes to standard items—there are too many people in Georgetown who can afford nothing else. So, what to do? I remembered a cabinetmaker hired by Q.C. who made some beautiful bookcases with glassed doors, etc. about three months ago. There was little thought then of our actually moving, but I asked for his card. In the recesses of my moldy old wallet I found it—Ivan Skeete, 20 Haly Street. We sent him a note, and his estimates for the whole job add up to something less than $200 B.W.I. Piece by piece, we're letting him undertake the project.

I had a couple of miserable days this week resulting from the faithful pursuit of profession. While gathering specimens for the G.C.E. exams, I must have stumbled into an infestation of the barely visible mite known locally as bête rouge. It's about the size of a pinpoint and invariably makes its way to the warmest and dampest parts of the body and then sets to work: nips a little puncture, injects a venom, then draws blood. Results: extreme itching sensation and large, dime-size scarlet welts around waist, "privates," rear end, ankles, and feet—lovely! By the time seventy or more welts had come up, I was in need of a dozen hands to scratch. I took a shower and that slowed them down—but only for a while. At one experienced person's suggestion, I went back to the shower and doused myself with ammonia—excruciating, but successful. Bête rouge, needless to say, makes picnics in the grass impossible here.

Well, the incessant rain has let up—so off to the P.O. with this.

Love to all,

Howard

July 19:

I do hope that once we move I can get out of my horrible Sunday routine. I get so tired of working just as hard on Sunday as on any other day. Ah well, we will have about half as much floor space there as we now have—and the better-planned rooms will help tremendously.

I've covered two pillows, and I intend to finish the third before retiring tonight. They will look very bright against the couch's brown cover, and they'll help to make it comfortable.

July 20:

Howard made the arrangements for our move today, with the one person who seems to do such things here. It will cost $30, and the men will come at 7:30 Saturday morning. We were told to have the refrigerator "serviced" beforehand—don't know just what that involves, but we shall inquire. The truck is an open one, and I hope they cover the furniture with canvas. We've been having such rainy mornings lately.

Tomorrow we go to a cocktail party at the S-Ds'. It is in honor of Mr. Martin-Sperry, who is leaving the colony soon. Mr. S-D told Howard it would be a mixed crowd—heaven only knows what that means. Mixed— in interests, occupations, skin colors?

July 21:

Such strange weather this afternoon. About an hour ago the wind began to blow wildly, and the sky grew dark with heavy bluish-gray clouds. I closed the windows and Mabel brought in the washing, and we got all set for a heavy shower. Apparently, however, the wind was strong enough to blow away the rain because the sky looks clearer now.

Must get dressed for tonight's outing.

July 22:

Made a major purchase downtown today—a mattress and springs, both the cheapest I could get. The mattress is straw, or "fiber" as the salesmen call it, which is cool as well as cheap—it cost $20. The springs were $36, and there is nothing special at all about them except that the four side pieces come off for easy storage or shipping. Also bought some shoes for Elizabeth, size 6 already! I wanted high shoes, but the only ones I saw at the three stores where I inquired were a size 4. As it was, I think I got the only size 6 in town.

The cocktail party last night was rather interesting. Quite a few people drank and drank and drank, and just before we left we had a rather impassioned discourse from one Tom Wieting on the horrors of French Guiana, Dutch Guiana, and certain parts of British Guiana. I met Mr. Fletcher, who is to be in charge of the Atkinson Field Board of Control—he was very pleasant, assured me that we'd really enjoy living there. He says there is no doctor stationed there but that there is a "dispenser" at the hospital who "would know what to do until the doctor could come." He, Mr. Martin-Sperry, and an unknown woman all said that we must meet some people named Jane and Jack Nichols—that we will undoubtedly enjoy them. He is chief engineer, I believe. (By a "mixed group," Mrs. S-D must have meant personalities: everyone there was English but the two of us.)

July 23:
This noon, just as we sat finishing our lunch, half a dozen men came with a dray for the furniture that we've been keeping for John and Margaret. The flat looks really barren now, and quite forlorn with most of the windows bare as well. Elizabeth woke up from her nap crying, and when I went in to her she had such a puzzled look on her face. I think she was wondering what had happened to the three wicker chairs that had been in her room!

July 24:
Washed two more pairs of draperies this afternoon. I will be glad to have that job all done.

July 24, 1953

Dear folks,

This place has suddenly changed from a comfortable, cozy apartment to a barren, obviously disturbed flat. No curtains, no pictures, no rugs, less furniture—but we're happier than we've been in a long while. As you said in your last letter, a move for the good makes you feel jubilant. Tomorrow we'll make a trip out with the rear half of the car filled to overflowing with miscellaneous, none-too-valuable items. These we'll leave with the rear seat cushions so that we'll have even more room for next Saturday, the date of the real move. Movers are scheduled to appear at 7:30 with an electrician close on their heels. The latter gent will "service" the refrigerator and disconnect the stove and then ride out in the truck to install the fixtures at Atkinson, returning to Georgetown with the movers. Incidentally, the bill to carry our worldly goods 30 miles in B.G. is $30—we still haven't become accustomed to what seem to us ridiculously low labor charges. The truck is not a van but a flatbed job with two-foot sides—looks something like a dump truck. Hope it doesn't rain! Valuables will go in the Morris, since no one trusts the casual laborers used by movers. If all goes well we should arrive at the Field by noon and be all in by 2.

Mr. Ivan Skeete, local cabinetmaker, is putting a bed together for us—we've purchased spring and mattress. After that comes a food safe, then a couple of clothes chests and chairs.

On Tuesday we went to a cocktail party given by S-D for Mr. Harold Martin-Sperry, local consul for the Netherlands and aspirant composer of light music. Our chief reason for going was to find out what items would be in his forthcoming furniture auction, but Mr. M-S had had a few before he arrived and wasn't in the mood. Otherwise the party impressed us as the tamest function we've attended at S-D's house. Only annoying factor was that is was all-white.

As I've been repeating in letter after letter, the term is about to end and, concerning next year's program, I'm getting a little worried. S-D has been saying all along, à la fait accompli, that I will have two men to help me with the biology program next year, that physics and chemistry will have an extra man, and that an adult-ed night program would be set up with subsidization from the local government. Now it appears one of the two men I was to have probably won't come (from England)—seems quite content where he is; the man for physics and chemistry is definitely out, which means the second man I'm to have will have to devote some time to those subjects, thus lessening his usefulness to me; and the night business seems quite doubtful for this year since the budget limits have already been set—not until next year can adequate financing arrangements be made. So—it looks like private students again and perhaps a once-weekly university-level lecture series for the University-College of the West Indies to help finances along.

Well, next week we have the usual term's-end staff meetings, then *Trial by Jury*, then we move, so you may not get a letter—or at best a shortie.

Love to all,

Howard

Saturday evening, July 25, 1953

Dear Mother and Daddy,

It's 8 p.m. and I've just finished the dishes. Howard is at the college rehearsing for *Trial by Jury*, which is to be given next Wednesday, Thursday, and Saturday nights. Saturday will be out, of course, as far as H. is concerned, since we will be newly installed at Atkinson Field then.

First, though, I'd better answer your questions, Mother. Yes, I think I'd better have the brown dress since I *must* retire the lavender, gray, and brown checked. They are falling apart. The skirts sound wonderful! I shall certainly be glad to have them. Thank you! Concerning Elizabeth's socks, I would say size 6. I bought her some shoes the other day, low, with one strap: not at all the thing I would have purchased if I'd had any choice, but I didn't. (Fogarty's had one pair of high shoes, size 4. Evidently high shoes aren't fashionable here.) Yes, I do like the square-toed socks. I bought E. two pairs of white socks here; they're rather heavy. At Bookers they had some like the ones you sent, more or less—a nice thin cotton, but they cost 98 cents, which seems awfully high to me. How much are they at home? I don't think Howard needs any shirts. Frances does them up beautifully, but I'm sure she beats them or uses a washboard; many of my things look a bit "gone." But since I'll be doing H.'s shirts from now on, I think they'll be all right. On the other hand, since the colored ones are so much easier than white, if the reductions are really worthwhile, you maybe should get two blue ones, please, size 16-35. His desperate need is for underwear—in the last week, three pairs of shorts have split down the seat—really! It is the old devil perspiration that just rots cloth even though we wash things much more frequently than at home. But I don't think we can wait for you to send them! This is a problem: undershirts here cost $1.67, shorts $2.17. Shorts aren't broadcloth but woven, like the shirts. Monday I plan to buy H. a few pairs of shorts and two undershirts; if such things are at all reduced at home, will you get half a dozen pairs of shorts and two more undershirts? I know they don't cost anywhere near as much there—the shorts, at least. Undershirts size 40, shorts size 34. Reminder—don't forget to wash or wrinkle things so that they can be called "used." Rough-dry will be fine.

We finally got a locksmith to open the trunk for us. Did I tell you this before? He came a total of three times and spent a couple of hours altogether; finally had to take the whole lock off. Charge: $1.50 B.G. In the trunk were Daddy's Gladstone, your black bag, and several pieces of my luggage. The only thing that was really a mess was the Gladstone—all moldy. I scrubbed it and left it in the sun, and it looks fine now. Something about genuine leather, I suppose. Some of the metal locks and corners are all tarnished and rusty—too bad.

I shall love to have the books. And I shall keep them! We gave nearly all the whodunits to Mrs. Patoir, who was very pleased and said her family loves them although she doesn't care too much for them . . . H. doesn't either, but I do!

Back to clothes. Yes, perhaps you should get a pair of shorts for me. I know Bee would love to, but after all, you have access to our bank account (not that that means too much, I suppose!), and she is so terribly sweet and generous that she'd probably buy $15 shorts with sequins or something, when all I want is denim. Size? I don't know—16, or a 27-inch waist. Brown or green if you have any choice.

Every day, Elizabeth grows so much more independent with this walking business. Quite often now she scorns the helping hand, and she spends more time on two feet than on all fours. In her bare feet she's remarkably steady, but in shoes she slips and slides. Not that she wears shoes often. Her molars are a bit bothersome, but two are through and this last week has been a happier one. The little dickens—twice this week she bit me on the shoulder as I was carrying her from her bath to the bedroom. I nearly dropped her—it hurt! Still have the bruise. H. said I should have been stern about it, but I was too busy yelling ouch and dislodging her grip. We have encountered a difficulty, easily remedied. When she eats bread and butter, her hands get greasy, and then she can't hold the cup because it's too slippery. I will make some little cuffs or bands of Turkish toweling to slip up on the cup—that should work. At present, I put the bread and butter in her mouth, but that's no fun for her.

We drove out to the airbase today with a load of bulky junk, none of which is very valuable. Always optimistic, I had hoped that the painting would all be done, but I should have remembered that B.G. isn't the most efficient place. Two bedrooms have been done, and they do look nice. It is a very pinkish ivory—not what I'd call ivory, but pleasant. Thank heaven we didn't say "pale blue" or "light green." Do hope they get it all done this week. The place reminds us of a nice residential neighborhood at home: houses well spaced with no crowding. While there, we saw two women, apparently English, about 30, chatting; one lives next door and the other across the street. One has a little girl about five, and as I said before, most of the houses right around ours show signs of children. We assume that theft isn't the problem there that it is here in town; nearly all the houses have chairs, hammocks, and tables underneath them, and we don't think they would be lugged upstairs and inside every night. After all, the only road in is barred by a gate and a guard, and only authorized persons are allowed in, which is nice.

I didn't get to put my shelf paper in. Oh well. While we were there, an Indian woman came to the back door and asked if we'd need any help. We told her to come back next Saturday and she can do the bathtub and washbasins—all pretty grimy—and scrub the kitchen floor and sweep out for us. I love to keep house, but scrubbing floors I can do without. Shall find someone to do it once a week, plus the stairs. Also the concrete underneath the house will need sweeping once a week or so, too, so we shall hire someone to do all that. By the way, many folks here are simply in a panic because one of the new Ministers has suggested that all domestic help should be paid $40 per month, two or three times what most of them get now.[52] Some of the men at school were discussing this, and H. was asked what we would do. He said that we didn't rely on help; one man replied, "You don't mean your wife does the housework—why, I've never heard of a white woman doing her own housework here." H. said, "Maybe not a white Englishwoman" and grinned, and the man smiled back. La de da, I bet we really do confuse some people here!

Something else I should have mentioned last week, but which is probably too good to be true: H. was talking to Ken Maudsley, who apparently knows this place from the governor on down and has just begun his third three-year stretch here; Howard mentioned the fact that we might be here a second two-year stretch and we wondered what the physical effect would be. Ken said that they were here for four and a half years once, and that they needed a vacation badly after that long. He went on to say that civil servants are generally given leave after three years (leave of six months), which we knew, but that sometimes after two years a leave of three months was given. Howard asked S-D about it, and he suggested we inquire after school starts this fall—after all, we've just barely been here a year. Ken said we might be granted $1500 B.G. for the leave; on the other hand, the new local wheels would cut out all money grants for leaves for civil servants. So we might be granted the leave but not be able to afford it. Hmm. At any rate, we'll see, because a vacation at home would make a whale of a difference in the way we feel about the second two-year business.

Monday I have a dentist appointment. If we had millions, I would import Dr. Grief for a week every six months! This is another man, a Dr. Tallim. H. made the appointment and said the office isn't too clean, but no place really is here, it seems. H.'s wisdom teeth give him a jolt every now and then, but we hate to have them taken out here where dentistry as an art isn't very far advanced.

At least we're healthy. Howard is pretty worn out. He needs this vacation and will enjoy puttering around our new home.

How I do enjoy the summer editions of *Good Housekeeping* and all their summer recipes. The only trouble is that they need "adapting"— nearly all of them call for frozen foods or bakery goods that we don't have. But the ideas are certainly fun. One day soon I shall have H. buy a can of wieners ($1) and I shall make some buns and we'll have hot dogs, by George.

My latest cookie variation: your refrigerator cookie recipe makes lovely filled cookies, in case you didn't know. I made some and used some pineapple jam that I'd concocted a few nights ago. They're very good, and the dough is just right! Amazing.

Well, my dears, I'm going to take the *Reader's Digest* and go to bed. Howard will be home at about 10, and it's 9 now. Elizabeth is sound asleep (she is wonderful about naps and bedtime) and the tortoises are all tucked away, too. Nighty night!

Love,

M.

July 26:

This noon a nice-looking couple came to see the flat. Frank Osborn, nephew of the infamous Miss O., was giving them a line about a one-year contract. They seemed a little stunned when we mentioned that the stove and refrigerator were ours. Tonight while we were eating, the man came back and asked for Howard's frank opinion on the place's worth. He said that Osborn painted such a rosy picture they couldn't quite believe it; also he asked about some stains on the floor and whether or not the place leaked. Howard told him the truth!

Scrubbed the last and largest of the braided rugs this afternoon and washed the last two pairs of brown draperies. I only wish I didn't have to iron them.

July 27:
Howard went to Mr. Martin-Sperry's auction today, and working a deal with Mrs. S-D, he bought four dining room chairs. Actually, he bid for the set of ten: Mrs. S-D had already bought the huge dining table, and she wanted six chairs, so it worked out well for all of us. They haven't been delivered yet, but Howard says they're nice looking and comfortable.

July 28:
Howard came home at noon with three of our dining room chairs and a very sad tale about the fourth. Mrs. S-D had arranged to have the chairs carted to their house, and upon their arrival Mr. S-D paid the cart man and that was that. Later they discovered that one had apparently fallen from the cart and been run over, for all the legs were broken as well as the seat. The man had carefully tied it together, and when he carried it upstairs it was concealed under another. Too bad S-D didn't check before paying. Now he says he didn't know what condition the chairs were in when his wife bought them! He is going to have it repaired at the vocational school but of course it won't be the same. H. is going to talk to him about it tomorrow—it seems to me they should keep it, but it is rather a delicate situation, I'm afraid. The three chairs that we have are really very nice. They are good-looking—very simple yet not the stark modern which is currently popular here. Rounded backs and seats are upholstered with a homespun-looking material that is mostly light brown with a few red threads in it. Just perfect with all our other colors. They were $12.50 each.

July 29:
The first performance of *Trial by Jury*. Howard dropped me off at the Ramsarans', and I had a little chat with Margaret and John before Mrs. McLaren and I went over to the school. I was surprised to find how ill Margaret has actually been: John hadn't given any indication to Howard of how serious it has been. Mrs. McLaren seemed tired out and upset, and I told her to plan on visiting us for a while once Margaret is on her feet again.

We enjoyed the performance, except for the fact that S-D (who conducted it) insisted on repeating the six main numbers as encores. It stretched out the operetta to a respectable length but was boring; rather quickly the audience cut down its applause appreciably after the first time through. Mrs. S-D supervised the costumes again, and they were attractive. Most of the boys did well. The bridesmaids were awfully cute, and several of them got right in the spirit of the thing so well that they really seemed to be girls. The boy who was Angelina was fine, a lovely soprano, but all the college people held their breath—his voice is just changing, and every once in a while during rehearsals it cracked! Not last night, though.

After the performance we had a cup of coffee with Mrs. McLaren, and it nearly did Howard in since he was sweltering after the exertion of playing.

Thursday evening, July 30, 1953

Dear Mother—

I've been in a daze lately, I guess, because now I can't remember what I've written and what I haven't. I was just about to write you that the bibs, washcloths, sponges, and Jumbo toy had arrived, and then today the package with the precious dresses arrived. I can't wait to see Elizabeth in the red-and-white nautical number—I held it up, and it will fit beautifully; the pink is a bit big. My pink I just adore! It looks cool as clover, and it fits perfectly—I let the hem out, of course, and the petticoat is so pretty. You certainly are the sweetest mother to send us such wonderful packages. We're saving Jumbo for the wading pool, which we shall probably christen, or launch or whatever one does, this Sunday.

We are so beautifully organized for this move that we shall accomplish it with the bare minimum of fuss and discomfort. Early this week I did the last of the curtains; since then we've packed books and what not. Howard took a load out today, so all that is left to go in the car is china, silver, glassware, and the kitchen things. We're told not to trust anything to the movers unless it is locked—the truck's driver is an employee of the couple who run the business, but the other men are just laborers picked up downtown. H. says the painters are through but for a little trim—he thought they'd finish it this afternoon. Tomorrow a plumber will check all the plumbing and fix the john seat, which is broken.

We are having fun being cagey and economical about all this. Last Sunday after dinner we sanded the hideous, tacky finish off the old table H. bought last fall; I waxed it today and it looks just lovely. We had to fill in two cracks, but they're scarcely noticeable. When we've settled and have more time, we may get around to sanding the legs and waxing them; they aren't in bad shape, but Howard's parental training is giving him a guilty conscience about leaving them as is.

Mr. Skeete delivered our safe and bedstead yesterday, and they are just what we wanted. The bed is simplicity itself: really no headboard to show at all. The lines are infinitely more attractive than those in the stores, which are so big and heavy and ugly.

Elizabeth has a determined streak that will carry her far; at this age, she sometimes tries and tries and tries and finally gets the toy that's almost up too high or the doll that's just beyond her reach. At other times, she tries and tries and we say "no-no" and she sits and howls until we present her with something new.

She's going to be a climber, I fear. Already she tries to climb into her chair or onto our bed. There's nothing she won't be able to do if she makes up her mind she wants to do it!

The poor Ramsarans are having one hell of a time. Margaret has been really sick—I hadn't realized how sick until last night. She has an infection in a breast, as a result of carelessness in the hospital. The baby has had some trouble, too—the brand of milk that Susan thrived on hasn't worked for Janet, and that sort of thing, which never helps. Mrs. McLaren is worn out. As soon as Margaret is up and able to cope with things, Mrs. McLaren will come out and rest up with us for a week or however long she cares to stay. I really think she'd be much happier with her brother in England; and we can see John and Margaret's side, too, for I'm sure it isn't easy for them.

Howard talked to Mr. D'Agrella at the Field today about the plumbing and other things. Mr. D. said, for one, that no one worries about burglars there—a big change from here in town, and a darned good one. Very few people sneak through the gate, and the occasional one who does is more interested in airplane parts than household goods. The men work right there: B.G. Airways is located there, and many who live at the airbase belong to that. There are many people still required to run the field and the airport itself; also the maintenance of the buildings. Mr. D. told H. that two American families live there. Three cheers for our side! One runs B.G. Airways; the other is the Nichols family—he is chief engineer, whatever that implies—the people mentioned by nearly everyone at the S-Ds' the other night as lovely folks whom we'd be sure to enjoy. They are grandparents of a baby about E.'s age; but lovely people are lovely without regard to age. We really don't know much about the Inn yet except that it is expensive, it is considered to be the resort here, that honeymooners go there, vacationers from town go there, etc. We've seen the outside, which looks quite nice—it was the officers' club, formerly. They serve meals, so perhaps we can have a meal out now and then. Don't worry about the small wading pool—I imagine all the other children use the swimming pool. We'll save E.'s for any other toddlers around.

I don't know whether it's a sign of ease or carelessness (that's silly—of course I know) but I very, very seldom refer to Messrs. Spock and *Better Homes and Gardens* anymore [for advice about parenting]. I am convinced that Elizabeth will let us know in no uncertain terms when she's ready for new things. She is so bright and alert and precious. Her latest occupation is putting and taking. She takes shoes from the floor and puts them on our bed; she takes my apron off the towel rack and puts it in her bathtub; she puts her toys in a chair or takes them out of the chair, depending on where she left them. She loves to carry toys from room to room, depositing them with anyone who is there. I think she is just ready for the yellow toy box—putting her toys away will be sheer joy at this stage. She walks much more than she crawls now—arms outstretched, she walks pretty steadily, and the little curl at the back of her neck joggles and bounces.

Mother, I'm seriously considering sending home the two jersey dresses and the blue pleated one. The dry cleaning here is just plain poor—they don't get things really clean. Consequently, the dresses I can't wash just aren't as nice as they should be. H.'s suits suffer, too—but he just about has no recourse. If I do decide to send them, I think you might as well keep them since I'll need summer clothes at home, eventually, and it's silly to have them here if I'm not wearing them. The blue may be a total loss. Will you ask a good cleaners if it can be dyed navy or even black? If it's going to cost a lot, might as well skip it since the dress wasn't expensive to begin with—just gorgeous.

After we are somewhat settled I shall write what will probably be a rather hysterical account of moving à la B.G. We are taking the tortoises with us; we feel that Testudo and Junior are becoming affectionate. They seem to like to have their heads scratched. We lost track of Little Jr. for three days this week—after being dormant all this time, he finally went exploring. But he's just too little, and we feel we might step on him accidentally, so he will go back to the bush.

Love to you and Daddy,
Marian

July 30:
We pulled our three trunks out into the open and I started to fill them up. Discouraging.

July 31:
Except for a fit of depression at noon today, we were well organized and got everything put together per schedule. All trunks loaded and the lids squashed down upon them; suitcases filled and locked.

ENDNOTES

11 Stabroek Market (10/1/1952): Marian noted years later, "Howard felt the crowded, dirty Stabroek Market was not a place where I should shop."

12 Thomas (10/6/52): An Afro-Guyanese in his fifties whom Marian later described as "a huge, smiling man who appeared weekly with his heavy, long-handled hand-powered buffer to 'bump' the polished floors."

13 Filaria (10/12/52): A parasitic disease in which microscopic worms spread by infected mosquitoes can cause elephantiasis as well as arthritis, abdominal pain, and "river blindness," filariasis was found among some 20 percent of Guianese in 1964. It is still classified as a "neglected tropical disease" in Guyana and several other areas of Central and South America, though drug treatments sponsored by the World Health Organization have made inroads in controlling transmission.

14 Sorrel drink (10/19/52): One recipe calls for 2 pints dried sorrel (hibiscus) flowers to be mixed with 6 pints water, 2 small pieces mace, and sugar to taste; let stand 24–36 hours, then strain and chill.

15 Burglars (10/21/52): A somewhat similar technique is described by Margaret Bacon in *Journey to Guyana*, her memoir of living in Georgetown for two years in the mid-1960s (her husband, the engineer Richard Tuckwell, helped Bookers construct Georgetown's first bulk sugar terminal): ". . . neighbours, tradesmen and passers-by all warned us about teef-men [thief men]. Apparently they were quite fearless, usually came at night, naked and covered with grease so that they were too slippery to catch, and armed with a cutlass."

16 Abbreviations for degrees (10/21/52): The letters denote rank within the British Honours System. The Most Distinguished Order of St. Michael and St. George (1818) honours service overseas or in connection with foreign or Commonwealth affairs. Gutch's rank in the order was Companion (CMG). The Most Excellent Order of the British Empire (1917) is awarded mainly to civilians and service personnel for public service or other distinctions and has a military and a civil division. In this order, Gutch's rank was Officer (OBE). Appointed B.G.'s colonial secretary (second in command to the governor), Gutch was standing in as acting governor until Alfred Savage arrived in April 1953.

17 Dear All (11/6/1952): Marian sent this particular letter to her parents, her sister, and her in-laws; the Irwins did not receive subsequent "Dear All" carbons.

18 Local sugar (11/9/1952): According to Noël Bacchus, there were two basic forms of sugar: coarse dark crystal (which may be what Marian used here) and pale yellow crystal. The latter was "the popular choice for limeade, tea tables, and social functions." For weddings, holidays, and other formal occasions, "only imported white sugar was considered for the elaborately iced cakes."

19 Winifred (11/11/1952): Winifred Grant. Marian later recalled: "She arrived one day to sell eggs; she soon came regularly and stayed to scrub the bare wooden floor of the kitchen and back steps. This was called scraping: she wet the floor from a bucket, scraped vigorously with a flattened piece of tin can, then wiped up the water with ancient rags. One day she asked shyly if she could take home an empty jar I had discarded. From then on, I saved for her my empty catsup bottles, jam jars, paper bags—all valuable containers."

20 Van Fleet letter (11/11/1952): Eisenhower, during a campaign speech, quoted from a letter in which General James A. Van Fleet complained that his training program had received insufficient official support from the Democrat-helmed Defense Department.

21 Mr. Rodway (11/17/1952): James Alwyn Rodway, an English master at Queen's; his father, James Rodway, one of the colony's foremost historians, wrote a number of books, including *A History of British Guiana*, a two-volume work published in 1891, and *Guiana: British, Dutch, and French*, from 1912.

22 F. H. Martin-Sperry (11/27/1952): Earlier that year, as president of the British Guiana Music Festival Committee, Martin-Sperry had overseen the colony's inaugural festival, performed at five sites in Georgetown (not at Queen's, which was in the midst of sitting final exams) and representing juried talent from all three counties. At the time, there was a hunger for culture throughout B.G.; Martin-Sperry noted in his remarks at the final performance that attendance for the festival as a whole numbered "more than 23,000 people."

23 Houses of Queen's College (12/16/1952): The house system, borrowed from British public schools, was intended to promote team spirit and solidarity. At Queen's the houses referred to groups of boys, of mixed ages and abilities, not to physical structures. Each house met weekly, and the system also provided an organizational framework for sports and other extracurricular events.

24 Eze Day (12/29/1952): In 1950 the colony's League of Coloured People invited Eze Ogueri II, a young Nigerian studying in the U.S., for a visit to promote cultural pride among the colony's black population, a step widely viewed as being politically motivated. Cultural links to their original homeland were weaker among B.G.'s blacks than among the other, more recently arrived ethnic groups, a circumstance exacerbated by Indian independence (1947), Mao Tse-tung's victory in China (1949), and the three-month colony-wide touring exhibition of the Our Lady of Fatima statue from Portugal (1950), each of which was for its respective group a source of pride. Ogueri, a tribal chieftain from Obibi-Ezena, was greeted as royalty in Georgetown and the colony's predominantly black villages during his seven-day trip. Upon concluding his graduate studies in the U.S. he would serve as a political affairs official at the U.N. and teach at Bethune-Cookman College before returning to Nigeria in 1958. Eze Day was celebrated from 1951 through 1954.

25 McCarran-Walter Act (1/8/1953): Refers to an unidentified editorial from a B.G. newspaper, probably denouncing the McCarran Act. Put into effect in December 1952, the act was intended to block immigration by enemies of the United States, notably those who had any affiliation with Communism. But until the repeal of some provisions in 1965, it also drastically reduced immigration to the U.S. from the British West Indies (including British Guiana) by limiting annual immigration to 100 people per colony—a steep drop from the previous provision, under which Caribbean residents qualified for immigration as part of Britain's quote of 65,000 per year.

26 Universal suffrage (1/11/1953): The rate of illiteracy among East Indians in the colony was thought to exceed 40 percent. Until 1953, not only were the landless and illiterate barred from voting, but also housewives with no income or property of their own, and domestic workers who earned less than ten dollars a month. H. R. Harewood, the registration officer, noted after Election Day that "about two-thirds of the total number of voters had not voted before at any election."

27 Unfavorable impression left by Americans (1/11/1953): The American presence in the colony had been an eye-opener for many Guianese. "A mythology of white superiority, carefully fostered by the British colonial administration, was eroded as assiduously by the American servicemen," writes Roy Heath.

28 South African man who antagonized Transport & Harbour Dept (1/12/1953): Allsopp may have been referring to the "Teare Affair." Col. Robert V. Teare, an Englishman, arrived in British Guiana in 1946 to assume the role of general manager of the Transport and Harbours Department. In late February 1948, railway and steamer workers went out on strike for four days to protest Teare's treatment of workers. As Odeen Ishmael writes: "Teare behaved like a tyrant, showed no respect for the workers' trade union, and imposed harsh discipline on the employees. He also dismissed a number of workers" and attempted to transfer union leaders to other parts of the colony with less than twenty-four hours' notice. The commission appointed by the governor to investigate the strike recommended that the workers be reinstated. Teare soon moved on to manage Bermuda's railway service.

29 Thomas accosted by policeman (1/16/1953): This altercation did not have racial roots; by the 1950s Georgetown's police force (other than the top rank) was almost entirely black.

30 Sanger-Davies's ambitions for new term (1/20/1953): Along with its focus on scholastic achievement, Queen's College aimed to broaden students' horizons through familiarization with the arts. M. K. Bacchus, a former assistant director in Guyana's Ministry of Education, writes that "In the 1950s, when there was an increase in the number of students coming from lower-middle and working-class homes, the Principal was very anxious to stress those extra-curricular activities, such as art, music, drama, and poetry, which would help prepare these young men to lead a 'cultured' life."

31 Brother in politics (1/23/1953): Lionel Luckhoo, a prosperous lawyer and active conservative in the colony's politics, was also president of the Man-Power Citizens Association, a union representing workers in the sugar and bauxite industries; its interests were described by the People's Progressive Party as "collaborationist" with the industry owners. In 1952, as an appointed member of the Legislative Council, Luckhoo introduced a motion to prohibit the "entry into the colony of literature, publications, propaganda or films which are subversive or contrary to public interest." Known unofficially as the "Dunce Motion," it was understood as an effort to pointedly rein in the PPP's wide distribution of socialist and anti-imperialist pamphlets, written by Marxist theoreticians in the Soviet Union, Eastern Europe, and the U.K., that were ordered from Britain, where they were available legally. The literature fanned the political consciousness and anti-colonial fervour of many Guianese; it was, Eric Huntley later said, "all we read." Luckhoo would be appointed to the Executive Council of the interim government in 1953. He served as mayor of Georgetown in 1955–56 and 1960–61, led the National Labour Front party in the late 1950s, and later held several diplomatic posts.

32 Brown Betty (2/19/1953): The Guianese version of a soda fountain cum hamburger joint, popular throughout the 1940s and 1950s. According to the "Nostalgia" columnist Godfrey Chin, who called it "our Mel's Diner," the shop introduced Popsicles, Fudgsicles, and Creamsicles to the colony in 1946.

33 Gardening classes abandoned (3/4/1953): From a letter to the editor, published on March 30, 1953, in the *Daily Argosy* in response to a front-page article in the March 20 edition of the *Q.C. Lichtor* titled "'Gardening' Abandoned After 26 Years": "Sir, I think this is a most distressing and retrograde decision to be made by the new principal, after so short a period of tenure of office. . . . The future of this colony is based on the expansion of its agricultural industries. There has been a consistent and all too noticeable tendency among rural folk [to] seek white collar jobs and spurn the soil which gives them sustenance. Queen's has always been accused by politicians especially of late, of catering for a select few and training a brood of snobs. Scientific agriculture and intelligent farmers are sadly needed in this colony. . . . Rather than abandon gardening, agricultural interest should have been expanded. . . . I would ask you, Mr. Editor, to read this scandal in the *Lichtor*. . . . I would ask you to read how an American biologist specially brought here at high cost has been required to waste time and money with soil conditions and practices of which he knows nothing. . . . For the good of the colony, I say please rescind that decision and let us give our boys a proper education with a true sense of values. Yours etc., 'Old Boy' " Marian's note in the scrapbook where this article was pasted: "We all wonder who wrote this—Howard and I agree with most of the points made, but wish the author had had the courage to sign his name."

34 Churchill talk on Queen Mary (3/25/1953): Queen Mary, the widow of King George V and the grandmother of the soon-to-be-crowned Elizabeth II, died on March 24, 1953.

35 AMM (4/24/1953): The Association of Masters and Mistresses, the teachers' association organized in January 1953 by Norman Cameron to bring together the six secondary schools that were recognized by the colony's government as, in Cameron's words, "entitled to admit Government scholars": Queen's College, St. Stanislaus College, Bishops' High School, Berbice High School, St. Rose's High School, and St. Joseph's High. Private secondary schools had their own union, and the Elementary Teachers' Association performed a similar role.

36 PPP wins seats in 18 of the 24 districts (4/29/1953): The socialist/Marxist PPP did not proclaim itself as Communist; however, some of its members supported Communism, it was labeled as such in the Georgetown press (which, owned and backed by conservatives whose interests lay with the sugar industry, was resolutely anti-PPP), and its leader, Cheddi Jagan, and his wife, Janet, had been identified as Communist activists in 1949 by the head of counterespionage in the British War Office. The tally of PPP seats would be reduced by one in May upon the court's finding in response to a petition that the election of the PPP candidate Frank Van Sertima to represent the Georgetown North district was void due to insufficiently guarded secrecy at the district's four polling stations.

37 successful professionals and businessmen (4/29/1953): Cheddi Jagan, the son of field workers on a sugar estate, had earned a degree in dentistry from Northwestern University before returning to B.G. with his American wife, Janet, in 1943; until their time was overtaken by their political activities—including his election in 1947 as a member of the Legislative Council as well as her co-founding in 1946 of the Women's Political and Economic Organization and election in 1950 to the Georgetown Town Council—they maintained his dental practice in the capital. L.F.S. Burnham, who upon his return from London in 1949 became a leading Georgetown barrister, joined forces with the Jagans and others—schoolteachers, doctors, lawyers, trade union activists—to found the People's Progressive Party in 1950. Among those elected, Cheddi Jagan was the only one with experience as a politician.

38 Janet Jagan née Rosenberg (4/29/1953): The false rumour that Mrs. Jagan was related to Julius Rosenberg, who had been arrested in 1950 and along with his wife would be executed in June 1953 for being a Communist spy, was so tenacious that it found its way into some of the obituaries for her husband in the US press in 1997.

39 Far better off than the poor devils in Kenya (4/29/1953): The Mau Mau uprising, the militant revolt against colonial rule in Kenya, had reached a pitch in October 1952 that led the British to send in troops and declare a state of emergency. In the end the greatest toll by far would be taken by the Kikuyus, the colony's largest ethnic group, but in January 1953 Mau Mau fighters had killed a family of white settlers, setting off panic among the colony's other whites. The massacre at Lari took place on March 26; Jomo Kenyatta had been sentenced to seven years' hard labour on April 5. Kenya's independence was ten years off.

40 St. George's Cathedral (5/8/1953): Perhaps the tallest wooden building in the world at a height of 143 feet, the Gothic-style Anglican cathedral dates to 1894. It was submitted to UNESCO for designation as a World Heritage Site and is on the Tentatives List.

41 B.G. made *Time* at last (5/9/1953): The election results galvanized the American press and Washington. In *The West on Trial*, Cheddi Jagan notes: "*Time* magazine referred to our government as the first Communist government being set up in the British Empire." But even while Jagan noted the "alarm" set off in the United States by the PPP's success at the polls, the May issue of the party's newspaper, *Thunder*, titled its note on the death of Joseph Stalin: "The Third Congress of the PPP Mourns the Loss to Mankind of J.V. Stalin." A photographic portrait of Stalin hung in his clinic. The American consul general, in his analysis of the election for the State Department, wrote that "it may be doubtful whether more than one or two of the central group of PPP leaders (some of whom may, for all practicable purposes, be called Communists) are solidly steeped in traditional doctrine. But they parrot Moscow phrases, they receive Moscow (or Vienna) guidance and funds, they maintain Vienna (and perhaps Moscow) contacts, and they profess support for some stated Communist objectives. Thus, whether ideologically they are Communists or not, some of these PPP leaders act and behave like Communists, and this is a hard political fact to be reckoned with."

42 Sir John Hawkins (5/17/1953): The sixteenth-century head of the Royal Navy was England's first slave trader, who accrued great wealth by selling kidnapped Africans to Spanish colonials in the Caribbean. He died at sea off Puerto Rico.

43 Washington State College (5/17/1953 letter): Renamed Washington State University in 1959.

44 Drew Pearson's column (5/29/1953): Pearson's syndicated column, The Washington Merry-Go-Round, of May 12, 1953, reads in part:
Washington.—While most of the Nation has been worried about Indochina, Korea and Europe, the state department has been exchanging frantic cables with the British foreign office over the surge of Communism in the Caribbean—just across from the Panama Canal. Both American and British authorities were stunned by the Communist sweep in British Guiana's recent elections. The Reds, parading under the banner of the People's Progressive Party, won 18 out of 24 seats in the House of Assembly. This means the Communists are in complete control of the legislature and will have a major voice in running this British crown colony. . . . The man responsible for the Red coup in British Guiana is Cheddi Jagan, a tough, ruthless Communist agent who studied dentistry in the United States but got his political training behind the Red Curtain. He is now Red boss of the House of Assembly, which means that Moscow, in effect, is giving orders to a British colonial legislature.

45 a huge marble "thing" (6/1/1953): A baptismal font.

46 Eve Leary (6/2/1953): Dating to 1825 and named for the widow of the eighteenth-century plantation owner Cornelius Leary on whose estate it was built, the Eve Leary garrison included the Parade Grounds, an officers' cemetery, military barracks, and the police commissioner's residence.

47 Letter from State Department (6/5/1953): The response from Howard's contact at the International Information Administration reads in part: "The Department of State is following closely the situation in British Guiana. On the basis of all available information concerning the recent elections in that country, the Department does not envisage the present situation as one of immediate threat to the safety and health of American nationals nor does the Department believe there is any cause for alarm for the safety of your family or yourself. . . . At the present time, there is no plan to evacuate American nationals from British Guiana nor to restrict them from going there. The responsibilities of the Department in British Guiana are carried out under the supervision of the Consul General at Port of Spain, Trinidad, Mr. William P. Maddox. You may wish to communicate with Mr. Maddox if you have any further questions."

48 steel bands (6/5/1953): "Introduced into British Guiana from the neighbouring island of Trinidad, the steelband first swept into popular favour in 1953 on the occasion of Queen Elizabeth's Coronation," wrote V. Jones in the special "Guianese Christmas" edition of Kyk-Over-Al in 1955. "Beating out popular patriotic airs, several combinations then paraded the streets, drawing thousands in their train and reaping rich reward when Governor Sir Alfred Savage permitted them entrance into Government House grounds and himself accorded appreciation of their high standard of music." Among those was the Chicago Steel Band, which played "Rule Britannia" and "God Save the Queen" for Lady Savage. By that time there were more than twenty steel bands in the colony. Often performing in costume, infusing classics like Gounod's "Ave Maria" with "tropical rhythms," the steel bands "impart[ed] the 'local' touch to any occasion."

49 The political situation here doesn't seem at all alarming (6/13/1953): Marian's remark was likely intended to allay her parents' concerns. Years later she recollected about this time and the weeks soon after: "The political situation increased our desire to move out of town. Agitation for independence in Georgetown began with name-calling; light-skinned people were increasingly jeered at on the streets. Safety and courtesy were no longer guaranteed by skin colour." Cheddi Jagan refers to "irrational anti-white feelings" stirred up by Burnham following the court's voiding of the election of Frank Van Sertima, and also to "a change in attitude of the workers following the election victory. . . . Their behaviour perhaps took on an exaggerated form. . . . 'You have got too big for your boots,' many housewives were overheard to have said to their now 'bumptious' servants."

50 the interminable paper changing (6/13/1953): Howard dried plant specimens in presses between sheets of newspaper that absorbed the moisture released from the plants. The papers were changed frequently to speed the drying process.

51 The ministers have been making the rounds (6/28/1953 HSI letter): "The changes we began to introduce now seem quite modest," wrote Cheddi Jagan in 1966, before citing a list of the PPP's objectives. "Apparently, we committed acts of omission and commission. . . . Our decision not to send delegates to greet the Queen in Jamaica was probably our main sin of omission. . . ." He then describes "the 'crimes' we committed," such as the repeal of the Undesirable Publications Act. "There was also the resolution passed by the House asking the President of the United States to exercise clemency in the case of Ethel and Julius Rosenberg, a 'sin' also committed by the Pope."

52 one of the new ministers has suggested that all domestic help should be paid $40 per month (7/25/1953): Striving to make good on the PPP's campaign promise to enact increased rates of pay for some groups of workers, Minister of Labour Ashton Chase appointed Jessie Burnham, a member of the House (and sister of L.F.S. Burnham), as head of a Domestic Servants Committee that would "investigate the conditions of employment and wages of domestic servants and washers," as Chase wrote in his 1954 pamphlet *133 Days Towards Freedom in Guiana*. He added, "These workers are about the most forsaken in our community."

The U.S. Army–built residences at Atkinson Field, including the Irwins', above, stood on pillars. Below, Elizabeth and Marian in the playpen Howard fashioned underneath the house.

Chapter 4

1953–1954: ATKINSON FIELD

August 1:

Howard and I got up at 5, and by the time Elizabeth was awake we'd put all the last-minute things in the suitcases, locked them, folded the bedding, etc. H. loaded the car while I fed Elizabeth, then we sat on the trunks for a while until 7, when we went over to the Ramsarans' for breakfast. Such a help. After that, we went back to the flat and Elizabeth, Testudo, Junior, and I retired to Elizabeth's bedroom, where we sat on the floor and played with the toys that I'd jammed into one shopping bag. Tortoises confused; Elizabeth quite content. Fogarty's sent two electricians to disconnect and then reconnect the stove; they came on a motorcycle and went all the way out to the Field on it!

The movers came just about when they were supposed to, and what a rough-looking crew. At least the men looked strong and stocky, not the spindly type we usually see around here. It didn't take them too long to load the truck, and with our car washer sweeping out the flat, we managed to get ourselves into the car just before the truck left. Lordy—there wasn't a spare inch of space in the car. The back was entirely filled, and Howard had left the seats in the new house on his last trip there. The big tortoises were each in a basket, and these were perched on the top of the suitcases, boxes, bedding, and mosquito nets. However, Junior managed to get out of his basket en route and, after scrambling clear across the width of the car, wound up with Testudo in her basket, where, in their excitement, they forgot their pleasant neat habits. Elizabeth was very good, although she wasn't too happy about sitting in my lap. I'd stuffed several toys in the glove compartment, and we opened and shut that for entertainment. I think she was a little confused by the move because she seemed quiet and subdued; of course, we were so wedged into the front seat with diaper bags, toy bag, and toilet seat tucked around my legs that she couldn't have squirmed too much!

Shortly before we reached the entrance to the airbase, it began to rain, really a heavy shower. It had stopped by the time we arrived at the house, and Howard unpacked Elizabeth and me and certain bits of necessary equipment and installed us in Elizabeth's new bedroom, where I tried to organize her lunch. The truck arrived, and as soon as all the furniture was unloaded, Howard brought Elizabeth's crib in and we made it up, then tucked her in for a nap. (Howard didn't even want us around those men; he said they were pretty dirty and crude of speech as well, so we stayed put in the bedroom.)

Elizabeth had a nap; we sorted out furniture and suitcases and boxes and got pretty well unpacked. Mildred, the maid from next door, came and scrubbed the bathtub and toilet and washbasin. All the fresh paint was still tacky, and in the kitchen, where the only workspace was a newly painted counter, we rapidly made a mess of the sticky paint.

August 2:

We had a thundershower around noon that really amazed me. The sky grew very dark, and we had lightning cracking around us. One bolt came down just across the street—caused a wonderful snapping sound. The rain made so much noise that several times I dashed back to Elizabeth's room to see if she was awake and frightened, but she slept beautifully throughout, enjoying the coolness.

During all of this, I was on my hands and knees scrubbing the bathroom and kitchen floors, and Howard was on his hands and knees going all over the other floors with a rag soaked in oily polish. It was the only way we could think of to get up all the dust that had accumulated; the floors are in bad shape and really need a thorough polishing, but this helped tremendously. We put curtains up in our bedroom and in the living room and look well settled.

August 3, 1953

Dear folks,

If the following is at all incoherent, it's because your son is pooped and not really up to writing a good letter. We're in the process of what the British call "settling in." Our new home makes the old one on Parade Street seem like a dump—it has surpassed all expectations.

First of all, the weather provides a delightful change—not as monotonous as on the coastal plain. Here the night temperature is near 65°, while the daily shade temperature high is probably close to 90°—a little warmer than in Georgetown but well worth it considering the cool night. On a sunny day the inside of the house does get pretty warm, but that's no problem with the cool, breezy paved area under the house.

As for the actual move, we had four of the brawniest men we've seen in Georgetown—reminded me of "Steel Vent—tough but oh so gentle." These fellows weren't exactly delicate in manner, but at least everything got here in one piece and without damage. It did rain, but they were supplied with a large waterproof tarp—so no water damage. And it's a good thing I'd made the two trips out here previously, for there wasn't an inch to spare when they finished loading the truck. Two electricians disconnected the stove and refrigerator in Parade Street and motorcycled out here to reconnect them.

Marian is forever raving about the merits of the American-style kitchen. Hardly a step is needed—and a maid would definitely be in the way. When our grant money comes in September we'll buy outright a small washing machine made by the British Hoover people for £32 ($160 local money, $95 U.S.). According to those who now own them, they pay for themselves in one year. Hand washing, then, is the only inconvenience Marian will have here, and that will extend for just six weeks or so.

We couldn't be happier. We find the close association with the sounds of nature ever so more satisfying than the street conversation in Georgetown. The bush is just a half-block away. As I think I've written before, the type of animal life most startlingly abundant here is the insect. Already we've been treated to a few local monsters of that realm: a grasshopper five inches long with feelers eight inches long; a moth with a head like so [drawing]; and a "horse"-fly measuring an inch and a half in length. Damn good thing we have screens.

Elizabeth, needless to say, is having the time of her life exploring this new world. We gave the playpen back to John and Margaret before we left, so now she has the run of the place—and with a place as long as this she's fast giving up creeping in preference to walking. It's a blessing to have doors though, for now and then we have to keep her out of a room. And each morning she spends at least an hour by herself—as always. The tub proved something of a surprise to her—overwhelmingly big. Downstairs she found a lot that was new: sand (definitely does not like to walk on it), concrete (not too sure), and her little wading pool (soon learned to love it!).

Well, I'd better bring this to a close. I'm in a state of contented fatigue—and can write no more.

Love to all,

Howard

August 3:

Howard began clearing off the land around our house; it is mostly sand, but in places the weeds had grown up into something resembling a very scrubby lawn. We decided it would look better if all the weeds were out, leaving just the white sand. There are amaryllis lilies and orchids, which the ants are supposed to leave alone; everything else, they eat. Howard moved some of the lilies so that they now form a border around the driveway.

We couldn't keep the tortoises in the third bedroom forever, so Howard built a sturdy pen for them just off the edge of the concrete under the house—their pen is under the eaves of the roof. All the neighborhood children were intrigued, as were some of their parents.

We blew up the little wading pool (sent by Mother) after Elizabeth's nap, and although she was a little fearful of it at first, she soon seemed to enjoy sitting in it and splashing.

Howard met some of our neighbors, the Englishes, who live across the street. He is with a firm making an aerial survey of the colony. They are English and have a three-year-old daughter, Elizabeth.

August 4:

While I did the washing, another neighbor came over—Zela Defreitas, with her little boy, Pete. The child is two and a half but is retarded mentally, is uncoordinated, and lacks the understanding you'd expect from a child that age. Zela is expecting a baby at the end of October and has two little girls who are six and eight. Learned from her that there is a case of measles across the street. She invited me to a card game, a weekly affair that all the women out here seem to enjoy.

We are thrilled to find the nights really cool here. Mornings seem to be pleasantly cool. Between 11 a.m. and 2 it gets frightfully hot, but underneath the house it seems to stay fairly cool. By 9 or 10 p.m. it is very comfortable again.

August 5:

Met still another neighbor, Jean Crooks, who lives behind us. She was taking her two children to a special movie at the Inn, a great occasion that happens only once or twice a year. We learned that movies are shown every Saturday night at the Inn, however.

August 6:

Learned to play samba at the card party. It is a game very similar to canasta, really just an elaboration of it. I was impressed by the fact that all eight women seemed to want to play cards, and no one used the gathering as an excuse to gossip about absentees. Everyone is friendly—such a change from town.

Howard collected some orchids from around the base and put them in a bed near the edge of our yard. Also some pretty little shrubs and a few plants for pots. Down in a swamp he dug up a little philodendron for my copper planter, and we're hoping that will live. I say "little" because so many of the plants are huge that it takes some looking to find one small enough for the planter.

August 7:

Howard made the hot trip into town with a great long list and came back with almost everything on it. Included were hammer and masonite for an L-shaped table, which Howard started in the workroom soon after he got back from town and had finished before dinner.

The afternoon was just plain hot; I felt mean and nasty and decided to drown myself in a shower. After washing my hair I felt considerably better. Elizabeth splashed in the wading pool for a while, and then we both were cool and comfortable—relatively.

Bought meat from the local meat man for the first time. Or rather, Howard did. The man has a truck in which he brings the meat, but usually the folks here go down to the police station to meet him since there is a better choice that way. His meat is just plain old cow, slaughtered that morning. Forty cents a pound for any of it, and there are no real "cuts"—just hunks.

Saturday evening, August 8, 1953

Dear All—

This letter is overdue, but the week has truly been a full one. We are just about completely settled—and very happily so. Things here are much better than we'd even hoped for, but more about that. Today I finished

Elizabeth's curtains and we got them up; the only thing left along that line is for me to even off the brown draperies in the living room. Floor length in town, they now dangle an inch or so below our sills! The painting was done when we arrived but was still tacky—the whole house is fresh and clean. We found out that the electrical current here is different than in town, so Howard had to take the phonograph in to have the speed adjusted. Cost: 58 cents! The cyclage is the same as in the States, but in Georgetown it is slower. He also bought a plumber's friend, and now all our washbasins drain properly. Biggest construction job was finished just last evening—an L-shaped table against the corner in our third bedroom, where H. now has all his botany equipment and stamp business. At the other end is my ironing board, and we have two trunks in there, too. When we can afford it we will purchase a single bed (old iron things don't cost much here, so we shall get one soon), and then it will be our guest room as well. Looks very neat despite the mental image all the stuff might imply. Howard also built a good pen for the tortoises—it is about three feet wide and seven or eight feet long, built in the sand right next to the concrete under the house, and under the eaves so they won't get soaked. My dears, the tortoises are the hit of the neighborhood!

About the neighborhood: it is lovely. There are families in nearly all the houses, but some are away on leave and others don't seem to mix much. A good many are very friendly, however. We know nearly all our neighbors and are on first-name terms with many—something never achieved in town. Next door, to our right, live the Warwicks with their Jennifer, who is about five or six. Across the street from them live the Englishes with their Elizabeth, who is red-haired and just three. Both of those men are working on an aerial survey of the colony, along with two others still unknown to us. To our left live the Defreitases, with Betty, eight, Annie, six, and little Pete, who is two and a half and a very sad child—very badly handicapped mentally, evidently. He is quite uncoordinated, doesn't talk, falls down a lot, is still fed from a bottle. Across the street from them live the Kings, with Tessa, who is about eight, and Brenda, whom I haven't really seen because she has the measles, as does Betty Defreitas. We're all waiting to see who is next! Behind us live the Crookses, with Wayne, five, and Donna, not quite two. There is also a precious child named Angela, who lives on the next street, and others who must live there, too, since I don't see them around any of the houses on our street. During the day we have all the children around now and then, checking to see whether the tortoises are awake and out of their house. The children are lovely: clean, healthy, courteous, and just plain cute. Actually they are filthy dirty much of the time—they all play wildly all morning, and then appear after 3:30 or 4 all cleaned up and wearing shoes and socks. Nearly all of them are English.

Their mothers are awfully pleasant, too. Every week they gather to play samba, a glorified canasta, and last Thursday I went next door to the Defreitases', too. My partner and I won! Sheer luck, since I'd forgotten about as much canasta as I've ever known. Everyone is friendly—more or less out of self-preservation; since there aren't many families here, I guess there is nothing to do but get along with the neighbors. Anyway, it is something I've really missed in the last year, and I know I'll enjoy a little casual chat now and then. Ah yes—Jean Crooks wears shorts around in the morning, too—something "no one" did in town. Everyone wears sundresses in the afternoon, for it is really, really hot here from 11 to 3. In the houses, that is— underneath it is cool and sometimes a little breezy. We will buy a couple of raunchy chairs to keep downstairs and perhaps put our hammock up. Elizabeth loves the wading pool and just sits there playing with Jumbo, the little seal, and a few other toys. We envy her! She is just beginning to accept the sand; she'll walk on it now when she has shoes on, and this morning she wiggled her toes in it for a while. She shrieked the first time we put her down on it!

To go back to the weather, joy of joys, it is cool at night and cool in the morning until 8:30 or so—I can drink two or three cups of coffee without melting into a puddle. Now it is 9:20 p.m. and pleasantly cool again. The first of last week it rained a lot and was really damp and chilly; I even had to cover Elizabeth at night. The heat of the afternoon isn't so bad as long as we know there will be relief. And after September it will cool off some anyway.

H. says I should say something about our food supply. A man comes around with meat (beef) once a week. We can get a fair variety of good greens from the hydroponic gardens here on the airbase. Some fruit is available at the ferry landing: the local farmers take their produce there to sell to people on the boat, and the families here hasten to pick up what they need. Howard will still have to get citrus fruits in town.

I forgot to mention all the clearing Howard has done in our yard. No one else bothers, and their yards are all a scramble of sand and weeds. Howard has weeded all around the house and has put in a few plants that he got in the bush—just to see if they will survive. If they do we'll put more in and make a sort of border around our plot. It really looks grand!

As perhaps you can tell from the typing, I'm getting sleepy. So, dears, enough for tonight.

Love,

Marian

Mother, Elizabeth looks just precious in the red-and-white dress you sent. She loves to putter around outside here—quite on her own, as long as one of us is downstairs, too. We can't leave her, because she tries to climb the stairs and manages to do so: a few days ago she fell down from the first step, cried mightily, and after a few hours was right back trying to go up again. Grand spirit!

August 8:

Bought some fruit at the ferry dock, or "stelling," this morning, but we were a little disappointed. No citrus fruit at all. Bananas, cucumbers (two for six cents), papaws, and a huge half of a Hubbard squash. From the hydroponic gardens we got lettuce, spring onions, crookneck squash, and the loveliest string beans we've seen in B.G.

August 9:

Howard began his collecting. It is a treat for him to be within ten or fifteen minutes of the plants he needs. He put up rows of string in the workroom and will hang damp papers over them to dry. The whole setup here is just perfect for his work, and I appreciate the fact that the mess involved is confined to a room that can be shut off from the rest of the house.

I finished Elizabeth's curtains and we hung them up. The yellow toy box is in one corner, with the little rug in front of it. We're still using a trunk for a bath table, and that plus the crib and a few pictures completes her room. It's amazing how the toys help!

August 11, 1953

Dear folks,

Well, now we've been here at A.F. for ten days and can say with some conviction that it's a hell of a lot better than Georgetown—from just about any point of view. Apologies for any repetition, but I was so shot when the last note was written that I scarcely remember what I said.

As a neighborhood, this place is as ideal as we could wish. All the people we've met (nearly everyone) are such nice, genuine folks—the kind we hoped to see more of in town. Most are white or near-white, either

British or Guianese. The children (mostly girls) come around and play and talk with Elizabeth and watch the tortoises.

Needless to say, your son is in seventh heaven with the bush practically within spittin' distance. I've been able to do quite a bit of collecting the last few days and, of course, will continue from now on. We've converted our third bedroom into a workroom—for my work as well as Marian's ironing. Eventually we'll get an old iron bedstead for guests. We've had one guest already—Rev. Bowen, the U.S.-educated Guianese pastor of the Lutheran Church who took Rodway and me up the Demerara River last year to one of his missions. Well, he comes to A.F. frequently to meet visiting ecclesiasts. He'll be out again this Friday and says he'll bring an American pastor with him, a man by the name of Hansen.

When I'm not collecting or otherwise working on botanical specimens, I work in our garden—real exclusive: nothing but orchids! There are some beautiful orchids growing on the savannah and in the bush, and since they're so easy to move and are relatively free of ant invasion, I decided they could well be massed in a border. They are interesting not only for their colors but also for their shapes. In bloom at the moment are a yellow one, a brown one, and a green one. The first is in a large cluster over four feet high. There is no clear limit as to the property that goes with this house, but I have taken about 20 to 30 feet all around the house for our use—that is, I've cleared and leveled and plan to plant it with orchids.

There's animal life galore here, too. Second to the ants are butterflies—in almost endless variety. Then I suppose come the reptiles, mostly as snakes and lizards, both attaining great size in some species. A couple of days ago I saw a snake that approached 12 feet in length and 6 or 7 inches in diameter. Not as bad as it sounds since nearly all of them retreat at human approach. One type of snake is ebony black except for the last quarter of its length, that portion having a canary-yellow hue—a very striking species. The largest found here is the anaconda, a constrictor locally known as the camoodi, which commonly exceeds 25 feet by 12 inches. Hope I don't come across one of them—they're dark green with emerald diamonds down the back. Some small (setter size) cats called ocelots come out at night in the bush, so are seldom seen. Wild peccaries (pigs) travel about the savannah in packs of thirty to fifty and can be mean if molested. They clatter their teeth when alarmed. And in the trees are monkeys and the howling baboon, which Marian shuddered at hearing for the first time this morning. When I drive off in the morning I commonly come across a few giant grasshoppers, which I am collecting for dissection purposes next year. They're huge fellows, up to nine inches long and three-quarters of an inch through—bright green with Chinese red exposed when they lift their membranous wings for flight.

As soon as we have a sunny late afternoon I'll take two rolls of pictures (ready and waiting). Funny thing, but each afternoon at about 4 it begins to cloud up, or at least it has so far this week. Pictures coming up, nonetheless!

Love to all,
Howard

Thursday, August 13, 1953

Dear All—

Just remembered that I should write today so that Howard can take the letters into town with him tomorrow. Mail goes from the Field into town to the post office and then back out here to the plane. Silly, isn't it! Elizabeth and Howard are downstairs, polishing the car. Elizabeth loves to grub around outside—she putters around picking up clothespins and old matches (when she can find them) and is as good as gold. I guess she's learned her lesson about the stairs because she ignores them now.

I have re-hemmed three of the six draperies. Counted our brass doorknobs this afternoon and found out that there are fifteen pairs, all badly tarnished. I've polished three pairs plus four light switches so far—and I must confess I never would have thought of them at all if I hadn't sat smack in front of a gorgeous, highly polished doorknob yesterday at our weekly samba game. Yesterday we played at Bridget Rodriguez's—she is Trinidadian. Makes a pleasant afternoon for me, and Elizabeth and Howard do beautifully. She behaves better for her daddy than for me, I do believe—no nonsense at all about spitting out the supper or impatient crying before the bath.

Measles is still around us; yesterday one mother had a little girl with a high fever, and another had a tearful and headachey little boy, and both were afraid they were doomed. All the children run from house to house playing with one another, so I guess constant vigil is the only thing to keep a child segregated. Last Sunday I read in Spock's book that measles in children of three or four can be very serious, even fatal. That frightened us, so Howard went into town Monday to inquire about the preventive shots that Spock also mentioned. First he went to Mercy Hospital but got no information other than that the shots aren't given here. Then, at Q.C., he ran into John Ramsaran and mentioned it.

It seems Susan had been sick and they'd called a Dr. Hanoman-Singh, who is a newly elected member of the House of Assembly.[53] So Howard went to the Ramsarans' house to wait for the doctor. When he came, he told H. that until a few years ago none of the temperate diseases were had here and that this is the first widespread measles epidemic in the colony. Mumps is going the rounds currently, too. He explained that measles never reaches the serious proportions in the tropics that it does in a temperate climate; that a child may be seriously ill with it here, but it doesn't approach the fatal state. The immune globulin treatment isn't used anywhere anymore, he said, because it often leads to jaundice. Knowing that it isn't too serious, we have relaxed a bit. So far as we know, E. hasn't been directly exposed to it (as the doctor said was necessary to catch it), and it may blow over soon.

We are certainly enjoying this house. Our living room will be complete when we get the two Morris chairs; as it is now it's fine for us, but company would be awkward. We have the radio against one wall, the bookcase against another, the couch against the third, and our dining room table against the fourth. The four chairs H. bought at the auction, E.'s little chair, and our small tables are scattered among these, and the effect is really pleasant. The two larger braided rugs are in here, and the small one is just inside our front door. The light brown rug I had at school is in front of the bookcase, and our copper candlesticks are on top of it—bookcase, not the rug. I try to keep this big table fairly neat. At one end I have the chafing dish; and at the third where I'm now sitting I have some stationery and stuff, which makes this end the "desk." Our brown and copper tones look cool against the cream walls. Oh yes—just inside the front door is the little copper planter with a small bit of philodendron that we're trying to keep alive. To the right of the door we hung the three little Van Gogh prints. The room has a personality that makes it at least a hundred times more pleasant than the one on Parade Street; maybe it is the absence of the hanging light bulbs!

From the outside, our house looks very, very long and simply huge. The eaves hang down about ten feet, protecting the screened windows from the gusts of rain that would otherwise blow right in. It is wonderful to have no opening and closing of windows to fool around with.

I do love the kitchen; I can feel efficient even at night when I mix up the bread. I suppose, Mother, I feel the same way about it that you did when we moved from G Street into the apartment: I get a huge kick out of standing in one place and moving a step to the right to reach the sink, one to the left to the refrigerator, and an about-face to the stove.

Our bathroom is colorful with the green linoleum, the green in the shower curtain, and our bright towels. Elizabeth loves the big bathtub, and I love the trustworthy toilet that *always* flushes without the tampering that was necessary in town. Good old American plumbing. We have achieved a necessary luxury: all of our towels and washcloths are hung with no double thicknesses. In the bathroom we keep just bath towels plus a washcloth for E. and one of those big sponges for us. No more smelly washcloths—I never would have guessed how quickly towels and such can get a sour smell. But now they have a chance to dry out.

The bedroom will look better once we acquire our chest and can remove the packing box that now holds comb, brush, and bottles. A bit quaint. Elizabeth's bedroom looks cute and bright now that I've put her curtains up. I put a washcloth and hand towel in her room with colors that match the yellow and melon in the rug and curtain trim. Howard added another bar between the jalousied partition and the floor, so she's unable to slither out now.

Our workroom is a joy. Howard brings in a batch of plants, most of them ant-ridden or sticky or infested with beetles or something, and he takes them right back there, away from Elizabeth and the rugs. The washbasin there helps, too, since so many plants either need to be washed or else leave H.'s hands a mess. Not that I don't appreciate the effort involved in H.'s botany, but it certainly is grand to have a room for his unrestricted use. I iron there, too, after dinner when it is reasonably cool.

Ha. H. rescued a thermometer that the Q.C. physics lab was discarding, and brought it home. Such a blow for my psychological warfare! The last few evenings as I've ironed, I've inquired—and learned that it is 82° or 80° even then. Mornings are around 70° and feel very pleasant; midday is 90° or so. H. says that in the sun it is about 140° at noon. Yes, checking with yesterday's paper, I see that the maximum temperature in the sun was 142.8°. Well, Mother, are you coming?

Homemade bread really tastes good. Howard threatens to live in isolation always so that we can't buy any. It is his first experience with the homemade variety, and he enjoys it as much as I do. We'll get fat, though, eating so many rolls and biscuits and coffeecakes!

Time for E.'s bath, then supper.

Much love to each of you,

Marian

Saturday afternoon, August 15, 1953

Dearest Mother—

Just a note. I wanted to get the house description off before it slipped my mind. It is a one-story frame house with galvanized, corrugated iron roof; elevated one story from the ground, on concrete posts. In case it makes any difference, we have front and back entrances, with wooden stairways, and a fire extinguisher (checked at frequent intervals by the Atkinson Field Board of Control) at our back door. As one might expect at an airbase, there is a fire department complete with shiny red engine. We have a hydrant right across the street, too.

Honestly, we are thanking our stars that we decided to move out here. We agreed last night that it isn't up to living in the U.S., but it certainly is an advancement over Georgetown. Let's see—we've been here two weeks, and so far I've spent two afternoons playing cards, several afternoons visiting on neighbors' doorsteps, and a couple chatting with the others on our steps. Last night we went across the street to the Englishes' and had a couple of drinks and talked—he is one of the air surveyors, you remember. He has collected some butterflies since they've been here—so much of the time the men can't fly at all because the weather is too bad for photography. He has some gorgeous specimens with iridescent blue wings—I hope Howard can catch some. People here use them in jewelry and like mosaics in pictures. Don't care for that, but a few would be lovely in a frame, I think.

Howard used one roll of film this morning—Elizabeth, the house, me hanging up the washing, and such. This afternoon we will try to catch E. in the wading pool and again after she's cleaned up a bit.

We shall wait eagerly for the package with slacks, shoes, shorts, and dish drainer! An early Christmas for us. I really do love the Keds—awfully comfortable to wear around all morning.

Must wash my hair—a good way of cooling off!

Love,

Marian

Thursday evening, August 20, 1953

Dear All—

Bee, you really were one up on me on the starching business. I've just started using it and am tickled to pieces to find that blouses I wear in the morning hold up for a couple of days, instead of wilting down like handkerchiefs within an hour of my putting them on. Elizabeth's thin dresses look better, too, but Howard refuses to let me use any starch on his clothes. I sneak a little into collars and cuffs on his good shirts, but he threatens all sorts of dire things if I go any further!

Monday we went into town for my dentist appointment; found the man an hour behind in his appointments so we didn't wait. Went to the Ramsarans' for tea and had a pleasant visit, but Margaret still isn't looking very well. I'm getting ahead of myself, though. Elizabeth didn't nap at all Monday afternoon before we left, and I was afraid we'd have a rough afternoon. But she fell asleep in the car about halfway there and slept all through the noise of getting into town. I carried her into the Ramsarans', said hello to everyone, and put her on a bed; Howard and I went to the dentist's office and then back, and she was still asleep! When she did wake up she had a good time playing with Susan. Margaret has lost pounds and pounds; she looks drawn and pale and hasn't any energy at all. Just before we moved, I had Howard suggest to John that they get Mabel to do the baby's wash in the afternoons as she had done for us. John said no, they couldn't afford any more help. That made me rather mad, thinking of Mrs. McLaren wearing herself out, so the day we had breakfast there (the day we moved) I played dumb and told Margaret that I didn't know whether or not H. had mentioned it to John, but that we thought they might find Mabel a help. Well, I don't know whose mind was changed, but Mabel comes in the afternoon and does the lunch dishes and Susan's and Janet's wash, which gives Mrs. McLaren time for a rest. She's pretty well tired out as it is.

Anyway, we all go back to town tomorrow morning, and I'll try the dentist again. We will leave at about 7:30, get there at about 8:30. We hope. My appointment is at 9, and after that Elizabeth and I will do some errands (her first time in the stores since we first arrived) while Howard shops in dirty old Stabroek and Yong Hing's. The Irwins sent us a nice giftie for our anniversary, and we plan to buy a couple of records and a couple of books. Elizabeth and I will look at books tomorrow if we have time.

We have adopted a dog. No name as yet; suggestions will be appreciated. He is largish, mostly black with a little brown and white. He's pretty old and is gray and also crippled in the hindquarters. He has nice brown eyes and is so grateful for any scrap of affection or food that we've just decided to encourage him. Tomorrow I shall purchase some flea powder and soap, and Saturday we shall bathe him. So far he is a perfect gentleman with Elizabeth; his tail interests her, but if she gets too friendly, he just walks away. There are quite a few strays here, but this pooch seems to be in the best condition—no skin trouble, and not as suspicious.

Howard is so busy with his collecting that we scarcely see each other except at meals and at night. He goes out almost every morning until noon, then after lunch he shuts the door of the workroom and concentrates on identifying what he's collected. He says progress is good, and this dry weather we're having now is ideal. The plants dry quickly and so do the papers; Mother, we'll love to read the papers you sent, but H. is even happier to have them for his plants. Our one-page newspaper doesn't go very far.

We had our floors polished—part done Tuesday, some Wednesday, and the rest today. All that remains is the kitchen, which we wouldn't polish if it weren't right in the line of vision from the front door. As it is, the unstained, unpolished kitchen looks like a storeroom or something, in contrast with the other floors, which look excellent.

Think I shall end this and go to bed. This morning we slept until 8:15, and last Sunday we slept nearly as late. I don't know what time Elizabeth wakes up, but she doesn't get us up until then. This weekend Howard is going to enclose some of our space underneath the house, making a large playpen for her.[54] She really does love her freedom here and runs to the door when she thinks it's high time we went downstairs. Just yesterday she ventured out into the sand; before then she'd avoided it entirely. We think she gets filthy, but the other mothers here just laugh and say, "Wait until she discovers sand and water!" Howard will put the hammock up this weekend, too, so we can relax downstairs during the hot part of the day.

Yawn!

Love,

Marian

Thursday night, 9:30, August 27, 1953

Dear Everyone—

Anyone with tired eyes might just as well skip this, because I know right now it won't be anything special! This is much too late for me to start a letter— we're usually on our way to bed by this time.

This evening Howard put the last nail in our grand playpen for Elizabeth— it really isn't just a playpen, since we'll all sit there. It is about 10 feet wide and about 18 feet long. Poor Howard strained his eyes, his back, and nearly his patience painting all the narrow little bars, but the effect is certainly pleasant. We thought green would look nice; the green turned out to be a vivid grass green that is almost too bright, but the strain of a second coat would have been too much for H. It looks neat and spacious, and the bars are high enough and close enough together that we don't see how Elizabeth could possibly get out. Bless her heart, we really do need it, for she's taken several tumbles off the steps; no bad ones, fortunately, since she rarely gets off the first step, but it is concrete at that. Yesterday, while I was across the street at the samba game, E. gave H. a very bad time. He was trying to work on the pen, and Elizabeth was pretty good for a while. Then she crawled under the car, got frightened, and wouldn't come out, so H. had to pull her out—hard on her knees. He had just cleaned her up (much grease, of course) and gone back downstairs, when she tried to climb the stairs and fell, bruising her upper lip. Pandemonium followed that, of course, and Howard said she cried all of the next twenty minutes or so while she was bathed and fed—until the Jell-O was put in her mouth. How she loves Jell-O! The bruise is nothing, and she was back again today trying to go up the stairs. Tomorrow she'll go into the pen; Howard will buy some paint tomorrow and we'll get it all painted on Saturday, so then we'll really be all set.

Two days ago he put our hammock up downstairs, and now I can scarcely leave it long enough to do my housework. It really is lovely downstairs even during the hot noon hours; yesterday and today I've read and dozed there while E. has been sleeping upstairs. Howard has built one large table that holds five seed frames and is going to make two more; ants devour everything that grows on the ground (there are about two exceptions—orchids and lilies), so people plant things in tubs or boxes and elevate them, putting the table legs in little pans of kerosene. A nuisance, but the ants are really terrors.

Bee, I love the blouse you sent! The embroidery is precious—but tell me, are the little yellow things carrots or pineapples? I said carrots, but H. was sure they were pines, as they are called here. At any rate, it fits perfectly and I shall certainly enjoy wearing it.

An interesting tidbit I picked up yesterday while playing cards is that our electricity is on a flat-rate basis here—no meters. The two-bedroom houses are charged $7 a month, so ours will be a little more, but nowhere near the $15 to $16 charges we had in town.

We are really wallowing in our enjoyment out here. Howard has fun working in the yard and doing odd jobs such as the pen, and I love the friendliness of the place. I know already that I would have no qualms at all about waking up neighbors in the middle of the night (when H. is in town after school starts) if the need arose. And Elizabeth is having a great time. Little Elizabeth English has been over here a lot the last few days, playing with our E. It gets quite complicated, for E.E. doesn't really realize that they both have the same name, and so she answers when we talk to our E. She is just three, and her speech is hard to understand but awfully cute. She's interested and curious and possessive, as I suppose most three-year-olds are, and fun to watch. I think she enjoys playing with someone younger than she is, for up to the time we came she played mostly with five- and six-year-olds.

A few days ago Howard told me that he thought I was crazy for trying to do everything myself; the upshot is that now Mildred is coming on Monday afternoons to polish our brass doorknobs. She's an expert at it, too—it took me an hour to do what she did in half that time, and the knobs looked better, too. Furniture doesn't get as dusty here—in fact I don't notice any film on things at all. The only nuisance is sand, which we all track in, in huge quantities. But that is easily swept up, and I don't bother with it more than once a day unless we're expecting someone. In other words, I'm simplifying my housekeeping. We get up at 6 or 6:30 here, and I get everything done by noon except the ironing, and night seems to be the best time for that.

When we were in town last week I bought Arthur Koestler's *Arrow in the Blue*, which I read and enjoyed very much, and Rachel Carson's other one— *Under the Sea-Wind*. Howard liked that but said he didn't think it quite up to the *Sea* [*The Sea Around Us*]. I've just started it. I also want to buy a Singer book on needlework that I think is excellent, and that will be my book-buying for a time. Fogarty's carries a very limited number of American books, printed in the U.K., and since they are the only ones I've read about, they are the ones I buy.

Well, kiddies, I'm off to bed.

Love,

Marian

Wednesday night, September 2, 1953

Dear Parents—

Oh boy. Today has been hot—95° in the shade. Howard, the old boob, says he doesn't even notice it, but I do—prickly heat like fury! Elizabeth hasn't been troubled by that at all lately, but if I dressed as she does I probably wouldn't either. Howard spent the day fetching leaf mold, muck from the river, and sand from our yard; mixing it together; putting it in the window box on our front porch; then he went out and got plants for it—ferns, little palms, and other small plants. Result: a lovely, cool effect. He finished painting the completed playpen a few days ago, and since then has been building seed frames. Everyone around here is astounded at his energy—and it is amazing to see the change in this place since we've been here. It really looks like home.

A few days ago a fireman came by on his bicycle to check our extinguisher. He told me that they are checked once a month—a routine started by "the Yankees" and that the local firemen continue.

Our big news of the week is that the new Fulbright people are coming on Sunday's plane. He is to teach geography—their name, the Merrill Pedersons, of Balaton, Minnesota, wherever that is. (We looked—it's barely on the map.) The S-Ds and son are coming out Sunday to spend the day; they're bringing a picnic lunch but will have tea and dinner with us. If the plane is on time, which it seldom is, the Pedersons will arrive at about 7. If the plane is delayed until later, the S-Ds will go on back to Georgetown, leaving us to meet the Pedersons. They'll spend the night here, at any rate, since it's easiest to plan that way, and besides we want to meet them. On Monday morning Howard will take them into town to the college, the bank, and such like.

This is the nicest neighborhood. We're borrowing two beds from the Kings across the street; Zela insisted on lending me six cans of milk until H. goes into town on Friday, and her maid is bringing me two pounds of sugar tomorrow from the village; and Jean Crooks brought over some powdered sugar this afternoon because I'd asked Zela if she had any that I could borrow. I wouldn't be borrowing so much, but tomorrow there is a Thing called a "bring and buy" sale, to be held under our house, as a matter of fact. It was to be held under the Crookses' house, but Wayne broke out in spots today. Anyway, I said I'd make cookies but I'm out of sugar. Chocolate frosted ones, I think, and some animal cookies with currant eyes, cherry tongues, and the like. Everyone brings something, and then we all buy and eat. The object is to raise money for some furnishings for the chapel, which is at this point little more than a room with benches, in the Guest House. Howard and I haven't been near the chapel, but it's fun to participate. We'll have the tables inside our pen, with the women selling from the inside and people buying from the outside. Somebody is making fudge, another lemon meringue pies, another curried chicken with roti (a mealy thing not too far removed from tortillas), another ice cream. Sounds as if we'll all get indigestion, doesn't it!

Mother, do you recall the blue crepe nightie you made for E.? A few months ago I made a little jacket from some of the leftover material, and now I'm using up the remains in a little sundress. I thought it would be great to have at least one sundress that wouldn't need ironing (for emergencies), and this will be sweet. I'm putting a little white eyelet ruffle around the top and on the top of the pockets. I've also cut out a little dress from that cute pink material with the blue kittens. Remember? I'm doing them by hand, although there are several sewing machines around here that I'm sure I can use if ever I want to.

Last Friday Howard picked up three batches of magazines—two large rolls, and the one with three *Coronets*. Thank you! We've just barely begun on them; chances are I'll keep them in reserve until school starts.

Did I say that Elizabeth is one of the few children left here who haven't come down with the measles? Our Elizabeth and the Englishes', and a few babies—five in all, I believe. We're holding our breath. Unfortunately, the Guianese are not quite as careful about keeping their children in as the English folks and we would be. Their attitude is, "You just can't keep a child in the house in this weather." Angela Bogardus (her daddy is one of the survey men) hasn't been seen except inside a car for two weeks now, although her mother says she's at the bad in-between age where she's too young to sit and look at a book and too old for blocks and dolls. Yesterday I'd just taken Elizabeth downstairs to the pen, and little two-and-a-half-year-old Donna Crooks came over—she's just barely over it, and the last time I asked Jean how she was, she said Donna still had a cold. Well, I hated to hurt Donna's feelings, but I didn't want to take a chance, so I brought Elizabeth upstairs. Jean came over for Donna, saying rather plaintively that "after all, it's been three weeks," etc., but there's never any point in taking a chance, is there. Jean hasn't had either of her children given any shots—no whooping cough, diphtheria, typhoid, or anything.

Mildred can't work for me until November because she has a new job, but she has secured the services of Bridget Rodriguez's maid, who will do my damned brass doorknobs, the stairs, and windowsills and baseboards. It occurred to me the other day that I don't enjoy windowsills and baseboards, yet they need washing every week—so I shall let someone else do them.

Mother, I'll bet you skipped a cute autobiographical story in one of the *Journals* you sent, by an American girl who married a Mexican. Called "My Heart Lies South," by Elizabeth Borton de Trevino. It is coming out in a book, it said. I giggled and giggled over it, and I know you'd enjoy it. There was a typical sexy illustration, which, I imagine, may have deterred you.

I think we'll have chicken pie for the S-Ds. Of course if I serve biscuits they'll think they are scones and wonder why on earth I serve them with dinner; and I suppose I shouldn't have salad since it isn't appreciated. Cold beets maybe. Vanilla ice cream with pineapple, and apricot sauce. Biscuits or not, I sure have the biscuit-making technique down pat! And bread—just routine now.

Mother, you should know me well enough to know that I love books by and about handicapped people. Don't you remember—Helen Keller and Clifford Beers and all the rest have always fascinated me. And the more we read about people with handicaps who have overcome them, the better. The children here, after the first day or so, haven't paid any attention at all to E.'s hands. And no one will, as long as we keep it in the proper light. I can say very truthfully that I think I'd feel worse about a child with crossed eyes—that always disconcerts me, though it shouldn't.

Howard stole my pen! Love and kisses,
Marian

Friday evening, September 4, 1953

Hello, Sweeties—

Oh boy. Rossini is blaring forth on the phonograph, and Howard and Pete are discussing everything from A to zed, as we say here. What a week.

To begin with, the food sale last Thursday was fun and took in over $50. My animal cookies were the cutest I've ever made, and all the children loved them. Friday evening the Englishes came over for a game of samba, and we talked and talked, and they took a big batch of the magazines home with them. Saturday we worked hard—cleaning up the house and the grounds for our big weekend. Sunday we worked even harder, right up to about

3:30, for we expected the S-Ds anytime after 4 for dinner; and we had to prepare our "guest room" for the Pedersons. The S-Ds arrived at 6, about five minutes before Howard and I were ready to give them up and eat by ourselves, for the Pedersons' plane was due in at 7. But we gave the S-Ds a drink, and I turned the oven off and the chicken pies kept hot. We had a lovely dinner—really chickeny pies, string beans, and ice cream à la Blanc with pineapple and apricot jam. Unfortunately, there were no compliments on it except from H. later on, damn blast these reticent British who neither give compliments nor expect them. Ah well.

Well, a rare thing happened and the Pan Am plane came in on time. We welcomed Agnes and Pete with open arms, and talked and talked for a long time after the S-Ds went back into town. What a joy to talk to Americans—we really do speak the "same language," figuratively as well as literally. Agnes is a grade-school teacher but couldn't be placed through the Fulbright deal because she doesn't have a degree. They are in their middle to late thirties; have lived fourteen years in Balaton, Minnesota, which has a population of 800; have rented out their house there, which has electric dishwasher, deep freeze, washer and dryer—everything but TV. Monday morning Howard took them into town and helped them get settled. They found a house, for $65 a month, and H. says it's good for Georgetown. He settled them at the Woodbine Hotel, where S-D had reserved a room for them ($24 a day), and got home around 6. Tuesday he went in to attend to a car license renewal and spent a few hours talking to the Pedersons. When he got home he said that Agnes seemed pretty depressed, so when we went into town Wednesday morning for my dentist appointment, we decided to bring them back to the base if they'd come. Well—they were very glad to come. Pete was in the Army in Europe, and there as well as in the South he had seen poverty, but Agnes hadn't, and it depresses her as it did me. Maybe because we are younger our reactions and adjustments came easier; and as H. says, nothing is quite as isolated as the Midwest. Agnes is a dear, and is what I'd call a typical-appearing grade-school teacher; but I feel more sophisticated than I have in ages. It is so good to talk to them about anything and everything: she and I have talked about E. more than I have to everyone put together here in B.G.— she just understands our attitude more easily than the others. Howard and Pete have covered almost everything; luckily, Pete is as enthusiastic as H. was, which makes it easier for Agnes to feel miserable—like me! Like I was, that is. (I don't know if it was moving out here or not, but I think I'm finally adjusted to this silly country. Happy, happy happy—such a lovely life!) The Pedersons have very simple tastes, so having them here has been just plain fun. They don't drink, and Agnes is far more worried about entertaining than I ever was. They didn't bring anything but clothes—cost including rail freight from Minnesota was prohibitive. Thank heavens we were able to.

Tomorrow H. will take them into town, and they will move into their house. They insist that H. live with them during the week—their house has two bedrooms—and I think it will work well, at least until they get the feel of the place. I am sending *Joy of Cooking* with Agnes, since she doesn't even have a cookbook here. They are sending for some things, but my goodness—how thankful I am that we came with our bits of home. It has been such a pleasure having them here with us, and throughout the year they'll be able to come out for weekends and holidays. As soon as their grant comes through from London (how familiar this sounds), they're going to get a car, so they'll be able to get around more easily. School begins next Wednesday. Howard will go in on Monday to get squared away.

My dears, the packages have really been a-coming. Evidently a boat came in; we've received a charming pink and yellow squirrel from Polly; the lovely skirt from you, Bee (three cheers, a size 14 fits fine!); the blouses and skirts from Mother—ho ho, I must move buttons over on those skirts, but the length is good (such pretty skirts, and the blouses all fit; goody for seersucker); books and magazines. I'm reading *Karen* now and can scarcely put it down—it makes our Elizabeth's future seem so clear and simple. And we have two more packages awaiting us at the post office—H. will pick them up tomorrow.

Yesterday morning I went downstairs for Elizabeth at orange juice time and found her sans shoes, sunsuit, and panties. Clad in her little pink socks, she was having a lovely time swinging her sunsuit round and round. Now that she's learned how, the clothes come off very easily, several times a day. Yesterday we lost a sandal temporarily in the john, but it dried out quickly. I'll swear she gets cuter by the day, and Agnes assured me that we aren't spoiling her. The dearest thing now is the way, after she eats her dinner, Elizabeth toddles into the living room to tell Howard good night. For months and months I've carried her in to tell Daddy "night-night," and a few days ago I let her walk; she went right straight to Howard, sat on his knee for a few minutes, and then we went off to bed. I do wish you could see her in her little long nightie, going to Howard with her arms outstretched, knowing he'll pick her up for a hug and a kiss. Wednesday in town was a long day for her, but she was good as gold. I took a hard-boiled egg, bread and butter, and an apple to scrape for her lunch as well as milk and water; I fed her at 11, a little early, and after we all had lunch we went downtown for a while. She went to sleep after about five minutes in the car and slept all the way home. Not a peep of discontent all day. Yesterday morning she seemed a little cranky but after her nap was just fine.

I have a thank-you note to write and a grocery list to make out, so this is the end. We love you all and miss you and wish like mad that you could come for a visit—all of you! Since this is the beginning of the second year, time will fly. Maybe we'll be home next summer—before long we should know.

Much love,

Marian

September 6:

Several days ago our dog got in a fight over a female. Being old and almost toothless, he got the worst of the fight and came home with a bad gash in one ear. We hoped it would heal, but it rapidly went from bad to worse; by yesterday it had become a wretched wound, and H. asked the local authorities to have him put to sleep. Although the dog's resistance was undoubtedly low, it seemed to both of us that the wound went bad far more rapidly than it would have at home.

Tuesday night, September 8, 1953

Dear Daddy,

The grind has begun again for Howard, but I think he's glad to be back at the college. You asked about his living arrangements in town—I guess I mentioned in my last letter that he'd be staying with the Pedersons. At this point we don't know if he'll be staying there beyond the first term. We'd be the very last to want to run a good thing into the ground; of course, he'll be paying them, and then he won't be there at all on weekends, so I don't think they'll see too much of him. It will be awfully nice for him to have meals similar to those I cook—the Pedersons prefer plain, wholesome cooking quite a bit like mine. No sweets though—they just don't care about them. I don't know how many nights a week he'll be teaching—I think it's three, and I'm not sure whether it's one or two hours per night. (H. will know.) The money gained thereby isn't really necessary; we figure that what he makes will amply cover his expenses living in town and the extra gas and wear and tear on the car involved in living out here. The night classes are to take the place, in H.'s time schedule, of the private tutoring he did last year. Actually, I think it will take fewer hours since everyone will be taught at the same time. He feels an obligation to teach these courses; you can't imagine the need there is here for science teachers. The Bishops' High School biology teacher is on leave in Merrie England now, so H. is the only one in the colony. But I'm not worried about his overworking; he says he will enjoy devoting the week to school and the weekend to Elizabeth, me, and the bush!

Several times today I have thought to myself, "What fun—no cigarette ashes, no pipe tobacco, half as many crumbs on the floor, and no sand to sweep up—and how dull!"

I don't think I'll get really bored. I enjoy reading and such too much for that. Elizabeth is great entertainment during the day, and the neighbors have all invited me to drop in if I get bored or lonely. Frank Defreitas will pick up the mail and paper each day from the Board of Control office, so if the weather is bad I needn't bother about that. Howard will take Betty and Annie Defreitas in to school each Monday and bring them out each Friday; it's a good arrangement. [During the week] they are living just a block or so away from the Pedersons, too.

The latest news is sort of staggering; according to the local finance man, there is no reason on earth why we can't take any amount of accrued savings from the colony, despite anything said by the Fulbright people. We intend to get something in writing—it sounds too good to be true. We don't begrudge any of our purchases—heaven knows our life has been much more pleasant here because of them—and just about now we're in a position to start saving. H. intends to open a savings account when the grant comes—we won't need to spend more than a dab of the $1,800.

Elizabeth sleeps soundly from 6:30 to 6:30, much to the amazement of the local people. They can't understand how she goes to sleep so early; their tots stay up until 8. My latest shock today was learning that babies are bathed in tap water (fairly cool) after they're about two or three months old—"It makes them stronger," I was told. Maybe they consider the dirt beneficial!

The little imp refuses to keep shoes on; today by using three safety pins I managed to make her sunsuit (and therefore her panties, too) escape-proof. Now she tries to put her shoes back on, but no luck yet. Carrie [Howard's grandmother] sent some little quilted bedroom slippers like those she made for Howard and me; Elizabeth certainly looked cute padding around in them tonight. So far, we've escaped the measles, and no one new has them either. Maybe the epidemic has quieted down.

Did I tell you before we moved in that all the kitchen shelves for pans and bowls are open? I was a bit worried about E. and the temptation involved, but I needn't have been. She plays with three lids and an enameled cup and leaves all the rest strictly alone—that accomplished with not too much "no-no"-ing. And she very, very seldom delves into our bookcase or the magazines on the end tables. Wastebaskets are in her domain, and she really enjoys emptying them, carting them around, dumping them upside down, etc. She still isn't talking but now says something like "gidgie gidgie gidgie," which implies a robust satisfaction with whatever is going on.

Mother commented recently on our thinness—don't worry, kiddoes. I'm afraid the illusion is merely photographic. I have a tummy and more muscles in my arms than ever before. I feel fine. Howard could be a bit heavier, but he too feels fine. We eat well and enjoy it; the only real change in our diet is that we don't crave in-between-meal snacks. And Elizabeth has a grand appetite. Really, we are in excellent health; this last year we've had nothing more serious than a cold or so each—no flu, sinus, or measles.

Think I shall retire.

Much, much love to you and Mother,

Marian

September 10, 1953:

In a speech before the House of Assembly, Forbes Burnham draws wild approval from the gallery when he says: "I hear the pratings in certain places about the possibility of our present Constitution being taken from us. Perhaps, who knows, that may be in their minds but I believe I am speaking for the Majority Party when I say that any such attempt will be met with as much force as is necessary in the circumstances." Cheddi Jagan later noted that Burnham's remark was made to counter an assertion by a member of the opposition who was "apparently . . . more informed of the Government's secrets than we."

In early September Governor Savage delivered to the Colonial Office one in his series of reports on the colony in which he wrote: "I have now toured all the densely populated areas and seen for myself the general conditions of life. There is indeed, as elsewhere, much fertile ground for communists. The vast majority of the people are not communists but there is no doubt that they felt the voice of the common people was not heard in the previous councils of state and they demanded a change. Unfortunately, generally speaking, the only leadership offered was the highly organized PPP party. . . . The party members are a very mixed lot ranging from labourers to professional men and owners of substantial property. The six opposition members are of poor quality. . . . The sugar estates are to a considerable extent the crux of the situation. It is there that the extremist is well supported. It is so easy for him to point to the dreadful housing and social conditions which exist (and to ignore the improvements) and compare them with the comfortable quarters and the neat compounds and the recreational facilities of the staff who are predominantly European. It is also easy for him to allege unfair profits being transferred to absentee landlords and to blame, as is done, the British Government for the conditions which exist. . . . There is a lot of racial feeling here. In spite of the nationalistic slogans, there is a deep distrust by the African of the Indian and a physical fear of the African by the Indian. Many Africans hate the white man, while the Portuguese are probably more responsible than anybody for racial feelings. . . . There is very little social contact between white people and others. At the Coronation Ball at Government House a group of 'whites' left early after a 'Paul Jones' [a musical-chairs-type of mixer]."

Friday, 12:15 p.m., September 11, 1953

Dear Mother—

Just finished lunch and Elizabeth is sound asleep. Got two nice letters from you and thought this would be the best time to answer them. You all may get more letters from me while Howard is in town—writing a letter, to me, is just about as good as a conversation.

H. went into town Monday morning and had to drive back out Tuesday because he'd forgotten all his school keys. I was snoozing and was startled by his appearance. He had a cold drink of orangeade, stayed about 15 minutes, and left. Then he drove out again Wednesday because he'd forgotten his bow, and there was a rehearsal for the *Trial by Jury* repeat performance that night. That time he stayed just long enough for a cold drink. He'll be out about 4:30 this afternoon with Mrs. McLaren, who will stay about ten days or as long as she wants. All reports from town say that Margaret is doing very well and, aside from still being thin, looks her old self again, but that Mrs. McLaren looks really exhausted. Yesterday I cleaned up our so-called guest room and made up one of our borrowed beds with both the lavender-and-white checked [wool] blanket and the quilt Carrie made; it seems ridiculous, but I know she uses one blanket in town, and it does get cooler here! Those two, with bedspreads, constitute the sum total of our bedding here.

Yesterday I made cookies. Remember the vanilla wafers? They hold up better here with a little additional flour, it seems. Put half a candied cherry in the center of each and they certainly look pretty. Also made some lemon cookies with the refrigerator cookie recipe. I still don't know just what I'll do about meals while Mrs. McLaren is here—she is used to having her big meal at noon, then tea, and then supper. I imagine I'll pad out our usual sandwich-fruit-cookie lunch a bit, have tea by all means, and then have more or less our usual dinner. She eats less than Elizabeth does anyway—about a quarter of what Howard and I eat.

If Elizabeth's hair weren't quite so thin I'd have cut it before now, but there really isn't much. We will love the seersucker sundresses; I washed my seersucker blouse the other day, hung it on a hanger to dry, and it looks just grand. I am enjoying the skirts and blouses—I must confess that I'm not too sure about wearing the strapless top—people here are essentially conservative, and so am I.

You know, Mother, I get amused at myself now and then. I catch myself feeling so very sorry for Zela and Frank and their little Peter; yet I am sure that numerous people waste time feeling sorry for us and Elizabeth. Of course the two cases are entirely different, except that either can happen to almost any parents. Zela says Peter can tell the sound of his father's Land Rover (British jeep) and gets excited when he hears it; he knows that if Frank has on slippers it's all right, but if he puts shoes on, Pete wants to go out, too. He darts away from the house, can't be outside (or inside either, I guess) without someone watching him. And some nights he cries and cries—a pathetic wail, not like a normal child's cry at all. The thing that peeves H. is why on earth Frank doesn't build, or have built, a good, high, strong playpen like the one he built for Elizabeth. Zela has said over and over that one like ours would keep Peter in, but he still runs around, down the street, up the street, and across the lots behind and in front of us. I asked her once why they didn't build a little stand way up high for the electric fan so that he couldn't possibly reach it, and she looked as if the thought had never struck them.

Your encouragement is always so welcome; not that we pine for it, but it makes a nice boost. Elizabeth is such a happy child, and I think she's pretty well behaved for her age, too. The neighbors all marvel at the way she plays alone in the big pen; she loves to have other little youngsters play with her, of course, but she's happy by herself. (That is courtesy of the baby books, which told me to teach her to play by herself at an early age when she began to crawl.) She seems to enjoy life completely and never cries except when startled or hurt. While she was eating her lunch I sat and read your letters and then told her that her grandmother Anna and all the other grandparents and her mommy and daddy thought she was the cutest child on this earth; she gazed at me steadily, grinned, and whoops—bang went the cup of milk right smack into the air! She spills so seldom that it startles her as much as it does me, but it's easily mopped up.

No, I didn't care too much for Mrs. K's explanations to Karen,[55] but evidently Karen was a very religious little girl—remember the Communion and Confirmation excitement. And in a very religious household, I think it would be a good explanation. But in ours we lean so much more toward matter-of-factness and objectivity. If today Elizabeth asked me why she was born without hands, my mind would go first to Howard's remarking on the little undeveloped leaf on the tree, then to the doctors' explanation of the failure of the hands to grow, and then perhaps to a bit of Miss B.'s theory about Elizabeth as an angel hunting a home to be born into where she would be loved—heavens, I don't know. I think it over now and then, but I suppose when she does ask me it will take me by surprise.

E.'s naptime is about over, so I think I'll flop down until she wakes up. Love and kisses to you and Daddy, and a big hug from Elizabeth—she can really hug now!

Marian

September 13, 1953:

From Governor Savage's report to the Colonial Office: "The new Constitution has operated now for roughly four months. It is a fact that the P.P.P. have no planned policy and except for Jagan, the new Ministers had had no experience of Government departments or of normal administration. I still think that it is true to say that they were themselves unprepared for their landslide victory at the polls and had expected to find themselves in the role of a strong obstructive and disrupting opposition. . . . I am rapidly coming to the conclusion that unless the opposition elements rouse themselves quickly . . . we shall have to go back on the new Constitution which would mean use of force. . . . At a recent meeting with the leading businessmen here I pressed the problem on them and the part that they could play in arresting the deterioration of the situation. Unfortunately, I feel that some of them, supported particularly by the Portuguese community, consider the best solution is to hasten the breakdown of the constitution and to press Her Majesty's Government to go back to a less liberal system."

Sunday night, September 19, 1953

Dear All—

The end of a pleasant, busy week. Or perhaps I should say the beginning of a less busy one! Mrs. McLaren came out last Friday (a week ago last Friday, that is) and will go back into town with Howard tomorrow morning. In years she is very little older than our mothers, yet her whole outlook is that of a much older woman; I wonder how much of it is due to the fact that she lived right in the midst of the two world wars. Heavens—how we've talked! Nearly every day we finished lunch at 2 and dinner at 8 or 9 or 10, just because we talked and talked and talked over tea and coffee. Thursday evening I hosted the samba party, which was fun—first time it had been in the evening since I've been going, and several of the women appreciated the coffee that I offered as an alternative to soft drinks. They stayed and talked until nearly midnight, and I think everyone enjoyed the evening. We did!

Monday I gave Elizabeth a little haircut—snipped off the one dangling lock and evened off the back. Mother, was your comment a gentle hint—remember a few weeks ago you mentioned a Dutch bob for Elizabeth? I probably should have done it before now but didn't think about it. However, Monday I asked Mrs. McLaren if she thought it should be cut, and since she said definitely yes, I went ahead and did it. Elizabeth looks much neater, naturally.

When Howard came out Friday he brought all sorts of packages. The dish drainer arrived, thank heavens, and thank you, Mother! Everything fits beautifully; I love the shorts. That material is certainly much cooler than denim. I think the sandals are very pretty and they, too, fit. My goodness— I've cut the buttons off the old lavender and have rolled it up rough-dry; the gray receives the same fate tomorrow after I wash it. They look really shabby and it's high time I retired them. Think I may put those buttons (plain little pearl ones) on the piqué blouses. Wore the halter one yesterday and H. was quite impressed. Very comfortable. It looks lovely with the skirt you sent, Bee.

The socks for Elizabeth fit now and will fit for a few months; the only snag is that she doesn't care to have shoes or socks on and removes them at the earliest opportunity. But when we go out they stay on, and I'm awfully glad to have such pretty ones. The ones available here are much heavier.

I've had a ghastly time this weekend with one of the burners on the stove. The switch is broken, so that if any of the burners or the oven was turned on, this hottest and quickest burner went on full blast. I endured it all day yesterday but nearly died today, so around noon H. pulled out some wires to disconnect that one burner. We hope he can get someone sent out from town tomorrow—probably can since they aren't as picky-pecky as at home.

Mr. S-D said last week that he'd had a letter from the U.S. Educational Commission that was written July 26 (sent regular mail from London, the tightwads) and states that they would give consideration to the idea of H.'s being given a second two-year contract. It said the board would meet the following week—so we more or less expect a letter with the results of their considering anytime now. Darn it all, we'll sure be glad to quit tossing this "will we stay or will we go" ball back and forth.

This coming Friday I have to go back to the dentist. I only had two cavities, but the silly man didn't want to do them both the same day. Little credit did he give to my telling him of the two-hour sessions I've had in years past. It should be quite a day. I shall have to ask around to find someone who is going to town on Friday, and ask if E. and I may please have a ride in. Then I guess I shall leave E. at the Pedersons' and go to the dentist—my appointment is for 10. I gather we shall all eat there; then, when H. goes back to Queen's, he will drop the two of us at the Ramsarans' for the afternoon. We should manage to get home by 4:30, so it won't be too long a day. We hope to bring home the small washing machine I've mentioned from time to time; supposedly they have arrived, but due to strikes, the ships haven't been unloaded yet.

We've really had an interesting two weeks here—the political pot has become a bit scorched. The sugarcane workers were out for three weeks; Lord knows the cost to the colony.[56] Sympathy strikes were enforced in many lines—the dockworkers, telecommunications, Transport and Harbours Department, milk processors, railroad engineers, bus drivers, and the slaughterhouse employees. All that lasted only 24 hours, and then they had to go back to work; the sugar field hands go back to work tomorrow, and negotiations will begin.

Almost bedtime, so I shall wind this up.

Love to all,

Marian

September 24, 1953:

Rumours had begun to fly. From a speech made at a public meeting by Minister of Labour Ashton Chase, erroneously attributed by the British to Minister of Education Forbes Burnham: "They say they are going to take away the Constitution from us . . . [but] we intend to fight to the end. I would like not to discuss our plans for the intended action which we will take, but will keep it a secret until it becomes necessary to put it into operation."

Fire was always a worry in Georgetown. "One of our main fears was the rioters would set fire to the wooden houses in the residential quarters," recalled John Gutch, "and one night I was rung up by a Guianese friend who told me that cans of petrol were being bought up for this purpose."

In his report on the colony of early September, Governor Savage had noted that "anti-white feeling is growing."

Sunday, October 4, 1953

Dear All—

Oh my, I am without inspiration tonight—I must have eaten too much dinner. For some reason I have been on a pie Thing lately. Friday I made one but unfortunately didn't notice until I'd filled the silly thing that the crust wasn't completely baked. So today I vindicated myself by making another, this one banana cream, with a delicious, thoroughly baked shell. Now, of course, I've half a pie left and Howard won't be here to help me finish it!

We certainly do enjoy our weekends here. Howard works hard all week and relaxes completely once he gets home. Night classes haven't started yet, but once they're under way he'll have them from 6 to 8 on Monday, Tuesday, and Thursday nights. The boys have asked him to continue the stamp club, so that will take up Wednesday nights. But the Pedersons go to bed early, so Howard does, too. Elizabeth is delighted to have him home; this afternoon, while I was snoozing in the bedroom, she and Howard were here in the living room. He dozed off and was awakened once by the wastebasket, which E. had plopped on his head; another time, he woke up because she was patting his hair!

Last week went by quickly for me. One evening Mrs. English brought back some magazines and we talked for a while; eventually I went to her house and returned with some whole wheat flour for bread. We hadn't known it was available here, but they beg it from one of the commercial bakers in town. Thursday night I played cards at the Crookses' house; left Elizabeth alone because their house is within wailing distance of ours.

We will certainly be glad when we hear from London about this contract business. The political situation has us wondering just what will happen in the next few years; the latest events aren't very encouraging, but it's hard to know where rumor and exaggeration take over. Talk going around at present is that "everyone" is leaving;[57] that people with money invested are willing to take a 50 percent loss just to get out; that old-timers just "can't stand" the colony any longer and are leaving. Actually, we doubt if very many people are really leaving; no doubt many would like to. Congressman Donald Jackson was here last week and told the press that the State Department is keeping a day-by-day check on the colony because of its vital defense position.[58] So far, we've heard nothing alarming from anyone in the State Department or the U.S. Educational Commission. The extra two years would be grand from the educational, professional stand; and now that we're living here at Atkinson it wouldn't be uncomfortable, either. I think we're pretty well adjusted to the climate, as a matter of fact. But if by staying that extra time we are leaving ourselves open to criticism, we wouldn't care to chance it. Are people you all know aware to any extent of B.G. and its socialist cast? The BBC has mentioned local goings-on several times lately, but we're wondering if the U.S. radio and papers make much of it. It is hard to see how the local ministers, our young troublemakers here, could do much damage; the country is so terribly poor that the three-week sugar strike is being felt by many to a great degree. The governor has control of the police and militia, and there just isn't the money to equip another force; unless, of course, money or guns or what have you were sent from abroad. Well, as we keep saying, maybe we won't even be offered the darned extension and then all our problems will be solved for us!

We have to get up really early tomorrow so H. can get back to town. He will be taking in Ann and Betty Defreitas, also Mrs. Correia (she and her husband run the hydroponic gardens and raise chickens out here) and her little girl. I didn't get to town last Friday, much to my disappointment, because, oddly enough, no one was going in that day. Try again soon.

Love to you all,

Marian

From Marian's later recollections:

As placid as our days [at the airbase] were, the situation in town, as elsewhere in the colony, was deteriorating. Restlessness increased. Jibes were replaced with threats, and old resentments turned into violence.... A worried next-door neighbor sent her husband over one night to move Elizabeth's crib into my bedroom. He then installed a hook and eye on my door—minimal protection, since the partitions separating bedroom from hall began 18 inches above floor level and ended 18 inches below the ceiling. However, there was real concern over an anticipated uprising.

October 6:

As I was hanging up my washing, Jean Crooks came across from her house to tell me some important news: somebody's brother in Georgetown had called to say that the government was to be overthrown either today or on Thursday, October 8. Last night her husband and two other men had driven into Georgetown to collect their children who go to school in town; they would have told me, she said, but they didn't want me to worry. Everyone is excited and rumors are numerous; I considered calling Howard in town, but Frank Defreitas said he imagined the lines were tapped. Unfortunately, at this crucial period, our radio is out of commission, so I can hear news only by running to one of the neighboring houses. The local radio station reports nothing of the tense situation, but the BBC broadcasts from London on Tuesday tell of destroyers and an aircraft carrier that are proceeding toward Trinidad.[59]

October 6, 1953

From the Los Angeles Times:

Navy Moves in Colonial Crisis; British Blame U.S.-Born Woman as Leader of Unrest in Guiana. London, Oct. 5—Britain tonight faces a crisis in her rum-and-sugar colony of British Guiana where the Governor is reported sparring with the left-wing government and even considering firing some of its members.

A British force of warships carrying troop reinforcements was reported heading for Georgetown, capital of the empire's only Red colony, in case of real trouble. . . .

A 32-year-old U.S.-born strawberry blonde with a flair for leftist politics was front-paged by London newspapers as the mainspring behind the colony's angry movement for greater independence. . . .

Georgetown dispatches said tonight official quarters denied categorically a report circulating there that the new constitution has been withdrawn. The dispatches added that there was an atmosphere of tenseness in Georgetown and the population feared big developments were brewing. Police have been alerted to face any possible emergency. . . .

The London Daily Mail splashed a picture of bespectacled Mrs. Jagan under the headline: "She wants to run a British colony."

October 7, 1953:

Ralph Champion, a reporter for the *Daily Mirror*, wrote: "I was the first British newspaperman to arrive in this 'crisis' colony and when I flew in yesterday, I was greeted with amazement. There seemed to be little idea that there was a crisis over alleged moves by the government's People's Progressive Party to convert the colony into a Red Republic."

A correspondent from London's *Daily Mail* related his radio-telephone conversation with a Mr. Whittingham, the colony's deputy police commissioner, who spoke from Georgetown, saying: "There are no demonstrations, there is no general strike, there is nothing abnormal happening here whatsoever."

October 8:

Howard drove out yesterday afternoon to see how we are faring and reported the situation in town as being tense but quiet. The thought of fires being lit in town is a frightening one here where the majority of houses and buildings are ancient and wooden; riots begun among cane workers with their sharp, broad-bladed knives could be disastrous. Howard was reassuring, however, and said that there was no talk of schools being closed as yet.

This morning he drove back into town—and the troops arrived. Five hundred Royal Welsh Fusiliers were brought here by three British warships to be stationed on various sugar plantations and other key spots where trouble is expected.[60]

October 8, 1953

From the Los Angeles Times:

> *British Moves Hit by Guiana Premier: Leftist Leader Declares Governor Asked for Warships and Troops to Take Rights. Georgetown, Oct. 7—Leftist Prime Minister Cheddi Jagan charged in the House of Assembly today that the Governor of this British colony called for troop-laden warships as a show of force here without consulting his elected minister.*
>
> *"The responsibility for whatever may happen is entirely that of the governor and those who have advised him," declared Jagan, fiery leader of the leftwing People's Progressive Party. . . .*
>
> *Jagan was blocked by the Speaker of the House, Sir Eustace Woolford, in attempting to introduce a motion calling for the withdrawal of the warships because they were likely "to precipitate incidents and endanger peace." . . . The People's Progressive Party said in a statement:*
>
> *"The BBC announcement that naval and military forces have been sent to British Guiana with the utmost dispatch has caused us much surprise. We cannot see any reason for such intimidation when all Guianese know conditions in our country are normal and peaceful."*
>
> *"There is no disturbance, unrest or violence. In this hour, when the (British) Colonial Office is trying to create hysteria and rob us of our rights, we ask the people of Guiana to remain calm, quiet and firm." . . .*

October 9:

This morning Governor Sir Alfred Savage announced over the radio the suspension of B.G.'s six-month-old Constitution, a drastic step that he said is necessary in order to break the grasp of the PPP ministers intent on turning B.G. into a servile state.

This afternoon Howard brought Agnes out with him; Pete considers the situation in town bad and wanted to get her out of the way. Howard doesn't think it that bad, but the worst moments came when the troops arrived and the expected outbursts failed to appear. With troops equipped to handle any rioting or disturbances, we feel quite safe.

October 9, 1953:

> Governor Savage's broadcast "was the first most Guianese heard" of the suspension of the constitution and declared state of emergency. Savage's announcement was accompanied by one from Chief Secretary John Gutch, in which he said the actions had been taken "to prevent Communist subversion of the Government and a dangerous crisis both in public order and in economic affairs. . . . It has become clear to Her Majesty's Government that the Ministers have no intention of making the constitution work, that on the contrary their sole object is to seize control of the whole territory and to run it on totalitarian lines. They have clearly shown they are prepared to use violence and to plunge the State into economic and social chaos to achieve their ends. Their next attempt to demonstrate their power might have been disastrous to the territory."
>
> Writing from Georgetown, a correspondent from London's *Daily Herald* reported: "I flew into this crisis city of palms and wooden houses late last night. And this afternoon, 18 hours later, I am still looking for the crisis."

October 11:

Saturday I baked cupcakes and more cupcakes for a fair held at the hospital to benefit the chapel; over $500 was made. Today Howard had a ghastly time with a wisdom tooth, and we made a quick trip into Georgetown to a dentist's office, leaving Elizabeth with Agnes. Worries, worries.

October 11, 1953:

Headline above a full page of photos in the Sunday edition of *The Daily Argosy:* "British Troops Land In Colony To Preserve Order"

From the Los Angeles Times:

Georgetown, Oct. 11—Ousted Leftist Prime Minister Cheddi Jagan flung back the charge of conspiracy at the British today and accused London of inventing a Communist plot as a "smoke screen to cover up Britain's attempt to scrap even our limited constitution."

He branded "just nonsense" Britain's charges that Jagan's left-wing People's Progressive Party was plotting to subvert this rum and sugar colony to Moscow-dominated Communism and establish a "dangerous platform for extending Communist influence in the Western Hemisphere." . . .

The PPP called a general strike today and said it would issue a statement tomorrow. But tomorrow is the Pan-American Day holiday and no effects of the strike will be felt before Tuesday.

The entire colony appeared calm.

Businessmen, big farmers and industrialists here cheered the decision and supported London's charges that the Communists had gained control of the PPP government, had attempted to convert the police, had tried to institute Red-tinged laws, had crippled the colony's $15,000,000-a-year sugar industry with a 25-day strike.

Washington added its support of the British action. A sign of the intense interest the United States was showing in events here was the presence of William Percy Maddox, the Consul General at Trinidad. . . .

To the question, "Are you or are you not a Communist?" Jagan blinked and replied, "That depends on one's interpretation of Communism." . . . Asked why his wife and others in his government had gone to these [Moscow-sponsored conferences in Eastern European capitals behind the Iron Curtain] if they were not Communists, Jagan replied: "Oh, we naturally need the help of outside forces, since the British government seems determined to deprive us of even the limited constitutional privileges we had, and now the United States, we understand, is supporting solidly London's viewpoint. We must look for friends where we can find them."

Tuesday p.m., October 13, 1953

Dear All—

Well, everything is pretty normal again. The newspapers are full of little articles about such-and-such a group declaring its loyalty to the throne, stories from various countries criticizing the British government for its unwarranted action, and pictures of the Royal Welsh Fusiliers smiling, talking with kiddies, and posing with their weapons. The only sign I've seen of the Fusiliers up here at the Field was a group of them sprawled beside a truck down near the end of our street. Pete was all set last week to send Agnes back to Minnesota, but Howard talked him into letting her stay; she came out here with H. on Friday and stayed through Sunday, when Pete came out. Pete thought that Georgetown was "ominously quiet" on Sunday; we thought it was just the ordinary Sunday lull. Of course if all this ruckus had happened after we'd been here one month, we might have been all set to move out, too! Pete talked to William Maddox, the U.S. Consul General in Trinidad, who was here over the weekend to size up the situation, and Mr. Maddox said he thought everything was under control and there was no need for worry; that the RAF had planes standing by, and that we Americans would come under the British airlift if such were needed.

Howard's wisdom teeth finally caught up with him, and he spent a rather miserable weekend. Saturday I phoned four dentists in town but none was in; finally I got some pills from the dispenser here and they at least put H. out of his misery for a while. Sunday things got bad enough that he and I went into town, leaving Elizabeth with Agnes, and finally we got hold of a Dr. Wong, who is supposedly the best dentist there is here. (When we first arrived, the Larthes told us that he was the "society" dentist and charged too much; now we take their endorsements with a grain of salt.) Most of the people here at the airbase go to him and think he is good. Anyway, he told H. he wouldn't do a thing without taking X-rays, a hopeful sign in this place, where action usually replaces investigation. He came in from his boat on the river to see H., took the X-rays, and gave him a prescription for some pills to tide him over. Unfortunately, drugstores in Georgetown aren't open on Sundays at 2 p.m. so we came home sans pills. To be safe, H. got some from the dispenser, which, happily, he didn't need. Today he was to have one tooth out and I guess another on Friday, with the last two coming out next week. It's a shame he has to have it done during school time, but I don't know how many times I told him to call the dentist during vacations; it just takes a jolt, I guess. I sent him to town with baked custards, custard powder, eggs, and Jell-O—he'll pull through nicely, I imagine.

Today was one of those rare off days with Elizabeth. She didn't eat all of any meal, twice turned over a nearly full cup of milk, and gave me quite a time with her shoe removal act downstairs. I shall blame it all on the lower right molar, which is poking through. We are beginning to brush her teeth, and it is quite something—she doesn't get the point at all yet, but I know now that she'll be able to brush them herself once she does get the idea. She holds the brush easily and sticks it in her mouth and chews on it. Darn it all, I sure wish we could buy meat for babies her age. I just can't get our local beef tender enough for her; even ground, it is still tough. I suppose a pressure cooker would do it, but such a nuisance. I gave her some liver tonight, but she just chewed it for a while and then out it came. I suppose if I ground up the meat from a lamb chop that would work.

I really don't mind these evenings alone. Elizabeth is grand entertainment all day long. We enjoy walking up and down the street or around the block in the afternoon; she loves her encounters with dogs, children, and various adults. After dinner I enjoy reading or sewing or writing letters. The neighbors look askance when I say I don't mind; last week I made a little toy dog for Elizabeth—a silly-looking aqua, two-legged animal with perky ears and tail. Fun for me—I'll put him away for Christmas.

And then I iron in the evenings—gads, the ironing! I think of the way we used to complain at home when summer and cotton dresses came around each year. Here it is worse than that all the time. The shorts and blouses I wear in the morning are really soaked with perspiration in no time at all, but I wear them two mornings before I wash them. Dresses I wear two or three afternoons. I do three dress shirts for Howard and four sports shirts, and a couple of Elizabeth's dresses. And we use more napkins because the ants get into them as soon as they get at all sticky or greasy. But I go into a sort of trance when I iron and really don't mind it; my mind wanders all over the country and the time goes quickly. Howard's lightweight shirts are just a snap to iron, too—I am being spoiled by them! We still don't have the washing machine; the crisis has held up the unloading of the boats, we are told.

Bee, the wrapping papers are charming! We were a bit appalled that you sent the package airmail; you really shouldn't, dear. We have learned patience, or perhaps just adopted a different standard of time, and don't fidget for packages as we used to. I'm awfully glad to have the sequins. Christmas, Christmas, Christmas. What do we want? For me, a book—any book! A set of bowl covers. For Elizabeth—I don't know what to suggest. Why don't you just go to one of the department stores' toy departments and ask what they have for the almost-two-year-old. Something non-breakable and fairly small, of course. H. will have to let you know his desires.

Now to do a spot of ironing, and then I shall retire. Don't know what our temperature is tonight, but I have on my pink sundress and am dripping all over!

Love to each of you,

Marian

Mother, did you ever send the Joy of Cooking *I wanted for Mrs. Patoir? Or the directions for making those toys? Neither received at this point.*

Monday, October 19, 1953

Greetings, All—

Can't figure out where this evening has gone—it's 9:30 now and I just finished washing my dishes. I guess it's because I made a pot of coffee with dinner, then sat and drank it for quite a while as I read. All last week, Bee, I amused myself with sequins, satin ribbon, and organdy—I still think I'm a frustrated kindergartner! Intended to "create" some more tonight, but time flies.

On Friday we will be invaded by 350 Scottish Highlanders, who will be quartered in the guesthouse up here. Another group will be stationed in town. I'm wondering if I need worry about being in the house alone with All Those Men nearby. Oh well, these open and airy houses would be wonderful in time of crisis—say "Boo" in a slightly raised voice even now at 9:30, and the whole neighborhood would hear and come running. Everything seems pretty quiet in town, although the police have been raiding houses like mad hunting for secret documents, Red literature, and such. Jagan and Burnham left today for England,[61] where they hope to plead their case; we're all waiting for the debate in Parliament to begin because more information is bound to come out then.

Poor Howard is having a hell of a time with his tooth extraction of last Tuesday. Dr. Wong said it was the worst he'd seen in years and years; it took well over an hour to get it out. No one here is equipped to use gas; Novocain is it. Pretty grim, H. said. He got along well enough, but last Saturday it began to swell, and by Sunday morning he couldn't open his mouth or close his teeth. So at 9 a.m. we went flying into town. When we got there, Agnes and Pete were still asleep, so we went to the Ramsarans'. H. called Dr. Wong and talked to his brother, who is a physician and who sent him to another physician (Physician Wong was just recovering from performing an operation), who took Howard's temperature (102°) and gave him a whopping big shot of penicillin. He was to have another today and one tomorrow, and then, the doctor said, if it was still bad he'd have to go to the hospital. We hope to heaven it doesn't come to that. Actually, the stitches are healing just as they should; evidently the draining has caused this infection. I don't think he's mentioned this to his parents, so if you talk with them, Mother, you might not say anything.

We had a lovely time at the Ramsarans'—at least Elizabeth and I did. Howard slept much of the time! We ate dinner with them at noon and then came back home at about 4. Elizabeth had a nap in the crib, with Janet asleep in the buggy. Janet is a cute baby—three and a half months old now and in the bubble-blowing stage. Elizabeth was fascinated with her; for a while Janet was on the floor, and E. sat by her touching her (trying to poke). E. and Susan had fun playing together; Susan seems very proud of Janet now and told me that she has two sisters, Elizabeth and Janet. Margaret looks very well; she's lost 22 pounds in the 18 months they have been here, but her figure looks fine. They urged us to stay the night; we all hated to have H. drive back out here feeling as he did, but he insisted. I knew that Pete would be glad to drive E. and me out, and we always could have taken a taxi—but Howard got stubborn and home we came. At least it gave me a chance to bake more custard and make more Jell-O for him to take back into town. If I weren't such a dodo I'd *know* how to drive, damn it.

Bee, after reading last week's *Time* and discussing the matter with Elizabeth, we have decided that she would *love* to have a set of the nursery-rhyme mobiles to dangle from the ceiling in her room. If they're available (as a set, the article said) anywhere, you'll be able to find them in Los Angeles!

I shall be frightfully glad when this month is over—it's too darned hot nearly every day. Elizabeth has broken out with prickly heat lately; last week she had a touch of fever and diarrhea, but we stopped it quickly. We've started taking showers before lunch; she gets a kick out of it although she doesn't like to get her head wet. I still give her a warm bath before supper, which she loves. I have a new girl, Lucille, who works for me once or twice a week; this morning she asked, "Madam, can you understand what Elizabeth says?" and laughed when I said not always. E. was most fascinated by the brass polishing and was talking a streak.

Sleepy, sleepy—guess it's bedtime. Cookbook arrived, Mother, as I thought it might!

Love to you all,
Marian

October 19, 1953

From Time *magazine:*

> *Kicking Out the Communists:... Last week, after six months of mounting frustration over the colony's Red-created unrest and subversive intrigues, Britain suspended the constitution and sent in troops to guarantee public safety. Said Colonial Secretary Oliver Lyttelton: "Her Majesty's government is not willing to allow a Communist state to be organized within the British Commonwealth."*
>
> *... Governor Savage quickly realized that he could never work successfully with the Reds. As soon as he let them repeal a ban on importing subversive literature, they brought in stocks of Communist propaganda. Then the new ministers fomented another big sugar strike that shut down the colony's main industry.*
>
> *... The U.S. State Department ... issued a prompt statement declaring itself "gratified" at the "firm action" against a Communist bid for power within the U.S.'s vital strategic zone.*

October 19, 1953

From Life *magazine:*

> *Face-Off in Guiana: The British act to end a pro-Communist regime. ... Instead of forming a government for the people it pretended to serve, the party set out through strikes and sabotage to destroy the new constitution and bring forth a totalitarian state. Anticipating a coup and acting with a bold dispatch reminiscent of bygone days of the empire, the British government decided to revoke the constitution. ...*

Sunday, October 25, 1953

Dear All—

A quiet Sunday afternoon—right at the moment, we'd never know there were over 300 soldiers within a block of us, but at times we hear them parading, and we can hear their bagpipes off and on, too. They (the Scottish Argyll and Sutherland Highlanders) arrived on Wednesday by boat right down at the Atkinson dock and marched up the hill (a mile, roughly) with bagpipes and drums. Here to stay "indefinitely," they brought trucks, Bren carriers (look like small tanks), and numerous American-made jeeps. Crates and crates and cartons and bags of supplies are around the buildings they occupy, as well as rolls and more rolls of barbed wire. The men marched up the hill at 10 Wednesday morning, and supplies were brought up immediately. But there were so many things that they kept on and on—nearly all night long the jeeps and tanks and trucks rumbled up the hill, about half a block from our door. It's disconcerting to hear so many people walking about after dark: we were used to quiet streets after 8 or 9, and now of course there is activity for an hour or so beyond that.

Thursday E. and I went into town with Frank Defreitas. He took us to Agnes's and then we went downtown, where I did a bit of shopping that had accumulated. Bought a Revlon lipstick and paid $3 for it, which seems shockingly high until you figure out exchange rates and duty and all that sort of thing.

We had lunch with the Pedersons, and then Howard took E. and me to the Ramsarans'. The previous Sunday they had said that we could stay with them any night, so we had arranged that E. and I would stay there Thursday night. Susan was all excited, and she and Elizabeth really did have fun playing together. Friday morning H. took us back to see Agnes for a while, and Susan cried and cried when we left. We had a most enjoyable time—the Pedersons, I'm afraid, are pretty dull going, but John and Margaret are good company and we all enjoy ourselves when we're together. I am sure that Agnes is a grand teacher for little kiddies, but she doesn't seem to have any interests except school teaching and crocheting. She doesn't read at all, but says Pete reads "a lot," which has turned out to be *Time*, *Reader's Digest*, *The Saturday Evening Post*, and the *American Education Journal*. Well, it still is nice to have Americans here.

Mother, the package with the dresses for Elizabeth arrived last week. Both dresses are too large, which pleases me since she has plenty in the present size. I love the navy blue one especially. Elizabeth is enjoying the sand pail and shovel tremendously and likes to bang them together. Yes, the cute yellow mittens did come with the shorts and dish drainer. I'm surprised that I didn't comment on them—such glamorous things for washing the vegetables!

Howard's tooth has finally calmed down; I suppose in another week or so he'll have the next one out. The remaining three are still bothering him, so he just can't put them off any longer than necessary. We nearly croaked when Dr. Wong, this character with a very high reputation locally, told H. that he usually gives a covering shot of penicillin when he removes a tooth surgically, but Howard "looked so healthy" that he "didn't think it was necessary." Nice to know, isn't it. We assume that next time he won't take that chance again.

Elizabeth has developed a habit that we hope is just a temporary phase of clouding up, pouting, and saying "hoo-hoo" in a soulful little sob whenever we say "no-no" about anything. Whenever she doesn't get her way, the little lower lip trembles and this funny little "hoo-hoo" business starts. It sounds so funny to us that we just laugh, and it never lasts long. She has several upper teeth on the way in, and they may be making her a bit cross. She also has prickly heat all over, still. Will be glad when it's a bit cooler and that goes away.

H. is going to ask Mr. S-D again to please write the U.S. Ed. Com. in London; we just have to know before long whether or not we'll be offered this contract. Surely they won't have to wait any longer to make up their minds, now that Parliament has agreed that the PPP is a bad lot.[62]

We're going out now to take some pictures of Elizabeth. We hope to get a good one that we will use to send out with Christmas cards.

Much love to you all,

Marian

Sunday, November 1, 1953

Dear All—

A pleasant, cool Sunday—and when I say cool, I mean the temperature is 83 degrees, damn it. But it really does feel cool(er), and we assume the showers of the past few days mean that our rainy season is about to begin. It still is hard to believe that Christmas is on the way, but this morning I made a trial batch of fruitcake, and if it seems to be good I may make more. We couldn't get candied pineapple or white raisins, and we couldn't afford brandy, so I juggled the other fruits a bit and used rum. Don't know how it will taste, but it is fun to try—it's got two more hours to go in the oven and I'm so curious that I can scarcely wait!

Yesterday we received the following letter from London—the U.S. Ed. Commission:

Dear Mr. Irwin,

Needling, pushing and prying on your behalf. Will be in touch with you at the earliest possible moment.

I think it a "damn shame" that you have heard no further since July.

Sincerely yours,

Richard P. Taylor

Exec. Sec.

As a matter of fact, we think it a damn nuisance that they haven't seen fit to answer Howard's letter or S-D's. This is the most human communication we've had from London thus far. Howard wrote to Dr. Gibbs of the College of Puget Sound education department and to Dr. Rubendall (the headmaster of Mount Hermon [the prep school Howard attended]), asking their professional opinions on the possibility of our being labeled "Red" or victimized in any way if we do choose to stay here another two years. The British government is certainly back in power, and we hear that new elections won't take place for another two years. We see no reason why we should be bothered by this when we get home, but it's hard to tell how the American public and the educators feel. Mr. S-D had a letter from the Colonial Secretariat here saying that from now on they intend to run the Fulbright positions on a one-year basis, and would he be interested in one of several different instructors. He took this to mean that they may not want us here for *two* more years, but of course we really don't know.

We read in today's paper that Marian Anderson is going to give a concert here on the 27th. The ads say, "First time world-famous artist to appear in B.G. at height of career," etc. etc. It will be given in the Q.C. hall, and I hope we can get there.

Getting back to the fruitcake for a minute, I remember someone here saying that it is apt to mold if kept long; so with that as an additional hazard, I'm planning to store it in a tin can with anti-ant tape around the can, and the can in the linen closet where our ever-burning light globe may keep the air a bit dryer. If it does start to mold I shall be furious, but at least I will have tried!

Howard is most interested in my new attitude toward the little red ants that bite and get into sweets and fats when given the opportunity. Sometimes after I wash my skillets, I evidently don't have them completely grease-free, and the little devils swarm all over them. A year ago I threw fits; now I just let them stay and eventually they leave, or if I need to use the skillet, I just put it on the burner. Uncomfortable for the ants, and the hotter it gets, the quicker they swarm up the handle, where I can neatly wipe them off with the dishcloth.

Howard's extraction is all nicely back to normal, but Dr. Wong wants to wait until a week from Monday to take out the next tooth. Poor H. is still being bothered by the remaining three, so the *only* thing to do is get rid of them as soon as possible.

Here at the airbase I spend much less time on the kind of futile cleaning that was required in town; we have less dust, but the sand is something of a mess. Elizabeth usually comes upstairs with two little shoes full, and I seldom remember to empty them before we get upstairs.

Bee, please tell Donna that the *Pat the Bunny* book is *the* thing in Elizabeth's life at the present. I have read it through with her several times on and off since it arrived, but Friday I nearly fell off my chair when I casually asked E. if she'd like to read *Pat the Bunny* and she walked right over to the bookcase where it is! She did it again yesterday, too, so it wasn't an accident. Picture books on the whole still mean nothing to Elizabeth, but it shouldn't be long before she enjoys them.

The little monkey understands so much of what we say. In the evenings I ask her if she wants a bath, and she runs right to the bathroom (or squeals and runs away if she's in a playful mood). I always think of her as being the best child possible, but yesterday H. catalogued some of the impish little things she does, and it makes me wonder! She loves to dangle her foot in the toilet while she sits on the john, and she pulls yards and yards of toilet paper if it is left hanging within her reach. She takes off her slippers and sometimes they go into the john if I forgot to receive them as she takes them off. Once in the tub, she loves to throw things out—duck, seal, fish, washcloth, sponge, giraffe, pony. That's good clean fun! She carries market baskets all over the house, also carton boxes; likes to remove my bedroom slippers and fusses when I won't let her play with them; and at present is in a phase of throwing her spoon on the floor and tipping over her milk. "Mamamama" comes easily; she still doesn't say "daddy" but she does talk a blue streak of words, phrases, sentences, and paragraphs, the meaning of which is clear as can be, with wonderful inflexion and emotion. The only thing she lacks is the knowledge of *our* words!

To pick up a spoon, sand spade, or toothbrush she uses both hands, and she has a wonderful grip. It's just plain hard to take something away from her. She tucks toys under one arm often to carry them around. She can carry the sand pail or a basket on her left arm; she loves to carry her shoes around, one hand stuck into each shoe. We take a walk often in the afternoon, sometimes just up and down in front of the house, and she picks up leaves and pebbles and examines them, sometimes handing them on to me. Sticks, grass, ants, and the occasional flower are all intriguing. She stares at the soldiers we pass and wants to pat any dog that comes to pay respects. When another child comes to play she is just delighted; she is very rarely unhappy about anything. Upper teeth are a slight bother now and the prickly heat has been bad lately, but even these things don't upset her much.

Five ex-PPP men are being "indefinitely detained" by the government up here at the airbase;[63] we have a most impressive barbed wire enclosed area where they are kept; not a mouse could get in or out, I'm sure. Everything seems very calm. The inquiry commission will commence the first of the year; after that there will be a new constitutional commission, followed eventually by a new election. The troops are to stay for two years, we are told, and officers' families may be brought out.

Love to each of you,
Marian

November 2, 1953

From Time *magazine:*

Sledge Hammer in Guiana: Clement Attlee, whose government had prepared the way for self-government in Guiana, had urgent questions to ask [Jagan and Burnham on their arrival in London]. He had been disturbed by Lyttelton's handling of other colonial revolts (in Kenya and Nyasa-land), and wanted to make sure that the two Guianans got their day in court. For close to three hours, Attlee ... and ten others of Labor's top command grilled the pair... Time and again, they put the direct question, "Are you Communists?," got only evasive replies. To a man, the Labor leaders were revolted by Burnham's doubletalk. "It's a tragedy," said one, "that such an opportunity should have been thrown away by such terrible men..." "Burnham is 20 times more astute than Jagan," said another. "His answers were so slick that sometimes you were almost caught by them..."

... Next day, in the House of Commons, the Laborites disowned Jagan and all his works, stoutly endorsed Lyttelton's pronouncement....

Tuesday a.m., November 3, 1953

Dear Mother—

How wicked I am today. Yesterday I had to clean up after the weekend, and I got both the washing and the ironing done, too. So today I am luxuriating in a clean-enough house and I'm ignoring the few things that were washed out this morning and that I could iron if I were really ambitious.

I think Elizabeth and I will take long naps this afternoon because she had a bad night last night. She woke up about 11 wheezing and coughing; in an upright position she breathed quite clearly, but as soon as I would put her back to bed she'd begin snoring again. About half past 12 I went to sleep, so I guess she did, too. This morning she is still a bit hoarse, sneezing, and such, so I guess we're in for a cold. The local ladies attribute it to the "change in the weather"—so far it just amounts to a bit more dampness and a little less heat; maybe it is enough to start colds going around.

Elizabeth and I are going full tilt now at this "reading" business. She needs plenty of supervision, but she seems to enjoy looking at the pictures and touching them. Just now we were looking at *Noodle*, and after I said "bow-wow" a few times while pointing to the pictures, she said "wow-wow," which is still her version of that word. I just cleared out some magazines from the space under our phonograph and transferred her books there from the bookcase.

Do you remember our mentioning Elizabeth's scowl, quivering lower lip, and the "hoo-hoo" that sounded so pathetic? Now, I find if I make a face and say "hoo-hoo," she giggles and thinks it a grand joke. Of course, Elizabeth has me so thoroughly bewitched that the slightest twinkle in her eye just captivates me. Sunday I consulted the *Better Homes and Gardens* baby book about the 18-to-24-month stage and was most interested to read that playing with and throwing food around is very common—once the child learns to get the food into his mouth he's out to learn something new, which is to throw it around. Following the book's advice, we now consider her through her meal when she starts that monkey business.

Later—Three p.m., as a matter of fact, and we've both had a little snooze. E. woke up once, all stopped up, but went back to sleep after I gave her two aspirin. Don't know how much they help a cold, but she seemed uncomfortable and I thought I might as well try them. I had a shower but I still feel sleepy.

Sure enough, I have a letter from each of you today. Mother, thank you for the stickers. Unfortunately, by the time I undid the envelope our lovely climate here had caused them to stick together—so I guess I shall steam them apart. On the top of your letter you have written something—"I'll order the—" bank? bark? Haven't the vaguest notion what it is, and for that matter I can't remember asking you to order anything for me! Oh dear. I'm very glad you're sending rubbers for Elizabeth—she adores splashing in puddles, but in just her little sandals it doesn't work too well. Many little children wear knee-high rubber boots called Wellingtons, but I think they must be awfully hot.

So hard to believe this is the third of November. Everything here is so timeless—it might as well be February or July, and I feel just plain cheated whenever I think about fall weather—especially the crisp Walla Walla type. (E. is standing here, holding *Pat the Bunny* and simply flirting with me, trying to get me to play with her. I explained that I was writing to you all but she wasn't impressed. . . . Just finished reading *P the B*.)

Everything seems very calm here. One of the five men being detained across the street is a vegetarian, and the army is giving him a special diet. I can just barely see the barbed wire of their enclosure through the trees. I'm really not worried; the first night they were here one soldier tried to break into a house in the other residential area, and now he is being court-martialed. We hear the army is going to be hard on him as an object lesson to the others.

Too warm to sit inside here any longer; guess I will take a chair and sit on our little front porch. We certainly do enjoy having the gate across the stairs; Elizabeth runs in and out all the time and likes to see the cars and people go by. By the way, after my nap this afternoon I brought E. in on our bed for a little while, and you should have seen her scrambling up and down the bed! Up, then down, in rapid succession. Too bad we don't have movie equipment.

Much love to each of you,
Marian

Monday, November 8, 1953

Dear All—

Health bulletin: Elizabeth's cold is about gone but for a cough and a slightly runny nose. She feels fine and is up to all her deviltry; I wish someone would write a book on child care in the tropics, because it's hard to know whether keeping a child warm and thus encouraging prickly heat is more important than letting her wear a sundress and *dis*couraging p.h. What a bother.

Howard will have another wisdom tooth out tomorrow. Dr. Wong is going to give him a penicillin shot before the extraction and two more on days following. Good thing, huh.

Marian, in a fit of something, had Howard cut off long hair to the point where all it can do is hang damply about the collar. I guess I'll have him bring a Toni home next weekend and do that. I shall probably regret having cut it, but there comes a moment when a haircut is the *only* thing that makes life bearable.

Well, we had a hint of bad news this weekend from Major Nicole, head of Civil Aviation and in charge of Atkinson Field now. He said that due to the shortage of housing for civil aviation and B.G. Airways people, we might have to move out. What a repulsive thought—we just hope we can stay here through Christmas. Two other families have been given the same sort of notice, so it appears to be a gentle warning. We keep telling ourselves that there is no point in counting our boobies before they're hatched, as Thurber says, but nevertheless it is a revolting thought.

Still no word from London. Talk about feeling "up in the air"—we will all have insecurity complexes in a few more weeks!

We've decided not to go into town for Marian Anderson's concert. Margaret invited us all to stay overnight with them; but Elizabeth does get a bit off her routine when she's away from home, and I wouldn't want to take her if she isn't completely over her coughing, etc.

Politically, everything seems pretty calm at present. Last Friday the governor made a speech about the structure of the interim government,[64] which will be in effect from the middle of December for about a year. Very dull going. The government is entirely appointive, and the governor will very definitely be in charge of it—much to the disappointment of many Guianese, who feel discouraged about the whole mess.

Am I too late to suggest a Christmas gift for Elizabeth? Howard tried here to find some children's records but, not surprisingly, there aren't any. We think she would love one—I don't know if they're all rhythmical or all story-type, but she gets a kick out of waving her arms to Rossini and would undoubtedly enjoy Babar or whoever is supposedly the best. She has *Pat the Bunny* down cold now and races through it patting the bunny and playing peek-a-boo and looking into the mirror at a wicked pace, eager to turn each page. She sits and does it all by herself, giggling away. She still won't sit still long enough for a story or poem to be read to her, but it won't be long now.

I'm sleepy!

Love,

Marian

November 15, 1953

Dear All—

Oh boy, 9:30 on a Sunday night and I should be in bed! We have music on the phonograph and Howard is working on his stamp albums, and at this point, 6 a.m. tomorrow seems a long way off.

Elizabeth's cold is all gone, but we unfortunately have a little problem that seems to have resulted from it—maybe it's just another phase. At the very slightest "no-no" yesterday and today, she's dissolved into loud, indignant wails. Yesterday she didn't eat much lunch at all because she was all worked up; today, after being told no when she wanted to touch the iron cord while I was ironing, she went into her loud sobs, watching carefully (according to H.) to see if I was looking at her. I paid no attention, and she stopped, ran out of the room, and came back with a book. Yes, Mother, the throwing-food-on-floor phase is long behind us, and she's been eating well for weeks. I think I did spoil her while she had that cold—after all, you, or I at least, can't let a child cry when she gets all choked up with mucous and coughs. Bless her heart, she does learn quickly. Today she has almost mastered the word "hello," starting with eye-o, eye-lo, and then to el-o, which certainly sounds cute.

Howard and I gave me a Toni yesterday, and for some reason nothing much happened. I think perhaps we put too much hair on each curler—I can think of nothing else we could have done, and the test curls seemed to indicate a long enough period. Disgusting after messing around with all that stuff and spotting our bathroom linoleum in the process. H. will purchase a refill and I guess we'll try again.

Howard's second extraction was a thing of joy, almost—a ten-minute business, and he ate a lamb chop for dinner afterward. He said it felt no worse than it had been feeling before it was taken out!

Nona English had a bad fall last week during a tennis game; the army medical corpsmen rushed to the fore and brought her home via jeep on a stretcher. They left rolls and rolls of bandages and cotton with her, and later assured one of the women that any time any of the children have a tumble (or anyone else), they'd be only too happy to be of service. There is a doctor stationed with them, so we're really prepared for anything along that line.

Everything is calm up here, and Howard says it is in town, too. The police raid PPP headquarters nearly every day, confiscating copies of their journal. Janet Jagan is still free, as are other PPP leaders—we wonder just why. The police can't locate the press that prints their pamphlets and papers—they've gone underground. The only active trouble this week was at two sugar plantations where the workers are still off. At one, an attempt was made to burn the manager's house: the butler found a pile of twigs and wood that had been lighted, but apparently the arsonists were in too big a hurry to leave and didn't stay to be sure the fire was really started. Military forces there have been enlarged as a result. On another plantation, grinding and distilling machinery in the factory have been destroyed, and many fires in the cane fields have been reported.

After our warning last week about moving out, Howard talked around to people in town and discovered that the housing situation is the worst it has been in years. The army has taken over all available housing;[65] such local wheels as the Attorney General and the Chief Justice are having to move out of their government-owned houses, and the Carib, the only nightclub, has been taken over as a permanent headquarters. We are told there is *nothing* available for such as we.

John says that if the Larthes come back, as they seem to be planning to do, and they [Ramsarans] can get no decent quarters, he will send Margaret and Mrs. McLaren and the children back to England, staying here alone to finish his contract, which ends a year from next April. If we really do have to move out of this house and can't find a decent place in town, we might have to do something similar, although we will do our best to resist leaving this place. And when we say "decent," we mean a house in a fairly good neighborhood, a respectable house. We can't see being uncomfortable in a little shack—it's not worth it. Well, kiddies, hold the thought that we can stay in this house—I'd hate to leave it for the nicest place in Georgetown.

I can't resist adding this. Howard pays the Pedersons so much a month for staying with them; mostly it's just to cover the food. Pete insists on subtracting the amount of room and board for the time they spent with us when they first arrived, plus the days Agnes was here a few weeks ago, from H.'s bill with them. Poor H. tried to explain that that was entirely different, that they were our guests, etc., but P. remained adamant! My word, how customs differ. Did I tell you that when Agnes came out with H. during the crisis scare, she brought her own sheets and towels and a new box of Tide, which she left with me because she'd used some of *my* Tide during their previous stay? Evidently hospitality means something else to them. Their arrival has pointed out many things to us: we feel fortunate that we came here armed with broad interests, good education, and the experience of living in various parts of our own country; all of these of course widened our outlook generously enough so that we can enjoy and appreciate the opportunity we have here. Still, ignoring differences in interests, outlook, and age, it is very satisfying to have fellow Americans in the colony.

Well, time for bed. That old alarm clock always shocks me in the morning; E. and I don't arise till close to 7 now on the days when H. isn't home!

Love to you all,

Marian

Tuesday evening, 8:30, November 17, 1953

Dear Mother—

Tuesdays we always get mail from home—what a blessing that we get letters regularly. I've got some mending to do—pants need new elastic all the time. I suppose it's a matter of perspiration around the middle.

You asked about our card games—actually there has only been one since I had everyone here in September. The fair kept everyone busy. Then the "crisis" dampened enthusiasm somewhat. Jean Crooks invited us a few weeks ago, but it was one of the first evenings of E.'s bad cold and she was sleeping badly—naturally, I didn't want to leave her. I think I can leave E. with Lucille to play cards in the neighborhood. E. seems quite fascinated with her and follows her around when she's here. I would still do the bathing and feeding.

About duty—we'll certainly let you know the amount if you want us to. Sometimes (rather rarely, actually) the customs men compute duty accurately, and then it does add up. Usually they don't bother to convert U.S. dollars to B.G. dollars: they charge duty on a $5 package rather than on the $9 or whatever it would be in local money. Or they chop part of it off.

We had a very pleasant day, Elizabeth and I. At lunch she began this funny little whimpering—so pathetic. I laughed, then she laughed, and we giggled happily at each other all during lunch.

This afternoon we had a walk around the block—quite a big block at that. We went down our street to the main road, which comes up the hill from the police station and dock and goes past us to the hospital. While we walked along that street, we were passed by about twelve of the B.G. volunteers, big Negroes who are now on duty guarding the detainees. As they marched by, E. just stood and stared. Then, by the next corner, one of the volunteers exchanged a "good afternoon" with me. I realized he was the electrician who connected our stove when we moved out here. He inquired if it was working well!

We turned that corner and started up the street that parallels our own. E. picked up a little flower from the street; I discouraged her from picking up a discarded cigarette package. On past the detainees' compound—they weren't outside, which was just as well, since I feel uncomfortable seeing anyone behind barbed wire even if they do belong there. At the next corner, we encountered about a dozen chickens and one turkey. Very noisy; therefore, very interesting.

Around the third corner, where four Scottish majors are quartered. Two men—orderlies, I guess—were sitting outside polishing boots. They came out to the street and gave E. a chocolate bar. I could scarcely understand them, but we were all happy.

Before we came in we had a swing out in the back and then checked on the puppies behind the Crookses' house. Home, bath, supper, bed. I would have gone crazy months ago in this country without Elizabeth.

To my mending now.

Much love—

Marian

Sunday night

Howdy, dears!

This is sort of a P.S., I guess.

Mother, will you please send us ten 10-cent airmail stamps? H. is going to be writing to some schools, etc. in the States before long, and if we enclose return envelopes we may get faster service. We still haven't heard from London. On the first of December H. will write London and tell them that if we haven't heard by January 1 we'll consider the matter closed and plan on returning home. We hope to hear before then, of course. Will you wrap the stamps in waxed paper so that none of the glued surfaces touch other stamps?

Elizabeth has now discovered the joy of pulling at my apron strings until the apron falls off. My only defense is a good knot.

There are a lot of mangy dogs around here—one of the few nice ones is a largish pooch, white with black spots, named Spot and belonging to the Crookses. He seems hungry for affection and now comes over whenever he sees E. and me outside. I pat him and say pleasant things while E. pats his back and tries to catch his tail. He is very good-natured and used to children—a bit smelly, but we overlook that. Elizabeth is delighted to see him.

Howard had a most interesting discussion yesterday with Mr. D'Agrella, chief engineer of the base. We've never seen them out anywhere—it seems they have interests similar to ours (reading, music), which they prefer to the drinking and cards—the limit of entertainment to nearly everyone on the base. We hope to get to know them better. The English families leave [the colony] December 8, and we'll miss them—especially their children.

Howard has a holiday on Wednesday—honoring the Queen's visit to the West Indies. And after this week, there are only three more until Christmas vacation! Whee—

Today was lovely, but all last week it rained hard much of the time. Really soggy.

Love,

Marian

November 28, 1953

Dear All:

Howard received a letter from Mr. Rubendall of Mount Hermon, answering some of H.'s questions. He said he thought the prestige attached to the Fulbright appointment would make a longer stay worthwhile, and that the Communist angle wasn't too alarming since the British are fully in control again. We're still waiting to get Dr. Gibbs's answer.

Elizabeth now enjoys going through a cute Little Golden Book called *I Can Fly* with me. On each page there is an illustration for such lines as "A bird can fly. So can I," "A cow can moo. I can, too," "Swish, I'm a fish," and "I'm merrier than a terrier." Her favorites are "Who's busy as a bee? Me, me, me!"—naturally the "busy" is said "bzzzzzzy" and she giggles delightedly. She repeats the "mooo" and manages a nice "ow" sound for "Howl, howl, howl, I'm an old hoot owl." Another book shows pictures of all sorts of common household objects with a little story tying them together; Elizabeth knows the bathtub and the shoes that are pictured. She says "ba," which means bath, and something like "soos" for shoes. As least we know that she means, and it is great sport for all of us. In the last few days she has begun "smelling the pretty flowers" like Paul does in *Pat the Bunny*; and this noon she sat on the floor turning pages of *Peter Rabbit* and chattering madly about it—or something—having a lovely time.

She loves to play with the pan lids, and when Howard leaves his dresser drawer open we are apt to find socks, handkerchiefs, tie clip, etc. all lined up neatly on the edge of the bed. How any little living thing can keep so busy is amazing—I guess she really needs her naps and good nights' sleep.

My poor old hair. I have finally developed a theory about me, Tonis, and the tropics. We tried another Toni last Wednesday when Howard was home, and it came out very well. The problem, ladies, is this: permanented hair needs to be dampened before it's put up in pin curls, and if I dampen my hair before putting it up, it doesn't get dry! I've tried putting it up just barely damp, and it doesn't work. Between 7 and 9 a.m. yesterday, my hair looked quite good; by 9, however, I was cleaning and therefore perspiring in earnest, and there went any curl, wave, or what have you. I'm just an old wet-head. So I shall wait patiently while my hair grows long enough to braid again. At present it is pulled back, held by a rubber band, and coolly off my neck. It's been raining and is cool—this morning at 8 it was 78°.

My, but it's hard to believe that last Thursday was Thanksgiving. Howard and I were going to celebrate it last night when he was home. I had intended to have chicken for dinner and make a pumpkin pie, but I decided that chicken was too expensive and instead of a pie, I made a truly gorgeous chocolate banana cake and lemon sherbet. The cake is awfully good—you wouldn't know about the bananas, but it has a lovely texture. And ground beef for dinner. We *will* have chicken for Christmas.

I have thought and thought about something to give the Ramsaran family and finally decided to get a few Christmas tree balls and decorate them with sequins. I'd think it awfully impractical if we hadn't succeeded in bringing ours with no breakage problem. The Larthes are definitely coming back, which means the Ramsarans will have to move come the first of the year. If they can't find a nice place in Georgetown, the ladies of the family will go to John's parents' home in Trinidad until his tour is up—a year from April.

I think I shall go flop on the bed for a while before E. wakes up.

Much love to each of you dear people,

Marian

424

[Christmas card, dated November 10]

Dearest Parents,

This is #1 card—I'm trying to generate a bit of spirit! We've bought a few toys for Elizabeth and I've made a few more; plus fruitcake; plus sequins and ornaments—but it still doesn't seem possible that we're so close to Christmas. Thank heavens we aren't as homesick as we were last year! Found our old copy of *The Night Before Christmas* in a trunk—it is so battered. I should get a new copy for E.—but I'm just sentimental about it. She will love Christmas this year, I know. Won't it be fun when we're all together for a Christmas again!

Merry Christmas and much love from all—

Marian

December 1, 1953

Hello, Mother dear—

I finished reading your nice long letter an hour ago, and since then I've been having my own "chat" with you while doing the dishes and a little ironing. There is one more dress to do—I've been putting it off since Sunday—but I'll start this, anyway. Elizabeth just had her orange juice and is now sitting on the floor looking at a book.

I'm glad to have your opinions on "spoiling" and colds or sickness—of course, it is only natural, isn't it, that a child should be a little spoiled. By now Elizabeth is long over her spell, and both cough and crying are behind us. Last Sunday Howard and I were trying to assess the success of our handling of E. in terms of the way the other children around here behave, and we feel we're doing pretty well. (I'd be more emphatic and say *damned* well, but then tomorrow she'd undoubtedly start throwing things or having tantrums!) For one thing, she knows well what is hers to play with and what isn't—sometimes she takes something knowing she shouldn't, but that is just teasing or testing to see what we'll do. Most of the time she plays strictly with her own toys and books and three lids in the kitchen; when you consider that we have magazines, records, books, ashtrays, and all the kitchen pots and bowls within easy reach, I think she does very well.

We're on a slightly different routine in the afternoons now: instead of always going for a walk, we sometimes stay under the house. Not in the playpen, however. She loves to dig in the sand and carry her little pail around, so often she digs while I sit on the steps. She roams around some, coming back to me or turning to see if I'm still around. I have just taken up the hem of the navy-and-white dress you sent, and taken two tucks under the arms. This sand business is fine, but it is foolish to put her in a light-colored dress that has to be ironed, because she does get a bit grimy. Good old seersucker. She is such a happy little girl—naturally she has her moments of anger and grief, but they certainly don't last long.

Yesterday was a Great Day. For the first time, Elizabeth tried and succeeded in putting food on her spoon and then getting it into her mouth. At lunch she started with stewed tomatoes, of all things, but was tickled pink with each little drop that she put in her mouth. Last evening she tackled the peas with great vigor and was terribly proud. My goodness, it really is exciting!

Your Thanksgiving dinner sounds wonderful. I can practically taste it!

Later—Dress ironed, lunch eaten, naps taken. Mama is bathed and more or less awake again; Elizabeth is playing in her room with door closed. She takes everything out of her toy box, bangs blocks in an enamel cup, sometimes makes a great racket, and generally has a grand time. She's usually there until 3, when she has a drink of milk.

The magazines haven't come yet, but today there was a package notice in the mail, and there was one last week that Howard didn't have time to pick up, so maybe they are here. We both enjoyed the one that you sent earlier.

Three cheers for the $500. Am I dreaming, or didn't you write a few weeks ago that it had come—or was it just that this payment would be coming? I can't imagine that it's *another* $500! Maybe it was wishful thinking. Yes, do pay off our debts to H.'s mother and to you all, too. There are many things we ask you to send that we really wouldn't if we didn't think we could pay for them eventually. Howard and I have mulled over the possibility of our landing a job in Florida or New England and then facing the problem of having all our stuff collected and sent from Seattle and Tacoma. Actually there isn't much big stuff, but I suppose it would cost quite a bit to send it so far—ugh. Well, every little bit counts.

This up-in-the-air feeling is a bother, and we'll both relax when we hear something. We feel a bit easier about the housing; Mr. D'Agrella told H. that he didn't think we needed to worry. Housing in town is rather awful at best, but the army is working day and night to finish a barracks so that they can move their men into it, freeing the clubs and such that they took over earlier. We really can't expect the college to do much about housing for us. H.'s salary is padded with the additional grant from London just so that we can find housing comparable to what we're used to (ha). For instance, John makes less than H.'s school salary of $420 per month, but he is granted government housing at 10 percent of his salary. We're paying 10 percent here, but actually the extra money is given us so that we don't have to depend on government housing. It's the government housing that is driving the Ramsarans crazy, for it makes them dependent on moving into houses on a short-term basis while the occupants are away on leave.

H. is having another tooth out today—hope it is as easy as the last one.

Elizabeth is cajoling me now to go downstairs; the wind is blowing and we may have a shower soon. She has piled a neat stack of books at my feet and is going through one saying "moo, moo, moo." She is *really* our pride and joy!

Downstairs we go—

Much love to you and Daddy,

Marian

We received the New Yorker *notice a few days ago—bless your hearts! I read it from cover to cover, and H. and I love to go through the ads. Thank you.*

December 7, 1953

Dear All—

It's damp, cool, and quiet tonight. While I bathed Elizabeth this evening it was raining so hard that we could scarcely hear each other. Now it is cooler, and the only drawback is the number of tiny little winged creatures that always appear in the evening after it has rained. A nuisance when you're trying to eat.

The Englishes, Warwicks, and Bogotas left last night. They told us that some B.G. Airways people are just panting to get into their vacated houses, so we won't be neighborless for long, I guess. The Englishes left with us a cute little potty chair outgrown by their Elizabeth, which H. is going to do over a bit so that our E. can use it just as a plain chair in her room. All it needs is a solid seat and a coat of paint. The Warwicks gave us a woven fiber rug about eight feet by ten feet for the playpen; they couldn't sell it because Harry had torn holes in it practicing his golf swing in the living room. It gives E. a nice place to sit downstairs. They also brought over odds and ends of jam, butter, milk, etc. at the last minute—there was quite a stream of people in and out last night!

On Friday H. brought out three packages from Mother—two large and one small—and one from Donna. He cleverly removed all traces, tags, and whatnot and would scarcely let me *touch* them. Happily, Howard has a "friend" at the customs counter now, a man whom he chatted with at Dr. Wong's not long ago. I guess they were discussing extractions; anyway, H. walked into the post office last week and was greeted by Lewis as an old friend. He took the parcel slips and hunted up the packages himself, saving loads of time. Took H. about fifteen minutes instead of the hour it generally takes at this time of year.

In the past week Elizabeth has made great strides in this self-feeding business. She feeds herself from a third to a half of her meal, simply crowing and gurgling with pride. She displays quite a temper when she tries two or three times to get something on the spoon and can't. Flings the spoon on the tray and shoves it away, endangering milk, dish, and food. Gets right over it as soon as I put the spoon back in the dish and get a little food on it. We're plugging away at the tooth brushing now—I was ready to put up a chart for myself and give myself a gold star for remembering E.'s teeth; finally, I have it embedded in my getting-her-up and putting-her-to-bed routines. I don't think it makes a bit of sense to Elizabeth. What *I* want to know from these people who say yes, by all means, start brushing baby's teeth when the first one appears, is this: *How* do you get the little imp's mouth open; what do you do about sore gums when teeth are about to appear; and how do you get the very idea of brushing across? I think I agree with those experts who say to wait until the child is two or so and wants to imitate.

I brought my fruitcake out of the refrigerator today to re-dampen the cloth in rum. Couldn't resist tasting it and my, is it good! Isn't it amazing what a few weeks of aging will do—makes all the difference in the world. Mother, I'll bet you chop the nuts, don't you. My copy of your recipe didn't say to chop so I didn't, but I should think the slicing would be easier if I had. With time and the rum-soaked cloth, however, the nuts are becoming soft enough to cut easily, but I was worried for a while.

Now to write a note to Howard and then to bed. I always forget to mention to him something that I need desperately, and the mail is rather uncertain; if I send a letter in to him Tuesday morning, he gets it on Thursday! Twenty-six miles away.

Much love to you all,
Marian

Thursday, 8 p.m., December 17, 1953

Dearest Mother—

Goodness, but I do get frustrated; always, just after I read one of your letters, I do wish so hard that we could respond and converse a bit more quickly than we can through the mail! Ann and Betty Defreitas just brought a few letters over. ("Daddy says he's *awfully* sorry he was so late, but he was doing reports—" They're sweet little girls, both in pajamas tonight.) And I just finished doing my dishes—*had* to finish reading a mystery over another cup of coffee, so it's a bit late for dishes.

I just knew that as soon as I wrote about how good E. is the spell would be broken. This week I found her in the living room with a *Time* and a *New Yorker* both minus covers, and I paddled her bottom. I've done this before and she hasn't peeped, but yesterday I was more emphatic and she sobbed bitterly, especially when I led her by the hand into the kitchen and closed the door behind us. Ordinarily when I'm working in the kitchen, she delights in closing the door, and ordinarily I open it quickly because it gets mighty warm with it shut. After about ten minutes I told her I'd open it if she'd behave herself, which of course she did. Today we haven't had any of that trouble, but about 5 this evening she fell into the bathtub (empty, thank goodness) and landed on that little head. Poor dear, it must have hurt! I read a few poems from *Silver Pennies* ("I met a little elf man once, Down where the lilies blow"—that is a short one and currently a favorite; she giggles at the end of it). In a few minutes she was over it, and we proceeded with bath, supper, and all.

Isn't it funny about you having so much rain in Tacoma and we have had practically none. Every fourteen years there is a drought here, we're told, and this is a fourteenth year. Driest December in seventy-some years, we read in the paper a few days ago. It's supposed to be just dripping at this time; it's all right with me if it stays like this!

This week I've been busy and have accomplished a great deal. Some chores such as scrubbing the shower curtain aren't too much fun, but nice to get them done. The little rugs I dyed came out well. Monday I made a little steamed pudding, and today I made a few Christmas cookies experimenting with Jean Crooks's cookie press. Will make more next week, I guess. Yesterday I finished E.'s dress, and it certainly looks sweet. It is the pale pink with tiny blue and red flowers—you bought the material, remember? I put the narrow blue rickrack around the neck, cuffs, and pocket flaps. And I spent last night listening to the static-y radio and creating a little doll for Janet. Nylon dishcloth body, pink nylon ribbon bonnet, and blue seersucker dress. Practical, and I think she came out quite well. The book Bee sent me on doll making has improved my technique tremendously. I am pleased with E.'s doll, too—the redhead with a blue dress.

I am wondering if I should cut bangs for Elizabeth. Her hair looks so blown and wispy, and I can't get a rubber band to stay on the little lock that should be kept in place. Howard has an innate distrust of bangs and says they look artificial, but I do love them on little girls—maybe I'll give it a whirl. If only I could get E. to sit still for five minutes when I want to cut her hair!

I fear I have neglected to allay your fears concerning a Christmas tree. I assure you, we would have a tree of some sort, even if I had to draw one on the wall with a green crayon! But we will have a live, pretty one that we spotted in the bush near the old U.S. Army rifle range. Last Sunday Howard partially dug it up; the worst comes this weekend when we try to get it home. It is big—about seven feet tall, I guess. 'Taint no fir, but it has a pretty shape and rather fine, broad evergreen leaves that are very graceful. Actually, it will be prettier than the wispy casuarina we had last year, even if that did look a bit more pine-like. Some people here have firs flown in from Trinidad, but H. is absolutely horrified by that idea—as a matter of fact, much of the White Christmas idea is a bit funny here, but everyone seems to overlook that. We shall put this tree in an old pot—half an oil drum—which we shall then disguise with paper or an old sheet. Since we have no playpen, H. will build some sort of little fence to protect the tree and Elizabeth from each other. She will love it, I know, and I guess we'll wait until Christmas Eve to put it up.

A note from Howard came with your letter, in which he says that John is going by boat to Trinidad tonight or tomorrow, to return after the first—to find accommodation for Margaret and the others. Too bad he won't be here for Christmas. Howard suggests having the ladies out for a few days instead of the one we'd planned on. It would be fun to have them out over Christmas—wonder if I could manage! John has also suggested that he and H. share a flat somewhere after his family leaves. I know H. would enjoy that. John is infinitely more interesting than the Pedersons.

H. also says that Mrs. S-D *insists* (capitals, underlined) that we stop by Monday afternoon when we're in town. Oh my. When she insists, you feel like a naughty ten-year-old. I think that is the chief reason she annoys me; she treats me like an adult, but she calls me "lass," which just *galls* me.

H. said he spent two hours at the post office sending off a batch of specimens to the National Herbarium and receiving four packages from his mother. It is a frightfully inefficient place. It's a good thing he is patient.

I've been sitting for a good ten minutes mulling over the idea of having the Ramsarans out— If I can get them to say yes, I'll have Lucille come Thursday morning to do the cleaning so I won't have that to worry about. It would be fun to have them here. I always like the idea of extra people around for Christmas, especially such good company. Have to scrounge around for beds.

Well, dear, I'd better hie off to the back bedroom, the workroom, or whatever we call it, and change the papers on H.'s drying specimens. And then to bed.

Love and kisses to you,
Marian

Boxing Day, December 26, 2:30 p.m., 1953

My Dears—

We had such a lovely Christmas that Howard and I were overwhelmed. Elizabeth, of course, had an ecstatic time while we opened gifts and was put to bed at naptime completely exhausted. But let's see, I think I shall backtrack and do this in chronological order more or less.

Howard's vacation started on Friday the 18th, and he came home with the beginnings of a cold. Luckily, it didn't develop into anything much, and Monday we all went into town. Elizabeth stayed at the Ramsarans' and played happily with Susan while H. and I did our shopping; the stores seemed hectic and wild after our peaceful life here at the Field, and I wonder just how big cities will strike me when we go home. Scare me to death, no doubt. Anyway, I managed to get nearly everything on my list, and Howard and I went back to the Ramsarans' for lunch. At that point they hadn't had any word from John but were expecting a letter the next day. We had a very good lunch somewhat marred by the fact that Elizabeth decided that she didn't like the strange crib, and howled and howled until H. rescued her. Little Janet was in the same room in her buggy, smiling happily and unperturbed by the strange loud roars. They already had plans for Christmas Day, so they're coming out next Monday for a night or two. We left there around 2:30 and bought a pair of shoes for Elizabeth—crepe-soled sandals—did a few more errands, and got home at 5.

Tired as we were, after dinner we went over to the chapel in the hospital to sing carols. A few days earlier, Frank had urged Howard to help in directing a group of the civilians who were entering a team to sing carols in competition with several army groups. Howard agreed; but unfortunately, Major Nicole was enjoying himself so much doing the leading that he just didn't relinquish control. (Major N. is the civilian head of civil aviation here. His favorite remark was "Never mind the words—it's the melody that counts." Also, "Let's adjourn and have a drink.") Anyway, the competition came off Christmas Eve, and the judges didn't show up until the last group was singing; apparently no one was taking it seriously.

We came home from the singing and decorated our tree; we were halfway through unwrapping the stack of overseas parcels when Frank and Zela came over. A little while later, Jean and Desmond Crooks and Jean and Trevor Darwent bellowed in; they were following a local custom of going from house to house for a drink and trying to pick up a few more people here and there. I'm afraid I resented it a bit, since frolicking doesn't seem the right way to spend Christmas Eve to me. Recognizing the rattle of one of the cans in H.'s box, Mother, I opened the chili chips and everyone enjoyed them. Lucky I had them to open!

Yesterday we got up around 7, our usual time, and after a quick look at the tree, I gave Elizabeth her breakfast and Howard and I had juice and coffee. We are just plain delighted with everything, big and little; there is nothing that isn't perfect. I wore the blue dress yesterday, and it is lovely! I had to let out one of the tucks to get more length (I know M. Dior says skirts are shorter, but my legs are still just as long), a simple job, and it is a lovely, flattering style. Elizabeth looks precious in her raincoat. We'll send you a picture as soon as we get some sunshine in which to take one.

Later—Sunday evening. Time does fly! The only item that doesn't fit is Elizabeth's rubbers. Her new pair of shoes are a size 7, and the rubbers just fit her feet without any shoes on. So Howard is mailing a little box with them tomorrow. I hope you can exchange them for a size larger.

I am madly in love with Elizabeth's toy dog, whom we've named Muffin. She gets the "Mu," no more. Isn't he precious! *I'd* just as soon sit on the floor and play with Muffin and the wonderful teddy bear that Donna sent her—such cuties. I have read through most of the stories in the book Daddy sent and think they are grand. They'll be fun to read to her. The pink dress is lovely, Mother; yes, it is too big now, but at her present rate of growing, it won't be for very long.

The books, Mother, have me all eager to crochet potholders and remake all my clothes and weave a rug (Bee sent the *Sunset Rug Book*). Next week I shall go into town and buy some yarn. The sewing book is just wonderful—it really does cover everything, doesn't it.

Howard says he'll write you himself. The ties and socks are handsome and certainly welcome. I didn't even look at either here this year, knowing from experience the stuff that is in the stores. I love the brown polka dots. What fun to have the [canned] fish and oysters—we'll probably hoard it for months. You dear, sweet, wonderful people: you don't know what fun we had opening all our lovely packages!

H.'s family sent lovely gifts, too. Mrs. Irwin sent me two Ship 'n Shore blouses, one brown-and-white checks, the other a red-and-white check with blue lines running through it. Also some gorgeous bath towels and little fingertip towels, *South Pacific* and *Oklahoma* [soundtrack recordings], two no-iron sports shirts for Howard, a Raggedy Ann for Elizabeth. Carrie sent E. a cute gadget to pull, a mother duck with three little ones behind— mama quacks as she is pulled. The Nortons sent E. a Playskool set of blocks, if the name Playskool means anything to you. It's about tops, I think. And other lovely things too—*everything* perfect. (Except, perhaps, some nylon shorts that H. fears may be too warm. They'll keep.)

Howard, bless his heart, gave me (us) an electric fan! Joy, joy—won't it be good to have when the weather gets warm again. (Howard kids the daylights out of me at night now—I creep into my new blue nightshirt complaining of the chilly dampness while he insists that it would be considered a warm night at home.) We gave E. a big ball, a picture book, a top, a gadget that rings a loud bell as it is pushed along, and the doll I made for her. I gave H. some undershirts, a stamp catalogue, "Variations on a Theme by Haydn" by Tchaikovsky and "Francesca da Rimini" (which I didn't know I knew until he played it for me), and some Yardley after-shave lotion. And Santa also gave me some Quelques Fleurs cologne and some bath powder. Dear old Santa!

Our house certainly looks pretty. The day before Christmas, Howard went out into the bush and came back with lovely big reddish berries; brown, fuzzy, hard fruits; greenish-white fruits that look like Bermuda onions, sort of. He tied them all into two long sprays, which we hung on either side of the radio. They look lovely. He knows just what will keep well, of course, and where to look for unusual flowers. He also brought home some orange flowers—tall spikes, and some yellow ones that I fixed. We took Bee's idea for hanging cards on ribbons, and hung ours on four yard-long strips—red, green, gold, and blue. Very pretty, and we had several compliments on them. H.'s sprays caused quite a sensation when the folks came in Christmas Eve. Everyone around here seems to be content with crepe paper streamers. We were very proud of our greens, also of the tree, which looks lovely. Seven feet high, it was boosted up another foot after Howard put it in a tub. (The five-mile drive home took an hour—our little car wasn't built to be a logging truck!) Any tree can be a beautiful Christmas tree if it is decorated with love and care, and ours was really charming with the little velvet angel on top and our own homemade ornaments on the branches.

The Ramsarans will be with us tomorrow. I really worked today to get ready for them. Howard cleaned out his back room and switched his paper-drying operations to a closet in E.'s room. We borrowed one bed from the Crookses and will get three more in the morning from the Board of Control. I made beautiful cookies with the borrowed cookie press, also cupcakes, rolls, and cinnamon rolls. We'll have smothered chicken tomorrow, with baked potatoes and string-beans-and-onions done in the oven. And ice cream on pineapple with apricot sauce for dessert. Good and simple; everything is ready to go into the oven or onto the table but the chicken, which H. will cut up for me in the morning.

Well, dears, I'm sleepy and tomorrow will be busy, too, so I guess I'll retire. Happy New Year and all that. It's hard for us to believe that 1954 is so close.

Much love to each of you and many, many thank-you's for helping to make our Christmas such a happy one. Wish you'd been here with us!

Love,

Marian

Mother, we're desperate! Please send three pairs white socks size 7 and three size 7½. There's nothing in town between 5 and 8½, and E. has just one pair now. Airmail, please!

H. would like you to please pick up a quart can of Sanford's Rubber Cement—send sea mail. Stationers' carries it. And H. says he spent about $20 on duty, which would be $12 U.S. Okay? Thanks, sweetie!

Mother, sweetie,

Please don't worry about us! We really don't need it, and you know perfectly well it does no good. Really, kiddo, your desire to see your family (us) is, I'm sure, coloring the way you look at our pictures. Howard, I admit, is thin—during this vacation I want to give him eggnogs and such; he should gain about seven pounds. His teeth, plus the fact that Agnes never serves very much, have done him no good this term. But I am frightfully healthy, as healthy as I can remember being. No kidding, that's the truth. I can tell by the way my clothes fit that I haven't lost weight. Naturally my face may look thin to you; I'm not your round-cheeked little girl any longer. Alas, my stomach is round, my legs are round, and I still have hips. All the pictures we sent home show me in sleeveless sundress or halter blouse; both show much more of arms, neck, etc. than sweaters, dresses, etc. do. You just see more—it's really just the same!

And the two years more are important, Mother. A Ph.D. is a very dear goal of ours, and if the work Howard is doing here can bring that a step closer, that's part of the work we're willing to do for it. That same goal will probably mean skimping once we're home; that's one thing we're not doing here. There has been next to no botanical work done here, and since Ph.D. requirements call for original work, it seems like the proverbial golden opportunity.

We both agree that a stretch of four years without a break would be too much, and we won't try that. But it isn't the climate that makes us feel that way so much as the feeling of isolation from the world as a whole—concerts, department stores, other biologists, etc.

Concerning housing, the sensible thing to do would be for Howard to get positive assurance from S-D that if we had to move out of this house, the school would furnish adequate quarters or agree to terminate the contract at the end of the first year.

But there are so many ifs about this scheming that if they all are ironed out it will be amazing. We love you all and respect your opinions, as I'm sure you know! But as you also know, in the end we'll do what we believe to be the best. I wish you had the money to fly down on a brief visit just to see our comfortable home and to see that we all are well—it would make a great difference in the way you feel. The only time I am bothered by the heat is when I try to hurry, so I plan my day accordingly (or try to. It doesn't always work, of course). And the only other "discomfort" is boredom, but I'm nearly always too busy to be bothered on that score.

Cheer up, sweetie, we're young, healthy, ambitious, and intelligent. We're a very happy family, and I know that being here has been and is good for me—I feel much more independent than before.

How about cashing in a coupon and dropping in for a visit?

Much love to you and Daddy—

Marian

Sunday, January 3, 1954

Hello, parents—

This is just a shortie to let you know we're all fine—I wonder why our letters have been so slow to reach you lately. I wrote several letters to Los Angeles that you should have received while you were all together; maybe they caught up with you before you left.

We did so enjoy having Margaret, Mrs. McLaren, and the children here. They came out Monday noon, and Howard drove them back Wednesday afternoon. Susan and Elizabeth had a wonderful time playing together; Janet is really angelic. She cried quite a bit when they first arrived, but after the first hour she didn't peep at all. As Margaret says, if it weren't for feeding and diapers, you wouldn't even know there was a baby around. Tuesday afternoon we all crowded into the car and went down to Madewini Creek, where Susan took off her shoes and waded for a few minutes, to her intense delight.

Thursday I felt absolutely pooped—partly the letdown after Christmas, partly just being tired. When you are on a schedule of four meals a day instead of three, it seems to mean spending the entire day in the kitchen either preparing or cleaning up. I suppose John is home from Trinidad now, but the last we heard they knew nothing yet about housing there.

Yesterday we drove out beyond Madewini Creek and came across another tortoise, which, of course, we brought home. Did I tell you that the Monday before Christmas we lost a tortoise? Junior was gone when we came home from town. Anyway, the Crookses found him over by the guesthouse, and yesterday they brought him back. So now we have three. The new acquisition is a female with more orange on her shell than the others have. She looks younger, judging by the roughish spots on her shell, which are similar to those of the little one we used to have.

I'm afraid "The Star-Spangled Banner" and Brahms's Lullaby are too small to play on this record player. It rejects before it will start playing— Howard says the one on the Westinghouse radio at home should take them all right, but we were disappointed. The two others are fine, however; I think there is half an inch difference or so.

It is rainy most of the time now; our rains were just late in coming. It is so damp that I hate to have E. sitting downstairs on the concrete, so she's been playing up here more lately. She plays in her room with the door closed while I do the dishes, clean, etc.; makes life much simpler and more pleasant for both of us. She is so delighted with all her toys and plays happily for long stretches.

The lights in our closets are a big help, and we don't have the smelly clothes we had last year. But the mattress and mattress pad feel damp to the touch and there is no possibility of getting them dry till we have some sunshine. None of my shoes have mildewed since we've been living out here.

Elizabeth is wearing her rosebud dress today, but she's almost outgrown it. It still looks sweet, though. The dresses H.'s mother sent will fit her for a short time; she looks like a precious doll in the pink one—haven't tried the other yet. They have big hems, so unless she gets bigger around the middle, they'll be all right for a while.

Must fix E.'s lunch, then ours. All sorts of letters to write this afternoon; next week yours will be longer!

Much love to you both,
Marian

January 4, 1954

Dearest Bee—

It's about 12:15; Elizabeth is sleeping and Howard is due home any minute from town. He really had to go into town for food today—out here, when we run out, we're really *out*. We wouldn't starve to death, but meat and green beans gets a little boring after a while.

How we do love the things you sent! They are all wonderful gifts, and if you want to know how much we appreciate them, just hop down here and visit us for a while in our pleasant but plain and rather dull surroundings!

The Ramsarans were here from Monday to Wednesday afternoon. Susan and E. had grand time playing together. Susan was simply thrilled over our big bathtub and enjoyed her baths thoroughly. They only have a shower, and Susan prefers a little oval enamel tub like the one we used to use for Elizabeth. Their Janet is the best baby I've ever seen—she is bathed and fed, and spends the entire day shaking a rattle and cooing and sleeping. Not that she is ignored, but she is just contented by herself. Wonderful. As usual, we enjoyed Margaret and her mother—it is a treat to have good conversationalists around!

Later—Tuesday, in fact. Howard came home hungry and I had groceries to put away, and then Elizabeth woke up and somehow the day was over before very long.

The telegram that Daddy sent on the day before Christmas arrived in Georgetown on the 26th and was mailed to us; we received it the following Monday. I hope a real emergency never comes, or we'd never even know about it! I was under the impression that there was a telegraph office here at Atkinson Field, but evidently I was wrong.

Talking to Zela and Jean Crooks today I heard more gossip about the army taking over all available quarters here. Twenty officers' families are coming out to the colony, but some are to be stationed in Georgetown, some in New Amsterdam, and some up here. So far, of course, nothing at all has been said to us about moving out; maybe they will ignore us and let us remain!

The rains came late, but I think they're making up for it now. Such a wet country. I must admit that the general feeling of dampness doesn't bother me as it did at first; I don't notice my clothes feeling damp when I put them on, yet I'm sure they are. E. and I walked up and down for half an hour yesterday afternoon, but some days it seems to rain all afternoon. When it does, we put a record on (H.'s parents sent us *Oklahoma* and *South Pacific*!) and bring in a basket of blocks and play.

Time to fix lunch. The bread won't be out of the oven for another fifteen minutes, which means that we'll have hot bread with lunch. Oh, for a Van de Kamp's [bakery] around the corner! No, I shouldn't say that because I really do love to bake. I bought a cookie press for myself with a little money I received for Christmas, so now I can really have fun.

Much love,
Marian

Friday, 8 January 1954

Dear Tom and Anna,

Marian has gone to bed on the heels of Elizabeth—both pooped from a day in town. We went in primarily to have E. get her triple-vaccine booster (diphtheria, tetanus, whooping cough); mission accomplished. Marian also wanted to shop a bit but found that nearly impossible, what with the stores nearly empty of decent goods and goodwill. Some were closed for annual inventory (pronounced in-VENT-ory here). We used the Ramsarans' as a base of operations and so had opportunity to hear the good news of John's securing a nice four-bedroom house for them in Port of Spain. At least they'll have a roof over their heads, which is more than they can hope for from military-pressed B.G. when Archie Larthe returns (to re-occupy the house they presently have).

There have again been nasty rumors about the military swooping and smiting about the Field for possible quarters for the batch of wives expected in a few months. This always alarms us a bit. But should we be pushed off, I shall inform the Education Department of that fact and ask that they find suitable housing for us. If they refuse, then the only alternative, considering current conditions, is for Marian and Elizabeth to go home, and for me to follow at the conclusion of the term in session. No one here at the base feels we will be given notice, and even Mr. D'Agrella, the chief executive officer of the base's civil affairs, concurs in that belief. Hope they're right.

Despite the rain, my fieldwork has been going very well indeed. In fact, the rain is a blessing insofar as bringing into flower plants which are dormant during the long dry spell. The College of Puget Sound and the U.S. National Herbarium (part of the Smithsonian) have duplicates (or are getting them) of all my collections, so that should anything happen to my sets, all work will not be lost. Additionally, the USNH verifies my identification gratis. Once I have (to my satisfaction, at least) mastered the flora of this area, I'll begin compiling data for my proposed advanced work in a university. All in all, things are going better than I thought they would.

Thanks for the wonderful, assuring bedtime reading. And more thanks for the fine pair of tie-and-socks sets so badly needed. And still more for the Chopin, Copland, and our beloved [Beethoven's] Ninth, which arrived today with the two children's records for E., all in good shape. You are the two most thoughtful parents-in-law a fellow could have—

Howard

Sunday, January 10, 1954

Hello, dear parents!

It is pouring! I woke up from a nap so cool that the idea of washing my hair was just too much. So I'll hope that tomorrow afternoon won't be quite so wet.

Since Howard has written the news, I shall confine myself to a mere note. When we were in town Friday I was very disappointed in not being able to find the materials I wanted to crochet some potholders. So this is request No. 1. Please purchase a steel crochet hook #7 and six balls of Knit-Cro-Sheen in various colors—brown, yellow, green, rust, whatever strike you as being "my" colors.

And please send a bottle of the New, Dry Purex or Clorox or whatever it is that I see advertised in all the magazines. I am being driven mad by my not-so-clean sheets, and in this weather there just isn't any sun to help. I don't care when we're coming home, that is something I've done without long enough. The only thing on the local market that would do at all is something called Milton, which costs 40 cents for about a five-ounce bottle.

All of this can come by slow boat, I guess, since the bleach is the only thing I'd like in a hurry, and I imagine that is too heavy to send by air. It is pleasant being able to ask for things when I know we have a bit of money there to pay for them!

We are tickled to death to have the records. I hope E. grows up to love "The Battle Hymn" as we all do! When I finish another letter we shall probably play them, since it is too wet to go out and they are a good source of entertainment. She loves to wave her arms in time to the music!

Yesterday we went out driving—and I had another first lesson in the fine art. It seems easier in this little car, somehow. We were way out on a dirt road, and I wove up and down it a few times and off into a balloon field for a while. Howard sat in the back holding Elizabeth; it sounds dangerous, but in our little car he was still practically breathing down my neck. Great sport; too bad it's raining or we'd go out again.

Thursday we cut E.'s hair—gave her bangs more or less against her daddy's wishes, but he now agrees that she looks much neater than before. Real cute, too! I decided there was no point in waiting longer for her hair to get thick enough to hold a clip or bobby pin. She is cuter every day!

Much love,

M.

Sunday, January 10, 1954

Dear Bee,

Just finished grinding up some hamburger and my hands smell like onions. We exist, meat-wise, on lamb chops, liver, hamburger, and Swiss steak. Good, but it surely gets monotonous. Howard bought a half pound of ham last week, the first we've had since we've been here. It costs $2 a pound, which is just too much to enjoy.

We were in town on Friday and picked up the mobile. Fascinating, isn't it! Elizabeth is quite taken with it, points and says something about it whenever we go into her room. The customs man was most puzzled; we all think it is lovely! Thanks, dear.

I wore my Dacron blouse to town Friday, and my, but am I pleased with it. Usually I arrive looking much the worse for wear, since E. alternately sits, climbs, and stands on me on the way in. But this, of course, doesn't wrinkle at all. Lovely!

There is a Chinese family moving into the house across the street, and a woman just walked over to our yard and picked our three sprays of yellow orchids! H. went across the street to tell her that they were private property, and all she said was that she thought they were growing wild. No apology. They are really lovely—small flowers about an inch long, but dozens growing on each plant. As if wild plants grow in neat rows!

E. and I had a five-minute walk up and down the street; now it's raining again. Drip, drip, drip.

Much love,
Marian

Thursday, January 14, 1954

Dear All—

Glad to get your letter today, Mother; we received two package notices this week, so perhaps one contains the little rubbers. Elizabeth will be awfully happy to have them, for we're confined to the house on a lot of afternoons when it is drizzly. Won't she have fun splashing in the puddles! About the two points you asked: I don't think you need to send more paper napkins, since they are available here. I haven't been able to find plain white ones in ages, so before Christmas we had some with Old King Cole on them, and then we finished up some with holly on them that H. bought shortly after we moved into the Parade Street place. I shall save the little pretty ones for a special occasion. A record for Elizabeth would be a lovely birthday present since it is something that just can't be had here. I have no idea at all what is available, though, so anything you choose will be fine. At this point she doesn't pay much attention to the words, but she loves the rhythm and waves her arms (to Beethoven and Rossini as well). But sooner or later the songs themselves will charm her, so it's nice to be prepared.

This afternoon we went out driving, to a bit of old abandoned taxi strip (no planes, no cars, no people at all now), and I went around one way making right turns, around the other way making left turns, and stopping, shifting, and starting on command. Poor Elizabeth got a little bored after a while; she much prefers to bounce over the dirt roads at a good clip. But she sat on the back seat with Howard, playing with some twigs and flowers that had accumulated there in the course of the week. On the way back we found another tortoise, No. 4, also a female. They are such funny creatures. Testudo comes out of the little house whenever we're down near their pen and seems to like to have her head scratched. Elizabeth seems quite fond of them all.

Tomorrow we're going in to town again. We'll have lunch with the Ramsarans and I will try again to do some shopping. Did I say that last week the stores were taking inventory and nothing much was available? Disgusting! I want to try to buy a pair of white Wedgwood candlesticks that I have seen at Bookers. This will be a Christmas present from some of H.'s East Coast relatives. Hope I have some luck.

I am all enthused about my latest project. I was prepared to make a small tablecloth of white, bound in brown tape, with brown and yellow daisies on it, when Howard scornfully said: Why *daisies* in *this* country? So he has drawn pictures of two local flowers (one is the red spike I mentioned at Christmas) and has two more to go, all flowers that we've enjoyed bringing home from the bush to have in the living room. I shall trace the drawings onto the cloth and do my best to embroider them, although so far, daisies have been just about my limit! He has four more little flowers in mind for the napkins, and if this turns out well at all we have ideas about other flowers that would look lovely on something else. Take me all year to do it, I imagine.

Elizabeth had no reaction at all from her shot last Friday, thank goodness. Dr. Kerry said she is as healthy as she looks; he commented on her fat tummy.

School starts next Wednesday, so E. and I will be, sob, orphan and widow again. We shall go back to our well-ordered existence in which breakfast dishes get done before lunchtime *every day*, and stories are read between 3 and 3:30, and mommy reads until midnight. Real giddy life, huh!

Love to you all,
Marian

Monday, January 18, 1954

Dear All—

Only one piece of important news this week, but the one for which we've been waiting these many months. Howard had a letter from London Saturday saying that our request for a third year has been granted, and that the fourth year must be applied for at the end of the present academic year, but the tone of the letter indicated that such a request would very probably be granted. Now all we have to do is find out when we can come home [on leave], either next summer or next Christmas. That, of course, depends on when they'll give us the money, and since that presents another precedent, it may take some time for the decision to reach us. Normally civil servants are eligible for four months' leave at the end of two years' service; Howard is asking for two months before the end of the full two years, so we'll have to hope for the best. Mr. S-D is anxious to have the request granted, of course, since it will be to the school's benefit.

Since we know now that we'll be here at least another 18 months, we will purchase the washing machine at first opportunity. Also today I borrowed a bigger crib for Elizabeth; Jean Crooks offered me Donna's a few days ago, but I told her we'd wait and see how long we are to be here. We'd like to buy it so we can paint it—it is a horrible shade of blue and badly scratched—but they haven't decided yet if they want to sell it. Since they're going on leave to Trinidad in March "maybe to stay," we may have to buy a new one then if they decide not to sell. Meanwhile, Elizabeth has more room to stretch out.

Yesterday Howard took the plane trip to Kaieteur Falls; I think I'll just copy some of his letter to his parents, since his descriptions are much more graphic than mine would be:

"Back from Kaieteur, and except for some airsickness, it was a delightful day. The weather was more favorable than we could have hoped for—rainless and sunny. I drove into town after a quick breakfast to the Pedersons' at 6:30. Agnes then drove Pete and me to the B.G. Airways ramp just south of town. At 9:30 we climbed into the two-engine six-passenger Grumman Goose amphibious plane, piloted by Mr. Harry Wendt, native of Wisconsin (now a naturalized Guianese), and descended the ramp, into the muddy Demerara. After taxiing about two miles upstream, he angled the plane around and with a roar and a swish, we were off. Georgetown looks infinitely better from the air than at ground level—I suppose most places do.

"Circling around to the Southwest, we passed over the sugar-rice-banana-coconut cultivation of the West Bank of the river, and off to the right was the brown muddy strip where the Caribbean laps Guiana's alluvium. It took just five minutes to pass over the agricultural strip paralleling the river, and then we were over unbroken tropical forest—a symphony of greens, as Edgar Mittelholzer once called it. Not a uniform color blanket, as our forests often appear from the air, but a crazy quilt of from near black-green

Howard stands on the precipice that juts out over Kaieteur Falls, a natural rock shelf just visible at the top right edge of the falls in the long-range vista below. The Pakaraima Mountains rise in the distance beyond the Potaro River.

to the palest chartreuse; rounded domes of canopy trees and star-shaped forms of palm crowns, all underlaid with "bush." Here and there splashes of color could be found: fiery red-orange of *Norautea guyanensis* (no common name—looks something like the Red-Hot Poker, only the spikes are borne on a high-climbing woody vine), yellow of various species of Cassia, and dull reds of various trees with colored foliage.

"In about twenty minutes' time we were over Bartica, capital of the Essequibo Province, which lies at the confluence of the Mazaruni River with the mile-wide Essequibo River. Bartica from the air looked like a small version of Georgetown, in about the same ratio as Puyallup with Tacoma. To travel to Bartica from Georgetown by coastal and river steamer takes 16 hours. Across the mouth of the Mazaruni from Bartica lies the penal settlement, B.G.'s Sing Sing or Alcatraz, beautiful from the air!

"About this time I was beginning to feel a little upset, for although the land was flat and the clouds were few, we had been bouncing, turning, and twisting—despite Pilot Wendt's best efforts to maintain a steady, true course. So I didn't look out of the window for a while.

"A quarter of an hour later I ventured to peek, and saw we were getting close to a low, broad falls still on the Mazaruni: Kaburi Falls, the pilot told us. The land was undulating, sort of a foothill or piedmont appearance. Nauseated again, I held head in hands and hoped for the best.

"Sometime later, Pilot Wendt sent a scrap of paper back saying we were about to enter Potaro gorge, so I played with luck and watched from the window. Across the horizon there appeared an escarpment of considerable height, extending as far as the eye could see—a sort of dark green stripe on a verdant field. On top of the cliff extended southward a flat plateau, almost like a terrace. Cutting into the plateau was the gorge and along its floor flowed the foamy, rapid Potaro River—the foam told us the fall was near. And as we rounded a right-angle bend, we saw Kaieteur in all her glory—how the two-cent stamps slight her real beauty! Pilot Wendt flew straight for the wall of golden spume—for the benefit of Pederson, who by now had negotiated himself and his movie camera into the copilot's seat, displacing the copilot into the cabin. Then, whoosh, and we banked right up over the brink. My poor stomach, fortunately empty, had taken enough, and I turned green. But after five miserable moments we had landed a mile upstream, and except for a case of the jitters, I was okay once again.

"We disembarked by walking a plank to shore and were greeted by an Amerindian family, stationed there by the Demerara Bauxite

Co. to tend a flow-checking device preparatory to the setting up of a hydroelectric plant. According to them, nine times as much water passes over the falls at the end of the rainy season as at its beginning, during any set period, of course.

"With Wendt leading and copilot Nash (an Indian) trailing with a case of drinks and a basket of lunches, we trudged the mile up to the brink. Wendt said the trail, which wasn't bad except for a little brook that flowed for nearly its entire length, was cut by him and Col. [Art] Williams, B.G. Airways' American-born head, when they opened the Kaieteur run in 1935.[66] We heard a distant roar, but as we approached we were disappointed to find it was just a gushing contributory stream, making its rapid, tortuous way to the Potaro. Just beyond there was a clearing of rock—and there was Kaieteur once again, this time on her own level, strangely quiet for so enormous and active a spectacle. I don't really know how to describe it except in dimension and color—pictures will probably do best; you'll have some in a couple of weeks. Statistically, the river, now nearly high, is about 200 feet across—maybe more for it's hard to judge. At the brink, which is not nearly so curved as Niagara's, the brown water becomes a golden yellow. At about halfway down its 750-foot descent, it becomes foam, creamy white, and much of it vaporizes to mist. At the bottom, which we couldn't see for all the mist, the water probably falls as a torrential rain over quite a wide area, hence the comparative quiet. It collects to form the lower Potaro in a mile-wide arena with walls rising to 1,000 feet. To the north from this gap extends the beautiful round-bottomed, completely green gorge. A strong wind blows down the gorge into the gap and up the face of the falls, so that only occasionally could we see the falls in its entirety; mist enveloped it much of the time.

"A beautiful rainbow extended for the width of the arena. So strong were the hues of the rainbow that the second one, always present in any rainbow but seldom visible, was clearly seen above. The color photographers had a field day. So did I, but along a different line. I took along two presses and brought them home filled. I was a little perturbed that relatively few plants were in flower, but then it would have been frustrating to have come upon multitudes with no means of getting them out.

"After lunch we walked part way around the fringe of the arena, to three new vantage points. One of them, the furthest, is the one from which the two- and thirty-six-cent stamp designs were cut. After due photography and collecting, we made our way back to a shelter—the 'rest house'—and chatted for a bit. The other four besides the pilot, copilot, Pederson, and myself were two pairs of lovebirds: an Argyll soldier and girlfriend and a Portuguese fellow from Georgetown and his mulatto belle. We had little to discuss with them; most of our conversation was with Wendt, who told of some of his experiences in twenty years of flying in Guiana.

"Later, we strode back to the brink for a last look and to use our remaining film. The lovebirds worried Wendt a bit when they decided to take a swim just fifty feet back from the drop-off. Reluctantly, we parted with Kaieteur and made our way back to the Goose.

"The takeoff was a thriller. Wendt taxied the plane upstream and, as before, roared downstream, lifting from the water just as we reached the brink—and up, up, up we went on that tremendous air draft. I decided not to look out the window on the way home, so just dozed off and contemplated the wonderful day."

Some day! I would love to see the falls myself, but the plane doesn't appeal to me too much; I think I'll stick with Pan Am's nice big ones.

We go to town tomorrow for the dentist; the road in takes an hour and a half now, thanks to the rain and the army's heavy trucks. It is really gucky, squishy mud, and whenever we have to get to one side of the road to let an oncoming car go by, I hold my breath until we're out of the goo and back on the hard, center portion. Ghastly.

I'm glad you all liked the snowflakes [organdy Christmas tree ornaments]; they weren't hard at all to make. I'll do more for next year if anyone would like them. Pinking shears plus a little sharp scissors did the cutting—just like paper dolls in first grade.

Sweetie, it *is* an ashtray—Howard and I can't quite figure out how it could possibly be a nutcracker, but if it works, use it as one!

Love to you all,
Marian

Saturday, January 23, 1954

Dear All—

Today our mail consisted of a letter from Daddy that was mailed in Tacoma on December 5. I guess it was sent by boat even though it was in an airmail envelope. We received the reprints you referred to, Mother, several weeks ago, but I think I may have forgotten to mention it. Harold Russell's book[67] came, too, and I did enjoy it. More power to him.

The YMCA, situated adjacent to Queen's College, in the 1950s

Elizabeth is saying more words nearly every day. She even makes sentences that sound like "It's a bow-wow," "It's a dolly," "It's a bear," etc. New words: egg (pronounced eggie), girl, yes, nightie, cat, apple (she's had precious little experience with apples, but there is a nice picture of one in one of her new books), and powder, which somehow comes out "bow-boo." Her table manners are coming along: she hasn't thrown her spoon on the floor in ages, and when she's finished she puts her cup in her dish and calls me to take them away.

Yesterday Howard brought out with him our long-awaited washing machine. As you remember, we were all set to get one as soon as we moved out here, but first H. had to order it, then the order got lost, then the political crisis kept the boats from being unloaded, and then we decided to wait until we heard how long we'd be here. It really is a cute little thing but seems to do a very efficient job. It is a Hoover, stands about three and a half feet high, and is about 20 inches square. Capacity is 8½ gallons of water and 6 pounds of clothes. It's right in the kitchen (rolls under the drain board in between washings), so now I can heat water conveniently for both washing and rinsing. It has a hand wringer but a pump for emptying. Cost: $189 local money. I've seen the new Easy machines in town but never dared to price them—they probably cost a young fortune. These Hoovers have a good reputation—the Maudsleys have had two and think they are grand.

On Wednesday Howard told S-D about our recent letter from London, and he said he'd write to the Colonial Secretary here right away to find out about our vacation money. He also said it might take awhile to get a reply since it is something of a new idea. Ah well, if there is one thing we've learned it is patience!

Howard is pleased with his accommodations at the YMCA, which is right smack across the street from Q.C. He has a clean room with two beds and three tables and a bathroom virtually to himself since the rooms are generally used only on weekends. There is a closet with a lock. He has breakfast and lunch in his room and tea and supper with the manager, his wife, and niece and nephew, a local Negro family. He says the food is very good and abundant, and he even had ham one morning for breakfast, which proves something. Evidently they are going out of their way to be pleasant and to make him feel at home. He pays $55 a month.

It's a good thing that I got into town a couple of times before school started, because Howard says he doesn't think I'd care to go in now. The condition of the road is ghastly, as it always is during the rainy season, but evidently it has been made worse this year by the heavy military traffic. It took Howard two hours to get home yesterday, against the fifty minutes in dry weather. It is a soft, sodden quagmire, full of ruts filled with water— some ruts two feet deep. He had to stop twice to help people get their cars unstuck; luckily he didn't have any trouble, but Monday he'll take a shovel in with him. There have been violent letters to the editors and wrought-up editorials, condemning the government for not doing something about it. Pan Am will probably complain, too, since it's the only way to get into town from the airport.

Twice last evening and several times today I had a mouse in the kitchen—a brazen creature, it practically stood and stared at me this afternoon. Scared me to death. Howard nailed a board over the place we think he was getting in—we don't leave any food out except at meal times, so I don't know just what he was doing. Hope that is the end.

My tablecloth is coming along beautifully and my embroidery, so far, is far better than I'd anticipated. Apparently, embroidery thread is one item that the local stores carry in great abundance and variety—nice to know.

Love to you all,

Marian

Just a few days ago we received the notice about our Time *subscription—thank you [for renewing it]—we'd be utterly lost without it!*

January 23, 1954: [68]

Everything is quiet now, politically. A committee is now sitting in Georgetown, studying changes for the Constitution. For about ten weeks we had five PPP men detained in a building a block away from us; the army put barbed wire around it, and there were guards night and day. These men have recently been released; Jagan and Burnham are still touring the U.K. trying to stir up sympathy.

The governor is expected to return tomorrow from the U.K., where he has been seeking investment capital to help revitalize B.G. Aside from the presence of Scottish soldiers (the Fusiliers were replaced in November by the Royal Argyll and Sutherland Highlanders, complete with pipes, drums, and kilts), the colony appears much the same as when we arrived.

The month of December was the driest in some eighty years, with scarcely any rain until a few days before Christmas. Since then the rain has been heavy, and the road between Atkinson and Georgetown almost impassable. Each day's paper brings new letters of disgust and protest and editorials demanding improvement. I heard today that the governor will be taken from the airbase to Georgetown by boat after his arrival tomorrow. So far Howard hasn't been stuck in the muck and ruts—we're hoping his luck continues.

We now hope the Ramsarans will be able to stay in the Larthes' house, for Archie has been transferred to Nairobi.

Two weeks ago we heard from London that Howard's request for an extension has been granted. We will be here until August of 1955; if we want to, we can apply for the fourth year at the end of this academic year. Right now we're waiting for approval by the Colonial Secretary of our request for leave next summer. The thought of two months at home is tantalizing.

Elizabeth feeds herself now, with assistance only when something is spilled or if she is very sleepy. She loves bananas, cheese, and bread and butter. She eats everything else with gusto, too. She loves to play in her own room: she stands in the doorway and waves bye-bye to me, then slams the door with immense satisfaction. Her vocabulary consists of about a dozen words, but such sentences as "Let's go downstairs and feed the tortoises" or "Will you bring Raggedy Ann to mommy?" bring instantaneous delighted action.

The rainy season forced Howard to turn two clothes closets into drying closets for his presses and for drying newspapers. The first has four 100-watt light globes to heat it, the second has two. Plants dry out in a few days as against the ten days to two weeks in the open room. The newspapers get dry instead of becoming soggier, as they did when hung in the open.

Patting the pet tortoises, February 1954

Tortoise population: We now have Testudo, Junior, and two new females found in the last month. Both are good-sized, one about ten inches long, the other slightly smaller. Both seem quite happy with their diet of bananas, lettuce, and other odds and ends of fruits.

January 29, 1954

Dear All—

Snow? What's that! It is so hard for us to picture snow and to think of being cold. It *is* nice not to worry about keeping E. covered at night. She has prickly heat on her arm and in back of one knee again—that's our winter for you.

As far as I'm concerned, there's no news at all this week. The road into town is going from bad to worse—H. says they've filled the chuckholes in with coconut husks, sugarcane stalks, rocks, old bones, *anything*. In the paper a few days ago there was a report that the road might have to be closed to all but essential traffic—and it is the chief road of the colony! They are now employing 100 men to repair it and extend the paving, and they estimate that they can do a mile a month. It is really not much more than a lane where there isn't paving—to pass a car, you have to get way over on

451

the side. And of the 100 men, probably not 40 really work on it—at least half of them stand and lean on their shovels, just stand, or sit down and relax. Very poor situation.

The picture of E. was taken in the playpen after the hammock fell down. Did I tell you that it collapsed with me in it? And E. on my lap? Good old concrete—not the softest flooring in the world. Elizabeth is wearing the sundress I made for her out of my old brown-and-white checked dress. She usually wears socks, but my policy is to put shoes on only after the day's first pair of socks has gone into the john, as it sometimes does.

Mentally, I've been all the way home and back about half a dozen times in the last week—such fun to think about and mull over all the things we'd like to do. Still no word about the money for our vacation. If we do get it and if everything goes according to schedule (ha), we'd like to leave about July 20. I do wish I knew how cool a temperate summer will feel to us. At least we won't be bothered by much baggage, because I imagine we'd be far more comfortable in the clothes we left behind than in the ones we have here. Elizabeth will need all sorts of things—coat, bathrobe, warmer dresses. Gosh, parents, if we do descend on you, would there be room for us? It was a bit crowded when E. was a really little girl—could you manage it now that she's crib-size and self-propelled?

I did so enjoy reading Barbour's column on advice to young wives— "lower standards," etc. Isn't it true, though, that if you read many women's magazines you get the impression that the standard is perfection—starched organdy curtains and starched kiddies and an exciting centerpiece to go with your exotic casserole and so on. And of course you always have half an hour for your beauty bath—oh boy, such gorp. I know I'm lucky, though, because Howard is absolutely undemanding about such things—he'd eat baked beans three nights a week for dinner if it made life simpler for me. As it is, when his back room gets about an inch deep in twigs, leaves, dust, string, used stamp hinges, etc. etc., he chides me for not doing my duty and sweeps it out himself. Dirty windows have never bothered me too much, but here we don't even have any to get dirty, and that is fun. I don't suppose I need to lower my standards—after all, we don't want to live in a mess—but it is fun to read that it's more important to spend time with your child than in cleaning house. Just the sort of thing I agree with.

All for tonight—much love to each of you,

Marian

Don't worry about the boxes arriving late—time isn't so important here!

February 1954:

Burnham and Jagan return from their side trip in India, where they were greeted cordially but received no official government support.

Saturday, February 7, 1954

Dear All—

This has been one of those weeks when, without Elizabeth and a good source of reading material, I would have gone bats. A routine is fine, but there's nothing like having it blown to hell-and-gone once in a while! As soon as we can really plan our vacation at home, things will pick up, I'm sure.

Mother, we don't think we want E.'s crib sent [to B.G.]. For one reason, she'll have to have something to sleep in while we're home. For another, we can buy one here for relatively little, probably much less than the cost of sending hers down. The little one that the Beckleses bought cost $58 local money, but it was made in England; I've seen locally made cribs in town for far less if we can't buy the Crookses' bed. Besides, all the metal parts would rust here—Margaret can scarcely get the moving side up and down on Janet's crib. E.'s little one has rusted some, too.

Bee, we can't think of anything more wonderful than having you pay us a visit. Howard says you'd probably have more luck getting a ship going to Trinidad and then flying on to B.G.—no boats to speak of come this far. And I really think the trip would only be worth the money if you could stop at ports along the way—especially Trinidad and maybe Jamaica. Poor old B.G. has frightfully little to offer the tourist. But wouldn't we love to have you here for a while!

This morning we witnessed part of a USAF jet demonstration—evidently the group went up and down the western part of South America, and B.G. was their last stop coming up the eastern side before going home. Six of them flew very low over the houses, and the screaming noise that followed scared E. to pieces—she was alone in the pen downstairs—and it made me put my hands over my ears. We went up to the airport to watch for a while, but as soon as we got there things stopped happening and all the planes had to be refueled.

Howard has been writing replies to the answers that came during the week, following his letters of inquiry to Nebraska, U. of Miami, and

UCLA. The U. of Miami doesn't offer the Ph.D.; Nebraska sounded good, but they asked for details of H.'s background; and UCLA said to write to Berkeley. He also wrote to the biology teacher he had in New York who first fired his interest in the subject, and an answer to that came also. This Mr. Patrie received his Ph.D. from Cornell in 1951, and wrote that he thought that school would be a good one for H. to look into. Seems they stress the taxonomic angle more than others do nowadays, and that's what H. is most interested in. But, as H. says, Mr. P. has been outside of New York very little, so he may just not know much about the other schools.

Margaret has a cold with fever, and the resultant extra work has made Mrs. McLaren look like grim death, H. says. He's worried about her. She couldn't even get up out of her chair to tell H. goodbye.

Off for a driving lesson—

Much love,

Marian

Tuesday, February 9, 1954

Dear All—

It's 1:30 p.m. and I wish I were napping: I flopped down on the bed at quarter of 1, then at 1 the man came dashing up the stairs with the letters and a paper—people so seldom run upstairs here that it startled me—and then as I finished reading them, Elizabeth woke up, so I shall just go without said nap today. Yawn.

I had about a dozen heart attacks yesterday watching E. go up and down the stairs alone. If we had a nice soft indoor stairway with a rug at the bottom, I suppose she'd have been going alone long before now. But our only stairs end in the concrete pavement, and I get cold chills thinking about her falling. Anyway, Nature and Progress, etc. have ganged up on poor me, and yesterday dear Elizabeth was truly hell-bent and determined to do it, either front or back stairs. So I sat at the bottom, and she went up about halfway, turned around and started back down. I told her she was a good girl and my! such a big girl and held my breath, and she came down upright and chortling with pleasure. Next time she went up higher, and after that she went all the way to the top and decided to bring Raggedy Ann downstairs. Holding the doll, she wasn't quite as well balanced, and when she was about two steps above me she stumbled and abruptly sat down on the stair behind her. She looked startled but continued down. Isn't it the hardest thing in the world to sit by and watch your child try something new and perhaps dangerous—probably you would say you just have to accept it and do your best to prepare the child for it.

Speaking of things new and dangerous, *no* one has commented on my startling news about learning to drive. What's the matter, kiddos—have I cried wolf too often? Aside from the fact that I panic when I have to shift from second to third (we have fourth, too, on our little wonder) and that we weave drunkenly if I take my eyes off the road and that as yet I don't know one signal from another, I do enjoy it and Howard, bless his heart, says no, he's not the least bit nervous. Elizabeth seems to have more confidence now and doesn't whimper as she did at first.

End of page; now to the bath; more later.

Saturday, February 13
Howard is using the typewriter, so—how I hate to write by hand now!

We are enthusiastic about having a house to ourselves [when we're on leave]—not that a short stay with you all wouldn't be lovely, but two months in cramped quarters, with a child, would be hard on all of us.

Just finished reading *River of the Sun*—makes B.G. sound really civilized!

Margaret has had dengue fever—Dr. Kerry had a hard time diagnosing it and a harder one convincing the medical officer that it was a correct diagnosis, for dengue fever hasn't been around here for ages. H. says the mosquitoes are terrible at Q.C. and, of course, the Ramsarans live right on the grounds. S-D says they'll do "something" about the mosquitoes, and the health department has been spraying—so we hope no one else gets it. Margaret ran a temperature of 102°–103° for two weeks, has lost much weight, and is still very weak. Haven't they had more things go wrong, though! The fever is fairly common in Barbados and there has been some recently in Trinidad.

Howard *has* gained back a few pounds—he gets four meals a day at the Y (tea included), a bit starchy but very good, he says. He's had ham more often there than we've had it all the time we've been here.

I'm sleepy! Off to bed—I do *much* better with a typewriter!
Much love to you both,
Marian

Saturday, February 20, 1954

Dear All—

I am sitting here in a cloud of steam of my own making. To get dressed up without having the dress stick to me will be a wonderful luxury. And I hate to have to mop my face all the time, but it's either mop or drip. The weather hasn't been bad lately—mostly clear. March is supposed to be the short dry season, then the rains start and reach their heaviest in June, after which they taper off again. Hot as the sun is, we really appreciate it.

This has been a Week. I suppose I should take it in order. Monday afternoon Elizabeth was coming down the stairs, lost her balance, fell, and knocked a tooth out. I was at the bottom, but it happened too quickly for me to catch her. She didn't cry much at all, and I found the tooth; apparently the whole tooth came out. It was a center bottom tooth. It hasn't bothered her: she ate her supper that night and slept well. We can't keep her off the stairs—she has to learn to navigate them sooner or later, but balancing is more important to her than to other children since she can't grasp the handrail for support.

Wednesday afternoon Howard drove out to see if E. was all right, since they had the afternoon off for the England–West Indies cricket match. Good news: Tuesday he received word that our leave has been granted! We want to make reservations to leave here July 20, allow a stopover in New York, and reach Seattle-Tacoma early in the evening of Thursday, July 22. We are allowed approximately $1,850 local money for Howard's and my fares home; we have to pay Elizabeth's. There is a chance, however, that hers may be paid, since there is a bill or something up now to grant children's leave passages. We shall hope so! Now we can all get excited, make plans, make new plans, etc. Fun!

Thursday we were subjected to an annual ordeal (annual out here—not in town)—a thorough spraying of the house by the Mosquito Control Service of the Medical Department. They came at 11 a.m., just the time I usually start E.'s lunch. I bundled her next door, where Zela was keeping Pete and her baby; the fumes—DDT—were terribly strong. The men were especially thorough in the bathroom, and I had to scrub the tub violently to get the oily film off. All the faucets, the mirror, the john, E.'s little seat—everything was drippy with the stuff. We had to take everything out of closets, cover furniture, etc. A real mess, but I guess it's worth it. Elizabeth ate her lunch, a trifle late, on the front porch. Great sport for her. I turned the fan on in her room, which cleared the air pretty well, and she slept as usual. Aside from a lingering smell, the only sign of it is a white film on the floors—hard to get off and very noticeable on our dark waxed floors. I guess we'll just have them polished and not try to get it off ourselves.

Jean Crooks and their two children left today for Trinidad, ostensibly just for six weeks' leave but they hope to make it permanent. The Darwents and their two older children also went, so our area seems quieter with the four children gone. Elizabeth will miss Wayne and Donna especially, since they came over here a lot to play with her, read her books, play with her toys, etc.

Oh yes, Thursday evening, just after I took Elizabeth's dish away from her, she decided to stand up and lean over the tray—a practice which always brings a stern "no-no" and which is taken as a signal that the meal is over. This time I only got one "no" out, and over she went with a loud clatter. Good thing it isn't a high chair, I guess. I extracted her from the upside-down chair and brought her into the living room to soothe; she stopped crying, and I diverted her with a few short rhymes. Then I said, "My, what a bang!"; E. said, "Bang, bang," and off we went to the bathroom. She didn't go to sleep quite as quickly as usual, and I heard her saying "bang, bang" for half an hour or so!

All for tonight. Won't it be fun to be home—I hope you'll have loads of cottage cheese and fresh fruits and ham and raw carrots and celery and potato chips. No lamb chops, please!

Much love,

Marian

I had another tragedy—almost forgot it. Remember my little yellow faille coat? I took it out Thursday, and for some odd chemical reason the tortoise shell button has caused the material in a four-inch radius around it to rot. Clear through lapel, lining, and through the coat's back. Nothing to do about it—the material just falls apart. Can't understand it, but the coat was only $11 or so, so I don't feel too badly—but I was planning on it for this trip home. Grrr.

Saturday, February 27, 1954

Dear All—

First, Mother, Elizabeth would simply love to have a little broom and dustpan for her birthday. She does her best with my big one, but generally it bangs her on the head. I think there would be plenty of time to send it by boat. Also could you find some of those great big crayons; she has trouble bearing down with the normal-size ones. She is terribly fond of all the older girls' pretty dollies, but we are holding off buying one for her because we're afraid it wouldn't last long. Besides, they are all imported from England and they seem awfully expensive for the plain little dolls that they are. But an unbreakable plastic doll she would love, if such things exist.

Howard had Wednesday, Thursday, and Friday afternoons off last week because of the international cricket here. A West Indies team is playing the Manchester Cricket Club, and it is the only topic of conversation. Not that we understand it. All the stores close at noon, and everyone who can afford to go, goes. Anyway, Thursday morning H. took us to town (he came home Wednesday noon). Elizabeth and I shopped from 9 to 11:30, and it was a bit too long for her. She was fine until 10, when I decided to go to Bookers' soda fountain and have something to refresh us. She ate a dish of ice cream while I had an orangeade. But she still was a little tired, and several times instead of coming along she sat abruptly down on the floor, only to stretch out full length on the floor when I asked her to get up. Believe me, there's nothing like hoisting a hefty tot under one arm when the other is laden with shopping bag, purse, and two boxes! One salesgirl popped a hard candy into E.'s mouth, and that was good for quite a while. Bless her heart, she really did very well. At 10:45 we went to Fogarty's and I bought three little picture books, and we sat and looked at them until 11:15.

After Howard picked us up we went to his room at the Y for lunch. I was very impressed with both the room and the lunch—there are two beds with dark green spreads, and the table is set with green-and-white checked cloth and napkins. It is all as clean as can be, and there is a nice bathroom with good toilet paper and soap. H. pays approximately $3 a day there, and at the guesthouse when we first arrived we had neither bedspreads nor clean table linens, nor decent toilet paper nor soap—for $12. Of course, the Y doesn't try to make a profit, but *still*. He is very happy with the setup. For lunch we had pork chops, cabbage, beans-and-shrimp, boiled potatoes, rice, and lettuce-cucumber-tomato salad; dessert was shredded grapefruit with peaches and cherries. He has a very nice maid named Hyacinth, an East Indian woman, whose job is to take care of all details for the wing in which H.'s room is located. Since he is the only one there, except on weekends and except for an occasional visitor during the week, he gets excellent service.

Mother, will you please call the College of Puget Sound and make arrangements to have a copy of H.'s transcript sent to Cornell? There is a charge, I think it's $1, so you'll have to send them a check or something.

The address is: Dr. Harlan P. Banks, Chairman, Botany Department, Cornell University, Ithaca, New York. I think it has to be sent directly from CPS.

Besides Cornell, H. is in the midst of correspondence with the U. of Texas about courses and requirements, etc. for a Ph.D. Whatever school he decides on, he will stop and visit "on our way" home. Not that Texas is exactly on our way, but if it is Texas, he will go by himself, since we imagine that it would involve stopovers and waits. He would try to go to Miami and then across to Texas. Since we think stopovers would be hard on Elizabeth, she and I will plan to go by way of New York. He is especially interested in Texas at present because some of the botanical groups that are found here are also found there—different species, but the same families. They have suggested an intensive study of one family both here and in Texas, then forming a thesis around the conclusions. But he is still awaiting replies from Nebraska and Cornell, so we shall see.

We have a set of pictures that should have been ready to go with this letter, but they weren't. Cricket, I suppose!

Much, much love to you all,

Marian

My tablecloth is done and I'm very proud of it. Doing the napkins now. Then I'll start E.'s little dresses.

Saturday, March 6, 1954

Dear All—

A rainy, coolish Saturday afternoon. Daddy, we got your cute letter while we were eating lunch, and thus inspired, I shall answer now instead of waiting till after dinner.

Mother, we snickered over your comments about excess baggage. We've learned a few things about traveling, and Lord knows that excess baggage is one. I don't imagine we'll have much (I shall probably eat that statement later!), but really, we'll probably be more comfortable in the clothes that are bulging out of the closets at home.

About the family plan [airfare] business, we are aware of it—but if H. wants to take the grand tour to Texas or other parts, it wouldn't do us much good on the way home. Coming back [to B.G.], yes. He says the clerks in the Pan Am office [here] are sure of one thing: the price of the fare to New York. On all other matters they hem, haw, turn pages frantically, and look distressed. One woman said "she thought" the family plan would apply to the flight out of New York that we wanted. Such a lack of confidence isn't very inspiring, and we thought we would write our detailed plans to you or H.'s father so that they can all be checked and verified before we start out.

Elizabeth is in a phase of some sort, I'm not sure what. She yelled throughout her nap periods on Monday and Wednesday, and on Tuesday and Thursday she wept a bit before going to sleep; today she stood up and started to wail as I left her, and Howard went and said, "All right, Elizabeth, that's enough of *that.*" He said she looked utterly shocked, but he stretched her out on her bed and by George, she was asleep in about five minutes. I have great difficulty in making my voice sound stern; I find that she only wails the harder if *I* go and tell her "that's enough," so I ignore her. Try to, that is. She has mighty powerful lungs and a strong voice. She is adding new words to her vocabulary at an astounding speed, even though interpretation is sometimes needed. Today she teased me for a while by insisting that Peter Rabbit was a bow-wow, but I'm sure she was spoofing. She also teases by asking for cheese, toast, cake, milk, or bananas when she has left before her such fare as eggie, carrots, etc. She raises her eyebrows and says "tcheese" and then giggles away when I laugh and say, "No, dear, you don't *have* cheese with your breakfast." Big joke!

Elizabeth has started again to walk up and down the stairs unassisted, please. If we start down hand in hand, and she decides to go alone, I just have to let go of her hand. If I don't, she pulls and pulls hard, and I'm afraid that she might get it loose and lose her balance. I must say it is mighty hard to watch her, but since it's inevitable there's nothing else to do. Thanks for the suggestions about a rug or mat at the bottom, Mother, but I don't think they'd do too much good. The stairs are wooden, except for the bottom one, which is concrete. When she did fall, she only landed on the wooden part but it, too, is hard. What we need is a carpet for all the stairs! I think her balance is as good as that of any child her age, but without a hand to grasp the handrail, she does have a disadvantage.

Mother, you musn't worry about my having to cook—I really do enjoy it. I get bored sometimes with our staples here: tough old cow that can be ground, stewed, or Swissed, and third-rate canned peaches (slimey) from Australia or New Zealand. And it would be nice to buy cinnamon rolls for Sunday breakfast or to buy ice cream on a lazy day. So when we are home, I may well go out of my head with frozen foods and cake mixes and ready-to-heat rolls. This would be hell for anyone who hated cooking; the local maids, I think, do everything pretty much alike.

It is 2:30 and time for me to take a shower and dress up like a lady for a while. Poor Howard had to bring test papers home to correct, and he's been at it so far all day. If you think he used to be busy at home, you should just follow him around here for a while!

Much love to each of you,
Marian

Saturday

Mother—

I am *so* pleased with the birthday things you sent—yes, I cheated and opened them with dinner. The lovely plastic bowls are wonderful—and won't they be good for E. when she starts "cooking." The towels are almost too pretty for the kitchen, but I shall love them there. And my rubber scraper has looked a bit gnawed for some time now. *Everything* is needed, too!

The box with bleach, crochet thread, and "used" dress also arrived— the dress is lovely. Very flattering, too. Needs pressing badly, but it still looks good on me. Will the rhinestones wash, do you think? I was quite overwhelmed! The crochet thread is in lovely colors—just what I would have chosen.

I used some of the Purex today, and I think I may be able to put new life into some of our washcloths that look so ghastly. Shall issue reports on the subject.

H. gave me a huge tin of Huntley & Palmer biscuits—a luxury for us. Also a tin of chocolates—even more a treat. What fun!

All my love,
Marian

Wednesday evening, March 10, 1954

Dearest Mother and Daddy,

Mother, I have been carrying on a silent conversation over the dishpan and the bread dough, so I shall just have to write you! I am eating my third piece of candy for the day, after telling Howard, quite honestly, last Sunday that I didn't even care for more than one piece per day. I've decided it's all a matter of habit, and probably a good one out of which to stay.

I am in the midst of a potholder, and it certainly is a good thing I started on something that unassuming. The colors are brown, ivory, and coral and they are lovely, but my first few rows are quite loose. The width has shrunk quite a bit, and I can't decide if it is from tighter stitches or perhaps I've been dropping some, somehow, at the ends of the rows. I may take it all out and begin again. I have two more napkins to embroider—H. still has to pick and draw one of the flowers for me. He doesn't quite approve of my beginning another "project" before I've finished the first, but with me it's much the same as making the bed while the clothes are washing or baking cookies while washing dishes. In fact I like to juggle several things around—it gives domestic life a certain bit of suspense. *Will* the cookies burn before I dry the silver? *Will* the biscuits burn if I take Elizabeth to the john?

I am convinced that Elizabeth read the chapters on two-year-olds in both baby books and now has them down cold. She really is a scream, and more and more fun. I don't need a TV! While I ate my breakfast this morning she dragged her chair in from the kitchen, then brought a book over and wanted to be put in the chair so she could read in comfort. A minute later, out for another book, and so on. Then when I said my breakfast was all gone, she popped out of her chair and brought me the big tray so I could clear the table. While I washed the dishes and clothes, she put her dolly to bed, said "nigh' nigh'" to her, and closed the bedroom door, also the doors to our room and the bathroom. Wednesdays and Thursdays are not busy days for us, so we spent nearly an hour at Zela's in their playpen, talking to Zela and Jean King and their children. Aside from Pete's tendency to throw things at E., which makes constant vigilance a necessity, and aside from E.'s overwhelming desire to swing in their rickety swing or sit on a wreck of a trike, it was a calm interlude. We came home for orange juice, then I pressed my pretty new dress and mended a few of Elizabeth's things. Elizabeth has been wonderful about staying dry lately—Sunday, Monday, and Tuesday nights she remained dry all of her own accord. And today she slept relatively late, until 6:45. This noon I put her to bed without a diaper, since she hasn't needed one at naptime for ages. Ho ho—she showed me!

She is alternately very independent and very dependent. Taking a walk is now a matter of playing tag—she just won't go the way I'm going. She will go to the door and say "walk, walk," and then as soon as we are started on a walk, she turns around and runs down the street in the opposite direction. If I go after her, she runs ahead laughing until I catch up with her; we walk a few paces in *her* direction, and she turns around and runs *that* way. Then, she'll run back to me with her arms outstretched to be picked up, we hug each other for a few minutes, and then she'll say "Shing, shing." With that she starts off for the swings, only to run away as soon as I get there. We don't spend as much time outside now as we used to, because it is just too tiring. However, she makes mighty good use of her time. I am truly thankful that there is so little traffic on these streets.

I am so enjoying all the birthday presents you sent. And everything looked so pretty in the box, Mother, so spring-like! Mrs. Worthen sent me a letter that arrived yesterday and wrote all about her daffodils and primroses and her new house. How I would love to have a great bunch of yellow daffodils sitting in front of me! Oh well, not everybody has bougainvillea in the front yard, as we do.

Have either of you read Tom Lea's *The Wonderful Country*? I bought it shortly after Christmas and finally got around to reading it (during a lull in our magazine supply). I just loved it and could hardly put it down to go to sleep at night. Reading is such a wonderful occupation. As long as I have something to read I really enjoy my evenings alone. When Howard is home he usually works at his stamp albums or mounts plants or does something else that encourages conversation, so I sew or crochet.

I always have enjoyed the simple life, and it's a darned good thing, because here we get it in a big dose. And yet it is very satisfying to know that we can get by so very well with our own bright ideas our chief entertainment. Granted, I would be far less happy without the books, magazines, and loving gifts that you all send: I always feel quite tipsy when faced with a bundle of reading matter or something new for Elizabeth. And we would both suffer from mental malnutrition if we had to stay too long without contact with the world—each in our own way. Howard concentrates so completely on his work at school that he isn't bothered as much with the absence of outside garden-variety stimuli (I have said over and over that a Northgate [store] out here would make every difference—good windows to look at and a good store to prowl through, not necessarily to buy anything!); but he says he does yearn at times for another biologist or kindred soul. We both think that living here will prove a big help when we do get home and are on a very small salary but have so many diversions available that are free—those store windows, a public library, congenial friends on the same (let's face it) intellectual or interest level, etc. (I wasn't really surprised, yet I was a bit shocked to read in the Whitman Management Audit that only six professors at Whitman receive more than $5,000 a year. H. says that Dr. Alcorn makes about that, too.) It's all very well to have high academic goals—but isn't it great that we don't crave Cadillacs and furs!

We still are juggling dates around, and Howard is waiting for a letter from Cornell before he makes that decision. It's after 9 so I shall hie off to bed.

Much, much love to you both,

Marian

Sunday, March 14, 1954

Dear All—

I guess I'm too old to eat two dishes of chocolate bread pudding comfortably; I really feel stuffed! I *love* chocolate bread pudding, however.

Guess what? Spotty is now ours to love, feed, and bathe. The Crookses are going to remain in Trinidad permanently, and Desmond is selling off furniture, plants, and miscellaneous items right and left. Zela said she would take Spot but she didn't want to have to bathe him, and she has said before that she really doesn't like dogs. She said she'd take him rather than have him become a stray; but naturally I said we'd love to have him. The Defreitases will feed him while we're away in the summer. He is a nice dog, very well mannered and wonderful with children. Howard and I gave him a bath today, downstairs with the hose, and he was a perfect gentleman about it all. We used Spratt's Germicidal Soap and good Lord! you should have seen the fleas. He looks very handsome now, however, and seems delighted with the affection that he gets.

When H. came home Friday he brought a box from you, Mother, with his birthday presents and the plastic bags for me. You have no idea how tickled I am to have the bags—months and months ago I stitched up all mine that had ripped, but they had long since ripped again. I have now discarded all but the two little tiny ones, and three medium-size ones that the Correias' chickens come in. And the bowl covers are most welcome, too.

We have two package notices here now, but Howard won't be able to get them until next week. He has tomorrow off, which is nice; Friday was the Q.C. Sports Day, and traditionally the following Monday is a holiday.

My potholder is coming along very well now; I analyzed the stitch-dropping business and conquered that, but like an old stupid I changed colors at the wrong end so that my stripes are not all the same width. I don't think it will affect the usefulness of the potholder as such, so I don't worry. I enjoy crocheting but, at this point, not as much as knitting. You're supposed to hold the hook just like you hold a pencil, and since I've always had trouble holding a pencil without getting a kink in my forefinger (the one that bends backward), I seem to have the same trouble with the crochet hook.

Today while Howard and I were snoozing after lunch, we heard a sound in E.'s bedroom (where she was playing) that sounded like a minor Kaieteur. H. went to investigate, and sure enough, Elizabeth had turned on the faucet and was having a gay old time splashing water all over the floor. We have to discourage it; if not, she'd inevitably put all her dollies in for a bath, or something equally hard to dry. She really gets enough splashing anyway, what with a shower and a tub bath every day and a session with the wading pool a couple of times a week.

Thursday evening I spent a delightful hour or so taking some clothes from a trunk and trying them on with an eye toward wearing or bringing them home in July. I tried on my beige shantung suit, which fits very well except that it's too big in the waist—I think I let out some tucks just after E. was born. The shoulders look sort of squareish for the current fashions, but it is such a pretty suit that I think I might wear it from New York to Seattle. I also tried on my beige-and-lavender wool skirt, and even put my beige cashmere on just for the effect. Nearly died of the warmth, but they both look just as nice as they ever did. I found my girdle in the trunk and pulled it and stretched it to see if the stretchiness has gone, but it seems to be all right. Haven't worn the thing since we've been here, but I'll probably need it at home. None of my clothes look very new or smart, but after a long trip, nothing would!

I had my white linen shoes half-soled, and they are quite rejuvenated. About a month ago I was astonished to find that I had holes in the soles, so H. took them into town to be fixed. Now my brown-and-white spectators need heel lifts, and if I can polish up the scuffed leather they'll look very good. The one thing that I will have to buy before we can leave is stockings. All mine have rotted, and I hate to think what will happen if some day, suddenly, I have to go someplace wearing stockings!

Back to the potholder for a while. Nice to know we won't have to get up before the crack of dawn in the morning!

Love to each of you,
Marian

Saturday, March 20, 1954

Dear All—

Howard is having the loveliest correspondence with the U. of Texas, and our latest communication from them was a letter that said, "I think it is safe for me to say that for a good man we can always find some means of subsidization." They sent a copy of the fellowship announcement, and heavens—they have a whole list of grants, fellowships, scholarships, etc. Sounds most encouraging. When last we heard from Cornell they hadn't received the transcript, so nothing new from them. Texas also sent the bulletin of their Graduate School—a 300-page book of just graduate school courses. Impressive—neither of us realized that it was such a large university.

My project today was to put the first coat of ivory paint on E.'s bed. We bought it from the Crookses for $10, a minor sum; H. said that the only beds available in town are English imports and cost from $50 up. So E. is back in her little bed for tonight, and it is a tight squeeze! The larger one will look much better painted—it was such a bilious shade of blue. And wonder of wonders, the first coat was actually dry this evening. At Christmas when I painted a little table for her, it took days and days to thoroughly dry out, but that was the rainy season and that must make the difference. I should wash our mattress pad before the rains come next month, but I'm putting it off out of sheer distrust of my wringer—I'm not sure it will go through. We'll see.

The affection we've lavished on Spot in the last week or so has made its mark; he has become playful and affectionate in his turn. He laps up kind words and would probably turn into an overgrown lap dog if I let him. He sleeps on the front porch at night; on the back porch is a wretched-looking mongrel that, because I speak kindly to him and rub his chin, has become a faithful follower. I feel very well protected when H. isn't home; both dogs bark loudly whenever anyone goes by at night.

H. has two and a half more weeks of school, then vacation. Time goes quickly!

Love and kisses to you all,
Marian

Sunday, 8 p.m., March 21, 1954

Mother—

You haven't mentioned whether or not you've purchased the patterns for E. that I wrote of a few weeks ago. I know you've been busy and going in a dozen directions. If you haven't, and don't think you'll have time to get to town, will you pass the request along to H.'s mother? I want a dress pattern (no frills), a nightie pattern, and a slip pattern—all size 2. The two nighties you made for her are just beginning to fall apart, so I *have* to make some more lightweight ones. Okay?

We had a chocolate banana cake with candles tonight—pretty! H. is very pleased with the socks and ties and will probably add a P.S. to my next letter. I love those pretty ties, too.

Love and a kiss to you both,
Marian

Monday, 10 p.m., March 22, 1954

Dearest Mother and Daddy—

Mercy! This long-distance business is frustrating when you really want to pick up a phone and chat. Zela brought over our mail an hour ago, then Jean King came over to borrow some books. So now I shall write a brief letter that can say nothing much—I'd like to know right *now* that Daddy is feeling much better, and that you, Mother, are all calm and not too busy with your Red Cross and Scouts work. Well, dears, you will be very much in my thoughts until we hear further news.

Elizabeth was just up to go to the bathroom—she is very good now about remaining dry all night but frequently soaks the bed at naptime, a gesture of independence and defiance, I think, since she hasn't slept then for a week or so. She has ceased to be a baby and is wonderfully unpredictable. I know she will love a real dolly. Raggedy Ann gets a workout these days—breakfast, lunch, dinner, orange juice, toilet, bed—at any and all hours of the day!

Spotty is snoring on the front porch, and it's time I turned in.

All my love,
Marian

Saturday, March 27, 1954

Dear All—

First of all, Daddy, I certainly hope you're feeling more chipper than you were when Mother wrote last weekend. By now I suppose you are home and enjoying Mother's bland diet instead of the hospital's. How I wish I could be right there to do anything that might make you feel better!

I'm practically finished with my second potholder; this one is yellow, round, with two red stripes and one brown. Great sport. Would anyone like a potholder or two for Christmas?

Howard had a most interesting chat this week with Foreign Operations Administration men who have just come to B.G. to survey the colony with the view of eventually supplying technical assistance.[69] Nearly all the men are Ph.D.s; H. met one at Q.C. and this man, a Dr. [Theo] Vaughan, was most intrigued at finding two Americans there. He invited Pete and Howard to his hotel room for a chat, but Pete couldn't go. Anyway, Dr. Vaughan asked H. to prepare a report on B.G. conditions for the prospective resident—the sort of information that we would have greatly appreciated before we came!

For the last few weeks we have been eagerly discussing the idea of mama going back to school as well as papa. When we do get back to the States, Elizabeth will be at the nursery school age, so we see no reason why I couldn't take a few courses at a time. The U. of Texas offers a master of library science degree which, according to the catalogue, sounds almost made to order for me. It ordinarily takes a year's work, but with a reduced load it would probably take two. It would give both of us such a good feeling to know that I would always be qualified to work at a pleasant job that I would enjoy; and the extra income would nicely pad out H.'s professional pittance. Howard says I should write them now; he sees no reason why I couldn't use our location here to some advantage for thesis material. And we wonder if I could do one or two of the prerequisite courses here, by extension. We are waiting to receive a general catalogue that would list all tuition and other fees and housing information, etc. Howard is writing the head of the botanical lab there to say he will come for an interview in July—it sounds from all correspondence to offer the best program for him. You can be assured that if Elizabeth weren't ready for school, I wouldn't think of being away even a few hours a day. You all know me better than that, anyway. But while Howard is at a university that offers a program of interest to me, it would seem just plain sensible to take advantage of it if at all possible.

Elizabeth learns new words daily—bacon is "baking," lunch is "yunch," lamb is "yamb," etc. The little mongrel that sleeps on our back porch is Poochie, and E. now says "Nigh'-nigh' Boddie" (Spottie) and "Nigh'-nigh' Pooch" along with her night-nights to Howard and me. She makes little sentences— "Cookie all gone," "Back to bed," etc. She loves the towel set that Donna sent for Christmas, and we use that alternately with another towel that has a horse, car, blocks, and ball on it. Biggest joke on us, however, is that she has, of her own accord, started calling the toilet the "toidy." We have scrupulously avoided calling it that because it is such a ridiculous name—but apparently the makers of her "Little Toidy" seat know their toddlers' vocabularies!

Tomorrow I bake a great big cake for Howard so that we can celebrate [his birthday] in style.

Love to you all, and special thought waves to Daddy,
Marian

Wednesday, March 31, 1954

Hello, dears!

It is quarter to 10 p.m., certainly a silly hour for me to start a letter. But Frank is going into town tomorrow, so if I give this to him to mail you may get it fairly soon.

Today was sort of horrible—I think it was warmer and more humid than usual. It rained a little after lunch, but not enough. I know that I felt quite awful and mean, and I think E. did, too, because she was much naughtier than usual, and I had to really exercise my patience—although she got spanked a few times as it was! Ah well, we all have our bad days. Mine got off to a bad start when I did the wash this morning and the lovely dress that Bee sent for my birthday proceeded to fade. It has a tiny little red piping that makes a sort of yoke in front, and that piping faded like fury, leaving pink spots on various parts of the dress and turning some socks and pants a delicate shade. Not that I mind that. The dress is a L'Aiglon and *shouldn't* have done it. I don't know whether to write Bee and ask if she's already paid for it, and send it back if the store would take it—or what. I know how she hates a fuss like that, so maybe I won't. It isn't really too bad, but sort of ruins it as the extra-nice dress it was. Grrrr.

Elizabeth fell down yesterday and skinned one knee, and fell down today and skinned the other plus bumping and bruising her forehead. A neighbor yesterday kept asking her if it hurt, and by George, if she didn't pick that word up in a hurry. Every time she even thought of her knee today, it "hurt."

Current problem: what to do with the [portable, child-sized] toilet seat on the plane. I don't think she'll be ready to do without it—but I may as well try. It's a little heavy to lug around needlessly, especially since, if she and I are on our own, we'll have other things to carry.

I finished the last napkin of my "Bush Flower" set and finished my second potholder, a distinct improvement on the first. And today I crocheted a little mat to use under a hot serving dish, and made it out of what was left of the orangey rug wool I used for hair on Elizabeth's last doll. It is nice looking, and maybe when we're home I'll get some less vivid color and make some large enough to go under plates.

Much love,

Marian

Sunday, April 4, 1954

Dear All—

Hard to believe it's April, eh? We keep muttering to ourselves, "Vacation starts next week, for three weeks; then not even a *full* term and we'll be going home." Sooner or later, I suppose, the reality of it will hit us, but it doesn't seem quite possible now!

We had a grand surprise this week—an unexpected visitor. Thursday night as I was reading the paper, I saw that Dr. [Ronald V.] Sires (Whitman history professor; parents, you remember Bee especially speaking of him) had arrived in B.G. on Tuesday for a four-day stay. I spent the entire evening [on the Defreitases' telephone] trying to get hold of Howard so that he could invite Dr. Sires to dinner. At 10:30 I did get him, and he had already tried to phone but couldn't locate Dr. S. Finally he did, and Dr. Sires accepted an invitation for dinner today. Poor old H. had to go into town this morning to bring him out, but of course it was all more than worth it because we had a lovely time. He is teaching at the University College of the West Indies, at Jamaica,[70] this year, on a Fulbright grant—we learned that last September but hadn't planned at all on seeing him. He remembered you well, Bee, and asked how you were and what you are doing. Didn't know me, but I didn't expect him to as I had no classes from him. It is just plain exhilarating to talk with intelligent Americans—we go for months and months, or I should say I do, out here especially—without talking to anyone who is really keen and educated (except the dear spouse, of course), and luckily I don't miss it much until we do find a contact, and then our spirits really soar. He was here only from 10:30 until 1, when he had to catch the plane to Trinidad, but we had great sport comparing Jamaica with B.G.—Jamaica seems to be a lot more pleasant all the way around. We had Swiss steak, baked potatoes, peas, summer squash, rolls, ice cream, and cookies. And Howard and I said again that we don't see how people can always eat their big meals at noon, because it is just much too hot to enjoy it then. Ah well, a nice change not cooking tonight!

I finished a cute blouse for Elizabeth today. It is white with a round collar and puffed sleeves, both trimmed with the little green rickrack I brought with us. She is very happy with it, and so am I. Next to do is the jumper and then the second blouse.

So pleased to get the cable, Mother, and to know that Daddy is home and feeling better. The cable was on H.'s desk when he arrived at Queen's on Tuesday, so it arrived promptly.

Elizabeth will, I suppose, always amaze us, and I am delighted with her latest accomplishment—pushing and steering the Taylor Tot. The pushing is nothing new, but the steering certainly is. It is hard to steer because the front casters are worn out, and it has a tendency to go around in a circle; it takes some continuous effort to keep it going in a straight line. But E. has now mastered that and has such fun taking her bear or doll or duck for a ride. If it does get off the road she just pulls it back; she can turn it around easily, too. So, for a while at least, I think we're over our walk crisis. I'm sure she'll be happy as long as she can really push it around the block when she wants to.

Well, dearies, I must write some checks and then totter off to bed. Tomorrow we arise at crack of dawn!

Much love and many kisses to all,
Marian

Friday, April 9, 1954

Dear All—

We don't know if B.G. is in the U.S. newspapers again, but the BBC has been devoting some time to us. Last week it became apparent that Jagan and his cohorts have begun their campaign of civil disobedience;[71] they were jailed for gathering together in a group larger than five persons (prohibited by the emergency regulations set up last fall), then, after being set free on bail, they proceeded to parade away from the police station and were picked up again for disrupting the peace. Bail was refused, and the ringleaders are still in jail, awaiting trial. The BBC reported "mobs" converging in Georgetown from the outlying sugar estates, but that sounds much more exciting than it actually was. There have been three estates closed down with strikes, and some of the workers have poured into Georgetown; the police had to use tear gas to break up one crowd, and the dock workers on one firm's wharf in Georgetown have struck because of that. Wednesday afternoon when H. drove out from town, he had a little incident;[72] driving through one of the sugar estates, he came to the drawbridge across a canal and had to stop as the bridge was up. A group of East Indian men sauntered up to the car, but as he saw them coming he rolled up the windows and locked the doors. They rapped on the windows and shook fists, and H. says he "put the transmission in reverse, raced the engine, let out the clutch—the car jerked violently and the men skittered away." I would have been petrified, but Howard maintains that the local people wouldn't dare to molest a white man. Anyway, he didn't have any trouble today, and the radio reported the situation in town "less tense."

Howard is involved in the construction of a large cabinet in which to store all his dried specimens. He has filled up one large closet and can't do any more collecting until he moves some of the plants out. It's a blessing we have our extra bedroom. This cupboard will have three light globes in it to keep it dry; the men at Fogarty's, where H. buys light globes, just can't figure out what we do with all the globes—he buys some nearly every week!

A little brown stray dog was killed just in front of our house this afternoon by a Bren gun carrier (small tank) that was barreling up the street—Spot was nearly hit (his passion is chasing cars, silly dog). I told H. that I thought the carrier was going much too fast, and I've seen big trucks go even faster; jeeps, too, and also one of the local residents. He is going to lodge a complaint with Major Nicole tomorrow. There are so many little children on these streets that a speed limit should be enforced. The men in the gun carrier didn't even stop after they hit the dog, which provoked me. She was killed outright, I think, at least she didn't cry out at all, so it wasn't too bad. Besides Spot and Pooch, we now have a pleasant male with a badly burned back and a good-looking female who is still shy, who have elected to spend most of their time under our house. Oh brother—you should hear them bark at night.

I'm enclosing the latest issue of the Q.C. paper; H. wrote the article on the Stamp Club, and do read the nice remarks about it in the editorial. Don't you just love the style? It reminds me of Daddy's old high school annual.

Much love,
Marian

[Howard's article in the Q.C. Lichtor *begins: "The Stamp Club has just passed its first anniversary which, in light of the brief histories of previous organisations of this type, is something of a record. Many of the present members were among those who attended the first meeting held in February 1953." A contributing cause was likely the "change of monarch" in 1953. The event necessitated a new stamp design, which made previous sets obsolete, "and obsolescence is the philatelist's delight." Referring to the club as "the only oasis" in a "desert of failures" of extracurricular groups, the editorial states: "It would be wise to find out the reasons for the continued success of this club and apply the precepts learnt to other organisations. We should try to emulate the zeal and enthusiasm of this society."]*

Howdy,

Many thanks for the King-Sized Card and ties and socks. The gray tie with red dog-heads has made quite a hit in the staff room at school.

Now for finances:

Expected for 1954:

1. Total Q.C. salary this year $5040 B.W.I.
2. Total Evening Tech Institute salary $600 B.W.I.
3. Fulbright grant (from London) as before
4. Mundt Act payments as before (i.e., the $500 U.S. will be deposited in the fall)

Item #1 may go up by 10 percent if the salaries commission, due to sit in a few months, recommends. Item #3 may be slightly reduced in the third contract (i.e., from September), but I've offset that possibility by giving a low figure for #2. O.K.?

Here's hoping you'll be fully fit soon, Tom, and a firm handshake for handling our home-fires finances so well.

H.

Monday, April 19, 1954

Dear All—

We haven't had any letters for a long time—missed our regular Friday and Monday deliveries because of the Easter holidays. Good Friday is a holiday, as is "Easter Monday," or the "Easter bank holiday" as it is called in England. Anyway, nothing much has happened except that the rain has come. Gads—it has poured and poured for a solid week, yesterday being the only exception. There are a few dry spells now and then, but the sudden downpours keep the humidity up real high. I washed this morning, and the clothes have scarcely lost an ounce of water although they've been "drying" all day.

We celebrated Easter by (1) each having an Easter egg, (2) having a leg of mutton for dinner (we got tired of roasts in town and have scarcely had any since we've been out here. It certainly tasted good), and (3) Elizabeth wore a new dress—the precious brown striped one, which her Granny Irwin asked that we give her for Easter. Howard spent most of Saturday, between rain, weeding our front yard, and continued it yesterday. A great improvement—the weeds really do flourish here.

Last Thursday we went into town, did some shopping, and had lunch with the Ramsarans. Had a good visit and didn't leave until 5—Elizabeth and Susan had a great time playing, and as soon as we left Elizabeth started calling, "Susan, bye-bye Susan"—and has kept on with the "Susan" ever since. I think we're going in again this Friday, so they'll have fun together again. Howard's vacation is half over, which is hard to believe—time goes so quickly. I was rather stunned with a new phase of Janet's feeding—her third meal of the day is tea, which for her consists of bread and butter and sponge cake. Mrs. McLaren and Margaret have given up asking me if E. eats chocolate yet; they give it to very young babies, whereas I still go on Spock's advice that chocolate before two years may be hard to manage. Not to mention tooth decay, etc. For that matter, tea is Susan's last meal of the day, too—and she gets the bread and butter and cake, too. Well, the English seem to be a hardy race despite it, so I shan't fret.

While at the Ramsarans', we were startled when Mr. S-D walked in the door without knocking and gave John some exams to correct as his holiday chore. Then he turned and said, "And Irwin, your holiday task is to meet Mr. Rock, our new master, who will arrive on Friday, Saturday, Sunday, or Monday; Mr. Beckles will greet him at the hotel." Well, H. finally met him yesterday, and unfortunately there was only one cab at the airport, a full one at that, so H. drove Mr. [R. D.] Rock and a British salesman into town. Rock is a Barbadian Negro who has been teaching only three months, in Barbados, and requested a transfer. Sounds strange, doesn't it. Even more strange, he wouldn't talk about it at all—hardly said a word during the hour's drive into town, and didn't even thank H. for driving him in! The salesman, on the other hand, had been all over the world, and he made the trip both interesting and worthwhile.

Elizabeth and I can get into the U.S. on birth certificates alone,[73] we have recently learned. Mother, don't you have a certified copy of mine in your safety deposit box? You might send it, please, if you have. I am going to write to get E.'s, and if there is a charge I shall have them bill you—so don't be alarmed if you get such a bill. I have to write the consul in Trinidad again, because I don't understand just how the authorities can believe that I am the same person the birth certificate was made out for. Name changed, no decent U.S. identification card, etc. We could get a passport, but that would cost money.

When we were in town Thursday I took E. with me to do just a little shopping. She did not behave very well at all, and it suddenly occurred to me that she and I would have a hell of a trip if I didn't do something now about this discipline business. Howard needs only tell her once to do something and she minds him beautifully. But it has been quite different with me, and although a certain amount of teasing is just fine, we've had too much. And without daddy along to maintain order, it could be a bad trip. Who in the world likes to see a child who doesn't take her mother seriously! So, in the last few days, I have tried out a new stern voice: instead of saying "No, Elizabeth," I now say "NO! ELIZABETH!" and if necessary back it up with a spank or two. I don't know if it's harder on me or on her, but it works, and I think I can be in control before long. She is so good about most things—she's back on a regular nap schedule again, and I often have to wake her up at 2; she eats all her food very well; and the toilet training is coming along—I don't think that will be a bother at all on our vacation, if I take the toilet seat along. We feel that this discipline is the only thing to work hard on now, and I'm sure we'll all be happier once she knows that I mean business. It's all up to me. Isn't it funny how you can read over and over in the books how a child should be raised and things you should do and shouldn't do, and then all of a sudden you realize that all is not going as smoothly as it should be. Well, only a conscientious parent even stops to assess the progress, I suppose, so I don't feel too badly. She is such a bright little monkey, it wouldn't take long for her to realize what an old softie her mother is—and really capitalize on it!

Well, dears, since I have a few more letters to write I shall cut this one off. Once H. is back at school and we are on our "last lap" before our vacation, won't time fly!

Much love to each of you,

Marian

Tom: forgot to add in my financial errata last time that uncle B.G. is paying out £400 ($1200 U.S.) toward our return leave passage. —H.

Sunday, April 25, 1954

Dear All—

Busy week! It's hard to realize that H. goes back to school on Wednesday and that the end of this month is so close. We will celebrate E.'s birthday on Friday the 30th so that daddy can be here; no party with little friends, just us. Two weeks ago when we were in town, E. had such fun playing with Susan's doll bed that we thought we'd buy one for her birthday. Howard looked all around last Friday, but the closest he could find was a doll pram for $24, which we thought silly. So today he put one together out of scrap wood, and I've just finished putting the second coat of paint on it. It's a bit rough, but I'm sure Elizabeth will love it. I'm also in the midst of making a patchwork quilt for it, and have pulled out some torn sheets to make little ones. We got some straw to stuff a mattress, so I'm all set, except for the time to do it all! We shall give her her presents as soon as H. gets home on Friday, and then we'll all have an early dinner together. I hope to have chicken, mashed potatoes, carrots, ice cream, and cake.

I asked Margaret if they'd be interested in coming out here for a while when we're gone, and she sounded quite interested. It would be a chore getting all of them and the necessary equipment into one little taxi, but I know they'd enjoy the change if it works out.

Howard received a booklet from the U. of Texas this week with all the usual information for freshmen, etc. Best news: housing is plentiful. The U. owns 600 apartments for married students, giving Texas veterans first preference. They have a hospital with 80 beds ("A beautiful new building"), physicians in attendance, plus a psychiatrist. They have an orchestra, air-conditioned science labs, the largest enrollment in the Southern tier of states—it all sounds rather stupendous, especially from this location. Dr. [Billie Lee] Turner, the man H. has been corresponding with, has written saying he'll be happy to meet H. at the airport, etc.

I also had a letter from Texas, but shucks—it appears that I would have to take a course in thesis research before doing any work on my own. So we'll shelve that idea for the time being. But it was, like the letters to H., very friendly and interested and not at all the formal spiel that he got from the other schools to which he wrote.

We learned Friday that the Pan Am schedules from here to New York will change the first of July, ho ho. As of yet, the exact change isn't known, but the man said he thought the planes would be leaving here at 6 or 7 a.m., whereas they have been leaving shortly after midnight. For me, early morning will be harder than midnight—dishes to wash, more last-minute packing. But for Elizabeth, it may be easier than the late hour. At any rate, the Neumanns [friends of Howard's family] will be there [in New York] to meet us, and I don't think they'd mind having to meet us at an odd hour. H. will have to go from San Juan to Miami to New Orleans to Houston, then to Austin, changing planes *and* airlines each time. Gads—what a trip. The Pan Am man wasn't quite sure how long it would take. The whole trip can be paid for here, thank goodness, since that will eliminate the travel tax at home. We thought we might have to buy H.'s return ticket at home but are reassured.

Elizabeth is a little parrot, copying everything we say, and we are about at the stage where it is necessary for us to refer to each other as Mommy and Daddy. H. called me "babe" once this afternoon, and Little Echo repeated it, which might not be so good some day! Parents, we shall refer to you as Grandmother Anna and Grandfather Tom and leave it to E. to abbreviate it according to her ability. And Bee, I think we'll be happier if E. calls you Auntie Bee, at least on this trip. She now knows all adults can be called auntie or uncle. Naturally she doesn't call many by name, but it is The Thing and heaven knows we'd hate to confuse all that in two months at home, since we'll be coming back here for a spell.

Well, kiddies, I'm sure there's more to tell, but I'm in a hurry to get that quilt done. E.'s asleep only so much these days!

Much love and kisses to you all,

Marian

Mother dear,

I thought and thought but could find no reason *here* why we should have been in your thoughts last Saturday and Sunday. You must not let your good imagination run away with you, you know! Perhaps I was thinking of home in terms of getting there: will our wool clothes be comfortable in July? Will E. take to these changes easily? Will I be able to carry all the Stuff that I shall probably end up carrying? Tut tut, Grandmother Anna! Everything is sailing along smoothly, and with this trip to look forward to, time is really flying.

About your house-hunting, Mother, I can't see any reason why you and Daddy would need more than a two-bedroom house, except on a rare occasion like this when we three plus Bee will be home at one time. We even think it best if you don't plan on having us stay with you, since the three of us living as a family unit *somewhere* might seem more normal to Elizabeth than if we stayed with you or anyone else. According to the experts, her present age is one of the worst for disrupting the schedule, so we'll try to keep it as normal as possible despite the drastic change. I hope you or Daddy will be able to babysit when we want to go out—I'd hate to leave a stranger with her. Of course, a lot of it depends on Elizabeth: if she seems to adjust easily to all the new faces and places, we'll have few qualms about leaving her; but if she isn't happy about it, we just won't.

Of course, please plan on E. and me staying with you until H. arrives: he's going to allow about a week in Austin, or several days—

Much love,

Marian

Saturday, May 1, 1954

Dear All—

Kiddies, I'm all tired out tonight, so hold your spectacles on tight—there will be typing errors for sure! It's 8 p.m., and after an exciting day Elizabeth has just now fallen asleep. But I shall go back to this morning, for today, as far as she was concerned, was her birthday. She woke up at 6, went to the bathroom and then back to bed. I had all intentions of sleeping until 7, but the dogs began to raise hell outside, so at 6:30 I said to H., "Let's get up so E. can open her packages." We all had breakfast, then brought out the packages and the fun started.

At Christmas, Elizabeth didn't know just what to do with the pretty packages. Times have changed. She knew perfectly well the pretty ribbon and paper were supposed to come off, and she tore right in. (H. and I had wrapped a few things in very much used paper, so she opened those all by herself.) The things you sent, Mother, are all lovely. Let's see: I shall take up the hem on the nighties, I think—aren't they sweet! Haven't tried on the blouse and skirt yet, but I think the straps will need a tuck; alas, the shoes are too small. This kiddo apparently has large feet for one her age, so I shall send them back. The pair we bought here a few weeks ago are 8's, but I think they maybe sized larger—it would be safer to wait to replace them until we are back, I think. I love the little books—all old favorites, aren't they; and *Hickory Dickory Dock* is just delightful.

But the absolute ultimate is the doll, christened Mary. I mentioned earlier the doll bed that H. made; we put four coats of paint of it, and I made the sheets, quilt, pillow, etc. and it looked really cute this morning. In went Mary. Out came Mary. Out came sheet, pillow, quilt, sheet, mattress pad, mattress. In went Mary. In went mattress, sheets (wadded), pillow, and quilt. Out they came. Out came Mary, in went mattress. And on and on—. I shall have to make a dress for Mary, since a diaper doesn't look too dressy. I hope she doesn't mildew; other dollies in the neighborhood have. I shall tuck her in E.'s heated closet every night, and maybe that will prevent it. Raggedy Ann is a bit "freckled" on her face, unfortunately.

Bee, I think the best thing to do with the broom set is to send it to Tacoma. If you sent it here, it would arrive just about the time we're ready to leave and then, no doubt, I'd have to tuck it in a suitcase. She will be wild about it; and since we don't have a carpet sweeper here, she can see a big one in action at home and get the hang of that.

We gave E. a little pink plastic tea set, a hard rubber sand bucket, and some hankies. Susan and Janet gave her some little lead animals—horse, colt, bull, cow, sheep, pig, dog, and man-on-horse. All small, and nearly identical to some that E. has enjoyed playing with at the Ramsarans'. By lunchtime Elizabeth was practically shot, and she was in a complete state before she fell asleep for her nap. Talk about overstimulation! Tonight, for the first time, we all had dinner together. We forgot about the chicken until too late, so we had Swiss steak, and E. ate that and cauliflower and string beans and sweet potatoes and ice cream and cake and milk. So did we. Then H. gave her a bath, and by 6:30 she was in bed, but as I said, it took her a long time to calm down!

H. checked with the Treasury this week and found that the official papers concerning our money have come through. All he has to do is make the arrangements with Pan Am and have them bill the government. If his fare and mine come to more than the £400 allotted, the balance will be taken from his salary in easy monthly payments. E.'s fare comes from papa's pocket.

Mother, will you purchase for me a pair of white Wedgwood candlesticks? The low ones, plain white, with the grape design. I can't get them here, darn it, so I told H.'s mother I'd have you get them for me since you can repay yourself from our bank account. Don't send them—I'll tuck them in somewhere on our way back.

The stray dogs are being rounded up this next week, so the three extras will go soon. They bark a lot and I can't say we'll be too sorry to see them go; it's fun having them around, but they are a nuisance. One of them tore the wide hem off one of my sheets a few weeks ago; after a few days I found part of the torn section in the sand, and then after a few more days I found the rest. After numerous washings, the bits are clean, and I'll sew them back.

Elizabeth and I went next door yesterday to a birthday party for Dianne Hosea, who is ten. Her father is a pilot for B.G. Airways—he and her mother are rather aloof, but maybe it's just British reticence. Anyway, it was a lovely party—about a dozen children, I think. Many little triangular sandwiches—tomato, egg, and cucumber. Plates of little cupcakes, some iced with chocolate, some with white icing. A large chocolate layer cake with little colored sprinkles on the top. And a traditional English birthday cake (like their Christmas cakes), which is a white fruitcake with almond paste on top, iced with white frosting. And lovely little biscuits; crepe paper bags with hard candy; cute hats, balloons, etc. I would love to know where she got the bright-colored candles for the birthday cake—I'll bet they weren't bought locally. E. was exhausted when we got home (a 4-to-6 party, well organized, too) and didn't get to sleep until late last night, either. Busy time for her!

Thanks for the patterns, Mother—I shall have H. buy some seersucker, and I'll make the nighties first.

All for tonight. Our thanks to all of you for making our little girl's birthday such a wonderful one. I'll bet she's having sweet dreams tonight!

Much love to each of you,
Marian

And many, many thanks for the score of the Ninth. My, what different proportions the last movement takes on when you have the words before you. Marian and I have already listened (and followed) through the final movement once and think there's nothing to do but learn the words. —H.

Saturday, May 8, 1954

Dear All—

Delightful news this week was that the B.G. government has come through with an increase for travel money for civil servants' leaves. The increase is from $960 to $1260 B.G. per round-trip ticket. This means that the amount we have to pay on this trip home will be limited to E.'s ticket, a mere $460, instead of some $800, which we were steeling ourselves to pay. Howard's gallivanting through Texas adds to the cost, but now we don't worry. His route has changed some since the last letter. It seems it would be both cheaper and somewhat faster if he went from here to Trinidad, then to Panama, hence to Mexico City, then to Houston, and finally to Austin. On the trip north he will go to Los Angeles and then up the coast (maybe Bee and H. could fly north together?). Both Panama and Mexico City are overnight stops, but since we don't know the hours or days, we have no idea how much time he'll have there. Alas, the tourist planes carry no toilet seats. (Tourist is the only available flight from here to New York.) Also, they aren't pressurized, which means that it will be colder up in the air and warmer on the ground. Lordy—do you think we should wear our longies?

Mother—please make a note of this. On your calendar. Important. Ready? During the month of June, please enclose in letters one stocking per letter. Not having worn stockings for months and months, my supply is almost nil. Each time I have to wear them, I put on at least three pairs, causing runs as I go. I guess I'm due for two new pairs, some decent light shade, whatever you like. Size is still 10½, I suppose, but you couldn't prove it by me. Imagine—I haven't worn my girdle since we've been here!

Problem for your legal and business minds. The ninnies at Port of Spain wrote and said that any documents with my picture and/or signature would do as identification. What besides a passport carries a picture? Wish I could think of something. Any ideas? I have our marriage certificate and our Last Will and Testament here, which have my signature both as it was and as it is, but I'd relax much more if I had something with a picture.

I forgot to say that we will have our tickets in a week or so, and not until we have them will we know times and dates definitely. Elizabeth and I will arrive in Tacoma on the 18th and H. on the 26th, as it stands now. Have just finished a gay little bag, gray with red apples and red binding, to conceal the Toilet Seat. It looks sort of raunchy—paint is worn off the metal and it is rusty in places, so we shall hide it from strangers' eyes.

"Wynken, Blynken, and Nod," "The Owl and the Pussycat," and "The Duel" are favorites of Elizabeth's now—she loves them, and I read them each about three times a day. She says "Blinken and Nod" and "Owl and Pussy," which is pretty good! Must get to my sewing.

Much love and kisses—

Marian

Saturday, May 15, 1954

Dear All—

Oh, confusion. Do we ever need that telephone; then I'd just call you up, Mother, and say "I've changed my mind," as simple as that. H. and I were talking last night about the success of my discipline campaign with Elizabeth (mother and child doing nicely, thank you), and he asked me why I thought it would be better for us to stay with you parents rather than going on to our own place. "Why"? I said, "Well, Mother and I could sit up until 3 and get caught up." "How about the little girl?" asks papa. "Oh dear," says mama, lamely. Obviously, it will be easier for her if we go to our "own" place. I keep forgetting that to Elizabeth, all of you dear people will be strangers. Despite the fact that we now talk about going to visit Grandmother, etc., naturally she really won't know you, and it may be hard at first. I had just been thinking that it would be easier (on me, and on you, Mother) if we went home with you, but I suppose you could have milk in one refrigerator as well as in another. Hell's bells—E. will probably prefer Carnation anyway.

Now for the latest on our tickets. Howard has made reservations for us to go first class as far as possible. As it now stands, we go from B.G. to Trinidad tourist class (an hour's flight) and wait overnight to catch the plane to New York. But—come this great change Pan Am is making the first of July, the local Pan Am men "think" that layover will be greatly shortened or eliminated. H. says they are quite vague about any details—they just sell tickets. Darned good thing he started this early, isn't it! H. stays overnight at Piarco (Trinidad, 20 miles out of Port of Spain) anyway, so it wouldn't be too grim. Then he catches a Constellation to Panama and stays overnight there. Then on to Mexico, on to Houston, and from there he goes by bus or train or piggyback (the local wizards don't know about local flights in Texas, think he might have to wait too long to catch one) to Austin. I'm glad we're going first class; I'd been wondering about the sort of food we could count on up to New York going tourist. As I remember from the flight down, it was ample and fine, but real meals would be better for E. We get 60 pounds' baggage allowance instead of 44, and I assume there will be toilet seats provided. Ah, luxury.

I borrowed Zela's sewing machine this week and nearly put my eyes out getting Things done. It is a portable and you turn a crank to make it go—no turn, no stitch. At least you can stop it quickly. It has the oval bobbin like the Ramsarans', which I find impossible to thread correctly, so I have to patiently stick the thread through all the slots instead of just "snapping" it in as should be done. I did two nighties for E., a slip and a dress, and took some tucks in my beige suit skirt.

Glad you like the book, Daddy.[74] The infant feeding fascinates me—a far cry from our diets. We can pore over it together, and I can at least identify some of the names even if the foods aren't available to you.

Much love,

Marian

Tom: $1.00 B.W.I. still equals 58 cents U.S. —H.

Saturday, May 22, 1954

Dear All—

Government functionaries can certainly be frustrating! When I wrote you asking about this identification business, H. wrote his parents asking the same thing, just to get more ideas. His father called the Passport Office in Seattle and was told that, as far as they knew, the only valid identification for entering the U.S. was a passport. H. has just composed a letter to the passport division of the State Department in Washington, quoting Mr. Miller in Trinidad and asking for the real scoop. On an information sheet that we have, it says that a passport application has to be filled out in the presence of some representative of the State Department—and that gives us horrible images of having to go to Trinidad in order to do that. Keep fingers crossed, please, everyone.

We have had a distressing day. On the first of the month, we were notified that all stray dogs were to be rounded up and disposed of; this we all considered a blessing, since the strays are a nuisance. Even the three who have hung around here were noisy and were terrible about running after bicycles, cars, children, etc. Anyway, last week a man came around armed with a sack of bread and a few ropes, to take away our three. I helped him put the ropes around two, and he led them off. Fifteen minutes later they were back, having chewed through the ropes. The next day the man returned, succeeded in retying one of the dogs; then, somehow, the dog turned and bit the man's hand, a rather nasty bite. And that was the end of that. In the last few days, the big brown female (ours) and another female have been in heat, and the dogs have all been going wild. Friday the army major who lives down the street said that he would send some men to help H. tie up the dogs, then they would take them away and shoot them. We agreed, and this morning H. put the three in the playpen and started to wait for the soldiers. The little dog slipped out through the bars, so H. put him in the car; he began to claw up the seats, so H. enticed him into the trunk and when he started to get just too excited, he put the dog to sleep with exhaust gas. We felt sad, but after all it is a humane way of doing it. The soldiers were to come between 9 and 9:30; at 11 they hadn't come, and the smaller dog had slipped out of the pen, so I let the big one out, too. About fifteen minutes later, along came the soldiers equipped with rifles, rope, and shovel. I gave them some fish scraps, and they suggested that we go upstairs, that they could handle the dogs. *Well!* The idiots. Apparently, they put the dish down, and as the dog was about to eat, they knocked him on the head with the shovel. Broke the dish, cut the dog's mouth, but not badly. Both dogs ran, men followed. Spotty going frantic in the house; E. ditto because Spotty was in the house. Soon the male dog was back on our doorstep; later this afternoon the big female showed up. No sign of soldiers. The cowards. Imagine—one could easily have held the dogs while the other put a rope around their necks. We were both upset, as were some of the neighbors who had watched all this from their houses. Before dinner, Howard went over to Major Nicole's (he's the man in charge of the Field, not the army major) and offered to pay to have the SPCA come for all the strays—we had been told that they wouldn't come up unless there were 50 strays. Thank heavens, Major N. said that arrangements have been made for them to come next Tuesday. H. says he was shocked to hear of the soldiers' cruelty (Major N. reportedly likes dogs better than children) but said the army has fouled up other things and that he doesn't count on them anymore. Distressing, as I say. I'm sure the dogs will be better off once they are put to sleep, but if it can't be done humanely we'd rather have them alive.

As we returned from a drive this afternoon, who should we come upon but the governor and party in their huge black Buick. It must have looked funny—our little car bouncing along the rutted road (H. said we mustn't hold up the Gov.) followed by this monstrous black car. Didn't see the governor but saw the back of Lady Savage's neck. Her hair is shingled up the back, by the way. Did I tell you that last week H. met the governor? He was correcting papers at school, and in walked the governor, accompanied by Mr. S-D in dirty, frayed shirt and horrible spotted trousers. His Excellency was inspecting some Technical Institute classes being held. He asked H. if our living accommodations were satisfactory out here—don't know how he knew we lived here, but H. said he was very friendly and interested.

I spent most of my evenings this week making some clothes for Mary, E.'s new doll. Panties, slip, dress, and nightie are cute, but a coat is sort of a patchy-looking thing. Mary is wearing the nightie at present, and I think we'll save the others until we start home. E. hasn't seen them yet, and they'd make a nice diversion, I think.

It rained and rained this week. Today was clear, thank goodness. Everything gets so repulsively clammy in the wet weather. I've washed all Howard's "heavy" shirts and now just have to iron them. We will bring them home, he will wear them, and we'll leave them. I also sent my beige suit to the cleaners, and it came out quite nicely. Washed one of H.'s sweaters, and it was so successful that I washed my brown cardigan and two cashmeres. They smelled; I hated to take them home like that, and I don't have too much confidence in the dry cleaners here—where would they learn how to clean sweaters, pray tell? Anyway, now they all look fine and smell fine. I have wedged suitcases into the closets and shall put all these clean clothes in them, hoping that the drier air will keep everything in good shape.

By the way, Mother, last week we sent off a box with some clothes—formals, mainly, and a few other things I've never needed here and never will. I reckon it will arrive about the time we do, but even if it comes earlier you needn't bother with it. Some of the things are rather repulsive and I shall deal with them myself. One of the things is that yellow two-piece of mine—remember? It has mildew spots on the top, and the local cleaners couldn't get them out. If the cleaners in Tacoma don't think they'll come out, I shall consider having the dress dyed. It would be worth it, if the dying isn't expensive, since the dress is still good and of an indeterminate style. Howard says please leave intact the $3 stamp on the box!

Elizabeth is minding me so much better than before, it is truly wonderful. I think we shall have that all straightened out by the time we set out. She is happiest now when helping; when we first go to the kitchen in the morning, she takes out her box of cereal from the cupboard and then mine, and puts them back when I'm through. She loves to carry things to daddy—a magazine or what have you. Now, whenever she sees a book or magazine on our bed, she triumphantly carries it back into the living room, places it on the table, saying "'Ank you, 'ank you!" as she does it. (She knows the value of "please" and "thank you," but "you're welcome" hasn't hit her yet.) Thursday afternoon it rained, so we couldn't go out; we played together, and I taught her to rock Mary as I sang "Rockabye Baby." How she loves that—you should see the way she holds poor Mary and swings from side to side!

Did I say that Agnes has gone back to Minnesota? Left without telling anyone goodbye. Pete now spends his time going to movies—takes in three different shows on Saturdays and most every weeknight as well. He's going home the week after we are, but won't say whether he's returning. He applied for the second year thinking he could get out of it if he desired; he received a letter that said they appreciated his application, and of course he understood that it was expected that grantees in the W.I. would stay for the second year. What a pickle—Agnes doesn't want to come back.

Bedtime. Love to all,

Marian

Received the December 26 New Yorker *yesterday—along with the April 10 issue. What happens to these delayed things? No* Time's *have been received in the colony for two weeks, and we can't figure it out!*

Saturday, May 29, 1954

My Dears—

Do sit down before you start this—otherwise you may collapse! This has been the week to end all weeks, and I shall take it chronologically.

Thursday we received an eviction notice. I got the letter, phoned H. at about 4 only to learn that he had been given notice to leave the Y—that wasn't unexpected, though, since Mr. Shepheard, the manager, died last week, and his wife must leave. Howard appeared here as I was washing dishes, read the letter from Major Nicole, and went over to see him. From the major he learned that we have to leave so that an army major can have the house at the first of July. Two other families and a bachelor also received notices; the Kings were already planning to move, the Armstrongs won't leave because he is representative for British West Indies Airways and KLM here. The bachelor is a B.G. Airways pilot, and he refuses to budge. Nicole all but sobbed and said that he had no choice, that political pressure was brought to bear; the army stationed in New Amsterdam has been quartered in the hospital. Folks there resent the fact that they don't have use of the hospital, and there has been a lot of agitation in that part of the colony lately. Nicole said there was no chance that we could stay on until mid-July.

Friday Howard changed E.'s and my reservations for June 25, letting us arrive in Tacoma the following Monday evening. These aren't confirmed, but the man said it isn't a busy time and he was quite sure they would be all right. Howard talked to all sorts of people in town:

1. The Government Housing Officer said that officially he had no houses on his list for civil servants. Unofficially he knew of a doctor who leaves for the UK in August or September for six months; he lives in a flat near the sea wall in town, a nice flat. Howard will call this man on Monday. Personally, I think our chances of getting the place are slight, because surely this doctor (he's the government malariologist) has good friends who desperately need housing.

2. H. succeeded in getting a room for himself at the Londonburg Hotel, sight unseen. He's lucky. It will be vacated Monday afternoon and he will move in Monday evening. He was told it is 20 by 20 feet, and he will share two showers and two toilets with four other men. I think he pays $80 a month. The other hotels wanted $250 a month, and they are all filled up anyway.

3. After talking to Maudsley and Beckles and learning that the army is to be here only until October, he decided to ask Major Kellway-Bamber, the local commander, if the major assigned to this house would be interested in renting our furniture, with the guarantee that they would be out the end of October.

Today he had the talk with Major K-B, and the major is to tell him tomorrow whether the October removal date is correct, and whether the major would like the furniture. It seems logical that he would, since none of the houses up here are furnished with stoves and refrigerators, and some have no furniture at all. The army men don't even want to come, because of the investment they'd have to make in furniture for such a short time.

Well, it begins to look worse and worse for Major Nicole. H. just came back from talking to Armstrong, and it seems that (1) a *Daily Chronicle* reporter was up here today talking to Kellway-Bamber, finding out why the army is kicking civilians off the base. (2) The Chief Secretary wrote Nicole today to find out what all the fuss is about—and the major replied that he had not told anyone the reasons for the eviction, that is, that it was to give housing to the army. The so-and-so told H. several times that it was for the army, and in the eviction letter to Armstrong he wrote it. This info comes from Alec Phillips, Nicole's secretary, a local man who "hates Nicole's guts," as Armstrong told it. Everyone up here seems to hate the man, all the local people whom he's treated like dirt. Phillips also told Armstrong that another neighbor, Lester Guyadeen, is being evicted. Guyadeen is an agriculture officer in charge of a banana plantation here on the base.

Both Armstrong and Vykes (the bachelor) say positively that the house Kellway-Bamber and wife occupy, known as the VIP cottage, is kept up with American funds, and with the understanding that it is to be used by Americans when necessary. With this in mind, H. has written the consul in Trinidad to see what they can do [for us].

Armstrong has the BWIA people behind him; they are writing to say that if Armstrong can't live on the base, the BWIA cargo will just pile up at the airport and won't get to town. Vykes has B.G. Airways behind him, and they say that if the government wants the gold dredge flown into the interior, they can jolly well let Vykes stay here. Guyadeen says that if he can't live up here, he'll quit the agriculture department and teach—he has two degrees. And they all seem to think that as Americans, we have a right to be up here and that Nicole won't want to stir up mud with us—there is something shady about houses that the B.G. government bought here for 50 cents a square foot with the intention of destroying them; they have never been destroyed. Other houses were bought for $1.50 a square foot for the government to maintain. Still other houses are still maintained by the U.S. government. But the houses that were to be destroyed have been a big bone of contention, apparently.

Howard thinks our real right to stay here is based on his being a civil servant. There is a rental ordinance that says you can't be evicted unless suitable quarters at comparable cost are available, and they aren't. Isn't it a mess?

What will we do? It's complicated. As far as I'm concerned, my job is to get everything packed up by June 25. I've already washed four rugs, two bedspreads, mattress pads, etc.—the weather was lovely today, and I know June is supposedly rainy. After we leave, H. will either move everything out (to the Ramsarans', bless their hearts) if that is necessary, or get the house into shape for the army major, or just plain lock it up if we are allowed to stay. If, while we're home, we find out we can't return to this house, or if the major is here, E. and I will plan to stay longer, and H. will come back to house-hunt or whatever is necessary. If he can't find housing, we would have to wait until the first of the year, when the Maudsleys go on leave, and then we could very probably have their house for the rest of the year. Unless we have real assurance that we can stay here, we won't apply for the fourth year.

We are waiting to hear from the passport people in Washington—H. is going to cable them Monday to urge them on. Hope the passport business doesn't foul up the works any more than the way it is now!

Can you parents find an apartment on such short notice? Mother, will you have two copies of the passport picture sent, with H. cut out if possible. Mother—did E.'s red shoes that we returned to you arrive? I'm wondering about the bedsprings that we included—have to have the crib ready for the dear child when she arrives.

The pictures must be regulation passport size—2½ by 2½ inches.

Howard just tells me that while he was at Armstrong's, he talked with an Argyll medical officer who was also there. This officer said that Kellway-Bamber has made it "abundantly clear" to Nicole that the army is perfectly willing to allow its men to stay in town; that he will provide transportation for them to and from the base; that the men don't want to come up here. Housing is so short here, the local government is evidently in a panic about where to house this army they've called out, and Major Nicole is apparently trying to bluff us out of these houses. Local gossip says he's toadying to the army in hopes of getting OBE when he retires in a few years.

On Wednesday, the statue of Queen Victoria that has stood in front of the Law Courts for 60 years was dynamited.[75] Blew off her head, mutilated her throne, and will cost 50 thousand to replace. On Monday, a pump house on a Bookers sugar estate was dynamited—not much damage done there. There are extra guards now around the electric company, the radio station, etc., and no unauthorized people are allowed to come into the airbase, as they previously were to have picnics, sightsee, etc. In New Amsterdam, attempts were made to blow up the bank, the police station, and another pump house. The governor is trying so hard to be polite about all this that nothing has come of it; the police keep tracking down clues, but they don't get anywhere. And now they're taking the army out of New Amsterdam, and that doesn't make sense to me. I suppose the governor will wait until the situation becomes unmistakably dangerous and then have the army get hot on it.

We test-packed all our suitcases today, and when H. weighed them at the airport E.'s and mine were within two kilos of the limit. H.'s had eight kilos to spare, so we'll transfer a little of ours to his just to be safe.

10 p.m. and bedtime—All this excitement! Won't it be fun to see you in a few weeks—Whee!

Much love to you both,

Marian

Monday, May 31, 1954

Mother dear—

Got your letter with all the stamps today—H. will be pleased!

About your house-hunting for us. I think in the letter I last wrote I said apartment, but of course a house will be better. *But*—now that our plans are so darned indefinite, don't you think we should aim for a place where, if necessary, E. and I could stay on until October or November? Moving about will probably be upsetting to E. so we should eliminate that if at all possible. Of course it all rests on what's available and what isn't.

Did I tell you we packed nearly all of E.'s toys into one suitcase, and she was quite upset that I didn't include Mary—she'll go right with us in the plane, of course, but E. didn't realize that!

Much love,

Marian

Sunday, June 6, 1954

Dear All—

A poor time to write, right after dinner—but I shall do my best. There isn't too much news: the housing situation is pretty much the same. However, Howard did talk yesterday with Mr. Guyadeen, the Agricultural Officer for this district who lives just down the street; he was given an eviction notice last Tuesday. He had talked with someone in the Colonial Secretary's office and had heard that Col. Sec. [John] Gutch was "much upset" about the letter that H. wrote. Guyadeen, also a civil servant, said he was going to write, too. It is becoming clearer that Major Nicole took it upon himself to remove residents, although he told H. he was at the mercy of the higher-ups. We hope to receive word this week.

Howard talked with Major Parnell, the officer scheduled to move into our house, and found him about 30, "sweet," with wife and three children. They would be overjoyed to move into our house until mid-October, when the Argylls are scheduled to leave. If we can get written assurance from Gutch that we can have the house back then, that's what we'll do. We'd really like to have it occupied, since things go to pot in a hurry here when they're unattended—mold, mildew, etc.

We had a letter from the consul in Trinidad saying they couldn't help us [with the eviction notice], since it didn't seem to be a case of discrimination against Americans. Also, the only buildings still owned by the U.S. are two barracks presently occupied by forces.

Howard talked to a Gerald Clark of the Foreign Operations Administration last week and was relieved to learn that the FOA men always travel in the Caribbean just on birth certificates. He said the customs men aren't fussy at all just as long as you look and sound American. That's good news—we haven't heard back from the Passport Division yet, but it sounds as if the chap in Trinidad knew what he was talking about.

Rumors have been persistent all week that a curfew would be imposed soon—10 p.m. to 4 a.m. Howard says that police now patrol the streets in pairs with fixed bayonets, as they did last October. Nobody likes the curfew idea, needless to say.

Howard will pick up Elizabeth's and my plane tickets Tuesday, since tomorrow is a holiday. We have two package notices, which I hope are for E.'s coat and the crayons, etc. from Bee. It sounds like a wonderful assortment, Bee, and I am most pleased with the notion of washable crayons!

I have done just about all the advance cleaning and putting away that I can do until we know definitely if the house will be occupied, or whether we have to vacate for good. If the Parnells are to come I shall get someone to wax the floors, since they haven't been done in ages; I won't put my clean rugs down, though, until we're back—if we are to come back. I've packed all the excess china, since we won't let the Parnells use that—or our linens.

Mother, the box with the mysteries and *Coronets* arrived, and I shall probably split trying to read everything before we leave. We were both fascinated with the *Consumers Guide*—are you and Daddy regular subscribers?

Spent hours and hours this week going through two cartons of letters that we finally had to get rid of—found a check for $15 from Mother, dated January 14, 1953. No. 2311, in case you're at all concerned—I shall tear it up.

All for now. Must reconcile the checkbook with the bank statement.

Much love,

Marian

H.'s mother wants to call me in New York, but I would rather wait to talk to you all in person. Truly—after all this time I'd probably go blank on the telephone!

Saturday, June 12, 1954

Dear All—

Nothing much to report—no word at all from the government about our house. So—Howard took down all the curtains this morning, and I will wash a few at a time. We are hoping that the action will result in our being allowed to stay! We also packed up the last of the boxes for storage at the bank. We will take them in next Saturday or the following Monday—it occurred to us today that I may have to make a trip into town just to get traveler's checks. It will have to be on Saturday, but if we do go in, it would give us a chance to see the Ramsarans for the first time since Easter.

Howard picked up all our tickets this week. Elizabeth and I leave here at 12:25 a.m. June 25 (ghastly!) and arrive in Trinidad at 2. We leave Trinidad at 8 a.m. Saturday the 26th, and arrive in New York at 6 p.m. Leave New York at 6 p.m. on Sunday the 27th, and arrive at Seattle at some wee hour Monday morning. Don't know the time, but it is a United flight #507. Okay?

Howard goes on the 16th, from Atkinson to Port of Spain to Balboa to Houston to Dallas to Austin. They cut out Mexico—I think there is a fuel stop but no layover. He will be in Los Angeles on flight #907 United A.L., having left Dallas at 1:30 p.m. on the 24th of July. Bee, will you call United and ask if H. can delay his flight from L.A. to Seattle, flight #675, from July 26 to July 27? In other words, can he make the change when he gets there—with just 24 hours' notice? Thank you. And if he can't do so, could you find out if there is another United flight at a different time that he could take? Confusing.

Well, kiddies, this is a poor excuse for a letter, but my heart isn't in it!
Much love to you all—
Marian

Friday, June 18, 1954

Dear Bee—

Your package arrived, and I am so tickled with everything! E. will love the coloring book and those large crayons. Many thanks from both of us.

We go to town tomorrow to do about traveler's checks and to have lunch with the Ramsarans. We will all go to the S-Ds' for a pre-lunch drink and I suppose we'll drop in on a few other people to say goodbye. Sort of difficult not knowing if we'll be coming back.

Howard talked to Gutch, the Colonial Secretary, this week—no chance of our coming back to this house, darn it. Now he will write the Fulbright people in London to see if they will let him break his contract for next year. Lordy, what a mess.

No books, pictures, or spare clothes in the closets now—we look frightfully bare.

H. is borrowing a truck from the Correias—the folks who run the hydroponic gardens here at the airbase. He'll take our furniture into town to the Ramsarans' the weekend after E. and I leave. Next weekend, that is. Very hard to believe we go in less than a week. I nearly got into a tizzy last night at 11:30 hearing the plane come in, projecting myself ahead a week!

H. says he doesn't know what time he reaches Los Angeles and will you please check.

Well, I'm off to press a skirt to wear tomorrow.
Much love to you,
Marian

Saturday, 27 June 1954: Londonburg Hotel, Georgetown

Dear Bee,

Sorry about all this confusion over my comings and goings. To answer your questions, this is where I stand:

I travel from Dallas to L.A. on American Air Lines flight #907, leaving Dallas at 1:30 p.m. (Dallas time) on July 24. According to my ticket, I'm to leave L.A. on U.A.L. flight #675 at 11:45 on the 26th, but I would like to change the day of departure to the 27th—same flight (seems to leave L.A. and probably gets to Seattle-Tacoma at good convenient times). This will give me time to make a brief stop in San Clemente [to visit his grandmother]. So please make the flight you reserved in your name effective, and cancel my original. U.A.L. should have a record of my reservation as it is listed as "cleared" on my ticket (#344090) in the Reservation Status column.

Well, sister-in-law, assure me that you have cool evenings in your parts—I'm apt to wander out on the roof and get drunk with the chill. Life in a Georgetown hotel is a far cry from being with my dear family—worse yet because at this time of year the mercury doesn't drop below 75 degrees, and that's around 4 a.m. Please excuse this atypical scrawl—I'm writing this on an inverted pulled-out top drawer in the bureau. Not even a table in this place. Need to get home for a while. The glitter of B.G. has long since worn off, and I'm getting a little fed up with the third-rateness of most everything here. Nuts about the good old U.S.A.!

Can't wait to see you folks.

Love,

Howard

ENDNOTES

53 Dr. Hanoman-Singh, who is a newly elected member of the House of Assembly (8/13/1953): A member of the PPP's Georgetown elite that hoped to check the Jagans' extremism, Dr. Robert S. Hanoman-Singh was a strong supporter of Burnham's. Immediately after the election, Burnham had attempted to push him forward to a ministerial appointment in place of one of the previously agreed-upon members; however, his name was dropped from the list before it was submitted to the governor.

54 This weekend Howard is . . . making a large playpen for her (8/20/1953): The need for the playpen became clear in light of some serious concerns not mentioned to Elizabeth's grandparents. From Marian's later writings: "The inviting white sand held too many insects, including scorpions and biting ants, to be safe for a small child playing alone. One morning I found a black widow spider in the laundry tub and gingerly caught it in an empty powdered milk tin to show Howard."

55 Mrs. K's explanations to Karen (9/11/1953): Marie Killilea, the author of *Karen*, answered her daughter's question about why she had cerebral palsy by explaining that God bestowed such suffering only on those He loved best.

56 The sugarcane workers were out for three weeks (9/19/1953): The object of the strike had been recognition by the Sugar Planters' Association of the PPP-led Guiana Industrial Workers' Union as the sole bargaining agent for all workers in the sugar industry. At that time, field workers (mainly East Indian) and factory workers (mainly black) were represented by the Man-Power Citizens' Association, which, with backing from the colonial government, largely protected the interests of the reform-averse planters. The lengthy strike brought the colony's entire sugar industry to a standstill; it was, in Clem Seecharan's words, "the single most important issue that impelled the British to suspend the Constitution."

57 Talk going around at present is that "everyone" is leaving (10/4/1953): Cheddi Jagan also overheard "some talk . . . of plans to evacuate the U.S. Air Base." Elsewhere he recollected, "during that day there was a great deal of excitement all over the capital. Georgetown was keyed up with the rumour."
  Some of the public had been taken aback by what they viewed as the disrespectful stridency of several PPP ministers, labeling them "kangalangs," or rowdies. Believing that Governor Savage was stalling on an issue, Sydney King was remembered to have said, "This confounded nonsense must stop." At the end of September, in an address before the House of Assembly, Burnham said, "Let us tell them they are wasting time to oppose us. . . . We are going to make laws to suit ourselves. They can never get the reins of government out of our hands and back into theirs. Let them know that." John Gutch was told that Burnham said of him, "He is going to crawl like an animal and eat the grass on the ground, that serpent." (In his memoir Gutch wrote, "We were seated

next to one another at Council meetings and I must admit that I, too, found it difficult to maintain feelings of friendly co-operation.") At a well-attended demonstration outside Government House on October 4, Burnham, the main speaker, said, "Her Majesty's Government will suspend this constitution over my dead body." The acrimonious outbursts broke with the customary decorum, and were later cited among the causes for suspending the constitution. Jagan retorted, "What was clearly political rhetoric—as later non-violence showed— has been selected as a serious charge by the Colonial Office."

58 Congressman Jackson . . . vital defense position (10/4/1953): Senator Jackson visited Georgetown as the guest of Governor Savage. American anxiety about B.G.'s stability is expressed in a telegram of October 1 from Consul General Maddox to the Department of State: "With PPP leaders pressing hard to establish complete control [of the] colony, consolidated Communist bridgehead [in] this area distinctly possible unless menace [is] firmly met."

59 the BBC broadcasts . . . tell of destroyers and an aircraft carrier that are proceeding toward Trinidad (10/6/1953): This was a gaffe in what was intended to be a secret action "in case the PPP might attempt a coup before their arrival," wrote Gutch in his memoir. "It was therefore a shock to hear on the BBC news, as I lay in bed with a touch of fever, that Winston Churchill had announced that a cruiser was on the way with reinforcements!"

60 500 Royal Welsh Fusiliers (10/8/1953): The Welsh Fusiliers had arrived "ready to open with all they had"; informed by an official party that there was no immediate alarm, the commanding officer told his men to change "from battle order to parade dress" before marching ashore.

61 Jagan and Burnham left today for England (10/19/1953): The trip was the PPP's idea, formed in response to the British government's announcement that a White Paper on the suspension of the constitution would be debated in Parliament. Jagan and Burnham hoped to counterbalance the testimony furnished by the opposition ministers, whose travel arrangements to London proceeded smoothly. In contrast, Jagan and Burnham encountered a network of international obstacles. "The governments of Trinidad, Barbados, Jamaica, and the United States indicated that we would not be allowed to pass (in transit) through their territories," Jagan wrote. U.S., French, and British airlines complied by refusing to book the men. KLM agreed to take them, but its flight from Georgetown required an overnight stop in Suriname, which that colony's government would not permit. In the end, Burnham and Jagan chartered a Dakota DC-3 from British Guiana Airways to fly the two of them to Suriname "at the prohibitive cost of $800."

62 Parliament has agreed that the PPP is a bad lot (10/25/1953): The British Government's White Paper on the suspension of the constitution had been released on October 20; it read in part: "It became clear by the end of September that British Guiana was facing a rapid deterioration in the efficiency of its administration, in its economy, and in its security. This deterioration threatened not only public order but the very livelihood of the people. . . .

After consultation with the Governor, Her Majesty's Government were driven reluctantly to the conclusion that the only course was to take steps to suspend the Constitution. . . . Her Majesty's Government realized the gravity of this step. Some Ministers had threatened violence, and tension was great. They and other extremists might have used this occasion for stirring up disorder. Her Majesty's Government accordingly decided to transfer to British Guiana the troops which were stationed in Jamaica and British Honduras to support the security forces and to ensure the maintenance of order. In the event, the action taken by Her Majesty's Government was greeted with widespread relief in the colony and there were no incidents beyond the General Strike which the PPP Ministers are attempting to organize."

The White Paper was soon widely criticized for propagandistically exaggerating signs of "Communist subversion" by the PPP. Its claim that the party had been trying to undermine the Boy Scouts and Girl Guides was among the charges that prompted James Giffiths, a member of the House of Commons, to remark, "Some things have been brought into this White Paper which, quite frankly, I think give the impression of scraping the barrel for evidence." London's *Spectator* noted: "It is one thing to encourage a strike and incite a riot; but it may be still another to plan a Communist coup. . . . The removal of democratic rights is not a matter which can, or should, be left to the imagination . . ."

Nonetheless, the charge of Communism had been leveled, and Jagan and Burnham did not win the support of the British Labour Party or prominent Caribbean leaders. As Reynold Burrowes writes, "It would seem that the PPP did not quite understand the international ramifications of its own actions, or the inability of a colonial government to coerce even some of their seemingly independent friends."

63 Five ex-PPP men are being "indefinitely detained" (11/1/1953): Martin Carter, Sydney King, Bally Lachmansingh, Ajodha Singh, and Rory Westmaas were detained without charge for flouting restrictions by holding illegal meetings at Plantation Blairmont on October 25. (Savage wrote to Secretary of State Oliver Lyttelton the following day, "police advise that most widespread fear of victimisation exists and in consequence some statements only obtained on the understanding that witnesses not required to give evidence in court. . . . I am therefore advised that if cases are brought, court acquittal appears inevitable. It is, however, becoming increasingly clear that extremist leaders are determined to undermine public order and police have statements to show there have been fresh acts of intimidation. In addition attempt was made to derail main line train in vicinity of Blairmont last night and it is reported that plan of incendiarism is likely to be carried out on Plantation Skeldon." Savage's proposed detainments were approved by London.) Lachmansingh was soon released due to ill health; the others were held until January 12, 1954, following a seven-day hunger strike. Looking back forty years later, Carter said, "we were very well treated. . . . And the chap that was in charge, Captain Anderson, was a very decent fellow. It was detention in a very civilized way. We could stay together and discuss things. My wife was allowed to see me and allowed to write." Phyllis Carter recalled smuggling letters in to her husband at the airbase and carrying his freshly composed poems out. His release came just before their first wedding anniversary.

64 Last Friday the governor made a speech about the structure of the interim government (11/8/1953): The governor had made his appointments to the interim government from among the elite and the middle-class members of the National Democratic Party, which had won just two seats in the 1953 election. The new government swiftly confirmed the colony's state of emergency. "Almost every form of political activity in which the PPP engaged," writes Reynold Burrowes, "was banned by the Government. All forms of assemblies, public and group meetings, even film shows were banned." Governor Savage assumed emergency powers while a new constitution was prepared.

65 the army has taken over all available housing (11/15/1953): The Argyll and Sutherland Highlanders stationed at the airbase were housed in the former U.S. Air Force hospital; headquarters in Georgetown was set up in an evacuated government office, with the officers' mess in the Mariners' Club, "an unsatisfactory building which was merely a rest house for merchant seamen while their ships were in Georgetown." Elsewhere, "troops could find themselves billeted in hotels not of high repute. In rural areas, cottage hospitals and buildings on sugar estates had to be made available. The Public Works Department laboured day and night to build four new barracks on Camp Road in Eve Leary exclusively for British troops. The governor named them 'Balaclava Barracks' at the formal opening on September 20, 1954."

66 Col. [Art] Williams, B.G. Airways' American-born head, when they opened the Kaieteur run in 1935 (1/18/1954): A pilot and mechanic from Wisconsin, Art Williams played a key role in the development of British Guiana's air transport. He arrived in the colony in 1924 and set himself up as a bush pilot, ferrying people and goods between Georgetown and a number of landing strips in the interior. He founded British Guiana Airways, the colony's first commercial aviation company, in 1938. After serving in the U.S. Air Force, Williams returned to the colony to continue his work and added several more planes to the fleet, including an amphibious Grumman Goose that could land in creeks. He and his business partner, Harry Wendt, sold B.G. Airways to the colonial government in 1955. By 1957 the colony's air transport network included twenty-one airstrips and forty-three water alighting areas.

67 Harold Russell's book (1/23/1954 letter): Russell's memoir *Victory in My Hands* was of particular interest to Marian because, due to injuries he suffered during World War II, his hands had been amputated. He earned acclaim for his role in *The Best Years of Our Lives* (1946), in which he portrayed a sailor who had lost his hands and dexterously used a pair of prosthetic hooks.

68 (1/23/1954): This is the final entry in Marian's B.G. journal.

69 Foreign Operations Administration (3/27/1954): The Foreign Operations Administration (FOA) was a short-lived agency founded in 1953 to centralize economic and military assistance programs—but not policy decisions—previously overseen by two other agencies. It was abolished in May 1955, after which its functions were transferred to the State Department and, for military matters, the Department of Defense. Dr. Theo Vaughan, an "agricultural

extension and community development specialist," was in charge of "assisting in carrying out self-help housing schemes."

70 University College of the West Indies, at Jamaica (4/4/1954): Opened in 1948 as a college of the University of London; achieved university status in 1962.

71 Jagan and his cohorts have begun their campaign of civil disobedience (4/9/1954): On April 1, Jagan's movements were restricted to Georgetown through 1957. As a form of civil disobedience, he violated the restriction on April 3; following his arrest, hearing, release on bail, and subsequent re-arrest for speaking to a gathering, Jagan was imprisoned for five months. Days before his release, Janet Jagan was charged with holding a public meeting and possessing a police riot manual; she was imprisoned through January 1955. The couple's incarcerations, along with the blacklisting of PPP members and the restriction of other PPP leaders to their home districts through 1956, effectively paralyzed the party. Meanwhile, Burnham was, in Jagan's words, "left out of the dragnet." Under obligation, like all PPP leaders, to report to the police at regular intervals, Burnham refused to comply, yet he was not arrested.

72 H. had a little incident (4/9/1954): Howard later recalled "the increasingly intense political strife in Georgetown, much of it directed against the English, for whom we were often mistaken." In a description more dramatic than the one Marian sent to her parents, he wrote that the men "began rocking the car as if they would overturn it."

73 Elizabeth and I can get into the U.S. on birth certificates alone (4/19/1954): The family had arrived in B.G. with a single passport for the three of them. Some accommodation was necessary as Marian and Howard would be re-entering the U.S. separately.

74 Glad you like the book (5/15/1954): *West Indian Cookery* by E. Phyllis Clark. From the chapter on feeding babies: "When breast feeding is impossible a mother can take animals' milk (cow's, goat's, [water] buffalo's, etc.) and make it as much like human milk as possible by adding water, sugar, fat, etc."

75 the statue of Queen Victoria that has stood in front of the Law Courts for 60 years was dynamited (5/29/1954): On Empire Day, 1954, as part of the PPP's campaign of civil disobedience, the marble statue's head was knocked off by the blast, as was the left arm holding the orb. The vandalism, which shocked the British, was met with lighthearted approval by Mona Williams and her Guianese classmates at Bishops' High School. The statue was shipped to Britain for repair.

7 Third Avenue, Subryanville

Chapter 5

1954–1955: 7 THIRD AVENUE, SUBRYANVILLE

Marian and Elizabeth were on leave from late June through October 1954. Howard completed the school term, then met up with them in Tacoma. He returned to Georgetown in time to begin the next term and set up house in Subryanville.

October 5, 1954, Tacoma, Washington

Dear Bee—

I should have stayed with you and "rested up" a while longer! Our pace here is getting just grim. I've been cleaning up this little house [in which the family stayed while on leave], doing windows and curtains, and helping Mother a little on the side. Yesterday we were in Seattle from noon until 8:30 p.m. tramping through the stores—including Magnin's, just for fun. I made our reservations for October 21—will arrive in Georgetown on the 24th.

When I got home from visiting you, I was greeted by a letter from Howard describing our [next] house.[76] Sounds wonderfully good. Three and a half years old, clean and light, three bedrooms, freshly painted. It is owned by the man [named Scargall] who has moved into the YMCA as general secretary. Right on the sea wall, the house has a good breeze—and plenty of mosquitoes, but H. has put up some screening on the bedroom windows. I'm awfully anxious to get back!

Had my eyes checked today—a little astigmatism, so now I shall wear glasses for reading. E. had her vaccination and a typhoid booster shot, so I think we're through. Damn well better be—we're just about broke. The lucky people who vacation in England get all their checkups free.

Nearly time to wake up the cherub. My, but I had fun staying with you! Many, many thanks again, sweetie.

Much love,

Marian

Wednesday, 10:45 p.m., October 27, 1954
7 Third Avenue, Subryanville, East Coast Demerara

Dearest Parents—

This will be brief—just to let you know we're settled safely. I'm sleepy! The flight [from Seattle] to N.Y. was fine, but we didn't sleep much. E. slept all the way from the airport to the Neumanns' house and didn't wake up until suppertime, then went to bed. Saturday she napped from 7:30 to 9:30. Idlewild was a frightful mess—hordes of pushing, shoving people— but Mr. Neumann was there to help with the bags and the *nicest* young Pan Am man weighed my three bags in at 40 pounds. My, I was pleased! [En route to Georgetown] we stopped at San Juan, St. Thomas, St. Croix, Antigua, Guadeloupe, Martinique, and Port of Spain. The stops were just for refueling and taking on passengers but they stretched out to over 30 minutes—everyone off the plane, of course. Tiring. We were three hours late but were given a lovely dinner at the Pan Am guesthouse at Port of Spain as consolation. E. was very tired but well behaved.

One of our Atkinson Field neighbors was customs inspector, and as I was first into the airport he just handed me a blank customs declaration to sign. No waiting in line to have passport checked either, as that official came to me. Didn't have to open any bags or make any currency declaration. Some nice young man also let E. go through the gate to where H. was waiting. So easy! It certainly pays to be pleasant to people (H. had bought a beer for the customs man shortly before our plane came in).

The house is amazingly nice. I moved some furniture around yesterday and think our living room is quite attractive. Will get pictures up Saturday. The four boxes H. mailed in Tacoma got here a week ago, so we're enjoying pin-up lamps, plastic dishes, and the new tablecloths—or should I have saved them till Christmas?

John and Howard had the best results from their exams last summer. Not surprising, but gratifying. Out of 55 candidates, H. had five failures. John had four out of 60; but some men had 50 percent failures.

Had tea at the Ramsarans' today—Janet is walking now. Susan and E. had great fun and exhausted each other completely.

E. is fine—head wet with perspiration much of the time and some prickly heat, but it doesn't bother her. She's full of zip. More in a few days—

Much love,
Marian

Sunday, October 31, 1954

Dear All—

Well, here we go again, with Vol. II, No. 1 [of letters from B.G.]. We're very satisfied with this house—it is just as comfortable as H. had written. Today we put up our pictures, so now it really seems like ours. The only casualties of the move seem to be my three pans and the can opener—we've looked everywhere and haven't found them. Yesterday I bought two new pans and what I hope will be a serviceable can opener (wall type, made in Chicago), so now I am sure the old ones will turn up! The house was partly furnished to begin with, and the Scargalls left their stove. It was a two-burner affair, both burners being the solid, slow-to-heat plate type. And the oven! A switch to turn to hot, medium, or low, plus a small thermometer set in the over door. I told dear, understanding H. that since we have our own stove it seemed only sensible to install it, so yesterday he and Ramphal (H.'s lab assistant) fetched it from the Ramsarans' and H. hooked it up. It is a small stove but proved to be heavier than anticipated, and Howard looked a little grim when he said he hoped I'd enjoy it!

Elizabeth eats at a small table in the corner of the dining room, and certainly does better than she was doing sitting with all of us. We blew up the small wading pool the other day and filled it with sand, and she loves it, of course. The only snag is convincing her that the sand stays downstairs in the "box," but I hope to win. Oh my—she's been such a handful that it is a blessing Howard is here to be firm. This morning she threw her sand buckets down the stairs, and after I told her that was not the thing to do she quickly threw down two books and a block. We spoke to her in firm tones. This afternoon just before her nap we told her she was not to wet the bed and H.'s influence won; she finally went to sleep, after throwing out of the bed all dolls, toys, sheets, mattress pad, etc. Bed stayed dry. When I went to take my shower she insisted on coming in, too, as I let her do a few times during the week. But I don't want it to become a habit, so today I said she would have to wait outside. She screamed, howled, etc., and H. took her in our room and closed the door, whereupon she began to kick, still screaming. She calmed down quickly and was reading when I emerged. I'm sure much of it is the aftermath of all the moving and upheaval, but she is really a little demon.

Last night we went to see *Martin Luther* and thought it excellent. Last Wednesday when we were at the Ramsarans', John had just returned from previewing it (he is on the local censor board) and in all the discussion, Mrs. McLaren said she'd be happy to come and stay with E. so that we could go. We shall have to get hold of someone to stay, but it is hard.

One note I love about this house is the fact that our two washbasins are Royal Doulton! Try and beat that.

Yesterday in the stores I noticed so many things that I'm sure are new since I last looked here: dish drainers in pretty colors, packages of colored rubber bands, a plastic child's dish similar to E.'s, musical books like E.'s *Hickory Dickory Dock* (I saw two, and bought *Silent Night*). There are some pretty dolls with the soft plastic skin. And the American can openers were a surprise, too. Mother, I bought a hairbrush for E., handbag size, which I think is just right for her—eight inches or so. Hope you hadn't already found one.

Also spotted Canadian-made Dutch Cleanser, and Howard bought cake mixes, also made in Canada. I've made up one and it's quite good. You add an egg and flavoring, and next time I'll add more than the one teaspoon of vanilla. I made it in the Scargalls' oven, with temperature unknown, and it rose to a volcanic-looking peak at one corner but the texture was still lovely. It all sounds like progress of a sort, doesn't it.

The screening Howard put up is just wonderful. It keeps out all but the smallest of insects, and they aren't as objectionable to me as the huge ones. We have quite a few little lizards here; they're our friends since they eat insects. Had a two-inch frog around the kitchen sink for a few days, but then Howard found it in E.'s bib as he was tying it on her and after he removed it the poor creature must have fled the house. Haven't seen many roaches.

Monday and Tuesday Elizabeth's head was just soaking wet with perspiration, and her face broke out terribly. Evidently she's adjusted now because her perspiration is moderate and her complexion back to normal. She and I are bitten rather badly by sand flies, but we use lots of powder and I don't think she's bothered much. She sleeps soundly, eats pretty well, and drinks canned milk without a question.

Dear me, I seem to be written out. Almost. I succeeded in removing the stains from H.'s three shirts (socks faded all over them once), and you should see the mountain of un-ironed shirts I faced when I got back! All under control now.

All for now. Hope to hear from you soon. No letter this week!

Love to all,

Marian

Sunday, November 7, 1954

Dear Family—

It strikes me, now that we really are settled, that I wrote nothing at all of our trip [back here] to Bee, and precious little to you parents. Since aspects of it struck me as funny, I'll start with the time we left Tacoma.

Elizabeth was a little frightened by the strangeness of the plane, even though she was well prepared for it all. She insisted on being held, didn't want to take off her coat or hat or me to take off my coat—and we were both perspiring after the bustle of getting on. We finally got settled, and she dropped off to sleep about the time we hit Portland. She slept as far as Denver, and then it seemed to me that she never did sleep soundly the rest of the flight. Hard on me, I might say, since I was dying to sleep! She reacted to the lavatories immediately and with great vigor—*no*. I don't remember what time we got into Chicago, about 8 or 9 I think, but she was a perfect lady, waiting until we got there and went to the airport restroom. We also stopped at Cleveland and used the facilities there. The poor child didn't sleep at all (not poor child—she was having a high old time opening surprise packages and eating goodies) until five minutes before we landed in New York. Then, of course, I had to wake her up and she was most unhappy about that. A gentleman sitting across the aisle offered to help so he carried the bag (it weighed 25 pounds, Bee, and both the grandfathers had serious doubts about how I would manage with it) and I carried E. Mr. Neumann wasn't there at the moment, so this nice stranger led us to the counter where we were to claim our baggage, and then offered to claim mine for me. I accepted, thanked him, etc. and he wouldn't take the money I offered him to tip the baggage men. He had a little girl E.'s age, he said, and two boys in an Episcopal school who were homesick and whom he was on his way to visit. Just as he brought my bags, Mr. Neumann strode up and we were set. Elizabeth went to sleep in his car, slept all the way to Bayside, and didn't wake up when I removed her coat, hat, and shoes before putting her to bed. I woke her for supper and put her back to bed right afterward. I slept well Friday night, too, and Saturday we puttered around. Thank goodness we arranged for that stopover!

The New York International Airport is just grim—*awful*. I suppose I wrote the parents about the huge crowd in the inadequate space at the check-in stands; they pushed and shoved with no regard for anyone else.

I'd still be there if Mr. Neumann hadn't been with us juggling all four bags and doing his share of the pushing. I even began to elbow a little when I thought a man was worming his way in front of us; in broken English he explained that he was just with a friend who was going. So I asked if he would move so that I could sit E. on the counter. She took a dim view of the idea, but there she sat, crying, while I dealt with the dearest Pan Am man. Really the dearest, considering that he marked our baggage weight as 40 pounds instead of the 100-plus that it was, and didn't even mention extra charges. He also told me which gate we'd be going through, and that enabled us to be first in line there, hence first on the plane. Elizabeth was simply dead and so was I, but as soon as she was settled she asked for a surprise package and was delighted with the tiny baby doll.

We reached Puerto Rico about 8 a.m. and only had half an hour there. The announced time was 20 minutes, so we dashed up the stairs (dashed—me dragging E. and the 25-pound bag) to the Pan Am restroom, plopped E. on the toilet, and changed from our knit dress and viyella jumper to cooler clothes. I had planned on brushing teeth and hair and doing it up right, but as it was I didn't even take time to go to the john. We hurried downstairs, and this time no gallant male helped me as I lurched down carrying both bag and E., who was insisting on being held. We were on a DC-7 from New York to Puerto Rico, with 93 aboard. At Puerto Rico we switched to DC-6s, two of them, each stopping at different islands en route to Port of Spain. That island-hopping routine is the limit, and if any of you ever dream of visiting us, do get a first-class ticket and avoid it all! We stopped at St. Thomas, St. Croix, Antigua, Guadeloupe, and Martinique before Port of Spain, and none of them had even decent toilet facilities. I was thankful E. had her own seat to use. At one place there was a questionable-looking roller towel, so we used mama's slip to dry our hands. The only good thing about the stops was the opportunity for E. to stretch her legs. "Now run!" I told her every time, and she ran as far as she could go in one direction and then turned around and ran back. I traipsed after her and stretched my legs, too. All those stops were supposed to be 30 minutes each, but somehow by the time we reached Trinidad we were three hours late. Instead of the scheduled box lunch, we were driven to the Piarco Guest House for a lovely buffet dinner, but E. was unhappy over her [stopped-up] ears so she didn't want to eat anything and I couldn't do much with her sitting in my lap. They had cold turkey, ham, deviled eggs, fresh pineapple, avocados, etc. Very nice. I did enjoy my iced tea! Back to the plane, and we endured the two hours to Atkinson somehow. Both tired by then—I was really too far gone to amuse E. satisfactorily.

Another kind man carried E. into the airport and by some strange fate we were the first in. A young East Indian who lived across the street from us at the airbase was the customs officer, and he handed me a blank customs declaration to sign and took my passport over to the official in charge of reading passports. I wasn't even asked about my U.S. currency, much less asked to sign that declaration. Our suitcases were checked off without being opened, and it wasn't long before we were in the car on our way into town. H. said later he'd bought Desmond (the customs man) a beer and told him that we didn't have anything much to declare. Desmond said he'd make it as easy as possible, and he certainly did!

Which gets us up to the present. We've been busy this week. Tuesday the Ramsarans came over and had tea with us, after a rather wild morning. It rained over four inches on Tuesday, most of it around the noon hour. Tuesday mornings the egg man leaves our eggs with Margaret, John supposedly takes them to H., who brings them home at noon. Well, John had forgotten and H. had forgotten to get them from Margaret. I had none yet had to bake something for the afternoon tea. At 2 p.m. H.'s lab assistant brought the eggs, and I whipped up a white cake mix, and the last of the cupcakes were just in the oven when the Ramsaran family came at 2:30. The cupcakes were delicious; I'd made pink icing in the morning and that touch really saved the day. Margaret very seldom has iced cakes for tea. Unfortunately on Thursday H. couldn't get more cake mix at Yong Hing's—I do hope it appears again as it is good and so easy.

Wednesday we went downtown and bought some Christmas presents and Christmas cards. Wednesday evening and Thursday we wrote cards like fury, and Friday H. mailed them just before the deadline. Sent off a box to Bee so you all had just better spend Christmas together! Elizabeth is all excited about Santa Claus, presents, etc.—as excited as she can be considering she doesn't really know what it's all about. The words "surprise" and "presents" do mean something, however.

At Howard's request I have spent some of the weekend cutting off the sleeves of seven shirts. I did one as a trial and must agree with him that the short sleeves look much neater than rolled-up long sleeves. Much cooler, too.

Today Howard made up a strong DDT solution and sprayed our bedrooms. He doesn't have many mosquito bites, but E. seemed to have a new one every morning and my arms are a sight. He sprayed in our wardrobe and encountered eight or ten in there, so following the spraying he installed two light globes, which will keep our clothes mildew-free and dry enough that the mosquitoes won't be encouraged. We also cleaned out some junk of the Scargalls' that was cluttering the garage, and hung clotheslines there. I don't think the rain ever will come in there, yet the breeze is good.

Tomorrow is a holiday, and Howard is taking Ramphal (the lab assistant) and Chan, a 6th-former, out to Atkinson for the day. He is also (1) taking the Frangos [chocolates] to Zela, (2) hunting a small shade plant for my copper planter, and (3) keeping his eyes peeled for a likely-looking Christmas tree!

We've asked Pete to have dinner with us this Wednesday evening. The Allsopps live just a few blocks away and we're anxious to have them over.

Oh yes—yesterday Elizabeth and I made fruitcake. We sampled it last night, and it seems too moist again. I didn't brush it with rum, just wrapped it up and put it away. Maybe it will dry out some of its own accord? Any suggestions? It looks lovely and tastes delicious but won't cut nicely into thin slices. Or does that come with age?

All for now. Much love to you all,

Marian

Sweet parents, I can never really thank you enough for the lovely summer you gave us. It was all such fun, and seems to have put B.G. back into proper perspective. Sure, we don't have everything here we'd like to have, but what is at home won't run away before we get back permanently.

And just being with you two and Bee was wonderful. It is so cute to hear Elizabeth speak of you all—Grandmother's rain hat (did it start to rain one day when you were in the park? So she told me) and Grampa Tom's car. Yesterday she patted a fender on our car and said "American car"—surprised, we said no, it was a British car but that Grampa Tom's car is an American car. And she does talk about the "pretty new house" and she spends lots of time making cookies (patting rubber bands).

Well, dears, must go press those seven shirts and put them away.

Love to you both,

Marian

Sunday, November 14, 1954

Dear All—

Did I mention that last week we got two of the boxes Mother and I shipped off? One had all my seersucker underwear in it, the other had lampshades and poppy seeds and other miscellany. The strange thing is that so far we've had no package notices for the other boxes. No, I'm wrong—the underwear and poppy seeds were in one box; the second box was Elizabeth's pram. Thursday we got a big batch of magazines and thought perhaps the boxes would be with that shipment, but evidently not. Howard is getting anxious about the record [he needs for the school's coming production of] *The Tempest,* which was sent airmail from Vancouver over a week ago. His mother sent the letter from the man who sent the record, and theoretically both letter and record should have arrived together. The play, if it comes off, will be given in less than four weeks.

Wednesday evening Pete had dinner with us and recommended his maid, Patrine, to us as a babysitter. He says she is honest and has initiative, and today she came by to see me. Thursday afternoon she will come by and play with Elizabeth for a while and get acquainted, and then we'll have her to call on when we need her. Except on Wednesday and Sunday nights when she "has to go to church." Pete says Agnes hopes to have her B.A. by the end of the year. She's doing two years' work in one, taking beginning French as an elective, and reading proof on the paper as well. She had to go back to school because the Minnesota laws have changed and teachers must have a B.A.

Last week the major topic of discussion was the report of the Constitutional Commission, and maybe you read about it in *Time.* B.G. will continue for the next three years with the same emergency government that we now have, and at the end of that time the situation will be reevaluated. The local people are bitter about it, anticipating military occupation for the next decade at least. But the Commission reported that PPP strength was great and the country unready for self-government.[77]

This week the report of the Hands Committee on Government Salaries was released, and it brought another kind of storm. All government salaries were reviewed and increases made to compensate for the higher cost of living. Howard's salary, at present $4800, was recommended boosted to $6720. We thought goody, goody! until Howard heard all the dissension and griping among the masters at Q.C. Some of the men object to the committee's recommendation that expatriate civil servants be granted money for their families' passages; many don't like the suggestion that expatriates should be provided with housing. A major gripe is that private companies will have to follow suit and grant raises, then prices will go up, and with the increased cost of living, the poor farmers and pensioners will be worse off than ever. So maybe we won't get our increase—at this point we certainly aren't counting on it.

Elizabeth has been so exasperating lately that last Sunday we checked in the baby books to see if something couldn't be done. Nothing to do but sit it out—she sounds like a perfectly normal two-and-a-half-year-old, but it sure is harder to live with than the books make it sound. She is contrary, she can't make up her mind, she whines, she clings, she is fiercely independent, she wants to help, etc. She is still wetting the bed but a few hard spankings from her daddy have convinced her she really shouldn't. She's just too stubborn to give it up gracefully. It's comforting to know it's normal, but we'll be relieved when this stage has passed!

She spent most of the morning in the wading pool today, splashing, drinking, and pouring from one bucket to another. Every day she spends some time in the sand box. Thank goodness we came back with that set of plastic dishes. She loves to mess around the sink while I'm washing them, and I think that, so far, we'd have broken about three china dishes. She's just about memorized four new books—two that were surprises on the plane, and two that Howard's mother brought over to Tacoma. I hear her whisper "When Jimmy was a baby," or "Daddy brought home three downy baby chicks," and away we go. Sometimes she'll put in all the words of a story that she knows, and other times she just sits and grins. Yesterday we made some cookies. I used the cookie press, and on some Elizabeth carefully placed two raisins. After a while she got bored with waiting for the pan to come out of the oven, so she began washing dishes, then decided to wash the hand towel in the greasy bowl that had held the dough. She had a fine time and ended up by putting everything in the drainer. It was rather messy, but since it couldn't hurt anything I let her splash.

All for now.
Much love to each of you,
Marian

Sunday, November 21, 1954

Dear All—

Tuesday afternoon was a school holiday because of a cricket match, so Howard took us downtown to do some shopping. I bought a lovely Minton plate that, with some spritz cookies, will be the Ramsarans' Christmas present. The pattern is called Lothian and consists of a border of ivy leaves and small yellow-gold flowers. Margaret's china has green and gold bands around the edge, and I thought this would go well.

Also bought a couple of picture frames. Remember the photograph you sent last year from Sun Valley? We framed that and now Elizabeth has it in her room on her dresser, plus a little snapshot of the Irwins. She's quite tickled to have them, needless to say.

We saw quite a display of Christmas ornaments in Fogarty's, so I bought a dozen little ones. They are quite ordinary—"traditional"—but pretty. More stuff around than I've seen here before. They had lovely Irish linen embroidered pillowcases at Bookers—and soaps and perfumes and all sorts of things that only come before Christmas. I also bought six dear wineglasses, but more about that later.

Howard was scheduled to record a talk on taxonomy to be given over the radio; the recording was to be made on Tuesday. Sunday he wrote the talk and Monday I madly typed it out, only to find that the whole deal is postponed until this Friday. He had a bad time figuring out what he could say about taxonomy that would interest women (it's for a program series called "Invitation to Women"), and finally settled on a large proportion concerning evolution, origins of life, etc. with taxonomy tucked on at the last.

We had the Sanger-Davieses to dinner last night and it was a rather odd evening. I asked them to come about 6, but she said that Joe was playing cricket and that they had to get some bridge in (part of a tournament) and how about 7:15 or so. I said fine, and H. and I agreed that they probably wouldn't show up until 8. Around 7:30 she called and apologized for being late and asked for directions to our house, which H. gave. He went down a few minutes later and opened the gate, turned on lights, etc. and then a little while later saw their car pass our turn. He got in our car and chased after them, caught up, and found Mrs. S-D walking, fighting mad. She blamed H. for giving wrong directions and was her usual charming self, but had calmed down by the time they arrived (close to 8!). We had spaghetti and garlic bread and salad, and I'd hoped to have Burgundy but they don't sell it here (I shall have to take up sherry in order to make good my investment in the wineglasses). It was all new to the S-Ds, and of course I don't know if they liked it or loathed it. I suppose I could have had a "joint" and been safe, but I decided that, what the hell, we eat English food at all their houses, why shouldn't they sample our style once in a while? Mr. S-D wore a suit, something of a concession for him, but it had a hole in a rather awkward place. And of course, he lounged with his foot in the chair. I always have such dreadful mixed emotions about them: in some respects they are friendly but I suspect that is chiefly because we're white, and in so many respects they are just plain crude.

Thursday is Thanksgiving and Pete is going to have dinner with us. Friday is Speech Day but all the ceremony comes at a bad time, so I think I'll skip it. The S-Ds are having a cocktail party afterward, starting at about 6, so I'll get Elizabeth in bed and then, if Patrine can stay, we'll go imbibe for a bit.

I finally finished the dresses for [dolls] Nancy and Mary and they certainly are cute. I suspect that I have more fun making them than E., at this age, has playing with them, but that's okay. Nancy's is a little pink print with white rickrack around the hem and plain bound neck. Mary's is the same print in yellow with two rows of blue rickrack around the waist. I'm now working on blue seersucker overalls for Dennis, plus a pink-white-blue striped seersucker shirt. Elizabeth will be just delighted with the pram—if she were a few years older I would suspect her motives in all the talking she's done lately about a pram! Sometimes a basket is her pram, sometimes the doll bed. She'll say, "We don't have a pram. We should buy one." So matter-of-fact!

We sent H.'s mother a silver filigree bracelet for her birthday, which is December 4. When you see it, Mother, let me know if you think anyone else would like one. They are made locally—also necklaces, earrings, etc. and it has taken me this long to decide if I like them. They're very delicate and some of the work is lovely but I guess I just don't like it for me.

All for tonight. Happy Thanksgiving, everybody!

Much, much love to each of you,

Marian

Sunday, November 28, 1954

Dear All—

I don't feel inspired tonight, but had better plunge in anyway. Our electric current was off from 1 to 5:45 this afternoon—the electric company was installing something new and it was announced beforehand that it would be off from 1 to 5. So we had dinner an hour late and now it's 8:30 and I guess it's too late to catch up on some ironing that I had, virtuously, planned on doing this evening.

The most cheering aspect of the week, as far as we're concerned, is that we seem to be over the bed-wetting hurdle. Spanking was obviously doing no good, so we thought and thought and now (I suppose it would be poorly regarded by professionals) we are using simple bribery. The reward is one small piece of candy if she's a good girl, and so far it hasn't failed. She still tells me that Baby Dolly wet the bed or Mary wet the bed so she knows that they won't get their candy, and we tut-tut together about that. So peace is restored, and I hope it lasts throughout the rainy season, which should be commencing in earnest any day now.

Wednesday afternoon we spent with the Ramsarans, and before the men came from school we indulged in what Margaret called "a good moan" over the S-Ds and their trying ways. It must be ghastly having to work closely with them, as John has to as director of this play [*The Tempest*]. Howard is having his own troubles. He's doing the music and has 45 different cues to get just right; for weeks and weeks, S-D has said that the amplifiers, speakers, and turntables were all ordered and would be put in "soon." Just the other day H. was talking to the electrician who'd come to install the wiring, and that man had never heard of the turntables that H. needs. The question now is whether the things are available here—two 78s and one LP, all manual. The play begins December 14 and even the two remaining weeks don't give much time for practice.

On Thursday, Patrine and Elizabeth spent an enjoyable afternoon playing in the sandbox and reading. I think she'll be fine to come at night, once E. is in bed and asleep, if we don't expect too much more. It is just too hard for me to leave Elizabeth with someone even for a dinner-bath-bed period, if I can't be sure she'll do it just right, and I can't quite see any local girls doing it as I would. (Mabel was certainly an exception.) Actually we don't need one often anyway.

We had a lovely Thanksgiving dinner, if I do say so. We had chicken with mushroom soup and sherry—how easy can a good dinner be! It is expensive here, but well worth it for special occasions. The soup is 48 cents here; veg. is 36 cents. It is Campbell's, made in Canada. H. bought Sandeman sherry at $5, which seems high to us but I don't have any idea what it is at home. Let's see—for dinner we also had scalloped eggplant, beans, and the lime Jell-O and pear salad. Did I tell you that recipe is in Rombauer? It calls for a little vinegar and ginger and I just recognized it by chance—it's one, Bee, that H.'s mother gave me and is delicious.

Friday was Speech Day and we got all gussied up in stockings and blue suit. His Excellency the Governor was there; also His Grace the Archbishop. S-D gave a longwinded oration about placing less value on the results of the external examinations, especially by employers, and more emphasis on the old virtues—honesty, reliability, etc. He also said the cooperation and eagerness shown by the staff and deputy principal had, he was sure, made the year a memorable one. We can't imagine a situation where much less cooperation and enthusiasm could exist, but he apparently is blind to that.

After the ceremonies a select crowd adjourned to the principal's house for cocktails. We had one drink and then picked Elizabeth up at the Ramsarans' house, where Mrs. McLaren had offered to take care of her. It was 7 and E. was practically asleep on her feet.

At the S-Ds' I had a chance to chat with Joy Allsopp, and I'm sure I shocked Margaret by greeting Richard by his first name. The poor Allsopps are at present under great suspicion by the English members of the staff. (To be accurate, I should say that Mrs. S-D asked, "Is Allsopp Red?" and that the Ramsarans will have nothing to do with them because of things said in the staff room, presumably anti-British and pro-Guiana.) He is apt to speak rather wildly and we know firsthand that he hates the British, but we've never heard anything overtly Communist from him. And Joy is a lovely girl and I do like her.

Elizabeth picks up new words and phrases all the time. Everything is "delicious" now since we've read that in a book. The other day I gave her apple juice for the first time since we've been back, and she said, "I love apple juice, Muvver," which tickled me immensely. I gave her a taste of ice cream yesterday as I beat it, and she "loved that," too. And the way she quotes from books is astounding, especially if she's trying to get my attention. When I'm reading to her, she may add a word here and there, but she says whole passages if she thinks it will get me interested. Usually it does.

Hard to believe that December is almost upon us. I finished a natty outfit for Dennis and made an apron for Elizabeth—a tie-around that won't be too practical but is just like mine.

H. received a letter from London—the fourth year is okayed, which—hurray!—means we'll keep on getting our subsidies. It was made clear that this is the final renewal. Guess they don't want us on the permanent payroll!

Much love to each of you,

Marian

Sunday, December 5, 1954

Dear Parents—

We got all excited last Friday because Howard received a package notice that said three packages had arrived; we assumed they would be the records, books, etc. that I sent off in October. Strangely enough, they were the three parcels from Mother, mailed almost exactly a month ago. It sets a record for quickness, I suppose, but we do wish those others would arrive. Mother, would you call the Sixth Avenue P.O. and ask to have an inquiry started? We mailed them on October 2, and we mailed seven boxes that day. Three have arrived, and of the remaining four, one is addressed to Mr. J. A. Ramsaran, one is addressed to Mrs. J. A. Ramsaran, and the other two to H., all at Q.C. I don't remember what day we mailed the last two but probably they're all stuck on some awfully slow boat.

Howard has scarcely been home at all this weekend. It developed last week that S-D just wasn't on the ball about getting an electrician to set up the switchboard for all the lights on the stage, so Howard and the chemistry master, Mr. Barker, decided to do it. Yesterday H. left the house at 7:30 to buy fruit and get the packages, and came back with them an hour later: two minutes at home. Back to school and to work until 11:40, when he came home, ate his lunch, and left in 10 minutes. He worked until 6:30, came home for dinner (half an hour), and returned until 9 or so. Most of today they worked, too, but at least the job is finished and it works. It all sounds complicated to me—Howard says it was more tedious than difficult. It burns me up to think that S-D just didn't bother to hire it done; Howard says he did it himself because he wanted to have some time to rehearse with it, and if it had been done by an electrician chances are it wouldn't have been finished until the night before the first performance. S-D expressed admiration at the way H. and Barker got "right down to work" and said that no English school master would do that; H. replied, "But, sir, I'm not English," and that was that.

Elizabeth is getting all keyed up about Christmas. I know I shall regret having started it so early, but I couldn't resist; next year, no doubt, I'll know better. She went around today swinging a little bag that was the "pack on her back, full of candy and toys." Life goes on smoothly; no bed-wetting. She told me this evening, "You did wet the bed once" as if it were a long, long time ago. (She still says "you" when she means "I.")

E. and I made fondant yesterday. Half of it we made into peppermint and wintergreen patties, which turned out very nicely. The other half, alas, we combined with candied cherries, citron, and dates and it just won't firm up. I added powdered sugar but that doesn't seem to help. At present, I think I'll melt it down someday and use it as a cake filling. It tastes lovely. I was surprised that our dirty, coarse sugar could turn into such nice fondant.

Howard says to please return the stamps on these letters. They are our new issue, and he has no canceled stamps yet. He would also like you to send down the new U.S. presidential issues, canceled, as you get them. Mother, you did nobly on those three packages. Such an array of stamps!

I am reading *The Age of Jackson*, although how we came to have a copy of it I certainly don't know. Very interesting but it certainly points up my inadequate grasp of U.S. history.

Much love to you all,
Marian

December 9, 1954

Dear Bee,

It is just 6:30 and dinner is over, dishes done, Elizabeth bathed and in bed—and H. gone out to another rehearsal of *The Tempest*. Gads, such a production. It will all be over in another week, but at this point a week is a long time away! Howard is doing all the sound effects, ranging from howling dogs to thunder to "God Save the Queen" at the end. He has three turntables to juggle and something like 40 music cues as well. Then he and one of the other men pitched in and built a switchboard for all the electrical fittings on the stage; they did this after giving up all hope of the principal hiring someone to do it. Took the entire weekend but it works and is done. Saturday night is the dress rehearsal and I am to help dress the boys then as well as for the four performances. Such fun, pinning and sewing a lot of nervous, sweaty boys into costumes. Oh well, it is sort of fun and I certainly haven't contributed much to the play as yet.

I was flabbergasted last night when H. announced that the Q.C. masters are planning a Christmas party, stag, to be held in the history room of the school. At first they were planning on one bottle of rum per every four men per hour, but eventually they got it down to a mere bottle per every four men, period. This is with the principal's sanction, too. Can you imagine having a drinkin' party in any school in the States!

Much love,

Marian

Sunday, December 12, 1954

Dear All—

I just finished ironing ten stiffly starched Elizabethan ruffs, two capes, and one pair of breeches with shirt. Am exhausted but will do my best to bring you all up to date.

At last, all the packages I sent in October have arrived. The records were all in fine shape. One of the boxes was completely burst open—Howard was given the contents in a mailbag! It had lots of Elizabeth's books in it, some new pants for her (four pairs), some socks (six pairs), brown candles, a toy for Janet, and some plaid bias tape. Missing is a little box of birthday candles and so far as I can remember, that's all. Can't understand why it all collapsed, but at least most of it arrived.

Last night was the dress rehearsal of *The Tempest.* I went over at 4:30 to help dress the boys, and although there was confusion it was certainly better organized confusion than prevailed at *Twelfth Night.* After the play, pictures were taken and it was 10 when we got home—a long, long evening. The play went quite well and the sets are really outstanding. All the electrical work paid off, too, for the lighting and sound effects are the best we've seen here. I had difficulty understanding lots of the boys, but most of that is just because I still have trouble with local pronunciation.

Our most interesting news this week concerns the house. Last Thursday night while Howard was at Q.C., Mr. Perreira (our next-door neighbor) called and explained that (1) he has bought the house (it is a duplex), and (2) if we want to stay here permanently we may. Friday when H. talked to him he explained that we would love to stay but felt some concern for the Scargalls. Mr. Perreira said that the old contract was null and void, that as the new owner he could choose his own tenant, etc. etc. Saturday afternoon Mr. Scargall came over and was perfectly affable about it all but said it came as a shock to them because they are fond of this house, too. Mr. Scargall's chief concern was [for us] to get a written statement from Mr. Perreira that we could stay until the end of May since that was our agreement with him. He strongly implied that Mr. P. might change his mind on a sudden whim and shoo us out, too. *But* since Mr. Perreira told Howard that they liked quiet neighbors (I guess we are) and said we could stay the year and a half we'll be here, we feel there is a bit of friction between the two gentlemen. H. has heard that Mr. Scargall isn't too considerate; they have three noisy boys and H. says Mrs. S. is a little crude, all of which may mean that the Perreiras just don't want the Scargalls living next door. We shall keep the Scargalls' furniture here, since they haven't room for it at present and we really do need some of it. We will really be delighted if it works out—it's such a nice house and the thought of moving again is just repulsive.

Did I tell you about the Christmas aprons I made for Elizabeth and me? They are of dark green Indian Head with triangular pockets that I outlined in red rickrack, gave a brown trunk, and decorated with embroidered ornaments. Real cute, and E. will be delighted, I'm sure.

One night last week I created some elegant ornaments by cutting a snowflake shape out of paper lace doilies, then scattering silver sprinkles over it. I've also had fun with the colored paper since that arrived.

Off to bed now.

Much love,

Marian

Sunday, December 19, 1954

Dear Family—

We lived through the week and the play went off with no more than the minimum of slips, so everyone was pleased and reasonably happy. Patrine stayed with Elizabeth three nights, and one evening she did my whole week's ironing, unasked! Amazing. Pete stayed on Wednesday night because that is Patrine's church-going night. After Christmas Margaret plans on washing all the costumes that were used, and I shall help with that. If you can imagine a bunch of boys, normally rather odoriferous, sweating profusely under the combined effects of stage lights, nervousness, and heavy garments, you can imagine the reek of the costumes. Charming task to look forward to! I nearly passed out pressing them between performances.

The staff's stag party was last night, starting at 8:30. Howard came home at 1 but the party was still going. He said it did great things for fellowship and goodwill and all that, and no one got out of hand. S-D was there and enjoyed himself tremendously, and John the non-drinker went and stayed until 12:30—H. said he seemed to be having a wonderful time.

I had a lovely time this morning making cookies, and my little helper alternately amused and exasperated me. We made spritz cookies and decorated them with red and green candied cherries, and then we made a batch of sugar cookies and cut them out in star and tree shapes. How Elizabeth loves to cut out cookies! The only trouble was that she didn't quite get the idea of leaving a little space between them, so every time I turned my back she chop-chop-chopped with the cookie cutter and crowed over her cookies. "You are a big help to Muvver," she said several times, and who has the heart to resist that! I put white frosting on the stars (she was in bed at this time) and sprinkled colored sprinkles on them. They all look pretty and now I feel anyone can drop in and there will be something ready.

The Maudsleys' transfer to Kenya has come through and they are mighty happy about it. There are seven staff men who want to move into their house, and most of them have already asked us if we want it, since I guess we'd be the logical first choice. Ken was quite alarmed when we said no. There may be a big battle about who gets the house, since in theory if one local man gets a government house (rent 10 percent of salary) the others should have the same opportunity. And the Ramsarans' house will be open for six months and those same seven men would like to get into that for even six months, to save on rent. We have heard nothing further about our deal here but assume that all is well.

Let's see—we go to the Ramsarans' on Christmas Day (hope we can pry E. away from her toys), and on Sunday we plan to snag Pete and have him come for a drink at least. On Monday the Allsopps are going to have dinner with us and that will be fun. Chicken and mushroom soup and aha! Ocean Spray cranberry sauce "grown and packed in the Pacific Northwest," which for me at least will make the meal.

This is such an exciting season, I just can't wait to see Elizabeth on Christmas morning! Shall write you all about it, of course. Merry Christmas to you all, and much, much love,

Marian

Sunday, December 26, 1954

Dear Mother and Daddy—

Christmas gets to be more and more fun, but it seems to take me longer to recover. My—such a busy time we've had. On Thursday Howard drove out to the airbase and dug up two trees—one for us, and one for the Ramsarans. He also cut some pretty greens and the orange spike-like flowers we had last Christmas. All this he did in the rain and I'm surprised he hasn't caught a cold.

Friday was busy. E. and I did a huge washing and baked more cookies and some sweet rolls. We all ate at the same time, and after dinner and E.'s bath we put out a sandwich, cookies, and a glass of cold water for Santa. You should have seen the enchanted but puzzled look on her face. We hung up the stocking and H. read *The Night Before Christmas* to her, and off to bed she went.

Our tree looks just lovely—lots of ornaments per square inch, but I love it that way. We unwrapped all the packages from home (carefully saving twine, wrapping paper, newspaper stuffing, and tissue padding for future use) and H. put up the pram. The doll swing arrived, in perfect shape—so did everything else. You all are much better packers than I!

Yesterday morning I awoke at 6 when the paperboy opened our gate, and eventually I woke up Howard. I dressed and started fixing breakfast, then woke up E. about 6:45. She emptied her stocking and we ate (H. fed E. nearly everything—her mind was not on food). She marveled at the fact that Santa was hungry and had eaten the sandwich and cookies and drunk most of the water. She said the tree was beautiful, and was smitten with the unwrapped pram from the first glance but was a bit doubtful at first of whether it was really hers.

After breakfast we began opening in earnest. Such fun! After about half the packages were opened E. became overwhelmed and retired to the sidelines with Nancy and the new doll clothes. Howard is so pleased with the records, and I nearly died at the cold meat fork "in absentia"—aren't you cute! The towels are really too pretty to use in our plain-Jane kitchen—I shall probably hem them and then put them away till we're back in pretty kitchens. My, they're pretty.

This morning, early, I had the blocks dumped on me in bed ("Make a post office—*please*, Mommy, make a post office!") and heaven help me, I had to sing "Farmer in the Dell" before washing my face. E. is delighted with the powder mitt, and the pajamas look awfully sweet on her. We've put the puzzle away for a quiet day, and we haven't really had time for books yet, either. That counting book has the dearest pictures.

By 10 a.m. on Christmas Elizabeth was exhausted, so we put her to bed, cleared up the papers and ribbons, washed dishes, and collapsed, too. We went to the Ramsarans' at noon and had a lovely dinner, and the children played hard. The Maudsleys came over for tea, after which we all played some games, had a drink, and came home at 7. A long, full day, and a happy one.

Today we recovered—E. splashed happily in the dishpan the Irwins sent, washing all her new dishes and pans. And the pram was constantly with her. Such a happy child!

Tomorrow night the Allsopps come for dinner, and I hope the Ramsarans can all come New Year's Eve. Howard goes a-traveling from January 4 to 7, up to the savannah at Orealla to collect some plant specimens, we hope, for his thesis work.

Much love from all of us, and many thank-you's for the lovely presents. I wish you were here!

Love,

Marian

Many thanks for the three Haydns and the Mozart 40th. Was the 55th ("The School Master") an accidental overside comparison? —H.

Tuesday, December 28, 1954

Dearest Bee—

My stars, such a Christmas! Howard and I had such fun getting everything set for Elizabeth, and of course she was enchanted by everything. But first—I love the pajamas and would like to wear them all day long! So cool.

We went to John and Margaret's at noon Christmas Day for a big dinner, followed by tea at 4, then a drink and more to eat. Stuffo! We got home at 7, E. all worn out. It was fun but we resolved to stay home on future Christmases, at least as long as there are little children. It just doesn't work out the way we like.

Sunday we relaxed, and yesterday we had Joy and Richard Allsopp to dinner. Richard still seems pretty PPP-ish; otherwise we had a fine time.

On Friday the Ramsarans are coming for dinner, which means coming at 5 so the children can play a little before bedtime. There will probably be bedlam before we manage to eat at 7:30 or 8. I shall plan an easy dinner!

By the way, you did mention, didn't you, that you'd sent off the steam iron? I still owe you for it, and now I'm getting anxious for it because my big iron, our school pal, has given out so many times that H. can no longer repair it. I'm using my travel iron but that's not too satisfactory and I know from experience that when used steadily something burns out quickly.

Two of H.'s relatives sent us checks, and today I had fun spending part of the money. I bought some Repartee cologne (Lenthéric) and some Rose Geranium soap, which should keep me going for quite some time. I do love nice soap. And a little blotter and inlaid box to keep pens, paper clips, etc. in. We've sent a lot of local stuff home but bought little for ourselves.

We'll be thinking of you on New Year's Eve—toast you with a chaste glass of sherry, or something!

Much, much love,

Marian

Saturday, January 1, 1955

Dear All—

Well, kiddies, Happy New Year. I'll bet you all have had a mighty busy time in Los Angeles; we've been busy, too. Let's see. Last Monday was Boxing Day and we had the Allsopps to dinner. Tuesday morning we went downtown and I bought some soap and perfume, gifts from some of H.'s relatives. Wednesday night Pete stopped by for a while. Thursday night H. and I went to see *White Christmas*, which, to us, just didn't quite have it. There was a gorgeous short about Norway in VistaVision that was worth the price of admission.

Last night the Ramsarans came for dinner, and it turned out to be a rather botched-up affair. We went on the assumption that all the children would go quietly to bed, leaving the adults free to talk, listen to records, etc. Ha! Elizabeth and Susan had supper together, and then Elizabeth went to bed and fell asleep quickly. Janet was terrified of the little crib and refused to be put in it, so Margaret and John took turns holding her. Susan went to bed, but halfway through dinner she got up again because Janet wasn't in bed and why should *she* have to go to bed if Janet wasn't, etc. So—we finished dinner with Janet on John's lap, eating a cracker and cranberry jelly and custard, and Susan on Margaret's lap, eating a Brussels sprout, cranberry jelly, and Floating

Island. They never did go to bed, and Susan managed to stay awake until midnight—quite something for a five-year-old. Janet dozed, but it couldn't have been much fun for the children or parents. Our dinner was good, and the Floating Island (dash of rum in the custard) entranced the children no end.

Today we took down the tree, mistletoe, red candles, leaves and berries, cards and ribbons, etc. and we feel awfully barren. The chief consolation is that once again we can open all the windows without fear of everything blowing down!

Elizabeth is having such fun with all the new toys. To date, she has constructed houses, post offices, churches, planes, tables, chairs, and beds with the blocks, and four little round rods have been Tammy, Janet, Betsy, and Susan all afternoon. At one point they were kissed goodbye and put on the airplane to go see Auntie Barbara in California.

Howard is all packed for tomorrow. He'll leave here at 7:30 a.m. and drive to Rosignol, where he trusts he'll catch the 10:45 ferry to New Amsterdam. From there he drives 50 miles over a questionable road to Skeldon, where he'll spend the night, leaving Monday morning by launch for Orealla [in East Berbice on the Corentyne River, adjacent to Suriname]. His equipment includes the usual presses for collecting plants, plus canned food, crackers, cot, net, band-aids, etc. We're holding the thought that the weather will be good at least part of the week: this is really the rainy season and he may have to sneak out between showers.

Howard's parents sent me the loveliest beige linen tablecloth with a wheat design in brown and gold. We used it Monday night, with my brown candles in the copper candelabra, and it was beautiful to behold; unfortunately, those new brown candles burned all the way down during dinner, due to the constant breeze. Last night my centerpiece was yellow and orange cosmos, chrysanthemums, marigolds, and gaillardia in the copper "water pan" of my chafing dish. I do so enjoy having flowers to play around with! I've had an arrangement in the living room with anthurium lilies (three), white chrysanthemums, and sprigs of red geraniums, tiny red zinnias and red balsam together with green leaves and some red berries. Sounds odd, but with an old dead branch and four tiny pottery birds, it has character and looks pretty.

Love to each of you,
Marian

Monday, January 10, 1955

Dear All—

My own personal after-the-holidays lull began with a jolt, of course, for Howard was gone until yesterday and E. and I really did lead the quiet life during the week. The whole week here was awfully wet—fortunately at Orealla there were only a few brief showers, so Howard was able to be out all he wanted to be. I wish he had the time to write you about his trip, but at this point that is unlikely so I shall give you the highlights.

He left here Sunday morning and drove to Skeldon, where he spent the night, all as planned. The launch was supposed to leave early Monday morning but it was 11 by the time it left. It took seven and a half hours to putt-putt the 50 miles up the river, and of course it was dark when they arrived at Orealla. H. had been told that the schoolteacher there could supply him with a cot and food. Luckily, he went supplied with his own; the schoolteacher was on vacation and his house was all locked up. The nurse was on vacation, too, and the priest was away, so there were no white people at all when H. arrived. He said the older men of the village all came up and bade him welcome, but the younger men would have nothing to do with him for a few days. All the villagers are Amerindians, 95 percent literate, and pretty well Westernized. The men cut trees and sell them to nearby sawmills, earning $100–$120 per month, which is better than most people here in Georgetown do.

Howard stayed in the rest house, complete with bats. A privy outside. No stove, so he heated his cans over a kerosene lantern. Because of the pirai [piranhas] in the river (they're carnivorous fish that delight in snapping off a toe or a finger), H. didn't plunge in but managed a shower of sorts with a bucket, propped up on a beam and tilted by a pull of a string. The weather was favorable, so he had good luck with his collecting and found four of the Cassias that he was seeking, plus seventy-some other plants new to his collection.

The return trip down the river took eight hours. Two Chinese men on board were apprehended by customs officials at the dock and turned out to be entering illegally from Suriname. The actual landing was enlivened by a crash with another boat in which a couple of windows were broken; the owner of the boat and the man at the wheel (helm?) thereupon began a long harangue in true Guianese fashion, and for fifteen minutes they cursed each other while the launch slowly drifted back out into the river. Howard stayed at Skeldon again Saturday night and got home about noon.

Monday evening I started reading *Gone With the Wind* and heavens! it's been ages since I've been so engrossed in a book. I came close to neglecting Elizabeth; couldn't stand to put the book down to nap after lunch, and read Monday and Tuesday nights until my eyes just wouldn't stay open. Nearly went blind, but such fun.

Tuesday we had tea at the Ramsarans', and I took E.'s new songbook over. They have a piano, which went on the blink shortly after their arrival here, and this fall they had it all repaired. Now, after having it back just a month, it's already lost its tone and some of the keys don't strike. Very discouraging. But still it was fun to have Mrs. McLaren play some of the songs that I couldn't figure out by myself.

Zela and Frank were in town and stopped by this afternoon. According to Zela, the old friendly atmosphere at the airbase has gone. The Black Watch now stationed there aren't as friendly as the Argylls were, and she says many of them just don't speak at all. There are only a few civilian families left, of course.

I'm finally getting around to putting up some curtains in our bedrooms. The same aqua ones that we started with on Parade Street, split in two for the Atkinson Field house, I shall now shorten for this place. With the strips that are left I intend to make a rug of some sort for our bedroom—I think I shall combine the aqua with some brown, and either braid or weave a small rug. Must consult my *Sunset Rug Book*! The Scargalls left us three rather awful blue and faded-black braided rugs, and as soon as I can substitute one of our own the happier I'll be.

Elizabeth is just gone on the subject of babies. The other day we dusted all the books in the bookcase, and of course came across the *Better Homes and Gardens Baby Book*. She looked at all the pictures and I'll swear she asked a hundred times, "What is that baby doing?" or, "What is that mommy doing?" There is one picture of a mommy taking baby's temperature, and there were some diagrams of the "mommy's tummy" where, I told her, babies grew before they were born. She was simply engrossed with the idea that she had been in my tummy, and vigorously patted her tummy with a thoughtful expression. She hugged some of the pictures as best she could; kissed some of the babies; and since then has been giving Janet, Betsy, Tammy et al. their bottles of milk. She helps Nancy walk, because "Nancy is just learning and might fall down" and on and on. I told H. it is a shame we can't produce a baby just this minute—it would be such a perfect psychological moment! She'd probably bop it on the head and have tantrums if one did suddenly appear, I suppose, in line with what the books say. It really is fun; of course, at the same time that she croons and rocks an imaginary baby in her arms, she will suddenly decide that she's riding on an airplane and start hugging a pillow that is the propeller. I believe she told me this morning, hugging away, that she did "just love this propeller." The neighbors' puppy came in the yard today and frightened her by jumping up, and she even cried and was quite rigid for a few minutes; but as soon as the puppy went away, out of our yard, she said, "We do love puppies," trying to convince herself that time.

Back to the curtains. School starts Monday—hard to believe the vacation is almost over!

Much love to you all,
Marian

Tuesday, January 18, 1955

Dear All—

It's just 6:30 but we're all through with dinner, dishes, baths, etc. and I think Elizabeth is already asleep. This is one of Howard's night-class evenings, so we all ate together early. Poor Howard says he does resent school this term—he'd so much rather be spending all his time on field trips. He's already started making arrangements for his trip to the Rupununi district during the Easter holidays and a trip to Brazil during the next summer vacation. It takes forever and a day to get things settled—he began in October making contacts and plans for this last weeklong trip up the Corentyne, and got the final okay on his plans from the District Commissioner who was helping arrange the boat trip just a day or so before he planned on going!

We went downtown this afternoon for some major purchases. Among them were a tablespoon for E. to use in the sandbox and two new toothbrushes for her. She gnaws on hers so they don't last long, but at least she doesn't mind the thrice-a-day brushing. Among other things, I noticed a tea set that I'd admired at Fogarty's in 1952, still there, same price. Bookers had a dresser set with spun-gold handles for $65 and I suppose that will remain for y'ars and y'ars, too.

My chief purchase was some material for my rug. Naturally, I couldn't get just what I wanted, but one learns to remain relaxed about such matters. I am having such fun with it. I am weaving it, using the twined-

Queen's College staff, 1954–1955. Standing, from left: Basil Eyre (English, History), Edmund Archer (Junior subjects), Stanley King (Junior subjects), Clement Yansen (English), Joseph Niles (Physics, Chemistry, Biology), Joshua Chung (Woodwork), Harold Persaud (Senior History), James Noel (Junior subjects), Edmund Wason (English, Scripture), Malcolm Boland (Chemistry, Biology, Zoology), Edward Burrowes (Art), Clarence Drayton (Senior Physics), Cecil Barker (Senior Chemistry), Ronald Rock (Latin). Seated, from left: Doodnauth Hetram (Senior Latin), Merrill Pederson (Geography), Richard Allsopp (Senior French), Howard Irwin (Biology), Doris Wan-Ping (secretary), Chunilall (Mathematics), Norman Cameron (Senior Mathematics), Vyvyan Sanger-Davies (headmaster; Chemistry), Edward Pilgrim (Mathematics), Jocelyn D'Oliveira (French), Lynette Dolphin (Preparatory Form, Music), Edwin London (Geography), George Narayan (English, Scripture, Mathematics), John Ramsaran (Senior English), Terrence Richmond (Junior subjects, Sports).

plaiting method if that means anything to you. It means that the warp threads are completely covered by the weft threads, which are twined around them. Clear? Well, it looks pretty and makes a heavy, firm texture. The main color is brown (surprise), and for that I'm using faded brown draperies. I also had some aqua and a little green material and I wanted to buy rose and gold, to make stripes. I wound up with pink and ochre but I think they'll look pretty.

For my birthday, Mother, I would love to have another tablespoon in our silver pattern, or some pretty sheets with yellow stripes or flowers or whatnot on them, or an operatic recording—not the whole opera, mind you—I just yearn for an aria now and then. However, in the box of "corruption" will you please include a scrapbook? I tried to find one today suitable for my growing number of clippings but found only icky little paper things. I would like something with firm covers (no cowboys or horses, as I saw today) and not too big. What would *you* put newspaper clippings in?

The last few days here have been lovely—no rain. What a relief. Sunday was simply beautiful, and Elizabeth played in the wading pool nearly all morning while H. polished the car and I read *Time*. Half the fun is having the hose turned on, and she managed to squirt it smack in her face a few times, without being bothered by it. Sunday afternoon we drove about 20 miles to a beach where H. had been before to collect plants. He was after more plants, and E. and I gathered up some shells. There was a stiff breeze, which was refreshing, but the beach was pretty depressing—just a mud flat, with a few shells here and there.

Elizabeth and I have been taking walks again, which we hadn't for quite some time. Everything is interesting to her, fortunately—the little wooden plank "bridge" over the trench, roosters, a cow, barking dogs, a donkey cart, a stick in the road. We live in one of the best sections of town, and true enough, if we turn to the left on Third Avenue, we can walk to the end of the block on pavement, turn left again and go one block farther, which takes us smack up the Public Road along the sea wall. That is the extent of the paved road around here—the Public Road is paved, but there is too much wild traffic on it to be safe [for walking along] without sidewalks. Along Third Avenue (the one-block paved stretch) there are some nice houses with pretty flowers. But if you turn to the right, away from the sea wall, you get right into another dingy group of unpainted, unkempt houses, fences strewn with ragged clothes [to dry in the sun], chickens playing at the doorstep, etc.

Well, we can't have everything and it is a pleasant house. Oh yes—H. saw Mrs. Scargall at the grocery store last week, and she says they are going to contest Mr. Perreira's right to keep them out. La ti da, here we go again, maybe.

The Ramsarans are going to come Thursday afternoon for tea, and if it's nice the little girls can have a "swim" in the wading pool. Heavens—what *shall* I do if Janet howls all the time they're here! All she needs is one good look at me and you'd think I'd beaten her at the least. Isn't it strange.

Well, I'm off to sprinkle clothes for tomorrow's ironing session. Elizabeth is fine. The pretty yellow dress is getting tight—hard to get the sleeves on and off. I tried on two of the size 5's you bought—the sundresses with the elastic in the backs, and if I take two-inch tucks in the shoulder straps she can wear them. She needs sundresses—sleeves are just too hot for me and I'm sure they are for her, too.

Much, much love to you all,

Marian

For Elizabeth's birthday, please send a xylophone that we can really play tunes on. Okay? For H.'s birthday, I think he'd like a subscription to Popular Mechanics. *He brings it home from school or buys it downtown—it tells everything from how to make a phonograph cabinet to electric hoes! For me—I could use a dresser scarf or two, here and now.*

Tuesday, January 25, 1955

Dear All—

Such a day we had today—Elizabeth is evidently on a new tack, and we had a grand total of four wet sheets, two wet mattress pads, three wet pants, two wet dresses, pajamas, and socks to contend with. I don't pretend to understand it, but we hope it passes quickly. At any rate, yesterday she stepped on my foot and said "Excuse me, Mommy" without being prompted, and we can't have everything!

Poor old Howard came back from the Corentyne with dysentery, which Dr. Kerry treated as a bacillic infection; it went away and came back, and so now Dr. K. has decided it's amoebic dysentery and is giving him a more powerful drug. In addition to that drug, he had to take an opium mixture and it's all he can do to stay awake through his classes. His diet is restricted to semi-solids, with no milk or butter or other fats. We hope it won't last long now—the drug (I forget what it is) was developed in the States just for this bug.

Howard spoke briefly with Mr. Perreira a few days ago, and Mr. P. is confident that the Scargalls won't get anywhere in their efforts to get back here. He also told H. that they'd been greatly bothered lately by the mosquitoes; we've had a few but not enough to be a real pest, thanks to our screens. Some nights we can see dozens flying around on the other side. Our current nuisance is some tiny gnats that can come through tiny cracks and other openings. They bite just enough to be maddening.

The Ramsarans came last Thursday, and Susan and Elizabeth had lots of fun going from the wading pool to the sandbox and back again. The weather has been lovely up to today and E. has gone "swimming" nearly every day. Janet was very timid and apprehensive and clutched Margaret's neck most of the time, but once toward the end of the afternoon she walked right past me without paying any attention, and we considered that progress.

We had fresh string beans from our garden tonight. Our gardener, a young East Indian named Doodnauth, started a vegetable garden for us on his own initiative, and Howard has since given him some money for seeds and things. He seems like a nice boy, is very shy, and only recently has he begun to smile as he says "Good afternoon" to me. He does lots of things without being asked—empties the wading pool and coils up the hose—and seemed very pleased when Howard asked him to come for two hours a day instead of only one.

My rug is nearly half done and I'm quite pleased with it. By the time it's finished I'll have used up nearly all the faded draperies, and I can think of nothing else they'd have really been good for.

Mother, do send me Ruth's fruitcake recipe. I have a hunch that the one I used is too rich for this climate, for when we finished it the first of this month it was two months old and still sticky and moist.

About H.'s Cassias, he hopes to get 90 Chamaecristaes, which is the sub-section he is interested in—about 60 here in South America, a dozen or so from Africa, Australia, and Asia (by mail), the rest from Texas and Mexico. Also he hopes to get as many of the remaining 300 Cassias as he can—he has 20 at present. I think I've written that the majority of the Chamaecristaes are found in Brazil. Howard received a reply this week from the director of the agricultural college in Minas Gerais state in Brazil, where the greatest concentration is found. H. has been offered free room and board and transportation in the area, and any help they can give concerning location of the plants. I hadn't realized before that there was such a bond between botanists—Howard has had such friendly cooperation from the U.S. National Herbarium, and now this help from Brazil. He says it's because so few people are interested in pure research, that when someone comes along who is, everyone knows how tough it is and is anxious to help.

Mother, the next time you send a box, will you include one or two black velvet belts one inch wide? Two dresses require them and they don't seem to stand up well. My waist is a snug 26 inches.

All for now. Much, much love to you both—

Marian

Tuesday, February 1, 1955

Dear All—

Gads—February already. Howard is out teaching tonight. At 7:30 there is a rehearsal for *The Mikado*, which is being given this Friday night. It's a Georgetown Philharmonic production, which means questionable quality. This is the first rehearsal that Howard has been to; he was told yesterday that four of the main singers had quit, and as far as he knows nothing has been done about the staging. It's to be given at Q.C., and of course I shall go. Curious about it all!

Howard is still having his troubles, but I think he's a bit better. He's to see Dr. Kerry again tomorrow. He still can't have any fats at all and is supposed to be on a semi-liquid diet. I've been giving him meat at dinner because he was losing weight on his soup-and-juice diet. Elizabeth has a cold. Not bad, just a drippy nose and she still hasn't learned how to really blow, so that is a nuisance.

We have a new addition to our family—Spotty. I'd wanted to bring him into town last fall, but Howard and I decided against it since our yard space is limited and he has always run all over the airbase. Last week Zela called and said that the latest circular sent by Major Nicole stated that dogs would have to be chained. They felt that Spot would not take kindly to that, and she asked if we wanted him. We had planned to go out Saturday anyway for Howard to do some collecting, so we brought Spotty home. Sunday we worried about him—he wouldn't eat, moped, etc. But yesterday and today he has been more at ease and today for the first time has assumed some of the watchdog character that we want. He barked at the gardener, and this evening barked when Mr. Perreira came home next door. Not too much barking, just a good signal. You should see the quantities of white dog hair that loom up on our dark floors! I shall buy a dog brush and try to get some of the loose hairs out that way. Elizabeth is just overjoyed about having him. She follows him everywhere just to sit near him; tries to feed him sand and can't understand why Spot can't "pretend" to eat it like we do. He is very good-natured, just walks away when he's bored with it all. I do hope it works out well—we'd love to keep him. Yesterday and today we've been for walks and he's pretty good about the leash.

Now for another chapter in the Perils of Renting Houses in B.G. Yesterday I took a check for our rent to Mr. Perreira, and sent a $5 check to Mr. Scargall for the rent of the furniture that is his. Last night Scargall called, told H. he was sorry that we hadn't sent him the $90 so that he could give Perreira the $85, which was how it was handled before Perreira bought the property. Howard told him we thought it best that we pay the owner ourselves; Scargall said that he would take his check to Perreira today. He also said that his lawyer said that Perreira didn't have a chance. Howard went next door to see what was going on, and Perreira told him that Scargall had already brought his check, which he, Perreira, had refused. He says that Scargall hasn't a leg to stand on. Well, it's their problem to thrash out but it keeps putting us in awkward positions. At any rate, H. and Mr. P. had a good talk about stamp collections—Mr. P. says that he and a doctor here have the "largest and best collections in the colony" and one of these days he'll get his B.G. collection out of the bank and bring it home for Howard to see. They are not friendly neighbors—we seldom speak at all, but they are quiet and just mind their own business. Several men have told Howard that they wouldn't want to live next door to the Perreiras; he's not popular. But he's done well in his business and owns property in all three counties—Demerara, Berbice, and Essequibo. We certainly can't complain—since they've owned the house we have been given a new garbage can two or three times as large as the old one, which had a hole in the bottom. Their gardener has cleared the weeds from in front of our gate, which makes it look very tidy even though they'll grow up again in a week or so.

Well, dears, I think I shall make a cup of coffee and peruse a *New Yorker* for a while.

Much love to each of you,
Marian

Tuesday, February 8, 1955

Dear All—

In half an hour we must turn on the radio and listen to a broadcast that Howard recorded months ago. So I shall write until then, listen, and then fall into bed. Mrs. McLaren came last night to have dinner with us and then she and I had a game of Scrabble; all in all we didn't get to bed until midnight—*much* too late for us. I do think Scrabble is fun—I want to try playing it in German or French once Howard has started on his reviewing of those two languages.

We got some valentines today, and the cute package of cards to make from Bee. Unfortunately, we haven't done anything clever about making cards and I shall just say Happy Valentine's Day and let it go at that. Elizabeth has several cards on her dresser, and although she thinks they are Christmas cards she is very happy with them!

We did so enjoy *The Mikado*. I thought I wouldn't be able to get to it—we have an American wonder-boy preacher here and Patrine has been attending his services faithfully. But at the last minute on Saturday night, Mrs. McLaren offered to stay with Elizabeth. They did a very good job—the only real sour note was the awful violin playing. Such wonderful music.

Spotty has settled down very nicely, thank goodness. He has quickly learned his way around the neighborhood, and we let him out for a run several times a day—he always comes home, especially in the evening when he expects his dinner. He looks so cute when we make a fuss over him—he's an affectionate dog and really revels in the attention.

Yesterday I cleared up a mystery. Do you remember my writing that we couldn't find the door chains, birthday candles, and a red sink stopper that we sent back here last summer? Ha! When I opened the Scrabble box, there they were. Now the only missing items are the towel racks, which we still haven't located.

Howard's innards have been better, and for a week he ate a normal diet, but today we fear a setback has started. Poor old dear, maybe he'll have to ignore milk and butter for a longer time.

Elizabeth has kept us busy. Last Thursday she and Spotty together discovered how to open the gate; about 5 p.m. I discovered them practically in the street, playing with the puppy from next door. H. bought a new hook that neither can manage. Friday she was washing dishes in the sink while I ran downstairs to get the clothes off the line; she came down, too, but

Elizabeth and Marian join Spotty outside the house, February 1955.

left the water running into the sink and the drain covered. I investigated after the gardener told me water was coming from the kitchen; water was streaming down over the sink, but thanks to our numerous cracks in the floor, it just drained right on through. Saturday E. fell down the stairs but just bruised a shoulder. Her cold is nearly gone. Today she said "Gran'pa Tom is a darling man" and she frequently asks about what Grandmother is doing. Stock answer: Red Cross meeting or baking cookies!

It's 7:30 now.

Love,

Marian

Many thanks to you both for the Saturday Review *subscription. I've had their card for several weeks but kept forgetting to mention it.*

We took some pictures Sunday—you'll be getting copies soon.

In confidence: I think I'm pregnant and have an appointment to see Dr. Bissessar on Friday. We certainly hope so!

Saturday, February 12, 1955

Dear All—

Well, kiddies, it looks as if you are going to be grandparents and aunt to another offspring! I saw Dr. Bissessar yesterday, and although he didn't give me a date, according to the *Better Homes and Gardens* book, I would say October 10. It seems odd to be planning so far ahead, but in view of all the time it takes to get things here, it really isn't too early. There are no ready-made maternity clothes here, and I don't want to make them myself—too hard getting to a sewing machine. The idea I'm leading up to is this: Mother, would you look around a bit and compare the cost of buying ready-made dresses and having Mrs. Phillips make some? If it would be cheaper to have them made (might be nearly the same cost but more a question of choice of style), I would allow Mrs. P. a month to do that, plus two months to send them, which brings us to the end of May, when I shall need them. More about clothes later on.

You are no doubt perishing to know what sort of facilities exist here. There is the Public Hospital, St. Joseph's Mercy Hospital, and a nursing home[78] that Dr. Bissessar operates. We've heard tales of all. Dorothy Larthe had a baby at the Public Hospital and said it was ghastly—it operates chiefly for those who can't afford anything better. Margaret and Zela both had babies at Mercy Hospital and their reports weren't too good:

Janet was brought to M. wearing some other baby's clothes (mother furnishes baby clothes worn in hospital); nurse failing to wash hands after changing diaper; water given baby in dirty bottle; flies, etc., in nursery; dirty bathtub for patients to use. Doesn't sound very inviting, does it. Zela also had a baby at Dr. Bissessar's and had told me a little about it. It is right on the main street of Kitty, with a theater two doors away. It is a small building with his offices downstairs, nursing home upstairs. We saw the downstairs yesterday—very old-fashioned but evidently clean. Tile floor and long horsehair sofa in waiting room. Facilities in examining room rather quaint—no toilet paper offered after taking of urine specimen; no paper or cloth put on the scales to protect one's bare feet from all the other bare feet that have already stood there. But he does have food prepared to the individual's taste, since there are so few patients at any time—a rather large point since I could say, "Please, no curry, no eddoes, no tannias, no cassavas," etc. Babies are kept in the mother's rooms, in separate beds, of course, with nets. I said that we weren't pleased with what we'd heard about the Mercy Hospital and hoped that in a smaller place there would be more personal supervision, and he said that though it certainly wouldn't be up to American standards, they did take all sanitary precautions. He charges $2 for each prenatal visit and $93 for nine days of "room and board" and delivery.

I'm sure I would have qualms if this were to be our first baby. But since, with Elizabeth, everything went so smoothly, I don't think we need to worry at all—you either. Dr. B. didn't advise me to take vitamins, but today H. went downtown and purchased some expensive little capsules that contain all the vitamins, plus copper, iron, and what-have-you.

The next time I see Margaret I shall ask her if her maid has a job lined up after the Ramsarans leave. Enid has asked before if I could use her—she'd like to work for me, and I know she is honest, reliable, etc. If not Enid then I'll get someone else later in the spring. After all, household help is one luxury that is available here and I shall take advantage of it when I need to—even though the words "help" and "luxury" are used very loosely!

Is the enclosed scrap of material called underwear crepe? Will you buy eight yards of it in white, and send it? The only seersucker-type material here is too rough for a baby.

I guess that's all on that subject for tonight. Howard is at school, in the midst of the final performance of The Mikado. Last weekend's shows were so successful that two more were scheduled for last night and tonight.

Elizabeth certainly picks up the words to songs I sing—yesterday she was playing downstairs and was excited about something—I could hear her running about saying "Wunderbar, wunderbar, wunderbar!" Lately she has spent quite a bit of time looking at *The Child's Garden of Verses*, and one of her favorites is "Dark brown is the river, Golden is the sand—" One of mine, too, which I suppose explains her preference! Did I ever mention Nancy's "down-down"? It is Nancy's toy, imaginary, and Nancy still plays with it now and then and we *still* haven't a clue as to what it is.

Joy Allsopp is working for the FOA here, and twice has invited us to their Wednesday night movies. The first time E. had her cold so we couldn't go. Howard went by himself last week, since we couldn't get anyone to stay, and Mr. Macaulay, the chief, had expressed his desire to meet H. several times. H. said he was embarrassed at the laughter at some local pictures—I guess there were four or five men and their wives there, and H. said they seemed very cliquish. One young man, a Negro, acted annoyingly superior, and another, an expert on something, didn't have a thing to say to H. We realize that we have made a greater effort *not* to feel or act superior than most people would—and H. has received compliments from Q.C. staff members who say they forget that we are visitors. What provoked H. most was that several important Guianese were there Wednesday—big wheels—and yet the Americans snickered and laughed unconcernedly. They are all from the U. of Maryland, and after reading about the scandals involving that school (in *Time* a few weeks ago) we wonder if perhaps it wasn't political pull of some sort that gave these men their government contracts. At any rate, we don't miss Americans as much as we did two years ago so it's no great disappointment.

All for now.

Much love,

Marian

I forgot to say that I feel fine.

Mother, I remember last summer you said you'd come here "if you were needed." I would never coax you to come because I'm sure you'd be warm (I shiver rather often in this breezy house!), but heaven knows we'd be happy if you would come. It would be an expensive trip and, except for us, dull as all get out. But I would certainly love to have you here! Please mull!

February 12–13, 1955:
The PPP splits into two factions, one led by Jagan and the other by Burnham, a stalemate that lasted until 1958.

Tuesday, February 22, 1955

Dear All—

Such a wet day today, but not much breeze so I am sitting here steaming away. Elizabeth's head has been wet all afternoon from perspiration—I think I'll wash her hair tomorrow regardless of her still-running nose. It might as well be wet from shampoo as from perspiration, and I'm sure she'd feel better.

So good to get your letters today. Bee, is your bird a talking parakeet? When we were at Atkinson, we used to have clouds of them fly over our house early every morning and every evening, chattering like mad.

Elizabeth is growing up so—this morning she "made" our bed for me, before I got to the bedroom. She'd gone through all the motions—pulled up the sheet, "smoothed" it and turned it back, and smoothed the pillows. When I walked in she said, "Mommy, put the bedspread on," so I did, and didn't touch it until this afternoon when I remade it. She was so proud of herself. She likes to clean the sink now, too, providing I let her use lots of cleaner. And she sometimes spreads the jam on Howard's sandwiches (still no fats; just jam). She does so well dressing her dolls, snaps and all, that it occurred to me yesterday that I should make her a couple of dresses with snaps up the front. She would love zippers but I can't put them in by hand. As I said, she does very well, until she comes to something that won't work as quickly as she'd like and then wham! throws the offending dolly across the room. The other day I heard a banging from the kitchen, investigated to find her picking up the doll swing and throwing it down the hall, picking it up and throwing again, mad as could be because she couldn't get Nancy to sit up in it. It never lasts long, but I hope she can outgrow it before she's school age if not sooner.

We have to move. If we wanted to we could rant about the ghastly housing setup here, but it doesn't do any good and anyway, we can move into the Ramsarans' house. They leave for England on May 31, and we don't know just when Mr. Scargall wants to come back here but I don't think he's in any big hurry. That is, we hope he will give us the first two days of June to get moved. We will move our screening promptly. The Ramsarans have several problems concerning their house, but Howard is confident that they won't be hard to remedy. One concerns the ground under the house, which, since it is unpaved, gets muddy and collects water during rainy weather and encourages mosquitoes. H. feels sure that the only trouble there is that they haven't cleaned out the drainage ditches around the house. Then they have lots of ants, even biting ants in their beds! We will douse the mattresses with DDT and get rid of them one way or another. At least it's a house. We can stay there until the end of December, and then, God willing, we'll find another place to move into for our remaining time here. Isn't it a rat race, though.

On Saturday we drove out to the airbase so Howard could do some collecting. We took a picnic lunch with us and gave Elizabeth quite a thrill— she was so eager to have the picnic lunch that she thought of little else all morning. We came back early in the afternoon, all had showers, and plopped into bed. It really is an exhausting trip, all 30 miles each way!

On Sunday we had lunch with Joy and Richard. We were to go at 10:30 so we could hear some records before lunch, but unfortunately at about 10:15 the electric company pulled what is becoming routine and left us without power. (A week ago Sunday it was out from 9:30 p.m. till 4:30 a.m., and ten days before that it was out for a couple of hours, too.) It came on again about noon Sunday (and went out again between 6:30 and 9 p.m.) so we had a little music but not as much as we'd all hoped for. Elizabeth went, too, and had a lovely time playing with their three dogs and a kitten. Their little house was awfully hot, and we were uncomfortably warm all the time we were there. Such a dreadful feeling, trying to look decent and perspiring freely!

I went intending to ask Joy about Dr. Bissessar, just to check, and I'm glad I did. She says she thinks he's old-fashioned and more interested now in politics than in medicine, and Lord help us, he has no facilities at all for surgery at his nursing home. Innocent that I am, I guess I just took it for granted that somewhere there was at least bare equipment for emergencies, but Joy said that if difficulties develop, off you go to the hospital.

She said that the fashionable place to have babies is Mercy Hospital, which we know, but said that all her friends have lately been going to another nursing home run by a Dr. Georges. One friend in particular, she said, had nothing but praise for him, and she's arranged for us to meet this girl and her husband next Saturday. Joy thinks this Dr. Georges is

Trinidadian, says he is youngish and that he does have a little "theatre" or operating room, that all his equipment is new, etc. He came here on appointment to the Public Hospital but was so popular with all his patients that he decided he could do better in private practice. We'll be very glad to talk to this girl and get some more details.

Howard is feeling fine again, but his experiments with butter haven't proved too satisfactory so he is still not eating fats. One of these days I shall provoke him into going to see Dr. Kerry again—I'd like to know if his fatless diet is necessary or if there is something he can take to really knock out that bug.

His planned trip to Mount Roraima (who has read *Green Mansions*?[79]) is shaping up, although for a while it was on-again, off-again. To go, one has to get a visa from Venezuela, and that involves five photos, medical certificate, good-conduct certificate from the local police, smallpox and yellow fever certificates—I guess that's all. Three other Q.C. masters are going, and H. estimates they'll have about 12 porters to carry their supplies. It's mostly uninhabited country, which is why he didn't want to go alone.

Mother, could you send us some more colored paper in a box someday? No hurry, but Elizabeth does enjoy coloring on it and pasting it, etc. She knows most simple colors now, but I believe she likes to tease—calls red blue, green yellow, etc.

Howard will be home shortly so I shall heat up the coffee and have a cup. I finished reading *From Here to Eternity* a day or so ago—what an awful book. I really liked the cleaned-up movie much better, just because it wasn't full of such filthy language, sadistic soldiers, etc. But I couldn't put the book down because the story was so interesting!

Much, much love to you all,

Marian

Tuesday, March 1, 1955

Dear All—

The iron arrived last week, and I'm tickled to have it. Thank you all! I haven't used the steam yet, chiefly because I haven't defrosted and therefore have no [distilled] water for it, but as soon as I get some I shall press some of H.'s slacks. He will appreciate the iron, too, I'm sure!

Howard received some microfilmed material from Dr. Turner at the U. of Texas last month. He tried just about everywhere to get it developed but no one would do it, and we haven't been able to locate a projector either.

So our latest project is copying it all—quite a task, and one which usually ends with me slightly hysterical. We sit at the dinner table, Howard peering through a microscope at the film, reading off the botanical descriptions and spelling when necessary while I madly type it out. We have worked up to quite a rate, but that's what makes me giggle after an hour and a half of it. It goes like this: "petiolar gland discoid, slender stalked; leaflets six to eight pairs, broadly linear to oblanceolate, 10 to 15 mm. long, 2 mm. wide, obliquely mucronulate, glabrous but ciliate, rather strongly several nerved, pedicels puberulent . . ." and on and on. We have 20 typed pages so far, and have done 19 out of a hundred or more filmed pages.

Last Saturday evening we went with Joy and Richard to meet Eva and Herbie Walker. We walked in the door and the three men settled in one end of the room, and we three settled at the other. We never did exchange more than "hello" and "goodbye" with each other, but I suppose it was because everyone knew the main reason for our visit and the men didn't want to intrude on such a delicate discussion! Eva raved about Dr. Georges, everything from the food served to his willingness to come whenever he's needed. I had an appointment this morning and was really impressed by him—he has a charming manner and a very nice way about him. He is tall, very dark skinned, I suppose between 35 and 40, and good-looking. He's terribly busy—makes three appointments every weekday morning between 8 and 8:30, then sees those who come without appointments. When I got there at ten to 8 this morning, there were half a dozen folks waiting already, and many more by the time I left at 8:10. I don't know if it was because I knew it was a ten-minute appointment (rather unnervingly brief!) that I forgot to ask several questions, but I did. I didn't ask about money, but Eva said that his standard delivery fee is $30, plus $5 a day at the nursing home. He agreed on October 10 as the date, prescribed some vitamins, and has requested a blood test, which we will take care of tomorrow.

Eva also told me that they insist that the babies wear wool booties! Heavens above, I just can't see it, and of course Dr. Hellyer told me that a baby's cold feet or hands didn't mean the child was chilled, just a sign of poor circulation. I know I shall run into all sorts of things like that and I don't suppose it would kill me to put booties on a baby for a week in the nursing home. Maybe Margaret will lend me some.

Mr. Scargall says we have to be out by May 31, so we shall be busy that day, I can see it now. We keep telling each other that there's no point in stewing about this moving business, but in the backs of our minds is a rather worrisome question: where to go in December after the Ramsarans come back? Houses just keep getting scarcer and more expensive, and if we can't find anything, the only answer would be for Howard to ship the rest of us home.

I can think of few things less appealing than taking a two-and-a-half-month-old baby on a long trip like that, going from the tropics to New York and Seattle in December, being away from Howard for a year, etc. etc. But if we did have to do that, would your precious little house be big enough to hold us? A separate apartment or house would be pretty expensive for ten or twelve months. We shall do as much as we can to stay here until summer, but after all we don't want to live in a dump and we keep hearing tales of awful shacks now being rented for $100 a month.

Elizabeth insisted on putting on her pajamas by herself tonight, and they were the pink ones you bought in Tacoma, Mother, the ones with the drop seat. With just a little help she got the arms and legs in the right places and insisted on snapping the snaps *all* by herself, which she did fairly quickly and quite easily.

All for now. Howard will be home in a few minutes, and then we'll go back to our Chamaecristae.

Much, much love to you all,

Marian

Heavens, Mother, I know how you must feel about coming down here. You might inquire at Moore-McCormack in Seattle—they go from Seattle-Portland-S.F. to Trinidad. Or you could go by train to New Orleans or Houston, then come direct to Georgetown. But with the possibility of our having to come home early, it might be better if you didn't try. We can always get someone to stay, and we'll have several months to pick and choose. I haven't found out about Enid yet.

Much love, dears,

M.

Tuesday, March 8, 1955

Dear All—

Elizabeth is in bed, chirping to herself. Just lately she has begun saying whole nursery rhymes, and with expression, too! She just finished "Ride a cock horse to Banbury Cross" and "Hey diddle diddle," her two favorites at the moment. I guess she just copies the inflections from the way I've said them over and over, but it does amuse me.

Last Thursday, after I defrosted, I carefully filled an empty rum bottle with the water that had dripped off, and later proceeded to steam some of Howard's slacks. I am simply delighted! It takes all the curse off pressing the crease in trousers, one of the jobs I have ignored quite consistently because I do so hate messing with a press cloth, damp cloth, etc. and not being able to see what I'm doing. I do prefer to iron cottons damp, with the dry iron, but the steam is just wonderful for the woolens, also for pressing out "sat-in" wrinkles in my dresses (not that I press them after wearing them each time, heaven knows—just on special occasions).

Mother's box of "corruption" arrived last Friday, with simply exquisite timing. I was feeling rather depressed at lunch, for no definite reason but probably because E. has been on an irresponsible bed-wetting spree lately that wouldn't even succumb to the candy reward. It's better now, and I know it is always just temporary, but it is so difficult having to wash sheets and mattress pads all the time. At any rate, Howard brought the box home at noon but had forgotten to bring it upstairs, until, as we finished lunch, he looked at me and said, "For heaven's sake, what is the matter?" Then he remembered the box, and what fun it was to look through all that stuff! I haven't opened the two birthday-wrapped packages, of course, but Elizabeth has enjoyed the toy catalogues (so have we) and we are excited about using the decorations on our "birthday parties," as E. says. I decided that I will make a birthday cake (chocolate, thank you, Mother; white for Howard—the spice mix we'll save for company) first for me, then for Howard, and we'll go through the routine of presents for us before her birthday comes around. She's much more used to opening things for herself than giving to others, so tomorrow H. is going to take her to town to buy something for me.

I crowed when I read a short article about dressing babies in one of the magazines you sent, and I may frame the sentence that reads: "It is normal for the legs and feet to feel cool, up to six months." Ha! I don't suppose I can get anyone here to believe it, but it bolsters my own convictions.

Daddy, we sent off a box by boat yesterday that should reach you by your birthday. Two-thirds of the contents is breakable, but since it was well packed in straw it should arrive safely. Please return the stamps. Poor H. was quite depressed that Bee gave all those B.G. stamps away, and said he hoped you two would succeed in keeping yours for him. It is hard to get used copies, and he relies on the families to return them.

Friday evening I went with Joy to the FOA office, where she works, to see two movies on the bauxite business. Both were interesting, and I met some of the FOA wives. One works with Joy. Another whom Joy doesn't know well at all seemed much more interesting, has five-and-a-half-year-old twin daughters and a one-and-a-half-year-old girl, too.

Yesterday we spent the afternoon at the Ramsarans'—first time we'd been together in over a month, for Susan has had two bad colds. Margaret told me that Enid will be delighted to work for me, so that's a relief. Margaret pays her $12 a month, and she comes six days a week for three hours in the morning. M. says one cannot expect her to do everything on her own, that she is "dreamy" and frequently forgets to dust a table or something, but when asked to go back and do it she is perfectly happy to, with no resentment. Margaret says she is completely honest, clean, speaks quite well, and is courteous. She had never worked before she came to Margaret, so I'm sure she's been quite well trained!

This morning we washed doll clothes. It always seems such a good idea to Elizabeth, until the moment when they're about ready to disappear into the suds; then she wants them. However, this morning they went on in and the dollies sat around in nothing all day. Tomorrow we iron the clothes, which means we'll spend a good half hour dressing them up in everything, too. It is fun, I must admit.

Mother, I've borrowed a pattern from Margaret to make a dress for E. that opens down the front. It is a very plain pattern, no style at all, but I shall trim it with something and it will do. Unless you've already bought a pattern, in which case send it on down and we shall have variety.

The family living next door to the Ramsarans has two little children, and Mrs. Persaud is expecting another shortly. Their little girl is nearly four, the boy about three, so once we're living there E. will have playmates at last. Margaret said they seemed just awfully eager to come and play, so they haven't been encouraging them—although she said they seem like nice children. But I think we will encourage them—neighbor children in my hair will be all right with me, as long as they are good playmates for Elizabeth. She really needs them.

On Sunday I finished my rug, and it lives up to all expectations. We think it very pretty—it is firm and thick and heavy, the colors are attractive and it lies nice and flat on the floor. If the thread I used to join the strips of material holds together, it should wear well.

Mother, I would love a book for E. about a second baby. She's so intrigued with books, she would love it, too. I have been feeling fine nearly all the time. With Elizabeth, I couldn't stand the thought of eggs for breakfast. This time, I feel rather repulsive around dinnertime—which does handicap the culinary processes somewhat. I can't stand the thought of eating some of our local greens—so-called cabbage and spinach and so on, which actually aren't too bad. However, the last few days have been better in that respect, and heaven knows I haven't been sick at all, just a "feeling." I miss cottage cheese and fresh milk—mixing up an extra quart of Klim plus Carnation plus water is a nuisance. And of course we always miss goodies like frozen peas, fresh carrots, cauliflower, salmon, frozen chicken pies, and the like, but we do not dwell on that. We have been getting some nice tomatoes lately and they do taste so good. Thomas brings me four fairly good-sized ones for 60 cents; Howard bought a pound at the market for 48 cents, and there were six smaller ones in that pound. I've been living on cheese-and-tomato sandwiches for lunch. Tonight we finished up some good meat loaf—stuffed the last of it into tomatoes and baked them—very nice. I get so provoked having to grind up beef; the only place I can attach my grinder is on a stepladder. Elizabeth climbs up to help hold the bowl, then as I grind with all my strength with one hand I try to hold the meat in the grinder with the other, also steady the bowl and keep the stepladder from skidding around. Last time the bowl of ground meat went flying in the air when E. momentarily forgot her duties and let go. Luckily, it was a plastic bowl and I scooped up the meat off the floor, pulled out a few dog hairs, and continued. All for now; Howard's due home any minute.

Much, much love,
Marian

Saturday, March 12, 1955

Dear Mother—

It was nice to get your unexpected letter on Thursday. We count on our Tuesday afternoon mail, but extra dividends are fun! Darn—I guess our birthday present to you didn't arrive on time. We sent a small package by air, in what should have been good time. Has it arrived yet?

I had such fun yesterday. After breakfast, Howard and Elizabeth presented me with a bottle of hand lotion that E. had wrapped and H. had tied with a card written by E. holding a pencil guided by Howard. She was so excited, and said "Happy birthday, Mommy" so many times! Howard has ordered a recorder for me (have you read the ads? "Make Mellow Music") but it hasn't arrived yet. The candles are so pretty—a better shade of brown

545

than the ones I bought—and such a pleasant luxury here. They burn down darn fast but look so pretty. And you have us all set to give a party now, with napkins and coasters and food!

And then of course I had to have a birthday cake, and it was the first decorating I've done in nearly three years. I made a chocolate cake, put strawberry jam between the layers, and used chocolate icing. Calories, calories, what the hell! Elizabeth and I decorated it and almost outdid ourselves—yellow flowers, green leaves, yellow candles, etc. *Such* fun. Howard sang "Happy Birthday" to me, and Elizabeth echoed the "Happy Birthday, dear Mommy" several times more (today, too).

This morning H. decided to go out to the airbase to collect plants, and we decided to go, too. We had to eat our lunch in the car, as it was pretty wet, but we stretched our legs several times and had books to read while H. worked. It is a hot, bumpy, tiring trip but it does come under the heading of "getting out," so every now and then I want to go. We all came in, showered, and had a rest before dinner.

Howard is fine now. He's been drinking milk and eating butter for a week with no ill effects.

I can get so excited thinking about this baby—it will certainly make time go faster! Howard wrote his mother asking if she would see about having the bathinette and pram sent down. In a way, it will be an extravagance, but I think a justifiable one. We will do all we can to stay here until June, and in those eight months the pram would be the most needed, and the bathinette—well, I lifted enough tubs of water around for E. to know it's tiring. And dressing and diaper changing, too. Heaven knows we have enough inconveniences that we can't do anything about. Having the washing machine will help a lot with baby clothes, and I don't imagine we'll have the trouble with sour-smelling bibs and clothes that we had before.

Dr. Georges prescribed some very expensive vitamins for me—$4.50 for a ten-day supply, and when H. tried to get a refill the other day he was told that the colony's supply has run out! *Such* a place. Am waiting for a new prescription.

Bought some material the other day for two new dresses for Elizabeth. I'm piping one with light green and trimming the other with dark green rickrack.

Must go do the ironing I should have done this morning.

Much love,

Marian

Tuesday, March 15, 1955

Dear All—

About 15 minutes before dinner was ready this evening, the postman brought five letters, a book for Howard, and some literature on GM trucks, and as a consequence the creamed cabbage got scorched a bit. You'd think we didn't hear from anyone for months at a time the way we tear into our letters!

The clothes sound pretty, and Bee, Howard got quite disgusted with me because I said I thought maternity shorts might shock people here and that I had decided to stick to skirts. His theory, like yours, is that one is free to wear anything one pleases in one's home, damn it! I'm sure I will end up wearing them, as skirts do feel warmer around the legs. The pink outfit sounds very pretty and I do love pink. Be sure to let Mother know how much our bank account owes you!

Dear parents, I'm so glad to know that you wouldn't mind letting us crowd in. (I hadn't really thought you would refuse us a pallet in the garage, or something.) Have I ever made it apparent that, at this point (that is, before H. goes to Brazil in August), we are planning that he will have to go back in August of next year and stay several months, perhaps until Christmas? There is the possibility that this summer he might get enough work done there to make another trip unnecessary, but H. groans and says he could live there for several years and not do as much [plant collecting] as he'd like to. Anyway, chances are that Elizabeth and I and Little X will be with you for several months then. As far as next fall goes, I certainly hope you can work it out to come, Mother. For some reasons it would be simpler if E. and I could return in September and stay, but there are too many reasons for not doing so. It would cost about ten times more money to have a baby in Tacoma than here. I know, money isn't everything, etc. etc., but there is a major difference to us between the $30 or so which it will cost here and the nearly $300 which little E.'s arrival cost. Granted, some of that is balanced out by peace of mind, certainty about hospital, etc. We think the arrival of another child would be easier for Elizabeth in these familiar surroundings, especially with her daddy close at hand. And gads, Mother, *if* we couldn't find a place to move into in December and if you were here to accompany us, still—a baby less than two months old just isn't old enough for that kind of traveling. At the moment, I can't get upset about all the moving. I suppose one gets hardened to it after a while, and it is just the order of the day in Georgetown. The most sensible thing is for us to plan on staying until June, hoping to get some fairly decent place to live. A hotel or boarding house would be out, with a tiny baby, but we could put up with quite a bit for a few months. I don't like the idea of Elizabeth being separated from her daddy for a year—she needs him too much. Of course, *I* would miss him, too, but I trust you understand what I mean—I wouldn't forget him in a year but Elizabeth might, and the poor baby wouldn't know him at all. Ah well, this is the topic that I suppose we shall cover and re-cover in every letter. Don't worry; we aren't anxious or upset. We've had awfully good luck getting nice houses so far, and if it continues, fine; if it doesn't, well, we *have* had good luck.

Bee, you have no idea what you've started! I was all set to buy an "opera, gems of" [record] yesterday, so we went down to the auto supplies store which H. had discovered is the new agency for HMV records here. It is a messy place, wet concrete floor, mostly motorcycles and bicycles and automobile tires in heaps, with a few refrigerators, radios, etc. roped off from the reach of the general public. They are in the process of building a new addition, so maybe that accounts for the mess. At the end of one counter is the Record Department, and of all things, they had no gems, just complete operas! They had one of the two records of *Bohème*, so that settled that. They also had *Il Trovatore*, *Traviata*, *Aida*, and a Rossini opera, which H. was encouraging me to choose. We got quite reckless, recalled some Christmas gift money that we were going to spend on another fan but never have, and bought *Traviata*, plus Brahms's Fourth for H. The recording is made in England but evidently from an American one—the NBC Symphony Orchestra conducted by Toscanini, with Jan Peerce, Robert Merrill, and Licia Albanese. It is just lovely, the only flaw being that the very end is too near the center of the record for our player, and it rejects with about one revolution left to go! Frustrating.

Some more pictures for you. The squash that Elizabeth and I are holding is one of Howard's favorite foods, and the only thing which at present I really gag on. Unfortunately, it comes from an extraordinarily healthy vine, and we are loaded with the damn things. I've given two to Margaret, and H. is now canvassing the Q.C. staff although he himself hates to give them up! The other pictures were taken at Madewini Creek, which doesn't show up well at all. It is Coca-Cola colored, golden where the sun strikes it, and quite lovely. In the picture where I am clutching E.'s sunsuit straps, she was intent on "feeding leaves to the water."

It pleases me so that Elizabeth is so fond of her books. She has poems and songs confused, and after she reads a poem or nursery rhyme she tells me she was "singing a poem," but since she enjoys them all I haven't corrected her yet. You know the "Dark brown is the river" poem of Robert Louis Stevenson? She is fond of that, and refers to Madewini Creek as the "dark brown is the river." Mother, do you remember the night we drove back from the Sheffelheims' singing "Come, little leaves—"? Elizabeth likes that, too, but we don't get very far with it because I've forgotten the words to most of it. Could you remember them for us? At any time during the day she'll say the first line of a poem or song, and then look so pleased when I finish it. We have started reading a story at bedtime—Howard does it on the nights when he's home—and it is a pleasant way to end the day.

Howard will be home from class soon, and perhaps he'll want to get on with the microfilm. From what we're doing now, it looks as if he'll be traipsing all over Florida, Texas, Mexico, etc. tracking down these blessed plants!

Much, much love to you all,

Marian

Tuesday, March 22, 1955

Dear All—

Look at what arrived today! Bee, I love the stationery and am certainly happy to have it. I've been planning on catching up on my letter writing while Howard is away next month, and now I can impress people.

Mother, the gray dress sounds just right, and gray is just as cool a color as any, and perhaps more practical than some. I shall certainly be glad to see these clothes when they arrive. My clothes, some of them, are beginning to feel tight, and I'm glad that I have two skirts with tucks in the waistbands that I can let out when necessary. Don't worry about our milk. I think the new powdered milk that dissolves instantly is nonfat, isn't it? It would be easier, but by this time mixing up milk is part of our routine, and after Enid starts doing the housework I'll have little enough to do to keep busy. As for the cottage cheese, there is a recipe for making it in one of my cookbooks but I have never felt quite up to the effort, even if the necessary rennin tablets are available here.

Elizabeth is over, and has been for ten days or so, the last siege of bed-wetting. She knows, I am quite sure, that she shouldn't wet the bed, and she does enjoy her candy when she's a good girl. After all, she is very good about it most of the time. In dry weather when the sheets dry quickly it is much less of a problem than in wet weather, and we've had rain, rain, rain nearly all month. Today was mostly sunny for the first time in weeks.

Sunday Elizabeth and I had a lovely time baking goodies, for the Ramsarans came yesterday (Monday) and had tea with us. We made a spice cake, orange bread, and butter cookies with the cookie press. Then, with some yellow and green icing left from my birthday cake, we put one yellow flower and one green leaf on each cookie (some circles, some bars) and they looked awfully cute and spring-like. I cut the cake into diamonds, triangles, squares, and rectangles and used the decorator to edge each piece with plain white icing. It was lots of fun and good, too, the only trouble being the number of cookies and the amount of cake left for me to eat!

We thought of buying scales so I could keep close track of my weight, but the only ones available are American made and cost about $30, which does seem sort of silly. I shall try to get to town once a week or so and weigh in one of the department stores.

Janet actually said hello to me yesterday and smiled at me several times, a distinct advance over previous visits. Elizabeth and Susan were very busy every minute but had a more peaceful afternoon than many. No tears, no jealousy, no selfishness apparent to us. Lots of giggles from Elizabeth's room.

I went to Dr. Georges this morning, since he had asked me to stop in after taking some new vitamins. I have four prescriptions for vitamins—general, iron, vitamin B12 for red blood cells, and Lord only knows what else, and we have spent about $18 on them; tomorrow H. picks up refills of them all to last me while he's gone, so with that $36 we will already have exceeded the cost of the delivery itself! Sort of topsy-turvy, isn't it? Dr. Georges says everything is fine. I went upstairs, at his invitation, and his nurse showed me around. There are, I think, three private rooms, one on the breezy side of the house, which is $6 a day, the other two being $5; and two semi-private rooms, which are $3. All the paint is fresh and clean, and the rooms are small but neat and clean. Actually I just peeked in so couldn't tell too much. I went up the back stairs, entering through the kitchen, and that, too, was clean, which means quite a bit in this country. The cook or maid there was cleaning up the breakfast things, and her uniform was unbuttoned over her stomach. Looked peculiar, but I suppose she wanted her comfort. The nurse was very pleasant, friendly, polite, and dressed in an immaculate white uniform. She showed me the delivery room, which, by

George, is air-conditioned! There is no gleaming tile, of course, and what I took to be oxygen tanks resting rather casually on the floor, and a crucifix on the wall—but if the essentials are there, which I guess they are, plus air-conditioning, that's good enough for me. I asked him about anesthetics and he said he prefers an injection that affects the involved area but leaves you conscious; but he can also use trilene or gas-and-oxygen if that is preferred.

We are hoping that Howard's trip to Mount Roraima next month can go as scheduled—if the rain continues there is some doubt, however, as to the condition of the airstrip in the interior. Unless it dries out enough, planes can't land. If that happens he'd go somewhere else, he tells me, but it would be too bad for all these plans to fall through.

E. and I will go downtown tomorrow to buy birthday presents for Howard.

Yes, we'll take Spot with us to the Ramsarans' house, although I don't know just what we'll do with him and their cat, Binky. We're having a great battle with fleas right now, and I don't know who's winning at this point. Little beasts!

I must open up Elizabeth's powder mitt and refill it tonight, since she has asked me to do it and I meant to do it last evening.

Much love to you all,

Marian

Tuesday, March 29, 1955

Dear All—

Nothing very momentous to record this week. The weather has changed, praise be, and we've had some sun, which is a huge relief. Howard hasn't checked with the District Commissioner yet, but at this rate there is every reason to believe the trip will come off on schedule. He is home tonight, correcting exams—the term is over April 6 and exams are being given this week.

Mother, I assume your birthday present never did arrive—Howard heard from Dr. Turner at U. of Texas today that the package of vials sent at the same time hasn't come, either. We suppose it is possible that the vials might have leaked and been confiscated, but can't figure out what happened to your little box. Perhaps it got sent sea mail by mistake—I hope so! At any rate, it wasn't too valuable. Yesterday H. mailed a little box of soap to you. I was so smitten with the pretty colors and fragrances that I bought several, and intend to send one to you, Bee, one of these days.

We celebrated H.'s birthday last evening with ice cream and cake for dessert. I guess I was a bit heavy-handed with the food coloring when I made the decorative icing, for the flowers were a bit garish, but the effect was all right, and as I told Howard, it did not look like a feminine cake! Sort of five-year-old-boy colors.

Bee, I can't believe you've been left out of much news! It seems to me that I ramble on about everything in my letters, but maybe not. Just to bring you up to date, the Ramsarans go on leave on May 31. Their six months doesn't actually begin until they arrive in England, some three weeks after leaving here. They will be due back here in December but won't know the exact time until they make their return reservations, for the shipping companies sometimes have to arrange passage before, sometimes after, the date on which the leave expires. So sometime in December we will have to move from their house, unless, as Margaret says, a miracle happens and John gets another appointment. But even then, we would have scruples against staying in their house, which rents at the government rate of 10 percent of salary, when we have a generous allowance for housing that the other masters don't have.

Howard will go to Brazil in August, planning on being back the first week in September. He will scout around and get as much as possible done there—the State University of Minas Gerais has offered him room and board and transportation within the area, and if there is someone there to interpret he'll be all set. He doesn't anticipate much language trouble, though—we've been told that most people he'll be in contact with can read and write English if they can't speak it.

Mother, the main reason I specified white plisse is because it won't fade. Some of E.'s blue and pink things got so washed-out looking, and then it is easier to remove stains from white. Now I hate to say "will you please send," having said it so often, but sometime will you include in a package some of those nice big diaper pins with the plastic heads? An assortment of colors, I guess. They're so much easier to use than plain safety pins.

We've been having a real battle with Spotty's fleas lately. On Saturday Howard spent nearly two hours giving him a good, thorough bath, and he (Spot) looked so handsome afterward. On Sunday afternoon E. and I took him for a walk, and what did the hound do but roll in numerous piles of manure! I was disgusted, and so was poor dear Howard, who had to bathe him all over again.

Thanks for sending the book, Mother. (*Childbirth Without Fear*, Bee.) I borrowed a copy from Zela last year and just had time to scan it. This is a new edition—the other had no pictures—and naturally, I shall read this with more interest! Howard has just looked at the pictures of the exercises and says he thinks I really should do them. Hmm. I guess I am just plain lazy about exercising.

Saw Joy and Richard this afternoon as E. and I were walking home, and I think Joy and I will go to a piano recital tomorrow night, leaving the men to correct their papers. She was given two tickets and invited me to go—don't know much about the man but it will be interesting anyway. On Thursday Pete is coming for dinner. It's hard to believe Easter is so near—I've bought some new plastic cups, a little scoop, and some spoons for E.'s sandbox, since the dogs chewed up most of what she did have, and the Easter bunny will leave her those plus one chocolate egg. Maybe I'll use food coloring to dye a few for her, too.

All for now—I must leave the dining room, because I keep interrupting H. and he says he *must* get this set of papers done tonight. I shall adjourn to the living room and read, in silence.

Much love to you all,

Marian

Gads, Mother—imagine a boat [trip] costing so much! I'm surprised, too. Heavens, it really wouldn't be worth that expense, since we can have help. No, I don't think I'd want anyone staying with me at night [while Howard is in Brazil]. I don't get nervous, if that's what worries you. The house next door is so close that in the dining room, one speaks very softly if one refers to one's neighbors. We'll have a phone. Enid, M.'s girl, is single, so I imagine she could stay if needed. But I would prefer it only in an emergency. She loves to cook, mostly Indian dishes, I imagine, but there will be no difficulty in showing her what to fix for H. and E.'s main meal (at noon, since Enid won't stay in the evenings) while I'm not home. H. can scramble eggs, heat up leftovers for supper. And Dr. Georges believes in getting patients up quickly, so I shouldn't be away for long.

Just think—if you don't spend $1,000 coming here, where you wouldn't even want to be, you can take me out to dinner at the Tacoma Club, you can buy me Chinese food and Mexican food (can you?) and all sorts of goodies when we do get back! There's something about being pregnant that makes me want to go out for dinner, and here we are without a single decent restaurant. I guess we're lucky to be able to afford one-inch-thick lamb chops, and who am I to complain about them!

Much love again,

M.

Tuesday, April 5, 1955

Dear All—

Such an evening. Shortly before dinner, Spotty fell off the back porch, happily landing in the vegetable garden and not on the rabbit hutch a few inches away. He got up, looking very sheepish and limping slightly, but of course we were all quite concerned and I used it as an object lesson for Elizabeth. Then, right after dinner, as E. got up from her table she lost her balance and fell against the corner of the big table, cutting her lip. To make her feel better, we opened the box from Mother, which H. had just brought home, and took out the new socks. Howard dashed off to school to enter grades, and E. had her bath a little later than usual. I got her into bed and then started perusing the clippings, etc. which were in the box, so—I just finished the dinner dishes, a bit later than usual. Mother, that's a cute little wire gadget for holding letters. It should help ease some of our mess on the desk—this week's letters in one pile, last week's letters in another, bills in another, old empty envelopes in another, etc.

Howard leaves for Roraima on Friday, and so far everything is going according to schedule. He has 180 pounds of rice in the car, and tomorrow $108 worth of groceries will be delivered here. Each man has his duties, and if the weather is good the trip should go off smoothly.

Last week we had a package from [Marian's aunts and uncle] Helen, Julia, and Henry, combination birthday and Easter for Elizabeth. You remember that I sent back the lovely dress they sent at Christmas because it was too small. My goodness, they outdid themselves. Included were all the clothes to make up a complete outfit. A lovely blue nylon dress, with many rows of narrow white lace making a collar effect around the wide, round neck; full skirt with a tiny corsage of pink flowers with pearls on them. The nylon will be warm, but it's not the sort of thing she'll wear except for parties, and I am pleased—it is too large! I shall set the buttons over in the back and it will be fine—should do a couple of years. Also, nylon panties and a stiff nylon petticoat, also with a little bunch of delicate flowers. A pair of the stretchy nylon socks—they are very easy for E. to manage by herself, and when we are in a cooler climate we may switch to them altogether. And to complete it, a little pearl necklace and bracelet—the bracelet has three strands, wired so that it grips her wrist. I took pictures—a whole roll—of her all dressed up, and you shall have copies as soon as possible. They also included a little apron, two Easter candies, and Easter cards from each with a snapshot inside. Very, very sweet of them.

I am getting all excited about E.'s birthday—tried to see what was in the packages you sent, but didn't have much luck. Guess they'll surprise mommy, too! We have another two package notices. Howard bought a tricycle the other day—it looks big, but heaven knows she won't grow any shorter.

The piano recital I went to with Joy last week was rather odd. The man, Professor Patrick Cory, reminded me strongly of Alec Guinness playing the role of an eccentric music teacher, and I derived much amusement from that thought during the evening. He stated after the intermission that the piano was ancient and awful, and undoubtedly that was no help, but I didn't think he played too well. He's been busy the last several months touring the West Indies judging music competitions and granting certificates for the examining board of the Royal Academy of Music, so he hasn't had much time to practice himself. But what really annoyed me was his little explanations—I thought he was terribly condescending to his audience, and it irritated me. Joy said it was nothing compared to the concert he had given the previous Saturday, when he was explaining a fugue and made his audience sing! Someone must have told him that a colonial audience knows nothing about music, and he took it literally. He played very ordinary pieces, repeating some that he'd played the Saturday before.

Yesterday afternoon we spent with the Ramsarans. Susan and Elizabeth had their tea at a separate little table, using a little tea set that was given to Margaret when she was six, and Mrs. McLaren told me, crossing her fingers, that nothing had been lost yet! Made me a little nervous, but the children had a fine time, devoured many cups of milk, enormous quantities of toast, cake, and bread and butter, and broke nothing. I, personally, prefer plastic dishes and a relaxed manner.

Today in the drugstore Howard met a youngish American Lutheran minister and his wife whom Pete had mentioned some time ago. He can't remember their name but thought they seemed very pleasant. They have invited us to their house Thursday evening, and I am eager to meet them, naturally. Howard said we had no one to stay with Elizabeth, and this man said they have a Mrs. So-and-so whom they could recommend highly, and they will send her to our house Thursday evening at 7; we will go to theirs at 7:30. Evidently they have a child or children—they live just a few blocks from us.

Last Sunday Elizabeth and I made some delightful Easter cookies. I can't understand why, but they tasted much better than the same recipe has before. Bunnies, iced in white with pink noses and whiskers and white rosettes for tails, and round, scalloped cookies also iced in white with pink edging or a small cluster of lavender and yellow flowers. I thought they were fetching, really very pretty, and E. has had such fun eating the bunnies—first the tail, then the nose, then the ears, all in order!

Heavens, Mother, don't give another thought to going to Port of Spain! Reason number one—if you got that far, within two hours and $50 of B.G., you would be obliged to see us in our habitat! Reason number two—I am holding the thought that we will be here until spring so that the trip would be simplified all the way around. One of the things I have been putting off until H. goes is a batch of letter writing—one to the Kessler Institute [regarding an evaluation of possible correction of Elizabeth's handicap]. It occurred to me that if we wanted to take E. there (New Jersey), it would save a lot of money to stop on the way home, if H.'s mother could meet us at New York and help steer us around. But New Jersey is one hell of a long way from Texas, and I'm also going to write the Texas branch of the Crippled Children's organization for information. Undoubtedly any work that is undertaken would have to be done over a period of time, and transportation would be an important item, wouldn't it.

Must write checks, go through the returned checks, and decide how much money I'll need while Howard is away.

Much love to you all,

Marian

Thank you for the stamps. H. also says thank you for the Popular Mechanics *subscription—if he had ten free minutes he'd write himself!*

Tuesday, April 12, 1955

Dear All—

Well, Howard got off safely on Friday morning, after a few hectic days of preparation. We waved goodbye, and Elizabeth knew all about Daddy's trip to collect plants, and I explained it over and over during the day, and all was fine. But—about 3:30, who drove up but Daddy, tired and disgusted. It had rained all night Thursday, and the interior airstrip was flooded—they were told this when they arrived at Atkinson at 10 a.m. Friday, but the pilot and other men could scarcely believe it because on Thursday it had been in fine shape. They spent a long time radioing back and forth, and finally decided, after the District Commissioner's aide radioed "If you try to land the plane you will crash," that it wasn't worth trying. So, back they came.

Then H. had to arrange for a plane to be chartered and Wednesday the 13th was chosen as the day. Last Saturday, the pilot phoned and said that he could take their food and supplies in on Sunday and the men in Tuesday, today. So at 7 Easter morning H. and one other man went down to the B.G. Airways ramp and sorted food, eliminating what wouldn't be needed on the shortened trip. And today, finally, they left. After all our farewells last week, we all felt a bit casual about it today, but Elizabeth asked several times where Daddy would sleep, was he eating his dinner now, were there other daddies in the plane, too, were there children in the plane, would the lights go on in the plane at night, and so on. So tonight I am Alone, and I always feel sort of purposeless when H. isn't here. Glad we have Spot, for he is good company after E. is in bed, even if he doesn't smell very good: he initiated a ghastly cycle, first rolling in manure and then having a bath and then rolling in some more to show his contempt of cleanliness. We decided yesterday that it is hopeless and are letting the odor wear off, but last night we nearly had hysterics when he decided to sleep under the bed. I'm glad we all love dogs! (Really, it's not too bad—most of the odor and all the mess wore off while he was in exile a day and a night downstairs.)

Bee, your package for E. arrived and H. picked it up today before he left. I am sure it will be a grand mess, but I am equally sure she will love smearing paint around with both arms. Freedom of expression and all that.

Mother, the dress hasn't come yet, and I hope it does soon—heavens! what if someone takes a fancy to it! Of course, our mail was somewhat fouled up over the Easter weekend, so we may get a package notice tomorrow. Speaking of being fouled up, I had carefully ordered just enough meat, greens, bread, etc. to last E. and me this week, and with Howard home all weekend we ran out of just about everything. Stores here are closed from Thursday night before Good Friday until Tuesday—Easter Monday being quite a holiday here. Everyone has drinkin' parties on Easter, and the traffic is ghastly. We stayed home and couldn't even have one drink Sunday because I'd forgotten to make ice. Tut tut.

This is not a consecutive letter. I keep jumping around! Elizabeth was intrigued with the idea of the Easter Bunny, naturally, and was impressed with the things he left for her. He left a new set of plastic measuring cups, a scoop, and a big funnel for her sandbox—thoughtful of the rabbit because she really needed them. And of course some eggs. I dyed the eggs with food coloring and got some on the counter and on my fingers. It washed off my fingers, but I had a few bad moments when she asked me "What's that?"

Sunday, looking at the counter. I said we'd spilled some coloring when we decorated Daddy's birthday cake, and changed the subject quickly.

We are delighted with the records you sent for Howard's birthday. You sent the Third, and we already have the First, Second, and Fourth (Brahms, Bee). I think it is lovely, and H. asked me to please say thank you for him. For his birthday, more or less, we bought two out of three records of *The Barber of Seville*—the third is on order and should arrive in five or six weeks. Silly way to buy records, isn't it! And a week or so ago, H. bought the Emperor Concerto "for me," which was certainly sweet of him: bless his heart, he's played it about a dozen times this weekend, listening intently and saying that he'd never really heard parts of it before.

I have been having fun with my recorder, which also arrived last week. The customs man at the post office didn't know what a recorder was, and only charged sixty cents duty instead of the high—30 or 60 percent or something awful—duty supposedly charged on musical instruments. It will take practice, and I shall have to learn scales and such, but it is fun and I can manage simple tunes, in C, like "Jingle Bells" and "Oh, Susanna." Howard is thinking seriously of selling his string bass [when we are back home] and buying a bass recorder. They are $90, lots, lots more expensive than my soprano one, but would be easier to keep around than H.'s monster. He says he won't have time for orchestra work for years and years to come, and would like to be able to play something at home. Anyway, yesterday after I'd been playing my tunes for a little while, I asked E. if she didn't think it was pretty. "No," said she firmly. I can see her point, of course, my playing being far from perfect; also I can't talk to her while I'm blowing away and she can't quite understand that.

We spent a very pleasant evening last Thursday with the Voesslers (I think that's the spelling; pronounced Vossler), the American couple I mentioned in my last letter. They are awfully nice, and it amuses me to think of how much ground we covered in one evening in comparison with the more reticent Guianese and English folks. They are Harriet and "Voss"; he is the son of a Lutheran minister and from San Diego. She is from Nebraska, daughter of farmers, had one year of college. They lived in Longview, Washington, for a spell and consider it the wettest, grayest spot imaginable! There is nothing stuffy about him—I have known no ministers and so didn't know quite what to expect. He is very down-to-earth but dedicated, informal, and intelligent. I imagine they are just about our ages, maybe a little older. They have four children: Linda is five, David four, Cheryl will be three on April 26, and Judy is four months. Can't tell you how it tickles me to have another three-year-old around for comparison. Makes me feel much better about some of E.'s foibles. They are attractive children, nicely brought up. On Saturday E. and I took a walk with them, and yesterday they all came over here and played for a while. It is rather annoying to think that they live just around the corner, and have for two years, without our having known them before!

Must quit now and write a note to the Irwins—they'd probably like to know the latest news about their wandering boy!

Much love to you all,

Marian

Had a nice note from H.'s mother today, in which she said, "I think it most remarkable that you are not bothered more with nausea," etc. etc. I have my ups and downs, but so much of the time I feel really wonderful.

But Mother, your saying that I sound in command of the situation really tickles me and I can just hear Howard snort! Of course I am in command of the situation! My only real problem here until it is time for us to return to the States is boredom, and there isn't much excuse for that now. Heaven knows I'm sorry you can't come, but it would be just plain silly at that expense; and once something is settled there is no point about wishful thinking for what can't be. Just call me the Pollyanna Kid!

When the dress does come, I think I can ask Pete to pick it up at the post office for me. He is on vacation now, of course, and I don't think too busy. He'll bring me any mail from Queen's, and he's always so willing to do any errands that need doing. I will order my groceries by phone, and Winifred will bring our fruit from Stabroek.

As I said, I should write the Irwins, so night-night.

M.

Saturday, April 16, 1955

Dearest Parents—

Dinner dishes done, E. tucked into bed. Halfway through *Traviata*—I told H. frankly that I enjoy these operas we've acquired as much for their happy associations as for the music itself. Just think of all those nice Saturday mornings with the radio blaring [broadcast from the Metropolitan Opera] and Bee and me cleaning our rooms. And later, everyone drinking coffee in strict silence!

YEARS OF HIGH HOPES

You'll be glad to know that the dress has arrived safely. Pete brought it today and he will pick up another package for me on Monday. Don't know what that one can be. Mother, I love the skirt and blouse! They're so pretty and cool, I can scarcely wait to wear them. E. wants me to wear them on her birthday—that's when she's going to wear *her* new dress, you know—but I haven't committed myself. Should probably wait a while before starting the maternity clothes. That skirt is certainly nicely made— tricky. Thank you, dear. H. will be pleased to have the 20-cent and 30-cent airmail stamps!

You'll be glad to know that the dress has arrived safely. Pete brought it today and he will pick up another package for me on Monday. Don't know what that one can be. Mother, I love the skirt and blouse! They're so pretty and cool, I can scarcely wait to wear them. E. wants me to wear them on her birthday—that's when she's going to wear *her* new dress, you know—but I haven't committed myself. Should probably wait a while before starting the maternity clothes. That skirt is certainly nicely made— tricky. Thank you, dear. H. will be pleased to have the 20-cent and 30-cent airmail stamps!

Thursday we asked the Voessler children to come wade with E., and they came, bringing three other youngsters and their mother. More Lutherans from Nebraska, these live in New Amsterdam. Nice folks—at one point there were six children in the pool at once! Lots of fun for all of us.

Margaret called today—one good day next week we will go with them to the Botanical Gardens for a picnic. Tea, I suppose she meant.

I've decided that about two weeks or so before we move, as soon as H. removes our screens, I'll hire Winifred and her eldest daughter to come for a day and clean. There will be lots of woodwork to dust that is inaccessible behind the screens, plus windows and *stuff*. Isn't it awful—I don't mind living with cobwebs, but I don't want to leave them for the Scargalls. I shall be busy enough packing dishes, books, etc.

Winifred is buying fruit for me—three limes for 4 cents, a medium-size luscious pineapple for 14 cents, three bananas for 8 cents, four or five oranges for 24 cents.

E. and I made up half a box of chocolate cake into cupcakes today despite my having found two worms in the mix. Don't we grow tolerant though.

I feel grand. Am getting caught up with sewing, letters, etc. High time!
Much love,
Marian

Tuesday, April 19, 1955

Dear All—

Nothing very exciting to report, as you might imagine. Elizabeth, Spot, and I have been very pleasantly busy, though, and I feel virtuous having written some letters that have been on my mind for a long time. I am also determined to finish the white napkins with the gold threads—I've done half, so I think I'll make it. I figure if I can get all caught up on my sewing and letters while H. is gone, I will be more or less ready to think about moving next month. Gads—such a thing to think about!

Let's see—I wrote the parents over the weekend, didn't I, and I said that the white skirt and blouse had arrived. On Monday Pete brought the other package up and this one had the clothes from Bee. Aren't they cute! Such a pretty shade of pink, and I love the polka-dot top. Elizabeth is quite thrilled, too, and eager for me to wear my new clothes. The shorts are sure big, and if I tried to wear them at present I think they'd fall off. The idea, I'm sure, is to avoid the skimpy look later on—jolly good, as we say when we wish to irritate the husband.

I have an oniony taste in my mouth from my salad. A few weeks ago H. brought me some olive oil—a real present since it's awfully expensive here and the only oil available for salad dressing. I've been enjoying salads since then, but it was a shock to see the state of my can of paprika when I first started making the French dressing. It is solid, gray on top. A lesser soul would have thrown it away immediately, but I dug around a bit in the can and found that it is still red underneath the gray part. The poppy seeds I brought back for rolls are still fine, but the sesame seeds have turned soft and look as if they might sprout, or something. I should have kept them in my closet with the light globe burning, I guess. Do you know that our light bills run about $35 a month? And everyone else shudders when theirs reach $14 or $15! We don't even tell people what ours is anymore—they look so shocked. It is one of our wisest expenditures; much of it is the numerous lights in H.'s plant-drying closets, of course, but our clothes never smell musty, and that is saying something.

Elizabeth and I walked by the Voesslers' today but Harriet wasn't home so we didn't stay; then, about 4:45, she stopped in here with the children and another young missionary's wife and her son. This girl is from New York, expecting a baby in June, and they've only been here eight months. They live in Berbice. They didn't stay long, and tomorrow afternoon we'll go over for a while.

Among my selected reading for Howard's absence I picked up a Jeeves story. I don't think all of it is funny, but I find myself laughing out loud rather often. Haven't had much time to read yet, though.

Thanks for sending the clippings. What good news about the polio vaccine!

Spotty is so funny, so thoroughly domesticated now and one of the family. He dances around and barks short commanding barks to be let out the gate, then 15 minutes or so later barks to be let it. He scratches on the door in the evening to come in, curls up, and sleeps contentedly. Follows me to the bedroom and sleeps under the bed or nearby. He seldom barks at outside noises now during the night, and only growls when the paperboy comes in the morning. He doesn't bark at all when Pete comes, or the gardener, or the postman, but I trust he'd bark at a stranger. At any rate, when he does bark he sounds quite fierce, and he is such a nice companionable dog.

All for now I guess. Back to Jeeves!

Much love to you all,

Marian

Tuesday, April 26, 1955

My Dears—

It was a treat getting so much mail today, and I decided a short answer written tonight would be better than a long one postponed until goodness knows when. I'm not in much of a letter-writing mood, but I shall blather on anyway. You all ask if I'm busy and if I'm lonesome. Lord knows I'm busy, and I haven't had time to be lonesome. Last week we saw the Voesslers on two afternoons, and on Friday E. and I went to the Botanical Gardens with Susan, Janet, Margaret, and Mrs. McLaren. Saw all the animals and then sat on a bench and had "tea." Lots of fun. Early Saturday morning Joy called and asked if I'd like to go with them to see *Robinson Crusoe*, a pantomime; I said I'd love to but explained about the babysitting situation and said I'd call her back. About 9 E. and I walked over to the Voesslers' to ask again where Mrs. DeSousa lives, only to find that Richard had already stopped by for the same information. He got her all lined up for me and we were all set to go; then Joy got the flu so another girl went with us. I enjoyed it very much, having heard a lot about English pantomime. Where did I get the idea that pantomime was just gestures? This had words, music—local jokes, etc. Written by two amateurs here, and quite good. Wonderful costumes.

We didn't get home until midnight, and all day Sunday I just waited until bedtime. Yesterday I still felt tired and achy, and this afternoon when I got up from a nap feeling worse than before I decided something wasn't right. I called Dr. Georges, and he suggested I come down to his office, so I called a cab and we went. He gave me a shot and some pills that he said had warded off the flu he thought he was getting a few weeks ago, so I expect to feel better tomorrow. Margaret asked us to come over tomorrow afternoon, but I rather doubt now that we will go.

Just to top everything off nicely tonight, something is apparently the matter with our water pump. I turn the switch and the pump starts, but no water comes up into the tank. How jolly. No water in the faucets, can't flush the toilet, etc. I expect to bring tears to Howard's eyes with my tale of woe when he returns!

Elizabeth was as good as gold until last Saturday, when she either decided deliberately to plague mama or else she started worrying about H.'s absence, or something. She has puddled in her bed at every opportunity, and has practically given up going to the bathroom. We've had puddles on chairs, on the floor, in the sandbox, and yesterday in my lap! And did she think that was funny—what a chortle. I haven't spanked her for that, but both Saturday and Sunday evenings I had to spank her for extreme dawdling and refusal to do as asked. I guess she needed the firm hand, because she has been respecting my tone of authority a bit more.

Harriet and the children came by yesterday for a little while, chiefly to tell me that she hopes to leave here on the 17th to return home. She has had a bad back since Judy was born, and now her doctor here advises her to return home for treatment. They're hurrying it up because another missionary's wife is leaving on the 17th and she would help Harriet with the youngsters. I certainly hate to see them go; she doesn't like the idea either, because her husband isn't due to return until next March. Our conversation was broken up by screams from the bedroom, where Cheryl had bitten each of Elizabeth's arms, hard. Poor Harriet felt much worse than Elizabeth, I know. There are still two little circles of tooth marks on each arm!

Thank you for the rubber bands, Mother. The postman brought most of our mail before lunch today, and Elizabeth ran up the stairs sure that there would be more birthday cards for her. Unfortunately, there weren't, but about 1:30 he came again and brought the cute one from Bee and another from Howard's aunt, and E. was quite satisfied. Howard will be very pleased to get the stamps, Bee.

There is something in Howard's and my makeup that made it natural and easy for us to accept Elizabeth's handicap, and has given us confidence in raising her—luckily, since we've been so far from specialists and whatnot. My worry, or concern, here has been all along "what do American mothers do—" with problems like temper and bedwetting and the like, just normal problems. Elizabeth's own special problems haven't worried us yet, since she has been able to solve most of them without even being aware of doing so.

On Saturday I was trying to read, and Elizabeth was looking through a box in which I keep cookie cutters, Jell-O molds, and a great assortment of junk. She came upon an extra sprinkler top [to be attached to a bottle for dampening clothes before ironing] and wanted to use it, so I sent her to the kitchen for an empty pop bottle. She sprinkled a doll dress, using imaginary water, and then I suggested that she go iron it. She took the silver ivy-leaf ashtray to use as an iron, ran back to the workroom to the ironing board, and proceeded to "iron" all her dolls' clothes. My, she was proud!

I think I shall retire with the new *Reader's Digest*. I can see nothing to be gained by staying up any longer!

Much, much love,

Marian

I got a letter from Mrs. Irwin today but don't feel like answering it. Maybe all the "news" in this letter would depress her—but if you don't think so, call her up and pass it on. Aside from an aching arm, from the shot, and a general blah feeling, I feel fine. Night-night, sweeties. I sure miss you!

Tuesday, May 3, 1955

Dear All—

It certainly is good to have Howard home again. He says the trip wasn't much fun—they had six days of rain at the start, and not enough time to cover the ground leisurely. He looks very thin (don't tell his mother!) and estimates conservatively that he lost ten pounds, but he says he feels fine nonetheless. They all suffered with bad blisters on their feet, and one man fell the first day of hiking and badly bumped a knee—he was in pain the rest of the trip. It sounds just plain grim to me. Some of their clothes and blankets never did dry out—you should have seen the clothes that came home! Talk about dirt. Howard was the only one of the six to actually ascend Mount Roraima, as two men weren't able physically to get up it, and the other three were temporarily cut off from the main party—they'd missed a turn in the all but nonexistent trail.[80] H. got some plants at the top of the mountain but didn't have time to do any collecting on the trail. He says it was worth it but that never again will he plan a trip with people he doesn't know and who aren't experienced campers. Some of the men never did accept their responsibilities enough to help with the camp routine.

I suppose I should backtrack a little, to say that the flu never did really develop, thanks to the shot and the pills. Tuesday night, after I finished my

Chunilall (far right), L. P. Cummings (center), and porters during the trip to Mount Roraima, April 1955.　　　　　　　　　　　　　　　　Photo: R. D. Rock

A porter, with plant presses atop pack and gas can (for Coleman lantern) in hand, before sheer-sided Mount Roraima. Howard's note: "Shade temp. here at mid-day was 95°, sun temp. 160°."　　　　　　　　　　　　　　　　Photo: R. D. Rock

Howard at Kamarang after two and a half weeks in the bush, just before takeoff to Georgetown.   Photo: R. D. Rock

letter to you, I crept into bed with a sweater on and the heavy blanket on the bed and had a good old chill for a while. The pump remained out of whack until 2:30 p.m. Wednesday, but I really wasn't in the mood to do much so I just sat most of the day. On Thursday I felt quite well again and that was a relief. I had told E. that I had a cold, since she has had a cold and knows more or less what that implies, and she was quite solicitous. She brought me hankies for my nose, which wasn't running, and hugged me, and after watching me take a pill she always wanted to know if mommy felt better, now.

On Saturday evening when H. got home, he did look rather strange—dirty clothes, canvas sneakers in shreds, helmet on head, arms burned a dark brown, nose and lips peeling, etc. I don't think E. even recognized him at first—after Howard went to take a shower, E. came to the kitchen and said something to me about "that man"; but by the time we both tucked her into bed, she seemed to be sure it was daddy, home again.

Sunday I tackled some of H.'s clothes (I still haven't got around to the denim slacks, mud-stiff socks, and blankets), then E. and I made her birthday cake and some cookies. We made up the angel food cake I've been hoarding for these last few months, and although it came out burned on top we just cut that off. My oven is so small—the pan really filled it up. We made plain sugar cookies, cutting them into animal shapes, and after our rests we iced them—horses, dogs, chickens, lions, and bunnies. The cake we iced pale pink and piped a darker pink border around the top. It was very pretty.

Yesterday Lucille came for the first time—did I tell you I had decided that I had too much else to do before we move and that I might as well hire someone to do the dusting and sweeping? And it is a major relief just to have someone else carry the garbage downstairs every day. At any rate, Lucille cleaned yesterday, which was fortunate, for I spent the morning making little sandwiches. This, of course, was after E. had opened all her presents and I was interrupted frequently to help get the new dolly's shoes back on, or to help her get on the new tricycle. We are all delighted with the gifts—the finger paints haven't been opened yet, and I may leave them until the rains start again and we have to stay inside. The rains are due soon, alas. The xylophone made a big hit and it does sound pretty; and the lovely books! I love the selections in the poetry book, and you just should have seen E. tonight when H. read, for the first time, the one about the new baby! She was practically pop-eyed when she came to the kitchen to kiss me goodnight, and Howard said she was quite speechless. Tomorrow I imagine we'll go over it picture by picture and word by word, a dozen times.

The toy clock is cute, but I'm afraid time doesn't mean much to E. as yet. She likes to turn the hand around, though. Let's see. The Irwins sent her a little doll with hair and *The Better Homes and Gardens Storybook* (at my request, since I'd heard good things about it. It's lovely—has "Little Black Sambo" and "Peter Rabbit" and some verses from "When We Were Very Young" and lots of others, all with the original illustrations. It has "The Story of the Live Dolls"—always one of my very favorites). Also a lovely little dress, a sleeveless sheer cotton with a design of pink roses, with an attached petticoat with two ruffles, one bound in pink and one in green. It has a black velvet belt and a tiny pink rose pinned on the shoulder. Really lovely. And of course she is fascinated by the tricycle and can scarcely keep away from it. Howard is in the process of blocking the pedals so she can reach them, and I think it will take her a very short time to get the hang of pedaling.

We had quite a party. I was a little embarrassed because John came along—I had specifically invited the little girls and Margaret and said we'd love to have Mrs. McLaren come, too; my embarrassment was because we hadn't asked the Voesslers' daddy, and it looked rather strange, but I'm sure they'll understand. It would have been much simpler without the men (and Howard had planned on staying in his workroom during the party, without shoes) because Margaret and I spent nearly all the time with the six children while they were eating. Perhaps English birthday parties always include tea for the parents. I think all the youngsters had a good time, and there was plenty of food. The angel food cake made quite a hit—it was new to the Ramsarans. The Voesslers brought E. a cute little red purse, and Susan and Janet gave her a set of tiny kitchen furniture—stove, refrigerator, sink, etc. Mrs. McLaren brought her two boats for her wading pool. At the time E. opened her gifts, Susan was downstairs playing in the sandbox; I suggested that E. go down and thank her, and she was so eager to do it that she tripped and fell down two stairs. Great howls and sobs, for by this time it was 5 or so and she was pretty tired. A little while later she fell downstairs on the gravel path, and more howls and sobs. About 6, just as the Ramsarans were beginning to prepare to leave, Richard Allsopp came by with a little box of chocolates for E. from Joy—so he sat down, and the R.'s couldn't leave gracefully for quite a while. Janet was exhausted, E. had just about had it, and Susan was having a fine time. The Voesslers had left earlier. I think it was 8 by the time E. got to bed. I forgot to say how cute Elizabeth looked when I brought in the cake and we all sang to her. She really beamed and giggled and looked simply delighted by it all. And she huffed and puffed and blew out the candles all by herself.

I feel fine—I shall put it in every week, in case it really does make you feel better. I really feel wonderful.

Howard's appetite is simply phenomenal; this noon I'd fixed some rice with a little meat in it, and mushroom soup, and he ate what I would have called three rather generous servings. Bless his heart, I'll feed him all he wants if we can just cover up his bones quickly. I hate to see ribs!

All for now—end of page.

Much, much love to each of you,

Marian

Tuesday, May 10, 1955

Dear All—

Well, it is obvious that we are going to move, because I've been stirring around and doing things that don't seem to get done otherwise. Last week I washed our bedspreads and the little rugs in Elizabeth's room and tinted the bathmat and her green rug darker shades. I don't have anything large enough to boil rugs in, so my dye jobs are always just tintings and they don't last very long. I also washed our bedroom curtains. Today I did the two brown rugs in the living room. Later this week I shall wash the curtains in the living room and workroom, which are the Scargalls', and leave them down until after the weekend. Howard is going to take our screens down then, and early next week Lucille will be busy dusting the louvers and washing the woodwork and windows that have been covered. I've packed all the brown-and-white dishes but the teapot, and I guess if H. has time next weekend he'll take that to the Ramsarans' and leave it. Most of the books have already gone. We look quite empty. Starting early to do all this is the only way—Howard has very little time during the week, and after puttering around all morning I've had enough. I told E. the other day, when we first started packing boxes, that we are going to move, that Mr. Scargall wants to come back and live here, that we will move to the R.'s, and that they are going on a long, long trip. She took it all in and asked where would we live when the Ramsarans come back from their trip! I airily replied, "We'll move to another house, dear," and changed the subject quickly. I thought little children lived in the present!

Mother, in your last letter you sure hit the nail on the head when you said that a child who refuses to be completely toilet trained feels a sense of power. You should just see the look on Elizabeth's face sometimes when she slips! Lately I've remembered to take her to the toilet periodically, over her vehement objections, and we've had no wet pants. Frequently we take a dolly along, and the doll has to go first—she always makes sure that I pull down the doll's damned pants—then she'll go, too. I don't think we need a book yet; I've read articles on the subject in various magazines, and at least one said that if your child was still untrained at four or five you might do well to seek professional advice. I know it isn't a matter of being physically unable to control it, and I'm sure there's no grave psychological block or such. I think she's trying to get away with any and all deviltry that I will take, and there is so little a mother can do about this. Tonight I asked her to get her shoes from the dining room and take them to her room—a daily request, since she generally takes her shoes off while she eats, and she took them one at a time and threw them in her nice clean bed. Laughing wickedly, she said, "Now I'm going to take off your dress and socks and panties and spank you." I asked her if she needed a spanking, and she said, "I do!" I told her I didn't think she did, and ordered her into the bathtub. She might well be termed a "spirited" child, and I guess we should be thankful for it, as we are.

I have begun wearing my new pretty clothes, and I must say they are certainly comfortable. There is a great difference between wearing skirts, with maybe the top button undone, and loose sweaters, and cotton dresses that all seem to fit snugly around the waist. Oh Mother, I am so tickled with the gray dress! That big box arrived last Friday. We opened the box while E. was finishing her lunch, and naturally her eye fell upon the pink booties and little white baby shoes. She asked about them, and I said they were for a baby, and that sometime we would have a baby to wear them. I thought it best to be vague—there's a long time to wait, and we should probably get settled from our move before we concentrate on the baby.

Howard should be home from his class in a few minutes; he ate at 5, so maybe I can entice him to eat a meat sandwich with hot gravy when he gets back. And some cake.

On Sunday evening Joy and Richard came over, and as arranged earlier she made Guianese chow mein to show me how. She says here it is used as a dish to use up leftovers—anything goes. She made it with regulation Chinese noodles, leftover chicken (mine), Vienna sausages, corn, string beans, a chopped onion, and strips of a thin omelet on top. Joy brought her bottle of soy sauce, and of course that by itself would make anything taste good. It was good, and we ate a lot.

Howard is on the front porch, finishing up a cabinet that will hold his stamp albums and duplicates. We will keep it in the living room, and of course it will have a small light burning in it. I guess we will also put our beat-up old dining table in the living room at the Ramsarans' house, too, since there is no desk and we always seem to need something to spread books, letters, papers, stamps, sewing, etc. out on. It is such a big, uninspired-looking living room that the more of our stuff we can put in it, the better.

I had better go sprinkle my ironing for tomorrow.

The best thing about this next move is that, once again, we'll have a decently short address. How tired I get of this one—it's just too long.

Much love to each of you,
Marian

Tuesday, May 17, 1955

Dear All—

This letter is mostly just something to wrap around Howard's pictures from Mount Roraima; I haven't much news. Aren't the pictures good! The tiny ones looked fair, but when we saw the enlargements we were both very pleased. I still wish you could see the Keds H. wore back—they are in ribbons, and although they should have been thrown away immediately somehow they are still with us. Howard threatens to have them cast in bronze, and I admit I can see his point.

He spent all weekend taking down our screens, washing them with the hose, and rolling them up ready to move. We look hideously bare and are just marking time now until we can do all the last-minute jobs before moving. Not much left to do.

The Voesslers came by Thursday evening for a while and we had a nice, last visit. They were supposed to leave today but at that point still hadn't received their passport from Trinidad. We will see Voss again, I imagine, and he said he'd like to go with H. the next time H. goes collecting out at the airbase. He is an awfully nice person, and I am sure he'll miss his family terribly.

Poor Pete has himself in a real pickle. Sunday evening while eating dinner, we heard the screech of brakes and looked out the window to see that Pete had rammed a girl on a bicycle, with his car, that is. As we watched, a crowd gathered and Pete and another fellow lifted the girl into his car, and he drove off. Pete has been charged with intoxication while driving; the girl has a fractured hip; and the story was in the most sensational of our three local papers today. Someone at school told H. that the tests used locally to establish intoxication are a farce: walk a straight line; comparison of handwriting, etc.—no blood test. So perhaps he hadn't had more than one drink. I think the case comes up June 9. He's all set to sell his car right away; Howard stopped by this morning and said he's completely unnerved, shaking, etc.

If you haven't already thought of it, you should start sending letters to us at Queen's.

Damn the mosquitoes! I think as soon as Howard gets home we'll go to bed and read—take refuge under the net!

Much love to each of you,
Marian

Glad you like the soap and [guava] jelly; kind of a funny present for you, Daddy, but we like the stuff. I am halfway through a week of staying in bed, on Dr. Georges's advice. There were a few signs that this baby might not stay put where it belongs, and he said the only thing to do is to stay in bed for a week and see. I asked if I should be worried and he said no, it was merely a precaution to take and that it might mean nothing at all. H. fixes breakfast and lunch; Lucille does breakfast dishes and cleans. Margaret's girl, Enid, comes in the afternoon, irons the necessities, and fixes dinner. It's a workable arrangement but I'm going mad—not used to enforced inactivity. We decided not to mention this to H.'s folks because they worry excessively, and I don't think I'll even tell Bee, since we think everything will be okay. I am writing it to you, trusting that you won't fret, because I love you two and always like to have your thought waves attuned to mine. I shall call Dr. Georges on Thursday and see if I can't at least do the cooking, even though I have to watch stairs and lifting, etc. Don't worry!

Wednesday, May 25, 1955

Dear All—

Thank goodness this week has been calmer than last—we seemed to go from one crisis to another there for a while. I mentioned Pete's accident last week, didn't I. We were getting disgusted with him for not trying to snap out of his doldrums after it happened, and then on Thursday Pete's landlady informed H. that Pete wasn't eating. Howard had been stopping by faithfully once or twice a day to see him, and Pete wasn't at all cordial, finally resorted to covering his face with a towel and refusing to look at people. The Mootoos, the folks whose house he lives in, were worried, and so were we. Howard went to see Pete's lawyer and talked him into going to see Pete, for he didn't realize how serious Pete's condition was. Thursday night Howard and a police inspector who used to be a neighbor of the Pedersons' went to see Pete, and Pete refused to believe that things were looking up. The girl he hit is still in the hospital, of course, but doing as well as can be expected, but Pete said, "They tell me she's all right," implying that she is worse off than ever. All day Friday various people tried to get various doctors to go see Pete, but most doctors are wary of going "out of town," as we are here in Subryanville, to see patients unless they know them personally. Finally someone recommended Dr. Georges as being one of the best men here to deal with mental disorders (there are no trained psychiatrists here), and on

Friday evening Howard took him to see Pete. Dr. Georges examined him with some difficulty, was worried about a bad cold that he said might go into pneumonia if Pete continued to avoid food, and said that Pete would be taken to the hospital on Saturday after being examined by one of the Public Hospital men. He gave Pete some pills to make him sleep, and they left—Howard got home to dinner about 10 p.m. On Saturday Pete was much improved—evidently the idea of going to the hospital startled him enough to force him out of his state. Dr. Georges stopped by on Saturday, and of course we don't know what he told Pete, but Pete was terribly impressed by the man, his personality, ability, etc. Aside from the fact that he refuses to drive and has his car up for sale, Pete seems all right now.

Wednesday evening when we were ready to retire, we called Spotty as usual but got no response; Howard found him downstairs in a corner near the garage, with what we feared to be a broken leg. Evidently he'd fallen off the porch again, this time with poor results. I thought dogs had more sense! Anyway, Thursday morning Howard took him to the livestock station at the Botanical Gardens (there are no private vets here) and the technicians decided it was just dislocated, snapped the bone in place, and put a cast on it. Spot seems absolutely oblivious of the cast, scratches his head with that leg, and trots all over using four legs. He's wary of the upper steps, though, and H. has had to carry him up the stairs these last few nights. Spot is filthy and needs a bath desperately, but of course we can't do that for two more weeks until the cast can come off.

While I am thinking of it, Mother, H. informed me that Q.C. has received both the April and May issues of *Popular Mechanics* and he hasn't; could you send a postcard and inquire?

Howard has been busy building cabinets lately: one for his stamps, one for his Cassias, and aha! one for me to keep in the kitchen, for salt, cereals, cookies, etc. We have been so disgusted lately with the salt turning to liquid overnight and the cornflakes that get rubbery almost as quickly. Each cabinet will have a light globe in it to keep the stamps unstuck, the Cassias free from mildew, and the Krispies crisp. Strange that it has taken us so long to think of some of these minor improvements. Next on Howard's list is a group of containers to hold our growing record collection. We have kept them all standing together on a shelf under the radio, but there are so many now that it's hard to get out what you want. We have over 50 twelve-inch records.

Lucille really slays me—I can't decide if she is merely dense, overawed, or perhaps just completely untaught. At any rate she'll only be with us for a few more days. She is so submissive with Elizabeth that E. is encouraged to do all sorts of wicked things that she never even thought of when I was wielding the broom. She has to date thrown a cleaning rag out the window, repeatedly thrown cushions on the floor, knocked my sewing basket onto the floor, thrown a pile of clean clothes on the floor and dampened them with my sprinkler bottle, etc. I've told Lucille that if E. is bothering her to lead her to me and tell me about it. So far, she hasn't. I hear E. laughing like a little fiend, and investigate and find something mischievous going on. One of the chief factors involved is that Lucille has no concept of the Toy. I'm sure she's never had any of her own, and heaven knows I don't blame her. The minute E. takes her tricycle to the living room and abandons it, Lucille pushes it back to the bedroom. E. asks to have her broom and dustpan to help, but as soon as she puts them down, Lucille thrusts them back into the closet. Yesterday Elizabeth was sitting in the living room looking at *The Little Engine That Could*, a birthday present that arrived just the day before yesterday. Elizabeth proceeded to tear up one of the pages, badly but not beyond repair, and Lucille was just standing there watching her! Today when H. came home for lunch he found the hose pouring water into E.'s wading pool, which had long since overflowed, flooding the grass and concrete—and Lucille standing there, watching it without making a move to turn off the faucet or ask me if it was meant to be on. I assume E. had turned it on. Ah well, at least she gets the cobwebs off the ceiling and the food spots off the wall around E.'s table, and, by George, she *does* run down the stairs with the garbage and the wastebaskets, so I guess it's worth it. Hope Elizabeth gets over it after we move. I shall have to make things clear to Enid and Elizabeth both.

All for now. Hope you all have a happy holiday on the 31st, while we slave away. The Ramsarans leave at 4:30 a.m. on Tuesday, we move in as early in the morning as possible—the good Lord willing, the movers will move quickly and the sun will shine—and the Scargalls move back into this house that afternoon!

Much love,

Marian

Parents, you'll be glad to know that I've had no more difficulties and trust they are all over. Dr. Georges advised me to stay quiet this week, so we've had Enid come in the afternoons again to fix dinner. I feel fine and shall just act the perfect lady during all this moving, and not budge a box or even carry anything downstairs to the car. Saturday morning Richard is going to help H. take stuff to the Ramsarans'—clothes from the closets, pictures, etc.

S-D informed H. the other day that Q.C. is going to get another Fulbright man next fall, a physics teacher. No more information yet but we hope to hear soon.

ENDNOTES

76 our [next] house in Subryanville (10/5/1954): From Howard's later recollection: "The house—actually the north half of a sprawling duplex—was very much to our liking, both in its general layout and its proximity to the coast, which spawned a breeze much of the year. We were close enough to hear the night-time calls of the thousands of giant toads, called crapauds locally, that lived in the grassy tidal flats."

77 the report of the Constitutional Commission; "unready for self-government" (11/14/1954): Governor Savage read the Robertson Commission's report to the Legislative Council on November 2. It was excerpted the following day in *The British Guiana Bulletin*, a weekly supplement published by the *Daily Chronicle* and sponsored by the colonial government as a public relations effort against the PPP. The report stated that the commission had been "driven to the conclusion that so long as the PPP retains its present leadership and policies there is no way in which any real measure of responsible government can be restored without the certainty that the country will again be subjected to constitutional crisis. We have no doubt that British Guiana, with its precarious economy, cannot afford another crisis of the kind that developed in 1953 and we can, therefore, see no alternative but to recommend a period of marking time in the advance towards self-government." According to the commission, "it cannot be denied that since India received her independence in 1947 there has been a marked self-assertiveness amongst [East] Indians in British Guiana." It added that educational and economic advances among East Indians "ha[ve] begun to awaken the fears of the African section of the population," noting "a tendency for racial tension to increase." It further identified "a very powerful communist influence" within the PPP and contrasted it to the "socialists," such as Burnham, which it described as "essential democrats" whose "preference at all times would have been that the Party should pursue its constitutional objectives by straightforward and peaceful means," thus pointing the way for Burnham to take control of the PPP.

78 nursing home (2/12/1955): Addressing convalescence rather than services for the elderly, a nursing home was a small, private hospital facility overseen by an individual doctor.

79 *Green Mansions* (2/22/1955): W. H. Hudson's popular work of fiction, subtitled "A Romance of the Tropical Forest" and published in 1904, was set in the remote Guiana interior that includes the sheer-sided, flat-topped Mount Roraima.

80 Mount Roraima trip (5/3/1955): L. P. Cummings, a master at St. Stanislaus College who was part of the three-week expedition, wrote about it in the school magazine. The trip began with a three-day boat ride up the Mazaruni, Kako, and Arabaru rivers, traveling by day and camping on the banks by night. Joining the party at Amigoi Landing were fourteen Amerindian droughers,

hired to transport equipment and supplies. "The next few days followed a pattern: we would strike camp at about eight, set off through the damp and narrow trail, across streams, through incredibly large swamps, up slippery slopes, stop at midday for a few biscuits, and walk again until about six. And all the time it rained incessantly. . . . We got so used to this rain that we would eat, talk and even take short naps in it." On Monday the 18th the men camped on the border between British Guiana and Brazil. "This part of the boundary is the summit of a very steep mountain, a mountain covered by superficial deposits of red lateritic clay. . . . The clay was slippery and treacherous, the slope was steep, the footholds were pools of mud. Each step had to be studied, for one false step would mean crashing down into the yawning valley to our right, or tumbling headlong down, down, downward to lie prone against any of the huge trees that rise like dripping sentinels on the slope." Cummings was among those who became separated from the party. He finally caught up with the others at the camp, which had appeared from a distance to be "almost against the vertical Roraima Wall," but, exhausted, he didn't ascend: "I glared at the huge box-shaped mountain that I had come all this way to climb. It had defeated me!"

Above, the Irwins' home on the college compound. Below, from the front, residences of the Irwins, Persauds, Camerons, Beckleses, and Sanger-Davieses. "The wood in the foreground is being used in the new houses," Howard noted.

Chapter 6

1955–1956: QUEEN'S COLLEGE COMPOUND

Tuesday, June 7, 1955

Hello, dears,

I trust my failure to write last week didn't alarm you all unduly—after all, we did move! By now of course we're pretty well settled, and the move itself last Tuesday went very smoothly. On Monday when we came over to say our farewells to the Ramsarans, Howard discovered that they were planning to go out to the airbase by bus, at 4 a.m. Good old John, the original worrywart, didn't trust any of the taxis to get them there and preferred the bus, which is about the ghastliest form of transportation you can imagine. As they were all just recovering from colds, Howard offered to drive them out instead of leaving them to the mercies of the witless bus drivers; so at 2:45 Tuesday morning we both got up and I made Howard some breakfast and had a glass of milk myself. I didn't need to get up, of course, but we'd both been sleeping lightly and I was hungry. H. drove Margaret, her mother, and the children (John shepherded the suitcases aboard the bus) out, and got back just before 8 a.m., just in time to bring E. and me over here. The movers arrived promptly and, thanks to Howard's good organization, succeeded in getting everything transferred to this house by about 10:30.

I was surprised to find this house in quite a mess. None of the drawers in Mrs. McLaren's room, now ours, had been completely emptied, so I had to take out the odd knitting needle and hairpin, etc. and dust them out. Ditto the kitchen cupboards. The counters in the kitchen had been covered with white plastic that was torn and stained, and the only other work surface is a table that is unfinished and very rough. Also, all the drawers in Mrs. McLaren's built-in dresser had lost their knobs, making it almost impossible to pull them open. None of the closet doors fit; we found lots of tiny 60-watt bulbs serving huge areas of space; the floors need polishing, woodwork everywhere needs scrubbing, etc. etc. Thank *goodness* for Howard! Already he's installed lights in our closets; put up my sink light; put in new drawer knobs; covered the kitchen counters and table with oilcloth and provided me with a little garbage pail; and he's in the process of building screens for our bedrooms. This house has such a lot of open wall space that we've decided against screening all of it, so he is going to do the bedrooms and a screen door for the hall, and we can at least sleep without nets. This house has oodles of ants—black ones that smell meat or sugar in an instant, and red ones that bite, and tiny little ones that just run about aimlessly. We had swarms of black ones in the shower one night, and Lord only knows what they find to interest them there. They constitute the only animal life, however, so I suppose we can consider ourselves lucky.

The only animals, that is, not counting Binky. Binky was originally the Larthes' kitty, inherited by the Ramsarans and now by us. I don't really understand cats, and of course this poor creature has Spot to contend with, too, so I don't imagine he's much happier than I am. He's used to eating meat, potatoes (boiled, preferably), and gravy twice a day, with milk for breakfast—cow's milk, that is, which is local parlance for Klim or Carnation unless they're mixed with bread. I give him raw meat once a day, in the evening, and to hell with boiling potatoes just for him! I think the Ramsarans always had table scraps in abundance, and we just don't have any. Elizabeth is quite taken with Binky, and he is a nice enough cat, I guess, good-natured at least. He is orange and white, sort of scrawny looking.

Elizabeth is completely happy here, I believe. She runs to the toilet when she needs to, hasn't wet her bed, and has been generally good about nearly everything. She and Indrani Persaud, the four-year-old next door, seem equally happy to have a new playmate, and I think they'll have fun together. Indrani's brother Bini is two and a half and shy. We've just barely seen him but I think he is intrigued enough to play with them now.

The only bad times we've had with Elizabeth were last weekend, twice when I asked her to cease doing something that was annoying me—once she was kicking me while I was sewing on the bed, and when I asked her to stop she continued. I marched her into the living room and told her to stay in there for a while with Daddy. She immediately started to follow me back; Howard told her to stay, and she said, "I won't" in a very determined voice. So Daddy had to plop her in a chair, impress her with the fact that one does not say "I won't" to one's parents, and she sat there howling with indignation and surprise for a minute or so. The other occasion was similar, and when told to sit in a chair, she said, "I don't want to" and had to be told that she must sometimes do what we want her to do. She resented that with gusto, for a few minutes, then sat quietly for a few more until lunch was ready. It's all very well to talk about reasoning, but this precious child evidently has a generous share of will, and if she really wants to do something forbidden, reasoning and substitution and sweetness-and-light do not work. However, most of the time she is happy to cooperate and help, and she dusts and helps make meatballs and feeds Binky and generally is as sweet as one could ask for. This strong-mindedness is a good character trait, heaven knows, but she has got to learn that she can't always have her way.

She enjoys being "Mommy," which makes me Daddy and Daddy, Elizabeth. She asks, "Where has Elizabeth gone?" and I must answer, "Why, Mommy, I think Elizabeth has gone to school already." And as I make her bed she'll say, "Daddy is making Mommy's bed." Or she'll suddenly be Binky, or Spotty, or Bitsy—or Spot and E. will both be Binky and "What will we do if we have two cats named Binky?" She delights in teasing me by saying she's going to cut me up, eat part of me, and put the rest in the refrigerator, and "then Daddy and Spotty and Elizabeth would have to get a new mommy." I pretend to be horrified, and she thinks that's just awfully funny. Lately, all the washing has consisted of Mommy's baby sheets, Mommy's baby apron, Mommy's baby shirt, etc., regardless of whether they belong to me or H. or E. Her mind flits from one thought to the next with tremendous ease, and out of a clear sky she'll ask a question pertaining to a story we've read or quote a few lines from something. She was so thoroughly prepared for this move ("Now Elizabeth, this chair is Mr. Scargall's and we'll leave it here, but *this* is ours and we'll take it with us," repeated for nearly every item) that I believe it has seemed entirely natural to her, and she's quite aware that some of these things are ours and some the Ramsarans'.

Looking back at the first page, I should add that the only reason I was surprised to find this house in less than apple-pie condition is that the Ramsaran family, all of them, are nuts on the subject of cleanliness. Heaven knows I can ignore cobwebs and I don't even see lots of things, but so many times I've seen Margaret or her mother exclaim in horror over some little curl of dust, or Enid's failure to sweep under a chest, or something similar. Ah well, at least it's the grime of friends!

On Sunday evening H. and I went to the Allsopps' for a special meal—real Guianese pepperpot. It's made with a pig's trotter or a cow heel, and beef, and the essential ingredient is something called cassareep, just what that is I don't know.[81] It is real peppery, served with boiled rice, and delicious. The advantage, in the pre-refrigerator age, was that a pepperpot would keep up to three months, with a daily boiling to keep it from spoiling, and meat added as needed. Joy also introduced us to a new fruit that she calls a Malaca pear and Winifred calls a French cashew, and that we think tastes like a rose smells when fresh, but when cooked is very nice. (Howard verifies that it is the fruit of the cashew.) It's a lovely plum color. Wish I could think of something to introduce her to! I wore my white linen skirt and blouse for the first time, and cheers! the skirt doesn't wrinkle. It's a beautiful dress and I feel really dressed up in it.

Much, much love to you all,

Marian

I'm feeling fine, and no ill effects from the move, thank goodness. Dentist appointment next week and I dread it! H. says it was a 25-watt bulb serving hall, shower, and john!

Tuesday, June 14, 1955

Dear All—

It poured much of the morning today, and now, at 7:30 p.m., there is no breeze and the air is at its muggiest. S-D is holding forth at the meeting of his Musical Society across the way at the school, which is just an hour or so of S-D blaring forth.

Yesterday morning I had my regular visit with Dr. Georges, and everything seems to be as it should. Today, finally, I went to the dentist, and he poked around a little bit and said I have no cavities. Nothing shatters my confidence in a dentist as much as being told that. However, he said my gums are slightly inflamed and he wants me to come back next week to treat them, and he said he might find something else then. Of course, since Dr. Greif patched me up last summer [in Tacoma] I have made a point of brushing my teeth four times daily, after meals, and that may have made some difference, but I can't believe it would make so much!

We had a real, genuine scare yesterday. Elizabeth tumbled off the back stairs, fell about eight feet and landed in gravel. Had she fallen about two steps farther up she would have landed on solid concrete. I don't know just what she was doing, probably leaning over the banister too far—it's hard to get information from a child. I was right in the kitchen, heard something land, and there was Elizabeth on her back in the gravel. One of the groundsmen was cutting grass near our house, and he came running just as I got to her; I sent him over for Howard (one of the compensations for living in the backyard of Q.C. is his nearness in emergencies). Poor E. was petrified and howling, and she'd cut her tongue a little but seemed otherwise all right, so H. took her upstairs. I kept her on our bed a little while, for she was quite shaken and nervous, but after an hour I dressed her again, and before lunch she was back in form, "scrubbing" the kitchen floor for me. She has two very small bruises on her back and one elbow was scraped a bit, and I found a tiny scratch on her head. As soon as H. saw she wasn't seriously hurt he went downtown and ordered enough wood to put up more uprights and two more rails on our stair railings, and by dinnertime yesterday they were up. Thank the Lord for the elasticity of children's bones! She scarcely referred to the incident today, except to say that "Spot didn't like it when he fell down the stairs, either."

Last Friday night Enid stayed and H. and I went to see *Sabrina*. We enjoyed it and noticed posters announcing that *Rear Window* and *The Country Girl* are both coming "soon," whatever that means. *The Living Desert* starts here this Friday and we're going to see that.

Howard has the screens nearly finished—all built, just needing a coat of paint on the frames. He hopes to get them up this weekend.

Yesterday Mr. Cameron, one of the Q.C. masters, asked H. if he and his wife could come call on us. To be polite, we asked them to come have tea with us tomorrow, but they can't make that—they'll come at 6. He is a man so filled with his own importance that any contact at all is a trial. But they are going on leave in December, and we would like to get their house here in the compound when they go. It's the house Margaret and John found in a ghastly state, but a house is a house and it is just a matter of hiring someone to clean it up if necessary.

All for now. I've started sewing baby clothes—such fun!

Love to you all,

Marian

Mother, will you buy a Scrabble set and send it, please, fairly promptly? H.'s nice young lab assistant wants one for his sister and can't get it here. If you take its cost and postage out of our account, H. will be reimbursed here. H.'s subscription to Popular Mechanics *came through practically the day after I wrote you. It never fails!*

And yet another little request (aren't we awful!): Would you phone the Public Library and get the address of the Ronald Press in New York? I'm to get a book for one of the men on the staff but cannot find the address of the firm anywhere here. Thanx. —H.

Tuesday, June 21, 1955

Dear All—

Time goes so quickly—I had to write down glacé cherries on my grocery list today so I would be sure and have them to decorate Fourth of July cookies, and it's so hard to believe we're nearly through June. We got lots of mail today, including a package notice, and at lunch, as I was speculating on what it might be, E. piped up and said maybe it was some toys for *her*. Don't they learn early! It turned out to be the box from Mother with baby shirts, diapers, and chili chips, and I was awfully glad that there were the two little books for E. because they pleased her immensely. Right on top, too! All those goodies, Mother—my problem shall be breaking down and opening that can of tuna fish!

Howard had a letter from Dr. Turner at the U. of Texas that relieves us all. He's been sending numerous vials containing plant buds in a fixative solution, and for some reason the last few batches hadn't been turning out at all well when Dr. Turner examined them. H. thought and thought and thought, and finally decided the villain in the piece was the metal liners in the caps of the little bottles he'd used for those shipments. Dr. Turner congratulated him on his "sleuthing," and from now on H. will use something instead of the metal liners, which, it seems, were attacked by the solution and the chemical result played the devil with the buds. Complicated, isn't it. Dr. Turner writes nice letters, mostly business; in this one he said he was sure we'd like Austin, that it's uncivilized enough for most people to be genuinely friendly yet civilized enough to have most of the amenities. I'm sure it will seem very civilized to us.

Enid is being married this Sunday, and I'd agreed to give her a week off starting this Thursday. However, yesterday she came with a bad cold, and today she didn't come at all so I may be without help for the next ten days. Heavens! Sweeping gives me a pain in the back, literally and figuratively, and I can't see doing more of it than absolutely necessary. To my way of thinking, that means the kitchen and dining room only daily, and the obvious parts of the living room without shifting furniture around.

I feel just fine and manage to keep comfortably busy without doing the house cleaning, and I am not one to dust the furniture with my last gasp just because it looks a trifle dusty.

I went back to Dr. Wong, the dentist, today, and he cleaned my teeth and poked around and I gather there are three cavities. He said I should use dental floss after each meal. I am really pleased with the difference all this brushing seems to have made. Next Tuesday when I go I am going to take Elizabeth along so she can get an idea of what it's all about and maybe have her teeth looked at, too. He has a nice manner and, as the father of eight youngsters, should have a way with children!

We're doing lots of talking about the new baby now, since I had to start the sewing, and Elizabeth seems quite thrilled by it all. Nancy [doll] has become her baby, and I change Nancy's diaper umpteen times a day. The Persauds' baby, not quite three months old, is a big help. E. has watched her drink her milk and have a bath, and was quite agog after watching the baby's diaper being changed. Mrs. Persaud is very sweet and apparently doesn't mind another youngster watching the proceedings. We take turns having the children over for an hour or so every morning, and then on most afternoons they play together some, too, but our hours are so different that it doesn't work out too well. They are downstairs from 5 to 6:30 or so, just about our mealtime.

Sunday I repaired the nighties and jackets that E. practically wore out—new ribbon and a few rips sewed up. I've finished two new nighties and two jackets, and have two more of each cut out. I think that, with the shirts, will be plenty. While I'm thinking of it, if anybody wants to send anything in the way of clothing, may I say emphatically no nylon, of course, and I'd really rather wait until we see what, or should I say which, the baby turns out to be. If we have a boy, I shall have to send out a frantic SOS for some of those cute cotton knit suits that I see advertised, for after a couple of months I believe a boy should be dressed like a boy. If we have a girl, we're all set.

We had a letter today from Margaret, and their leave hasn't started out too well. The afternoon of their arrival in London, Janet came down with dysentery and was taken to the hospital. She'd been there five days when M. wrote and was due home the next; poor Margaret said each day they'd been to see her (unknown to Janet) and each time she'd been crying. She'll be two in July, a bad time for the upheaval of the sea trip and then being sick on top of it. Mrs. McLaren is having sinus trouble, but the others are well and Susan is delighted by everything.

Thanks again for the package, Mother—I'm sure I enjoy the "surprises" as much as Elizabeth does! Oh yes—H. said the twine was all off the box, the customs declaration off too, so he had to open the box and take everything out. At that, the man was in a friendly mood and the duty came to seventy-some cents!

Much love to you all,
Marian

Thursday, June 23, 1955

Dear Mother—

No news since I wrote Tuesday, but I just remembered something I meant to ask you before. A request, but I don't think you'll mind. I decided it might be a good idea to buy a new doll to present to E. after I've left to have the baby—to give her something to think about other than my being gone. At any rate, Nancy is in sad shape and if she lasts until October I'll be grateful. Last Saturday I looked here for a doll, but the stores don't even try to stock them except at Christmas and I didn't have much luck. They had a cute boy doll but I think a girl is more fun for E.; and a sweet baby doll but Mary is still in good shape—not as popular as Nancy!

So, will you please purchase for me a girl doll, about 12 inches high—plastic skin. Washable. No real hair (the sweet doll with hair, from Howard's grandmother for E.'s birthday, is a fright now! Hair all pulled off, or almost so). I don't know how well you recall Nancy and Dennis and Mary, but the first two didn't last nearly as well as Mary, whom I expect was more expensive. Hell's bells, you know the sort I want—cute and durable. I'd like to have time to make a dress or so for the doll, so if you can send it soon I'd be very pleased.

Elizabeth and H. have such fun together—he bathes her and puts her to bed every night but Tuesday and Thursday, when he teaches. They have real routines—

H: "What's in here?", patting E.'s tummy.

E: "Sup." (laughter)

H: "What did you have for supper?" (We all have had the same thing ten minutes previously)

E: "Eggie, custard, carrots, cheese," etc. etc.—the more improbable the more she giggles, and of course the point is to avoid saying what she really did have!

Must sprinkle some clothes to iron tomorrow. I've quit ironing sheets, dishtowels, and H.'s shirts—and it seems to have cut my ironing in half. And my washing has gone down to twice weekly instead of three times, principally because E. has decided not to wet the bed anymore (I hope a permanent decision). No wet sheets since we moved—a novel twist on the moving-unsettled-insecure theory! Bless her heart, she's sure sweet.

Love to you both,

Marian

Tuesday, June 28, 1955

Dear All—

We've had a busy day. Elizabeth and I went to the dentist today, and I am relieved to say that it was a pleasant, successful trip. She walked around and looked at everything, and watched while he filled one of my teeth. I'm sure she didn't miss a gesture. We took Nancy along and a couple of her books, but she only looked at them for a few minutes—Dr. Wong was much more interesting. And then it was her turn, and she sat in the chair, eyes wide but not visibly upset, and opened and closed as he told her to do. No cavities, thank goodness. She practically leapt out of the chair when he was through and she walked quickly out of the office, so she was a bit unnerved but on the whole quite composed about it.

We had our usual early Tuesday supper, and after H. went to school E. and I rinsed the dishes off and walked over to see Mrs. Patoir. I'm glad we went—she's going to the hospital on Saturday for an operation and will be grateful for some of the magazines Mother sent. The magazines arrived about a week ago, and I've had fun looking at them but am always glad to pass them on. Two of her three oldest daughters are in Canada and the other in Germany, and one of her little girls has been seriously ill with nephritis. The house was just as bad as ever, and she as untidy as ever, but just as friendly and very glad to see us.

Last Thursday evening I was in a mood—I didn't want to sew on the baby clothes, didn't want to read. I moped around for a while and finally got out the handkerchiefs and appliqués that Bee sent me for Christmas. I did the blue fish, the two little clusters of flowers, and the strawberries and am tickled pink with the way they came out. They look just darling, Bee, and I was completely cheered up by the time I'd finished.

Work has started on the [duplex] house being built next door to us. Didn't I say last week that they intend to get it done by the end of September? They probably won't, the way things work here. We may get one [unit], but H. has to apply to the Colonial Secretary and Go Through Channels and Lord knows what all.

We are in the midst of a double financial blow. The B.G. civil servants have just been granted a raise to cover the increase in the cost of living—we would have been given about a third again as much as we get now. But starting with this fiscal year, the local government no longer pays H.'s salary; it all comes from the U.S. Educational Commission, and it won't raise our money since the £1000 is standard for teachers in the colonies under the Fulbright program. There was just one ray of hope—the man who wrote said that since H. is such an exception to all established rules, having been here so long, they might reconsider our case. The other blow: the $1000 grant under Public Law whatever-it-is has been cut to $500 for all Fulbright teachers and lecturers in the colonies; completely cut out for other Fulbrighters! Snarl.

Last Wednesday E. and I washed baby clothes—gads—what quantities! At least it looks like a lot now. At any rate, I shouldn't have to worry about drying diapers in the oven or any other such nonsense.

The screens are up, but the screen door in the hall dividing the bedroom end of the house from the rest isn't done so we're still using nets. Poor Howard is so busy during the week, he just doesn't have any time for carpentering then.

Elizabeth will be so glad to have the new records, Mother. Just in the last few days I've seen a change in her receptiveness when I've played her records—yesterday she sang along a little bit with the record, and in the afternoon while I was playing some songs on my recorder she said the words along with them—the first step in "singing," isn't it.

Enid is supposed to come back to work tomorrow and I certainly hope she does. We're a little bit dusty, under the beds especially, and the shower needs scrubbing and the wastebaskets are about ready to overflow. I cannot see making a trip downstairs just to empty wastebaskets, but the time has nearly come.

All for tonight.

Love to you all,

Marian

Tuesday, July 5, 1955

Dear All,

It is another warm, muggy evening—a very buggy one, too. It poured this morning and we've been steaming gently ever since. Howard has a cold, not surprisingly as there are lots of boys absent now with them. So far E. and I show no signs at all of getting it and I hope all the vitamins we take will serve their purpose.

Last Friday night we were treated to our first experience with one of the noisy clubs behind us. There are two, the Portuguese Club and the Teachers' Club, and they are right across the trench from us—say half a block away. Naturally they hold dances, and the noise they make is one of the chief gripes of residents of the Q.C. compound. There was a small orchestra, and it was so bad that we winced all evening long—Howard especially. The string bass sounded like a heavy bag being thudded against the floor, and aside from the instruments carrying the melody, all the others just tootled around making noise. Awful. They started about 8, and at 12:30 they stopped—only to start again fifteen minutes later, with much foot stomping and "audience participation." It went on until 2 or so, and although Elizabeth's room is the closest to it she didn't even stir. We hardly slept. On Saturday they tuned up once again in what sounded like a rehearsal session for the band, but then about 10:30 people began stomping again so we had a little more noise.

I went to Dr. Wong today for the last time. Yesterday I saw Dr. Georges and all is as it should be. Have I said that he's never so much as weighed me or said boo about gaining? I find it very refreshing! In fact it is enjoyable to get away from the American craze for dieting—all the calorie counting and slimming recipes sound sort of foolish here.

Joy came by yesterday after lunch and we had a long visit. She brought me a bottle of cassareep, the essential ingredient of the pepperpot I mentioned a few weeks ago, so sometime soon I shall have to get Enid to purchase a pig trotter or a cow heel and try it out! Joy also told me where I can get an inexpensive wicker rocker. I decided we had to have a rocker before the baby comes, and H. and I were going to hunt for a secondhand one, but this will do beautifully. I hope she and Richard can come have dinner with us on Sunday but I can't decide what to have.

Howard is through with school here on July 29 and hopes to leave for Brazil as soon as possible—early in the next week. He'll be away for a month, returning in the first week of September. I shall miss the Ramsarans and the Voesslers more than ever while he's away, and the Persauds are going to be gone, too, which leaves me practically to the mercies of Mrs. S-D and Mrs. Cameron. The only other family in the compound seems nice but they are just occupying the Beckleses' house while the B's are on leave, and since they have nothing to do with Q.C. it's a bit hard to get to know them. Their name is Wilson-Hodgkinson or something awkward, but they're friendly. Shall have to work on that a little, I think.

Don't worry about sending a scrapbook, Mother. At the time I asked you to I didn't know that there were any available here as nice as the ones H. used for the clippings. One like that will do, and I'd forgotten about it, too. As for a gift for the baby, since you underlined the word "gift" I gather you mean something permanent like a spoon or cup, rather than a plastic pantie or something! I can't think of a thing we need, having silver spoons and plastic cups and the heavy china steam dish. Of course if we could tour the baby departments together I would see loads of things to tempt us, but I don't really know what is around. Why don't you wait until the baby is here and you can decide on something definitely feminine or masculine.

I don't think I told you that by sheer accident of local merchandising I was able to match the plastic I bought two years ago to cover the little crib mattress, and bought enough to make a new clothes bag for the baby. Remember the plastic one with the Humpty Dumpty face? This is yellow with cute little animals on it. What is now our workroom will be turned into the baby's room, but we can't see doing much to it for the short time it will be used. It is a large room, the largest of the three bedrooms, and has three trunks and the ironing board in it now, plus a bookcase with a torn skirt over the front that Margaret evidently used as a dressing table. I couldn't see buying material for curtains, but after mulling it over I remembered some cheap gray stuff I bought for curtains when H. was using a room out at the airbase on weekends before we moved there. They were big enough to cover large widows and give him privacy. I pulled them out of the trunk, and luckily there are three whole ones left, which will take care of the windows, splitting one to curtain two little windows up high on the wall. The fourth curtain has had a large chunk cut off for something else but what remains will be just enough for the skirt on the bookcase. Tomorrow I shall buy some rickrack—whatever color they can give me enough yardage in—and over the weekend make up the curtains.

My other inspiration came Friday night as we tried to sleep amid all that music. Howard painted ivory a five-pound Kim can, a small tobacco can, and the top to a plain pint jar. I found some pretty gift paper one of you sent, and from it cut out enough designs (baby-in-hammock, baby-in-rose, baby-in-slipper, etc.) to encircle the Klim can and the tobacco can and the glass jar. Howard made a neat slit in the jar's top, and that is now my cotton container—you know, pull out as much as you need and keep the rest clean. The Klim can is a cute small wastebasket, and the tobacco can is just the right size to hold cotton-on-toothpick swabs. I still have to paint over the cutouts with clear nail polish to make them waterproof. I was pleased with the way they came out—really nice-looking and practical, too.

I am sweltering. I think I shall sit and read awhile and try to cool off!

Much love to each of you,

Marian

Thursday, July 7, 1955

Dear Parents—

Do I always start a letter by saying it is a sticky, warm evening? It must be because I always sit down to write just as soon as the dinner dishes are done, and I'm sure the dishwater contributes to my own personal humidity!

Elizabeth has had a good day with pronouns today, I am very pleased to say. We've had such a time with you, me, I, etc. At lunch today she said, "Mommy, you're sitting on your apron," which was quite correct on all counts, and later on she referred to herself as "I." Dr. Spock says pronouns often don't get straightened out until a child goes to school so I suppose we're about on schedule. She has taken lately to (1) snorting like a horsie on the slightest provocation, frequently after being reprimanded, (2) calling H. "Howie" or Howard, or tonight "Honey Howie," which I am not guilty of—at least in her presence! She has once again become choosy about eating and has rarely finished her dinner lately. Lord knows she is not starving, so we ignore it and let her leave her table, withholding dessert, which doesn't seem to upset her at all. She has also just learned how to climb out of bed and into bed all by herself, so for the last two mornings we've been awakened by her clear call, "I'm hopping out of bed by myself. I'm hopping out of bed by myself." And then she comes and peeks in our door and says in a loud voice, "Is Mommy awake?"

I don't know just how much I've written you about our homecoming plans. We decided some time ago that it would be better on all counts for Elizabeth, the baby, and me to leave before Howard, thus enabling us to leave calmly and get out of all the packing mess. Then it seemed logical to have us go home early enough so that H. could do all that packing during the Easter holidays. We thought it would be a big help if H.'s mother could meet us in New York and help with the business of visiting the Kessler Institute—by "help" I mean someone to hold the baby and leave me free to concentrate on E., and also someone to help us get around from place to place. We thought that it would be fun for her to see some of the New York friends and relatives, and in addition she would know her way around New York and New Jersey. Howard wrote proposing all this, and we received an answer saying that the Irwins thought we should all go to the Kessler Institute even if it meant inconvenience here; that the children and I should wait until H. is able to leave.

Evidently we didn't make it clear to them that that would be next to impossible. In the first place, we would have to move into a hotel for about a month in order for Howard to be free to pack, crate, sell, etc. We couldn't stay with friends, as Mrs. Irwin suggested, because no one here short of the governor and a few bigwigs has a house big enough for that. And a hotel would be most difficult—I won't go into details, but they involve Guianese cooking and Elizabeth, no hot water and the baby, no way of washing diapers clean, no sterilizing, and on and on and on, not to mention confusion. And the good Lord knows that moving from here isn't like moving in the States, where you call the company and nice men come and pack up and away you go. (All right, that's simplified, but you get the point.) We shall have to pack every sheet, spoon, and dish ourselves, also H.'s pressed plants, books, tricycle, etc. And since most of it will have to be done after we've gone, it will take Howard quite a bit of time to do it. Then he has to do about the shipping arrangements, and that sort of thing is just plain slow here—efficiency is an unknown word. I'm trying to prove a point that you probably grasped way back when we first mentioned it.

The Irwins have relatives on Long Island—H.'s aunt and uncle, and their son's family as well, whom everyone agrees would be only too happy to meet and help us in every way. Fine. The only thing is I don't know them.

Don't either of you have any dear old friends in New York? Then, Mother, you could go visit said old friend, meet us, hear what the Kessler doctors say, and help us get on to Tacoma. The Irwins felt it was very important that Howard be in on that consultation, and heavens—we agree. Unfortunately, it isn't possible and the next best thing is for him to go by himself on his way home, and talk to the doctors then. But I would like, if possible, to have someone else along. I know my limitations, and I think that juggling a baby, comforting E. in a strange situation, and then trying to soak up everything I see and hear as well is a little beyond me!

Well, dearies, will you two mull it all over and see what you think? I am perfectly confident that I can manage to get to New York with ease. (Comparative, that is!) And it would be so expensive for someone to come, say, to Puerto Rico to meet us. There are always nice folks on planes who will help, and we'll be relatively fresh and untired. But I do think I could use help at the New York end, since we definitely want to stop at the Kessler Institute.

Joy and Richard are coming Sunday for dinner, and I finally decided to make individual tamale pies but the grocery didn't have cornmeal or beefsteak today. I shall have to send Enid downtown tomorrow to prowl about and buy some. Mother, I could have sworn that I had your recipe for tamale pie, but all there is in my cookbook is a note that says it's as easy to make it for twelve as for six. No recipe. Mrs. Rombauer doesn't say a word about ground beef but as I remember it, that's what you used. She says chicken, or leftover meat in cream sauce, which doesn't sound right to me.

Lynette Dolphin, the Q.C. music mistress, is going to have tea with us on Monday. Don't know yet just what we'll make for that. I have a few glacé cherries left so whatever it is should end up looking pretty!

All for now, I guess. Oh yes—we had creamed tuna tonight, with Roman Meal muffins. Delicious! Elizabeth was a bit slow about eating and asked what kind of fish it was. I told her it was creamed tuna like she had at Grandmother's, and did she remember? "Yes," she replied, but I'm afraid it really doesn't mean a thing. She generally says yes nowadays!

Much love to you both,

Marian

Tuesday, July 12, 1955

Dear All—

I wonder if this letter will catch Bee in Tacoma. That new white coat sounds lovely—Should I hope the weather is cool enough that you can wear it? The tropical-weight baby clothes sound intriguing—just remember that I'll only need lightweight clothes for the first six months or so, and that I've made six seersucker nightgowns and six jackets.

Why on earth don't the doll makers think realistically and produce a doll without hair for three-year-olds! Bobbed hair, I suppose, will have to do. Is the wig firmly attached? I've seen ads for dolls with "rooted Saran hair," I think that's what they call it. Are they more expensive? I shall enclose a separate list of little things that I am sure E. would love. I had planned on buying some stuff so that she could have something to open each day, but that sort of thing just isn't available here. The only thing on the list that she hasn't had is the beads, but I think she'd enjoy stringing them. Dr. Georges told me that with a normal delivery five days is the usual length of stay.

Howard has made plane reservations to leave here for Brazil on August 3. So far he's not sure just exactly when he'll plan on returning.

Sunday morning as I was in the midst of making tamale pie and baking cupcakes, Mrs. S-D came to call. I was in my shorts, and she certainly gave me a good hard look as she said good morning, but as H. says, what I wear in my own home is my own business. At any rate, we were soon distracted. H. met her downstairs as she arrived, and as they came upstairs together he suggested that her dog might remain outside as he wasn't sure of Spot's whereabouts. "Oh no," said she, "it will be quite all right." It was just dandy—Spot resented Zegyl's presence and in no time at all we had a rip-snorting dogfight in the living room. Elizabeth stood in the dining room door and gaped; Mrs. S-D swatted the dogs with a newspaper; Howard got bitten trying to break it up; Spot bit Zegyl; blood flew. The rest of her call was spent mopping, bandaging, scolding, etc. Their dog has no manners at all, and unfortunately she believes him to be well trained.

We had a good time with the Allsopps; for dinner we had the tamale pie, salad, poppy seed rolls, and butterballs. Floating Island for dessert. The rolls and butterballs made quite a hit, especially as the poppy seeds aren't available here and they do spruce up rolls, I think.

And then yesterday Miss Dolphin came to tea, and E. was quite excited about helping with that. I put the bread-and-butter in my breadbasket so she could pass it easily, which she did, and she also took the sugar bowl to Miss D. After we'd talked awhile we went for a drive, leaving H. at home, and saw some of the new housing projects that are going up in the south part of Georgetown. Low-cost housing for the very poorly paid, and sort of middle-class housing, too. Paradise compared with the hovels from which they came; modern architecture, brightly painted, with toilets, etc. for each unit.

We had a letter today from Lester Hirsch, who is to come to Q.C. in September to teach physics. He's a teacher at the East Los Angeles Junior College, and his letter was informal if not almost breezy. Refreshing. He said his family would come later but didn't specify how much family.

I guess that's all for tonight. H. is out rehearsing for a Philharmonic concert Friday. E. seems to be getting a cold. Hope it doesn't develop.

Love to all,

Marian

Thursday, July 21, 1955

Dear All—

Happy Birthday, Bee—hope you received our package. Howard says please return the stamp—I think it is a $2 one or something that he really wants back!

Elizabeth's cold developed just enough to give her a cough, so after being up with her an hour or so for a couple of nights we took her to Dr. Georges last Saturday. He prescribed something that did the trick and she is fine again. Howard is over his cold finally, but on Monday was hit hard with an attack of dysentery that sent him to Dr. Georges. He felt like dying on Tuesday but is just about over it now, although he still is eating a simplified, no-fat diet. Dr. Georges is such a peach, and it is a relief to both of us to have a doctor we can rely on—he even goes out at night when necessary, which is a lot more than some doctors here will do. I am fine—no flu, no cold, no diarrhea. Too disgustingly healthy!

Mother, I'm so glad you found a doll without hair! Would you send me a pattern for doll clothes for a 15-inch child? I suppose I could enlarge the one I have, but with a pattern that fits, doll clothes are such a cinch to make. I'm sure I'll have to end up making a coat for the doll to fly home in!

And speaking of flying home, maybe I never did say that Howard and I agreed shortly after we came back last fall that the tourist flight from New York down just isn't worth the savings. Too many stops. And although it isn't merely a question of our making up the difference in price this time—we foot the whole bill for getting E. and me home—we will go first class all the way. That will mean a few hours' stop in Trinidad, which won't amount to anything because the accommodations are very good, and a stop at Puerto Rico for customs examination. And if we fly first class from

New York to Seattle we will be fed on the plane, and that of course would save juggling box lunches, milk bottles, etc. Unless, of course, someone meets us at New York to fly the rest of the way home with us—then I'd be willing to spend my $1.50 for two bologna sandwiches (dry) and save on the cost!

The construction next door proceeds at a staggeringly slow pace. At this point they have nearly finished the cement posts on which the house will be built. I shall be relieved when they finally finish mixing the damned concrete. It is done by hand, practically under our front windows, and that grating noise of the shovels scooping the sand, cement, and gravel together gets on my nerves. The men have to get water from the faucet in our front yard, and they used our front walk until H. complained. Now they take a slightly longer route but keep away from our driveway and walk. We also had to complain about their parking their bicycles under our house, using our house as a shelter, and urinating wherever they felt the urge. H. protested to S-D and we have had no more trouble along those lines. S-D says the contractors now think the house won't be done until December—we think even that is an optimistic estimate, if they continue at the present rate.

And finding houses seems to get harder and harder—we're beginning to worry about getting one for Mr. Hirsch. H. spoke with Mr. Macaulay of the FOA today and asked if they had any places lined up that might do. Mr. Macaulay said they have four technicians waiting for houses, and they're willing to pay $175 per month! The U.S. government pays for it, so they don't worry, but it's hardly the same with us poor old Fulbrighters, and $100 is a lot for us to pay. Makes us wonder just what will happen to us in December.

Mother, I hope you're not sick and tired of being asked to send things. Howard needs a pair of brown shoes and of course he can't get his size here. Would you please buy a pair of dark brown, 12B, plain round toe? His black shoes, which are so comfortable, are Winthrops, and perhaps you could get the same thing in brown. You have said that all makes of shoes you buy for Daddy are made on the same last and so fit him—I'm hoping the same will be true for H. He wants the plainest that's made—no wing tips, no perforations, etc., and if you could smear a little mud on them, scratch the soles, and call them "used" it would save on the duty.

Much, much love to you all,
Marian

Wednesday, July 27, 1955

Dear All—

Today was the last day of the school term, so Howard will have a few free days before leaving next Wednesday for Brazil. He's been horribly busy, as always near the end of a term, and I suppose he'll need this next week to catch up on odds and ends. Tonight he's gone to see the parents of a boy who is just entering Queen's (his father is an FOA man), who has, I believe, finished the seventh grade in the States and who took the exams given to his age group here at Q.C. two weeks ago in order to find his place in the school—only to flunk all but one. Not his fault, really, for included were algebra, geometry, biology, and Latin, none of which the boy has had at all yet. And after that meeting, H. goes to school to participate in a final fling, sort of a farewell party for Pete. The last H. told me, however, was that Pete had said he wasn't going to attend, so I don't know just what the score is. One of the boys leaving school presented the masters with a case of Scotch, so the party will be a good one, I imagine.

Howard's week has also included installing a microphone for S-D; showing an American math teacher from Brooklyn (a young, attractive Negro girl—the object of appreciative glances from the masters) around the school—she's had three years' experience and makes $4700!; prodding Richard into getting the Q.C. newsletter out—Richard is staff adviser, was provoked at the editor, and sulkily refusing to do anything about printing. And then he's involved in translating some German advertising pamphlets for a businessman downtown. A month or so ago he brought home a letter that one of the Q.C. masters had brought in hopes that one of the language teachers could make out German. Howard showed it to me and we struggled a whole weekend over it. The man was most grateful, and last Friday H. brought home pamphlets about raincoats, milk pitchers ("They keep the milk fresh"), and all sorts of odds and ends.

The bathinette and pram are due to arrive here tomorrow, so H. can take care of the customs and whatnot before he leaves. The boat was supposed to arrive on the 25th, so we hoped to get them today but didn't. We also visited the Cottage Industries shop, a branch of the local Social Welfare Department, where all sorts of basketry, woodwork, and such are sold. Cheaper than what we've seen elsewhere. The baskets they have are lovely, and I bought a very attractive one for shopping. We also bought a cute wide-brimmed hat for E.—whether she'll wear it is debatable, but at least she can shade her face now if she wants to. The hat was 90 cents, the basket $3.75. Their wooden dishes and ashtrays were the same old stuff, and they had some lamp bases made out of local woods—pretty wood, poor design. We are mulling over the idea of having a lamp base made to order; there is a woodworking shop downtown that does such things. There was also a tray with the lovely blue butterfly wings set in, but it was large and too expensive. I want a small one sometime before we leave here. Do you remember the gorgeous one of Mrs. Metzler's? None of the work here compares with that in intricacy, but it is still pretty.

Yes, Enid is back. She is rather poor at housework—invariably forgets to put things back after she's removed them to dust, and of course that doesn't mean she does move everything in order to dust. H. was missing a red ballpoint pen for a month, and we finally found it under a chair cushion that is supposed to be removed twice a week for dusting purposes. However, she is honest, clean, and has a nice way with Elizabeth. For one thing, she keeps track of E.—I won't need to worry at all about Elizabeth wandering away unnoticed while I'm gone. She's also good about running errands on her bicycle, which is handy for me and a relief for Howard.

Maybe we've never described the setup here in the Q.C. compound. The school is a long, narrow building, most of it only as wide as one-classroom-plus-corridor, for ventilation purposes. And behind it in a row are the five houses now up, to which two duplex units are being added. The principal's house is the largest and has a veranda all across the front that juts out slightly ahead of the other houses. I don't imagine this was done intentionally, but the S-Ds delight in watching everything and everyone that goes in and out of the remaining four houses. They are obnoxiously curious, and every time a car, bicycle, or footsteps go by, their heads pop up over the veranda railing to see whose house is involved. Next down the line is the vice-principal's house, followed by Mr. Cameron's, the Persauds', and ours. For B.G. the houses are considered real nifty, and I suppose if we worried more about money we'd be glad to be here if only for the 10 percent government housing rate. As it is, I wouldn't have one on a bet if there were any other place to go. There is noise. On Friday night, for example, there will be a concert at Q.C. by the Policemen's Choir. They rehearsed until nearly 11 last night, they rehearsed this afternoon, and they're just tuning up now. We can hear every note clearly. The same extends to school plays, various meetings, table tennis tournaments, basketball games, and Lord knows what all.

Compound residents are subject not only to the usual school noises—the boys really yell, but that is mostly during the day and doesn't bother me—but also all rehearsals and performances that are put on at Q.C., which has the largest and "best" hall in Georgetown. And from behind we get rip-roaring parties at the Portuguese Club or the Teachers' Club once a month or so. Think of our open architecture—there are no solid walls at all—and don't imagine I'm exaggerating when I say that the Teachers' Club might just as well be holding a dance in Elizabeth's bedroom as across the trench, for all the noise we get.

Our dining room is tiny and gets the benefit of the late afternoon sun, so it doesn't cool off until 7 or so, which is too late to help us much. From its one large window we look smack into one of the Persauds' bedrooms, and frequently one of their youngsters hangs out the window at their house and watches us eat our dinner. From our living room windows I can see into the Q.C. auditorium—through it in fact to the doors of the Staff Room, and if I'm watching closely I can see Howard walk out of the Staff Room, across the auditorium, down the stairs, and out the door.

Between the school and the houses is a boggy field, unfit for anything other than donkey and sheep grazing, for it floods in wet weather and breeds mosquitoes, and in dry weather it's full of holes. No effort has been made to do any landscaping around the college—it is quite a disgrace. There is a gardener who is supposed to keep the grass cut around the houses, but since Mr. Cameron is in charge of the gardeners, this man spends nearly all his time tending the Camerons' garden. We have weeds over a foot high, and Mr. C.'s grass is cut weekly. If we really felt this was "our" house we'd hire someone to keep up a garden, but it's not worth it. Spot enjoys himself thoroughly here, and the freedom to run is good for him. He's still too fat, though, because he's turned scavenger and goes to each back door hunting for bones and bread crusts. Our chief current problem is mud. He roams through the fields, of course, and his whole underside is more brown than white. And the mud he tracks into the house! It's a good thing we love him!

Elizabeth uses real long sentences now, all the time. At lunch she sometimes says, "Oh Mommy, you mustn't sit with your feet folded (crossed) like that, they must be flat like mine." Or, "Oh Daddy, you forgot to put salt and pepper on my food!" She'll miss Howard while he's gone—especially first thing in the morning, when I can't respond very well to her chatter, jokes, requests, etc. I'm sure she would enjoy receiving picture postcards from you all now and then. She got one from Susan today, with lovely soldiers and Buckingham Palace on it, and was she thrilled!

All for tonight. The policemen are in good voice, but they have a couple of soprano guest soloists and a violinist I could do without!

Much love,

Marian

Tuesday, August 2, 1955

Dear All—

Three letters from Mother today, and one from Bee. I must say I spent all morning, after receiving Mother's first two letters, wondering what on earth it was that Bee was getting all set to do, but when the postman brought the last one, plus Bee's, this afternoon, all became clear. My dear family, I think it is a splendid idea for Bee to be ready to leap aboard a plane. My only doubt is that I shall have the strength of character to resist sending a cable saying "Come," just for the joy of a good visit! Actually, neither Howard nor I had worried about emergencies; once it was decided that Mother couldn't come in October we just quit thinking about it. However, it is very nice to know that you are set to come, Bee, and I do hope the typhoid shots bother you as little as they did me.

Howard leaves tomorrow, and I am sure he'll be glad to leave! He's spent the past weekend doing all sorts of last-minute things, like detecting a leak in E.'s sandbox, purchasing new sand, taking clothes to the cleaners, mending a chair of Elizabeth's, and so on. He spent most of Friday getting the pram and bathinette through customs here—you just wouldn't believe the fol-de-rol that requires. Inquiring the first of last week, he was advised to buy a customs entry form and take it to Customs House, which he did on Friday. Once there he was directed back to the wharf, back to the stationery store to buy *another* form, back to Customs House, off to buy another form, and back to the wharf. He had to pay just a dollar or so in duty, and had to sign a form swearing that we wouldn't sell or give them away here. If we want to get rid of them we have to destroy them! Looks like we'll tote them home with us. Anyway, I'm so glad we asked the Irwins to send them. The bathinette is so nice and high, and so much easier for me than the trunk and chest we used with Elizabeth. Elizabeth was practically hysterical with interest, and I hope that by the time the baby is in or on them she'll accept them as just more furniture!

Howard is over his flu, by the way, and feeling fine. I never did get it. Elizabeth is fine now and doesn't even remember to cough when she desires attention.

Had a short note from Mr. Hirsch today, in which he said that he has a 20-month-old son. Just having a child will provide some common interest, I trust, no matter what they're like. His family will be coming later, after he locates housing. Ha. The man doesn't know the score yet.

Howard looked at a house on Saturday after Joy passed along a tip from Mr. Macaulay, the FOA head. (She works there as his secretary.) It was a flat priced at $130, which is too high for us, and H. stopped off at the FOA to tell their housing people that we weren't interested (he was hoping it would do for the Hirsches). The woman, an American, wife of one of the U. of Maryland men, gave him hell for trying to get the house away from *them*, for the owner had telephoned the FOA to say that it was available. This is common practice here among people who have good housing to rent, and since the FOA expect a constant stream of technicians they have a constant need for housing. Lord knows they can pay more than we can. The house a-building next door is going so slowly that we can't believe it would be done by December, and we are once again mulling over the idea of my coming home with E. and the baby in the cold of December. We have even begun applying the positive approach—New York in December isn't as cold as New York in January or February, we could be met at the airport with coats, etc. What a mess.

Went to Dr. Georges this morning and as usual everything is fine. He asked me to send a urine specimen to him every week from now on, which makes me feel better about his not wanting to see me more often than once a month. He also took a blood sample for a blood count; I think he is thorough as well as charming, and I certainly have confidence in him.

Don't worry about my being lonely. I have a feeling we're going to get all sorts of attention, some of which we could just as nicely do without. Mrs. S-D told H. that she would take us out for a drive, and Mr. Cameron told him that he would keep his eye on me, and Lord knows I could do without *that*. Ah well, good intentions, etc. We shall be polite. Lynette Dolphin also said that she would stop by, and I imagine Joy will, too. This Thursday night I'm going to see a production of the Georgetown Dramatic Club in which Richard has a part. Next week a touring company from England is presenting *Hamlet*. Week after that is a ballet recital of a local girl who has been trained in the U.K. and U.S., plus a man who is chief male dancer with the Met Ballet Corps or some such. She is supposed to be quite good. All these things are at Queen's, which is convenient; convenient up to a point, since there are several nights devoted to each and we shall have loud applause from all. Let's see—last Sunday we stopped by the Allsopps' and I borrowed eight books from Joy—*Gone with the Windsors* and *A King's Story* among them. I'm all set!

Mother, the records for Elizabeth arrived last week. Unfortunately "Davy Crockett" was broken clean in two, but we just love the Robert Shaw record. It is lovely, and H. and I and Elizabeth are all delighted to have it.

Elizabeth will start to hope that I stay away for weeks and weeks when she catches on to this toy-a-day business! The list sounds wonderful, and don't worry about forgetting the pencils, for goodness sake. I can just see Enid spending a morning helping E. with the four doll dresses, or mopping up after bubble pipe operation. She will be only too happy to assist, I'm sure.

Elizabeth has finally picked up another habit of mine (isn't it a shame that mothers can't be *perfect* examples) and now calls us "sweetheart" and "darling." "Oh no, sweetheart, I want to read that book," she says as I try to clean up the room. We are now on a campaign to get her to say "Mommy, dear," or "Daddy, darling," as we think that sounds a trifle better. It sounds rather cute to hear her (at least I thought so at first; H. has better immediate reactions to such things) but I shudder at the thought that she might refer indiscriminately to adults in that way, and that wouldn't be cute. Imagine Mr. S-D dropping in and sitting down with feet in chair (as I'm afraid he does), and little Miss Know-It-All saying, "Oh no, darling, we mustn't put our feet in the chair." I'd die.

I also have some sewing to do while H. is gone. Do you remember my saying before E. was born that I thought it would be nice to make something for each child so that, when child was grown, he could have something to show his children and say, "Look what your dear old grandmaw did, kiddies"? It sounds dreadfully sentimental, but I still like the idea. I wove the white coverlet for Elizabeth, and after spending much thought on what would be useful, appropriate, and attractive for this child, I decided on a mosquito net. Rita Webber gave me one for E., which I threw into a washing machine in a stupid thoughtless moment, thereby ruining it. I have purchased netting, will cut it into a size to fit over the pram, and bind the edges in white ribbon. In each corner I shall embroider a cluster of three flowers—all local, and one is a cassia of Howard's—which are yellow, blue, and red. It should be pretty—H. drew the flowers for me the other day, and the designs are very good, delicate, and small.

Near the end of the page so that's all for tonight.

Much, much love to each of you,

Marian

We've been enjoying broiled steak lately—made edible with Adolph's Meat Tenderizer. It sure ruins the oven, though. But today I had Enid clean the mess for me and I must say, I did enjoy that! There are some household chores I'd just as soon never do.

Tuesday, August 9, 1955—10 a.m.!

Dearest Mother—

Just read today's letters and since our little dab of ironing is done I shall sit down and have a chat with you. This may sound like one big complaint but I shall at least get my gripes off my chest!

I am hot—the breeze seems to have left us more than usual these last few days, and of course with no wind we steam. After lunch I lie on the bed, windows open, fan blowing right on me, and drip like a melting ice cube. Poor old E. sits in her bed, nothing on, and perspiration simply runs off her. It won't go on forever, I trust!

Enid didn't show up this morning, darn it. Just when I think we're all set with her, something happens. I'm counting on her to come tomorrow night so I can see *Hamlet*, and I hope she's not sick. I still think Enid is the best bet to stay with Elizabeth in October—otherwise I'd go back to Lucille, who came every day on time.

We've had a four-day Youth Conference at Q.C., which started Friday. Thank the Lord, it ended this morning. Every night something noisy went on until about 11, then the Youths took another hour or so to calm down and go to bed. Night before last they were entertained by the Police Choir, which ended by singing popular calypsos—and the audience got so excited that there was yelling, stomping, and loads of applause. They quieted down at about 12:30, but I could swear that at 4 a.m. some boys started singing again! They were really up by 6 each morning. Last night we had a dance at the Teachers' Club plus a dance at Q.C., and I nearly died. Tried cotton-in-the-ears but it didn't work—and I was afraid I might not hear E. However, she sleeps peacefully through all that racket! A blessing, to be sure. The Q.C. revels ended at 12:30. At 2 the Teachers' Club blared forth "God Save the Queen" and finally we had peace and quiet.

You know me. If I feel grumpy today it's because I feel as if I hadn't had a good night's sleep in months!

We sent a check for $37 to the Irwins—cost of sending pram and bathinette. H. said they will be insulted, but I talked him into sending it for they never *did* say they would pay for the shipping, and I said they could tear up the check if they felt that strongly.

The magazines arrived last week. Very interesting article called "Children Are No Picnic" or something like that. It said tension, strain, arguments, etc. are a normal part of family life and we should expect them. I remember so few squabbles between Bee and me—it is hard for me to believe that quarrels are inevitable! Also enjoyed Spock's article on traveling with children, but I don't think I got any new ideas from it.

Mrs. Cameron dropped in last Wednesday evening—she said nothing that she hadn't said the last time she and her husband came, except to tell me graphically how ill she gets on ships and planes. She asked if I was going to "get" the baby here (common local expression—no one has a baby, you get one), and I said, "Oh yes," and added that it was due in October. "Oh? October? This year?" said she. Heavens! I've snickered over that ever since.

I've been meaning to write for several weeks that E. has almost entirely stopped using her toilet seat. Talk about perseverance—she practically fell in the first few times but was stubborn enough to refuse her own small seat and try again. She's awfully nonchalant about it now—waves her arms sometimes—and if she loses her balance I imagine she'll go in again. She's quite pleased, as she should be.

Time to fix lunch. Elizabeth loves melba toast—my pet substitute for crackers, which aren't very good here. And tomato soup, which we are having frequently while H. is gone. Wish we had some good fresh tomatoes!

All for now. *Much* love to you and Daddy,
Marian

Thursday, August 11, 1955: Viçosa, Minas Gerais, Brazil

Dear Bee,

It isn't often that I write you, but I must give you some tangible evidence of my presence here in Brazil, at the Rural University of Minas Gerais State, some 200 miles north of Rio.

It's a sort of scholastic diamond-in-the-rough—Brazil's best Ag. School situated in some pretty unfavorable country. Founded by one Peter Rolfs of St. Augustine, Florida, in 1921, its organization is pretty much along American lines—even to a cafeteria food service, which is indeed a novel idea to Brazilians. While nearly all the teaching was done by Americans back in pre–World War II days, the present staff (of 45, to 300 students) is made up of Brazilians together with émigré Germans, Russians, Japanese, Bulgarians, and a handful of American women (including the founder's daughter), these last doing home ec. All speak Portuguese, although many didn't know a word of it when they arrived. On the whole they have been very friendly and accommodating. I have become a good friend of Alberto Maestrai (Italian plant physiologist—my age) and Chataro Shimoya (Japanese cytologist—about forty-five), both of whom speak a bit of English. If we make a real linguistic effort and talk simply, we can make ourselves understood.

The university buildings are arranged around the usual quadrangle and extend for miles—widely scattered—up and down a rather narrow valley, the valley of the Doce ("Sweet") River. Many of them are stables and barns set in pastures and hillside orchards, but all are yellow stucco-faced brick, and none, not even the dorms or this guesthouse, has heat. When the temperature dips to 40 degrees each night this time of year (winter), a little heat would be appreciated! After living in hothouse-climate Guiana, arising in a 45-degree morning, with everything icy to the touch, is pure torture. Back to B.G. for me! Am I spoiled!

I've taken some photos, copies of which we'll pass along soon after I get back to Georgetown.

Bye for now.

Love,

Howard

Wednesday, August 17, 1955

Dear All—

Our big surprise came last Sunday when Howard arrived home! He says it is winter down there, and although he saw lots of cassias, there were none in flower or with buds. But he spent five days at the university (really an agriculture and home ec school) and made arrangements with the cytologist there, who will send him the buds when they appear. This man is a Japanese-born, Sorbonne-trained Brazilian citizen, and he and Howard managed to carry on most of their conversations in French using Latin for technical terms. The work Howard is doing is just his line, and he will be happy to help out; Howard in return is to send him some orchids from B.G. for he is making a similar study of them. The university has 300 students and was founded by an American in the 1920s. There are two

American women there now who are teaching the home economics, and the founder's daughter is the rather rugged matriarch of the place. She was kind enough to let H. take two hot baths in her apartment; poor Howard was cold nearly all the time, for the buildings have no heat, and at night the temperature got down to nearly freezing and of course the buildings didn't heat up until afternoon. No hot water in his guesthouse, or he probably would have spent all his time in a hot tub! He considers the trip a success, short as it was, as he never could have accomplished by letter the arrangements that he and this Japanese fellow worked out.

I wish he had time to write you about the trip. He had an unexpected night's stay in Belem on the way down, due to a wrong date given in the schedule. He went into town to the "best" hotel, where for some unknown reason the clerk didn't want to give him a room. This was at dawn, and H. was tired, so he persisted and finally the clerk gave in; when H. left the next day he complained about the bill, which had charged him for two days' stay, and although the manager intervened in H.'s favor, the clerk was none too happy about it. Howard didn't care about that, but on the way back he had another night to spend in Belem, and when he went back to the same hotel and the clerk again refused him a room, he decided it wasn't worth arguing about again and went to the next-best hotel. All filled up. That left him with the No. 3 hotel, where he got a room with three beds and a table. A drunk wandered in, his key to the room next to H.'s having unlocked Howard's door as well, so Howard had to stand a chair-on-a-table in front of the door to act as burglar alarm. He says there were great noises of bottles and glasses and furniture being moved around, and the whole place seemed so questionable that he didn't even use the shower. I'm glad I stayed home.

He decided that most Brazilians in the cities look like suspicious characters, and one of the men at the university agreed that they are— "immature citizens" I think is what he called them, and they just live from one day to the next, getting a little money in the easiest possible way.

Nearly all H.'s flying was done in a Cruzeiro do Sul plane, a DC-3, which, not being pressurized, was hot as the dickens every time they landed and cold as ice each time they rose above the clouds. The crew drank beer constantly during the flight, with one crewmember asleep in the back most of the time.

Have you seen ads for the Hotel Amazonas in Manaus? There is always an ad in our edition of *Time*, and it sounds like a real plushy place, "in the middle of the Green Hell" and so on. H. had a night in Manaus and decided to try the place just for fun. It turned out to be right in the city, three blocks from the river. According to H. the only claim the hotel has to being a really first-rate establishment is the paper band they seal their toilets with which says, "This toilet sterilized on such-and-such a date." The rooms were nice but undistinguished, for 600 cruzeiros a day, which is about $8 U.S., the cheapest room available. When he went to the dining room that evening for dinner he was prepared for a whopping bill, and was rather ready to complain after he'd had a horribly meager meal consisting of jellied consommé, two slices of roast pork with dry bread crumbs (some sort of dressing, I gather[82]), and jellied fruit for dessert. This was all, no vegetables, and was all that was on the menu for the evening. Cost—27 cruzeiros, or about 20 cents! Strange, eh?

Going back to last week, I was able to see *Hamlet* after scurrying about much of Wednesday morning to find someone to stay with Elizabeth. Finally got Mr. Cameron's maid to come. I enjoyed the play, but it was hot and the chairs at Q.C. are terribly hard and it seemed like an awfully long evening.[83] I got home at 12, and then couldn't really get to sleep until 1, for the fire department had stationed a truck right outside our house and the men couldn't get the thing started for ages. For each of the performances, the fire truck came, connected hoses, and remained alert during the play; the fire department had decided that the Q.C. fire defenses weren't adequate and with such big crowds they preferred to play it safe. Splendid idea.

Tomorrow night we're having an FOA man out to dinner. He's a bachelor, and although I haven't met him yet, he and Howard have become quite well acquainted and H. likes him. Friday night we go to a ballet recital at Queen's.

Elizabeth was very pleased to receive the postcards yesterday, and she says she remembers the park. I think she does—she associates it with pigeons, bread crumbs, and so on. She has started to sing lately, and you would love to hear her. Of course she's too young yet to manage the tune, but she says the words in a singsong voice and follows a tempo of sorts.

Thank you, Mother, for getting H.'s shoes. I'm glad you didn't have to search for them! The Scrabble game came and E. and I picked it up last Saturday.

The house next door is proceeding at a slightly more brisk pace, and Howard and I are allowing ourselves to be slightly hopeful that it might be finished in December. It appears that the house will be two stories, with the ground floor of cement blocks.

Bee, thanks for your offer of more stationery, but since I have about half left I don't think I need more right now. My letter-writing output has gone way down—in fact I run down so early in the evenings that I can't even read late anymore. When we were at the airbase and H. was gone during the week, I used to love to read until midnight or so, but now times have changed and if I stay awake until 10 I'm doing well. It's now 9 p.m. and I'm ready to go to bed!

All for now.

Much, much love to you all,

Marian

Wednesday, August 24, 1955

Dear All—

I just wrote another letter and my creative ability is at low ebb, so I shall just blither on a bit and let you know that all is well. It is still warm, but Howard came home yesterday with a new fan—bigger than our other one, and the kind that revolves, so we are more comfortable. The little fan is now in E.'s room, and I more or less take the new one with me from room to room. About the noise here at Q.C., Mother, everyone loves to complain about it. It is one of the favorite topics of conversation.

Elizabeth is still on her song-learning streak and now sings "Eliza Jane, Eliza Jane, oh Eliza Jane" over and over and over. Also "Old MacDonald," "My Grandfather's Clock," "Old Susan with a banjo on my knee," and others. You should hear her rather dirge-like rendition of "with a chick here, with a chick here, here a chick, old MacDonald had a farm, ee ei ee ei o." But, by George, as far as she's concerned, she's singing!

We had quite a Thing with her this evening. I called her and told her it was almost time for dinner (she was downstairs) and E. said she wanted to have a swing, so I told her she could have one swing and then come upstairs. Five minutes later I told her it was time to come up, and she started crying, said she hadn't had her swing yet (we'd heard the squeak and knew she had) and so on. She came upstairs and cried and cried, resented the fact that she had to go to the toilet, told H. "I won't wash my hands" and continued to howl. We put her in her room to calm down, and a few minutes later Howard went back to tell her she could come have her dinner—but she said she didn't want it. We went on eating, and then I went back to suggest that her dinner was "ready," that we were having fish just like Binky had except he ate the head and we were having the body, etc. etc. She pulled herself together, proceeded to eat all her dinner and even forgot to complain about the skins on the tomatoes, and appeared to be making an effort to be as pleasant as possible. She gets so darned stubborn now and then, when she can't have her way, that she really needs firm handling.

We expect Mr. Hirsch soon—maybe tomorrow. Yesterday we put up the bed in the workroom, removed our trunks, and generally straightened it up. Elizabeth was all prepared for us to turn the room over to the baby when it arrives, but the idea of someone else sleeping there really bewildered her, and I still think she rather expects Mr. Hirsch to bring a baby along with him!

Howard and I were horribly disappointed by the ballet performance last Friday. We had evidently expected just too much, but all the advertising led us to believe we would see a real professional show, and several discriminating friends told us we should see this girl because she is really good, etc. Actually she herself was pretty good, but her partner, "The World Famous" George Chaffee, was scarcely graceful. His main sin, to us, was the way he smoothed back his too-long hair after each spin—ugh! Then, at the intermission, Mrs. Taitt (the ballerina's mother and a self-proclaimed benefactress of the Arts) announced over the loudspeaker that two more performances would be given, due to popular demand, and thanked the audience for the "generous support given my daughter and Mr. Chaffee." The dance routines weren't spectacular, the show lagged horribly, and various vocal solos between the dances were quite bad. The newspapers gave it rave notices—"Ballet at its best," etc. etc., due to Mrs. Taitt's influence. Again, ugh.

Love, M.

Wednesday, August 31, 1955

Dear All—

I am all excited about tomorrow being September 1—from then on we can think of this baby in terms of "next month." Oh boy! I am feeling fine, but it gets harder and harder for me to get up from my afternoon nap. I have extended the time from 2 to 2:30, and these last few days 2:45 has sneaked up on me. Fortunately, Elizabeth doesn't have any objections—several weeks ago we gave up insisting that she stay in bed for her rest. Now we close the door, and about fifteen minutes later she hops out of bed and plays contentedly in her room, singing to herself.

We got a telegram yesterday that we assume to be from our new Fulbright man, saying he will arrive tomorrow morning. Oddly, it was unsigned, but since we expect no one else I guess we're safe to assume it is he. We are planning to have the S-Ds over for a drink Friday evening, and if it works out I shall finish the last of the goodies from Mother. Heavens, that sounds like a hint for more, which it really isn't; I just want you to know that they are greatly appreciated. Not being able to find any suitable crackers to put the fish on, I make little melba toast rounds, triangles, and squares, which turn out fine as long as something good is put on them. Howard bought a bottle of Canadian Club today for $6, about $3.50 in your money—isn't that quite a bit less than what you'd pay? He and I are completely happy with rum, but Mrs. S-D always looks somewhat distressed when offered it so this time we'll make her happy. We undoubtedly should invite them for dinner, too, but what the hell, I don't intend to knock myself out. I'm sure they'll understand, anyway.

We want Lester to stay with us, over the weekend at least, until he gets his feet on the ground, but we shall live simply and not try to have anyone else in. If he is anything at all like the other American men we have entertained, he will be no trouble—and his letters sound very informal. When we had Denver Green, the FOA man, to dinner, H. and I were both a bit sorry that he turned out to be no conversationalist at all, but he was a treat for me nonetheless. First, he arrived early, a real change from the half-hour to hour lateness that is considered quite fitting and proper here. When H. went to the kitchen to fix some drinks, Denver came along; he proceeded to examine our washing machine and the cupboard H. made for salt, sugar, and cereals, and he stepped out on the back porch to look at the trench. Then, my dears, he actually commented on the food! There is something about preparing a meal for guests, then having it eaten with nary a comment, good or bad, that is rather unsettling. We have had quite a few people eat with us from time to time, and apparently the British just don't comment on what they're eating. A few exceptions now and then, but rare. And we had a good laugh, because I had debated over a leg of lamb or a meat loaf and decided on the meat loaf; at dinner I asked Denver if he liked lamb and he replied no with great emphasis. He is a bachelor and has a hard time getting what he wants to eat, and hadn't had any ground beef for the more-than-a-year he's been here.

The FOA is the Foreign Operations Administration, just recently changed to the International Cooperative Agencies and put under different control in Washington. They are here to advise in all phases of development—agriculture, soil conservation, flood control, livestock development, village planning, and housing. Besides the administrative officers, there are technicians and experts, all of whom are from the University of Maryland. Heavens, don't you all read *Time*? There is frequent mention of the work they do.

We have a man now who brings me an extra six eggs every weekend and a chicken every other Sunday. I have even learned how to cut up a chicken! The ones he brings are frozen but still have heads and feet attached. You should have seen E. examining the chicken's eyes a few weeks back—gave me the creeps!

About names for the baby—if a boy, James Wilson. If a girl, Dorothy Campbell.

All for tonight. I am in the middle of *The King's General* and want to finish it. Isn't there an old English ballad about Sir Richard Grenville? And I don't mean Sir Patrick Spens.

Much love to each of you,
Marian

Wednesday, September 7, 1955

Dear All—

I guess in my last letter I said we were expecting our new Fulbright man on Thursday. Howard drove out to the airbase to get him, and since then we have been helping him get settled. Americans are so refreshing! We are already better acquainted with him than with many folks we've known for two or three years. His name is Lester Hirsch, he is about forty, and in 1953 was in Tokyo with a U. of California group—he had very posh accommodations and unfortunately was expecting a somewhat similar deal here. He's been married for five years, and his wife (who is about my age and very attractive, according to pictures) and little boy will come as soon as he can get a house. We've spent some time looking at what is available, and the poor man was utterly shocked at one $70-per-month hovel we looked at. We have all decided that the only thing he can do is wait for one of the new houses to be completed here at Queen's.

Before we even sat down to lunch that first day he spotted a *New Yorker*, and of course that is always a bond—he is an ardent fan. He is staying with us, but in the next few days he will move to the Londonburg Hotel, where H. stayed before going home on leave. He is an awfully nice person and we are hoping he can adjust to being here—Lester says if we hadn't been young and inexperienced we never would have stayed here, and I can appreciate that age makes a big difference. Then, too, the other Fulbrighters he has known were in the Visiting Lecturer category, and they apparently aren't really put to work as the Teachers are.

I went to see Dr. Georges this morning and all is progressing as it should. I am to go back near the end of the month. Elizabeth will be able to come visit the baby and me, and his visiting hours are 11 to 1 and 4 to 7. I talked with his nurse a minute, and she gave me a list of things to bring that includes chemises and booties (!); also baby powder, soap, oil, diapers, washcloths and towels, and binders. I keep thinking I should have a bed jacket for modesty's sake, but the thought of an extra layer makes me cringe so I guess I shall ignore it. I have two nylon nightgowns that are in good shape but hot (that's why I don't wear them often), plus the pink seersucker that you gave me, Bee, which is scarcely pink any longer, and the blue nightshirt and the short pj's. What the hell. Does someone want to send me a pair of short seersucker pj's, preferably tailored (to cover a bra)? Nylon just isn't very comfortable.

I love, Mother, your remark about a rattle being the only thing you could find suitable for the climate. I would love some rosebud diapers if the baby is a girl, but we have an ample supply of plain ones and at this point we hate to accumulate more stuff that will have to be brought home. Which sort of applies to Christmas, while I'm thinking of it. At least for H. and me, will you all try to hold yourselves down to a few small things? Howard needs brown and gray socks, and he is especially fond of the Dacron ones that look heavyish but which he says don't stick to his feet. Elizabeth will need socks, panties, pajamas. H. will also be able to use some handkerchiefs—I prefer that he has colored ones. Elizabeth would probably like more records, since she is really interested in songs and singing now.

E. is standing at my elbow, trying to get me to sing while I type. Her rests have become quite a farce—today she moved her dresser all over her room, just to test her muscles, I guess. She has been having such fun with Howard, going over to school with him now and then or driving to town with him when he does an errand. I foster it as much as possible because I just don't feel like taking her for walks, yet she needs a little diversion. She is all primed for my departure and knows that Enid and Daddy will take care of her. I trust that will go smoothly. All for now.

Much love to you both,
Marian

Wednesday, September 14, 1955

Dear All—

Lordy—it is just 9:30 a.m. and so hot. Spotty is panting, Elizabeth is perspiring, and I am a soaking mess. How horrible it must be to be here and be overweight—part of my discomfort is just the regular seasonal heat, but part is the extra twenty or so pounds I am lugging around. For not much longer, thank goodness. Elizabeth is standing on a little chair at my side, making comments about the typewriter, which naturally fascinates her, so any incoherence on my part will be understandable!

The building next door is coming along, and one unit really looks like a house now. The kitchen is small, and the living-dining area, an L-shaped room, is a fairly compact size. Upstairs are three bedrooms and we can't quite figure them out yet, as two of them look very large and one more like a closet. There is still no upstairs floor, no wiring or plumbing, no paint, no closets or cupboards. Supposedly they will be done in six weeks. We have absolutely no guarantee at all of getting a place there. S-D hasn't yet drawn up his "point system" for awarding the houses, but practically half the staff wants one. Lester has told the principal that if he doesn't get one of the houses he will throw up his job and go home, since there just isn't anyplace else he'd bring his family to. I should think we'd have a good chance of getting one, but S-D has a couple of new Englishmen coming this fall, and if they have families, well, he is partial to Englishmen and we just don't know how we'd stand. You may yet have the children and me on your hands come December or January!

Today is the first day of school. It seems strange to hear the babble of boyish voices again—it has been comparatively quiet here these past six weeks, with only the rough talk of the workmen as they mix concrete under our windows.

We have a package notice today, which may be the box from Mother with the things for E. She will certainly get a bang out of them.

Really, this is ridiculous. I have just been interrupted to please sing "Ten Little Indians," and I find that this letter amounts to nothing. Ramphal just came by to pick up the package downtown, and Elizabeth is now downstairs. Enid came late today, and I dispatched her immediately downtown with my grocery list and asked her to buy some tomatoes and carrots. E. has decided that she loves raw carrots—for such a long time she didn't want to chew anything, and I do like to encourage her. We had creamed cabbage last week for the first time in several months, and she lapped that up, too, although the last time I made it she wouldn't eat it at all. In this morning's paper I noticed an ad for Birds Eye frozen strawberries, raspberries, peas, sprouts, and beans. No prices given, but I shall check. Gad—strawberries! Mother, write me how much you pay for said items at home so I shall know whether or not they are just too much here.

Elizabeth continues to sing, and now she knows practically all the songs in her songbook—at least to recognize the first few words of each song. We wake up in the mornings to her voice, and when she's by herself she sings most of the time.

This is a poor excuse for a letter, but at least you know I am well and that we're all still here.

Much love to you all,
Marian

Tuesday, September 20, 1955

Dear All—

My, my—we've been showered with packages since I wrote last week. The big box arrived with the toys for Elizabeth, and I let her open the fish, which now hangs on the wall above her bed. She was very pleased, and I didn't say much about the other packages but just put them away in a drawer. She said we would keep them until her next birthday, wouldn't we, and I didn't disillusion her. Then we got the box from Bee with the cute little suit, and Elizabeth was simply tickled with that—I had to unsnap the pants several times and show her how they will go on the baby. She gets a big kick out of pretending, of course, so I had "one leg here," and "one leg here," and "the tummy here." Yesterday Howard brought home two packages of books, one from each of you, and once again Elizabeth was quite ecstatic. She sat in a chair undoing the tissue paper, and then said, "Oh, *look* at this!" She does love books, and naturally we've already read through them a couple of times. I am so glad to have a new supply of books on hand and have put three of them away to read while at the nursing home. Of course with the baby in the room right with me, I won't have to worry much about long hours with no entertainment! And we have a package notice here now that is probably the pj's, etc. from Mother. Thank you, thank you, thank you—this is as much fun as Christmas!

Ah yes, Christmas. Will you please include in our box a large bottle of Adolph's unseasoned meat tenderizer? We have been enjoying delicious steaks made out of our old tough beef, and I am nearing the end of my bottle. Also, please include my old faithful brown velvet hat—I think I shall want it when we finally leave.

We are hoping to see *The Country Girl* on Saturday night. We have told each other that we should go see a few movies before the baby is born since we won't be able to afterward, but there have been very few good ones around recently. I don't think I ever mentioned that we saw *Brigadoon* a few weeks ago and simply loved it.

Lester had dinner with us last night. He's a sociable person and we all enjoyed it, but he had to leave rather early to go back to his hotel and prepare for his classes today. Howard is holding his breath and, I imagine, saying prayers that he will turn out all right, for Lester has said that the boys make him feel ill at ease. And unfortunately he has a lack of tact concerning the Guianese, which certainly will make him unpopular unless he realizes it soon and changes his tune. He alludes in their presence to "curious Guianese habits," etc. and is making no effort at all to meet other staff members. They are very anxious to become acquainted, and ask H. where he is, is he ill, why doesn't he come to the staff room, etc. It's slightly embarrassing for H. Lester is forty and uses his age as an adequate reason for not paying attention to some things we've told him.

Not that we haven't made our own blunders now and then, but on the whole we've been so cautious, and done our best not to hurt local feelings. And the men at school have at several different times remarked to Howard on how well we have fitted in and how no one resents us. That is something of a feat for foreigners, too. I'm sure it's easier for us, though, for we came with no preconceived ideas about the place or the job, whereas poor Lester thought he would be treated as an honored guest and perhaps given one course to teach if he wanted to—not plunged into a full, heavy schedule.

Friday night we are having a Mr. Little out to dinner—he is a botanist, and I guess working here with the FOA, although he will only be here a few more weeks. He must be from Kansas or Oklahoma, somewhere where drawls grow thick!

I have a suitcase packed with all but the last-minute items and am practically ready to go have this baby right this minute. Don't think we have discounted the probability of jealousy, Mother. We have done everything we can think of to prepare Elizabeth for this new creature, and certainly nothing should come as a surprise to her. The questions that child asks! A few days ago she found a little pamphlet Dr. Georges had given me some months ago that gives the scoop on having a baby. Included are several diagrams of the birth process, and E. was fascinated, naturally. "What's *this? What's this?*" I explained that they were pictures of Mommy's tummy, and here was the baby; here the baby was coming out; and here the baby was all born. She pored over it for several days but seems to have forgotten it now. Today she asked me all about the baby's binders—*why* did the baby have to have a little Band-aid on its navel? I decided that even a simplified explanation would be too much, so just told her that when the baby is first born the navel is like a little cut and needs a bandage. A few hours later, Nancy appeared with a torn Kleenex that was *her* bandage over *her* navel.

I briefed Enid yesterday, and together we went over the two pages of lists, schedules, notes, etc. that I have posted on the kitchen wall. For two weeks from the time I leave, she will be here from 8 to 3 and do the baby's washing, iron the bare necessities, fix the main meal at noon, etc. I said we might want her for longer but we'll wait and see how things work out. H. will do the regular washings and fix breakfast and supper.

On Saturday afternoon we all went to the zoo and had a wonderful time. The animals were all hungry, apparently, and more active than usual. Elizabeth's favorites were the monkeys, who were chasing each other, swinging on a rope, and clambering all about their cage. Also she laughed and laughed at a bird—about pigeon size—that was pecking angrily at its enamel plate, scolding it, trying to pick it up in its beak, and so on. They have some beautiful parrots, too, and she always likes them.

All for now, I think.

Much love to each of you,

Marian

Tuesday, September 27, 1955

Dear All—

The package I mentioned last week did contain the pajamas, Elizabeth's pants, and the present for the baby, and we are very pleased with everything! The pj's are very pretty, Mother, and the white material is the same stuff as the baby suit Bee sent—an interesting new finish, isn't it. E. was delighted with her pants and they are a very good size, but I still think that for Christmas the next largest size would be wisest.

She has displayed great interest in the baby's package but of course we are saving it to open after the baby is here. Elizabeth is to bring it the first time she comes to visit us. I am really relieved to have the pj's and know I shall enjoy them. Thank you!

Not much news. The only thing on my mind is this baby, and now I find my first thought each morning as I come to is how many days are left!

Last week we had the hottest day in eighteen years—on Thursday it was 93 degrees, and on Friday it was 90. Everyone was complaining, dripping, and miserable. Each day was broken by a heavy shower, part of the hurricane that has done so much damage to the islands near us. At least to us the rain was a relief, and now our weather is back to its usual 87 or so.

Mr. Little, the botanist, had dinner with us Friday evening, and the only thing that made the evening passable was that he and H. could discuss botany. Mercy, such a shy man. He sat at first plucking at the cushions and pulling his fingers, only glancing up once in a while to dart a look at us. Later he relaxed a bit, and we learned that he was brought up in Muskogee [Marian's parents' hometown]. He didn't recognize your names, but since he would have been about five years behind you in high school, that isn't too odd. Maybe he was shy then, too! His wife is a botanist, and apparently he just doesn't have much else to talk about. He is a research botanist with the U.S. Forest Department in Washington and knows many people in the profession, so Howard enjoyed talking with him about that.

Elizabeth is delighted to have Indrani home again, although Indrani is now enrolled in nursery school for two hours in the morning so that their playtime together is limited to afternoons after the Persauds have tea and before we have dinner—which usually amounts to an hour. They get along together quite well. Elizabeth is quick to suggest what to do, but fortunately Indrani has a mind of her own and doesn't always agree. I'll be glad when Susan and Janet are back, and heaven only knows Elizabeth will be, too.

All for tonight. S-D and his Music Society are doing madrigals across the way and I am distracted!

Much love to you all,
Marian

Thursday, September 29, 1955

Dear Parents—

I wish this were the letter saying that our baby has arrived, but it hasn't and it isn't, so relax. I saw Dr. Georges this morning, and he says everything is fine and it won't be much longer.

Well, kiddies, we've had a blow today. Howard learned that the first two units next door to us have already been allocated to government officers other than Q.C. staff. His source also said that the first ones will be done in December, not October, and the other building will be finished in February, not December. After lunch H. went downtown to check with the Government Housing Officer to see if he would confirm this, and the man said no, the houses haven't been allocated yet. So H. went back to his first informant and asked to see the letter that he'd been told about earlier. He did see the letter, which stated that the first two units *have* been allocated and that the second two "may" be allocated to Q.C. staff. A most grievous blow.

After mulling the situation over, we decided the only thing to do is to take a very firm stand. Howard has just written a letter to S-D, applying officially for one of the new units or other suitable housing, and stating that if we aren't given suitable quarters by the time the Ramsarans come back he will be forced to resign and return home. S-D, by the way, is not the one responsible for allocating the houses. Somebody higher up in government circles does that. Howard feels it would be an unnecessary sacrifice for him to complete the year if we three had to go on home in December; we have had enough uncertainty about housing here. He is also writing to the U.S. Ed. Com. in London, informing them of his decision, and we will see what they have to say.

If we aren't successful in getting one of these new places, our only other hope is a slim one that the Ramsarans might not come back. We know they hoped against hope to get another, more interesting post somewhere else, and I have written Margaret asking if they know yet when they'll be back, outlining our problem. If they are returning, we shall have to get Elizabeth and the baby and me packed up as early in December as possible, giving Howard as much time as we can to sell and pack up our belongings here. The school term ends December 16 and he says now he doesn't think he could manage to get home for Christmas, but it might work out.

In view of all this confusion, it seems unwise to us for you all to send any Christmas boxes. Why don't we wait and see what happens, and if we are still here, you can send a few little things to Elizabeth and the baby by air at the last minute and we will all be delighted. I have just written this to the Irwins, so you can hash it all out over the phone. Will you pass all this on to Bee? We wouldn't want her sending off a box that wouldn't reach us.

Will you please hunt up my beige wool dress with three-quarter sleeves, the one that zips up the front, and send it off with the brown hat I mentioned a week ago? I will feel more secure if I have something in which to meet the wintry blasts of New York, if necessary. Don't bother to send a coat—I think we could arrange to have one sent to New York and have someone meet me there with it. I'll have enough to carry without a nice woolly coat, if this all comes to pass. I have the belt here that goes to that dress, so don't try to find that.

If the government doesn't care two hoots whether we stay, and if H.'s resignation goes through, we would naturally have to find someplace to stay in Tacoma or Seattle or somewhere, depending to some extent on what kind of a job H. could find and where he could get one. It seems to us that the best plan would be for me to bring the children to your house, and try to find an unfurnished place after H. arrives and finds a job. It would be rather cramped for a while, wouldn't it—could you manage? Then we could gather up our scattered furniture, live with it through July, and have it all there for Howard to pack up and tow away to Texas. Which would find you all cramped again, with us.

If he crates up our stuff here in December for shipment to Texas, we would have to have someone to receive it. Do you know anyone in Houston or Galveston who could keep numerous trunks, crates, and barrels for a period of six months or so for us? Howard said even New Orleans wouldn't be too far a haul. Storage would cost a lot, we fear.

What a mess. We can at least be grateful that the baby isn't due in December, for two months should give both baby and me time to get somewhat organized. Are you going to write back insisting that someone (Bee) meet us somewhere to help? It seems so awfully expensive to me. And I'm not convinced it would be necessary. Anyway, that would depend on our states of health, strength, and temper, I suppose. Bosh. I'm sick of thinking about it. All for tonight, dears.

Lester had dinner with us last night, and it seems he is having marriage difficulties. Thank goodness we don't have that. Everything else seems uncomplicated compared with that!

Much, much love,

Marian

October 11, 1955

Storkgram by Western Union
Mr. and Mrs. T. C. Sterne
Girl born 10th 9 lbs 6 oz blonde 21 in both doing well.
Howard

Tuesday, October 11, 1955
Saint Michael's Nursing Home
224 New Market Street, Georgetown

Dearest Parents—

Had we known October 10 is a holiday here we'd have picked another day! The wireless office was receiving messages but refused to send any, so H. had to wait till today. I'm on my back so forgive the scrawl.

Let's see. Sunday evening at 10 or so I felt twinges. I was afraid they might just be wishful thinking, but they were regular enough so that we came here to the nursing home at 11. The nurse gave me an injection to speed the process, and by 1:15 Dorothy was born! I was startled—didn't realize it could be over quite so quickly. I had no anesthesia, although I had expected a local of some sort—however, it was so brief that just as I was ready to ask for something please, the baby was born. Quite a sensation—and her first cries were so gurgly and waterlogged! Now Mother, don't worry about me and my "suffering"—it has already receded to the "interesting experience" category, although I don't think I'd recommend it to my friends. *Wonderful* not having gas; I wouldn't recommend that, either. (*Aren't* I the woman of experience!) I have a few stitches for which Dr. G. gave me a shot of some charming anesthetic that acted quickly and wore off equally fast with no ill effects.

Dorothy is pink, no bruises or other signs of a rough time. I don't think she is as pretty as E. was, but she is cute—her mouth is a pretty shape, little nose, flat tiny ears, and her eyes—I have scarcely seen them open but I think they are blue. Her fingernails need cutting.

My room is small but has three windows (good cross-ventilation), an electric fan, washbasin, and Dorothy. What a treat getting to know your child before she's thrust into your arms to take home. I am up a little today—can use the washbasin for tooth brushing, etc. Walked from the delivery room back to my room after D. was born, I might say! I feel grand.

Yesterday Elizabeth practically fell into the bassinet trying to get a good look at D., who slept all the time E. and H. were here. I think she's tickled to have a little sister like Susan, Indrani, Julie, et al.

Later—4:15. H. and E. are here, D. is still sound asleep, to E.'s disappointment. E. is delighted with Peggy, her new doll. Everything is going fairly smoothly at home, I gather.

End of page—lots of love,

Marian

October 12, 1955
Saint Michael's Nursing Home

Dear Bee—

Well, here I am, sitting on edge of bed with fan blowing hair into lipstick, Dorothy fussing in her bassinet a few feet away, and Mario [Lanza] singing "Noel" from the house next door. The little one arrived promptly, without much fuss. . . . By 1:15 Dorothy was one of us, howling away. No anesthesia at all, which wasn't what I'd expected, but I can't complain. I couldn't quite believe it was all over so quickly. Very nice not having gas fumes to bear, and quite an experience hearing the first gurgly cries.

I am quite comfortable here. The food isn't just what I'd like but for Guianese cooking it is not bad. There are only two or three other patients here at present, but lots of outside noises—dogs, cats, roosters at night, and a parrot at dawn. D. did her share last night, too.

What a scrawl. I'm on my back now with the stationery box resting on my flat stomach. Oh joy!

Much love,

Marian

Friday, October 14, 1955
Saint Michael's Nursing Home

Hi, Dears—

Glad to get your wires. This will not be a formal letter—I luxuriated this morning with four cups of coffee and now I'm jittery, per usual. Silly, but fun. I feel wonderful—proud of Dorothy and Elizabeth and Howard and just full of all sorts of elemental, basic joys. I feel so happy it's a pity I can't bottle up some of it and save it for a less buoyant day!

Dorothy is a dear—she is practically on a four-hour schedule but sleeps close to seven hours at night. Now she wants three or four ounces at a feeding—remember how we kept track of E.'s two- and three-ounce feedings? Yesterday D. was awake for the first time while H. and E. were here. She cried (hungry) and needed her diaper changed, and oh my! wasn't Elizabeth engrossed in that. She went into ecstasies about Dorothy's wee little eyes, wee little nose, wee little hands, wee little bottom, etc.

H. is tired—goes to bed at 7:30 after a full day. Enid is busy all the time she's there, but H. still has charge of supper, dishes, and E.'s bedtime routine. Elizabeth raised hell the first day or so—took the clean laundry out of the basket, put it on the floor, and said, "Mommy lets me do it." She took the baby clothes out of the dresser and said, "Mommy said I could use them for dolly clothes." She opened my dresser, took out all the surprise packages, opened them, and took them to her room. Little monkey. H. spanked her, retrieved the presents, and explained that presents are given but not taken. That afternoon they didn't come see us, and Elizabeth has behaved much better since.

Well—I just now called Q.C. to leave a message for H. ("more diapers—hurry") and spoke to Richard Allsopp, who didn't even know I'd had the baby! I'd wondered mildly why Joy hadn't come to see us because I know she is always going to see her friends who have had babies.

I'm having trouble nursing Dorothy, although I have plenty of milk. Ordinarily I'd never write about such delicate matters, but I assume you might be interested in such details and I'd discuss it with you if you were here! (Heavens—H. just brought the diapers. This is certainly conveniently close to home, and H. was told at school to take off anytime it was necessary. There's a lot to be said for such informality.) I felt miserable on Wednesday, but H. searched the town and succeeded after difficulty in buying a breast pump from a wholesale drugstore. Wouldn't you think they'd have one here and for sale in any drugstore? No nipple shields available, it seems. This *place!* Dr. Georges is such a peach and encourages me to keep on trying, but it is a nuisance. I really did want to nurse this baby, especially with an eye toward traveling in December. Much simpler than bottles. Well, we shall try.

Yesterday morning, just as I rang my bell for more coffee, Dr. Georges walked in, asked if I was through with my tray, and proceeded with the most courteous air of the good host to take my coffee pot to the kitchen! Bee asked recently if he is French or English or what—I thought I'd told all of you that he is a West Indian Negro. He didn't stop in last evening as he usually does, and said this morning he'd spent most of the evening with an old woman who has been dying slowly for weeks and finally did last night; then when he got home he found four more calls waiting for him. Doesn't sound unusual for a doctor, I suppose, but here it is—most won't accept night calls at all. Some demand payment on the spot, others won't go out of Georgetown proper to such distances as Kitty or Subryanville. Dr. Georges is doing well financially—he's now a director of a new beer company, just setting itself up—all local capital. I hope he makes a lot of money and lives to enjoy it!

All for now.

Much love,

Marian

Tuesday, October 18, 1955

Dear All—

It's 7:30 p.m., Dorothy has just been tucked into her pram, and I hope she'll be contented to sleep for a while. She has been quite an angel today, sleeping and eating and sleeping some more. She wants four to five ounces of milk each time now, and I suppose we'll be giving her cereal before she's three months. She sleeps three or four hours at a stretch during the day and about seven through the night.

So far we've had very smooth sailing with Elizabeth, who delights in tucking a blanket around Dorothy when it's breezy, or wiping up the milk that dribbles down her chin, or helping to put away the clean clothes. (Goodness. Dorothy interrupted, letting me know she hadn't had enough milk. I heated up another bottle, and she consumed two and a half more ounces—total: seven.)

I am so sleepy that I must go to bed, but shall answer a few questions that you asked in the letters we got today. We sent cables to Carrie and Bee as well as to the grandparents, but are wondering whether either was received since no mention was made.

Mother, we paid to have our household goods sent down here and will have to pay to send them back. Don't know if storage charges in Texas would equal the amount to have it shipped to Tacoma. If we did have it sent to Tacoma, H. wouldn't be able to get it all in a small trailer.

Howard had a letter from the U.S. Educational Commission in London saying they had taken up the matter of our housing with the Colonial Office, and the Colonial Office said they would immediately send a plea to the B.G. government asking that all assistance be given us. Daddy, Howard says it is not a matter of S-D being willing to let him go. If he does have to resign, he resigns his Fulbright award and just informs S-D of the fact; he doesn't need to wait for S-D to accept it or decline it or whatever.

If we do come home in December, I think Elizabeth's brown coat will fit. I've tried it on her, and with the hem and sleeves let down it would do to at least arrive in; probably wouldn't be nearly warm enough for a Puget Sound winter.

I know I forgot to tell you how cute Elizabeth was the night we went to Dr. Georges. I had of course told her beforehand that the baby might decide to be born at night, in which case we'd all get up and we would put her slippers on, and she and Daddy would take me and leave me at Dr. Georges's, etc. etc. So on Sunday night, when we woke her up to say that the baby was almost ready to be born, she hopped out of bed and we put on her slippers per schedule. Then, as we were going out the door, she went to the bookcase and got out a book—always when H. took me in the mornings she had brought a book to read while they waited in the car—and then as we walked downstairs she noticed all the stars in the sky. H. says that on the way back, she didn't say boo about me or the baby, but was still smitten with all the stars, more than she had ever seen before.

Daddy, Howard wants to know if it is the Toscanini recording of Beethoven's Ninth that is so good. It is available here and if it is the good one, we'll get it for our Christmas present to ourselves.

I have a horrible feeling that this letter doesn't quite make sense. I'm nearly asleep! You will forgive me, I know. I feel real fine, wonderful, dandy, etc. and have to lose about two inches around my waist. Not too bad considering that I never did weigh myself more than two times the whole nine months!

Much, much love,
Marian

Thursday, October 27, 1955

Dears—

We're breakfasting, D. is sleeping. I'm just too busy all day to write, and too sleepy at night. Knew you might worry if you didn't get a letter of sorts!

D. is doing fine—keeps me hopping all day but sleeps well. No complaint at all. She varies between three and four hours and from three and a half to seven ounces.

E. is doing fine, too. Seems really happy about D. aside from occasional sulky spells. H. is busy at school with a forthcoming science exhibition and tests to correct right now. Letter from Dr. Turner at Texas—H. could enter at February and get $1400 per nine-month school year as a lab assistant. Dr. Gibbs, placement man at the College of Puget Sound, wrote and said he was quite sure he could place H. at midyear in some kind of teaching job. No news here about a house, but the school secretary says she thinks we'll get Mr. Cameron's house. He can't legally leave it vacant. No news from Margaret—maybe they aren't returning.

I'm feeling wonderful—doing everything but the twice-weekly washing, which H. does. Enid does the cleaning of course.

Much love—*must* have my coffee!

Marian

Monday, October 31, 1955

Hello, dears—

It's not quite 6 a.m.—Dorothy woke up shortly after 5 (her last bottle last night was at 8—not bad, is it!) and I hate to go back to sleep for only half an hour. This will be my most peaceful moment all day long, no doubt.

We heard from Margaret on Saturday and she says we can plan to be here for Christmas. John will be back in time for the second school term but she plans to remain in England for a while—she didn't say how long. We are reasonably sure of getting Cameron's house, but he leaves on January 12. The next step is to find out from John and Margaret whether we can remain here until then, or possibly until March or April if she really is postponing her return. That's too much to hope for, no doubt.

So—will you pass the word on—you may as well send our Christmas packages here.

I went downtown last Monday and will go again today—left D. crying, E. peeking through the door of her room where she was "resting," and H. starting to do a mammoth washing. He has free time Monday afternoons and I'm glad to get away for a little while. They've got Christmas toys, etc. in the stores and now that I know we'll be here I must do some shopping.

Elizabeth is fine—I detect no difference in her behavior since Dorothy's arrival. She still tries to get away with murder now and then, but most of the time she's cooperative and/or busy. She plays quite a bit with the youngsters next door and they get along well.

The house next door, still under construction in August 1955 (above), and later nearly complete (below).

Dorothy still eats quite a lot—last week I started vitamins, today I'll give her orange juice for the first time. We've been for a few short walks but the sun is too hot until 4:30 or 5 and then I should be in the kitchen. Mrs. S-D brought her a lovely pink dress one day last week—hand smocked and embroidered.

Time to start breakfast. Love from all of us,

Marian

Saturday, November 5, 1955

Dear Bee—

You are not forgotten, although you're probably wondering! It is 6:15 a.m. and H. is quite sensibly still asleep. Dorothy has just finished a bottle and Elizabeth is lying in bed singing "Jingle Bells" and "Stand Up for Jesus," so I may have only a few minutes of peace.

Our thoughts are with you frequently and we certainly hope your problems are straightening out. Uncertainty is hard to live with—not your uncertainty, but a lack of control over future events is what I mean.

I hear E.'s door opening. Hmm. On Friday H. mailed a big box to you for Christmas. It weighs 19 pounds and is bulky so you'll have to fetch it from the P.O. with a car if it isn't delivered to your door. It includes Mother's and Daddy's gifts, too—I assume you'll all spend Christmas together.

Dorothy is awfully cute and very amenable most of the time. Her fussy time is our dinner hour, but we let her roar at one end of the house while we eat in relative quiet at the other end. There is much to be said for having a little baby in a big house—mere distance lessens the nerve strain, at times! However, she doesn't cry much at all except for that period. She is also very obliging about sleeping all morning while I wash dishes, do the bottles and her washing, and other such tasks. I think it is too bad people have to have first babies—the second is so much easier!

It seems that now we'll be able to stay here until next spring and summer. Mr. Cameron has agreed that we can move into his house after he leaves on January 12, and we hope to remain in this house until then. The new house next door is just about finished but we don't know who will get it. It wouldn't be too convenient for us—they put in a kerosene stove instead of wiring the kitchen for an electric stove, and since the bedrooms are upstairs it would mean much more stair-climbing (with a baby) than our present arrangement. The Camerons' house is identical to this one. If we move into it we will take down numerous fringed curtains and fringed lampshades and try to eradicate the atmosphere of what H. calls "little Egypt."

It's due partly to the unsettled housing situation, I suppose, but we are getting tired of this place. Mighty tired. Howard is chafing under the restrictions with which he works and I am bored with the lack of outside diversions. Not that we ask very much, but B.G. has so darned little.

Elizabeth is beginning to pester me, Dorothy is peeping about something—surely not hunger—and I'm hungry. H. is still asleep, bless his heart. He's got to go out to the airbase today to collect some stuff for a forthcoming science exhibition at Q.C. and it's always a hot, tiresome trip. Must go comb my hair and placate the baby!

Much, much love,
Marian

Tuesday, November 8, 1955

Dear All—

I am being terribly optimistic to think I can get more than one sentence written, because Dorothy is due to wake up any minute and probably will when she realizes I am writing a letter. They get smart very soon about such things! Howard is sleeping, Elizabeth is next door playing. It is 4:30 p.m.—fancy that, a letter written after breakfast!

This morning at 4 Spotty woke up and was sick, so H. and I had to get up and clean that up. We went back to bed, but the light had aroused Dorothy so at 4:30 I had to feed her, and then fifteen minutes later, after I'd tried to doze off again, I had to go in and quell at attack of hiccoughs. By then it was 5 and I should have stayed up but didn't, and if we didn't feel ghastly at 6 when it was time to get up! Took cold showers, which helped some.

Dorothy drinks five ounces at nearly every feeding now, and generally goes at least four hours. At night, she eats at 7:30 or 8:30 or 9:30 and lasts through until 5 or 6. She scarcely spits up at all—only twice so far. She fusses mightily between 5 and 9 p.m., roughly, between the feedings near those hours. So it is a good excuse for me to sit and hold her and tell her how cute she it—this, of course, after our dinner is over and the dishes done. If she's howling while we eat she just howls. It is amazing what you learn after the first baby! We always knew we held Elizabeth too much, but it is a vicious habit once it is started. Dorothy is so calm and so good (most of the time) and I am sure it is a reflection of our more relaxed attitude.

Then, too, there is a little marvel known as Woodward's Gripe Water— isn't that a name! I remember how shocked I was when I saw Margaret giving such a concoction to Janet. Anyway, it was recommended by Dr. Georges's nurse and we got some. It cures hiccoughs practically on contact and is supposed to be equally helpful for indigestion, teething, flatulence, etc. I asked Dr. Georges just what is in the stuff and he said he believed it was mineral water, sweetening—all very harmless but effective. It is used widely on the Continent, and he said it is a staple remedy throughout the West Indies.

Elizabeth is as happy as ever. Every once in a while she drops a question about Dorothy's origins. At breakfast the other day she asked who made Dorothy and where, and of course you know how dull-witted I am at that hour. I answered the first question quite calmly and simply, but glanced at H. for help on the second. "At Mr. Scargall's house," he said. It interests me that she is still thinking actively about all this.

Later—Wednesday, 7:30 p.m.: Howard is lulling D., who thinks it is time to eat right *now*, and E. is in bed singing herself to sleep. I shall finish this up and then feed Dorothy. My, my, these *are* busy days. Dorothy woke up at 5, and I had a cup of coffee as I fed her, then stayed up and read the morning paper for a few minutes before getting dressed. Five a.m. is a nice hour here—it is completely dark at 5 but begins getting light just about then, and I enjoy watching the sun come up. Good thing, isn't it!

The enclosed birth certificate is an extra that we wish you would put away in some safe place (don't forget where you put it!) in case we ever need it. We have already sent two other copies to Trinidad and soon should get an official document from the Consulate there. We have another certificate here—I'd hate to have to try to get one in a hurry at some later date! All for now, I think.

Love to you all,

Marian

We're having a nice FOA couple, the Sparks, over Friday evening—he's a drainage and irrigation specialist. We all ate ice cream at their house the Saturday before D. was born. Have to have Joy and Richard over soon—need some diversion!

Tuesday, November 15, 1955

Dear Parents—

It's 3:45 p.m. I'm sitting on the front step with Spot and "our" stray dog panting at my neck. D. is sleeping (I hope for a while) in the pram, E. is playing with Indrani, and I am trying to get Christmas cards written and keep paper from blowing away. I have done everything I intended to do today, including the ironing, but didn't get anything made for dessert. All week we've had good biscuits for dessert but today we're out. We shall all split an apple. Indrani is talking to me and I am somewhat distracted. Oh boy.

Big news: The second half of the new house is ours. S-D told H. yesterday. It should be finished in another week or so—we hope to move in on Sunday, November 27, with the help of six Q.C. boys to carry our stuff. The downstairs floors haven't received their final layers of concrete, all the upstairs windows aren't in, and all the painting isn't done. Glad D. isn't crawling yet! E. is now sitting behind me playing fire engine. A Mr. Digby, of the police department, and his family have moved into the first half. D. is crying.

H. thinks there may be a connection for our stove—hope so. Small convenient kitchen. Three medium-large bedrooms and one tiny one for D. The third large bedroom will be for trunks and ironing. The Sparks told us Friday that they rent a considerable amount of furniture from a local department store for $25 a month. We need to get a bed for E., dining table and chairs, and sofa and chair so will try to rent. If we can't rent, will make do or borrow. No more buying. Sure will be glad to be settled before Christmas. The house actually has some character—quite "finished" inside, which most B.G. houses aren't. But the stair railing is a three-inch pipe! Inside stairs, that is. I'll keep the bathinette in the dining room—no room downstairs anyplace else. D. will spend the day downstairs in the pram and I hope to eliminate some stair-climbing that way.

D. is thriving on her new diet, which includes a dab of mashed bananas twice a day—will substitute cereal for one meal later this week. She seems to love it and apparently she needed it. She is happy most of the day and really easy to have around. We are all having lots of fun with her. E. gave her the "little kiss" you sent. She is so affectionate and helpful. Glad we have the Persaud children for her to play with—very good for her. Wish I could collect my thoughts—too many voices claiming my attention.

Howard is napping. He has a science exhibition on the weekend we plan on moving, and the following weekend he takes some boys out to the airbase for a four-day field trip. I don't know if we'll be able to concentrate on Thanksgiving. I've got some aged mincemeat in the cupboard—left from last Christmas—so maybe we'll have a pie. H. and I got a good laugh out of Bee's trouble with the ants. We've learned to ignore so darn many bugs.

Much love,
Marian

Tuesday, November 22, 1955

Dear All—

I feel as if I'd been writing a soap opera lately: Will we move? Will we leave? Wait till the next installment! This one *does* it, kiddies. Our pleasant plans for moving into the new house went up in smoke last night.

We were awakened at slightly after 4 this morning by the Digbys' daughter, Madeline, who was calling our names and asking us to please phone the fire department as their house was on fire. H. phoned and Madeline came upstairs, followed shortly by her mother, who was attired only in a flimsy housecoat. Howard got through to the fire department after some delay, then went to help Mr. Digby salvage what they could—they brought armloads of silver and some clothes over here before the fire got too bad. I found enough clothes for Mrs. Digby to make her decent at least, and she said that she'd been awakened by a loud noise, seen the light in her wardrobe flickering and upon opening it, discovered it ablaze. The fire department arrived in due time, and proceeded to drive into the school yard instead of jogging into the road that comes by all the houses—the new one being at the very end of the line. Mr. Wilson-Hodgkinson finally went over and told the driver to back up and swing around; the driver didn't understand, so Mr. W-H ended up by leading the fire truck on foot.

By that time, the fire had spread throughout the upper story and flames were pouring out the windows of what was to be our bedroom, too close to this house for comfort. I went in to close Elizabeth's window to keep the sight of the flames out, and she roused and asked what was the pretty color. I told her everything was all right and to go back to sleep. Dorothy never did wake up. The firemen put the fire out rather quickly once they got started, but H. said they had water pouring out of two unattended hoses while men were trying to set up the third hose. The Digbys' car was parked in front of the house and the hoses got tangled in its wheels, so H. and some other men picked up the rear end and skidded it away—it was locked, of course.

Word got around quickly that it was the Digbys' house, and since he is Assistant Commissioner of Police and a VIP, all sorts of policemen were around. By 6 a.m. someone had taken Mrs. Digby and Madeline home with them, and of course the fire was out long since. After things cooled off enough they went into the house and salvaged more stuff. The place is a total wreck—the only part relatively unscathed is the living room on our side. H. says it looks as if they'll have to tear it down and start all over. Approximately 40 thousand dollars gone!

It gives us the willies to think that in another week we would have been seriously involved. As it is, it leaves us just where we were a couple of weeks ago, planning on the Camerons' house. The Persauds have said that if necessary Agatha and the children could remain in Berbice (they always go there to Harold's family for all vacations) after school reopens and Harold returns, so that we could stay in their house until we get the Camerons' cleaned up. I loathe the thought of moving into the Camerons' house, but with plenty of disinfectant and DDT we should be okay. Winifred is a good scrubber so I shall hire her to do the dirty work.

Does all this make sense? It is 7:30 p.m. and nearly time to feed Dorothy. She has responded to the excitement by being fussy allll day. I've been up since 4 with a half-hour rest after lunch. I have been answering E.'s questions all day—Why did the fire burn? How will they fix the house? Where will we be for Christmas? Why are they taking the furniture out? Why did Mr. Digby leave the dishes here? Why did you say "It's all right" when you closed my window last night? and so on. Then she nearly sent us into hysterics at lunchtime by suggesting in a firm little voice, "Let's go home."

Poor Howard is stiff and tired—while trying to move the car last night he slipped and landed on his back in a huge puddle, nearly drowning himself. It poured much of the night and the ground around us is sodden and flooded. Add to that the messy piles of sand, gravel, sawdust, junk; the empty cement barrels; the impassably rutted muddy road in front of the new houses, and you can get an idea of the vista from our windows. I guess I didn't say that the fire evidently started in defective wiring. The Digbys' side of the house was finished in a hurry, men working night and day, and evidently the wiring wasn't inspected as carefully as it should have been.

An aerial view of the college, taken shortly after the Digbys' fire, shows reconstruction of the house under way.

Two weeks ago the roof on the new addition to the Government Technical Institute, which is in the process of being built, caved in—one begins to wonder about B.G.'s building standards.

As I started to say, poor Howard is so involved getting the Science Exhibition (his botany part) ready for Friday evening that he is at school now working with the boys.

Yesterday Dorothy and I had our six-weeks' checkup and we're both fine. Damn good thing. Dorothy weighs 11 pounds 14 ounces.

The records came yesterday, Mother, and thank you so much! Elizabeth and Indrani and Bini were quite wide-eyed over "Davy Crockett," and I can't wait until E. has learned to sing it. I like the lullabies—I put them on while I feed Dorothy.

Sorry I forgot *all* about your wedding anniversary! Belated felicitations, etc. Gads, there is just too much going on around here.

Later—Dorothy is fed and I hope asleep for the night. At the present rate we're going we will ignore Thanksgiving this week—although I'll probably suffer last-minute pangs and make that darned mince pie up. The FOA people invited us to a cocktail party Thursday evening but that is not a good time for me and D. is too young to leave with anyone and

Howard is too busy. This Friday is the Q.C. Speech Day and the S-Ds are having an open house afterward, but I had to decline that, too, for the same reasons, and H. has his exhibit to tend to so he can't go, either. Don't really care about either.

Must go downstairs and get the clothes off the line. This damp weather is the nuts. Even the diapers were slow to dry today!

Much, much love to you all,

Marian

November 27, 1955

From an editorial in the Daily Chronicle:

Two years have gone by and we are no better off than we were before the political debacle. We have had more houses built, we have had a few self-aided schemes, a little of this and a little of that, but the population is increasing faster than ever, unemployment is increasing and the cost of living continues to rise. We submit to marking time politically, and even here we expect the time where the economic development of the country is concerned. Must we continue to live as we are living or should we say existing? Let there be an end to this nonsense.

Thursday, December 1, 1955

Dear All—

Busy, busy days. We did have that pie on Thanksgiving Day, but since Howard was frantically busy getting his exhibition prepared, we didn't linger over any festive meal. Friday was Speech Day; following that the Exhibition opened and continued Saturday, Monday, and Tuesday. E. and I went over Saturday morning intending to see all the exhibits in an hour (I left D. asleep with Enid) but didn't get beyond the zoology and botany. Saturday afternoon we went back to finish but spent an entire hour on the physics displays. The boys had all worked so hard and were so eager to explain their displays, which were excellent. Howard and his boys had probably worked harder than any of the others, since the botany exhibit is more difficult to make interesting to the general public, and since his purpose was to show what the boys study and learn in their botany courses. His boys made big diagrams and murals showing how plants reproduce, bacteria, microscopic plants, and so on—very neatly done. Howard made two trips to the airbase to get specimens—fungi, mosses, ground orchids,

Marian, holding Dorothy, with Elizabeth and Spotty, November 1955

etc., and they were effective and helped add atmosphere. The boys did all the assembling with little assistance from H.—he was too busy making other displays for the room. The zoology exhibit was good and interesting because they had borrowed animals from boys—turtles, tortoises, a rabbit; and also borrowed some specimens from the British Guiana Museum. The physics displays were all models of different things—steam engine, telephone, a radio in a matchbox, various effects of magnetics—interesting, but not exactly what the boys learn in their classrooms. We never did get to the chemistry exhibit—I was planning to go over Tuesday afternoon, but Howard came home after lunch and collapsed with what I now call End-of-the-Term Dysentery, and since he felt like dying for a few hours I stayed home.

Added to the work involved in the exhibit was a great deal of nervous tension caused by others on the staff who failed to realize the work done by the boys and science masters. Mr. Cameron, senior master and deputy principal, said he thought "too many men were spending too much time on this exhibit," and took offense when H. said they'd be glad to close it down anytime he suggested. The principal accused Mr. [Joshua] Ramsammy, one of H.'s fellow biology teachers, of neglecting his class, and denied having told the Science masters they would be relieved of their classes during the exhibit. He was quite vehement, and H. had to talk back and say that he *had* said they wouldn't have their classes. Poor old Howard, who does hate bickering and petty quarrels, had all this and some other nonsense, too.

He feels fine today and is going on the field trip that has been planned for this weekend. He is taking 35 boys, two masters, and Ramphal (H.'s lab assistant who graduated from Queen's a year ago and is such a pleasant, intelligent boy) and they will go out to the airbase tomorrow and return next Monday. I think they will be using the Boy Scout camp out there for shelter. They are split into two groups for purposes of food buying and cooking, and H.'s group purchased a sensible amount of food that will be easily prepared. The other group is taking eggs, chicken (one for nine boys), and other goodies that they will probably regret since they'll be doing all their own cooking.

Dorothy is doing beautifully and is smiling at us more and more. She looks so darned cute when she smiles—her eyes light up and she makes squeaky noises as if she's trying to talk. She has taken to sleeping on her stomach and is happy for much longer periods that way. A few nights ago she was fussy off and on all evening, and I had to feed her at 11, which is much later than usual. But the next morning she slept until 8:30, then after her bath and milk she slept again until I woke her at 2:30!

Don't I get a lot done when she's asleep—I do enjoy getting my ironing done by daylight, and reading or sewing in the evening. I'm trying to get a little doll made for Dorothy for Christmas, and so far I have head, body, and two arms. Elizabeth asks eagerly each day if I've finished the dolly, so I try to get a little more done on it so she can see progress. It is hard to believe that we are into December now, and soon we'll have to think seriously about cookies and fruitcake.

Mother, H. read an ad yesterday for the Robert Shaw Chorale record *Christmas Hymns and Carols*. Will you buy it, please, and send it off airmail? We are enjoying all the choral music and would love to have this record, too. I trust that when we ask you to get things for us you pay yourself back out of our account—that's understood as far as we're concerned!

We got a letter from John a few days ago saying that they won't be coming back. At the time he wrote he hadn't received the final word on his new appointment, but it seems likely that he wouldn't have written at all if it weren't all set. So, after innumerable crises, it looks as if we'll be able to stay here. John asked us to sell his furniture and pack up their belongings for them—no small task, actually—but of course we can't do anything until he notifies Sanger-Davies.

Glad to know the meat tenderizer is on its way. Even gladder to know someone thinks I look too thin! Howard has reached the point where he is watching what he eats—some of his trousers are getting a bit snug. As for me, I would like very much to lose some weight around the hips and stomach, but I'm too lazy to exercise ("don't have the time") and dieting is too great a problem here. After all, Dorothy isn't quite two months yet—maybe some of it will reshape itself.

The Persauds will leave a few days after school closes on December 16, and Elizabeth will miss them more than ever now that she's become accustomed to playing with the children. We will all miss the Ramsarans, of course, but I'm sorriest of all that E. won't have Susan and Janet to play with. Have I asked you before if there are any children or grandchildren near E.'s age that she could play with once in a while when we're staying with you?

I think if I'm smart I'll go have a shower now while Dorothy is still asleep and E. is "resting." Elizabeth is still my helper and does more and more all the time. Yesterday she carried off a diaper to the toilet, and although I had visions of the diaper going down the drain, she flushed the toilet and shook and cleaned the diaper all by herself. All at her insistence, mind you—it is one thing that I do a bit neater myself, but who am I to discourage help unless it's just impossible!

Much love,

Marian

Wednesday, December 7, 1955

Dears—

Oh boy—do we have confusion! We heard from John yesterday; he is taking up an appointment as lecturer in English at the University College of Ibadan, Nigeria. He is flying, and Margaret and the children will go by boat in January. They are in a hurry to have their belongings sent and furniture sold, so here we are with a furniture sale added to our already busy routine. In our living room we have all the regular stuff plus stove (ours, which we intend to sell now, with our two chairs; we're buying the Ramsarans' five-piece living room suite, dining table, and chairs), refrigerator, food safe, dresser, pram, two beds. Also our dining room furniture, since we have to gather all the Ramsarans' possessions somewhere before we can begin to pack them up. They have dishes, kitchen utensils, books, linens, and all the other necessities scattered around, crowded into closets and packed away in the maid's room downstairs—it will be a job just to get it all rounded up. As I told H., it's a good thing that they were our good friends. I would resent all the mess and labor if the people involved were strangers.

We intend to stay on in this house. We feel there is no real reason why we shouldn't be allowed to do so, but this morning the school secretary whispered in H.'s ear that he should promptly apply to the Chief Secretary for permission to remain here, since she thought perhaps S-D might be planning to shift us to Cameron's house and put a new man on the staff in here. Nuts to that—we are going to stay—squatters' rights and all that. We really don't anticipate any difficulties, however.

Elizabeth is fine, busy as usual. Yesterday morning I'd left Dorothy on the bathinette after her bath while I warmed her bottle, and when I went to get her I found E. standing beside her on a chair, feeding her "orange juice" out of her dolly bottle. The orange juice consisted of a few drops of juice plus water, highly unsterile. I tried to explain it all to E. without hurting her feelings—she does so want to help. When we put the teddy bear quilt on the floor for Dorothy to lie on in the afternoons, E. delights in turning D. over, tucking a blanket (unnecessary) around her, bringing her a teddy bear to play with, etc. I keep a close watch, darting back and forth from kitchen to living room, and keep telling myself that babies are very hardy little creatures. A little rolling from back to stomach won't hurt Dorothy, and it sure makes Elizabeth feel important.

Howard's field trip went off quite well, despite the fact that none of the boys were at all experienced in such things. Before they went, someone asked if they would "dress for dinner"! They got back Monday around noon, in the middle of a heavy shower. In fact, between 11:30 and 1:30 there were three inches of rainfall! It's winter.

Dorothy responds readily now to us when we talk to her, smiles and gurgles, and looks so eager to talk to us. Over the weekend while H. was gone I just had to let her cry in the evenings while I put Elizabeth to bed and did the dishes, and thereby discovered that after she cries between her 6 and 9 p.m. feedings, she goes off to sleep by herself after the last bottle. Up to then Howard had been rocking her to sleep every evening, but not since.

All for today. I've got things to do! Much, much love,

Marian

Did I mention the Q.C. art exhibit last week? H. and I were much impressed by the works of one boy, and bought two of his pictures, oils, both scenes in the Botanical Gardens. We've been looking for some local pictures for quite a spell and are glad to have these.

Two boxes arrived from you today, also one from H.'s mother—you might let her know. H. too busy to write right now.

Thursday, December 29, 1955

Dear All—

I don't think I've written for quite a spell—perhaps I'd better go back to the week before Christmas and bring you up to date.

The Sunday before Christmas we managed to clear all the Ramsarans' stuff out of our dining room—heaven only knows how many hours Howard spent crating their belongings. We also got our own curtains put up, a considerable improvement. On Monday Elizabeth went next door to the Persauds' for a little party with Indrani, for the Persauds were to leave on Tuesday for their usual vacation stay in New Amsterdam. Elizabeth came home at 5 utterly exhausted but quite full of cake and ice cream. I thought it was very sweet of Agatha to hold the party, for she had all their packing and whatnot to do in order to leave the next morning. Tuesday Howard went downtown and purchased a little book for Dorothy to give Elizabeth—I nearly forgot that!—and also some seersucker, as I had had the brilliant idea of making seersucker tablecloths and napkins for E. She does like to change from her plastic placemats, and then, too, I had to have something for Spot and Binky to give her! So Tuesday evening I sewed. Wednesday Howard went out to the airbase for our tree and greens, and came back with a tall, slender one for us and a cute little one for Elizabeth. Wednesday night I made a little "angel" for E.'s tree while H. fashioned three big sprays out of the green leaves, berries, and pods—during the evening we were "entertained" by a group of simply awful carol singers who stood in our driveway, right under our windows. Neither of the sleeping children heard them. Thursday evening I finished the tablecloths. Friday I washed clothes, washed E.'s and my hair, and that evening ironed most of the washing. More carol singers, children this time, so the discords weren't quite so horrifying.

Saturday was A Day. We had decided to have our Christmas dinner on Christmas Eve, and I had my day all planned out so that we would eat at 5:30. The morning was spent with my usual routine—Dorothy's bath, diapers, etc., but after lunch I baked some cinnamon rolls, made ambrosia (with an eight-cent coconut), stuffed the chicken, and put it in the oven. We were running our second ad in the papers to get rid of the Ramsarans' pram, stroller, and piano and a couple of people came to see the piano. About 3, while Howard and Elizabeth were busily wrapping gifts in the dining room, a man came to inquire about the piano. I thought from his voice he must be either Canadian or American, but when E. came into the room and he said "Hello, punkins" I was sure he was an American! From Oregon, it turned out, and a minister here for the Church of God. Howard came in and we sat down to chat, and it was nearly 5 by the time he left— he's a very nice young man and we all enjoyed the visit, but there was the chicken just about done and all of us in very unfestive attire. In rapid order I got the carrots and potatoes on to cook, washed up some pans, started the gravy, mashed the potatoes, set the table, and consumed a drink. Howard wanted to save me a rush and suggested that we not get dressed up, but I couldn't see it and he meekly put on a shirt and tie, bless his heart. It takes a lot to get H. to wear a tie in this country. Elizabeth got all excited as I put on her blue nylon party dress ("It's fun to get dressed up for Christmas, isn't it, Mommy!" repeated at least a dozen times). I didn't have time for a shower but put on my pretty white pique dress and combed my hair and washed my face and hands. We sat down at eat a few minutes before 6, with candles on the table. Elizabeth loved it all, of course, and the dinner was very good—we had a five-pound chicken, the biggest we've ever seen here in B.G. Usually we are lucky to get a three-pound chick.

Elizabeth had her bath, hung up her stocking, and helped fix a peanut butter sandwich and a thermos full of coffee for Santa. Howard read her *The Night Before Christmas* and she skittered off to bed, exhausted.

Howard removed his clothes with a sigh of relief and, clad in shorts, began to do the tree while I did the dishes. We were just beginning to put the ornaments on when Ramphal came by, and he helped us. About 10:30 Mrs. S-D came by with little gifts for E. and D., and I guess Ramphal left about 11. Then we got out all the boxes and undid the brown paper, and as happens every year, Howard scolded me as I scrutinized each gift—he accuses me of poking, prodding, and other unfair practices, but really I just love to gaze at the lovely papers, ribbons, and cards. Everything looked so very pretty, and we had a huge pile of presents under the tree. We got to bed about midnight.

Christmas morning I was awake first, then Dorothy, and as I was changing her diaper Elizabeth appeared and wailed, "But you didn't let me wake you up" (I had promised her she could do that). So I sent her in to wake up Howard, and we all said "Merry Christmas" very formally, as I had been telling her for weeks we would do on Christmas morning, and we proceeded to the living room. Elizabeth noticed Dorothy's stocking right away, and after gazing at the tree for a few minutes she got her stocking and began on that, while H. fed Dorothy and I fixed breakfast. E. kept repeating "Now wasn't that thoughtful of Santa to bring me what I needed!" Dorothy went back to bed, the stocking was emptied (Santa *did* bring things E. needed—two new toothbrushes, talcum powder, dolly soap, etc.), and we had breakfast. After that we sat down near the tree to open the gifts, and Elizabeth was just confused enough by it all to thank Santa for *everything*. We told her who sent each gift, but as far as she was concerned, Santa was very thoughtful to bring us these things that we needed.

We had to interrupt our session to bathe and feed Dorothy, and it was about 11 a.m. before we'd finished. Howard was just folding up the papers and collecting the ribbons when Lester dropped in, and he stayed for a sandwich. Mr. Digby (the burned-out ex-neighbor) stopped by with a baby doll for E., dressed in a white dress and jacket that Mrs. Digby had knitted. I was terribly glad we'd had our dinner the night before, because I didn't feel like doing any more than shoving leftovers into the oven. Good leftovers, at that!

And the presents you all sent us! My word, it is just plain hard to thank you adequately. Those darling socks for Dorothy. The plastic glasses for E., which had me fooled for several minutes—I couldn't imagine why you would send real glass! Those lovely dresses and blouses and skirts! The dresses are much too large, of course, but Elizabeth had to try them on ("But Mommy, I'm sure I can wear them afterward." After what, I don't know). The pink and blue skirts I will shorten a bit and she can wear them now; heaven knows she is growing fast. I love my tile and the lazy Susan and the dish drainer attachments, and I'm anxious to try the hurricane lamps—I'll bet they're the answer to candles in this windy place. Howard is very pleased with the new records and the handy little tray.

Bee, I love the gold necklace, bracelet, and earrings. They are just exactly what I wanted! The Alice in Wonderland party is lovely but I shall have to keep it until I, at least, have read the book. Elizabeth's hairclips are the sweetest I've seen, but I think she is most pleased by the Bo-Peep apron. Dorothy enjoys the "octo-puss" already, for I tie it to the side of her crib and she gurgles at it as she clutches a leg. The dear little medal she will wear on our trip home if not before, and she'll appreciate it at an even later date. We are delighted to have a good pencil sharpener in the family. Where did you hear of the *Carmina Burana* record? It is certainly interesting. And our whole Christmas was enhanced by the Robert Shaw record, which arrived, I think, the Wednesday before Christmas. Also our thanks for *Time* and the *Saturday Review*, parents, which as you know are quite an integral part of our existence!

Christmas night there was a dance at the Portuguese Club behind us, and it ended at 5 a.m. with "God Save the Queen." I didn't hear much of the racket, but Howard did; they set off more than thirty firecrackers—big loud ones—over a period of an hour or so, but fortunately neither Elizabeth nor Dorothy was really disturbed. Neither was I, just poor Howard, who lay there counting them! Then at 5 it was raining so the merrymakers couldn't leave when the dance ended, so they all sang Christmas carols with great gusto. The day after Christmas is Boxing Day, and on that night the Teachers' Club had *its* fling. Again, I was too sleepy to be disturbed, but H. wasn't. That one ended early, at about 2:30 a.m. Thank goodness the children sleep soundly. Tuesday night we had Joy and Richard to dinner, and Joy brought me a little magazine that is all about Guianese Christmases of the past, and so interesting that we've bought some extra copies to send to you all.

Last night H. went to a stag cocktail party that developed into a serious-minded political discussion, completely unaffected by small, weak drinks. (Howard had ten or twelve rum-and-gingers, fruit-juice-glass size, and came home as sober as if he'd been attending an economics lecture.) Next

Sunday, New Year's Day, we are to have dinner with the Sparks, Elizabeth and Dorothy, too. On January 6 (Friday) Howard and the three other biology masters are going out to the airbase to study the insects and other wildlife. They'll be back the following Monday.

I am beginning to make lists, lists, lists and otherwise get in the spirit of going home. Howard gave me a nice passport case which looks much more respectable than the worn envelope I used before. We are planning, more or less definitely, that E., D., and I will leave here on April 5, reaching New York on the 8th. We both thought that Pan Am had changed its schedule to eliminate that two-day wait at Port of Spain, but H. got a new schedule yesterday and either they never did change or else they've gone back to the old one. H. says to allow one day to get to New Jersey and another day to get back to New York, so I shall write the Kessler Institute and see if we can get an appointment for the 11th; also I would like to know how much time we should allow there.

Enclosed is an aerial view of Q.C. taken by a boy a few weeks ago, just after the fire next door. We've bought quite a few views from him, as they are all good and show what the city looks like. Howard is now writing a key so you'll know what you're looking at.

All for now. Time for bed.

Much, much love to you all,

Marian

Well, Mother dear, this is probably the first in a long series of notes pertaining to our arrival in April. Tomorrow H. will mail two boxes containing some stuff we will need in Tacoma and which we can't possibly take with us. They include two blankets and a quilt for Dorothy's crib (which we don't need here anyway), the teddy bear quilt, and two crib sheets, which I think I can do without here. Also some warm nighties. And some of Elizabeth's pet toys and books which she won't miss here, having many left, but which she will like to have in Tacoma—we'll bring a few dolls in our suitcases but the bulk of what is left here will go straight to Texas. I have given E. a big buildup about seeing the dollies as soon as we get to Grandmother's house—she will expect to see them all lined up in her room waiting for her!

Now for some questions.

1. Will you please find out from a doll hospital or whatever they're called how much it would cost to give Mary a new body? E. is very attached to her, and her head is as good as new, but she looks as if she has the plague all over

her body—black mildew spots, most unattractive. E. is not content to leave Mary behind, but I certainly hope we can get her a new body fairly reasonably.

2. How much do new strollers cost? Elizabeth's is so beat up, it would need new paint and a new canvas seat, and we are wondering if it would be simpler and nearly as expensive to buy a new one for Dorothy rather than ship E.'s. I think we paid about $16 for it. Any possibility of renting or borrowing one to use in Tacoma, thus eliminating one small item from the stuff to transport to Texas?

3. How much do driving lessons cost? Is there someone in the Lakes district who does it? I have sworn to H. that I will get a driver's license in Tacoma, before we get to Texas, and he has sworn back that I had just better.

4. Our washcloths are practically threadbare in the center and some of our towels look rather straggly. I shall bring them all back to use on camping trips if nothing else, but I would like to get some new ones for everyday use. (H.'s mother sent me such pretty ones for Christmas a year ago that I feel I must save them for company!) My point is this—if the savings to be had during the January sales are considerable, I would like you to get four sets for me. Or are there similar sales in August? I would enjoy buying them myself if there are!

I guess we'll have Dorothy vaccinated early in March so she'll be all over that before we leave. I've got lots of sewing to do—lots of everything to do.

Dorothy is so cute—she gurgles and blows bubbles and wrinkles up her nose when she smiles. I've had to wake her up every night for several weeks to feed her, and in another week or so we'll see if she can go through the night without the extra bottle. Haven't weighed her since she was six weeks old but we know she is gaining well—it's just plain fun taking care of her.

Saturday, December 31, 1955

Howdy—

When we had Joy and Richard to dinner the other night she brought us a copy of this *Kyk-Over-Al*[84] and I thought it very interesting. I asked then about traditional Guianese Christmas dinner, and they said until recent years everyone who possibly could had a turkey, ham, roast beef, pepperpot (the hot stew, with all sorts of meat), plus vegetables, Christmas cake, etc. Joy said in her family each one could have his favorite dish on Christmas Day—cabbage soup for one, salad for another, fried plantains for another. She said her grandmother spent the entire morning in the kitchen—not hard to believe!

People still cook a lot ahead because making calls on Christmas Day is traditional also and no one has time to cook. Joy helped put this issue out and I think you'll enjoy it.

All for now—Happy New Year!

Love,

Marian

Monday, January 2, 1956

Howdy, Bee! Thought you'd be interested in this issue of *Kyk-Over-Al*. Many of the old traditions have pretty well died out, but Christmas food is still the big thing. Guianese fruitcake is really alcoholic—very dark, wet, and potent.

We spent a very quiet New Year's Eve—I ironed, and then did some mending while H. read aloud from Kinsey's book on men. We had three parties going full blast behind us—a steel band at one, and they didn't break up until 4 or so. It was really noisy but the children slept through it all.

Much love,

Marian

Hi, there, Bee,

The *Carmina Burana* is an intriguing record. We put it on first without reading the annotation and couldn't make much of it. After reading the notes through and replaying, we began to feel the pulse of the melodies. I suppose this could be used as evidence against us, but then this is the 20th century!

Marian is itching to get home. Thank the Lord for the children or she might not be sane—poor dear. How about chiming in on my major theme without variations: She must learn to drive while in Tacoma. There must be no escape through excuse. O.K.?

All the best in '56.

Love,

Howard

Thursday, January 5, 1956

Howdy, dears—

We had a letter from H.'s mother today saying that because April 14 is their wedding anniversary, she'd like to be home then. So we plan now to leave here on March 29, arrive in New York on April 1 and probably arrive in Tacoma on Saturday the 7th. I still haven't managed to find the time to write the Kessler Institute but must this weekend. As soon as I hear from them, we'll make our plane reservations. So many times it takes *ages* to get things done from this end!

Quite a snappy typewriter ribbon this is, eh! [Its ink is blue.] Howard bought it for eight cents, so we hold no hopes for its long-lasting qualities.

The draft is the first that we will send you, one a month until Howard leaves. We went to the Treasury Department today and received permission to send $300 BWI a month, and we shall do so as long as our local account can take it. Every once in a while we get a cold chill thinking about devaluation, and of course they could up and tell us we can't take anything out—so we'll send what we can as we can.

The thought that we now leave in March makes me somewhat giddy. Of course I thoroughly enjoy the planning, the sewing, etc. as long as there is time enough to do it all. I think there is, but with only two or three clear hours a day to sew, I must get busy.

Now, here are some more specific questions, requests. Mother dear, how would you like to be an Easter bunny? Checking the calendar we find that April 1 is Easter Sunday, and the day we shall leave Trinidad for New York. Elizabeth has been interested in Easter ever since last year and would be very disappointed if she learned that it was Easter and the bunny had ignored her. Since the only candy eggs available here are chocolate, which would melt, and since I won't be able to hard-boil the real thing, will you please purchase a small, easily packable basket and some candy eggs of various sizes (not too many) and send them the first of March or so? A small airmail package I would gladly pay for. Also, a yellow chick and that sort of stuff. I suppose we'd have to discover the basket in our bag after we were safely on the plane; the plane leaves Trinidad at 7:30 a.m. or thereabouts, and an Easter basket found by her bed in the morning would probably delay us too much. The eggs should probably be sent in a jar so they won't get sticky on the way.

Item 2. Can you borrow a playpen from someone? I don't know just when Dorothy will start to crawl, but she sure manages to scoot around in her bed now. Howard is going to make a small playpen just to get her used to the idea (the *Better Homes and Gardens* book says baby should be put in playpen between three and four months) and Lord knows I wouldn't want her on the prowl with all your pretty things around!

Item 3. I was on the verge of buying more outing flannel here to make E. another nightie, but remembered the two pretty pieces I bought and left at your place. Would it be asking entirely too much of you to make up one into a nightgown? No frills necessary, of course. I think those two Carter's nightgowns will come only to her knees, she's grown so. But she does need at least two to get started, and I can always make another once we are there.

Tuesday we had Mr. and Mrs. [Laurence] Keates to tea. He is new at Queen's, here to teach Spanish for the first time. Spanish is to be taught here for the first time, that is. He is English, his wife Portuguese. They are about our ages and she is expecting a baby in February. They ended up staying for dinner and more talking—they are in a boardinghouse, no housing being available, and I suppose they're happy for a change of scenery now and then. They'd like to move into our house after we go, but how they'll be able to take care of the baby in one room for six weeks or so is more than I can imagine. We'd go mad, I know that!

Howard leaves tomorrow for his four-day jaunt into the airbase bush with the other Q.C. biology masters. He seems to be very casual about the possibility of ant bites, wasp bites, etc., but I wouldn't enjoy it.

While he's gone I hope to go through the three trunks and eliminate *some* stuff. It is so hard to know just what we should keep—Howard and I are both inclined to keep everything that has some use left, but I suppose we could buy new replacements at home for many items without spending much. There are always folks here eager for the castoffs.

Almost 8 p.m. and I must hem Elizabeth's new blue skirt. Such pretty skirts! The pink and blue ones both needed to be shortened about an inch, but size five is otherwise just right for her now.

All for now. Much love,
Marian

Monday, January 16, 1956

Dears—

Yes, I *know* I didn't write at all last week, and this won't get to you until next week, and I just hope you didn't worry! I keep getting busier and busier and I just hope to have a lull one of these days before too long. Right now I should be doing the washing, but the workmen are connecting the water pipes next door and our water is shut off for two hours. I would like to be taking a nap, but I'm doing this instead and having a cup of coffee as well. Howard will come home at 2 and I shall go downtown to buy ribbon to bind the hem of E.'s brown coat, buttons for a dress, and so on. I hope to find some disposable diapers; if not, you shall hear from me, Mother!

From January 6 to 10 Howard was at the airbase with the other men—I wrote you that they were going out. A highly satisfactory trip, except that Mr. Boland was attacked by wasps and suffered some discomfort. Yesterday Howard and Mr. Ramsammy went by air to Orinduik, on the Brazil border, and did some collecting there. Howard had a chance to go there on October 10 but didn't, so we were glad this opportunity came up. He has a little sunburn and his arms are covered with bites of the savannah fly, but otherwise he's dandy.

Elizabeth is still wrapped up in Christmas, and every day we pretend it is Christmas Eve and wrap presents, or that it is Christmas morning (in which case we *all* wish *everyone* a Merry Christmas, dog and cat included). We have prepared and eaten numerous Christmas dinners, and so far she's going strong. For Christmas I gave her a Little Golden Book called *Animal Friends*, all about Miss Kitty, Mr. Pup, Brown Bunny, Tweeter Bird, Poky Turtle, Fluffy Squirrel, and Little Chick. Much of the time recently we, the family, have been Miss Kitty (me), Mr. Pup (E.), Black-and-White Bunny (Spot), Tweeter Bird (Binky), Poky Turtle (new tortoise H. brought back from airbase), Fluffy Squirrel (H.), and Dorothy is Little Chick. The last is the easiest to remember, since I even called her that at times before the advent of the book. Sure as fate, I forget at the wrong time that Elizabeth is *not* Elizabeth but Mr. Pup, or even to complicate matters more she is sometimes a Monkey and sometimes a Baby Elizabeth and sometimes a little boy named Jimmy! There are moments when it nearly gets me down, this business of feeding worms to Dorothy, and bones to Elizabeth, and switching in mid-meal to carrots for the Fierce Bad Rabbit or something. Complicated it is, but such fun.

Dorothy is just plain cute. I know now what people mean when they talk about babies being fun. Take away the uncertainty that I suppose most mothers feel about their first, and taking care of a baby is just great sport. Dorothy coos and gurgles and blows bubbles with gusto, and enjoys banging away at a rattle. The octopus is a real favorite—all those legs are just perfect for a baby to grab hold of and chew. She has slid easily into a four-hour, five-meal schedule, and although I've tried once she apparently isn't ready to give up the 10 p.m. bottle. We've tried several kinds of baby foods, but so far the only ones she enjoys are applesauce and carrots—this is in addition to Pablum and mashed bananas, which she likes. Elizabeth is tickled pink to scrape up what Dorothy leaves, so we don't waste anything!

Have I written anything about Mr. and Mrs. Keates? They came for tea one afternoon two weeks ago and stayed for dinner. She is expecting a baby in February and is rather nervous about it—her first, and she is really a tiny girl, only about five feet tall. She came over one day last week, after lunch, and we had a good time talking. After school the men came over and we all had tea. Long ago we signed an agreement not to sell or give away our pram and bathinette, but we are going to lend them to the Keateses (for an indefinite period). We'll give them the pram as soon as their baby is born, for Sita (she is Portuguese—did I tell you that?) wants to use that instead of buying a bassinette, and after I leave with E. and D. they will use the bathinette.

They are living in one room in a boardinghouse, and the one room has no real breeze, and she is miserably hot most of the time. She learned English as a child and speaks it very well so language is no problem in conversation—she is intelligent and has a good sense of humor. Nice people to know—I feel rather badly that we didn't meet them before Christmas, since she said last week they spent Christmas in the boardinghouse. Her husband and one of the Q.C. teachers went through the university together in England, and the Keateses came here more or less under the proddings and suggestions of this teacher. We expected that he would make himself responsible for entertaining them at first, but apparently not.

I have finally finished making the nightgown for Elizabeth that I cut out in November. Today I started cutting out a jumper—plaid Viyella, I just love that material—and I shall get that done as soon as possible. If someone wants to give E. a sweater for her birthday, she could use one. I hope to buy some dye today to dye her lovely white sweater brown—it has some stains on the sleeves from bananas and I hope dye will cover them. A red sweater would be pretty. Do they make short-sleeved cardigans? Using her arms as she does, long sleeves get so messy so fast. The second jumper will be green, with two flowered blouses.

Mother, do you want me to send the lavender-and-white checked blanket to Tacoma or shall we put it in a trunk and send it to Texas? I think you said you didn't need it, but I don't remember for sure.

I would certainly enjoy a shower but guess I'll have to wait until I get home from town. I'll need it more then anyway! As always, it's hard to believe that this is January. Lovely sunny day, nice breeze. Howard and I think that we'll have to spend the rest of our days in a sunny climate—the Northwest's rain would never appeal to us now. I think he would enjoy teaching at the University of Hawaii, but so far he is noncommittal. Must go change my clothes now.

Much, much love,

Marian

The Persauds' baby, Denise, refuses to be left alone! She is about ten months, I guess, and since we've been here she has cried whenever she's left. Of course as she gets older she gets stronger and louder. They seem unaware of the fact that they could break her of the habit. Imagine—their third child at that. But perhaps they think we're just as crazy to put E. to bed at 6:30—theirs all stay up until 8:30 or so.

Elizabeth "wrote" you a long letter yesterday but decided at the last minute not to mail it. She "called" you on her phone instead—"We'll see you the end of March."

Monday, January 23, 1956

Dear Mother—

I am about to have my after-lunch rest, that is, a cup of coffee, while I do the washing and write to you. Split-level thinking, I call it. Dorothy is asleep and Elizabeth is resting, so while I time the washing machine I shall collect my thoughts and write. You say you're excited about our coming home? Every time I look at the calendar I get a jolt!

We had a letter from you and one from H.'s mother today, and now that we know what flight she is taking from New York to Tacoma, Howard will make our reservations. It is early, but the United man in Seattle said there would be heavy traffic due to Easter so it is best to make the reservations early. She wanted to know about a coat for me—I would like her to take my good beige coat, since the tweed is in rather sad shape. The lining is at any rate. I plan on wearing a cool dress since we'll have a couple of hours at Puerto Rico and there is no point in melting there—I shall shiver in New York, perhaps, from plane to airport, but that will only be a few minutes. Elizabeth's coat is all pressed, and all I have to do is stitch the ribbon and sew the hem. I have several sweaters and bonnets for Dorothy (all sorts of sweaters—two pink wool, one pink nylon, one white cotton, and one green wool) and I shall have a blanket with me to wrap her in.

Damn. There is a roller outside smoothing out the new gravel road in front of the new houses, and of course it *always* has to go by our house when Dorothy is asleep. She is awake now, but perhaps she'll drop off again. I get so sick and tired of the noise—men shouting, donkeys braying, wheelbarrows squeaking, hammering, the scritch of cement being mixed by hand, and the awful racket that we had last week of shovels full of gravel being dropped into wheelbarrows and trundled away. There were 13 tons of gravel in our front yard to be removed in this fashion, and I suppose they've taken a third of it away. I try not to think about it, but it peeves me when it wakes up Dorothy!

I don't feel so silly about asking you to send an Easter basket for Elizabeth since you thought of it first! Did I tell you I found a dear little white bunny for Dorothy? The knit nighties for E. will be lovely, as will the bunny slippers and robe. She looks awfully pretty in green, I think, if you have any choice.

Kyk-Over-Al means "looks over all" and is the name of the first Dutch settlement in the colony, a fortress really, on an island about 100 miles up the Essequibo River.

I am wondering if H.'s mother would have room to bring my Viyella robe to New York. She wrote that it would probably be chilly and damp there, in which case my shortie pj's might not be quite enough. Also, if we will be there a full week I will need a sweater and skirt to sit around in. If she doesn't have room you could mail them. Rust color sweater and brown skirt with brown, green, and rust stripes, please.

We are thankful that we didn't have to move into the Camerons' house. Mrs. Wilson-Hodgkinson came by this morning to borrow some paint remover and gave me an idea of its condition. All the drains were clogged up with gooey muck. There were four broken windowpanes in the living room. The back porch and top stairs were rotten. There were thousands of roaches, two to three inches long. Some of the Camerons' dishes were packed away with food left in them. The dresser drawers all had bobby pins, crumbs and bits of food, mice droppings, etc. in them. The kitchen stove had only one burner working, and when they had the electrician out to fix it he found that in the oven, the space between the bottom element and the floor of the oven was packed with crumbs, bits of burned waxed paper, rice, etc. Mrs. W-H said she thought the oven switch was black enamel, but on touching it, it turned out to be smothered in black grease.

But almost as bad as that is the S-Ds' hospitality. They invited the Wilson-Hodgkinsons to stay with them after the Beckleses came back and before the Camerons left. The Wilson-Hodgkinsons accepted reluctantly, but with a ten-year-old girl and a huge German shepherd pup, they had little choice. They furnished their own drinks, bread, butter, and other groceries including meat for two dinner parties that the S-Ds gave, and when they were ready to move out Mrs. Wilson-Hodgkinson thought they should offer to pay a little something toward the electricity used. She asked Mrs. S-D about it, and *that* dear lady said she thought $80 was about right. Imagine! Our light bill for a whole month is never more than $35.

Howard has repaired and painted two of our three trunks and will do the third one today. We are hoping to be able to send them to Houston since the Irwins have some friends there who might be willing to open them and stand by for the customs men. Dr. Turner said we could use his garage to store the stuff until H. gets to Texas, but it occurred to Howard that probably the boxes, etc. couldn't leave the port until the customs men have seen them. He is checking on this point.

Now let's see. I have just brought Dorothy's washing upstairs and it needs folding. I just emptied the third trunk so H. can take it downstairs. D. is asleep and E. is now out of bed and playing in her room. We use my kitchen timer—she stays in bed until the timer "bings," in an hour, and then she plays in her room until we tell her it is time to get up. She is awfully good about it.

Dorothy is just fine—couldn't ask for a better baby. She eats Pablum, all flavors; bananas, papaw, a few vegetables. Four meals a day now, no 10 p.m. bottle. At least I hope not—we may have to go back to it. Saturday morning she woke up at 5:30, Sunday at 4, today at 6:30. Must hang up the clothes.

Much love,

Marian

Did I mention dyeing a sweater? I bought some dye but it says to boil and I have qualms about boiling wool. Since E. has a new sweater now I think I'll let a professional dye the old one!

After dinner—H. went to the Pan Am office today and learned that there is a tourist flight leaving Trinidad on Wednesdays at 7 a.m. that stops only at San Juan. So—now we plan to leave here on March 27, Tuesday, at 10 a.m., stay overnight at Piarco, and leave early Wednesday. *Much* easier than the other, and we save about $75 U.S. We will keep our Wednesday date at Kessler Institute since the Easter weekend would foul up an earlier appointment. H. made our New York-to-Tacoma reservations for April 6 arriving at 5:30 a.m., like we did before. Jolly! Although we'll be anxious to get to Tacoma, I'd love to have time to see a little of the New York area and this may be our only chance for quite some time. The Neumanns have plenty of room and I don't think it will put them out to have us around for a few extra days.

Must feed Dorothy and get on with my sewing.

Much love,

Marian

About the Easter basket—We'll be at the Neumanns' on Easter Sunday. But I suppose you'll have already mailed the eggs by the time you get this. If not, perhaps H.'s mother could tote them to New York for me. Doesn't make too much difference—just so Elizabeth has her Easter basket!

M.

Dear Anna & Tom,

Well, soon three-quarters of this family will be with you. Are you all set to be Mr. Pup, or Santa's helper, or Mr. McGregor? Good!

I just want to thank you for the Brahms and Elgar. The latter makes particularly interesting listening, as we have another disk of the "Serenade for Strings" with New Symphony strings, Anthony Collins conducting, and you know how fond I am of comparing interpretations.

Thanks for stamps.

H.

Wednesday, February 1, 1956

Dear All—

No news to speak of, but since H. wants to send another draft to Tacoma, I thought I should at least try to fill up a page! By the way, Howard has ordered an electroplating outfit and asked to have it sent to you all in Tacoma. So don't be afraid to accept it if it comes.

Elizabeth will be very happy to receive the Valentine's Day blouse. We are working overtime trying to convince her that Christmas is really over. So now we spend much time discussing Valentine's Day, all our birthdays, Easter, etc.—and jokingly tell her that Christmas is all over so it *can't* be Christmas Eve. I never would have thought that I'd be one to discourage the Christmas spirit, but in January it begins to pall a bit.

She has had such fun lately playing with Rooney, the huge German shepherd pup of the Wilson-Hodgkinsons. Rooney is about ten months old and full of pep, and likes to play with Spot as long as Spot's strength and temper hold out. Elizabeth gets a kick out of seeing them play together, and when Rooney gets a little frisky with her she tells him he must be polite, and "Oh, Rooney, you are a silly pooch" and other phrases she has picked up from us. He could knock over an adult if he half tried, but he is fairly gentle with Elizabeth, and only a couple of times has she been knocked over. She treats it as something of a joke (the first time she was a bit apprehensive, not surprisingly) and trots upstairs to say that "Rooney tried to eat my head." She hands him sticks, which he tries to eat, and that delights them both. Lately he has become awfully interested in sand pails and yesterday he crunched up a plastic measuring cup, eating about half of it. Today he came over and barked downstairs, and E. immediately left her upstairs interests and ran down to play with Rooney.

We were glad to get your letter, Daddy, and spent an hour or so mulling over your suggestion [to come later]. Alas, it is out of the question but completely. Aside from the complexities of selling and packing, one of our chief reasons for going home in March is so Elizabeth's hands can be done—if possible. Of course the Kessler people could only say that they can't say anything at all until they see her, but we would certainly like to have anything necessary done this summer. And when you made your suggestions, were you aware that H.'s school term isn't over till August 1? Arriving in Tacoma the middle of August, packing up that stuff, and getting to Texas by the first of September would be virtually impossible since we would like to see families, friends, etc. in Tacoma and arrive fairly rested in Austin. With Howard, he *must* be in good shape to start. You weren't suggesting that we shouldn't come so early because you don't want us around all that time, were you? If the kiddies get you down, dears, we'll camp in the garage. Okay, Mother, relax. We already have our tickets and will be in Tacoma early in April anyway.

The green jumper is finished and a much better job than the plaid. I should always try out a pattern in unbleached muslin, I guess, before tackling the real thing.

As I said, there's no news. Dorothy is darling—she is so happy that after she is fed there is some danger of being sprayed with a fine mist of peas, papaw, cereal, or what have you because she starts to blow contented bubbles before her mouth is completely empty. Enid didn't come today—wasn't feeling well. Hope she appears tomorrow since Sita Keates is coming to spend the afternoon.

Howard will add a note on business matters.

Love to all,

Marian

Howdy Tom,

Sorry to bother you again with matters financial, but taxes, like death, must be reckoned with, so they say!

I believe I wrote about all this before, but what with the very busy time we've had around here the last few months, it may have been overlooked. Anyway, I have not been paid by the local treasury since 15 Sept. '55. From that date forward, all funds have been (and will continue to be) from the London Fulbright office. This, of course, changes the tax picture.

According to local Tax Authorities, my liability to local taxation ceased with my last paycheck from B.G. Treasury. According to London, "it is not usual" for persons receiving Fulbright moneys from London to be taxed by any government. The next step, I think, is to see how Uncle Sam looks on all this. Could you find out? Am I still to be exempt because I've been so many days (can't recall exact now) away from Continental U.S.? Could it be that we may be tax-free? Fingers are crossed!

Should you be interested, I'm enclosing also my last year's income tax assessment sheet. This year's income is approximately the same (in B.W.I. dollars, of course).

Sincerely,

Howard

Monday, February 13, 1956

Dear All—

Very poor of me not to write at all last week, but I really didn't have anything to report. At the moment, Dorothy is asleep and Elizabeth is having a tea party with her "family," so I shall use what time I have. Speaking of E.'s family, we sent off another box today containing the green toilet seat, a scrapbook, a few dresses, and Mary. The toilet seat is to use upstairs, Mother, when I decide to start training Dorothy. It is in rather grim condition, so you can hide it away when you have company if you want to.

Dorothy had her vaccination a week ago Saturday, along with the first of three triple immunization shots. The worst of the vaccination is over now, and we noticed very few ill effects from it—the chief reaction seemed to be in extra sleeping. Dr. Spock says not to cover a vaccination, and I remember Dr. Hellyer's nurse saying to take off the Band-aid as soon as we got home. But Dr. Georges covered D.'s, said to leave it covered for two or three days. I took the Band-aid off the second day, but on Saturday when I took her back to get the certificate he had the nurse cover it again, rather tightly. After a day I thought it looked too tightly covered, so now I have it loosely covered with a Band-aid—about the best compromise I can figure out. As H. says, if you disregard the doctor's advice you have no recourse if something does go wrong. I think the vaccination will calm down soon, however. He did it on her back, at about the waistline.

Elizabeth has been vaccinating her dollies steadily since Dorothy's was done. She is so busy! She talks to herself much of the day, as I suppose is natural for a child who plays alone, and I do love to hear her. She can count objects up to eleven now, quite well except she says "five, seven, six" instead of the correct way.

I have finished my sewing for Elizabeth and have done what little needs to be done to my own clothes. I took the hem up on my brown wool dress and replaced a button on my green jersey. I am now getting somewhat involved in doll clothes—pure fun for me or I wouldn't bother. I have quite a stock of "surprises" for E., which she may not need for entertainment, but I think it is best to be prepared. If Dorothy is fussy (I know now that she won't like being held all that time, unless she changes her mind on that score between now and then!) I can entertain her, and keep E. happy with new things to do. I remember [from a previous flight] a cute little four-year-old girl who was equipped only with a doll and who was horribly bored and so grateful to borrow some of E.'s books.

Elizabeth is standing right by me whispering that I should drink my tea before it gets hot. I think it is time to quit this for now and grind some meat for dinner. Elizabeth was delighted with the Valentine cards that came this afternoon, and I know she is excited over the package she will open tomorrow.

Tuesday p.m.: It is right after lunch, more or less. Dorothy woke up at 3:30 this morning, very wet and very messy so I had to turn on the light to change her—then, naturally, she had to eat, and threw this day's routine all to heck. I promised Elizabeth that we would make some special cupcakes for Valentine's Day, so we had to decorate them before she went to bed for her rest. Now all is quiet—dishes washed, cupcakes decorated, Elizabeth happily in bed. Dorothy decided not to eat at noon—so perhaps she'll have a nap for a while. Everything is under control but the ironing, which I shall tackle in about ten minutes.

Sita Keates is coming over tomorrow to spend the afternoon with me. She is to go to the hospital on Thursday, and on Saturday the doctor will give her something to start the baby on its way. It isn't due for another week but she is very tiny and the baby is big enough, the doctor says. Enid is all lined up to do their baby's washing, and will work for them when they move into this house, as it seems they will. They will buy much of our furniture, which will simplify Howard's work.

Did I ever thank you for the candy? I saw the little red box just now as I put the cupcakes away, and I can't remember. It surely was good. We controlled Elizabeth's intake sensibly, Howard controlled his own very sensibly, and I ate most of it. It was just lovely to have it.

Glancing at the bookshelf above this desk I see that Enid was busy dusting today, and succeeded in disorganizing all of Howard's carefully arranged books. Everything is upside down. I just hope it is all there someplace!

Dorothy is crying and I suppose I'd better be on to my ironing. By the way, Mother, what will we do about Dorothy's washing? I can always do it by hand but I'd rather not if you can work out something. Or did you ever buy a washing machine?

Much, much love,

Marian

Has the second draft from H. arrived?

February 18, 1956

Dear Bee—

We are simply delighted with your wonderful news—so very, very happy for you and for Chris, too. I can't imagine a nicer brother-in-law!

Your special [delivery] arrived just as we were finishing dinner—a shiny red truck with "Royal Mail" on it and the Royal Cipher, very posh looking. We didn't know it was possible to send specials! Anyhow, as soon as H. got Elizabeth in bed he went down to send you a cable and pick up a plane schedule. School is out July 25 but H. is so fed up he hopes to leave earlier, since he would only have three classes of little boys to give final tests to (the older boys get special ones from London). He is sure he can be in Los

Angeles [for Bee's wedding] by the 24th of July (2 a.m.!), and hopes to be able to make it by the 17th. We shall work on it—you go ahead and make your plans. Heavens, if we were any closer I'd pick up the phone, call you, and run up a huge bill!

This has been a long, hard week. Howard has had tensions at school—S-D has been unreasonable about all sorts of things concerning the staff. Elizabeth had a temperature and was ill Wednesday evening but fine on Thursday. H. spent Thursday fighting off a bug of some sort, and now I'm trying to get rid of a cold. Dorothy is fine, thank goodness.

H. just returned with schedule—he could leave here on July 14 and reach Los Angeles on the 17th. He stopped in to see Lester and they may just leave early whether or not S-D likes it!

I wish I were closer so I could keep up on all the details. Do write!

Much, much love,

Marian

Monday, February 20, 1956

Dear All—

Well, aren't we all excited and happy for Bee and Chris! I'm so glad we'll be able to be there [at their wedding]—as I wrote Bee, parents, Howard will do his best to make it. He is so fed up with S-D that he doesn't give two hoots whether the principal approves his leaving early—he intends to leave here about the middle of July.

My cold is about gone, thank goodness. I went downtown this afternoon to do some shopping while Howard did the washing for me—it is so nice to have an afternoon away now and then!

Regarding our leaving next month and Howard getting bored in the hotel, I guess I have neglected to tell you all that dear H. is somewhat anxious to get rid of us so that he can start spending his weekends at the airbase. He intends to write a paper on the flora of the area, compiling all the work he has done in that region since we've been here, hoping to get it published after we're settled in Texas. Also, he, Ramphal, and Ramsammy are going to go to Lethem during the Easter holidays, to collect there.

And, speaking of settling in Texas, we received the news last week that we won't get University housing. The woman in the housing office wrote that they haven't been able to place non-veterans for several years, let alone out-of-state non-veterans. Dr. Turner must have been confused when he told H. that there wouldn't be any difficulty in getting university housing for us. The woman suggested that H. write to the Austin Housing Authority requesting an apartment in a city housing project. Doesn't that sound grim! We are now waiting to hear just what they have to offer.

Mother, can you find a smallish fork and spoon for E.? (Didn't Bee and I have a set?) I won't bring hers. And do you still have that Tippy Cup you bought for E.? You were going to return it to the store, but maybe you never did. I'll bring D.'s if you don't have one.

We went real wild yesterday and bought a marble-top washstand. People still use them here for washstands, and we had to buy a pitcher, slop jar, etc. along with it but shall offer them to Winifred. I am completely smitten with the top, which is in good shape and has a sort of splash board across the back consisting of four dark red tiles with a green design, set in a graceful frame. The cupboard itself is just the right size to hold LPs—it is on legs that I'm not wild about.

If H. were home I'd be snarling at him. He took the blue ribbon off the typewriter and attached the black, which doesn't fit. He called it an "outrigger" ribbon and it doesn't reverse and rewind automatically. I'm tired of it.

Anyway, H. will build a frame and box to ship the marble top home in and we figure it will be a bargain even with shipping costs.

All for now. Your birthday present is on its way, Mother.

Love,

Marian

About E.'s hands. We hope (and doubt) that there is someplace in Texas where it could be done. Going back and forth from Austin to New Jersey or Seattle would add up—that assumes training and changes would necessitate return trips. We will have it done at Kessler if it can be done on this trip—can't afford the B.G.–Tacoma–New Jersey–Austin business, I'm afraid. Damn it, won't we all be glad to know what, when, where and how much!!

Mother—

Will you please try to buy a carrying "sling" or something for me to use on the trip home for Dorothy? There is a picture of one in the Better Homes and Gardens *book and it looks sensible—keeps mother's arms free. Since I'll be carrying a diaper bag and the brown canvas bag plus Dorothy—and I'd like to be able to grab E. if necessary—I'd like to have one of these slings. Look and see—maybe we could make one?*

M.

Wednesday, February 28, 1956

Dear All—

No real news, except that your letters about Bee's wedding and our coming home get me so excited I almost pop! With this month all but gone, I am practically counting the days until we leave. Needless to say, Elizabeth is all prepared and would be ready to go tomorrow if we said the word.

So glad to know you're going to get a washing machine, Mother. An automatic will be a real treat after our little hand-wringer job. Not that I should disparage it, since we trust it will serve us faithfully for a few more years.

In case anyone at all is interested, the percale sheets you bought for me, Mother, are not holding up as well as I had hoped. At the corners the selvage is tearing away from the sheet, and I have several small rips in the middles of sheets. Shouldn't sheets wear better than that?

Howard asked Mr. Beckles to inquire of the principal concerning his early departure, and the word is that the principal would be "only too happy" to let Howard go on July 12. This, we think, will mean he reaches Los Angeles on the 17th but he has yet to check with the Pan Am office. We'll be glad to know just what date to shoot for, since he doesn't want extra time in Los Angeles and yet he may have to arrange a stop in Austin. Oh well, one bridge at a time and all that, I guess. Anyhow, getting back to Queen's, some of the men feel that the principal will be happy to see H. go since Howard does not always back the principal's plans as S-D feels his European staff members should.

Howard got permission for me to bring out $1,000—we had anticipated some trouble, and Howard was all ready with a sob story about my having to pay board and room for self and kiddies, etc., but the man at the Treasury Department didn't bat an eye. He would, however, like me to look up two books for him and send them after I'm settled in Tacoma—naturally, I'm happy to oblige since Howard will have to bring out the rest of our funds and we don't want any snags there.

We have all our vaccination certificates, Dorothy's birth certificate, and so on, and all that remains is to get traveler's checks. I am still wondering how far our 88-pound limit will go. We shall pack everything a week in advance so H. can have it weighed, just to be sure. A nuisance, but worth it.

Dorothy had her second diphtheria, whooping cough, and tetanus shot on Saturday and this one didn't bother her at all. She is simply in love with

Elizabeth and smiles every time she sees her. Elizabeth responds nicely, of course, and is only too happy to entertain Dorothy (for a few minutes) or to bring her a rattle. She still loves to cover Dorothy, and given a chance she'll tuck a blanket around D.'s feet in no time flat. Dorothy is still a model baby—I get up about 6:30 to feed her, and she scarcely howls at all now unless I make her wait too long. Just lies and splutters happily to herself. She eats at 10 and at 2, and right after she's fed at 6 or so in the evening she goes to sleep. Elizabeth still goes to bed happily between 6:30 and 7, depending on what time we're through eating, and it is a blessing to get them both tucked into bed early. There is nothing like a peaceful evening!

I am just about through with my doll clothes binge. Elizabeth hasn't seen them yet, but I hope she'll be pleased. Did I tell you about the cute hat I crocheted for Peggy? Elizabeth simply loves it, but especially enjoys putting it on her teddy bear and her bunny. In fact it's silly to say I hope she'll be pleased, since she will no doubt be fascinated and insist on my dressing everyone up over and over and over again!

All for now—

Much love,

Marian

Monday, March 5, 1956

Dear All—

Our house has that torn-apart look, and are we ever sick and tired of packing. Even Elizabeth has caught the spirit and her pet new phrase is "Won't we be glad to get settled in Austin!" We still haven't had an answer from the housing people and we're hoping we *will* get settled in Austin.

Elizabeth eats all her meals at her little table, at the same time as we do, except when it is inconvenient and then she eats alone. I expect we will want to feed her her supper earlier than you all are used to eating— we get both Elizabeth and Dorothy fed and in bed between 6:30 and 7. I imagine the folding card table takes up more room than one of your tray tables, and the latter would do fine, I'm sure. You have a rug in the dining room now, don't you? For a child who eats quite neatly (as I really think E. does), she manages to spill an awful lot on the floor. If you do borrow a Baby-Tenda (that name makes me gag always), where would you put it? I foresee much flung Pablum as soon as Dorothy starts eating in a high chair or such, since she already tries her best to smear goo all over me. I had thought we might be able to use the youth chair for Dorothy, using a belt or scarf to tie her safely in. Haven't I heard of people putting a big square of oilcloth or plastic on top of their good rugs and under their children's high chairs?

My Lord, won't you be happy to get rid of all our stuff and Bee's, too. I shall be delighted to help pack books or anything else—I only wish I could be closer right now! I get so frustrated thinking about all that must be going on, and letters seem so vague.

Dorothy has a tooth! I was pulling octopus fuzz out of her mouth this afternoon and discovered it, and had I been more alert I might have been searching for it several days ago since she has been very noisy and fretful between her 10 and 2 o'clock meals lately. Elizabeth is now concerned about Dorothy's chewing up the nipples on the bottles, since I have told E. *she* mustn't chew on her doll bottles.

Elizabeth threw me into a mild panic as I washed dishes this morning by asking, "How do people breed?" Stalling madly, I asked, "What did you say, dear?" and finally deduced that she meant "breathe," especially how do people breathe when they have colds.

Howard has packed up most of our brown-and-white china and nearly all of our books. He has little spare time at present, since the annual Sports Day is to be on Friday and each afternoon there are heats to be run off, etc. which demand his presence. As soon as we leave he has tests to give and correct, a tiresome chore. The Keateses are buying nearly all of our furniture, but so far we have had no buyers at all for the remaining stuff. Howard will advertise it after we leave.

I am trying to use up food, and it seems as if the only things I have too much of are rice and syrup. Both cheap, but it hurts to throw it out. And Elizabeth just adores rice. And syrup, for that matter. As far as food for the kiddies is concerned, Mother, Elizabeth eats most things with relish and I don't think she'll be any problem. Dorothy consumes Carnation milk at an astounding rate—we buy case after case—also egg yolk, strained fruits and vegetables, and Pablum. All for now.

Much love,

M.

Mother, will you please let me know what our Central Bank balance is, including this draft? Hope you had a pleasant birthday. E. & I discussed the matter and were sure you had ice cream and cake. ("How many candles, Mommy?")

Tuesday, March 6, 1956

Dear Bee—

Glad to get another letter and *so* glad you said what you and Chris would like [as a wedding gift]. Only sensible to state preferences, don't you think.

Enid is not here. How I loathe having to depend on someone else. House is dirty. What the hell. We leave on March 27.

Next Monday is a school holiday. I plan to go downtown to get my traveler's checks and will scout around for something special for you. Don't know if there's any local silver but will see. How about a stuffed alligator, about three inches high, standing on its hind legs with a light globe in mouth? That would be different!

Diapers are rinsing and I should hang them up now. This is really just a note—I'm so very happy that you and Chris are happy. Howard and I are simply silly-happy—whether it is in spite of or because of being in B.G. I'm not sure! Heaven knows we'll be glad to be settled someplace for more than nine or ten months.

The weekend of the 20th will suit H. fine if only he doesn't have to stop in Austin to see about finding a house. Then he'd have to skip Los Angeles, I'm afraid. Money, money, you know. Hope that date works out all right for you two.

Darn—I must hang up the clothes. The sun is so hot and bright and fine for them but not for me—150 degrees is too much. All for now.

Much love,
Marian

Wednesday, March 14, 1956

Dear All—

Dorothy is asleep, Elizabeth is resting, and here I am with a small pot of tea. It is one of those rainy days when it just *should* be cool but isn't really.

Elizabeth is now all over a stomach upset which began about a week ago—diarrhea, throwing up, etc. Dr. Georges said to give her only fruit juices for two days, and prescribed some medicine, and she is fine again. I do hope we can all keep from getting colds or other bugs now.

Friday morning we discovered three little kittens under some old dead branches out in the backyard near the trench. Elizabeth was nearly beside herself

A New Age Society party, March 1956. The Irwins are in the back row, centre right.

with excitement, and was all set to name them, but I said firmly that Daddy would take them downtown as soon as he came home, which he did. The RSPCA finds homes for all the animals it can, but cats are too plentiful here and they said they'd put them to sleep. I told E. that the people would find nice homes for the kitties, and she accepted their departure without question. After all, as I told her, one cat, one dog, and two tortoises are enough for a single family!

Saturday evening Howard and I went over to the school for a New Age Society dinner party, which was held in the Q.C. dining room. Howard gave a talk on Reproduction to the Society during the past year, and so we were asked to this dinner. It was fun but we left early since we were concerned about Elizabeth.

Mother, I'm glad you mentioned the price of secondhand washing machines in your letter last week. We've been here too long, I think, and will have to adjust our thinking to U.S. prices when we get home. Laurence Keates is eager to buy our Hoover for $90, which is half what we paid for it, and with that converted into U.S. money we should be able to get something. Our portable machine has its advantages, and its smallness is one if we end up in small quarters, but we can find another to fit, no doubt.

We didn't make much fuss over my birthday, since E. was on her juice diet and couldn't have eaten any of the cake that she and H. were going to make. It seemed unnecessarily cruel to make it and then not let her have any, so we all had Jell-O. She was so excited when she and Howard brought my presents that as I picked up each one she said what was inside! She gave me some very pretty silver earrings ("just like Grandmother's"), and Dorothy gave me a silver napkin ring, and Howard a tray decorated with those lovely blue butterfly wings. I wish I could put it in a suitcase and let you all see it, but I'm afraid it is too heavy.

Mother, you suggested we try to get university housing. That is just what we were recently told we couldn't get, if you follow me. However, Dr. Turner wrote and said that he personally thinks the City housing project is superior to the university's, except for the fact that it isn't all U. personnel living there. He said he would make arrangements for us to get one if we desired, and we do. Hope that gets all settled. We also heard from the customs people at Houston, and H. has to go in person in order for our stuff to be let in duty free. That means a couple of days spent in going to Houston and transacting that business and getting back—he may want to leave Tacoma during the last week of August.

All the reports of snow in Tacoma and floods in New York make me a trifle nervous. Each time I tell Elizabeth that she will be wearing warm dresses and sweaters and coats, she says, "But what if I'm too warm?" She can't even imagine being really cold.

Howard packed all our brown-and-white dishes and then went to see about insurance—alas, they said they had to know exactly what breakables are in each container, so he unpacked the barrels, listed the contents, and packed them again. You'd think we'd learn. At least I've kept a list of the trunks' contents as I pack. We had a letter from Margaret yesterday saying they would start to unpack their things in a few days, and we are feverishly waiting to hear how their dishes arrived.

I have told E. that next week we will invite Bini and Indrani over for a little party. She has such fond memories of her birthday party last year and can recite all the details of it. We will make some fancy cookies, have ice cream and juice, and Elizabeth can wear her blue nylon party dress—and all added up, that undeniably equals a party!

All for now, I think.

Much love,

Marian

Marian and the children left British Guiana on March 27, 1956, some months before the end of term at Queen's. For those final months, Howard took a room in Georgetown at the Londonburg Hotel, "a run-down, unimpressive place on Main Street, badly in need of paint, obviously listing to the south," as he described it a few years ago. He chose it because it "had a reputation for good food and low rates. The proprietor, Murdock, was a Scotsman whose principal preoccupation was rebuilding a big sailboat (actually a yacht) that he hoped to refloat in the Demerara and on it take his family back to the Old Country. Unlike the stiff formality of the Park [Hotel] and even the Tower in those days, the Londonburg was informality itself. The boat was a-building in the backyard, with the help of sundry old and young hands, and produced an almost continual din of conversations punctuated with whoops of victory over some impediment or other. All of this was visible from the open-sided dining room. Beer and rum flowed, especially on Saturday nights. Against this festive atmosphere outside, there were people of varying interests as registrants in the hotel. One was a cranky old duffer who had difficulty walking down the three flights of stairs to eat, and every now and then would bellow for help. On other occasions there would be banging on the pipes with wails for 'Water! Water!' Rates were not posted, so each of us negotiated our rate according to length of stay, how many meals would be taken each day, and what the bookkeeper thought she could get out of us (she was the proprietor's wife). There was also a night watchman who paraded through the halls, mumbling some unintelligible tale of his past, but every once in a while would shout bloody murder and beat his head on the walls, doors, floor, which I took to be epileptic fits. All of this was sort of peripheral to me . . . it provided earthy comic relief from the quasi-formalities of school life at Q.C."

Saturday, 21 April 1956: Londonburg Hotel, 62 Main Street, Georgetown

Hello dearest,

Back again to Murdock's menageries after a busy week at Lethem and vicinity. I was greeted by no less than twenty pieces of mail, your three letters being most welcome for a tired traveler.

We had a very good trip—in fact one of the best. Such a difference having along people who are as interested in this sort of work as I am. Ramsammy makes very good company—he wears well. In all, we collected about 350 plant specimens and Ramphal got a goodly number of insects, despite a nagging cold. Thanks to Mr. Cosson, the District Commissioner, we were able to mix some "pleasures" with business and went visiting a few of the ranches near Lethem. He drove us out into the north savannah to the ranches of the Harts, the McTurks, and the Gorinskys. All are colorful frontiersmen who have done well in cattle rearing, and in sidelines as well. [Caesar] Gorinsky, for example, works with Louis Chung in the tropical fish line and has brought down a couple of young mining engineers (the Haack brothers[85]) from Wisconsin to do some diamond prospecting. All these men (the ranch owners, that is) and others are married to the numerous Melville sisters, daughters of the original pioneer who married a "buck." All look Indianish but are tall. Taken as a whole, the Rupununi seems peopled by the descendants of a relatively few original settlers, and they don't seem keen on encouraging young pioneers to come into the area. They have a good thing and are not going to share the wealth willingly.

That fifteen head of cattle is all one square mile of territory can support was surprising to me, so lush was most of the savannah—even at this time, the end of their long dry season. But the problem seems to center around quality of grasses rather than quantity, and because of the drought-flood-drought-flood extremes of water presence, introduction of better grasses is not nearly as easy as it sounds.

The roads were surprisingly good, permitting jeeps to travel between 40 and 50 m.p.h. Because of their very hard riding qualities, Willys jeeps have given way to the long-wheelbase Land Rovers, which certainly do ride well.

We stayed at the Government Rest House in Lethem itself. Like most of the town's scattered buildings, this one was built by a Brazilian contractor from Boa Vista and bears all the marks of such rural Brazilian house construction as I saw last summer: stuccoed walls, arches between rooms, appliquéd floral medallions in the nature of a huge Wedgwood design here and there on inside walls, much use of stripes, predominance of yellow, light blue, and light green in interior decorations Our food was cooked by a colored woman, for which we were glad. We were also glad we took our own stuff, for prices were very high in the two local shops (loaf of bread baked in Lethem: 36 cents). We had electric lights at night from 6 to 11, and within an hour after sunset the walls were black with insects—a field day for Ramphal!

On the local scene, the Keateses moved into No. 5 [on the college compound] without incident. After our thorough DDT-ing, the flea menace has largely abated, although they (the Keateses) had some difficulty getting the whitish powdery residue off the newly polished floor and finally, after scrubbing it with kerosene, had to repolish. Binky continues to hang around, and pointedly avoids Enid, so great is the attraction of that house and not hers.

Our table (during my absence) was sold for $15, but the crib and food safe still remain. It seems, according to Laurence, someone responded to the ad in the paper by looking the stuff over and giving verbal assurance he'd take all. Sensibly, Laurence took names and addresses of all callers (several came after this fellow). The man in question did not reappear, and when questioned by L. (who took the trouble to look him up), he said he had changed his mind. Thereupon, L. went to the others, whom, of course, he'd told the stuff was sold, in hopes of rekindling their interest. That's where the matter stands at present.

John sent me a short note along with some stamps and a draft for the first payment on the London-Lagos shipping bill. Another £25 is due. No news in his letter, save implied enjoyment of his work.

School reopens Wednesday, and then I'll begin counting the weeks in earnest—twelve in all! The principal has given heartening approval to my proposal concerning the establishment of a Q.C. Field Research Station at Atkinson Field, but details, especially as concerns security, must be worked out. I'll pay a visit to Major Nicole soon. Thank heavens Ramsammy will be here. I have unreserved confidence in him as a successor. I feel now I *should* step out. Boland is planning on getting out of teaching. Niles has retirementitis. Low, who comes as I leave, is untried.

Well, it's time I stop. I'm about to send E.'s birthday gift. I wanted to get it off yesterday, but another Elizabeth had her birthday then, together with attendant celebrations and, of course, a holiday. My, how I miss my family!

Right now I'm concentrating on regaining some lost pounds—you know, the usual after-effects of a grind in the field. My arms and face are as brown as a tabletop, and at present I'm enduring the messiness of moulting!

All my love,
Howard

Friday, 18 May 1956: Londonburg Hotel

Hello, darling,

I've been trying to get a letter off to you for the last three days, but my time is overfitted—and how it flies!

I gave my talk to the Science Society last night, but instead of the thirty or so who usually turn up, there were over a hundred, some coming from Bishops' and a considerable number from the evening classes. It was really too large a crowd for a room that is designed to hold thirty to thirty-five. The charts I made could be seen only by those in the first few rows and even the photos magnified and projected by the epidiascope were not clearly visible at the back. However, I think the talk went over pretty well, particularly as its subject matter was applicable to the syllabus of anyone doing biology or botany.

I ducked a request to take part in a debate concerning arts vs. science programs in schools, but agreed to serve as a judge.

Richard asked me some time ago to give a talk before the A.M.M. and I have decided to give an account of the Roraima trip in two weeks, using Rock's pictures and emphasizing the interesting aspects of natural history seen. That will make it an easy chore for me and it will be soon out of the way.

The stamp collection was airfreighted to you Tuesday and you may have already been informed of its arrival at the airport. If not, you might quote the number underlined on the enclosed airway bill when you inquire. The cost was double the estimate because of the classic mistaking of Washington State for D.C.

Enid is proving to be disappointing to Laurence and Sita. They suspect her of overcharging for greens and meat. For a while Sita had her working full days, but Enid would often sit down and read. When asked why, she simply said she was tired and had to rest. Without asking, she takes rice and bits of meat home to Binky (whom she has managed to keep). Finally Sita told her that she'd better look for work elsewhere. Enid then shed many tears and announced she is pregnant. No further news on that score.

Mr. and Mrs. [Clement] Yhap had Ramsammy and me around to their new house a few nights ago and we had a very pleasant time. While their means are limited, they do like classical music on LPs. They keep an immaculate house and have done much to fix up and finish off the shabby work done by the contractor. The roof still leaks badly and now the color in the downstairs floor comes off and is tracked throughout. Clem has put shelves in every closet and cabinet, and had to replace all clothes poles and towel racks. They had a bit of a messy time with the septic tank, which, because of a plugged outlet, overflowed several times. However, they're happy as clams over having a new house at 10 percent of salary—and who wouldn't be!

Received a letter from John (with the second draft for £25) in which he said they are excited about going on summer leave to England for three months. Seems as if they only just got to Nigeria. However, his description of the intense heat (90- to 97-degree days with humidity of 85 percent, and never below 72 degrees at night) makes B.G. sound very moderate indeed, and no doubt there is a real necessity for frequent relief. He is enamored with his work, feels much happier away from B.G., which he describes as "an unhappy dream, an experience of a past incarceration—except for the fact that I'm still being asked after by the Income Tax Collector and the Loan Office."

At times I get provoked with the shabby service in this fast-declining hotel, with the barefaced promiscuity, with having to plough through drunks in order to reach the dining room each evening, with the terribly biased criticisms of our country by half-tight Englishmen—but a look at the calendar gives reassurance that on the vehicle of work and plenty of it I'll soon be winging on home to you.

Bye now,

Howard

Tuesday, 22 May 1956: Londonburg Hotel

Darling,

Back to school again after the long weekend. Such wet weather. It has rained most of each day for over a week. Last night about 1 a.m. a high wind accompanied by downpour sprayed in through a one-inch crack— the window over my bed was open—and I awoke soaked. So I repaired to the adjacent room (empty; the one I used to be in) and spent the rest of the night there. At least there's one advantage to having the hotel more empty than full!

I, too, certainly miss doing things our way! Here we eat at 7 to 8 p.m., and that just about shoots the evening. Back to 5:30 for us at Texas! I really shouldn't, but I'm beginning to get the jitters about all this rushing around that's to come between July 1 and September 1. I do hope it will be possible for us to get away for a few days together.

Re your writing Margaret, you'd better wait until I get their London (summer vacation) address.

Needless to say, I am pleased as punch that you're coming along well with your driving lessons.

Don't worry too much about the Londonburg cuisine. It's only healthy for husbands to complain of food that's not of their wives' preparation! The trouble with it is that it's not yours. But there is enough of it.

Good night, dearest—
Howard

When Howard left British Guiana in July, he carried with him this handwritten letter for Marian:

Demerara: 11.7.56

Dear Madam:

Greetings: It is our hope that the reaches of this letter would not fail in finding yourself, Miss Elizabeth and Miss Dorothy very well, your presence is still greatly missed by us, the spirit of Charity, Kindness, Patience and Love for the unfortunate which you manifested here cannot be forgotten. It is our wish that God would ever bless you and your posterity in this life, also all your undertakings. We were sending a gift of some lovely eggs for you all but Mr. Irwin said that he is not coming home directly so they might spoil. Every day we were expecting to hear from you but we attribute it to your long absence from home, cause you to be very busy or you have lost the address.

All join in sending their regards for the home circle and still expecting one of these good days to see you in B.G.

Yrs Truly,
Winifred Grant

ENDNOTES

81 cassareep (6/7/1955): This native Guyanese molasses-like syrup is made from the boiled juice strained from grated cassava.

82 dry bread crumbs (some sort of dressing, I gather) (8/17/1955): This was most likely toasted cassava meal, or farofa, a culinary accompaniment ubiquitous throughout Brazil.

83 *Hamlet* (8/17/1955): In his review for *Thunder*, Martin Carter wrote that the production was "culturally significant but artistically weak. . . . Among us, as we know only too well, there is far too much gushing and uncritical acceptance of anything novel or well publicized. . . . May I add that the applause at the end of the play on the first night served also to awaken some of the members of the audience."

84 *Kyk-Over-Al* (12/31/1955): A joint effort by the British Guiana Writers' Association and the British Guiana Union of Cultural Clubs, the magazine had been launched in 1945. A. J. Seymour, a Guianese civil servant and poet who was affiliated with both organizations, was its founding editor, a role he continued for 16 years. The unlikelihood of the journal's longevity, but also the need for such a publication, is described in a note in the first issue by James W. Smith, who just the previous year had initiated the founding of the B.G. Writers' Association: "At present, the British Guianese writer suffers from a multiplicity of handicaps which may be summarised as follows: The total absence of Publishing Houses. Restricted Printing facilities. The high cost of Printing. The absence of sound and constructive literary critics. A limited reading public. There are five large printing houses in the city of Georgetown, and of these, three run daily newspapers. . . . When the author realises that he has to cater for a very small reading public within the colony and that any hope of a foreign market is negligible, the majority of his works remains unpublished." In a memoir, Seymour writes of the journal's role in "form[ing] a rallying point, consciously or unconsciously, for a growing home-centred outlook which builds national feeling by providing roots." With the goal of promoting all of the arts in the colony, *Kyk-Over-Al* published critical work as well as original prose and verse. Seymour describes the special Christmas edition as a "collaboration with Joy Allsopp."

85 the Haack brothers (4/21/1956): Donald Haack and his brother, Bob, arrived in B.G. in 1955 as diamond prospectors in the Rupununi district. To support the early stages of their mining, Don Haack worked as a bush pilot, and he eventually launched an air charter service called Guyana Wings. In 1970, as Burnham's government made moves to take over the privately owned company, Haack left the country. He later published three memoirs of his adventures among the Rupununi's cattle ranchers, prospectors, and Amerindians; his wife, Janet, also wrote about the years the couple and their children spent there.

Main Street, 1994

Chapter 7

1994: A RETURN, AND REFLECTIONS ON THE INTERIM

Marian never went back to Georgetown, but I did. On July 28, 1994, Howard and I flew to Guyana in a hot, fully booked DC-7, on the sole flight scheduled to make the five-and-a-half-hour trip from J.F.K. that day. The plane touched down at Timehri Airport—formerly Atkinson Field, later renamed Cheddi Jagan International Airport—after nightfall. As it happened, we had not been seated near windows and saw nothing of the place until we emerged from the plane to walk down the portable metal stairway. In the steamy darkness, we passed a pool of rainwater on the tarmac, where huge toads crouched in the beams of light cast from the low-slung building nearby. Inside, a young woman seated at a scuffed wooden podium methodically stamped our passports and motioned toward the rough wooden baggage rack, which was woefully inadequate for the dozens of hulking suitcases being unloaded from the plane. The building was crowded with exuberant travellers and those greeting them.

Our cab ride from the airport resembled the one described in Marian's first journal entry of 1952 and in every other visitor's account that I've read. The road, paved but still deeply rutted, which cars still shared with donkey-pulled carts and unencumbered livestock; the pedestrians casually stepping clear of oncoming traffic; the occasional waft of the stink of fermentation that Michael Swan identified in 1955 as "fresh molasses"; the startling evidence of poverty in the worn, gray housing along the route, particularly in Albouystown, clearly within city limits: despite the intervening decades and the transition from colony to full-fledged nation, none of this had appreciably changed.

After breakfast on our first morning, Howard and I walked around the city, and within an hour or so I was dripping with perspiration, parched, and spent. The equatorial heat and glare bore down. I found it hard to think, or even to be engaged with my own impressions. We returned to Hotel Tower and sat in a courtyard by the pool, where Howard had a beer and I quickly drank a litre of bottled water. Somewhat refreshed, we took a cab to the Botanical Gardens and zoo. Strolling through the grounds, I saw a crumpled banknote scudding along the asphalt path, a Guyanese dollar bill. Reflexively, I picked it up and handed it to a child walking our way. The girl, perhaps six or seven years old, took it from me, but she gave me a sceptical look that told me she was the wiser one in this transaction. Inflation had made a mockery of Guyana's currency. I'd offered her something worth a fraction of a penny. The exchange rate was $1 U.S. = $138 G. By Guyanese standards, Howard and I were affluent simply by having the choice of being there.

We sat on folding chairs in the currency exchange bureau across the street from our hotel for some time that afternoon before anyone was free to take our traveller's cheques. In the centre of the room were desks from different eras—oak, steel, laminate—piled with teetering mounds of manual and electric typewriters and a few computers, none of which was apparently fit for use. A woman came over to attend to us. She sat down next to each of us in turn with a clipboard and a stack of forms typed two to a page. Using a wooden ruler, she scored a page and ripped it in two, then stapled the parts together and between them inserted a sheet of carbon paper. She asked for our passports and wrote out by hand our names, addresses, and so on. We followed her as she carried the stapled forms and our cheques to a polished wooden booth at the front of the cambio, a cage with bars across the tiny window, inside of which a clerk manned the machine that counted out currency. The largest denomination was $500 (approximately $4 U.S.); in exchange for a traveller's cheque of $100 U.S., I came away with well over thirty bills.

The next day, after renting a car, we drove up Thomas Road to Queen's College. Though open, the building was nearly empty; a handful of people were setting up for the first of the sesquicentennial events. We climbed to the third floor and gazed out at the Atlantic: low tide; dark brown mud. The poor condition of the school unsettled us. Downstairs, the door to the biology laboratory was chained and padlocked, but through a gap Howard could see the bookshelves built by Ivan Skeete.

Across the yard stood the line of smaller buildings on pillars, one of which was the last house where my family had lived all those years earlier. My father and I had already seen the building on New Market

Street where I was born—then St. Michael's Nursing Home, now Creation Cuts, a hair salon—and the two other residences in the city. The well-maintained house in Subryanville seemed not to have aged at all, but the first one, on Parade Street, where he and Marian had rented the second-floor flat, was in sad shape, the paint having almost entirely worn off the weather-beaten wood. The house number, 124, was crookedly scrawled in black paint on one side of the building. The trunk of the traveller's palm was still standing, but the tree was dead. A small girl peered out from the tower window as we snapped a few photos of the house and yard, where a jaguar pelt was strung up on a line to dry in the sun.

The house on the Queen's compound was now being used as an adult education classroom. As we approached it we heard voices, then the scraping of chairs and the din of many feet on the plank floor, and a dozen young women emerged and streamed down the steps, their class just over. We went up. I was overwhelmed by the experience of walking into that house, my first home. I felt—silly as it sounds, since I was just five months old when we moved back to the States—as if I could almost remember being there, as if the play of light and shadows through the jalousies had rekindled some infant memory. I couldn't take in the spatial relationship of the house to the school or the layout of the rooms, and I was so transfixed by my perceptions of sun and shade that I didn't think to ask Howard to clarify any of it for me. Looking around, I saw daylight through chinks in the boards that formed the walls.

Howard and I were quiet as we left Queen's. We drove to the sea wall and looked out at the mud. A single ship was anchored far off in the deep water. The sun blazed. Only a few other people were about. We sat on a bench, one in a string facing the shore, made of sturdy moulded plastic in colours long ago muted by the unrelenting glare, each back panel decorated with what I remember as a relief of the crown.

On the opening day of the sesquicentennial events the Queen's auditorium looked full, with perhaps a thousand people sitting in row after row of white plastic chairs. The appearance of the crowd mirrored Guyana's population, with a seemingly infinite number of shades of dark skin. Howard and I may have been the only blond whites. Students had used palm leaves and marigold flower heads to decorate the walls flanking the stage with plaques that spelled out "QC." Crepe paper streamers in the school colours—gold and black—festooned the proscenium. Lynette Dolphin, long retired from Queen's but still very much on the scene, recognized Howard and sat next to me. Dark and trim, in a turquoise dress, she was gracious and seemed ageless. Clearly pleased to be with us, she seemed intriguingly unsurprised that we were there. I reminded Miss Dolphin that when I was born she'd given me a tiny gold pendant of the arms of the colony, which I still had. She laughed; that Guyanese custom for ensuring a person's return had apparently worked. And she reminisced about her young charges during her career as Prep Form mistress, the scamps playing timeless pranks, occasionally stumbling, or perhaps jumping, into the water-filled trench near the school, then wheedling permission to go home and change clothes.

After the lengthy program—during which, in the heat, I nearly fell asleep—Howard and I glanced at the souvenir T-shirts, mugs, pens, and booklets for sale. One table was devoted to a newly published work by Laurence Clarke, *Queen's College of Guyana: Records of a Tradition of Excellence (1844–1994)*. At a historical exhibition I saw two staff photos taken during Howard's tenure. He looked young, tall, lanky, pale as ivory.

Upon our return from a chartered flight to see the cascades at Orinduik and the startling, remote beauty of Kaieteur Falls, after we had viewed so clearly from the air the still-productive grid of plantations that had justified the colony's existence, Georgetown felt confining. It was unsafe, we were told more than once, to walk around the city after dark, which at the equator falls heavily at six o'clock, so we usually had our dinner in the hotel dining room. Often, during the day, we drove. We went out to the airport to locate the house at Atkinson Field; we crossed the pontoon bridge that spans the Demerara. Along the smooth, recently completed road to Linden, we pulled over so that Howard could get a close look at some roadside specimens growing in the white sand; "these old friends," he called them. One day we headed east, looking for Guyana University but continuing well past the point when we knew we'd missed it, all the way to Mahaica. We passed through a coastal area of coconut palms, tall old trees and some short, newly planted groves. A hawk swooped low in front of us to tug off a hunk of meat from road kill, a small alligator. Pale yellow canna bloomed at the flooded foot of the palms.

We came to a village. In a fleeting moment as we drove through it, I watched a dark-skinned woman in an indigo-coloured dress as she sat at an open window eating a slice of yellow papaw, a study in repose heightened by a sudden silence: we'd outstripped the reach of electrical power. I remembered the conversation I'd had with the East Indian cabdriver with whom I waited while Howard got his driver's license. He told me he lived with his family in "the country," where they used an open-pit latrine and fetched water. He said that once people moved away they didn't like to return to rough country life. But he explained: "You are a perfect stranger, but if you had difficulties and your car broke down, we would give you a meal to eat, we would give you a place to sleep." That kind of habitual, uncalculating generosity was, he said, why he preferred the countryside to Georgetown.

One evening had been set aside for Queen's College alumni and faculty to attend a cocktail reception hosted by President Cheddi Jagan, himself an "old boy." At 5:30 Howard and I left our hotel for Government House, walking the three blocks down Main Street's central promenade, the pathway built over a Dutch canal that, bordered by masses of vivid canna and low-pitched flamboyant trees, conjured the old descriptions of Georgetown as the "garden city of the tropics." Shaking off the panhandler who'd latched on to Howard with an intricate tale of woe almost the moment we set out, we passed through the ornate wrought-iron gates to the building and joined a reception line off the veranda to shake hands with Janet and Cheddi Jagan. Both in their mid-seventies, they seemed fatigued and strikingly unpretentious, polite but in no way standing on ceremony. Cheddi wore a shirt-jac, no necktie. My father introduced us, explaining that Georgetown was my birthplace; the Jagans didn't warm to the detail. The reception was held outdoors on the grounds adjacent to the building where governors had lived during colonial days and which was now the Jagans' residence. The lawn was crowded. More people had come to this than to the other Queen's events; this one was free. After the sun set promptly at six, spotlights mounted on the building shone onto the guests. The night was sweltering, and perspiration glistened on all our faces. A steel drum band played outdated pop hits ("Yellow Bird," "Bésame Mucho") as waiters brought around large, heavy trays, men carrying the drinks—fruit punch, coconut water, beer, white wine, served in thick glass tumblers—and women the canapés: pineapple chunks skewered with cheese cubes, pineapple with sliced chicken franks, baked cheese sticks, small meat tarts. A point was being made in that all the food was locally produced; no imports. We ran into a former woodwork master, Joshua Chung, and his wife, and James Ramsahoye, a former student of Howard's who, I would learn from Marian's letters, had portrayed Antonio in the 1953 production of *Twelfth Night* and whose 1996 book about Burnham's duplicity was inspired by his impressions while attending these very Queen's anniversary events. Now a geologist based in Trinidad, Ramsahoye was pessimistic about Guyana's bauxite industry (the country was just then being confronted with China's rock-bottom prices). The thick crowd made the event almost impossible to navigate. Howard and I left after about an hour and crossed Main Street to have dinner at the Park Hotel.

In its day, the Park was Georgetown's most exclusive gathering spot. Its Victorian details and grand proportions still evoked that past, but the place was desolate; when we walked in there were no visible guests and no other diners. Perhaps later they would arrive, as we had, from across the street. The rumpled East Indian concierge-waitress seated us and then admired my blouse. We ordered food and wine, and she disappeared, returning some time later to tell us that the bar was closed. Again she left us. When she reappeared we asked for water. Bringing two small glasses full, she told us conspiratorially that the man was, after all, in the bar, so we ordered two glasses of white wine. Back she came: no more wine, but she did have something to offer, though exactly what it was her whispering manner and her patois and perhaps her vocabulary prevented us from grasping. She assured us it was good, so we ordered two. She returned with a glass of ice, two goblets, and two small screw-top bottles of cream liqueur. We waited quite a long time before she reappeared with our rice and curry. The food was adequate but, like the demeanour of the waitress, seemed incongruous with the setting in what had once been a formal colonial dining room, its ten or twelve round tables still perfectly set with neat tablecloths over pleated skirts. Despite the whirring ceiling fans, we were both dripping in the heat. This was our first night outside the highly air-conditioned restaurant in our hotel. I'd had no idea the nights could be so oppressive.

After dinner we poked around the silent building, stepping into the enormous ballroom, peering out from the second-floor veranda that overlooked Main Street, where colonial officials and planters once sat in high-back wicker chairs and tut-tutted about B.G. Empty and practically unattended, the Park seemed at that moment more a relic of a bygone age than a functioning hotel. (The building burned to the ground in 2000.)

Back at the Tower, Howard and I said good-night and I walked out to the courtyard on my way to my room. A spotlight illuminated the one tall palm near the pool, and a dozen or so small bats flew gracefully in and out of the halo around its fronds, searching for insects.

On our last night with the car we drove to a residential neighbourhood near the hotel to have dinner at an Indian restaurant whose advertisement in the daily newspaper had caught my eye. We were shown to seats on the second-floor balcony. Pots of rabbit's-foot fern hung near our table, suspended from the roof's overhang. I drank in the sounds of the street—a handful of rowdy, bantering kids, a motorcycle circling around, the honk of an occasional car, the convivial patter between the man who watched the parked cars and a passerby, a few vendors calling out as they came by with trays of cigarettes and fruit. Dogs barked indifferently; lights were flicked on and then off in adjacent houses. Here was Georgetown's intimacy at its beguiling best. A breeze ruffled the ferns. The small vase of imported carnations and baby's breath decorating our table was an irrelevant luxury. We ordered prawn curry, lamb vindaloo, matar paneer, then finished the meal with masala tea served with cream and what the menu described as "colony gold" sugar.

On our way back to the hotel, I heard the crapauds—the enormous toads—make their distinctive, flutter-tongue call. Again, bats flew around the illuminated branches of the Tower's palm. Unseen frogs made the sound of a rusty gate swinging open and closed, open and closed. I had mixed feelings about leaving. It was time to go home, but since I couldn't fathom the circumstances under which I might return, I felt melancholy as the end drew near. I yearned for something I couldn't name, a sense of belonging in a country that itself lacked coherence and had none to spare. Without knowing it, I'd been touched by the abiding sadness of my birthplace.

~

Once my film had been developed, I studied the photographs—six rolls' worth. The sun, the glare, the almost visible, stifling heat. A few women sitting under broad-canopied trees next to tray tables on which they'd set a few papaws, packets of cigarettes, or a half-dozen bottles of Banks beer; a cow reclining in the shade on a patch of grass nearby. A boy acting as a lookout while perched on heaped bags of rice, transported by horse-drawn cart. A man standing on a busy sidewalk in downtown Georgetown, whacking coconuts with a cutlass to sell to thirsty passersby. Tattered cabins set back from the road, raised on cinder blocks and roofed with rusted corrugated steel, some—called "parlours," Dad had told me—selling beer or the extra-fizzy Coca-Cola bottled in Guyana. The expanses of flat, unmanicured land, evocative of pockets of America's rural South but flavoured with the occasional Hindu temple, Muslim mosque, or vestige of colonial Victorian gingerbread. Despite the appealing immediacy of nature, these scenes were not so much picturesque as backlit with near-despair.

In 1994, having never left the political arena, Cheddi Jagan had been in office for two years. The country was reeling from decades of economic ruin. The minimum wage was $5,500 a month, the equivalent of about $40 U.S.—more or less what Howard and I spent on dinner each night in the hotel dining room. During his two decades in office Forbes Burnham had nationalized Guyana's industries and rejected foreign investment, steeply lowering his countrymen's standard of living while he, meanwhile, amassed considerable personal wealth. Upon his sudden death, in 1985, he left the young nation saddled with a foreign debt of more than $2 billion U.S. and an unemployment rate nearing 40 percent. Now Jagan had agreed to foreign investment in lumbering, gold mines, and diamond mines, but unregulated practices had begun to raise environmental concerns. (A year after our visit, a major cyanide spill at the Canadian-operated Omai gold mine tinted a stretch of the Essequibo River red, killed fish, and made newspaper headlines worldwide.) Ecotourism was just coming into its own when we were there; in its brochure, Hotel Tower advertised what it called "the first purpose-built nature resort in Guyana," set up along the white sands of Madewini Creek. The country's eligibility for international compensation in exchange for its protecting its mammoth rain forest from development lay some years ahead. It was an innovative scheme promoted by the future president Bharrat Jagdeo in which stasis was flipped into a global asset, inaccessibility into a virtue, and on which Guyana's prospects may yet hang. But Guyana's privation was not only financial.

For a brief time, following Jagan's return from the United States in 1943 and Burnham's from London six years later, the two men, along with Janet Jagan and a handful of others, had worked together to press the

British for immediate reforms and push emphatically for independence, forming the People's Progressive Party in 1950. Jagan drew support primarily from the East Indian community on the sugar estates, on one of which he'd been raised, and Burnham had a strong base among the blacks in Georgetown, his home ground. Their uniting of the colony's two major ethnic groups was unprecedented. As the election approached, the party's frequent public meetings drew large mixed audiences and inspired a sense of euphoria. "They did wonderful things for us all at first," wrote Richard Allsopp in 2005; "everything they said and did seemed so natural and correct to us." Suspension of the constitution, however necessary it had been deemed by the panicky Colonial Office, was just one in a series of crushing blows to that optimism.

It is possible to view the PPP's volatile 133 days in office as representing a conflict of purpose; the head-on collision of Britain's plan for the gradual withdrawal of its colonial presence with the PPP's insistence on its immediate exit. The denouement became much more complex. With the arrival of the Royal Welsh Fusiliers in October 1953, British troops established a presence throughout the colony that lasted for the next thirteen years. A fissure in the PPP leadership between Cheddi Jagan and Burnham, pricked in 1954 by the Robertson Commission report, split the party's fragile alliance, setting the stage for decades of rivalry between the two ambitious men and the political polarization of the populace along racial lines that persists to this day. When Jagan was elected prime minister in 1961, just after the Bay of Pigs debacle, the United States, fearing that his inflammatory socialist rhetoric signaled the coming of a second Soviet satellite in the Americas, undertook a disastrous covert program of violent insurgency on Burnham's behalf. Declassified documents show that President Kennedy ordered Jagan deposed; to that end, the CIA joined the AFL-CIO to fund strikes and promote arson and rioting in the colony between 1961 and 1964 that caused death and injury, significant loss of property, and a cataclysmic deepening of the gulf of mistrust between racial groups. Emigration picked up. In 1961 the British tried to allay the Kennedy administration's fears: Jagan "is a confused thinker and his mind is clogged with ill-digested dogma derived from Marxist literature. But he has learnt a good deal in the last eight years; he has not, since 1957, proved as difficult to deal with as he was earlier," wrote Foreign Secretary Alec Douglas-Home to Secretary of State Dean Rusk in August; yet, although the two powers came to an apparent agreement, within weeks the Americans were discussing plans for "converting the UK to a program of direct anti-Jagan action." By February 1962, Rusk had written to Lord Home that "it is not possible for us to put up with an independent British Guiana under Jagan. . . . Partly reflective of ever growing concern over Cuba, public and Congressional opinion here is incensed at the thought of our dealing with Jagan. . . . Current happenings in British Guiana indicate Jagan is not master of the situation at home without your support. There is some resemblance to the events of 1953. Thus, the continuation of Jagan in power is leading us to disaster in terms of the colony itself, strains on Anglo American relations and difficulties for the Inter-American system." Finally acceding to U.S. pressure, the British agreed to postpone their departure, citing British Guiana's instability, and to orchestrate the implementation of an electoral change to the colony's constitution, as advocated by Forbes Burnham, that would favour him in the coming election. And Burnham, upon attaining the role of prime minister and guiding the colony to national independence in 1966, went on to cripple Guyana with policies of corruption and violence, staying in office through force and flagrantly rigged elections. "We misunderstood the whole struggle down there," said Arthur Schlesinger, Jr., in 1994, recalling his years in the White House with Kennedy. Jagan, he said, "wasn't a Communist. The British thought we were overreacting, and indeed we were. The CIA decided this was some great menace, and they got the bit between their teeth." The British, wishing to maintain good relations with the United States and to wash their hands of the colony, had acquiesced. British Guiana had outlived its usefulness.

But the problem did not originate with suspension of the constitution. British Guiana had lagged behind other parts of the British West Indies, some of which had taken steps toward political and constitutional reform as early as the mid-1940s. That Governor Savage had arrived in Georgetown from Barbados just two weeks before the 1953 election meant that he had insufficient time to master the complexities peculiar to British Guiana that underlay the PPP's sweeping victory. His sincerity of intent was lost on the PPP ministers, who were consumed with pent-up nationalist fervour. The ministers faced their own challenges; having expected to carry on as the opposition, they had wound up as the majority and now had to lead. As the constitution described it, it was a role for which they were unprepared. Instead, the party misconstrued its sudden change in stature, viewing its winning of 51 percent of the popular vote as a mandate to impose its political platform. The governor resisted. The ministers' rancour mounted. "They continued to hold public meetings on Saturday nights," recalled Richard Allsopp, "explaining to the public the difficulties they were having with the governor, the government, the permanent secretaries and all the senior administrative officers, and we were cheering and cheering not realizing that they should be getting on with the business of government and managing those people who were giving them difficulties."

The diversity of leaders within the PPP, whose alliance had won its success at the polls, created another complication. As Sydney King (now Eusi Kwayana), one of the men detained at Atkinson Field, down the street from my parents' house, said much later, the PPP's victory "was too quick"; the party's philosophical and interracial coalition hadn't yet had time to coalesce. Its leaders were young, in their twenties and thirties. Inexperience, naiveté, and dogmatism left them subject to the agendas of outside forces. In 1953 and the years to come, the PPP's militant leaders did not grasp how resoundingly the trappings they'd borrowed from Communist ideology alienated Western interests. The party newsletter, *Thunder*, edited by Janet Jagan, looked to the Soviet Union as "the motherland." Even after they had assumed positions in government, the legislators continued to lead strikes. They didn't recognize the contradiction between forging bonds with the Communist bloc and lobbying simultaneously for U.S. support in their drive for independence from Britain. "Our party was like a boy with short pants adapting to the role of a man in a very short space of time," said Eric Huntley, a founding member of the PPP, in an interview in 1994. Ashton Chase, another leader, later bemoaned the party's "amateurish displays." "It was absolute nonsense to try to establish communism in British Guiana . . . without having independence," he said. "The extremists in the party took a course of action that provoked the British to react."

The innocence, or obtuseness, endured. A few years after winning the 1957 election, Premier Jagan railed against Britain just when the Colonial Office was preparing to hand him Guyana's independence. In April 1961, days after the Bay of Pigs incident, he championed Castro. That fall, despite preparatory briefing by PPP advisers, Jagan was unable to offer a coherent reply when asked point blank on a live American TV news program whether he was a Communist. "I do not believe in capitalism," he said. "Life in the Soviet Union is growing day by day better and better. . . . We want to know how this is done." President Kennedy had watched the program and asked him to pay a call. At the White House, Jagan made evasive remarks that convinced the Americans of his Communist allegiances, yet he was astounded by Kennedy's subsequent refusal to provide aid. He was unable to modulate his views, oblivious of the harm his outbursts unleashed, insensitive to the self-restraint and judgment that politics required. Burnham, carefully eschewing Communist ties and so perceived by the U.S. as the lesser threat, was bankrolled to succeed him. There's no disputing the symbolic significance of Burnham's early years in office for blacks in Guyana and beyond; it still rings out in a remark he made to an *Ebony* magazine reporter in 1967: "I am proud of the fact that I am black, and I have an automatic sympathy with black people all over the world." But after the British had left, sometime during Guyana's participation in the era's heady black nationalism, his moderate pose collapsed. By 1973 he had assumed absolute control. "In Guyanese parlance he became a snake," writes James Ramsahoye. "He shed his skin and was now looked upon as dangerous and fearful. . . . It was a great betrayal. To many middle class Negro Guyanese and others, Burnham became a totally incomprehensible disappointment."

"Things are rough here at every level—political, economic, social," wrote Janet Jagan, with some understatement, to her cousin in Chicago in 1983. "I still work every day. I often do my own housework and cooking. Cooking is no easy task as so many foods are hard to get."

"The shops had bare shelves," Shiva Naipaul wrote in 1980 of his visit just after the Jonestown fiasco. (Burnham had welcomed the People's Temple to Guyana as a taunt to the U.S., where Jim Jones had begun to draw mounting scrutiny; President Burnham gave the People's Temple a twenty-five-year lease for its 3,852-acre compound at a gift rate of 25 cents per acre for the first five years, and turned a blind eye to what went on there.) "Hungry children and adults combed the garbage dumps. . . . Emigration was turning into a stampede." On the plane to Georgetown he meets an Englishman who had lived in Guyana for years and was returning to fetch his family and take them to Barbados, where he'd found a new job. He tells Naipaul the town has shortages of cigarettes and sugar. "Everywhere you look in the world's first and only Cooperative Socialist Republic you'll see sugar-cane fields," the man says. "But still we have shortages of sugar. Quite a feat." Guyana was importing its sugar from Guatemala.

A Guyanese man visiting Georgetown in 2005 after a long absence told the Trinidadian writer Nicholas Laughlin about Burnham's boycott of American imports: "We used to say he banned all the white things, flour and milk, and even cement to build, and white paint for houses, and toothpaste. You couldn't buy Colgate in Guyana. People used to smuggle it from Suriname and Brazil. . . . And milk was the worst. Because we hardly have dairy cows in Guyana, and in those days we didn't have refrigeration to store it. People used to line up for hours at the shops if they heard they had some milk, just to buy a little bit for their children."

When Burnham's nationalization policies threatened local businesses and the economy soured, emigration rates rose. As the violence, corruption, and hardship ratcheted up, so did the flight of Guyanese—to Jamaica, Trinidad, London, Toronto, New York. The trend did not end; by 2005, 89 percent of Guyanese with college degrees had left the country, a phenomenon described in *The Economist* magazine as a haemorrhage. In 2013 Guyana's rate per capita of emigration was the sixth highest in the world. It's not hard to see why some look back on the early 1950s in British Guiana as a sort of golden age.

Much of the recent literature about Guyana centres on Jagan and Burnham, and they do make for a compelling juxtaposition: the utterly dedicated, upright, blinkered ideologue and the whip-smart, shrewd, cynical opportunist. The men, so different in makeup and distinct in their agendas, each made a real contribution, although those have largely been eclipsed by their extreme limitations as leaders. Their longevity sealed the bitter rift that has outlived them both.

But they are just two people. There are so many other Guyanese, so many other voices.

For some, emigration was necessary in the search for a broader horizon, one that would allow for a more complete view. The historian Clem Seecharan grew up on a sugar estate in Berbice, then arrived at Queen's College on scholarship at age fifteen. In 1986 he immigrated to Britain with twelve dollars in his pocket. He is now emeritus professor of history at London Metropolitan University. "I felt there was an intellectual void in me," he said in 2007 of his Guyanese schooling. "The yearning to know and to better understand Guyana was there, but there was really no history on the place that had shaped me over the years for me to look at." Slowly, thanks to his contributions and those of others, that history has begun to appear, a promising step toward a cohesive national identity.

~

When, thirty years after moving to England, the novelist Roy Heath returned to Georgetown in the 1970s to visit his godparents, he felt a "fusion of time," a sensation that seems akin to my own, far more limited experience there in 1994. "The past was as immediate as the present," he writes. "Rather, the past was incorporated in the present, in such a way that a new, undifferentiated time emerged, neither past nor present." This was, for me, a signal aspect of the place.

In 1994, on arriving in Georgetown, I was absurdly underinformed. I knew little about Guyana's history or circumstances, about the turmoil of recent decades that it had just survived. I struggled to comprehend its crushing financial burdens, but, sheltered within the communion of Queen's College, I did not find a way to see the gulf of mutual mistrust, the unhealed wound still aching among its people. I did not understand how isolated the country still was, or how subject to the intractable realities of rain and sea—or even how much was missing from my personal picture of it. I sent my mother a postcard of the National Library, but it didn't occur to me, and Howard didn't mention, that he and Marian had been inside that building many times and had checked out perhaps dozens of books from its shelves. And she didn't tell me either; I discovered that detail, like so many others, only after her death, in 2001, when I read her letters to her parents. They opened up a lost chapter, a whole world.

For all that British Guiana had been invoked during my childhood as something of a family touchstone, my parents had never said much about their life there. The three and a half years in Georgetown had been a boon to my father, launching his career in tropical botany. For my mother, British Guiana had been part of a time that did not last, the beginning of "years with small children and high hopes." That description comes from a memoir she attempted during the 1980s, not long after she and Howard divorced. Like many women of her time, she found that the ground had shifted beneath her feet. Her compliance as a young wife in acquiescing to the hardships of life in B.G. had come to astonish her. Unspoken emotions finally found words and demanded expression. In the unfinished fragment of a memoir, I read, after her death, what she'd never written her parents.

The domestic demands in B.G. and her physical discomfort had surpassed anything she'd anticipated, but as she looked back, the real blow had been that she'd felt so terribly alone. Life on Parade Street in particular, so rich on the pages of her letters, had been hard on her. Her inexperience showed. She was marooned and couldn't get her bearings. "I felt it impolite to gripe in public, and my husband's absorption in his work, and his eagerness to continue, made it hard for me to complain at home. I persevered." Her life was almost completely circumscribed within the flat. "Eventually we reasoned that huge educational differences between the teachers and their wives kept them from offering hospitality to me—college educated, wealthy by their standards. The men had professional equality; among the wives, the social distances were enormous. As Americans our status was more elevated than we were accustomed to. Any modest diversion helped, but still, in the first strange months I frequently wept in frustration and loneliness. Howard would pat my shoulder and remind me that we were there for a good cause: our future." That future necessitated his frequent absence, often in remote surroundings. She wept a lot: "buckets," she wrote. "Elizabeth was thriving, Howard was exhilarated, and I was miserable." From one address to the next, she almost visibly matures in her letters, but I never heard my mother recall Georgetown with any pleasure. She found it hard to understand why I would want to go there in 1994. Still, I can't picture the woman I knew her to be without the broadening resilience and inner resources she acquired during what even she called those "nourishing" years.

A person's relationship to place is a complex thing, a shifting accrual of elements learned, lived, and looked back on. "I so clearly remember the moment I arrived in Guyana," Jock Campbell, of Bookers, told Clem Seecharan in 1994; then a man of eighty-one years, Campbell was recalling events six decades behind him, at the very beginning of his career, when he worked for a few months at the company's wharf on the Demerara River and a year and a half on Plantation Albion, in Berbice, in the colony where his family had held land since the 1780s. "The smell, absolutely everything; it was the most extraordinary thing to feel that this was my spiritual home, then the extraordinary contrast between the romance, the vision and the reality; but enough closeness for me to try to turn the vision into reality. It was very odd; it was almost like a sort of spiritual experience."

Despite my own ignorance and all that had happened in Guyana over the years since my birth, I felt some of that startling, telescoping connection in 1994, attributable, I suppose, to my return to a point of origin—because if Georgetown would in hindsight become a source of estrangement between my parents, it was also where our family, the one that includes me, took shape. The connection intensified as I read my parents' letters and was transported, outside of time, to a place both foreign and familiar. It seemed to me as I followed them over those many months, through events that unspool like well-crafted drama, that their life in British Guiana had consisted of an expansive, rippling joy, the joy born of effort and reach, and an unspoken, unconsoled anguish—a combination that, I find, suits the place.

EPILOGUE

Upon their return to the United States, the Irwins' lives continued at a hectic pace. They exchanged Christmas cards with the Allsopps and the Ramsarans, and Marian sent my sister's and my outgrown clothes to Winifred Grant for use by her children—two surviving letters of thanks from her are dated 1959 and 1963—but the primary bond of shared experience had been removed. Family life and Howard's career were demanding, and new affiliations streamed in.

In the fall of 1956 the family settled in Austin, where four years later Howard earned a combined master's degree and Ph.D. in botany at the University of Texas. Upon graduation he was offered a job as a research associate in tropical botany at the New York Botanical Garden, in the Bronx, and the family settled in a suburb outside New York City. At the Garden, Howard reported to Bassett Maguire, the head curator of the herbarium, whose concentration in tropical botany had brought him to British Guiana; the two men discovered that they had missed meeting at Kaieteur Falls in 1954 by a single day. Howard assisted Maguire in lengthy collecting trips throughout Guyana, Suriname, and northern Brazil, then shifted his focus to the savannah region of central Brazil and led his own three-month-long expeditions there over a period of twelve years. Although during his eighteen years at NYBG he was promoted to executive director and then president, and went on to direct Clark Garden on Long Island, his greatest fulfilment lay not in administrative achievement but in taxonomic fieldwork.

In 1978 Howard and Marian's marriage came to an end. Howard remarried and now lives with his second wife, Anne, on Cape Cod, where he served as a board member on a number of conservation and town planning organizations, edited the 1996 edition of *America's Garden Book*, and for thirteen years wrote a weekly column about gardening for a local newspaper.

In the 1970s Marian joined the Riverdale-Yonkers Society for Ethical Culture and found deep sustenance within that group, serving variously as its membership director, head of the children's program, board member, and president. Her affinity for volunteer work had begun with leading Brownie troops and directing Girl Scout camps, and would continue as she chaired committees in the Bronx involving elder services. She also wrote poetry and had several pieces published. Following her divorce, and after earning a master's degree in social work, Marian worked for fifteen years at Riverdale Senior Services in the Bronx, where her dedication and resourcefulness were commended by the New York City Council in 2000 with a Women of Achievement Pacemaker's Award. She held her job until ten weeks before her death in 2001. Among the things she left behind for her daughters were the ten quilts she'd sewn in the past decade, all of them pieced by hand.

The medical procedures envisaged to ameliorate Elizabeth's handicap did not come to pass. As a pre-schooler, Elizabeth—who now goes by Liz—became adept using prostheses, which she eventually abandoned in favour of direct contact with knife and fork, pen and pencil, sewing needle, steering wheel, and garden trowel. After completing college she taught early childhood special education for two years before earning a master's degree in social work in 1978. Liz now works as an intake counsellor at a hospital and a private psychotherapist in Milwaukee, where she lives with her husband. Visits from their two children, along with his four from a previous marriage and a generation of grandchildren, keep the couple's household in a state of happy turmoil.

While working on this book, I found that some of the people who figure in Howard's and Marian's letters were important to the colony in ways my parents did not remark upon and may not have perceived. Several had fascinating backstories that were not mentioned. Others went on to have distinguished careers. The following list, although incomplete, adds another facet to this book's portrait of mid-century Georgetown. Each name is followed by the bracketed date of the letter in which it first appears.

Dr. Vincent Roth [September 12, 1952]

Born in Australia, Vincent Roth (1889–1967) was reunited in 1907 with his father, Walter Roth, a government medical officer stationed in the North West District of British Guiana. Following a stint in Georgetown as a newspaper reporter, Vincent worked for twenty-five years for the Department of Lands and Mines, a post whose requisite travel throughout the interior gave him a deep knowledge of the colony. In later years he rebuilt the British Guiana Museum after its destruction during the 1945 fire, contributed as librarian and editor to the *Daily Chronicle*, founded the zoo, and served as a nominated member of the colony's Legislative Council. Taken aback by the scant awareness among Guianese of their homeland's long history, he persuaded the *Chronicle* to publish inexpensive reprints of more than a dozen historical books about the colony, which he oversaw as editor, and contributed his own compilation of a *Who's Who in British Guiana*. His two-volume memoir, *A Life in Guyana*, was published by Peepal Tree Press in 2003.

John Ramsaran [September 15, 1952]

After serving in the Royal Air Force, John Ansuman Ramsaran (1914–1991) married Margaret McLaren in 1945, and the couple lived with her parents while he studied English and Latin at King's College and Hindi with Sanskrit at the School of Oriental and African Languages, London University. Having obtained a teaching position in the Overseas Educational Commission, Ramsaran hoped to return to his native Trinidad but was invited instead to British Guiana. In a 1988 personal essay, "My Colonial Inheritance," he recalls the period of the family's stay there as "one of the most disturbed politically in the post war history of that unhappy country." He continues, "There was a strong anti-white feeling against expatriates in the capital, as a result of which my wife and her mother, Mrs. McLaren, were placed in a very embarrassing position; though I must admit that I myself encountered no hostility." He writes of teaching Shakespeare and Chaucer at Queen's, as required by the Oxford and Cambridge Board: "These we read closely and, I think, with pleasure; but I had returned to the Caribbean with the feeling that something vital was being omitted from the literary studies of the generation of schoolboys I was teaching and learning from at Queen's College." Ramsaran taught at the University College of Ibadan, Nigeria, through 1967, then moved to Swansea University College in Wales. He retired in 1981 to complete *With Both Hands*, an unpublished autobiography.

Herbert Allsopp [October 8, 1952]

W.H.L. Allsopp and his brothers grew up in Charlestown, a crowded, poor section of Georgetown. Returning to the colony in 1948 with a master of science degree from the University of Wisconsin, Allsopp joined the Department of Agriculture and Fisheries and soon focused on combating the widespread habit of discarding bycatch (he coined the word to replace the derogatory "trash fish") inadvertently caught by fisheries while trawling for higher-valued scaled fish or shrimp. The wasteful practice lowered the stocks of the less-remunerative species by millions of tons of fish per year while depriving cash-strapped shoppers of the rich protein of scaleless fish, which accounted for six of every ten fish found in British Guiana's coastal waters. To counter entrenched cultural and religious prejudices against eating the plentiful catfish, gillbacker, menari, and other "skinfish," Allsopp collaborated with Sam Chase, the colony's "King of Vaudeville," in a campaign that was kicked off in June 1950 with a Skinfish Feast, at which Chase performed "Eat Skin Fish," a calypso composed upon request by Norman Cameron. Praising the entertainer in *Kyk-Over-Al*, Allsopp wrote that Chase "reaches a level of popular understanding that perhaps cannot be otherwise scratched." Allsopp earned a Ph.D. from the University of Washington in 1959; he oversaw worldwide fisheries programs and was the first regional fisheries officer for the continent of Africa from 1966 through 1972. He next joined the Canadian International Development Research Centre, then opened his own company, Smallworld Fishery Consultants, in Vancouver in 1983. Since then, his bycatch campaign has grown into a globally recognized concern, and bycatch is now increasingly processed into food products in the developing world.

Betty and Cliff Evans [October 19, 1952]
Betty Jane Meggers (1921–2012) and Clifford Evans (1920–1981) conducted dozens of trips over their decades of field research in South America and were the first archaeologists to look closely at how ancient Amazonians lived. Their book *Archaeological Investigations in British Guiana* was published in 1960. "Cliff and I complemented each other," Meggers later recalled. "I was more interested in theory, and he was great at technology." Meggers was long affiliated with the Smithsonian and was at the time of her death the director of the institution's Latin American Archeology Program.

Doodnauth Hetram [October 31, 1952]
Hetram had served in the Royal Air Force before his arrival at Queen's College in 1951 to teach classics. In 1963 he became the school's first Guyanese headmaster. He retired in 1969. In his honour, the school

annually awards the Doodnauth Hetram Shield for Best Academic Achievement by a Fifth Form Student.

Vyvyan Joseph Sanger-Davies [November 12, 1952]

The last "imported" headmaster of Queen's College, Sanger-Davies (1908–1995) is remembered as an innovative administrator who introduced various programs that allowed for a greater number of students at Queen's and other schools to study the sciences, thereby equipping a generation of specialists who would be on hand during the colony's transition to independence. (The evening classes for "external" students were one such program.) Known by schoolboys in later years as "Sputnik," he retired from Queen's in 1962. Sanger-Davies had completed his education at Cambridge in 1930 and married the following year. He taught at Sedbergh School, in England, for sixteen years before receiving his appointment as headmaster of the School of Science at Bathurst in Gambia, West Africa, where he was also colony commissioner for Scouts and choirmaster of the Pro-Cathedral Choir. In 1993 he published *Gambia's First Teacher of Science.* He died in Banbury, Oxfordshire, England, in 1995; his wife, Nancy, preceded him in 1981.

Lynette Dolphin [November 17, 1952]

A graduate of Bishops' High School, Lynette de Weever Dolphin (1916–2000) was at the centre of efforts in the colony to promote musical culture. Having learned piano and begun accompanying soloists from her youth in the West Coast village of De Willem, Miss Dolphin arrived in London to study music in 1939, just as war broke out against Germany. She came home to British Guiana after suffering an injury when the house she'd been living in was bombed. Returning overseas after the war, she earned a teaching diploma at the Royal Schools of Music. Back in Georgetown, she organized the Schools' Music Festival in 1942 and was the first secretary, and later longtime president, of the British Guiana Music Teachers Association, which was founded at her home on Waterloo Street. Her years of teaching at Queen's began in 1943, resumed upon her return from London, and ended in 1969. Miss Dolphin had by then been tapped as the first chairman of the National History and Arts Centre (later the Department of Culture), a post she held for twenty-five years. In that capacity she directed the first Caribbean Festival of Creative Arts (Carifesta) in 1972. She also compiled six books of songs, the last of which,

Twenty Amerindian Folk Songs, she completed less than a week before her death. In an affectionate profile published in the *Stabroek News* during Queen's sesquicentennial, Terry Holder recalled Miss Dolphin's frequent travels on behalf of the Department of Culture. "And wherever she has gone, whether on the street in Canada, or while waiting for a train in London, it's always the same: 'Miss! Miss! What are you doing here?' and they all remember when they sang in the choir and what they sang."

Celeste Dolphin [November 17, 1952]
Like her elder sister, Celeste Dolphin was an active promoter of culture. In addition to writing *Children of Guiana*, a booklet for young readers (with illustrations by Marjorie Broodhagen) published in 1953 that describes the colony's different ethnic groups, she was a producer and the first organizer of *Broadcasts to Schools*, a government radio program initiated by Governor Savage in 1954 that served isolated communities in the interior and largely focused on Guianese themes. She also hosted *Talking About Education*, a nightly radio show, and later served as the editor of *Kaie*, a government-sponsored magazine that published literary pieces. E. Linford Dolphin, the sisters' father, was a strict disciplinarian after whom a government school in Georgetown was named.

Norman Cameron [December 12, 1952]
Born in New Amsterdam, Norman Eustace Cameron (1903–1983) entered Queen's College at age thirteen. He earned the prestigious Guiana Scholarship in 1921 and received a master's degree in mathematics from Cambridge University. In response to the discrimination he experienced in England, he returned to British Guiana imbued with ancestral pride and a drive toward community uplift that took many forms: founding his own school, the Guianese Academy, at which he taught from 1926 to 1934; writing plays; forming literary and other cultural groups; publishing books, including *Guianese Poetry* (1931), the first collection of its kind, and the two-volume *Evolution of the Negro* (1929, 1934). He made a point of publishing his works in the colony rather than abroad and was known to sometimes sell them door-to-door. Returning to Queen's in 1934 as a teacher (known as "Nebu"), he served as deputy principal from 1958 to 1962 before joining the University of Guyana in 1963. In 1951 Cameron published *A History of the Queen's College of British Guiana*, a fact-filled account of the school's development and contributions to the colony; a

remembrance in *Kaieteur News* upon the book's reissue in 2009 quotes Cameron as saying, "Mine has been a full life and complex with notable contradictions."

Dorothy Taitt [December 17, 1952]

Recalled in 2003 by the *Stabroek News* as "subversive in the positive sense," Dorothy Taitt (ca. 1896–1956) was a linchpin in advancing musical culture in Georgetown. Known as a forceful, competitive woman, she taught singing at Bishops' High School and was the founder of the B.G. Philharmonic Society, which included a choir as well as the orchestra (one of just two in the colony during the 1940s and 1950s). The orchestra rehearsed in the house she shared with her husband, Dr. Jabez Taitt, and their seven children. (The building, which dates to the 1840s, is now the home of Cara Lodge, an upscale hotel.) Dr. Taitt, a Barbadian who served as a government medical officer in Georgetown and the Corentyne, travelled widely with his wife, and their experience of racial discrimination in the United States during the 1930s is thought to have prompted Mrs. Taitt to promote self-confidence in her children and other Guianese through involvement in the creative arts. As the host of an amateur-hour radio program, *The Aunt Tabita Show*, she encouraged young talent. She was a co-founder of the B.G. Union of Cultural Clubs, and she brought into the management committee of the Philharmonic such pillars of the colonial establishment as Alan John Knight, the Archbishop of the West Indies; Sir Frank McDavid, the colonial treasurer; and W. J. Raatgaver, a prominent member of the Georgetown Chamber of Commerce—no small feat in the capital's class- and colour-conscious society. Mrs. Taitt also served Georgetown as town councillor and may have had a hand in awarding British Council scholarships. Her daughter Helen's School of Guiana Ballet and early plans for a History and Culture Week are affectionately recalled by then-student Mona Williams as a "vision . . . of blending Guianese and European arts." Helen went on to have a successful career touring the Caribbean, the United States, and Europe.

Richard Allsopp [January 9, 1953]

Stanley Reginald Richard Allsopp (1923–2009) was a Queen's College alumnus; in the contest for the Guiana Scholarship of 1941 he was bested only by his classmate Forbes Burnham. After studying French and education at the University of London, Allsopp returned to the colony to teach at

Queen's. He was the first Guianese to be named deputy headmaster, a post from which he stepped down upon Sanger-Davies's retirement in 1962, later explaining that he felt he'd been "fighting a losing battle" in upholding academic standards and that "racial and political divisions had become patent in my staff-room and were evidenced in my school." Having earned in London a master's degree in 1958 (his dissertation was the first to focus on a single English-related Caribbean language) and a Ph.D. in 1961, he turned down Prime Minister Burnham's invitation of a vice-chancellorship at the University of Guyana and in 1963 accepted a post as lecturer in English at the College of Arts and Science in Barbados, soon to become part of the University of the West Indies. There he introduced linguistics to the program, and his affiliation with the school continued through 1995. He is the author of *The Dictionary of Caribbean English Usage* (1996), a pioneering work on behalf of whose completion over twenty-five years Allsopp visited eighteen countries and interviewed thousands of people. He later remarked that despite their differences, Burnham "independently saw the value of the work as an instrument of integrative regional education and offered the support of both the Government and the University of Guyana. That Government's unconditional support, totalling over US$100,000 in the five years 1975–1980, made possible the bulk of data collection on location throughout the region, so giving a solid base to the work." The book earned Allsopp the Guyana Prize for Literature in 1998, and he was the sole West Indian included on the board of the New Oxford English Dictionary.

Joy Allsopp [January 12, 1953]
In addition to her collaboration with A. J. Seymour in editing the special Christmas 1955 issue of *Kyk-Over-Al*, Joy Allsopp was a contributor to the journal (sometimes under her maiden name, Joy Small) and is now known as part of the "first wave" of Guyanese women writers. She wrote short stories, a collection of which was published in book form, as well as several children's books, at least one of which was based on Amerindian legend. Several years after moving to Barbados with their daughter, Disa, Joy and Richard divorced. Joy and her second husband, Anthony Bland, a lawyer and university professor, lived for many years in St. Peter, Barbados, where she painted and sculpted. She died in 1996. The couple established the Joy and Anthony Bland Charitable Trust to provide scholarships and grants to students of law at the Cave Hill, Barbados, campus of the University of the West Indies.

Cecil Barker [March 18, 1953]
Captain C. E. Barker ("Bup"), the chemistry master who was stage manager for *Twelfth Night* in 1953 and with whom Howard rewired the lighting and sound system before the production of *The Tempest* the following year, was also commanding officer of the Queen's College Cadet Corps. He had joined the corps as a student in the early 1930s. Commissioned as a 2d lieutenant in 1942, he received the rank of captain in 1944 and held it until his retirement. Captain Barker earned his bachelor of science degree from London University, after which he returned to Queen's to teach. In 1964 he was appointed deputy headmaster of the school, a post he would retire in 1968. Long before he created the sets for *Twelfth Night*, Barker's flair for art took expression in his design for the original cover of *Kyk-Over-Al*, published in December 1945. He died in New York in April 1998.

Premnauth J. Ramphal [April 21, 1953]
Ramphal, known as Raj, was among a group of eleven Queen's students whose dreams of studying medicine were threatened by the school's lack of a biology master for the three years preceding 1952. Then, as he recalled in a letter to me in 2014, "out of thin air appeared a Fulbright Scholar and Biology was back on the curriculum." Ramphal convinced the other boys that "it was in our best interest if we could persuade this strange new being in our midst, an American, who had unexpectedly entered our world, to tutor us privately, outside of our regular Sixth Form time table. . . . None of us anticipated difficulty with the academics involved, but guidance we needed as the Labs were entirely new ground for us." Ramphal approached Howard, who agreed to meet with the boys the next day. "We all arrived on time, worried that some hitch might have developed in the interim especially with respect to fees, which not all of us were in a position to cover. The subject of fees did not arise then or ever. Thereafter, we met once or twice a week outside of regular school hours and we all took our special tutoring seriously and we all eleven gained the credit at the end of the school year. Without your father's guidance, I doubt any of us would have." Following his graduation from Queen's, Raj accepted Howard's invitation to work as lab assistant.

Ramphal referred to the nickname the students gave Howard "almost at the moment of his arrival": the Slengery Man. "In the Guyanese idiom, this describes a tall, lanky, loose-limbed man with a long stride. Not far off the mark, was it?" He remembered Marian as "tall, blonde, always immaculately dressed in high heels. She was Hollywood personified. She intimidated me and I avoided her as much as I could."

Ramphal is part of a notable family. His father, James I. Ramphal, was a barrister, intellectual, and co-founder of the privately run Modern High School in Georgetown; he was also the first Guianese to be appointed assistant secretary of labour and was enlisted by Governor Savage in 1954 to serve in the interim government as commissioner of labour. Raj's eldest brother, Shridath Ramphal, who had been appointed Crown Counsel in 1953 at age twenty-five, would serve under L.F.S. Burnham as attorney general and later as general secretary for the commonwealth from 1975 to 1990; he was knighted in 1970.

Raj Ramphal relocated to Ontario, where he opened a medical practice. He and Howard rekindled their acquaintance in the 1980s, and with his family Ramphal visited Howard and Anne in Cape Cod in 1993.

Martin Carter [November 1, 1953]

One of the five PPP leaders held at Atkinson Field following the suspension of the constitution in October 1953, Martin Wylde Carter (1927–1997) is remembered as Guyana's foremost poet. Among the works he wrote during his three-month detainment at the Field were those published in 1954 as *Poems of Resistance*, including "This Is the Dark Time, My Love" and "I Come From the Nigger Yard." "To read Carter's poems," writes Nicholas Laughlin in *Caribbean Beat* magazine, "is to encounter a sequence of lines that have become the everyday possessions of many ordinary people in Guyana and elsewhere in the Caribbean, possessions no less everyday for being lyrics of rare power and rhythm. . . ." Carter grew up as a child of civil servants in the colony's mixed-race middle class. A graduate of Queen's College, he worked as a clerk and schoolteacher before serving as chief information officer of Bookers from 1959 to 1966. Carter was among the PPP leaders who resigned in 1956 as part of the party's "ultra-left split." Upon Guyana's independence he joined Burnham's cabinet as minister of information and culture, and he served on Guyana's delegation to the U.N. General Assembly from 1967 to 1970. "I thought that anything that could bring about a diffusion of tension was worth fighting for," he recalled in 1995, "because no one who had not lived out here could have imagined what was going on at that time. Then the very trees almost failed to sprout." Thereafter, he returned to Bookers and gave lectures at the University of Guyana as part of its Creative Arts

Department. He was awarded the Guyana Prize for Literature in 1989. Carter eschewed materialism and is said to have never owned a wallet.

Sydney King [November 1, 1953]

Sydney Evanson King (1925–), who in the 1960s changed his name to Eusi Kwayana in tribute to his African heritage, has described himself as "a non-believer in white domination." A founding member of the PPP, he was one of the ministers ousted from office in 1953. Held at Atkinson Field, with Carter and the three other PPP leaders arrested for spreading dissension, he was upon release restricted to Buxton, his home village, where he'd been a schoolteacher when he first met Cheddi Jagan in 1947. The two men, neither of them a part of the Georgetown scene, had worked closely together for years. However, their loss of contact following King's release from the airbase, and Jagan's incarceration, created a rupture, which deepened to the extent that in 1956 King resigned from the PPP as part of the "ultra-left split." He allied himself with Burnham and served as General Secretary of the People's National Congress until he was expelled in 1961 for making public his aim to see the party become multiethnic. King went on to found the African Society for Racial Equality, followed by the African Society for Cultural Relations with Independent Africa. He was still a supporter of the PNC and the volunteer chair of several PNC committees until 1971, when he severed all ties over mounting government corruption and repression. ("Freedom was closing down," as he put it recently.) He then co-founded the multiracial Working People's Alliance, which became a political party in 1979. He was described in 1977 by Thomas Spinner in *The Nation* as "one of the most fascinating people in the entire Caribbean. . . . Considered incorruptible, he exerts a massive moral authority." Also a writer, playwright, and songwriter, King composed the party songs of the PPP, PNC, and WPA.

Dr. Reginald H. Georges [February 2, 1955]

A native of the Virgin Islands, Dr. Georges studied medicine in Edinburgh before providing government medical services in Georgetown, Bartica, and Suddie, British Guiana. After resigning from public service, he opened his own private practice, for which his wife, Mona, served as financial manager. He went on to open St. Michael's Nursing Home on New Market Street, where I was born. Dr. Georges died of a brain tumour in 1957; my parents told me that what may have been a flare-up during the early stages of his illness accounted for his absence at my delivery. After his death, his wife taught for four years at St. Gabriel's School in Georgetown, then relocated with the couple's three children to Trinidad. She died in 2000.

Harold Persaud [June 7, 1955]

The Persaud family lived in the house next door to Howard and Marian's on the Queen's College compound. Nicknamed "Bats" by students, Harold Rabindranath Persaud was a senior history master. He was a charter member of the board of governors of the University of Guyana and was named Permanent Secretary to Prime Minister Cheddi Jagan in the new government of 1961. According to *Across Three Continents*, a memoir by his cousin Joseph S. Persaud, he was "forced to flee to London" in 1965, where he remained until his death in 1992.

Joshua Ramsammy [December 1, 1955]

Having grown up in the rural Corentyne sugar belt at a time when only half of East Indian children had any schooling at all, Joshua Reuben Ramsammy (1928–2009) began attending Queen's College in 1943. "Josh's ambition, unlike a number of us who aspired to medicine, was always to be a Science teacher," recalls his schoolmate Harold Drayton, "with a University education that would equip him to teach at Queen's." After graduating, he taught science at a secondary school in Grenada before winning a scholarship toward an honours degree in zoology at the University of Edinburgh. He extended his studies through a year's postgraduate program that qualified him to teach botany and zoology at the certificate level, then returned to Queen's in 1955 as a senior biology master, where he remained for six years. Known as "Swami," he is remembered by students as a quiet, enigmatic man who stood up to school propriety by wearing a goatee and, in place of the customary suit and tie, a khaki bush jacket (he wore a tailored white version on formal occasions such as Speech Day). He left Queen's in 1962 for a post as the founding principal of a high school in the Corentyne and hired several recent Queen's graduates to staff its science program. Ramsammy next served the Ministry of Education, where plans were under way to create the University of Guyana, and he helped conceive the school's four-year biology curriculum. He received a Ph.D. in 1969 from Dalhousie University in Nova Scotia, then returned to Georgetown to teach at UG. There he joined a group of activists concerned about the repression taking hold under the PNC. The group chose the name Ratoon and eventually became part of the Working People's Alliance party. An outspoken critic of the PNC, Ramsammy was shot in broad daylight in the capital's downtown in 1971, the first in a series of searing acts of unattributed, unpunished violence that culminated in the assassination in 1980 of the WPA's best-known leader, Walter Rodney. Ramsammy survived the attack largely because his brother Herman, then a doctor at St. Joseph's Mercy Hospital, saw that he was properly cared for. Upon hearing that Ramsammy's wife, Ruby, had received phone calls threatening to "finish him off," friends and colleagues established a 24-hour security vigil outside his room for the twelve days he was hospitalized. Nonetheless, following his convalescence, Ramsammy chose not to emigrate but to remain in Guyana, where for the next two decades he continued undeterred in fulfilling his lifelong goal of teaching, upholding his stand on issues, and weathering, in Nigel Westmaas's words, his "sojourn with Guyanese political and social decay." After retiring from the university in 1990, Ramsammy served as pro-chancellor from 1999 to 2005. He was awarded the Cacique Crown of Honour in 1996 in recognition of his contributions to education, environmental advocacy, and "struggle for the restoration of democracy in Guyana."

Sita and Laurence Keates [January 5, 1956]
With his arrival at Queen's in 1955, Laurence Keates (1929–2012) introduced Spanish to the school's curriculum, a step toward the colony's goal of embracing a "continental destiny." He also taught French and Portuguese and became head of the Modern Languages faculty in 1958, his final year at the college. While in Georgetown, Keates frequently gave talks and reviewed books on Radio Demerara. Upon leaving B.G. he accepted a position teaching English at the University of Lisbon; after receiving his master's degree from Birmingham in 1959, he moved to Leeds University in 1961, where he remained until retiring in 1989. He and Sita had four children.

SOURCE NOTES

Preface
"You'd be surprised what goes with you: Wilson Harris, quoted by Andrew Salkey in *Georgetown Journal* (London: New Beacon Books, 1972), p. 81

Chapter 1
The Past as Prologue
A new constitution for the colony: Reynold A. Burrowes, *The Wild Coast: An Account of Politics in Guyana* (Cambridge, Mass.: Schenkman Publishing Co., 1984), pp. 36–37; Raymond T. Smith, *British Guiana* (Oxford: Oxford University Press, 1962), pp. 164–65

many Guianese felt the new constitution's provisions failed to go far enough: Smith, p. 170; Burrowes, pp. 37, 39; Thomas J. Spinner, Jr., *A Political and Social History of Guyana, 1945–1983* (Boulder, Colo.: Westview Press, 1984), p. 34

Catching the British and even most of the party leaders themselves by surprise: Smith, p. 174; Spinner, p. 36; Clem Seecharan, "Cheddi Jagan: The Marxist Leader in Guyana and the Cold War," *The Guyana Examiner*, May 2013, p. 30

founded in 1844 . . . opened its doors: Winston McGowan, "A Concise History of Queen's College," *Queen's College Sesquicentennial Souvenir Magazine*, 1994, p. 10

enrollment was up to 459: Ibid.

"it was a Queen's boy: James W. Ramsahoye, *A Mouldy Destiny: Visiting Guyana's Forbes Burnham* (London: Minerva Press, 1996), p. 37

"Whether coincidentally or otherwise: Editorial, *Stabroek News*, July 31, 1994

sometimes looked back on . . . as a golden age: Frank Birbalsingh, *The People's Progressive Party of Guyana, 1950–1992: An Oral History* (London: Hansib Publications, 2007), p. 135

salaries were relatively low; some technical people had turned down appointments: Michael Swan, *British Guiana: The Land of Six Peoples* (London: William Clowes & Sons, 1957), p. 57

the city's system of piped water: Swan, *British Guiana*, p. 14

DDT: Kenneth S. Davis, "The Deadly Dust: The Unhappy History of DDT,"

American Heritage, February 1971; C. B. Symes and A. B. Hadaway, "Initial Experiments in the use of DDT Against Mosquitos in British Guiana," *Bulletin of Entomological Research,* January 1947, pp. 399–430

curtailed the incidence of malaria, which had been endemic in the colony: Symes and Hadaway, "Initial Experiments in the use of DDT Against Mosquitos in British Guiana," *Bulletin Entomological Research,* 1947

"virtually a bridge to the grave": Denis Williams, quoted by Clem Seecharan, *Sweetening "Bitter Sugar"* (Kingston, Jamaica: Ian Randle Publishers, 2005), p. 381

"frequent debilitating bouts of malaria: Roy Heath, *Shadows Round the Moon* (Glasgow: William Collins Sons & Co., 1990), p. 42

"When I first began to look at people: Dr. George Giglioli, quoted in Seecharan, *Sweetening "Bitter Sugar",* p. 397

The incidence of malaria among schoolchildren: Cheddi Jagan, *Forbidden Freedom* (London: People's Books Co-operative Society and Lawrence & Wishart, 1954), p. 23

population, at 748,000: Guyana Population and Housing Census: 2012, Preliminary Report, Bureau of Statistics, June 2014

Mobile, Alabama, gets 67 inches: science and technology, nbcnews.com

Georgetown lies as much as eight feet below sea level: Jagan, *Forbidden Freedom,* p. 13

"Inhabited and productive British Guiana: Jock Campbell, quoted in Seecharan, *Sweetening "Bitter Sugar",* p. 317

for fifteen years served as chairman of Booker Bros., McConnell & Co.: Campbell became chairman of Bookers in 1952; Seecharan, *Sweetening "Bitter Sugar",* p. 306

By far the largest grower: Swan, *British Guiana,* p. 85

"carefully structured, stylized constraints: Noël Bacchus, *Guyana Farewell* (New York: Noël Bacchus Publishing Co., Inc., 1995), p. 33

East Indians . . . held civil service posts only on an exceptional basis: Under colonialism, civil service posts were open only to Christians, a rule that disqualified the majority of East Indians. As estimated by Dwarka Nath, in 1943 just 10 percent of civil service jobs were held by East Indians. Raymond Smith, in his book of 1962, noted that the group was "still seriously underrepresented" in the civil service, among other areas. both, Smith, p. 112

"represented the ambitions of a class: Heath, p. 22

At twenty-three Heath found her viewpoint eccentric: Heath, p. 250

"some of the oldest and most attractive: Heath, p. 228

"All we knew of each other: Bacchus, p. 155

"Something as simple as a separate classroom: Bacchus, p. 158

For one boy per year . . . government-paid scholarship: Jagan, *Forbidden Freedom*, p. 76

no college-level facilities: Cheddi Jagan, *The West on Trial: My Fight for Guyana's Freedom* (St. John's, Antigua: Hansib Caribbean, 1997), p. 200; Jagan, *Forbidden Freedom*, p. 76

criticized its favoring of the humanities: Swan, *British Guiana*, p. 21

common practice in the colony to hire from abroad (at better salaries): McGowan, "A Concise History of Queen's College," p. 10

"What is a birch, please: Mona Williams, *Bishops: My Turbulent Colonial Youth* (Wellington, New Zealand: Mallinson Rendel Publishers, 1995), pp. 46–47

tells of being taught to cook with imported carrots: Williams, p. 89

The curriculum at Queen's was broadened somewhat in the 1950s: McGowan, p. 10

"the plight of Guyanese in being so deeply conditioned: Frank Birbalsingh, "Bacon brings home truths in 'Journey to Guyana,' " review of *Journey to Guyana* by Margaret Bacon, *Indo Caribbean World*, January 22, 2014

"The opportunities that we considered special: Bacchus, p. 159

Chapter 2
1952: Loyola Guest House, 157 Waterloo Street

Endnote 1: Atkinson Field: Odeen Ishmael, *The Guyana Story: From Earliest Times to Independence* (Exlibris, 2013), p. 364; Lloyd Kandasammy, "A Brief History of Civil Aviation in British Guiana," *Stabroek News*, June 24, 2004; H. S. Irwin reminiscence, 2000, collection of editor

Endnote 2: H. S. Irwin correspondence, 1952, collection of editor

Endnote 3: Botanical Gardens: *Georgetown Botanic Gardens Illustrated Guide* (British Guiana: Department of Agriculture, 1934), pp. 5–6. Vincent Roth opens zoo in 1951: *Vincent Roth: A Life in Guyana, vol. 2: The Later Years, 1923–1935*, ed. Michael Bennett (Leeds, England: Peepal Tree Press, 2003), epilogue, p. 289

Endnote 4: "Hardly anyone in that room: Michael Swan, *The Marches of El Dorado: British Guiana, Brazil, Venezuela* (Boston: The Beacon Press, 1958), p. 19

Endnote 5: "the light-skinned clerk: Heath, p. 136

"store clerks and bank tellers were a uniform tan: H. S. Irwin reminiscence, 2000, collection of editor

"Portuguese, Chinese, and pale others: Williams, p. 104

Endnote 6: M. S. Irwin correspondence, May 1953, collection of editor

Endnote 8: "The biology laboratory was not used: M. S. Irwin memoir fragment, collection of editor

"As biology had been suspended: H. S. Irwin reminiscence, 2000, collection of editor

Endnote 9: Ubiquity of Bookers: Seecharan, *Sweetening "Bitter Sugar"*, pp. 91–93; "Nobody in their senses: Jock Campbell, quoted in Seecharan, *Sweetening "Bitter Sugar"*, p. 227

Endnote 10: M. S. Irwin memoir fragment, collection of editor

Chapter 3
1952–1953: 124 Parade Street

Endnote 11: M. S. Irwin memoir fragment, collection of editor

Endnote 12: M. S. Irwin memoir fragment, collection of editor

Endnote 13: George J. Burton, Ph.D., "Attack on the Vector of Filariasis in British Guiana," *Public Health Reports*, Vol. 79, No. 2 (February 1964), pp. 17–143; also cdc.gov/parasites/lymphaticfilariasis/index.html. For more about the disease in British Guiana, including the film *Filariasis in British Guiana*, made in 1963, see nlm.nih.gov/hmd/collections/films/medicalmoviesontheweb/filariasisessay.html.

Endnote 14: recipe, Carnegie School of Home Economics, *What's Cooking in Guyana* (London: Macmillan, 1973), p. 222

Endnote 15: burglars who coat themselves with grease: Margaret Bacon, *Journey to Guyana* (London: Dobson Books, 1970), pp. 28–29

Endnote 18: "the popular choice for limeade: Bacchus, p. 122

Endnote 19: M. S. Irwin memoir fragment, collection of editor

Endnote 22: Mr. Martin-Sperry and the colony's inaugural music festival: Lloyd Kandasammy, "A Brief History of the British Guiana Music Festivals," History This Week, *Stabroek News*, November 10, 2005

Endnote 24: Eze Day: Burrowes, pp. 41–43; "From Tribal Robes to Pin-Stripe Suit," *The Harvard Crimson*, February 2, 1955. Ogueri at the U.N. and Bethune-Cookman College: *Jet*, April 10, 1958, p. 20

Endnote 25: McCarran Act's limit on West Indian immigrants: Holger Henke, "Early and Contemporary Patterns of Anglophone Caribbean Migration," paper presented at the 24th Annual Caribbean Studies Association Conference, May 1999, Panama City, Panama, p. 2, ufdc.ulf.edu/CA00400205/00001

Endnote 26: voting restrictions on housewives and domestic workers: Jagan, *Forbidden Freedom*, p. 42. "About two-thirds of the total number of voters: H. R. Harewood, quoted in "PPP Wins 1953 General Elections—but loses candidate at elections petition," reproduced in Guyanese Chronicle Online, March 14, 2010, http://guyanachronicle.com/ppp-wins-1953-general-elections

Endnote 27: "A mythology of white superiority: Heath, p. 188

Endnote 28: "Teare behaved like a tyrant: Ishmael, p. 404; David Granger, "Joseph Pollydore, Eminence Grise: A Tribute," *Stabroek News*, March 9, 2003

Endnote 29: Police force almost entirely black by 1950s: doc. 1, Internal Colonial Office Memorandum on Availability of Forces to Prevent Disturbances in British Guiana, May 23, 1953, and doc. 35, Colonial Office Note on Forces Available, undated but most likely early October 1953, guyana.org/govt/declassified_british_documents_1953.html

Endnote 30: "In the 1950s, when there was an increase: M. K. Bacchus, *Education for Development or Underdevelopment? Guyana's Educational System and Its Implications for the Third World* (Ontario, Canada: Wilfrid Laurier University Press, 1980), pp. 167–168

Endnote 31: Lionel Luckhoo: Colin A. Palmer, *Cheddi Jagan and the Politics of Power* (Chapel Hill: The University of North Carolina Press, 2010), p. 99; Seecharan, *Sweetening "Bitter Sugar"*, pp. 133, 230; Smith, pp. 170, 180; Spinner, p. 56. "Entry into the colony of literature ("Dunce Motion" excerpt): as quoted by Philip Reno, *The Ordeal of British Guiana* (New York: Monthly Review Press, 1964), p. 15. "All we read": Eric Huntley, quoted in Palmer, p. 159

Endnote 32: "Our Mel's Diner: Godfrey Chin, "The Best of Everything Guyana 1945–1985: Food and Drink and Eating Houses," *Stabroek News*, February 4, 2007

March 1953—Jagan lone protestor: Brindley Benn, quoted in Birbalsingh, p. 58; the council's youngest member: Spinner, p. 25; the Legislative Council "hastily rushed through a Bill: Jagan, *Forbidden Freedom*, p. 60; distributors of banned materials were subject to a stiff fine: Jagan, *The West on Trial*, p. 120; a central issue during the last weeks of the election campaign: Smith, p. 170; Reno, p. 15

Endnote 33: Letter to the editor, *Daily Argosy*, March 30, 1953, collection of editor

Endnote 35: "entitled to admit Government scholars: N. E. Cameron, quoted in "Teachers of Recognise[d] Secondary Schools Plan Assoc.," *Daily Chronicle*, January 31, 1953, collection of editor

Endnote 36: PPP leaders supported Communism: Swan, *British Guiana*, p. 135; Rory Westmaas, quoted in Birbalsingh, p. 70; Robert Moore, quoted in Birbalsingh, p. 108; Moses Bhagwan, quoted in Birbalsingh, p. 119. Jagans identified as Communist activists: Cary Fraser, *Ambivalent Anti-Colonialism* (Westport, Connecticut: Greenwood Press, 1994), p. 116. Election results surprise British and Americans: Ishmael, p. 427; Fraser, *Ambivalent Anti-Colonialism*, pp. 124–125; Spinner, p. 36. Van Sertima: "PPP Wins 1953 General Elections—but loses candidate at elections petition," reproduced in Guyanese Chronicle Online, March 14, 2010; Jagan, *The West on Trial*, p. 137

Endnote 37: leading Georgetown barrister: Swan, *British Guiana*, p. 133; Cheddi Jagan was the only one with experience as a politician: Burrowes, p. 33

Endnote 38: Janet Jagan rumoured to be sister of Julius Rosenberg: Larry Rohter, "A Guyana Favorite: U.S.-Born Grandmother," *New York Times*, December 14, 1997

Endnote 41: "*Time* magazine referred to our government: Jagan, *The West on Trial*, p. 138. "The Third Congress of the PPP Mourns: Sheecharan, *Sweetening "Bitter Sugar"*, p. 216; portrait of Stalin: Swan, *British Guiana*, p. 135

"it may be doubtful: Dispatch, Maddox to U.S. Department of State, May 4, 1953, cited in Fraser, *Ambivalent Anti-Colonialism*, pg. 160

Endnote 44: Drew Pearson column of May 12, 1953: Drew Pearson, The Washington Merry-Go-Round, as reproduced in *The Southeast Missourian*, May 12, 1953, http://news.google.com/s?nid=1893&dat=1 9530512&id=A2EoAAAAIBAJ&sjid=qNYEAAAAIBAJ&pg=3770,5042 801&hl=en

May 30, 1953—Ministers marched from the PPP's office on Regent Street to the legislature a few blocks away: Burrowes, p. 50; "I had to push my way through: John Gutch, *Colonial Servant* (Padstow, Cornwall: T. J. Press, 1987), p. 102; "The decision on attire: Jagan, *The West on Trial*, p. 118

Endnote 47: "The Department of State is following closely: Correspondence to H. S. Irwin, collection of editor

Endnote 48: "Introduced into British Guiana: V. Jones, *Kyk-Over-Al* special "Guianese Christmas" edition, 1955, p. 237. Also Lloyd Kandasammy, "Pan Portrait: A Celebration of Guyana's Cultural Heritage," *Stabroek News*, February 19, 2004; Godfrey Chin, "The Forties in British Guiana—

Our Age of Innocence," godchin1@aol.com

Endnote 49: "The political situation: M. S. Irwin memoir fragment, collection of editor; "irrational anti-white feelings: Jagan, *The West on Trial*, p. 137; "a change in attitude of the workers: Jagan, *The West on Trial*, pp. 137–138

Endnote 51: "The changes we began to introduce: Jagan, *The West on Trial*, pp. 119–120. For a full account of the PPP's progress before suspension of the constitution, see Ashton Chase, *133 Days Towards Freedom in Guiana* (Kitty, British Guiana: B's Printery, 1954).

Endnote 52: "investigate the conditions of employment and wages: Ashton Chase, *133 Days Towards Freedom in Guiana*, p. 12

Chapter 4
1953–1954: Atkinson Field

Endnote 53: Dr. Hanoman-Singh a strong supporter of Burnham's: Brindley Benn, quoted in Birbalsingh, pp. 62–63. His name was dropped from the list: Ishmael, p. 429; Jagan, *The West on Trial*, p. 118

September 10, 1953—"I hear the pratings: Spinner, p. 41; "apparently more informed: Jagan, *Forbidden Freedom*, p. 57; "I have now toured: Report on British Guiana by Governor Alfred Savage, undated but from early September 1953, doc. 12, guyana.org/govt/declassified_british_ documents_1953.html

September 13, 1953—"The new Constitution has operated: Letter from Governor Alfred Savage to Secretary of the Colonial Office Thomas Lloyd, September 13, 1953, doc. 15, guyana.org/govt/declassified_ british_documents_1953.html

Endnote 56: The object of the sugarcane workers' strike: Seecharan, *Sweetening "Bitter Sugar"*, pp. 78, 81, 144. "the single most important issue: Seecharan, *Sweetening "Bitter Sugar"*, pg. 220; Fraser, *Ambivalent Anti-Colonialism*, pp. 128–129

September 24, 1953—"They say they are going to take away: Jagan, *Forbidden Freedom*, pp. 57–58; "One of our main fears: Gutch, *Colonial Servant*, p. 104; "anti-white feeling is growing: Report on British Guiana by Governor Alfred Savage, undated but from early September 1953, doc. 12, guyana.org/govt/declassified_british_documents_1953.html

Endnote 57: "some talk . . . of plans to evacuate: Jagan, *The West on Trial*, p. 137; "during that day: Jagan, *Forbidden Freedom*, p. 7; "This confounded nonsense must stop: Burrowes, p. 62; "Let us tell them: Palmer, p. 32; "He is going to crawl: Gutch, p. 103; "Her Majesty's Government will suspend this constitution over my dead body: Burrowes, p. 62; "What was clearly political rhetoric: Jagan, *Forbidden Freedom*, p. 58

Endnote 58: Senator Jackson visited Georgetown as the guest of Governor Savage: Ishmael, p. 448; "With PPP leaders pressing hard: Fraser, *Ambivalent Anti-Colonialism*, p. 129

"As placid as our days [at the airbase] were: M. S. Irwin, memoir fragment, collection of editor

Endnote 59: "in case the PPP might attempt a coup: Gutch, p. 104

October 6, 1953—*Los Angeles Times*: "Navy Moves in Colonial Crisis

October 7, 1953—"I was the first British newspaperman: Jagan, *The West on Trial*, p. 126; "There are no demonstrations: Jagan, *Forbidden Freedom*, p. 83; Spinner, p. 44

Endnote 60: "ready to open with all they had: "The Iron Fist in a Velvet Glove: The Caribbean 1948–1969," in Riots, Rebellions, Gun Boats and Peace Keepers, britains-smallwars.com/RRGP/Caribbean.htm; "from battle order to parade dress: Ibid.

October 8, 1953—*Los Angeles Times*: "British Moves Hit by Guiana Premier

October 9, 1953—"was the first most Guianese heard: David Granger, "British Regiments in British Guiana," *Stabroek News*, November 2, 2008; "to prevent Communist subversion of the Government: Statement by Her Majesty's Government read by John Gutch and broadcast on Radio Demerara, October 9, 1953, doc. 44, guyana.org/govt/declassified_british_documents_1953.html; "I flew into this crisis city of palms: Jagan, *Forbidden Freedom*, p. 10

October 11, 1953—*Daily Argosy*, Sunday edition: "British Troops Land In Colony To Preserve Order"; *Los Angeles Times*: "Red Plot Invented, Says Ousted Guiana Premier

Endnote 61: Jagan and Burnham's trip to London: Burrowes, pp. 56–57; "The governments of Trinidad, Barbados, Jamaica, and the United States: Jagan, *The West on Trial*, p. 128; "at the prohibitive cost: Ibid.

October 19, 1953—*Time*: "Kicking Out the Communists; *Life*: "Face-Off in Guiana

Endnote 62: "It became clear by the end of September: British Government White Paper on the Suspension of the Constitution of British Guiana, VI. 42, October 20, 1953, doc. 69, guyana.org/govt/declassified_british_documents_1953.html. Claims of "communist subversion" by the PPP: Jagan, *The West on Trial*, p. 136; Reno, p. 22. "Some things have been brought: House of Commons debate, October 22, 1953, Hansard HC Deb

22 October 1953 vol 518 cc2159–283, http://hansard.millbanksystems.com/commons/1953/oct/22/british-guiana; Smith, p. 176. "It is one thing to encourage a strike: *The Spectator*, October 23, 1953, cited in Fraser, *Ambivalent Anti-Colonialism*, p. 162. Did not win the support of the British Labour Party or prominent Caribbean leaders: Burrowes, p. 57; Reno, pp. 22–23; Jagan, *The West on Trial*, p. 130. "It would seem that the PPP: Burrowes, p. 58

Endnote 63: "Police advise that most widespread fear: Telegram from Governor Savage to the Colonial Secretary, October 26, 1953, doc. 82, guyana.org/govt/declassified_british_documents_1953.html; Lachmansingh was soon released: Jagan, *The West on Trial*, p. 150; "we were very well treated: Bruce Paddington, "The Poems Man," *Caribbean Beat*, March/April 1995; His release came just before their first wedding anniversary: Phyllis Carter obituary, *Stabroek News*, February 7, 2010

November 2, 1953—*Time*: "Sledge Hammer in Guiana"

Endnote 64: governor made his appointments to the interim government: Palmer, p. 56; Spinner, pp. 55–56; "Almost every form of political activity: Burrowes, pp. 69–70

Endnote 65: "an unsatisfactory building: "1st Battalion, The Argyll and Sutherland Highlanders History: British Guiana 1953–1954," argylls1945to1971.co.uk/AandSH_BG1953to54.htm; "troops could find themselves billeted: David Granger, "British Regiments in British Guiana," *Stabroek News*, November 2, 2008

Endnote 66: Col. [Art] Williams, B.G. Airways' American-born head: Smith, p. 76; Lloyd Kandasammy, "A Brief History of Civil Aviation in Guyana," *Stabroek News*, June 24, 2004

February 1954—Burnham and Jagan return from their side trip in India: Jagan, *The West on Trial*, pp. 150–151

Endnote 69: "agricultural extension and community development specialist: House of Commons debate, December 15, 1954, Hansard HC Deb 15 December 1954 vol 535 cc1764–5, http://hansard.millbanksystems.com/commons/1954/dec/15/united-states-experts

Endnote 71: restriction of PPP leaders: Brindley Benn, quoted in Birbalsingh, p. 61; "left out of the dragnet: Jagan, *The West on Trial*, pp. 155–160; Burnham's refusal to comply: Burrowes, p. 72

Endnote 72: H. S. Irwin reminiscence, 2000, collection of editor

Article and editorial on the Stamp Club: *The Q.C. Lichtor*, April 6, 1954, collection of editor

Endnote 74: "When breast feeding is impossible: E. Phyllis Clark, *West Indian Cookery* (Edinburgh: Thomas Nelson and Sons, 1953), p. 243

Endnote 75: statue of Queen Victoria dynamited: David Granger, "British Regiments in British Guiana," *Stabroek News*, November 2, 2008; met with lighthearted approval: Williams, pp. 109–110

Chapter 5
1954–1955: 7 Third Avenue, Subryanville

Endnote 76: "The house—actually the north half: H. S. Irwin reminiscence, 2000, collection of editor

Endnote 77: a weekly supplement published: Palmer, p. 77; "driven to the conclusion: *The British Guiana Bulletin*, November 15, 1954, collection of editor; "it cannot be denied: as quoted in Spinner, pp. 57–58; "a very powerful communist influence: as quoted in Jagan, *The West on Trial*, p. 162; pointing the way for Burnham: Fraser, *Ambivalent Anti-Colonialism*, p. 169; Spinner, p. 58

February 12–13, 1955—The PPP splits into two factions: Burrowes, pp. 85–86

Endnote 80: L. P. Cummings, "Some Roraima Experiences," *St. Stanislaus Magazine*, vol. 13, November 1955, pp. 14–19

Chapter 6
1955–1956: Queen's College Compound

Endnote 83: "culturally significant but artistically weak: *Thunder*, August 20, 1955; reprinted in "A Martin Carter Prose Sampler," *Kyk-Over-Al* special issue 44, May 1993, pp. 66–67

November 27, 1955—Editorial in the *Daily Chronicle*: "Two years have gone by: Ishmael, pp. 481–82

Endnote 84: "At present, the British Guianese writer: James W. Smith, *Kyk-Over-Al* vol. 1, no. 1, 1945, pp. 30–31; "form[ing] a rallying point: A. J. Seymour, *Growing Up in Guyana* (Georgetown, Guyana: Labour Advocate Printers, 1976), p. 53; "collaboration with Joy Allsopp: Seymour, p. 57

Londonburg Hotel "a run-down, unimpressive place on Main Street: H. S. Irwin correspondence, 2002, collection of editor

Letter from Winifred Grant dated July 11, 1956: collection of editor

Chapter 7
1994: A Return, and Reflections on the Interim

"fresh molasses": Swan, *British Guiana*, p. 8

Park Hotel burned to the ground in 2000: (on May 6, 2000) Nigel Williams and Iana Seales, "Muneshwers Gutter by Fire," *Stabroek News*, December 20, 2003

Burnham amassed considerable personal wealth: per Eusi Kwayana, quoted in Shiva Naipaul, *Journey to Nowhere: A New World Tragedy* (New York: Simon & Schuster, 1980), p. 41

foreign debt of more than US$2 billion and an unemployment rate nearing 40 percent: Ramsahoye, p. 152

cyanide spill at the Canadian-operated Omai gold mine: Anthony DePalma, "Monkey Jump Journal: Will Cyanide-Tainted River Ever Be Seen as Safe?" *New York Times*, September 16, 1995

"the first purpose-built nature resort: Tower brochure, 1994; collection of editor

international compensation in exchange for protecting its mammoth rain forest: Erica Gies, "Guyana Offers a Model to Save Rain Forest, *New York Times*, December 8, 2009; Erica Gies, "Climate for Conservation," *Américas*, June 2009, pp. 6–12; Nazma Muller, "Forest Economics," *Caribbean Beat*, September/October 2012, pp. 82–83

The party's frequent public meetings drew large mixed groups and inspired a sense of euphoria: Birbalsingh, p. 135; Smith, pp. 171–172

"They did wonderful things: Richard Allsopp, "Why I Left Guyana," September 27, 2005, jonoguyana.blogspot.com/2005/09/why-i-left-guyana.html

President Kennedy ordered Jagan deposed: Palmer, pp. 266; U.S. government officials say "the Jagan papers are a rare smoking run: a clear written record, without veiled words or plausible denials, of a President's command to depose a Prime Minister"; Tim Weiner, "A Kennedy–C.I.A. Plot Returns to Haunt Clinton," *New York Times*, October 30, 1994

The CIA joined the AFL-CIO to fund strikes and promote arson and riots: Palmer, pp. 233, 251–252; Spinner, pp. 91–98, 101–102; Seecharan, "Cheddi Jagan," p. 45

Jagan "is a confused thinker: Message from Foreign Secretary Home to Secretary of State Rusk, August 18, 1961, doc. 246, guyana.org/govt/declassified_documents.html#246

"converting the UK to a program: Memorandum from the Director of the Bureau of Intelligence and Research (R. Hilsman) to the Deputy Under Secretary of State for Political Affairs (U. A. Johnson), October 17, 1961, doc. 258, guyana.org/govt/declassified_documents.html#258

"it is not possible for us: Telegram from the U.S. Department of State to the Embassy in the United Kingdom, with instructions from Rusk to deliver message to Home "as soon as possible," February 19, 1962, doc. 264, guyana.org/govt/declassified_documents.html#264

"We misunderstood the whole struggle: Arthur Schlesinger, Jr., quoted by Tim Weiner, "A Kennedy–C.I.A. Plot Returns to Haunt Clinton," *New York Times*, October 30, 1994

B.G. had lagged behind: Fraser, *Ambivalent Anti-Colonialism*, pp. 110–111; Rita Hinden, "The Case of British Guiana," *Encounter*, January 1954, pp. 19, 22

insufficient time to master the intricacies: Palmer, p. 311; Cary Fraser, "The PPP on Trial: British Guiana in 1953," *Small Axe*, March 15, 2004, p. 31

PPP having expected to hold forth as the opposition: Spinner, p. 36; Smith p. 174

misconstrued its sudden change in stature: Fraser, "The PPP on Trial," pp. 22, 31, 39, 40

"they continued to hold public meetings: Allsopp, "Why I Left Guyana"

PPP's victory "was too quick": Eusi Kwayana, quoted in Birbalsingh, p. 48

The party newsletter, *Thunder*, looked to the Soviet Union as "the motherland": David de Caires, quoted in Birbalsingh, p. 148

contradiction in forging bonds with the Communist bloc while also lobbying for U.S. support: Cary Fraser, "The PPP on Trial," p. 35

"Our party was like a boy with short pants: Eric Huntley, quoted in Birbalsingh, p. 75

"amateurish displays: Ashton Chase, quoted in Birbalsingh, p. 44

"It was absolute nonsense: Ibid.

In 1957, Premier Jagan railed against Britain: Seecharan, "Cheddi Jagan," pp. 36–38

In 1961 Jagan championed Castro: Seecharan, "Cheddi Jagan," pp. 34, 38, 42

Jagan was unable to offer a coherent reply: Cedric Joseph, quoted in Birbalsingh, p. 180; transcript of *Meet the Press*, October 15, 1961; Seecharan, "Cheddi Jagan," p. 41; Palmer, p. 256; Spinner, pp. 83–84

Jagan made circuitous remarks that convinced the Americans of his Communist allegiances: Seecharan, "Cheddi Jagan," pp. 40, 42–44; Spinner, pp. 84–85; Palmer, pp. 247–248, 256, 269

he was astounded at President Kennedy's subsequent refusal: Lloyd Best, quoted in Birbalsingh, p. 89; Palmer pp. 256–57

Burnham, perceived by the U.S. as the lesser threat: Seecharan, "Cheddi Jagan," p. 43–45, 56–58; Palmer pp. 251–252, 261–63, 269, 283–285, 290–291

"I am proud of the fact that I am black: quoted by Era Bell Thompson, "Profile of a Prime Minister," *Ebony*, April 1967, p. 128; effect on black Guyanese: Fr. Andrew Morrison, quoted in Birbalsingh, p. 166

"In Guyanese parlance he became a snake: Ramsahoye, p. 66

"Things are rough here: Janet Jagan personal correspondence, displayed and read aloud as part of *Thunder in Guyana*, a 2003 documentary film by Suzanne Wasserman

"The shops had bare shelves: Naipaul, p. 40

Burnham had welcomed the People's Temple: Eric Banks, "The Legacy of Jonestown," *Wall Street Journal*, December 13, 2008; Naipaul, pp. 47, 64–67

president gave the People's Temple a 25-year lease: Guyana government Lease of State Land, posted by Steven War Ran, "The Jonestown Guyana Land Lease" (blog), July 17, 2013, stevenwarran.blogspot.com/2013/07/the-jonestown-guyana-land-lease.html

"Hungry children and adults: Naipaul, p. 40

"Everywhere you look: Naipaul, p. 18

Guyana was importing its sugar from Guatemala: Ramsahoye, p. 129

"We used to say he banned all the white things: Nicholas Laughlin, "He waited for an hour in the lounge of the Georgetown Club," Imaginary Roads 1.8 (blog), May 4, 2006, http://nicholaslaughlin.blogspot.com/2006/05/imaginary-roads-18-he-waited-hour-in.html

a phenomenon described . . . as a haemorrhage: "Fruit that Falls Far from the Tree," *The Economist*, November 3, 2005

Guyana's per capita rate of emigration: Rawle Lucas, "Guyana and Its Human Resources," *Stabroek News*, September 15, 2013

"I felt there was an intellectual void: Seecharan, quoted in John Mair, "Clem Seecharan: History Man," *Caribbean Beat*, January/February 2007

"fusion of time: Heath, p. 134

"years with small children and high hopes: This and the following quotes from M. S. Irwin, memoir fragment, collection of editor

"I so clearly remember the moment: Jock Campbell, quoted in Seecharan, *Sweetening "Bitter Sugar"*, p. 50

Campbell's family had held land since the 1780s: Seecharan, *Sweetening "Bitter Sugar"*, p. 18

Epilogue
John Ramsaran

"one of the most disturbed politically: John Ramsaran, "My Colonial Inheritance" from Frank Birbalsingh, *Jahaji Bhai: An Anthology of Indo-Caribbean Literature* (Toronto: TSAR Publications, 1988), p. 98

"These we read closely and, I think, with pleasure: Ibid., p. 99

Herbert Allsopp

Chase "reaches a level of popular understanding: W.H.L. Allsopp, "Sam Chase as an Educationist," *Kyk-Over-Al*, vol. 3, no. 12, Mid-Year 1951, p. 41

Betty and Cliff Evans

"Cliff and I complemented each other: Colleen P. Popson, "First Lady of Amazonia," *Archaeology*, May/June 2003

Lynette Dolphin

"And wherever she has gone: Terry Holder, "Miss—From 1943 to 1969," *Stabroek News*, July 31, 1994

Norman Cameron

"Mine has been a full life: Petamber Persaud, "Norman Cameron, part two," Kaieteur News Online, November 22, 2009

Dorothy Taitt

"subversive in the positive sense: Dr. Vibert Co. Cambridge, "Dorothy Taitt: An Exceptional Guyanese Woman," *Stabroek News*, December 7, 2003

"vision . . . of blending Guianese and European arts: Williams, p. 110

Richard Allsopp

"fighting a losing battle: "Professor Richard Allsopp, January 23, 1923–June 3, 2009," *Stabroek News*, June 7, 2009

"racial and political divisions: Ibid.

Burnham "independently saw the value of the work as an instrument of integrative regional education: Ibid.

Joy Allsopp

E-mail to editor from Disa Allsopp, August 2014

Premnauth J. Ramphal

Correspondence to editor from P. J. Ramphal, April and September 2014

Martin Carter

"To read Carter's poems: Nicholas Laughlin, Bookshelf, *Caribbean Beat*, July/August 2006

"I thought that anything that could bring about a diffusion of tension: Bruce Paddington, "The Poems Man," *Caribbean Beat*, March/April 1995

Sydney King

"a non-believer in white domination: Eusi Kwayana, "The death of Stetson Kennedy . . . : Reflections on My Encounter With Him and the Aftermath," August 28, 2011, http://thekwayanas.com/What_They_Carried_Out_of_Africa/TERROR_IN_THE_USA_files/The%20death%20of%20Stetson%20Kennedy%20at%20age%2094%20was%20announced%20in%20Florida%20on%20August%2027.htm

"Freedom was closing down: Vanessa Narine, "Following Eusi Kwayana's Testimony at Rodney Commission of Inquiry," *Guyana Chronicle*, May 31, 2014

"one of the most fascinating people in the entire Caribbean: Thomas J. Spinner, Jr., "Guyana: Old Scars Break Open," *The Nation*, December 31, 1977, p. 724

Harold Persaud

"forced to flee to London: Joseph S. Persaud, *Across Three Continents: An Indo-Guyanese Family Experience* (Bartlett, Ill.: Palm Tree Enterprises, 2002), pp. 8–10

Joshua Ramsammy

"Josh's ambition, unlike a number of us: Harold Drayton, "Joshua Reuben Ramsammy: A Celebration of His Life and Work," *The Scribbler* (Toronto Chapter, Queen's College Alumni Association), July 2009, p. 9

his "sojourn with Guyanese political and social decay: Nigel Westmaas, "In the Diaspora—A Memory of Josh Ramsammy," *Stabroek News*, February 16, 2009

"struggle for the restoration of democracy: cited by Derick Ackloo, "Remembering Dr. Josh Ramsammy, CHS Alumnus and a True Patriot," Chandisingh High School Alumni Blog, February 12, 2009, http://chs-jccss.org/blog

BIBLIOGRAPHY

Memoirs

Bacchus, Noël Compton. *Guyana Farewell.* New York: Noël Bacchus Publishing, 1995.

Bacon, Margaret. *Journey to Guyana.* London: Dennis Dobson, 1970.

Browne, Cyrill. *Backtracking Through Georgetown, Guyana.* Pittsburgh: Rosedog Books, 2006.

Dathan, Patricia Wendy. *Bauxite, Sugar and Mud: Memories of Living in Colonial Guyana, 1928–1944.* Ste-Anne-de-Bellevue, Quebec: Shoreline, 2006.

Gutch, John. *Colonial Servant.* Padstow, Cornwall: T. J. Press, 1987.

Heath, Roy. *Shadows Round the Moon.* Glasgow: William Collins Sons, 1990.

Persaud, J. S. *Across Three Continents: An Indo-Guyanese Family Experience.* Bartlett, Ill.: Palm Tree Enterprises, 2002.

Persaud, Yesu. *Reaching for the Stars: The Life of Yesu Persaud*, vol. 1. Georgetown, Guyana: Caribbean Press, 2014.

Ramsaran, John A. "My Colonial Inheritance," in Frank Birbalsingh, *Jahaji Bhai: An Anthology of Indo-Caribbean Literature.* Toronto: TSAR Publications, 1988.

Roth, Vincent. *A Life in Guyana*, 2 vols. Leeds, England: Peepal Tree Press, 2003.

Salkey, Andrew. *Georgetown Journal: A Caribbean Writer's Journey from London via Port of Spain to Georgetown, Guyana, 1970.* London: New Beacon Books, 1972.

Seymour, A. J. *Growing Up in Guyana.* Georgetown, Guyana: Labour Advocate Printers, 1976.

Williams, Mona. *Bishops: My Turbulent Youth.* New Zealand: Mallinson Rendel Publishers Ltd., 1995.

Other Books

Bacchus, M. K. *Education for Development of Underdevelopment? Guyana's Educational System and Its Implications for the Third World.* Waterloo, Ontario: Wilfrid Laurier University Press, 1980.

Beebe, William. *Jungle Peace.* New York: Henry Holt, 1918.

Birbalsingh, Frank. *Jahaji Bhai: An Anthology of Indo-Caribbean Literature.* Toronto: TSAR Publications, 1988.

———. *The People's Progressive Party of Guyana, 1950–1992: An Oral History.* London: Hansib Publications, 2007.

Burrowes, Reynold A. *The Wild Coast: An Account of Politics in Guyana*. Cambridge, Mass.: Schenkman Publishing Co., 1984.

Carnegie School of Home Economics. *What's Cooking in Guyana*. London: Macmillan, 1973.

Clark, E. Phyllis. *West Indian Cookery*. Edinburgh: Thomas Nelson and Sons, 1953.

Da Costa, Emilia Viotti. *Crowns of Glory, Tears of Blood: The Demerara Slave Rebellion of 1823*. New York: Oxford University Press, 1994.

De Barros, Juanita. *Order and Place in a Colonial City: Patterns of Struggle and Resistance in Georgetown, British Guiana, 1889–1924*. Montreal: McGill-Queen's University Press, 2002.

Emmer, P. C. *The Dutch Slave Trade, 1500–1850*. New York: Berghahn Books, 2006.

Evans, Clifford, and Betty J. Meggers. *Archeological Investigations in British Guiana*. Smithsonian Institution, Bureau of American Ethnology, Bulletin 177 (U.S. Printing Office, Washington), 1960. archive.org/stream/bulletin1771960smit/bulletin1771960smit_djvu.txt.

Fraser, Cary. *Ambivalent Anti-Colonialism: The United Stated and the Genesis of West Indian Independence, 1940–1964*. Westport, Conn.: Greenwood Press, 1994.

Henfrey, Colin. *Through Indian Eyes: A Journey Among the Tribes of Guiana*. New York: Holt, Rinehart and Winston, 1964.

Im Thurn, Everard F. *Among the Indians of Guiana*. 1883. Reprint, New York: Dover, 1967.

Ishmael, Odeen. *The Guyana Story: From Earliest Times to Independence*. 2005. guyana.org/features/guyanastory/guyana_story.html.

Jagan, Cheddi. *Forbidden Freedom: The Story of British Guiana*. Watford, Herts: People's Books Co-operative Society and Lawrence & Wishart, 1954.

———. *The West on Trial: My Fight for Guyana's Freedom*. 1966. Reprinted with a new epilogue, St. John's, Antigua: Hansib Caribbean, 1997.

Kirke, Henry. *Twenty-Five Years in British Guiana*. 1898. Reprint, Westport, Conn.: Negro Universities Press, 1970.

Lyttelton, Oliver. *The Memoirs of Lord Chandos: An Unexpected View from the Summit*. New York: New American Library of World Literature, 1963.

Morrison, Fr. Andrew, SJ. *Justice: The Struggle for Democracy in Guyana, 1952–1992*. Georgetown, Guyana: Red Thread Women's Press, 1998.

Naipaul, Shiva. *Journey to Nowhere: A New World Tragedy*. New York: Simon & Schuster, 1980.

Naipaul, V. S. *The Middle Passage: Impressions of Five Societies—British, French and Dutch—in the West Indies and South America*. New York: Random House, 1962.

Palmer, Colin A. *Cheddi Jagan and the Politics of Power: British Guiana's Struggle for Independence*. Chapel Hill: University of North Carolina Press, 2010.

Ramsahoye, James W. *A Mouldy Destiny: Visiting Guyana's Forbes Burnham*. London: Minerva Press, 1996.

Reno, Philip. *The Ordeal of British Guiana*. New York: Monthly Review Press, 1964.

Rodney, Walter. *A History of the Guyanese Working People, 1881–1905*. Baltimore: Johns Hopkins University Press, 1981.

Rodway, James. *Guiana: British, Dutch, and French*. 1912. Facsimile of the first edition, Elibron Classics, 2005.

Seecharan, Clem. *Sweetening "Bitter Sugar"*. Kingston, Jamaica: Ian Randle Publishers, 2005.

Smith, Raymond T. *British Guiana*. London: Oxford University Press, 1962.

Spinner, Thomas J., Jr. *A Political and Social History of Guyana, 1945–1983*. Boulder, Colo.: Westview Press, 1984.

Swan, Michael. *British Guiana: The Land of Six Peoples*. London: William Clowes & Sons, 1957.

———. *The Marches of El Dorado: British Guiana, Brazil, Venezuela*. Boston: Beacon Hill Press, 1958.

Vatuk, Ved Prakash. "Protest Songs of East Indians in British Guiana," in *Thieves in My House: Four Studies in Indian Folklore of Protest and Change*. Varanasi, India: Vishwavidyalaya Prakashan, 1969.

Articles

Ackloo, Derick. "Remembering Dr. Josh Ramsammy, CHS Alumnus and a True Patriot." Chandisingh High School Alumni Blog, 12 February 2011. http://chs-jccss.org/blog/2011/02/12/remembering-dr-josh-ramsammy-1928-2009.

Adamson, Alan H. "Monoculture and Village Decay in British Guiana: 1854–1872." *Journal of Social History* vol. 3, no. 4 (Summer 1970): 386–405.

Alexander, Robert J. "Confusion in British Guiana." *Dissent* vol. 6 (Autumn 1962): 402–409.

Allsopp, Joy. "Philip Pilgrim's Legend of Kaieteur." Articles and Reviews, 1955, *Kyk-Over-Al*, reproduced in April 1986 nos. 33 and 34 (Anthology of Selections from nos. 1–28). University of Florida Digital Collections, George A. Smathers Libraries, Digital Collections. http://ufdc.ufl.edu/UF00080046/00022/101j.

Allsopp, Richard. "Why I Left Guyana." Guyana Resource Center, 27 September 2005. jonoguyana.blogspot.com/2005/09/why-i-left-guyana.html.

Allsopp, W.H.L. "Sam Chase as an Educationist." *Kyk-Over-Al* vol. 3, no. 12 (Mid-Year 1951): 117–119. University of Florida, George A. Smathers Libraries, Digital Collections. http://ufdc.ufl.edu/UF00080046/00005/38x.

Banks, Eric. "The Legacy of Jonestown." *Wall Street Journal*, 13 December 2008.

Beharry, Inderjeet. "Short History of the development of English Freemasonry in Guyana 1780–2004." Proceedings of the Heritage Lodge, November 2005. http://heritagelodge730.ca/1GuyanaFreemasonry.htm.

Benjamin, Joel. "The Lesser-Known Tradition of Guyanese Fiction: A Preliminary Bibliographical Survey, Part 2." *Kyk-Over-Al* no. 31 (June 1985). University of Florida, George A. Smathers Libraries, Digital Collections. http://ufdc.ufl.edu/UF00080046/00021.

Bhagwan, Moses. "Being Indian in Guyana: The Challenges." Commentary, GuyanaCaribbeanPolitics.com, 12 August 2006. https://guyaneseonline.files.wordpress.com/2013/being-indian-in-guyana-the-challenges-moses-bhagwan.pdf.

Birbalsingh, Frank. "Bacon brings home truths in 'Journey to Guyana.'" Review of *Journey to Guyana*, by Margaret Bacon. *Indo Caribbean World*, 22 January 2014. http://www.indocaribbeanworld.com.

———. "Cameron unearths important steps in QC's development." Review of *A History of the Queen's College of British Guiana (Guyana)*, by N. E. Cameron. *Indo Caribbean World*, 11 November 2009. http://www.indocaribbeanworld.com.

———. "Order and place in a colonial city." Review of *Order and Place in a Colonial City*, by Juanita De Barros. *Guyana Chronicle Online*, 23 April 2013. http://www.guyanachronicle.com.

———. " 'With Both Hands'—Biography of an unanchored man." Review of *With Both Hands: The Story of Trishanku, a Self-Study*, by John A. Ramsaran (unpublished). *Indo Caribbean World*, 5 May 2010. http://www.indocaribbeanworld.com.

Boyea, Samuel. "Dent in the Crown: Leftists Win in Guiana." *The Nation*, 5 September 1953, 193–194.

British Guiana. The British Survey Popular Series. London and Hastings: F. J. Parsons, and the British Society for International Understanding, April 1953.

The British Guiana Bulletin no. 37, supplement, *Daily Chronicle*, 3 November 1954.

Brotherson, Festus, Jr. "The Foreign Policy of Guyana 1970–1985: Forbes Burnham's Search for Legitimacy." *Journal of Interamerican Studies and World Affairs* vol. 31, no. 3 (Autumn 1989): 9–35.

Burnham, L.F.S. *The Challenge*. Guyana Ministry of Information and Culture, ca. 1972.

Burton, George J. "Attack on the Vector of Filariasis in British Guiana." *Public Health Reports* vol. 79, no. 2 (February 1964): 137–143.

Cambridge, Dr. Vibert C. "Dorothy Taitt: An Exceptional Guyanese Woman." *Stabroek News*, 7 December 2003. http://www.landofsixpeoples.com/news304/ns3120716.htm.

———. "W. Herbert L. Allsopp: Mobilising entertainment for social change in the early 1950s." *Stabroek News*, 10 October 2004. http://www.landofsixpeoples.com/gycreperjs.htm.

Chase, Ashton. *133 Days Towards Freedom in Guiana*. Kitty, British Guiana: B's Printery, 1954.

Chin, Godfrey. "Art Williams: Aviator pioneer." Godfrey Chin's Nostalgia 485, *Stabroek News*, 16 May 2010. http://www.stabroeknews.com.

———. "The Best of Everything Guyana 1945–1985: Food and Drink and Eating Houses." *Stabroek News*, 4 February 2007. http://www.landofsixpeoples.com/news701/ns0702049.html.

———. "The Forties in British Guiana—Our Age of Innocence," Nostalgia 430. https://guyaneseonline.wordpress.com/2010/06/05/the-forties-in-british-guiana---our-age-of-innocence.

Christie, Pauline. "Focus on Creolists: Richard Allsopp." *The Carrier Pidgin* vol. 26, nos. 1–3 (January–December 1998). http:www.scl-online.net/srrallsopp.html.

Cummings, L. P. "Some Roraima Experiences." *St. Stanislaus Magazine* vol. 13 (November 1955): 14–19.

Davis, Kenneth S. "The Deadly Dust: The Unhappy History of DDT." *American Heritage* vol. 22, no. 2 (February 1971).

DePalma, Anthony. "Monkey Jump Journal: Will Cyanide-Tainted River Ever Be Seen as Safe?" *New York Times*, 16 September 1995.

Distance Education (brief history of the Broadcasts to Schools unit). http://www.education.gov.gy/web/index.php/ncerd/item/243-distance-education?tmpl=component&print=1.

Dolphin, Celeste. *Children of Guiana*. British Guiana, 1953.

Drayton, Harold A. "Joshua Reuben Ramsammy: A Celebration of His Life and Work." *The Scribbler* (Toronto chapter, Queen's College Alumni Association), July 2009, 9–11.

"Dr. Richard Allsopp—honored for Literary Achievement." *The Scribbler* (Toronto chapter, Queen's College Alumni Association), Spring 1999, 3.

The Economist. "Fruit that Falls Far from the Tree." 3 November 2005.

Eder, Richard. "Kennedy Refuses Aid to Guiana; Ties to Reds Termed Reason." *New York Times*, 9 July 1963.

"Eusi Kwayana." http://www.unity4power.org/EUSIKWAYANA.html.

Farrier, Francis Quamina. "Houses of culture: Wooden cultural iconic edifices of Georgetown." *Stabroek News*, 19 August 2008. http://www.stabroeknews.com.

1st Battalion, The Argyll and Sutherland Highlanders, History, British Guiana 1953–1954. http://www.argylls1945to1971.co.uk/AandSH_BG1953to54.htm.

Fraser, Cary. "The 'New Frontier' of Empire in the Caribbean: The Transfer of Power in British Guiana, 1961–1964." *The International History Review* vol. 22, no. 3 (September 2000): 583–610.

———. "The PPP on Trial: British Guiana in 1953." *Small Axe* 15 (March 2004): 21–42.

"From Tribal Robes to Pin-Stripe Suit: Eze Ogueri, Candidate for a Ph.D., Is Already a Nigerian Chief at 24." *The Harvard Crimson*, 2 February 1955.

Georgetown Botanic Gardens: Illustrated Guide. Georgetown, British Guiana: Department of Agriculture, 1934.

Gies, Erica. "Climate for Conservation." *Américas* vol. 61, no. 3 (June 2009): 6–12.

———. "Guyana Offers a Model to Save Rain Forest." *New York Times*, 8 December 2009.

Granger, David. "British Regiments in British Guiana." *Stabroek News*, 2 November 2008. http://www.stabroeknews.com.

———. "Joseph Pollydore, Eminence Grise: A Tribute." *Stabroek News*, 9 March 2003. http://www.landofsixpeoples.com/news301/ns303097.htm.

———. "Society: Waking the Dead," *Stabroek News*, 29 July 2010. http://www.stabroeknews.com.

Gupta, Girish. "Multiethnic Movement Emerges in Guyana to Counter Politics-as-Usual." *New York Times*, 17 January 2015.

Haynes, Andre. "Josh Ramsammy passes away." *Stabroek News*, 12 February 2009. http://www.stabroeknews.com.

Hergash, Harry. "Indians Attitude to Education During and Immediately After the Indentureship Period in British Guiana (Now Guyana)." *Guyana Journal*, May 2013. http://www.guyanajournal.com.

Hinden, Rita. "The Case of British Guiana." *Encounter* vol. 2 (January 1954): 18–22.

Hinds, David. "Eusi Kwayana: A Biographical Sketch." Hindsight, 12 September 2008. http://www.guyanacaribbeanpolitics.com/commentary/hinds_091208.html.

Holder, Terry. "Miss—From 1943 to 1969." *Stabroek News*, 31 July 1994.

"The Iron Fist in a Velvet Glove: The Caribbean 1948–1969." Riots, Rebellions, Gun Boats, and Peace Keepers. http://www.britains-smallwars.com/RRGP/Caribbean.htm.

Jagan Janet. "Reminiscences of Cheddi Jagan by Janet Jagan: Cheddi Jagan, the Man." Cheddi Jagan Research Centre. http://www.jagan.org.

Jones, V. "Steelband Magic." Special Christmas issue, *Kyk-Over-Al* vol. 6, no. 21 (1955): 236–237.

"The Jonestown Guyana Land Lease" (blog), 17 July 2013. http://stevenwarran. blogspot.com/2013/07/the-jonestown-guyana-land-lease.html.

Kandasammy, Lloyd. "A Brief History of the British Guiana Music Festivals." *Stabroek News*, 10 November 2005. http://www.landofsixpeoples.com/ news504/ns5111050.htm.

———. "A Brief History of Civil Aviation in British Guiana." *Stabroek News*, 24 June 2004. http://www.landofsixpeoples.com/news402/ns406242.htm.

———. "A Brief History of the Performing Arts, 1950–1955." *Stabroek News*, 26 April 2007. http://www.landofsixpeoples.com/news702/ns0704265.htm.

———. "Pan Portrait: A Celebration of Guyana's Cultural Heritage." *Stabroek News*, 19 February 2004. http://www.landofsixpeoples.com/news401/ ns4021914.htm.

Kilduff, Marshall, and Phil Tracy. "Inside Peoples Temple." *New West Magazine*, 1 August 1977, 30–38.

Kramer, Jane. "Letter from Guyana." *New Yorker*, 16 September 1974, 100–128.

Kwayana, Eusi. "The death of Stetson Kennedy . . . : Reflections on My Encounter With Him and the Aftermath," 28 August 2011. http://thekwayanas.com.

Laughlin, Nicholas. Review of *University of Hunger: Collected Poems and Selected Prose*, by Martin Carter, ed. Gemma Robinson. *Caribbean Beat* no. 80 (July/ August 2006).

———. "He waited for an hour in the lounge of the Georgetown Club." Imaginary Roads 1.8 (blog), 4 May 2006. http://nicholaslaughlin.blogspot.com/2006/05/ imaginary-roads-18-he-waited-hour-in.html.

Laurence Keates (obituary). *Yorkshire Post*, 18 June 2012.

Lernoux, Penny. "Tyranny in Guyana: Jonestown Nation." *The Nation*, 15 November 1980, 510–512.

Life. "Face-Off in Guiana." 19 October 1953.

Lucas, Rawle. "Guyana and Its Human Resources." *Stabroek News*, 15 September 2013. http://www.stabroeknews.com.

"Lynette Dolphin Passes On." *Stabroek News*, 9 February 2000. http://www. kaieteur.com/qcsite/news/articles/dollo.htm.

Maguire, Bassett, with an introduction by Celia K. Maguire. "The Lost Worlds of Guayana: A Search into Their Origins and History." New York Botanical Garden, Bronx, NY: *Brittonia* 48(3) (16 October 1996): 346–354.

Mair, John. "Clem Seecharan: History Man." *Caribbean Beat* no. 83 (January/ February 2007).

Mangar, Tota C. "The 1953 Parliamentary Elections in colonial British Guiana." *Stabroek News*, 1 June 2006. http://www.landofsixpeoples.com/news602/ns6060150.html.

Matthews, Lear. "Continuing the Tribute to Past Guyanese Teachers." *Guyana Cultural Association of New York Inc. On-line Magazine*, December 2012.

McDonald, Ian, and Nigel Westmaas, eds. "A Martin Carter Prose Sampler." *Kyk-Over-Al* no. 44 (May 1993).

"MI5 files reveal details of 1953 coup that overthrew British Guiana's leaders." *The Guardian*, 26 August 2011.

Moodie, Graeme C. "Questions on Guiana: Dr. Jagan in Britain." *The Nation*, 28 November 1953, 447–448.

Muller, Nazma. "Forest Economics." *Caribbean Beat* no. 123 (September/October 2013): 82–83.

Naipaul, V. S. "A Handful of Dust: Return to Guiana." *The New York Review of Books* vol. 38, no. 7 (11 April 1991).

Narine, Vanessa. "Following Eusi Kwayana's Testimony at Rodney Commission of Inquiry." *Guyana Chronicle*, 31 May 2014. http://guyanachronicle.com.

Niblet, Michael. "Guyana Classics Series, part 2: *Kyk-Over-Al, Volumes 1–7 (1945–51)*." Review. *Guyana Chronicle*, 2 February 2014. http://guyanachronicle.com.

Omawale. "The Josh Ramsammy I Remember." *Kaieteur News Online*, 16 February 2009.

Paddington, Bruce. "The Poems Man." *Caribbean Beat* no. 13 (March/April 1995).

Pauly, Daniel. "On bycatch, or How W.H.L. Allsopp Coined a New Word and Created New Insights." *The Sea Around Us Project Newsletter* issue 44 (November/December 2007): 1–4.

Pearson, Drew. The Washington Merry-Go-Round (syndicated column), 12 May 1953.

Perera, Judith. "'Whitewash' Charged in Guyana River Disaster." Albion Monitor/News, 3 December 1995.

Persaud, Petamber. "Norman Cameron (1903–1983)," parts one and two. *Kaieteur News Online*, 8 November 2009 and 22 November 2009. http://www.kaieteurnewsonline.com.

———. "Preserving Our Literary Heritage: 'The Children's Story' and Guy de Weever." *Guyana Chronicle*, 13 May 2007. http://www.landofsixpeoples.com/news702/nc0705128.html.

———. "Preserving Our Literary Heritage: The Distaff Side of Guyanese Literature." *Guyana Chronicle*, 12 March 2006. http://www.kykoveral.blogspot.com/2006/03/distaff-side-of-guyanese-literature.html.

"Phyllis Carter, December 9, 1932–January 28, 2010." *Stabroek News*, 7 February 2010. http://www.stabroeknews.com.

Pidduck, Angela. "Mona K Georges" (obituary). http://www.sputnick.com/angela.

Pilgrim, Billy. "Lynette de Weever Dolphin: A Tribute." *Stabroek News*, 20 February 2000. http://www.qcguyana.org/In_The_News/articles/doltrib2.htm.

"PPP Wins 1953 General Elections—but loses candidate at elections petition." Reproduced in *Guyana Chronicle Online*, 14 March 2010. http://www.guyanachronicle.com.

Popson, Colleen P. "First Lady of Amazonia" *Archaeology* vol. 56, no. 3 (May/June 2003).

"Professor Richard Allsopp, January 23, 1923–June 3, 2009." *Stabroek News*, 7 June 2009. http://www.stabroeknews.com.

"Queen's College." Editorial, Sunday Stabroek. *Stabroek News*, 31 July 1994, 6.

Queen's College Sesquicentennial Souvenir Magazine. Georgetown, Guyana: The Free Press for the Queen's College Old Students' Association, 1994.

"Remembering outstanding female classical musicians." *Guyana Times International*, 1 November 2013. http://www.guyanatimesinternational.com.

"Report of the British Guiana Constitutional Commission 1954 (Robertson Commission Report)." http://www.guyana.org/govt/robertson_report.html.

Rohter, Larry. "A Guyana Favorite: U.S.-Born Grandmother." *New York Times*, 14 December 1997.

Romero, Simon. "Can Ghosts Bring Life to Jonestown Cult Compound?" *New York Times*, 2 May 2010.

Seecharan, Clem. "Cheddi Jagan: The Marxist Leader in Guyana and the Cold War." *Guyana Examiner* vol. 1, no. 1 (May 2013): 26–70.

———. "Internal and External Factors in the Shaping of the Indo-Guyanese." *Guyana Examiner* vol. 1, no. 1 (May 2013): 3–25.

———. "Whose freedom at midnight?: Machinations towards Guyana's Independence, May 1966." *Stabroek News*, 3 September 2008. http://www.stabroeknews.com.

Sethi, Anita. "The Holes in History." *Caribbean Beat* no. 117 (September/October 2012): 64–67.

"The Shaping of Guyanese Literature..." (tribute to A. J. Seymour). *Guyana Chronicle Online*, 28 December 2013. http://www.guyanachronicle.com.

Smith, James W. (addendum to "Message by... N. E. Cameron, M.A., President of the British Guiana Union of Cultural Clubs"). *Kyk-Over-Al* vol. 1, no. 1 (1945): 30–31.

Spinner, Thomas J., Jr. "Guyana: A Dream Deferred." *The Nation*, 31 December 1973, 717–720.

———. "Guyana: Old Scars Break Open." *The Nation*, 31 December 1977, 723–724.

Stapleton, Darwin H. "The Short-Lived Miracle of DDT." *Invention & Technology* vol. 15, no. 3 (Winter 2000), 34–41.

"The Suspension of the British Guiana Constitution–1953 (Declassified British documents)." http://www.guyana.org/govt/declassified_british_documents_1953.html.

Symes, C. B., and A. B. Hadaway. "Initial Experiments in the use of DDT Against Mosquitos in British Guiana." *Bulletin of Entomological Research* vol. 37, no. 3 (January 1947): 399–430.

Thompson, Era Bell. "Profile of a Prime Minister." *Ebony*, April 1967, 124–134.

"Thousands Leave in Guiana Unrest." *New York Times*, 13 March 1962.

Time. "For the Record." 6 July 1962.

Time. "Kicking Out the Communists." 19 October 1953.

Time. "Liberty Deferred." 15 November 1954.

Time. "Old Leftist, New Game." 1 September 1961.

Time. "Sledge Hammer in Guiana." 2 November 1953.

Tracy (Minn.) Headlight Herald. "Agnes Pederson, 90." Week of 11 July 2007. https://www.headlightherald.com/archive/2007/obits28.htm.

United Kingdom. *Parliamentary Debates*. Commons, vol. 518, cc2393–404 (23 October 1953).

———. *Parliamentary Debates*. Commons, vol. 521, cc1624–763 (7 December 1953).

———. *Parliamentary Debates*. Commons, vol. 532, cc212–4 (2 November 1954).

Weiner, Tim. "A Kennedy–C.I.A. Plot Returns to Haunt Clinton." *New York Times*, 30 October 1994.

Westmaas, Nigel. "In the Diaspora: A Memory of Josh Ramsammy." *Stabroek News*, 16 February 2009. http://www.stabroeknews.com.

———. "Recording Guyanese Political History: Memory, 'Archives' and Narrative Overlook." *Stabroek News*, 30 December 2010. http://www.stabroeknews.com.

Wilkinson, Bert. "Guyana Lifts Ban on 'Cyanide River' Mine." Albion Monitor/News, 18 February 1996.

———. "Guyana Seeks to Shield Gold Miners from Mercury Ban." Inter Press Service News Agency, 26 November 2012.

———. "Guyana to Examine Gold Mining Damage." Albion Monitor/News, 5 May 1996.

Williams, Nigel, and Iana Seales. "Muneshwers Gutter by Fire." *Stabroek News*, 20 December 2003. http://www.landofsixpeoples.com/news304/ns312202.htm.

Wishart, Ian, with Doreen Roberts. "Lynette Passes On." Queen's College of Guyana Association (UK) Newsletter no. 21 (April 2000). http://www.qcguyanaalumny.org/Getting_Involved/chapters/london/newsletter_archive/news200004.html.

Woolford, Hazel. "A History of Political Alliances in Guyana: 1953–1997." *Guyana Chronicle*, 30 April 2000. http://www.guyanaundersiege.com/Historical/Political%20Alliances.htm.

Film and Television

Jagan, Cheddi. Interview by Ned Brooks. *Meet the Press*, NBC Universal (transcript, vol. 5, no. 40), 15 October 1961.

Roopnaraine, Rupert, dir. *The Terror and the Time*, Part 1. Feature documentary film, 72 min, produced by the Victor Jara Collective. New York: Third World Newsreel, 1979.

Wasserman, Suzanne, dir. *Thunder in Guyana*. Feature documentary film, 50 min. New York: Women Make Movies, 2003.

INDEX

Persaud, Harold, *527*, 544, 590, 598–99, 620,
  632, 637, 650, 702
Plaisance, 324
Policemen's Choir, 173, 598, 603
Portuguese Club, 589, 599, 642
Potaro River, *444*, 445–46

Queen's College, 12, 15, 19, 20, 24, *32*, 33ff, 47,
    633, 643
  history of, 21–22, 29–30
  class structure, 54–55
  staff, 1954–55, *527. See also individual names*
  Fulbright grantees
    Merrill Pederson, 325, 386, 389ff
    Lester Hirsch, 595–96, 601, 609ff
    unnamed math teacher from Brooklyn, 597
  staff party, 517, 519
  houses and house feeds, 168, 171, 262,
    361n23
  art exhibit, 639
  Literary and Debating Society, 162, 190,
    201, 223, 317, 321
  Musical Society, 582, 617
  The Tempest, 509, 513, 516–17, 699
  Trial by Jury, 213, 216, 259, 261, 325ff
  Twelfth Night, 188, 190, 194, 210ff, *248*, 517,
    699
  Q.C. Lichtor, 363n33, 473
  Science Exhibition, 633–36
  sesquicentennial, 19, 21, 676–78, 696
  Speech Day, 163, 165, 167–68, 512, 514, 634, 702
  Sports Day, 464, 662
  Stamp Club, 176, 178, 190, 194, 199, 203,
    218, 223, 225, 269, 280, 301, 316, 327, 329,
    340, 400, 473
  residences on compound, 19, 314, *578*,
    598–99, *626*, *633*, 677

Radio Demerara 126, 177, 195–96, 199, 202,
  269, 284, 313, 489, 511, 703
  Olga Lopes-Seale, 196
Ramphal, Premnauth 273, 287, 503, 507–8,
  583, 613, 636, 641, 658, 667, 699–700
Ramsahoye, James, 680, 686
Ramsammy, Joshua, 636, 648, 658, 667–69, 702–3
Ramsaran, John, 50, 52–53, 92, 117ff, 135, 142,
  163, 166, 174–75, 178, 181ff, 188, 195ff, 211ff,
  228, 230, 232, 239, 244, 248–50, 254, 261,
  263–64, 271, 274, 276, 279, 285, 297, 301,

306, 314, 319, 321, 331, 334, 337, 345, 349,
  355, 357, 369, 371, 378–79, 382, 398, 408–9,
  411, 420, 424, 427, 430–31, 434, 436–38,
  442, 450, 455, 474–75, 479, 483, 489, 492–93,
  502–3, 507, 513–15, 519ff, 525, *527*, 536,
  538, 542, 544, 550–52, 555, 568–70, 574–75,
  579–81, 583, 590, 618, 625, 637ff, 668, 670,
  691, 693
Ramsaran, Margaret, 50, 52–53, 55, 92, 117ff,
  138, 140ff, 163, 166, 168, 174–75, 178, 182–
  83, 186, 188, 194ff, 201, 203–4, 211, 214ff,
  220, 223–24, 230, 232–33, 238–39, 244, 247,
  249–50, 253, 255–56, 259, 264, 269, 271,
  274–76, 279, 285, 297, 301, 306, 314, 319,
  321, 330–31, 337, 345, 349, 355, 357, 369, 371,
  379, 382, 395, 398, 408–9, 411, 418, 420, 424,
  427, 430–31, 434, 436–38, 442, 450, 453–55,
  474–76, 479, 483, 489, 492–93, 502–3, 507,
  511, 513–15, 518ff, 525, 529–30, 535–36, 538,
  541–42, 544, 548, 550–52, 555, 560, 562,
  568–70, 572, 574–75, 579–81, 583, 585, 590,
  618, 625, 629, 637ff, 665, 671, 691, 693
Rock, Ronald D., 475, *527*, 669
Rodway, James A., 146, 148–49, 151, 155, 211,
  213, 361n21, 377
Rosignol, 523
Roth, Vincent, 41, 77n3, 692–93
Rupununi, 44, 183, 526, 667, 673n85

St. Cuthbert's Mission, 102–5, 120, 121, 150
St. George's Cathedral, 154, 284, 300, 304–5,
  365n40
St. Joseph's Mercy Hospital, 275, 378, 535–36,
  539, 703
St. Michael's Nursing Home. *See* Georges, Dr.
  Reginald H.
St. Stanislaus College, 22, 364n35, 576n80
Sandbach Parker, 75–76, 177
Sanger-Davies, Nancy, 198, 210–11, 214–16,
  219, 223, 225, 227–28, 230ff, 236–37, 242ff,
  288, 292, 306, 345, 349, 355, 357, 386,
  388–89, 430, 493, 511ff, 590, 594, 598, 601,
  610, 627, 634, 641, 652, 695
Sanger-Davies, Vyvyan J., 140–41, 164,
  176–77, 187–88, 190, 194, 199, 203, 210,
  213–14, 222–23, 228, 230, 234, 236–37, 239,
  244, 246, 248–49, 259, 261, 263, 278, 286,
  288ff, 305–6, 310, 313, 315, 317–18, 321–22,
  325, 329, 348, 350, 353, 355, 357, 362n30,